S0-ABT-434

Why Do You Need This New Edition?

Here are six great reasons.

1. **The introduction includes a new sample essay** that shows you how to annotate, outline, and analyze essays in detail according to the six steps for critical readings.

2. **More than 40 new** readings and images reflect today's topics from tweeting to *The Hunger Games* to bullying.

3. **Three new chapter themes include** Chapter 4, "That's Entertainment? Amusing Ourselves"; Chapter 5, "The Social Animal: Connecting in a Digital World"; and Chapter 9, "Brave New World: What Can Science Do?" provide you with compelling topics to write about.

4. **New writers are included in this edition with selections from noted authors such as** Robin Dunbar, danah boyd, Joseph Turow, Glenn Loury, and Peggy Orenstein.

5. **A new feature called "Modern Scholar"** highlights one reading in each chapter drawn from an academic journal. These readings provide you the opportunity to explore a topic more deeply.

6. **New ads** have been added to Chapter 2, with accompanying critical advertising chapter. Each ad and its accompanying critical thinking questions that encourage you to take a closer look at the effects of advertising on our culture.

The Contemporary Reader

The Contemporary Reader

ELEVENTH EDITION

Gary Goshgarian

NORTHEASTERN UNIVERSITY

PEARSON

Boston • Columbus • Indianapolis • New York • San Francisco
Upper Saddle River • Amsterdam • Cape Town • Dubai • London • Madrid
Milan • Munich • Paris • Montreal • Toronto • Delhi • Mexico City
Sao Paulo • Sydney • Hong Kong • Seoul • Singapore • Taipei • Tokyo

Senior Sponsoring Editor: Katharine Glynn
Assistant Editor: Rebecca Gilpin
Senior Marketing Manager: Sandra McGuire
Production Manager: S.S. Kulig
Project Coordination, Text Design and
    Electronic Page Makeup: Element LLC
Cover Designer/Manager: John Callahan

Cover Image: (clockwise from top left):
    Andy Lim/Shutterstock, Jim Barber/
    Shutterstock, Anthony Hall/Shutterstock,
    Peter Elvidge/Shutterstock, IKO/
    Shutterstock, alexwhite/Shutterstock,
    Aaron Amat/Shutterstock
Senior Manufacturing Buyer: Roy Pickering
Printer/Binder: R.R. Donnelley
Cover Printer: R.R. Donnelley

Credits and acknowledgments borrowed from other sources and reproduced, with permission, in this textbook appear on the appropriate page within text [or on pages 473–482].

Library of Congress Cataloging-in-Publication Data

The contemporary reader / [edited by] Gary Goshgarian. — 11th ed.
    p. cm.
Includes index.
ISBN 978-0-321-87189-3
    1. College readers.   2. English language—Rhetoric—Problems, exercises, etc.
3. Report writing—Problems, exercises, etc.   I. Goshgarian, Gary.
    PE1417.C6523 2013
    808'.0427—dc23

                                                         2012023118

10 9 8 7 6 5 4 3 2 1—DOC—16 15 14 13 12

                              Instructor's edition ISBN 10: 0-321-87239-8
                                               ISBN 13: 978-0-321-87239-5
                                    Student edition ISBN 10: 0-321-87189-8
                                               ISBN 13: 978-0-321-87189-3

www.pearsonhighered.com

Contents

1   Fashion and Flesh: The Images We Project   45

My Hips, My Caderas   47

Alisa Valdes

"In Spanish, the word for hips is *caderas*—a broad term used to denote every-thing a real woman carries from her waist to her thighs . . . [and] the bigger, the better. . . . In English, hips are something women try to be rid of."

Weight of the World   50

Niranjana Iyer

"In India, I'd been above average in height. In the States, I was short (so said the Gap). From a tall, thin Women's, I had morphed into a petite, plump Misses'— without gaining or losing a smidgen of flesh."

Strong Enough   53

Wendy Shanker

"We don't owe anyone an explanation when it comes to the choices we make about appearance. Yet here we are, dieting and sweating and cutting and spritzing and waxing and sucking and shooting and plucking, hoping to look less like our-selves and more like Halle Berry or Angelina Jolie or Anna Kournikova, thinking our problems will be solved."

Modern Scholar: Body Image, Media, and Eating Disorders   56

Jennifer L. Derenne and Eugene V. Beresin

"Throughout history, the standard of female beauty often has been unrealistic and difficult to attain. Those with money and higher socioeconomic status were far more likely to be able to conform to these standards. Women typically were will-ing to sacrifice comfort and even endure pain to achieve them."

Culture Shock: Get Real Ad   63

Out-of-Body Image   64

Caroline Heldman

"What would disappear [from their lives] if they stopped seeing themselves as objects? Painful high heels? Body hatred? Constant dieting? Liposuction? It's hard to know."

The Natural Beauty Myth   68

Garance Franke-Ruta

"Only in America do we think that beauty is a purely natural attribute rather than a type of artistry requiring effort."

---

downy skin and into their bloodstreams through the books and magazines they read, the television they watch, the trends they analyze like stock reports, and the celebrities they aspire to be."

"Boys use [video] games to experience fantasies of power and fame, to explore and master what they perceive as exciting and realistic environments (but distinct from real life), to work through angry feelings or relieve stress, and as social tools." But are these violent games putting boys, and society as a whole, at risk?"

"View many rap music videos and it is blatantly obvious that women are 'used' for the mere delight of the male rapper and his friends (and male viewer-ship). Put simply, it is painfully clear that women are mere sex objects; and this is predominately true of gangsta rap music videos."

"This isn't a Superman-vs.-Hulk stumper or anything; if you have even a passing acquaintance with Stephanie Meyer's *Twilight* or Suzanne Collins' *The Hunger Games*, you know that, unless Edward or Jacob came to her rescue as they are wont to do, Bella is going to get stomped."

"After the '08 crash, the empty promises of false prosperity became dark lessons in reality; *The Hills* no longer offered valuable lifestyle instruction but rather became a failed era's gross artifact. . . . [Now, we watch] *Jersey Shore*."

"The current boom may be a product of the changing economics of the television business, but reality TV is also the liveliest genre on the set right now. It has engaged hot-button cultural issues—class, sex, race—that respectable television, including the august CBS Evening News, rarely touches."

"These reality TV shows wouldn't be made if we didn't watch them, so why do we watch them? Either we find them entertaining or we find them so shocking that we are simply unable to turn away. I'm not sure that the latter is an entirely defensible reason for supporting such programming; turning away is as easy as hitting a button on the remote control."

"One can oppose affirmative action and still believe that the racial composition of a student body is a relevant factor among many for a university to consider in the construction of its educational mission. One can critique particular policy instruments without rejecting the notion that racial justice is an appropriate goal."

"Racial characterizations have trumped the achievement ideal; people born into a non-white race, whatever their accomplishments, have been unable to change their racial status. Worse, race has often been their most defining characteristic, affecting most, if not all, aspects of their being."

"Today, the picture is far more complex. To take the most obvious example, whiteness is no longer a precondition for entry into the highest levels of public office. The son of Indian immigrants doesn't have to become 'white' in order to be elected governor of Louisiana. A half-Kenyan, half-Kansan politician can self-identify as black and be elected president of the United States."

"Maybe it's time to admit the obvious. We don't really care about diversity all that much in America, even though we talk about it a great deal. . . . What I have seen all around the country is people making strenuous efforts to group themselves with people who are basically like themselves."

"[As a black man in my 20s, I've] incorporated into my daily life the sense that I might find myself up against a wall or on the ground with an officer's gun at my head."

"I realize that in recent years, profiling has become a dirty word, synonymous with prejudice, racism, and bigotry. But . . . in the debate I said,

'Profile me. Profile my family,' because, in my eyes, we in the Muslim community have failed to police ourselves."

"Can we reasonably expect Americans who are themselves collectively targets of surveillance and suspicion to trust the very agencies spying on them? . . . Rather than view law enforcement agencies as protectors, they are viewed as persecutors."

---

8 Family Affairs: Marriage in Flux 391

"Fundamental changes in the expectations, meanings, and practices defining American family life have characterized much of the twentieth century. . . . Consequently, concern about the family has moved to the center of the political arena."

"Share my life with this wonderful man, absolutely. But walk down the aisle and exchange rings—the tradition baffles me. I didn't expect my small refusal to matter much to anyone."

"Although some people hope to turn back the tide by promoting traditional values, making divorce harder, or outlawing gay marriage, they are having to confront a startling irony: The very factors that have made marriage more satisfying in modern times have also made it more optional."

"Words matter. They deeply affect us and others. Living with your 'boyfriend' is not the same as living with your 'husband.'. . . Likewise, when you introduce that person as your wife or husband to people, you are making a far more important statement of that person's role in your life than you are with any other title."

As same-sex couples march down the aisle in New York, Andrew Sullivan reflects on his own pursuit of happiness.

Alex Kuczynski

"We were not disturbed by the commercial aspect of surrogacy. A woman going through the risks of labor for another family clearly deserves to be paid. To me, imagining someone pregnant with the embryo produced by my egg and my husband's sperm felt more similar to organ donation, or I guess more accurately, organ rental. That was something I could live with."

Jay Newton-Small

"The sperm boom gives rise to a lot of complicated legal and medical questions. Could a remote biological heir seek a paternity declaration against a donor father and later make claims against Dad's estate? When a donor settles down and finally has kids he wants to raise, will those children want to meet their scattered tribe of half siblings?"

Einer Elhauge

"How does one address the terrible specter of a broccoli mandate? . . . Let us suppose one can concoct one by arguing that some hypothetical Congress might rationally think that the failure of some of us to eat broccoli makes us less healthy in a way that raises costs for others in our insurance pools. . . . Does this ensnare us in a logical trap, forcing us to modify existing constitutional limits, to add a ban on purchase mandates?"

Art Caplan

"Since most Americans say they do want to donate when they die . . . , and since most families, when asked, do consent to donation by a loved one, why the poor donor card rates? The answer, in part, is that the Department of Motor Vehicles is not the best agency to recruit organ donors. . . . Asking people to do something nice for others when they have been stewing in a long line, getting angrier and angrier while they wait is not conducive to altruism."

Martin Binks, PhD

"What role does blame play in our debate over placing obese children in foster care? While we are not technically blaming the obese child, could it still be seen as blaming a secondary victim, the obese child's parent for being unable to combat on behalf of their child, the very same contributors to obesity we all agree are out of the direct control of any individual?"

▶ **Childhood Obesity Warrants Removal of Child to Foster Care 469**

Susan Brady

Taking severely obese children away from their parents is a clear warning to parents about the consequences of parental actions. Losing your child to the system due to an inability or unwillingness to control their obesity is a real threat. But would it work? And is it right?

▶ **Why Fat Cannot Make You Unfit to Parent 470**

Summer Johnson McGee

"But will [a child's] health status be improved when he is yanked from his family and put into foster care? Almost certainly not, as studies have shown multiple negative mental and physical health consequences from being in foster care including 35% of children increasing their BMI while in foster care."

Rhetorical Contents

CAUSE AND EFFECT
Telling Why

Preface

Like its predecessors, the eleventh edition of *The Contemporary Reader* comprises many new readings and addresses several new issues. The nature of the subject matter covered necessitates constant updating to keep abreast of trends in popular culture, media, and society. However, despite such changes, the book's foundation remains the same: It continues to provide a collection of well-written, thought-provoking readings that students can relate to, readings that stimulate classroom discussion, critical thinking, and writing.

The Contemporary Reader, eleventh edition, is contemporary in more than just the selections. The introduction includes strategies for critical writing. Likewise, the apparatus reflects the latest and most effective rhetorical theories and practice. Preceding each reading is a headnote that helps orient the student to the topic and the reading. The critical thinking and writing questions following each essay help students process the text, encourage the flow of ideas, and promote class discussion. Where appropriate, we have included a directional cue in italics before certain writing questions, such as "Personal Narrative" or "Research and Analysis," to help students focus their critical writing. In Viewpoints articles, a feature continued in this edition, authors explore different aspects of the same issue.

What's New in the Eleventh Edition?

- **The introduction has been updated.** The introduction, "How to Read and Write Critically," has been updated with a new sample essay that is annotated, outlined, and analyzed in detail according to six proven steps for critical reading. As in the previous editions, this new introduction emphasizes the relationship between reading, thinking, and writing.

- **More than 40 new readings** have been added exploring a wealth of contemporary subjects, including selections from such noted writers as Robin Dunbar, danah boyd, Joseph Turow, Glenn Loury, and Peggy Orenstein.

- **Three new chapter themes** have been included. Chapter 4, "That's Entertainment? Amusing Ourselves"; Chapter 5, "The Social Animal: Connecting in a Digital World"; and Chapter 9, "Brave New World: What Can Science Do?" encourage class discussion and writing about today's important topics.

- **A new feature, "Modern Scholar,"** had been added. In response to requests, we have added a scholarly essay to each chapter on the respective topic. Many of these readings are drawn from scholarly journals and books and are designed to provide challenging readings for students' more analytical consideration of a topic or issue.

- **New images** appear in the widely assigned advertising chapter. Chapter 2 includes new ads. Each ad is supported with critical thinking questions that ask students to closely analyze the affects advertising has on our culture.

Chapter Topics

Although we have repeated or retooled the most popular chapters from the previous edition and added three new chapters, the themes of all the chapters were chosen to reflect a wide spectrum of issues that affect us all. Most importantly, they capture some of the conflicts and paradoxes that make our culture unique. From fashion and advertising to the cult of celebrity to medical ethics to the economy and family, ours is a culture caught in conflicts. We are a people who crave the modern yet yearn for the past. We harness technology to the hilt and reminisce about how things used to be simpler. We are as much a society steeped in traditional values and identities as we are one that redefines itself in response to trends and subcultures.

A Closer Look at Chapter Themes

The nine thematic chapters in this edition span issues that encourage students to consider their place in the world and their impact upon it. In many cases, topics in different chapters overlap an issue with another perspective. For example, some readings in the celebrity culture chapter address issues connected to gender, and pieces in the chapter on debt connect back to essays in the chapter on consumerism. A description of the contents, themes, and issues addressed in each chapter is featured at the beginning of the section.

Variety of Readings

In addition to extensively revising the chapter themes, we include many different types of readings. Expository communication comes in all shapes and models. This book includes newspaper stories, editorials, political cartoons, advertisements, academic essays, magazine articles, television interviews, Internet articles from "e-zines," student essays, humor columns, and a lot more. Students will read academic articles, personal narratives, objective essays, position papers, political arguments, and research reports.

Advertisements

Chapter 2, "Consumer Nation: Wanting It, Selling It," one of the most popular chapters in previous editions, has been updated with several new readings. Ads are accompanied by specific questions to help students closely analyze how advertising—and the particular ad at issue—affects us. The questions should spark lively class discussion about the art and craft of advertising. Beyond that, they encourage students to increase their visual literacy and critical thinking by closely focusing on particular print ads and making new associations and discoveries.

Viewpoints

The Viewpoints articles bring the traditional pro–con debates to a more focused level and aim to help students explore the different sides of a focused issue, such as body stereotyping, human cloning, or a particular aspect of advertising. The questions following these readings aim to help students consider multiple sides of an issue and move toward a collaborative discussion rather than a heated debate. In many cases, several points of view are presented to encourage discussion and exploration of the topic.

Culture Shock

Images are everywhere—and more and more, all of us need to be able to understand and evaluate those images critically. Images sell, they amuse, they provide information. The Culture Shock features found throughout this book reflect the kind of images that confront us every day—cartoons, advertisements, statistical maps, and charts—and the questions that accompany them encourage students to analyze the arguments being made visually and rhetorically.

Updated Introduction to Critical Reading and Writing

The premise of the new edition of *The Contemporary Reader* is that effective writing grows out of effective thinking, and effective thinking grows out of thoughtful reading. We intertwine these three concepts in the new introduction, featuring sections that discuss both critical reading and critical writing. The introductory chapter illustrates the process in a detailed, sample analysis of columnist Matt Ridley's essay, "Internet On, Inhibitions Off: Why We Tell All." The sample analysis demonstrates systematic approaches to critical reading and then continues this exploration into the Critical Writing section.

Critical Thinking and Critical Writing Considerations

Following each reading are critical thinking and critical writing questions that help students connect to the reading, analyze its points, and place themselves within the context of the issue. Writing assignments encourage students to expand their critical thinking, respond to the text, and research issues in greater depth.

Group Projects

Active communities work together, accepting multiple points of view and interacting with different identities, values, ideas, races, social outlooks, ethnicities, and educational backgrounds. In an effort to develop students' skills for working and learning together, and to expose them to different points of view, group projects accompany each reading. These exercises emphasize collaborative research, topic exploration, group writing, and problem solving. They also may encourage students to incorporate resources outside the classroom—to search the Internet, explore pop-culture sources, interview people, and conduct observations—to explore further what they have read.

Supplements

MyCompLab is Pearson's all-in-one online site for composition, with a wealth of interactive resources for writing, research, and grammar. Access to this site is available packaged with this Longman text at no additional cost, or it may be purchased at http://www.mycomplab.com. Longman's open access Web site for composition resources, http://www.longmancomposition.com, includes an array of materials about writing and research. Pearson English also offers many other supplementary items—some at no additional cost, some deeply discounted—that are available for packaging with this text. Please contact your local Pearson representative to find out more.

Instructor's Manual

The *Instructor's Manual* includes suggested responses to the critical reading questions in the text and offers ideas for directing class discussion and eliciting student response.

Acknowledgments

Many people behind the scenes deserve much acknowledgment and gratitude for their help with this edition. It would be impossible to thank all of them, but there are some for whose help I am particularly grateful. I would like to thank all the instructors and students who used the first ten editions of *The Contemporary Reader* and have remained loyal to its concept and content. Their continued support has made this latest edition possible. Also, I would like to thank those instructors who spent hours answering lengthy questionnaires on the effectiveness of the essays and who supplied many helpful comments and suggestions for the preparation of this new edition. For this edition, these include Cheryl R. Johnson, Lamar University; Cindy King, University of North Texas; Lisa Mott, Santa Rosa Junior College; John Panza,

Cuyahoga Community College; and Susan Van Rossum, Atlantic Cape Community College.

Foremost, I would like to thank Kathryn Goodfellow for her invaluable help in locating material, writing the apparatus, and putting together the *Instructor's Manual*. Her keen ability to identify topics and pieces that matter to today's students helped make this edition extraordinary. I would also like to thank Amy Trumbull for her help in securing permissions for the readings featured in this volume. Finally, my thanks to the people of Pearson, especially my editor, Katharine Glynn, who helped conceptualize this edition, her able assistant, Rebecca Gilpin, and Teresa Ward for her assistance in coordinating the Instructor's Manual.

Gary Goshgarian

The
Contemporary
Reader

Introduction
How to Read and Write Critically

What Is Critical Thinking?

Whenever you read a magazine article, newspaper editorial, or piece of advertising and find yourself questioning the author's claims, you are exercising the basics of critical reading. You are looking beneath the surface of words and thinking about their meaning and significance. And, subconsciously, you are asking the authors some of the following questions:

- What did you mean by that?
- Can you back up that statement?
- How do you define that term?
- How did you draw that conclusion?
- Do all the experts agree?
- Is this evidence dated?
- What is your point?
- Why do I need to know this?
- Where did you get your data?

You are also making some internal statements:

- That is not true.
- You are contradicting yourself.
- I see your point, but I do not agree because….
- That's a poor choice of words.
- You are jumping to conclusions.
- Good point. I never thought of that.
- That was nicely stated.
- This is an extreme view.

Whether conscious or unconscious, such responses indicate that you are thinking critically about what you read. You are weighing claims, asking for definitions, evaluating information, looking for proof, questioning assumptions, and making judgments. In short, you are processing another person's words, rather than just accepting them at face value.

Why Read Critically?

When you read critically, you think critically. Instead of blindly accepting what is written on a page, you begin to separate yourself from the text and decide for yourself what is or is not important, logical, or right. And you do so because you bring to your reading your own perspective, experience, education, and personal values, as well as your own powers of comprehension and analysis.

Critical reading is an active process of discovery. You discover an author's view on a subject, you enter into a dialogue with the author, you discover the strengths and weaknesses of the author's thesis or argument, and you decide whether you agree or disagree with the author's views. By questioning and analyzing what the author says with respect to other experiences or views of the issue, including your own, you actively enter into a dialogue or a debate and seek the truth on your own. The result is that you have a better understanding of the issue and the author.

In reality, we understand truth and meaning through interplay. Experience teaches us that knowledge and truth are not static entities but the by-products of struggle and dialogue—of asking tough questions. We witness this phenomenon all the time, recreated in the media through dialogue and conflict. And we recognize it as a force for social change. Consider, for example, how our culture has changed its attitudes concerning race and concepts of success, kinship, social groups, and class since the 1950s. Perhaps the most obvious example of changed attitudes regards gender: Were it not for the fact that old, rigid conventions have been questioned, most women would still be bound to the laundry and the kitchen stove.

The point is that critical reading is an active and reactive process that sharpens your focus on a subject and your ability to absorb information and ideas; at the same time, it encourages you to question accepted norms, views, and myths. And that is both healthy and laudable, for it is the basis of social evolution.

Critical reading also helps you become a better writer, because critical reading is the first step to critical writing. Good writers look at another's writing the way architects look at a house: They study the fine details and how those details connect and create the whole. Likewise, they consider the particular slants and strategies of appeal. Good writers always have a clear sense of their audience: their reader's social makeup, gender, and educational background; their political or religious persuasions; their values, prejudices, and assumptions about life; and so forth. Knowing your audience helps you to determine nearly every aspect of the writing process: the kind of language to use; the writing style, whether casual or formal, humorous or serious, technical or philosophical; the particular slant to take, appealing to the reader's reason, emotions, ethics, or a combination of these; what emphasis to give the essay; the type of evidence to offer; and the kinds of authorities to cite.

The better you become at analyzing and reacting to another's written work, the better you will analyze and react to your own. You will ask yourself questions such as the following: Is this argument logical? Do my points come across clearly? Are my examples solid enough? Is this the best wording? Is my conclusion persuasive? Do I have a clear sense of my audience? What strategy should I take: an appeal to logic, emotions, or ethics? In short, critical reading will help you to evaluate your own writing, thereby making you both a better reader and a better writer. Although you may already employ many strategies of critical reading, the following text presents some techniques to make you an even better critical reader.

How to Read Critically

To help you improve your critical reading, use these six proven, basic steps:

1. Keep a journal on what you read.
2. Annotate what you read.
3. Outline what you read.
4. Summarize what you read.
5. Question what you read.
6. Analyze what you read.

To demonstrate just how these techniques work, we will apply each of them to a sample essay, "Internet On, Inhibitions Off: Why We Tell All" by Matt Ridley, which appeared in the February 18, 2012 issue of *The Wall Street Journal*. This piece works well because, like all of the pieces in this book, it addresses a contemporary issue, namely, that online communication may alter our inhibitions, and presents opportunities for debate.

Internet On, Inhibitions Off: Why We Tell All
Matt Ridley

1   It is now well known that people are generally accurate and (sometimes embarrassingly) honest about their personalities when profiling themselves on social-networking sites. Patients are willing to be more open about psychiatric symptoms to an automated online doctor than a real one. Pollsters find that people give more honest answers to an online survey than to one conducted by phone.

2   But online honesty cuts both ways. Bloggers find that readers who comment on their posts are often harshly frank but that these same rude critics become polite if contacted directly. There's a curious pattern here that goes against old concerns over the threat of online dissembling. In fact, the mechanized medium of the Internet causes not concealment but disinhibition, giving us both confessional behavior and ugly brusqueness. When the medium is impersonal, people are prepared to be personal.

3   Arguably, the Catholic Church has long recognized this, which is why the confessor is separated from the priest by a grill or curtain. To get people to open up about themselves, psychoanalysts used to ask their patients to lie on a couch looking away from the doctor. Most of us have experienced the phenomenon whereby we

talk more freely about something intimate when walking or driving with a friend, facing forward in parallel. In interrogation scenes in movies, the interrogator often stands up and walks behind his victim at crucial moments in the conversation.

4   Why is this? Why do we become more honest the less we have to face each other? Posing the question may make the answer seem obvious—that we feel uncomfortable about confessing to or challenging others when face to face with them—but that begs the question: why? This is one of those cases where it is helpful to compare human beings with other species, to set our behavior in context.

5   In many monkeys and apes, face-to-face contact is essentially antagonistic. Staring is a threat. A baboon that fails to avert its eyes when stared at by a social superior is, in effect, mounting a challenge. Appeasing a dominant animal is an essential skill for any chimpanzee wishing to avoid a costly fight. Put two monkey strangers in a cage and they keep well apart, avoid eye contact and generally do their utmost to avoid triggering a fight. Put two people in an elevator and the same thing happens—with some verbal grooming to relieve the tension: "Cold out there today."

6   Deep in our psyches, the act of writing a furious online critique of someone's views does not feel like a confrontation, whereas telling them the same thing over the phone or face to face does. All the cues are missing that would warn us not to risk a revenge attack by being too frank.

7   The phenomenon has a name: the online disinhibition effect. John Suler of Rider University, who coined the phrase, points out that, online, the cues to status and hierarchy are also missing. Just like junior apes, junior people are reluctant to say what they really think to somebody with authority for fear of disapproval and punishment. "But online, in what feels like a peer relationship—with the appearances of 'authority' minimized—people are much more willing to speak out or misbehave."

8   Internet flaming and its benign equivalent, online honesty, are a surprise. Two decades ago, most people thought the anonymity of the online world would cause an epidemic of dishonesty, just as they thought it would lead to geeky social isolation. Then along came social networking, and the Internet not only turned social but became embarrassingly honest. The greatest perils most people perceive in their children's social networking are that they spend too much time being social and that they admit to things that will come back to haunt them when they apply for work. ◆

Keep a Journal on What You Read

Unlike writing an essay or a paper, journal writing is a personal exploration in which you develop your own ideas without set rules. It is a process of recording impressions and exploring feelings and ideas. Journal writing is a freewriting exercise in which you express yourself without restrictions and without judgment. You do not have to worry about breaking any rules, because in a journal, anything goes.

Reserve a special notebook just for your journal—not one you use for class notes or homework. Also, date your entries and include the titles of the articles to which you are responding. Eventually, by the end of the semester, you should have a substantial number of pages to review, enabling you to see how your ideas and writing style have developed over time.

What do you include in your journal? Although it may serve as a means to understanding an essay, you are not required to write only about the essay itself. Perhaps the article reminds you of a personal experience. Maybe it triggered an opinion you did not know you had. Or perhaps you wish to explore a particular phrase or idea presented by the author.

Some students may find keeping a journal difficult because it is so personal. They may feel as if they are exposing their feelings too much. Or they may feel uncomfortable thinking that someone else, perhaps a teacher or another student, may read their writing. Such apprehensions should not prevent you from exploring your impressions and feelings. If you must turn in your journal to your teacher, do not include anything you do not want others to read. Consider keeping a more private journal for your own benefit.

Reprinted below is one student's journal entry on our sample essay:

> After reading Matt Ridley's essay, originally published in *The Wall Street Journal*, I'm sure many people breathed a sigh of relief. I know I did. Maybe the information one reads on social media sites and blogs can actually be trusted. Maybe the personality profiles found on social networking sites like Facebook are more likely than not to accurately reflect the personality and background of the writer. Maybe the Facebook profile of new acquaintances accurately projects who these people are. According to Ridley's piece, people are generally open and honest on these sites.
>
> Ridley's article contains interesting examples of the way anonymity encourages honesty rather than deception. He points out that the impersonal nature of online communication even discourages inhibition. He makes interesting parallels between this and the Catholic confessional and the couch of the psychiatrist. In both cases, eye-to-eye communication is blocked. One is less aware of being judged and feels somehow safe to reveal what one might normally conceal.
>
> But if I were to advise my parents that they had no need to fear who I might meet online, I'm sure they would be extremely skeptical. And the more I think about it, they would be correct. Yes, as Ridley points out, people are more honest online whether in surveys or responses to blogs. But that doesn't preclude crazy or unethical or the dangerous people misusing information online.

Yes, I think Ridley's main idea that most normal people tend to be honest online is probably true. But one cannot generalize to include all people. I still say, beware. There are many people who deliberately use online communication to mislead, manipulate or even harm others. A healthy skepticism is still the best policy.

Annotate What You Read

It is a good idea to underline or highlight key passages and to make margin notes when reading an essay. If you do not own the publication in which the essay appears, or choose not to mark it up, make a photocopy of the piece and annotate that. You should annotate on the second or third reading, once you have an understanding of the essay's general ideas.

There are no specific guidelines for annotation. Use whatever technique suits you best, but keep in mind that in annotating a piece of writing, you are engaging in a dialogue with the author. As in any meaningful dialogue, you hear things you may not have known: things that may be interesting and exciting to you, things with which you may agree or disagree, or things that give you cause to ponder. The other side of the dialogue, of course, is your response. In annotating a piece of writing, that response takes the form of underlining or highlighting key passages and jotting down comments in the margin. Such comments can take the form of full sentences or shorthand codes. Sometimes "Why?" or "True" or "NO!" will be enough to help you respond to a writer's position or claim. If you come across a word or reference that is unfamiliar to you, underline or circle it. Once you have located the main thesis statement or claim, highlight or underline it and jot down "CLAIM" or "THESIS" in the margin.

The Ridley essay is reproduced here in its entirety with sample annotations.

Internet On, Inhibitions Off: Why We Tell All
Matt Ridley

1   It is now well known that people are generally accurate and (sometimes embarrassingly) honest about their personalities when profiling themselves on social-networking sites. Patients are willing to be more open about psychiatric symptoms to an automated online doctor than a real one. Pollsters find that people give more honest answers to an online survey than to one conducted by phone.

Opens with broad generalization. Not sure I agree.

I'd like to see supporting research. Suspect many exceptions.

Interesting!

2   But online honesty cuts both ways, Bloggers find that readers who comment on their posts are often harshly frank but that these same rude critics become polite if contacted directly. There's a curious pattern here that goes against old concerns over the threat of online dissembling. In fact, the mechanized medium of the Internet causes not concealment but disinhibition, giving us both confessional behavior and ugly brusqueness. When the medium is impersonal, people are prepared to be personal.

Do rude critics change ideas or opinions as well as attitude?

New idea rebuts old way of thinking.

Main thesis statement

Pithy statement. Paradoxical at first glance.

3   Arguably, the Catholic Church has long recognized this, which is why the confessor is separated from the priest by a grill or curtain. To get people to open up about themselves, psychoanalysts used to ask their patients to lie on a couch looking away from the doctor. Most of us have experienced the phenomenon whereby we talk more freely about something in parallel. In interrogation scenes in movies, the interrogator often stands up and walks behind his victim at crucial moments in the conversation.

Is this practice in the Catholic Church?

I disagree. Check friends if generally true.

4   Why is this? Why do we become more honest the less we have to face each other? Posing the question may make the answer seem obvious—that we feel uncomfortable about confessing to or challenging others when face to face with them—but that begs the question: why? This is one of those cases where it is helpful to compare human beings with other species, to set our behavior in context.

Rhetorical questions. Draws reader in.

Check definitions— "beg the question."

Check definition.

5   In many monkeys and apes, face-to-face contact is essentially antagonistic. Staring is a threat. A baboon that fails to avert its eyes when stared at by a social superior is, in effect, mounting a challenge. Appeasing a dominant animal is an essential skill for any chimpanzee wishing to avoid a costly fight, Put two monkey strangers in a cage and they keep well apart, avoid eye contact and generally do their utmost to avoid triggering a fight. Put two people in an elevator and the same thing happens—with some verbal grooming to relieve the tension: "Cold out there today."

Compares human behavior to other species. Vague references. Could use specific reference – studies, etc.

True!

6   Deep in our psyches, the act of writing a furious online critique of someone's views does not feel like a confrontation, whereas telling them the same thing over the phone or face to face does. All the cues are missing that would warn us not to risk a revenge attack by being too frank.

Parallel between animal and human behavior. But what are the clues?

7   The phenomenon has a name: the online disinhibition effect. John Suler of Rider University, who coined the phrase, points out that, online, the cues to status and hierarchy are also missing. Just like junior apes, junior people are reluctant to say what they really think to somebody with

Technical terminology.

Look up research of John Suler. Key to argument.

authority for fear of disapproval and punishment. "But online, in what feels like a peer relationship—with the appearances of 'authority' minimized—people are much more willing to speak out or misbehave."

8   Internet flaming and its benign equivalent, online honesty, are a surprise. Two decades ago, most people thought the anonymity of the online world would cause an epidemic of dishonesty, just as they thought it would lead to geeky social isolation. Then along came social networking, and the Internet not only turned social but became embarrassingly honest. The greatest perils most people perceive in their children's social networking are that they spend too much time being social and that they admit to things that will come back to haunt them when they apply for work.

Definition

Widely held belief debunked.

Not so sure.

Downside of too much honesty.

Outline What You Read

Briefly outlining an essay is a good way to see how writers structure their ideas. When you physically diagram the thesis statement, claims, and supporting evidence, you can better assess the quality of the writing and decide how convincing it is. You may already be familiar with detailed, formal essay outlines in which structure is broken down into main ideas and subsections. However, for our purposes, a brief and concise breakdown of an essay's components will suffice. This is done by simply jotting down a one-sentence summary of each paragraph. Sometimes brief paragraphs elaborating the same point can be lumped together:

- Point 1
- Point 2
- Point 3
- Point 4
- Point 5, etc.

Such outlines may seem rather primitive, but they demonstrate how the various parts of an essay are connected—that is, the organization and sequence of ideas.

Below is a sentence outline of "Internet On, Inhibitions Off: Why We Tell All." It identifies the points of each paragraph in an unbiased way. The purpose of summarizing is to better understand the author's point and how this point is constructed.

Point 1: The author provides three examples of individuals being more open and honest on online sites than in more traditional person-to-person interactions.

Point 2: When using online communication, which is inherently impersonal, people tend to be uninhibited. In these circumstances, people exhibit behavior that is sometimes confessional and at other times brusque if not rude.

Point 3: Four examples are given that illustrate communication that is open and uninhibited due to a mechanized or impersonal format of communication: (1) the Catholic confessional, (2) the psychoanalyst's couch, (3) conversation while walking without eye contact, and (4) interrogation scenes in movies.

Point 4: The author poses the question: Why is it easier to be honest when we do not have to face each another? He suggests that comparing human behavior to that of other species will put our behavior in context and thus enlighten us about this topic.

Point 5: The author cites patterns of animal behavior such as that of monkeys and apes and compares them to patterns of human behavior. For monkeys and apes, face-to-face contact is an antagonistic gesture and staring is a threat. Two monkeys in a cage will keep apart, avoid eye contact, and avoid the stare that could trigger a fight.

Point 6: The author follows the discussion of animal behavior with an explanation of human behavior and human attempts to avoid threats. Online communication omits the clues and warnings that face-to-face interaction might have. Thus, online, free of the cues from our audience, we feel no threat and, therefore, are free to unleash a harsher critique than we would in person.

Point 7: The author cites a name for this phenomenon: "online disinhibition effect," coined by John Suler of Rider University. Suler explains that online cues as to status and hierarchy are missing. Thus, the senses of fear of disapproval and punishment are minimized. People are willing to be more blunt, even misbehave.

Point 8: The author points out that with the introduction of the Internet came the fear that Internet communication would "cause an epidemic of dishonesty" and lead to "geeky social isolation." Instead, the opposite seems to be emerging in two extremes: Internet flaming and its benign equivalent, online honesty.

At this point, you should have a fairly solid grasp of the points expressed in the essay and the author's position on the issue. This exercise prepares you to critically evaluate the essay.

Summarize What You Read

Summarizing is perhaps the most important technique to develop for understanding and evaluating what you read. This means reducing the essay to its main points. In your journal or notebook, try to write a brief (about 100 words) synopsis of the reading in your own words. Note the claim or thesis of the discussion or argument and the chief supporting points. It is important to write these points down, rather than passively highlighting them with a pen or pencil, because the act of jotting down a summary helps you absorb the argument.

Now let us return to the sample essay. In the following paragraph, we offer a summary of Ridley's essay, mindful of using our own words rather than those of the author to avoid plagiarism. Again, you should approach this aspect of critical reading impartially: summary is not your opinion—that will come later. At times, it may be impossible to avoid using the author's own words in a summary; but if you do, remember to use quotation marks.

In this essay, Matt Ridley makes some general comments about the tone and content of online communication. Ridley observes two trends: When communicating online people tend to be more blunt and harsh in their remarks than they would be if they were communicating face-to-face with another person. On the other hand, people often tend to be more open and honest online than they might be one-on-one. Ridley refers to studies of animal behavior, pointing out how apes establish supremacy and threaten weaker group members by staring. Simple eye-to-eye contact subdues and inhibits the reactions of a would-be challenger. Online territory is completely neutral and contains no social cues to what kind of behavior is expected or to whom one is actually responding. This leads to the "online disinhibition effect," a term coined by John Suler of Rider University.

Although this paragraph seems to do a fairly good job of summarizing Ridley's essay, it took us a few tries to get it down to under 100 words. Do not be too discouraged when trying to summarize a reading on your own.

Question What You Read

Although we break down critical reading into discrete steps, these steps will naturally overlap in the actual process of reading and writing critically. In reading this essay, you were simultaneously summarizing and evaluating Ridley's points, perhaps adding your own ideas or even arguing with him. If something strikes you as particularly interesting or insightful, make a mental note of it. Likewise, if something strikes you the wrong way, argue back. For beginning writers, a good strategy is to convert that automatic mental response into actual note taking.

In your journal or in the margins of the text, question and challenge the writer. Jot down any points in the essay that do not measure up to your expectations or personal views. Note anything about which you are skeptical. Write down any questions you have about the claims, views, or evidence. If some point or conclusion seems forced or unfounded, record it and briefly explain why. The more skeptical and questioning you are, the better reader you are. Likewise, note what features of the essay impressed you: outstanding points and interesting wording, clever or amusing phrases or allusions, particular references, and the general structure of the piece. Record what you learned from the reading and the aspects of the issue you would like to explore.

Of course, you may not feel qualified to pass judgment on an author's views, especially if the author is a professional writer or an expert on a particular subject. Sometimes the issue discussed might be too technical, or you may not feel informed enough to make critical evaluations. Sometimes a personal narrative may focus on experiences completely alien to you. Nonetheless, you are an intelligent person with the instincts to determine whether the writing impresses you or whether an argument is sound, logical, and convincing. What you can do in such instances, and another good habit to get into, is to think of other views on the issue. If you have read or heard of experiences different from those of the author, or arguments with opposing views, jot them down. Similarly, if you agree with the author's view, highlight the parts of the essay with which you particularly identify.

Let us return to Ridley's essay. Although it is theoretically possible to question or comment on every sentence in the piece, let us select a few key points that may have struck you, made you question, or made you want to respond. Refer to your point-by-point outline to assist you in this exercise.

Paragraph 1: Ridley's essay opens with an endorsement of the assumption that people are more open and honest when communicating online or creating social-networking profiles. If one disagrees with this assumption, either because of personal experience or general knowledge, the entire premise of the piece is weakened. If, however, one agrees with this assumption,

Ridley's argument is more compelling. I personally question the honesty of people in the instances Ridley cites: social-networking sites, communication with online doctors, and responses to online pollsters.

Paragraph 2: Ridley makes an interesting point showing how conventional wisdom feared that Internet communication would be dishonest and withholding. He observes that the opposite has happened and that the Internet can be a place of brutally honest communication. Ridley's concluding sentence is concise and punchy, expressing the counterintuitive principle underlying his argument: "When the medium is impersonal, people are prepared to be personal."

Paragraph 3: Three examples of communication that avoid eye contact and, arguably, yield more honest responses. I find these examples to be familiar and convincing that the lack of face-to-face communication can enhance communication. But if one seriously considers each of these in any real depth, they seem shallow. One might be honest in a confessional because of ingrained religious convictions; but on a psychoanalyst's couch, one might make things up and even delude oneself; in the case of an interrogation, truth may emerge out of sheer terror and mental exhaustion. In other words, these situations are so complex that the way Ridley tosses them off seems rather oversimplified.

Paragraph 4: Here Ridley invites the reader into the discussion asking, "Why do we become more honest the less we have to face each other?" The obvious answer is we don't have to face each other, so we are more honest. He points out how this begs the question. According to the definition, "begging the question" is passing off as true an assumption that needs to be proven. How, in fact, can we prove that not facing one another makes us more honest? Ridley proposes to use examples comparing humans to other animal species to prove his point.

Paragraph 5: Now Ridley comes to the core proof of his argument. In this paragraph, he does not cite anecdotal evidence about honesty or the impulse to be brusque or even rude in the impersonal online world. Instead, to illustrate his point he references animal behavior patterns that parallel the human patterns of interaction. He points out that in the primate world, "face-to-face contact is essentially antagonistic. Staring is a threat." Monkeys in a cage will "keep well apart, avoid eye contact and generally do their utmost to avoid triggering a fight."

Paragraph 6: Extrapolating from the primate world example, Ridley explains that online we do not feel the threat of a face-to-face confrontation. We receive no clues of aggression from the person to whom we are responding. Thus we feel free to be more aggressive and assertive than if we were talking to an individual on a phone or in person.

Paragraph 7: To support his observations, Ridley makes reference to the work of John Suler of Rider University who coined the term "disinhibition effect." Ridley uses direct quotations from Suler's work. However, Ridley does not explore Suler's thinking in depth and leaves the reader wanting to know more about this phenomenon.

Paragraph 8: In concluding, Ridley points out the irony that what prognosticators feared most about online communication, dishonesty and geeky isolation, have not transpired. He ends on a comic note that "the greatest perils" of social networking are spending too much time socializing and admitting to things that could hinder future job searches.

Analyze What You Read

To analyze something means to break it down into its components, examine those components closely to evaluate their significance, and determine how they relate as a whole. In part, you already did this by briefly outlining the essay. However, there is more. Analyzing what you read involves interpreting and evaluating the points of a discussion or argument as well as its presentation—that is, its language and structure. Ultimately, analyzing an essay after establishing its key points will help you understand what may not be evident at first. A close examination of the author's words takes you beneath the surface and sharpens your understanding of the issues at hand.

Although there is no set procedure for analyzing a piece of prose, there are some specific questions you should raise when reading an essay, particularly one that is trying to sway you to its view:

- What kind of audience is the author addressing?
- What are the author's assumptions?
- What are the author's purpose and intentions?
- How well does the author accomplish those purposes?
- How convincing is the evidence presented? Is it sufficient and specific? Relevant? Reliable and not dated? Slanted?
- What types of sources were used: personal experience, outside authorities, factual references, or statistical data?
- Did the author address opposing views on the issue?
- Is the perspective of the author persuasive?

Using the essay by Ridley once more, let us apply these questions to his article.

What Kind of Audience Is the Author Addressing?

Before the first word is written, a good writer considers his or her audience—that is, their age group, gender, ethnic and racial makeup, educational background, and socioeconomic status. Writers also take into account the values, prejudices, and assumptions of their readers, as well as their readers' political and religious persuasions. Some writers, including several in this book, write for a target audience of readers who share the same interests, opinions, and prejudices. Other authors write for a general audience. Although general audiences consist of very different people with diversified backgrounds, expectations, and standards, think of them as the people who read *TIME, Newsweek,* and your local newspaper. You can assume general audiences are relatively well informed about what is going on in the country, that they have a good comprehension of language and a sense of humor, and that they are willing to listen to new ideas.

Because Ridley's essay appeared in his column entitled "Mind and Matter" in *The Wall Street Journal,* he is clearly writing for particular audience. According to a 2007 report from that newspaper, the average age of its readership is 53; most readers hold college degrees; and nearly 50 percent are female. It is also known that most readers are well-informed, spanning the politically liberal to moderately conservative. A close look tells us more about Ridley's audience:

1. The language suggests at least a high school education and most likely a college education.

2. The references to the "old concerns over the threat of online dissembling" and the reference in the closing line of the essay to parents of children involved in social networking suggest a mature audience of 35 years old and beyond.

3. The references to evolving social attitudes toward the Internet, traditions in the Catholic church, practices in modern psychotherapy, anthropological research, as well as academic studies imply that the readers are culturally informed.

4. The slant of Ridley's remarks assumes an open-minded and critically thinking reader who enjoys challenging conventionally held ideas.

5. The level of language takes for granted a highly educated, well-read, and curious audience capable of skepticism and independent thinking. They will listen to Ridley and may or may not agree with him.

What Are the Author's Assumptions?

Having a sense of the audience leads writers to certain assumptions. If a writer is addressing a general to a highly educated audience, as Ridley is, then he or she can assume certain levels of awareness about language and current events, certain values about education and morality, and certain nuances of an argument. After going through Ridley's essay, the following conclusions might be drawn about the author:

1. Ridley assumes that his readers have a familiarity with the history of the Internet. He also assumes his readers are knowledgeable about the various debates regarding the benefits and dangers of social networking, of addiction to online activities, and the impact of online communication on the nature and style of human communication.

2. Ridley assumes his readers are well educated and read widely.

3. Ridley assumes his readers are highly curious and enjoy synthesizing material from different fields such as science,

anthropology, primate research, religious customs, and psychotherapy to explain everyday human behavior.

4. Ridley assumes his readers are familiar with academic research
   and he is able to casually allude to the work of John Suler at
   Rider University.

5. Ridley assumes his readers are curious about the nature of online
   communication but that they are not extremist in their views.
   They do not see online communication as a threat, nor do they
   view it as perfection. They are open-minded and somewhat detached in their approach to analysis. There is no sense that he is
   addressing an audience with extreme or radical views.

What Are the Author's Purposes and Intentions?

A writer has a purpose in writing that goes beyond wanting to show up in print.
Sometimes it is simply the expression of how the writer feels about something;
sometimes the intent is to convince others to see things in a different light; sometimes the purpose is to persuade readers to change their views or behavior. We
might infer that Ridley intends:

1. To inform his readers how past fears that the impersonal nature
   of online communication would result in dishonesty and misrepresentation have not materialized.

2. To make the observation that online communication today tends
   to be honest (people are generally honest when profiling themselves on social-networking sites) and that communication can
   also be candid to the point of being "harshly frank" (called online
   flaming) and producing an "ugly brusqueness."

3. To explain why humans tend to be more honest when not in face-
   to- face contact.

4. To compare the behavior of human beings with that of other species such as primates for whom face-to-face contact is antagonistic
   and a means of establishing dominance and control.

5. To introduce the term "online disinhibition effect" coined by John
   Suler of Rider University.

How Well Does the Author Accomplish Those Purposes?

Determining how well an author accomplishes such purposes may seem subjective, but in reality it comes down to how well the case is presented. Is the thesis clear? Is it organized and well presented? Are the examples sharp and convincing? Is the author's conclusion a logical result of what came before? Returning to Ridley's essay, let us apply these questions:

1. Ridley's driving purpose is to explain why humans are more honest when they do not have to face one another and feel uncomfortable when challenging others face-to-face. Every point he makes is done to illuminate this purpose.

2. Ridley offers many examples to prove his points, calling on general cultural knowledge, primate studies, academic works, and commonsense observations. He refers to so many different sources and studies that the examples are intriguing but sometimes diluted.

3. Ridley's writing style is packed with information, robust, and always interesting.

4. Occasionally the linkage between Ridley's main points and the examples given is weak. The reader must fill in a lot of information.

How Convincing Is the Evidence Presented? Is It Sufficient and Specific? Relevant? Reliable and Not Dated? Slanted?

Convincing writing depends on convincing evidence; that is, it depends on sufficient and relevant facts along with proper interpretations of facts. Facts—such as statistics, examples, personal experience, expert testimony, and historical details— are pieces of information that can be verified. A proper interpretation of the facts must be logical and supported by relevant data. For instance, it is a disturbing fact that the national average for SAT verbal scores for the high school class of 2011 fell three points to 497, the lowest on record. One reason might be that students are spending less time reading and more time socially networking online or watching TV than in the past. Whatever the reasons, without hard statistics that document the viewing habits of a sample of students, such interpretations are shaky: the result of a writer jumping to conclusions.

Is the Evidence Sufficient and Specific? Writers routinely use evidence, but sometimes it may not be sufficient. Sometimes the conclusions reached have too little evidence to be justified. Sometimes writers make hasty generalizations based solely on personal experience as evidence. How much evidence is enough? It is hard to say, but the more specific the details, the more convincing the argument. Instead of generalizations, good writers cite figures, dates, and facts. Instead of paraphrasing information, they quote the experts verbatim.

Is the Evidence Relevant? Good writers select evidence based on how well it supports their thesis, not on how interesting, novel, or humorous it is. For instance, if you are claiming that Alex Rodriguez is the greatest living baseball player, you should not mention that he was born in New York City, went to high school in Miami, and dated Madonna and Cameron Diaz. Those are facts, and they are very interesting, but they have nothing to do with Rodriguez's athletic abilities. Irrelevant evidence distracts readers and weakens an argument.

Is the Evidence Reliable and Current? Evidence should not be so dated or vague that it fails to support your claim. For instance, it is not accurate to say that candidate Jones fails to support the American worker because 15 years ago she purchased a foreign car. Her current actions are more important. Readers expect the information writers provide to be current and specific enough to be verifiable. A writer supporting animal rights may cite cases of rabbits blinded in drug research, but such tests have been outlawed in the United States for many years. Another may point to medical research that appears to abuse human subjects, while it fails to name the researchers, the place, or the year of such testing. Because readers may have no way of verifying the evidence, the claims become suspicious and will weaken your point.

Is the Evidence Slanted? Sometimes writers select evidence that supports their case and ignore evidence that does not. Often referred to as "stacking the deck," this practice is unfair and potentially self-defeating for a writer. Although some evidence presented may have merit, an argument will be dismissed if readers discover that evidence was slanted or suppressed. For example, suppose you heard a classmate state that he would never take a course with Professor Sanchez because she gives surprise quizzes, assigns 50 pages of reading a night, and does not grade on a curve. Even if these statements are true, that may not be the whole truth. You might discover that Professor Sanchez is a dynamic and talented teacher whose classes are stimulating. Withholding that information may make an argument suspect. A better strategy is to acknowledge counterevidence and to confront it—that is, to strive for a balanced presentation by raising views and evidence that may not be supportive of your own.

Let us take a look at the evidence in Ridley's essay, applying some of the points we have just covered.

1. Ridley is writing a general information and opinion piece. He is making observations and connections to entertain and inform his readership. He is not writing an academic essay, nor is he using so-called hard or scientific evidence. Thus, is it useful to evaluate

the evidence he does use, keeping in mind that this is a tour de force of creative connection, not a scientific thesis. Nevertheless, let's look at some of the evidence he does use and the way he uses it. In his opening paragraph, Ridley makes the point that "people are accurate and . . . honest" about their personality profiles on social-networking sites; patients are more open with online doctors than real ones; and people are more honest on polls conducted on the phone. All these are given as evidence. Yet note that none of these claims is supported with reference to particular studies or outside sources. These are widely accepted beliefs—yet beliefs that could be challenged. These claims are persuasive but not conclusive and could certainly be challenged.

2. Notice the examples Ridley gives in paragraph 2 regarding instances where a certain degree of anonymity ensures truth telling—e.g., Catholic confessional, the psychoanalyst's couch, and interrogation techniques. These are very general pieces of evidence based on cultural knowledge—evidence a typical reader of Ridley's column would be familiar with and would accept without extensive proof.

3. Ridley is not arguing with his reader but rather putting together a range of information that cleverly and creatively supports his ideas.

4. Ridley's use of evidence falters in the section describing primate behaviors. Here the reader might like some reference to the sources for this information such as well-known books, articles, or journals on animal behavior. References to scientists and supporting research would be helpful. The reader might take Ridley's word that face-to-face contact is antagonistic in the primate world. However, if names of books, studies, or authors were provided, someone wanting verification or more information would have resources to consult.

5. Ridley's argument is logical, nonemotional, and one-sided in the sense that he does not entertain or introduce opposing points of view.

6. Ridley's argument works not because any one particular piece of evidence is totally convincing, but because the accumulation of multiple pieces of evidence is convincing.

7. A tone of confidence and wide-ranging exploration of ideas infuses the essay.

What Types of Sources Were Used: Personal Experience, Outside Authorities, Factual References, or Statistical Data?

Writers enlist four basic kinds of evidence to support their views or arguments: (1) *personal testimony* (theirs and others'), (2) *outside authorities,* (3) *factual references and examples,* and (4) *statistics.* In your own writing, you should aim to use combinations of these.

Personal testimony cannot be underestimated. Think of the books you have read or movies you have seen based on word-of-mouth recommendations. (Maybe you learned of the school you are attending through word of mouth.) Personal testimony, which provides eyewitness accounts not available to you or to other readers, is sometimes the most persuasive kind of evidence. Suppose you are writing about the rising abuse of alcohol on college campuses. In addition to statistics and hard facts, quoting the experience of a first-year student who nearly died one night from alcohol poisoning would add dramatic impact. Although personal observations are useful and valuable, writers must not draw hasty conclusions based only on such evidence. The fact that you and a few friends are in favor of replacing letter grades with a pass-fail system does not provide support for the claim that the student body at your school is in favor of the conversion.

Outside authorities are people recognized as experts in a given field. Appealing to such authorities is a powerful tool in writing, particularly for writers wanting to persuade readers of their views. We hear it all the time: "Scientists have discovered . . . ." "Scholars inform us that . . . ." "According to his biographer, Abraham Lincoln . . . ." Although experts try to be objective and fair-minded, their testimony may be biased. You would not expect scientists working for tobacco companies to provide unbiased opinions on lung cancer. And remember to cite who the authorities behind the statements are. It is not enough to simply state "scientists conducted a study"; you must say *who* they were, *where* the study was conducted, and even who paid for it.

Factual references and examples do as much to inform as to persuade. If somebody wants to sell you something, they will pour on the details. Think of the television commercials that show a sports utility vehicle climbing rocky mountain roads as a narrator lists all its great standard features: four-wheel drive, alloy wheels, second-generation airbags, power brakes, cruise control, and so on. Or cereal "infomercials" in which manufacturers explain that new Yummy-Os have 15 percent more fiber to help prevent cancer. Although readers may not have the expertise to determine which data are useful, they are often convinced by the sheer weight of the evidence, like courtroom juries judging a case.

Statistics impress people. Saying that 77 percent of your school's student body approves of women in military combat roles is much more persuasive than saying "a lot of people" do. Why? Because statistics have a no-nonsense authority. Batting averages, polling results, economic indicators, medical and FBI statistics, and demographic percentages are all reported in numbers. If accurate, they are persuasive, although they can be used to mislead. The claim that 139 people on campus protested the appearance of a certain controversial speaker may be accurate; however, it would be a distortion of the truth not to mention that another 1,500 people attended the talk and gave the speaker a standing ovation. Likewise, the manufacturer who claims that its potato chips are fried in 100 percent cholesterol-free vegetable oil misleads the public, because vegetable oil does not contain cholesterol, which is found only in animal fats. That is known as the "bandwagon" use of statistics, appealing to what people want to hear.

Now let us briefly examine Ridley's sources of evidence:

1. The premise of Ridley's argument is that the average person is less inhibited and more forthright when communicating online than he/she would be in a face-to-face situation. To establish this premise, Ridley uses personal testimony in a generalized sense. He does not draw on the personal testimony of a particular individual, but that of the general public. For instance, he cites the notion that patients are more open to online doctors and more open with online pollsters. These examples establish the thesis of his essay.

2. Later in the piece, Ridley uses commonly held cultural examples to illustrate the power of impersonal settings to encourage openness—the Catholic confessional and the psychoanalyst's couch.

3. Ridley supports his point by citing factual references and examples from animal research. This is the core of his argument. However, had he cited particular studies or named researchers, his argument would have been stronger.

4. He further supports his thesis by citing the work of academic John Suler of Rider University. He quotes Rider offhandedly, "But

online, in what feels like a peer relationship—with the appearances of 'authority' minimized—people are much more willing to speak out or misbehave." Notice how Ridley initially paraphrases Suler's ideas and then inserts a quotation with imprecise attribution.

5. Ridley does not use statistical data, though such evidence is always useful.

Did the Author Address Opposing Views on the Issue?

Many of the essays in this book will, in varying degrees, try to persuade you to agree with the author's position. But any slant on a topic can have multiple points of view. In developing their ideas, good writers will anticipate different and opposing views. They will cite alternative opinions and maybe even evidence that does not support their position. By treating alternative points of view fairly, writers strengthen their own position. Failing to present or admit other views could leave their perspective open to scrutiny, as well as to claims of naïveté and ignorance. This is particularly damaging when discussing a controversial issue.

Let us see how Ridley's essay addresses alternative points of view:

1. Ridley demonstrates how attitudes toward online communication have changed. He cites an opposing view though one he is careful to point out was in vogue two decades ago and has since been proven inaccurate: "Two decades ago, most people thought the anonymity of the online world would cause an epidemic of dishonesty, just as they thought it would lead to geeky social isolation. Then along came social networking, and the Internet not only turned social but became embarrassingly honest."

2. Other than this example meant to establish historical context, Ridley does not introduce alternative points of view into his column. It is, after all, a column based on his opinion.

Is the Perspective of the Author Persuasive?

Style and content make for persuasive writing. Important points are how well a paper is composed—the organization, logic, quality of thought, presentation of evidence, use of language, tone of discussion—and the details and evidence. Turning to Ridley's essay, we might make the following observations:

1. Ridley presents his argument well. The essay appeared in *The Wall Street Journal*, so Ridley assumes his readers are well-educated and interested in current cultural trends. To inform and entertain them, he refers to various forms of evidence that his readers should find interesting.

2. The kinds of evidence Ridley references tend to be general in nature. Those on animal studies are not documented or specified. If one wanted to do some follow-up reading on the subject, the source would not be available. Similarly, the reference to the work of John Suler is not documented.

3. Ridley relies to some extent on the authority of his voice. Because his discussion is general in nature, he can assume his readers trust in his expertise.

4. Ridley's style of writing is clear, concise, and engaging. The title of the piece "Internet On, Inhibitions Off: Why We Tell All," illustrates the lively and punchy quality of his prose.

By now you should have a fairly clear idea of how critical reading can improve your comprehension of a work and make you a better writer in the process. Make critical reading part of your daily life, not just something you do in the classroom or while studying. For example, as you wait for the bus, look at some billboards and consider how they try to hook their audience. While watching TV, think about the techniques advertisers use to convince you to buy their products. Try to apply some of the elements of critical reading as you peruse the articles and editorials in your favorite magazine or newspaper. The more you approach reading with a critical eye, the more natural it will become, and the better writer you will be.

What Is Critical Writing?

Critical writing is a systematic process. When following a recipe, you would not begin mixing ingredients together haphazardly. Instead, you would first gather your ingredients and equipment and then combine the ingredients according to the recipe. Similarly, in writing, you would not plan, write, edit, and proofread all at the same time. Rather, writing occurs one thoughtful step at a time.

Some writing assignments may require more steps than others. An in-class, freewriting exercise may allow for only one or two steps: light planning and writing. An essay question on a midterm examination may permit enough time for only three steps: planning, writing, and proofreading. A simple plan for such an assignment need answer only two questions: What am I going to say and how am I going to develop my idea convincingly? For example, suppose you are asked to answer the following question: Do you agree with Ridley's assertion in "Internet On, Inhibitions Off: Why We Tell All" that the impersonal nature of online communication leads to greater honesty and that this honesty might be in the form of Internet flaming or its benign equivalent, online honesty? You might decide to answer with the statement, "His observations about why we are honest on the Internet are convincing. But he seems to dismiss the real dangers of Internet flaming or uninhibited and angry online communication, which can be very tasteless and cruel." Or you could decide to answer, "Ridley seems to assume social networking has made the Internet a safer and more benign place than it really is. Online bullying, for example, is still rampant." You could then develop your idea by comparing or contrasting your own experiences in school with Internet flaming, or by presenting data or information that challenges or supports his argument.

A longer, out-of-class paper allows you to plan and organize your material and to develop more than one draft. In this extended version of the writing process, you will need to do the following to create a strong, critical paper:

- Develop your ideas into a focused thesis that is appropriate for your audience.
- Research pertinent sources.
- Organize your material and draft your paper.
- Proofread your paper thoroughly.

These are the general steps that every writer goes through when writing a paper. In the following sections, the use of these strategies will be discussed to help you write most effectively.

Developing Ideas

Even the most experienced writers sometimes have trouble getting started. Common problems you may encounter include focusing your ideas, knowing where to begin, having too much or too little to say, and determining your position on an issue. Developmental strategies can help promote the free expression of your ideas and make you more comfortable with writing.

Although your finished product should be a tightly focused and well-written essay, you can begin the writing process by being free and sloppy. This approach allows your ideas to develop and flow unblocked onto your paper. Writing techniques such as brainstorming, freewriting, and ballooning can help you through the development process. As with all writing strategies, you should try all of them at first to discover which ones work best for you.

Brainstorming

The goal of brainstorming is to generate and focus ideas. Brainstorming can be a personal exercise or a group project. Begin with a blank sheet of paper or a blackboard and—without paying attention to spelling, order, or grammar—simply list ideas about the topic as they come to you. You should spend at least 10 minutes brainstorming, building on the ideas you write down. There are no dumb ideas in brainstorming: the smallest detail may turn into a great essay.

Let us assume, for example, that you decide to write a paper supporting Ridley's assertion in "Internet On, Inhibitions Off: Why We Tell All." Brainstorming for a few minutes may provide something like this:

- Ridley dismisses the fear of two decades ago that the online world would be a place of geeky isolation. But isn't that still a major problem?

- Also, Ridley makes it sound that because of social networking most online honesty is, as he says, "embarrassingly honest" but not cruel or brutal. I still see a huge amount of cruelty online. Find newspaper articles to support. Sensational cases in which tormented victims of online bullying or exposure committed suicide.

- Look up the term "Internet flaming."

- Ask classmates if they experience the "online disinhibition effect."

- Headlines include many stories about Internet bullying leading in some cases to suicide. Ridley doesn't address any of this.

- Ridley focuses on what causes one to be uninhibited online. If possible, try to find some of the animal studies he refers to.

- Read John Suler's article and see if he finds the Internet as benign a place as Ridley. I found Suler's article listed as Suler, J. (2004). *CyberPsychology and Behavior*, 7, 321–326.

- Check with fellow students to find out if they instantly understood the references to the Catholic confessional, the psychoanalyst's couch, and interrogation strategies.

- Do students find it easier to harshly critique another student's paper online as opposed to face to face in the classroom?

You may notice that this brainstorming example has little structure and no apparent order. Its purpose is to elicit all the ideas you have about a subject, so you can read your ideas and identify an interesting topic to develop.

Freewriting

Like brainstorming, freewriting is a free expression of ideas. It helps you jump-start the writing process and get things flowing on paper. Freewriting is unencumbered by rules—you can write about your impressions, ideas, and reactions to the article or essay.

You should devote about 10 minutes to freewriting, keeping in mind that the goal is to write about the topic as ideas occur to you. If you are writing on a particular topic or idea, you may wish to note it at the top of your paper as a visual reminder of your focus. Structure, grammar, and spelling are not important—just focus on the free flow of ideas. Above all, do not stop writing, even if you feel that what you are writing is silly or irrelevant. Any one idea, or a combination of ideas, can be developed into a thoughtful essay. The following is an example of a freewriting exercise:

In this essay Ridley is presenting an opinion about the nature of online communication. He focuses on the fact that people are more honest when communicating online. He attributes this to the fact that online communication is impersonal. No direct face-to-face meeting or confrontation tempers one's response. In this impersonal format, one can be brutally honest, often referred to as "Internet flaming." Or according to Ridley one might be benignly honest. I found this interesting. But it seems that Ridley overlooks the more brutal aspects of online flaming. In fact he never addresses it. Having followed many news stories recently in which victims of online bullying have committed suicide and having seen the surge in anti-bullying campaigns I wondered why Ridley didn't pay a little more attention to this. I also know of efforts in Congress to introduce bills that would make Internet flaming and harassment a felony. I would have to say however, that Ridley provided fascinating background material as to "why we are more honest the less we have to face each other." His examples of how various primates intimidate and control one another simply by virtue of their fierce stares was instructive. It made me think about how all the subtle clues—glances, gestures, facial expressions—that cue us about how to react to another. I thought Ridley's piece was most successful in analyzing why we are uninhibited in our online communication. But

I felt he was less successful in evaluating the consequences of this uninhibited behavior. At the end of the essay he points out that all parents need to worry about regarding their children's online communication is that they spend too much time being social and might say things that will haunt them when applying for work. I think every one would agree that the Internet is not all that benign. In fact it can be a nasty place.

Ballooning

There are many names for ballooning, including *mind mapping, clustering,* or *grouping.* These techniques all provide a more graphic presentation of ideas, allowing writers to visualize ideas and the connections that stem from them. Ballooning is particularly effective if you already have a fairly clear idea about your topic and wish to develop it more fully.

Write your main topic in the center of a large sheet of paper or a blackboard and circle it. Using the circled idea as your focus, think of subtopics and place them in circles around the center circle, connecting them to each other with radiating lines; remember to keep the subtopics short. Continue doing this until you feel you have developed all the subtopics more fully. When you have finished this exercise, you should be able to visualize the connections between your main topic and its subpoints, which will provide a starting point for your essay.

Narrowing the Topic

Although brainstorming, freewriting, and ballooning help list and develop general ideas, you still need to narrow one idea down to something more manageable. Narrowing a topic can be quite a challenge: you might like more than one idea, or you may be afraid of limiting yourself to only one concept. Nevertheless, you must identify one idea and focus on developing it into an essay. Choose an idea that will interest you and your audience. Remember that if you do not like the way one idea begins to develop, you can always go back and develop another one instead. Once you identify your topic, you are ready to develop the thesis statement for your essay.

Based on the freewriting exercise described earlier, and additional idea development using ballooning techniques, we will follow a student who has decided to write her paper on the serious consequences of lack of inhibition on the Internet. The idea stems from a response to Ridley's essay, but it will develop into a thesis that uniquely belongs to the student.

Identifying Your Audience

Identifying your audience is one of the most important steps in organizing your essay. Knowing what your audience needs and expects from your essay will help you compose a convincing, effective paper. The following questions can help you identify the expectations of your audience:

- Who is my audience?
- What do they already know about my topic?
- What questions do they have about my topic?
- What do they need to know to understand my point?
- What is the best order in which to present information?
- How do they feel about this topic?
- Why would they want to read my essay?

Based on these questions, our student determined that her audience would be her teacher and fellow expository writing classmates. All of them would be familiar with Ridley's article and would have discussed it to some extent in class. As members of an academic institution as well as users of the Internet, social media, and all kinds of online communication, they should be familiar with the points Ridley makes about online communication and issues of Internet flaming as well as confessional-like honesty. The intended audience may also have different opinions on the issue, so supporting evidence—both from Ridley's article and some outside research—would be necessary to help our student make her point effectively. Because the essay would be about an issue that directly concerns both teachers and students, it should generate some level of personal interest to engage readers.

Developing a Thesis

A **thesis** is a type of contract between the writer and reader. It makes a claim or declaration and tells your audience exactly what you are going to discuss. It should be stated in the opening paragraph with the rest of the paper developing and supporting it.

As you write and develop your paper, your thesis should guide you as clearer and more precise thoughts evolve. Do not be constrained by your first thesis: If your paper is changing as you write, your thesis may change. Remember to go back and revise the thesis so that it matches the points made in your essay.

Although the thesis represents the last step in developing the topic for your essay, it is only the beginning of the actual writing process. For her paper, our student worked out the following sentence to help develop her thesis:

The effect of inhibition on online communication is a double-edged sword. Inhibition can foster benign honesty and openness on social media like Facebook. On the other hand, inhibition can unleash vitriolic and caustic diatribes often referred to as Internet flaming. More needs to be done to sensitize young people as to the damage done online by remarks or reactions qualifying as harassment, bullying, and even harsh criticism. Such cruelty, even disguised as humor, can have devastating even deadly effects.

Understanding Your Paper's Objective

Before determining how to research or organize your paper, consider what you are trying to achieve by writing it. Your objective may be *to inform*, *to describe*, or *to persuade*. To define your purpose, you should first determine your objective and then identify what you need to do to accomplish this objective. This helps you determine what you need to put in the body of your paper.

Writing to inform involves anticipating the questions your audience may have regarding the topic and how much background they will need to understand it. Once you have developed a list of questions, you can determine what order will best present the information that will answer these questions.

Writing to describe also involves answering some questions. First, you must identify what is important or relevant about the topic you intend to describe. Then you should determine what information is vital to conveying what is important. List these elements and order them in a way that presents a clear view of the experience to the reader.

Writing to persuade presents a perspective on an issue and attempts to convince readers to agree with it. You must provide reasons and supporting evidence to persuade your audience that your perspective makes sense. Although you might not sway all readers to your point of view, you should make enough of a case to allow them to understand your argument, even if they might not agree with it.

The first step in persuasive writing is to determine your position and to identify the objections others might have to it. Remember that there are many different reasons readers may not agree with you. By identifying the arguments against your position, you are better able to address them and thus support your own argument in the process. Three primary kinds of arguments are used in persuasive writing:

1. *Arguments based on disputed facts or consequences*, such as the claim that the building of a gambling casino generated revenue for a bankrupt town, created jobs, and improved the quality of life there.
2. *Arguments that advocate change*, such as arguing for a lower drinking age or changing how the penal system punishes juvenile offenders.
3. *Arguments based on evaluative personal claims*, as right or wrong, ethical or immoral, or favoring one thing or idea over another—such as arguing that physician-assisted suicide is wrong or that supermodels contribute to the development of anorexia nervosa in young women.

The key to effective persuasive writing is to support your perspective with statistics, factual data, and examples. Although your opinions drive the essay, your supporting evidence is what convinces your audience of the validity of your main point.

Researching

Research can involve a few or many steps, depending on the type and length of the paper you are writing. In many cases, simply reviewing the article and applying the steps of critical reading will be the final step you take before organizing your paper. For longer research papers that require outside sources, you will probably need to tap into library resources or look for information online.

Research may even involve taking surveys and conducting interviews. For her paper on the dangers of uninhibited communication online, our student decided to find John Suler's article, locate a primate study that Ridley might have referred to, and interview fellow students about their online experiences.

Selecting Sources for Your Paper

The best place to look for sources for your paper is the library, either at your local library or online. Most libraries have their holdings archived on electronic cataloging systems that let you look up books by author, title, and subject. Although books are a rich source of information, they can be dated and are sometimes inappropriate for essays addressing contemporary issues. For such papers, journals and periodicals are better. With all the different ways to do research, gathering useful and appropriate information can be overwhelming. Do not be afraid to ask the librarian for help.

For many people, the Internet has become the first avenue of research on a topic, and it can be an extremely useful way to locate information on contemporary issues. In addition to Web sites, newsgroups and bulletin boards can aid your research process. Remember that the Internet is largely unregulated, so you should surf the Web with the careful eye of a critic. Simply because something is posted online does not mean it is accurate or truthful. Whenever possible, take steps to verify your sources. When you do find a good source, write it down immediately. Many students lament the loss of a valuable resource, because they forgot to write down the title of the book or Internet address. A good technique is to write down your sources on index cards, which allow you to add sources, and to arrange them alphabetically, without having to rewrite, as you would with a list. You can also write down quotes for your paper on these cards for quick retrieval, and use them to help write the Works Cited section at the end of your essay.

Documenting Sources

Sources help support your ideas and emphasize your points. It is very important to cite any sources you use in your essay. Whether you quote, paraphrase, or use an idea from another source, you must identify the source of information. Documenting sources gives credit to the person who did the work, and it helps locate information on your topic. Even if you rewrite information in your own words, you must still document the source, because it is *borrowed* information. Failure to document your sources is called **plagiarism,** which is presenting someone else's work as your own, and it is considered a form of theft by most academic institutions. The following checklist should help you determine when to document your sources:

- When using someone's exact words
- When presenting someone else's opinion
- When paraphrasing or summarizing someone else's ideas
- When using information gathered from a study
- When citing statistics or reporting the results of research that is not your own

It is *not* necessary to cite dates, facts, or ideas considered common knowledge.

Organizing Your Paper

There are many ways to organize your paper. Some students prefer to use the standard outline technique, complete with Roman numerals and indented subpoints. Other students prefer more flexible flowcharts. The key to organizing is to define your focus and plan how to support your thesis statement from point to point in a logical order.

Drafting Your Essay

When writing your essay, think of your draft as a work in progress. Your objective should be to present your ideas in a logical order; you can address spelling, grammar, and sentence structure later. If you get stuck writing one paragraph or section, go on and work on another. Depending on how you write, you may choose to write your draft sequentially; or you may choose to move from your thesis to your body paragraphs, leaving your introduction and conclusion for last. Feel free to leave gaps, or write notes to yourself in brackets, to indicate areas to develop later when revising. Do not make the mistake of thinking that your first draft has to be your final draft. Remember that writing is a process of refinement—you can always go back and fix things later.

Writing Your Introduction

For many students, the hardest part of writing an essay is drafting the first paragraph. Humorist James Thurber once said "Don't get it right, get it written." What Thurber means is just start writing, even if you do not think it sounds very good. Use your thesis statement as a starting point and build around it. Explain what your essay will do, or provide interesting background information that serves to frame your points for your audience. After you have written the first paragraph, take a break before you revise it. Return to it later with a fresh outlook. Likewise, review your first paragraph as you develop the other sections of your essay to make sure that you are meeting your objectives.

Turning back to our student paper, an introduction might look like the one that follows. Note that the introduction works with the thesis statement developed earlier, and it builds in a few more ideas.

The world of online communications—whether it be in the

form of emailing, social media, blogging, tweeting, texting, online reviews or evaluations—is an impersonal world. Unlike face-to-face communication—replete with gesture, expression, posture, voice, tone and words—the world of online communication is an impersonal universe where lack of inhibition can flourish. Some critics like Matt Ridley feel that social networking has humanized the Internet and see that lack of inhibition as a conduit to more genuine and honest communication. Others, however, like John Suler of Rider University have studied the less benign aspects of online communication known as Internet flaming, the unleashed vitriol often expressed online. In my opinion, the overlooked fact is that the world of online communication allows for harassment, bullying, and personal exposure to damaging comments. My research on the topic including interviews with friends and an examination of attempts to make Internet flaming illegal convince me of the seriousness of this issue. I believe that more needs to be done to protect users of the Internet whether in the form of education, legal action, or social censure.

Developing Paragraphs and Making Transitions

A **paragraph** is a group of sentences that support and develop a central idea. The central idea serves as the core point of the paragraph, and the surrounding sentences support it. There are three primary types of sentences that make up paragraphs: *topic sentences, supporting sentences,* and *transitional sentences.*

The core point, or the **topic sentence,** is usually the first or second sentence in the paragraph. It is the controlling idea of the paragraph. Placing the topic sentence first lets the reader immediately know what the paragraph is about. However, sometimes a transition sentence or some supporting material needs to precede the topic sentence, in which case the topic sentence may appear as the second or third sentence in the paragraph. Think of the topic sentence as a mini thesis statement; it should connect logically to the topic sentences in the paragraphs before and after it.

Supporting sentences do just that: they support the topic sentence. This support may be from outside sources in the form of quotes or paraphrased material, or it may be from your own ideas. Think of the support sentences as proving the validity of your topic sentence.

Transitional sentences link paragraphs together. They make the paper a cohesive unit and promote its readability. Transitional sentences are often the first and last sentences of the paragraph. When they appear at the end of the paragraph, they foreshadow the topic to come. Words such as *in addition, yet, moreover, furthermore,* *meanwhile, likewise, also, since, before, hence, on the other hand, as well,* and *thus* are often used in transitional sentences. These words can also be used within the body of the paragraph to clarify and smooth the progression from idea to idea. For example, the last sentence in our student's introductory paragraph sets up the expectation that the paragraphs that follow will explain why language sensitivity in educational materials is a good idea. It forecasts what will come next.

Paragraphs have no required length. Remember, however, that an essay comprised of long, detailed paragraphs might prove tiresome and confusing to the reader. Likewise, short, choppy paragraphs may sacrifice clarity and leave the reader with unanswered questions. Remember that a paragraph presents a single, unified idea. It should be just long enough to effectively support its subject. Begin a new paragraph when your subject changes.

Use this list to help keep your paragraphs organized and coherent:

- Organize material logically, and present your core idea early in the paragraph.
- Include a topic sentence that expresses the core point of the paragraph.
- Support and explain the core point.
- Use transitional sentences to indicate where you are going and where you have been.

Let us see how our student applies these ideas to the second paragraph of her essay.

To better understand inhibition in online communication, it is helpful to begin with some historic background as to how the Internet was once viewed. We can, as Matt Ridley suggests in his *Wall Street Journal* article, "Internet On, Inhibitions Off: Why We Tell All," think back to two decades ago. At that time, fears regarding the Internet were that those addicted to it would become socially isolated geeks or that there would be an "epidemic of dishonesty." It seems to me that most people would admit that these two trends have persisted though, perhaps, not to the extent earlier feared. Instead, I think it is the role of inhibition on the Internet that is now the focus of concern.

In an article entitled "The Online Disinhibition Effect" published in *CyberPsychology and Behavior* in 2004, John Suler outlines the reasons people often feel unrestrained in what they write online. He talks about "dissociative anonymity" or the fact that many people you encounter online can't tell who you are. Thus, who you are is unknown. When acting out hostile feelings, a person communicating anonymously online does not have to take responsibility for those actions. Through evidence collected by interviewing many students on campus about this issue, I hope to demonstrate just how prevalent hostile communications are online.

Concluding Well

Your conclusion should bring together the points made in your paper and reiterate your final point. You may also use your conclusion as an opportunity to provoke a final thought you wish your audience to consider. Try to frame your conclusion to mirror your introduction—in other words, be consistent in your style. You may wish to repeat the point of the paper, revisit its key points, and then leave your reader with a final idea or thought on your topic.

Conclusions are your opportunity to explain to your reader how all your material adds up. In a short essay of about three to four pages, your conclusion should begin around the penultimate paragraph, winding down the discussion. Avoid the temptation to simply summarize your material; try to give your conclusions a little punch. However, it is equally important not to be overly dramatic, which can undercut your essay. Rather, conclusions should sound confident and reflective.

Notice how our student concludes her essay, making references to her final point as well as to the paper against which she is arguing, the essay by Matt Ridley. Based on her conclusion, we may infer that she has supported all of her final points within the actual body of her essay. Note, too, that she must revise her original thesis statement since some of her ideas have changed.

In conclusion, it appears that yes, Internet flaming and vicious online communication is a serious problem. In the body of my paper, interviews with my fellow students as well as the analysis of work by people like Matt Ridley and John Suler have demonstrated how damaging, disabling, even deadly Internet flaming can be. But the examination of laws proposed with the attempt to make such online destructive bullying illegal has convinced me that the solution to this problem is not a simple one. While online bullying clearly needs to stop, laws to prevent it are virtually unenforceable. There is the danger of stifling free speech and the difficulty of establishing intent and degree of damage. According to Eugene Volokh, the Gary T. Schwartz Professor of Law at UCLA School of Law, most cyber-bullying can be "effectively handled by parents, educators and other community members." In rare events where the bullying rises to the level of a crime, laws against criminal harassment and felonious assault can be evoked. Thus, while I am convinced that cyberbullying and Internet flaming are unacceptable in a civilized society, I conclude that education and social censure are the best ways to control it.

Editing and Revising

Once you have drafted a paper and, if possible, spent several hours or even a day away from it, you should begin editing and revising it. To edit your paper, read it closely, marking the words, phrases, and sections you want to change. Have a grammar handbook nearby to quickly reference any grammatical questions that may arise. Look for things that seem out of place or sound awkward, passages that lack adequate support and detail, and sentences that seem wordy or unclear. Many students find that reading the essay aloud helps them recognize awkward sentences and ambiguous wording. This technique may also reveal missing words.

As you read, you should always ask if what you have written refers back to your thesis. Keep the following questions in mind:

- Does this paragraph support my thesis?
- What does my reader need to know?
- Do my paragraphs flow in a logical order?
- Have I deviated from my point?

As you revise your paper, think about the voice and style you are using to present your material. Is your style smooth and confident? How much of yourself is in the essay, and is this level appropriate for the type of paper you are writing? Some writers, for example, overuse the pronoun *I*. If you find that this is the case, try to rework your sentences to decrease the use of this pronoun.

Using Active Voice

Although grammatically correct, the use of the passive voice can slow down the flow of a paper or distance the reader from your material. Many students are befuddled by the active versus the passive voice, confusing it with past, present, and future tense. The active voice can be used in any tense, and, in most situations, it is the better choice. In the active voice, you make your agent actively perform an action. Consider the following examples:

Passive: In "Internet On, Inhibitions Off: Why We Tell All" in order to explain why face-to-face communication represses hostility, examples from the world of primates are given by Matt Ridley.

Active: In his essay "Internet On, Inhibitions Off: Why We Tell All,"
Matt Ridley provides examples of animal behavior to explain human
behavior.

Passive: That social networking will make the Internet benignly honest is predicted by Ridley.

Active: Ridley predicts that social networking will make the Internet
benignly honest.

Grammar and Punctuation

You probably already have a grammar handbook; most first-year composition
courses require students to purchase these invaluable little books. If you do not
have a grammar handbook, get one. You will use it throughout college and probably throughout your professional career. Grammar handbooks can help you identify problems with phrases and clauses, parallel structure, verb-tense agreement, and
the various forms of punctuation. Most have useful sections on common usage mistakes, such as when to use *further* and *farther* and *effect* and *affect.* Try not to rely
on grammar-checking software available in most word-processing programs. You
are the best grammar checker for your essay.

Proofreading Effectively

The final step in preparing a paper is proofreading, the process of reading your
paper to correct errors. You will probably be more successful if you wait until you
are fresh to do it: Proofreading a paper at 3:00 A.M. immediately after finishing it is
not a good idea. With the use of word-processing programs, proofreading usually
involves three steps: *spell checking, reading,* and *correcting.*

If you are writing your paper using a word-processing system, you probably
have been using the spell checker throughout the composition process. Most word-
processing systems highlight misspelled words as you type them into the computer.
Remember to run the spell checker every time you change or revise your paper.
Many students make last minute changes to their papers and neglect to run the spell
checker one last time before printing it, only to discover a misspelled word as they
turn in their paper—or when it is returned to them. Keep in mind that spell checkers can fix only words that are misspelled, not words that are mistyped that are still
real words. Common typing errors in which letters are transposed, such as *from* and
form and *won* and *own,* will not be caught by a spell checker, because they all are
real words. Other common errors not caught by spell checkers include words incom-
pletely typed, such as when the *t* in *the* or the *e* in *here* are left off. Reading your
paper carefully will catch these errors.

To proofread correctly, you must read slowly and critically. Try to distance
yourself from the material. One careful, slow, attentive proofreading is better than

six careless reads. Look for and mark the following: errors in spelling and usage, sentence fragments and comma splices, inconsistencies in number between nouns and pronouns and between subjects and verbs, faulty parallelism, grammatical errors, unintentional repetitions, and omissions.

After you have proofread and identified the errors, go back and correct them. When you have finished, proofread the paper *again* to make sure you caught everything. As you proofread for grammar and style, ask yourself the questions listed above, and make corrections on your paper. Be prepared to read your essay through multiple times. Having only one or two small grammatical corrections is a good indication that you are done revising.

If your schedule permits, you might want to show your paper to a friend or instructor for review. Obtaining feedback from your audience is another way you can test the effectiveness of your paper. An outside reviewer will probably think of questions you had not thought of, and if you revise to answer those questions, you will make your paper stronger.

In the chapters that follow, you will discover dozens of new and updated selections, both written and visual, that range widely across contemporary matters; we hope you will find them exciting and thought provoking. Arranged thematically into nine chapters, the writings represent widely diverse topics—from the ways we construct beauty, to what makes us want to buy something, to the way the Internet is changing our lives, to the ethical issues surrounding human reproduction and gene technology. Some of the topics will be familiar, others you may be encountering for the first time. Regardless of how these language issues touch your experience, critical thinking, critical reading, and critical writing will open you up to a deeper understanding of our culture in the twenty-first century.

Approaching Visuals Critically

We have all heard the old saying: "A picture is worth a thousand words." Our daily lives are filled with the images of pop culture that influence what we buy, how we look, even how we think. Symbols, images, gestures, and graphics all communicate instant information about our culture.

Now more than ever before, ours is a visual world. Everywhere we look, images vie for our attention: magazine ads, T-shirt logos, movie billboards, artwork, traffic signs, political cartoons, statues, and storefront windows. Glanced at only briefly, visuals communicate information and ideas. They may project commonly held values, ideals, or fantasies. They can relay opinion, inspire reaction, and influence emotion. And because the competition for our attention today is so great, and the time for communication is so short, visuals compete to make an instant impression or risk being lost.

Consider the instant messages projected by brand names, company logos, or even the American flag; or the emotional appeal of a photo of a lost kitten or dog attached to a reward notice on a telephone pole. Without the skills of visual literacy, we are at the mercy of a highly persuasive visual universe. Just as we approach writing with the tools of critical analysis, we should carefully consider the many ways visuals influence us.

Understanding the persuasive power of visuals requires a close examination and interpretation of the premise, claims, details, supporting evidence, and stylistic touches embedded in any visual piece. Just as when we examine written arguments, we should ask ourselves the following four questions when examining visual arguments:

1. Who is the target *audience*?
2. What are the *claims* made in the images?
3. What shared history or cultural *assumptions* does the image make?
4. What is the supporting *evidence*?

Like works of art, visuals employ color, shape, line, texture, depth, and point of view to create their effect. Therefore to understand how visuals work and to analyze the way visuals persuade, we must also ask questions about specific aspects of form and design. For example, some questions to ask about print images, such as those in newspaper and magazine ads, include:

• What in the frame catches your attention immediately?
• What is the central image? The background image? The foreground images? The surrounding images? What is significant in the placement of these images? What is their relationship to one another?
• What verbal information is included? How is it made prominent? How does it relate to the other graphics or images?
• What specific details—people, objects, locale—are emphasized? Which are exaggerated or idealized?
• What is the effect of color and lighting?
• What emotional effect is created by the images? Pleasure? Longing? Anxiety? Nostalgia?
• Do the graphics and images make you want to know more about the subject or product?
• What special significance might objects in the image have?
• Is there any symbolism embedded in the images?

Because the goal of a calculated visual is to persuade, coax, intimidate, or otherwise subliminally influence its viewer, it is important that an audience be able to discern the strategies or techniques employed. To get you started, we will critically analyze two types of visuals: advertisements and editorial cartoons.

Images and Advertising

Images have clout, and none are so obvious or so craftily designed as those that come from the world of advertising. Advertising images are everywhere: television, newspapers, the Internet, magazines, the sides of buses, and on highway billboards. Each year, companies collectively spend more than $150 billion on print ads and television commercials—more than the gross national product of many countries. Advertisements make up at least a quarter of each television hour and form the bulk of most newspapers and magazines. Tapping into our most basic emotions, their appeal goes right to the quick of our fantasies: happiness, material wealth, eternal youth, social acceptance, sexual fulfillment, and power.

Yet most of us are so accustomed to the onslaught of such images that we see them without looking and hear them without listening. But if we stopped to examine how the images work, we might be amazed at their powerful and complex psychological force. And we might be surprised at how much effort goes into the crafting of such images—an effort solely intended to separate us from our money.

Like a written argument, every print ad or commercial has an audience, makes claims and assumptions, and offers evidence. Sometimes these elements are obvious, sometimes understated, sometimes implied. They may boast testimonials by average folk or celebrities, or they may cite hard scientific evidence. Sometimes they simply manipulate our desire to be happy or socially accepted. But common to every ad and commercial, no matter what the medium, is the assertion that you should buy the product.

Print ads are complex mixtures of images, graphics, and text. So in analyzing an ad, you should be aware of the use of photography, the placement of the images, and the use of text, company logos, and other graphics such as illustrations, drawings, sidebar boxes, and so on. You should keep in mind that every aspect of the image has been considered and designed carefully, even in those ads where the guiding principle was minimalism. Let us take a look at a recent magazine ad for Altoids.

Altoids Ad

When analyzing a print ad, we should try to determine what first catches our attention. In the accompanying Altoids ad, the image of the soldier—featured floating on a solid, pale green background—pops from the page. This is a calculated move on the part of the ad's designers: The soldier fills the center of the page, and the image is arresting—we stop and look. Ad images are staged and manipulated for maximum attention and effect; the uncluttered nature of this advertisement forces us to look at the soldier and the little tin he is holding in his hand.

The person featured in the ad is almost comic. He is wearing an ill-fitting uniform, he sports thick glasses, and he lacks the chiseled quality of many male models commonly used in advertising. This comic quality, coupled with the text under the ad, appeals to the viewer's sense of humor.

What Is the Claim?

Because advertisers are fighting for our attention, they must project their claim as efficiently as possible to discourage us from turning the page. The Altoids ad states its "claim" simply and boldly in white letters against a pale green background below the central photograph. In a large typeface, the slogan and claim come in two parts. The first two sentences presumably come from the soldier: "Thank you sir! May I have another!" The second statement tells us more specifically what the soldier wants: the curiously strong mints. It is interesting to note that the actual name of the product, Altoids, only appears on the little tin held in the soldier's right hand.

Let us take a closer look at the intention of framing the claim in two sentences and at how the layout subtly directs us. The first statement is intended to tap into our shared cultural expectations of what we know about military service. Soldiers must shout responses to their superiors and thank them even for punishments. For example, after being assigned 20 pushups as disciplinary action, a soldier is expected to not only thank his sergeant for the punishment but to actually ask for more. The ad twists this expectation by having Altoids be the "punishment." In this ad, the soldier is actually getting a treat.

The indirect claim is that the reader should also want these "curiously strong" mints. The word *curiously* is designed to set the product apart from its competitors. *Curiously* is more commonly used in British English, and the parent company for Altoids—Callard & Bowser-Suchard—has its roots in England. Viewers familiar with the mint will enjoy the ad for its comic appeal. Those readers who are unfamiliar with the product may wonder just what makes these mints "curiously strong," and curiosity is an effective hook.

Another possible claim could be connected to the scenario leading to the soldier's receiving the first mint. We know that soldiers are supposed to shout back responses to their commanding officer, often face to face. Perhaps his commanding officer was appalled at his recruit's bad breath and "punished" him with the directive to have a mint. The claim is that even at extremely close range, Altoids fixes bad breath.

What Is the Evidence?

The Altoids tag line, "the curiously strong mints," implies that other mints are simply ordinary and unremarkable. Altoids are different—they are "curiously strong" and thus, presumably, superior to their bland competition. Referring back to the possible scenario that led to the soldier's first mint, viewers might presume that if a commanding officer would "treat" his company's bad breath with this mint, it must be good.

Around the language of advertising, we should tread cautiously. As William Lutz warns us in his essay, "With These Words I Can Sell You Anything" (pages 127–138), we hear promises that are not really being made. The Altoids text does not say that they are in fact better than other mints, just that they are "curiously strong." What does the word *curiously* really mean? According to Lutz, such words sound enticing, but they are really telling readers nothing meaningful about the product.

What Are the Assumptions?

The creators of this ad make several assumptions about the audience: (1) that they are familiar with the phrase "Thank you sir, may I have another"; (2) that they understand who is depicted in the ad—a soldier at boot camp; and (3) that they want to have fresh breath.

Altoids Questions

1. What cultural conventions does this ad use to promote the product? What does it assume about the viewer? Would it work in another country, such as France or China? Explain.
2. This ad lists a Web site. Visit the Altoids Web site at www.altoids.com. How does the Web site complement the print ad? Who would visit this site? Evaluate the effectiveness of having companion Web sites in addition to printed advertisements.
3. Would you try Altoids based on this advertisement? Why or why not?
4. How does this photograph capture your attention? Can you tell at a glance what it is selling? Where is your eye directed?

Deciphering Editorial Cartoons

Editorial cartoons have been a part of American life for over a century. They are a mainstay feature on the editorial pages in most newspapers—those pages reserved for columnists, contributing editors, and illustrators to present their views in words and pen and ink. As in the nineteenth century, when they first started to appear, such editorial cartoons are political in nature, holding political and social issues up for public scrutiny and sometimes ridicule.

A stand-alone editorial cartoon, as opposed to a strip of multiple frames, is a powerful and terse form of communication that combines pen-and-ink drawings with dialogue balloons and captions. These are not just visual jokes but visual humor, which comments on social and political issues while drawing on viewers' experience and knowledge.

The editorial cartoon is the story of a moment in the flow of familiar current events. And the key words here are *moment* and *familiar.* Although a cartoon captures a split instant in time, it also implies what came before and, perhaps, what may happen next—either in the next moment or in some indefinite future. And usually the cartoon depicts a moment after which things will never be the same. One of the most famous cartoons of the last 40 years is the late Bill Mauldin's Pulitzer Prize-winning drawing of the figure of Abraham Lincoln with his head in his hands. It appeared the morning after the assassination of President John F. Kennedy in 1963. There was no caption, nor was there a need for one. The image represented the profound grief of a nation that had lost its leader to an assassin's bullet. But to capture the enormity of the event, Mauldin brilliantly chose to represent a woeful America by using the figure of Abraham Lincoln as depicted in the sculpture of the Lincoln Memorial in Washington, D.C. In so doing, the message implied that so profound was the loss that it even reduced to tears the marble figure of a man many considered to be our greatest president, assassinated a century before.

For a cartoon to be effective, it must make the issue clear at a glance, and it must establish where it stands on the argument. As in the Mauldin illustration, we instantly recognize Lincoln and identify with the emotion. We need not be told the circumstances, because by the time the cartoon appeared the next day, all the world knew the horrible news. To convey less obvious issues and figures at a glance, cartoonists resort to images that are instantly recognizable and that we do not have to work at to grasp. Locales are determined by giveaway props: airports have an airplane out the window, the desert is identified by a cactus and a cow's skull, and an overstuffed arm chair and TV represents the standard living room. Likewise, human emotions are instantly conveyed: pleasure is a huge, toothy grin; fury is steam blowing out of a figure's ears; and love is two figures making goo-goo eyes with floating hearts. Characters may also have exaggerated features to emphasize a point or emotion.

Mort Gerberg, in his essay "What Is a Cartoon?" (*The Arbor House Book of Cartooning*, HarperCollins, 1989), says that editorial cartoons rely on such visual clichés to instantly convey their messages; that is, they employ stock figures for their representation—images instantly recognizable from cultural stereotypes: the fat-cat tycoon, the mobster thug, the sexy female movie star. These images come to us in familiar outfits and with props that give away their identities and professions. The cartoon judge has a black robe and a gavel; the prisoner wears striped overalls and a ball and chain; the physician dons a smock and forehead light; the doomsayer is a scrawny, long-haired guy carrying a sign that reads "The End Is Near." These are visual clichés known by the population at large, and we get them.

The visual cliché may be what catches our eye in the editorial cartoon, but the message lies in what the cartoonist does with it. As Gerberg observes, "The message is in twisting it, in turning the cliché around."

Graduation Resistance Cartoon

Consider Mike Keefe's cartoon shown here. The cliché is a young graduate on his graduation day. We know that from the familiar props: the cap and gown, the bespeckled professor at the podium, the gowned professors in the background, and the rolled diploma. The scene is familiar to anyone who has attended a commencement ceremony. The twist, of course, is that instead of the graduate walking proudly across the stage, he is dragged by security guards as he begs those assembled to stop the ceremony. He does not want that diploma! The issue, of course, is the harsh reality of the current job market and the uncertainty many graduates face in a turbulent economy.

The cartoon's joke is in the twist—the gap between the familiar and the unexpected. The familiar is the graduation ceremony; the unexpected is the screaming student.

What Is the Claim?

The claim in this cartoon is that students enjoy a special grace period in college and that graduation marks a student's entry into the real world with all of its responsibilities and economic demands. Most of us can understand and sympathize with the student's fears.

What Are the Assumptions?

This cartoon assumes that viewers will know the meaning of a commencement ceremony and what happened before it and what happens after the student receives his

Mike Keefe/PoliticalCartoons.com

diploma. The cartoon also presumes that the reader will be aware of current economic challenges in the United States and why the student would be reluctant to graduate.

What Is the Evidence?

This cartoon was published in June of 2008—during graduation month and during a period of particular economic uncertainty in the United States and in the world. The unemployment rate in the United States was around 7 percent—a rate that continued to rise even months later. Graduates faced the most severe economic downturn since the Great Depression. Clearly, for students comfortable with college life and the respite it affords many of them from financial responsibility, the prospect of entering the job market under such conditions was particularly discouraging.

As you review the various visuals throughout the text, approach what you see with the critical eye of a skeptic. Many of the techniques used in reading critically can be applied to visuals. Consider the ways symbolism, brand recognition, stereotyping, and cultural expectations contribute to how such illustrations communicate their ideas. Try to think abstractly and take into account the many different levels of consciousness that visuals use to communicate. Consider also the way shading, lighting, and subject placement in the photos all converge to make a point. "Read" them as you would any text.

CHAPTER
1

Fashion and Flesh
The Images We Project

Pick up a magazine. Turn on the television. Watch a movie. Every day we are bombarded with images and messages telling us that slim is sexy, buff bodies are the best, and beauty means happiness. The right labels mean success and respect. The right look means acceptance. And overwhelmingly, we buy into these messages.

We live in a society caught up with images of ourselves, a society seemingly more driven by the cultivation of the body and how to shape and clothe it than by personal achievement. In fact, so powerful is the influence of image that other terms of self-definition are difficult to identify. In this chapter, several writers grapple with questions raised by our cultural preoccupation with flesh and fashion: Are we our bodies? Can our inner selves transcend the flesh? Do the clothes we wear express the self we want to be? Where does all the body-consciousness pressure come from? Some essays in this chapter recount people at war with their bodies due to cultural pressure. Other essays are accounts of people rising above the din of fashion's dictates to create a sense of self that is authentic and rooted in personal happiness. And some explore the cultural trends that help direct contemporary fashion.

The first three readings in this chapter address how we, as individuals, are influenced by cultural pressure to conform to a culturally driven ideal. In some cases, this ideal can vary from culture to culture, creating mixed messages. In "My Hips, My Caderas," Alisa Valdes examines such cultural differences that define beauty, as she tries to balance her sense of body image between her Hispanic and white roots. Niranjana Iyer continues this examination of cultural values in her essay "Weight of the World," in which she explains how she became overweight just by changing time zones. Then, in "Strong Enough," Wendy Shanker describes how the media drive us to diet and conform despite our inner voice that tells us that we are in control of our bodies.

The next section of readings addresses how cultural pressures, especially from advertisers and the fashion industry, are influencing how young men and women feel about their bodies. The first essay, "Body Image, Media, and Eating Disorders," is a scholarly article by Jennifer L. Derenne and Eugene V. Beresin that discusses the connection between the media, body image, and social status. Next is an essay by Caroline Heldman exploring the distortions many young women have about their bodies in "Out-of-Body Image." Then, Garance Franke-Ruta disagrees with critics of media-driven ideals of beauty in her editorial "The Natural Beauty Myth," as she challenges the concept of "natural beauty" and asserts that being beautiful takes hard work. Many women feel that men are free from the social pressures associated with body image. It may come as a surprise to some people that many men, like women, are concerned with body image. The next two essays explore the connections between male self-perception, body image, and advertising. First, Ted Spiker provides personal insight, as well as critical analysis, of the pressures men face but rarely talk about in "How Men Really Feel About Their Bodies." Then, in "Never Too Buff," John Cloud reports the disturbing trend that many men, and even young boys, are struggling with—the cultural pressure to achieve physical perfection.

Finally, the Viewpoints section ends the chapter by taking a closer look at body art. Beth Janes explains her motivations and regrets regarding her choice of body art in "Why I Rue My Tattoo." Another view comes from a blog post from *Salon* magazine "Reading Tattoos: What X Can Learn From Y," in which the writer describes how her experience with her daughter taught her something she didn't know about this art form.

My Hips, My Caderas
Alisa Valdes*

The saying "Beauty lies in the eye of the beholder" may be better expressed as "Beauty lies in the eye of the culture." A feature or characteristic that one culture finds unappealing may be considered beautiful in another. Physical beauty seems to be largely a subjective thing— some cultures artificially elongate the neck, others put plates in their lips, and others prefer tiny feet or high foreheads. As a Latina woman with a white mother and a Cuban father, Alisa Valdes explores the challenges she faces straddling the beauty preferences of two cultures.

1 My father is Cuban, with dark hair, a cleft in his chin, and feet that can dance the Guaguanco.

2 My mother is white and American, as blue-eyed as they come.

3 My voluptuous/big hips are both Cuban and American. And neither. Just like me. As I shift different halves of my soul daily to match whichever cultural backdrop I happen to face, I also carefully prepare myself for how differently my womanly/ fat hips will be treated in my two realities.

4 It all started 15 years ago, when my hips bloomed in Albuquerque, New Mexico, where I was born. I went from being a track club twig—mistaken more than once for a boy—to being a splendidly curving thing that Chicano men with their bandanas down low whistled at as they drove by in their low-riders. White boys in my middle school thought I suddenly had a fat ass, and had no problem saying so.

5 But the cholos loved me. San Mateo Boulevard . . . I remember it well. Jack in the Box on one corner, me on a splintered wooden bench with a Three Musketeers bar, tight shorts, a hot summer sun, and those catcalls and woof-woofs like slaps. I was 12.

6 My best friend Stacy and I set out dieting right away that summer, to lose our new hips so boys from the heights, like the nearly albino Tim Fairfield with the orange soccer socks, would like us. In those days, I was too naive to know that dismissing the Chicano guys from the valley and taking French instead of Spanish in middle school were leftovers of colonialism. Taking Spanish still had the stigma of shame, like it would make you a dirty wetback. So Stacy and I pushed through hundreds of leg lifts on her bedroom floor, an open *Seventeen* magazine as a tiny table for our lemon water, and the sound of cicadas grinding away in the tree outside.

7 In Spanish, the word for hips is *caderas*—a broad term used to denote everything a real woman carries from her waist to her thighs, all the way around. Belly, butt, it's all part of your caderas. And caderas are a magical sphere of womanhood.

*Alisa Valdes, *UnderWire MSN,* April 2000

In the lyrics of Merengue and Salsa, caderas are to be shaken, caressed, admired and exalted. The bigger, the better. In Spanish, you eat your rice and beans and sometimes your *chicharrones* because you fear your caderas will disappear.

8   In my work as a Latin music critic for a Boston newspaper, I frequent nightclubs with wood-paneled walls and Christmas lights flashing all year long. I wear short rubber skirts and tall shoes. There, I swing my round hips like a metronome. I become fierce. I strut. In the red disco lights, my hips absolutely torture men. I can see it on their faces.

9   "*Mujeron!*" they exclaim as I shimmy past. Much woman. They click their tongues, buy me drinks. They ask me to dance, and I often say "no," because I can. And these men suffer. Ironically, this makes the feminist in me very happy. In these places, my mujeron's hips get more nods than they might at a pony farm.

10   In English, your hips are those pesky things on the sides of your hipbones. They don't "*menear,*" as they do in Spanish; they "jiggle." In English, hips are something women try to be rid of. Hips are why women bruise themselves in the name of liposuction.

11   My mother's people hate my hips. They diet. My aunt smokes so she won't eat. And in the gym where I teach step aerobics—a habit I took up in the days when I identified more with my mother's than my father's people—I sometimes hear the suburban anorexics whisper in the front row: "My God, would you look at those hips." Sometimes they walk out of the room even before I have begun teaching, as if hips were contagious. In these situations, I am sad. I drive home and examine my hips in the mirror, hit them for being so imprudent, like great big ears on the side of my body. Sometimes I fast for days. Sometimes I make myself puke up rice and beans. Usually I get over it, but it always comes back.

12   Sociologists will tell you that in cultures where women are valued for traditional roles of mother and caregiver, hips are in, and that in cultures where those roles have broken down and women try to be like men were in traditional societies—i.e., have jobs—hips are out.

13   So when I want to be loved for my body, I am a Latina. But most Latino men will not love my mind as they do my body, because I am an Americanized professional. Indeed, they will feel threatened, and will soon lose interest in hips that want to "andar por la calle come un hombre" (carry themselves like a man).

14   When I want to be loved for my mind, I flock to liberal intellectuals, usually whites. They listen to my writings and nod . . . and then suggest I use skim milk instead of cream. These men love my fire and passion—words they always use to describe a Latina—but they are embarrassed by my hips. They want me to wear looser pants.

15   In some ways I am lucky to be able to move between two worlds. At least my hips get acknowledged as beautiful. I can't say the same for a lot of my bulimic friends, who don't have a second set of standards to turn

> *In the gym where I teach step aerobics—a habit I took up in the days when I identified more with my mother's than my father's people—I sometimes hear the suburban anorexics whisper in the front row: "My God, would you look at those hips."*

to. But still, I dream of the day when bicultural Latinas will set the standards for beauty and success, when our voluptuous caderas won't bar us from getting through those narrow American doors. ◆

CRITICAL THINKING

1. Valdes notes that sociologists conjecture that in cultures in which women adhere to the more traditional roles of housewife and mother, hips and voluptuous forms are considered beautiful. Evaluate this theory and its implied inversion—that in societies in which women hold jobs outside the home, small waists and hips are culturally preferred by both sexes.
2. Does the author view the transformation of her hips from her "track club twig" physique to her more womanly shape as a positive or negative change? How does her writing reveal her feelings?
3. In paragraph 6 Valdes describes how she and her best friend Stacy worked out to reduce their hips. How does she connect these efforts to other practices of her youth, such as taking French in middle school? Explain.
4. Valdes writes, "My mother's people hate my hips." Who are her "mother's people"? Does it seem strange that she would refer to her relatives this way? Compare her description of her mother's side of the family to that of her father's side of the family.
5. How can driving men wild with her hips make "the feminist in [Valdes] very happy"? Why does she consider this ironic?
6. How does Valdes's mixed background create conflict in her life? How does she deal with this conflict?
7. Valdes uses striking, vivid language in her essay to describe the two cultures she straddles. What particular words and phrases work especially well in conveying her message?

CRITICAL WRITING

1. *Exploratory Writing:* Valdes writes, "In cultures where women are valued for traditional roles of mother and caregiver, hips are in." If beauty is a cultural creation, how is it constructed? Write an essay exploring the idea that social politics influence our cultural sense of beauty.
2. *Narrative and Analysis:* Write a short essay describing the parts of your body you find especially appealing and why. Does your culture influence your perception of your body? What outside forces influence your sense of physical identity? What changes would you make if you could? Explain.
3. *Research and Analysis:* In your library, newsstand, or bookstore, locate at least two fashion magazines from cultures or ethnicities different from yours. Compare how beauty differs between the two and from your own. How are the models similar and different? Is beauty based on universal principles with a few deviations, or is it a social construction based on individual cultural factors? Write an essay detailing your conclusions, using your magazine research and personal perspective as support.

GROUP PROJECTS

1. In her article, Valdes implies that white women feel more pressure to be thin than Latino women do, because Latin culture holds women to a different standard of beauty. In small groups, explore the idea that beauty is culturally determined—that is, that what one group may find beautiful, another may not. Can you find any evidence that the all-American image of beauty is changing?

2. Have each member of your group interview a man or woman from another country to ask the following question: "What characteristics are considered physically beautiful in your culture?" Descriptions may be of both men and women or of only one sex. Compare your notes with the group. What traits are universally admired and what traits are not? Report your findings to the class.

Weight of the World
Niranjana Iyer *

Beauty is a cultural construct. In some areas of the world, such as the Pacific Islands and India, a more plump shape is considered healthy and beautiful. In the next essay, Niranjana Iyer explores the definitions of beauty in two cultures and the challenges she faces as a "slimmigrant." And as Western media permeate even the most remote corners of the world, the battle of the bulge has gone global.

1   Like several million people on this planet, I weigh 15 pounds more than I'd like. But my 15 pounds appeared overnight, after an airplane ride from my home in India to Boston.

2   As a child in Chennai, I was considered worryingly thin. My mother sluiced an appetite stimulant down my throat at dinnertime and force-fed me cod liver oil once a week—to no avail. As I grew into a slim teen, Ma would point to my collarbones as evidence that I was wasting away, but I was unmoved. If my figure didn't quite match the voluptuous Bollywood heroine standard, well, my salwar kameezes (flowing tunics worn over drawstring pants) fit me fine. Rare was the woman who wore pants in Chennai, which was far too hot for anything but the lightest and loosest of clothing.

3   Then I moved to New Hampshire for graduate school and began a life in denim.

4   The body that I had considered normal was now revealed to be anything but. My jeans showed no mercy; every untoned millimeter of my belly hung over my waistband like an overbite in search of an orthodontist. Pants widened my hips, shrank my legs and made my waist disappear. In India, I'd been above average in

height. In the States, I was short (so said the Gap). From a tall, thin Women's, I had morphed into a petite, plump Misses'—without gaining or losing a smidgen of flesh.

5   There ought to be a dictionary entry for those who enter the Western world to find that their bodies are thin no more. My vote goes to "slimmigrant"—for an immigrant who discovers that he or she needs to shed a dozen pounds to be considered unfat.

6   My quest for assimilation began with a whimper. I forswore mayonnaise, peanut butter, cheesecake, and tortilla chips—delicacies I'd never sampled before coming to America. I

> *There ought to be a dictionary entry for those who enter the Western world to find that their bodies are thin no more.*

stopped going to those $9.99 Indian buffets with their unlimited helpings of butter chicken. For the first time in my life, I visited a gym, where my whimpers became shrieks of pain.

7   My extra poundage, however, was like a cockroach; it might disappear for a while, but it could never be eradicated. Potluck lunches, Thanksgiving dinners, and snow days made sure of that.

8   Two years ago, on my 30th birthday, I resolved to remain plump forever rather than go on another diet. And to escape my new homeland, which considered me overweight, I resolved to take a holiday in Chennai, where salesgirls would hint that garments would drape better if only I were wider, my aunt would insist that I was scrawny, and my mother would feed me restorative spoonfuls of clarified butter. I booked my plane tickets.

9   Slimmigrants, beware!

10   Satellite television and globalization had changed the city I grew up in: in the five years I'd been away, skim milk had replaced the heavy cream of middle-class India, and those cushiony Bollywood heroines had been supplanted by supermodels whose hipbones could shred lettuce.

11   It seemed that every girl in Chennai was wearing trousers (and the girls' waists seemed no bigger round than a CD). The neighborhood video-rental store had become a fitness center. Even my aunt had bought a stationary bike (which she rode very competently in her sari).

12   My mother said she was glad to see me looking so nice and healthy. Time to go on a diet, I realized. I opted for the Mediterranean one—I love pizza. ◆

CRITICAL THINKING

1. Is beauty a cultural construction? Why are some physical characteristics admired in some cultures but not in others? Can you think of any physical traits that Americans esteem that other cultures do not?

2. How much do the opinions of others influence your personal view of your body and your concept of beauty? Was the author of this piece influenced by her family members? By American constructs of beauty? Whose opinions mattered more, and why?

3. At the end of her essay, Iyer notes that the city she grew up in had changed as a result of "globalization." What does she mean? How does she feel about this change? How can you tell?
4. What decision does the author make regarding her weight and her constant dieting? What words does she use to describe her weight and her struggle to meet the expectations of her new culture?
5. Is body size part of who you are? Do we try to pretend body size doesn't matter, while feeling that it really does? Explain.

CRITICAL WRITING

1. *Exploratory Writing:* Write about a time in your life when you received criticism or praise for your appearance. What did people notice about your body? How did it make you feel? How did you react?
2. *Research Writing:* The author of this piece, who is from India, makes a reference to the actresses from "Bollywood." Research Bollywood on the Web and find out more about famous actors and actresses from India. What similarities and differences do you notice between Bollywood and Hollywood?
3. *Exploratory Writing:* As the author explains, in India plumpness had always been a sign of health and beauty. Write an essay in which you explore the social and psychological aspects of this idea. What would your life be like if the Indian view of beauty and health were embraced by Western culture? Would you be more comfortable in your own skin or, like the author, encouraged to eat more spoonfuls of clarified butter? Explain.

GROUP PROJECTS

1. With your group, select two or three non-Western countries and research the cultural perspectives of beauty and health for each. (You may wish to ask international students for their perspectives on this topic.) How do the standards of beauty in the countries you researched compare with Western definitions? In your opinion—and supported by your research—what role, if any, does American popular culture play on body image in these countries?
2. Research fashion trends from two different cultures, such as the United States and Japan or England and India. Consult popular media online for each culture, including fashion magazines, popular television programs, and movies. What common themes can you find in both cultures? What differences seem distinct to each? Share your evaluation with the class to promote discussion on similarities and differences between each culture and what messages are conveyed to youth about beauty, self-confidence, and self-identity.

Strong Enough
*Wendy Shanker**

> Sometimes the pressure to conform to media-driven body images can sneak up on us in unexpected ways. When others expect people to look and act a certain way, nonconformists may find themselves in an unwanted spotlight, the subject of ridicule. Wendy Shanker, author of *The Fat Girl's Guide to Life,* describes one such incident, and how the experience led to much soul searching. Why do so many people—even strong ones—still do backflips to try and look like someone they are not?

1 "Are you a lez?" he asked.

2 "What?" I asked, taken aback.

3 "ARE. YOU. A. LEZ." he repeated, enunciating each word as if I was deaf instead of confused.

4 I didn't know what to say. I pulled away.

5 "Well, you must be." He got up from our not-so-secluded spot behind my cabin and snuck back across the lake.

6 That's how a 14-year old boy responded to me at summer camp, a 14-year old girl, when I said I didn't want to have sex with him. Couldn't be that I didn't want to. Wasn't ready to. Or worse, wanted to . . . just not with HIM.

7 I assume his pride was injured. I'm sure he felt rejected (though possibly relieved). Maybe he was expected to come back to his crew with a story that he wasn't going to be able to tell. So he lobbed what was at that time the teen girl equivalent of "fag" at me: lesbian.

8 By the next day, no one in my cabin would talk to me. 'Cause everyone at camp knew I was a LEZ.

9 I'm not gay. But as a fat girl, lots of people assume I am. My theory is that most people are confused by a fat woman who is not on a diet. If I am fat, I'm not doing my evolutionary job, which is to make myself attractive enough for men to want to have sex with me. Being fat is an insult to male egos. It makes dating and mating difficult. I've even met fat guys who have the audacity to share that resentment. So why would I choose to be fat? I must be gay!

10 My straight girl friends with short haircuts tell me they often get the same treatment. By not keeping their hair long and straight (and blond), some men sense it's their subtle way of saying no to our current beauty standard. "How dare you pull a Mia Farrow!" Short hair isn't sexy to a certain kind of man, or to the woman who desires that dude.

11 I believe the same issue was at the heart of the Don Imus controversy. We now know the words by heart, but the subtext got lost. Sure, his comments about the Rutgers women's basketball team were another example of racist, sexist insults from a white dude with a microphone. On a more subtle layer, I saw it as "lez" thinking: "Here's a group of talented, successful, strong young women who seem to have

---

*Wendy Shanker, *Feminist.com*

other priorities in life than making themselves attractive enough for me to want to have sex with them. How dare they? Ah, I know a way to bring them down to size, to collectively voice the thoughts of other men who may feel threatened just like me." Voila, Nappy Headed Ho-Gate broke loose on the airwaves.

12   What I heard was two mouthy men talking like they were scared of the Rutgers players, threatened by their physical appearance. Were they trying to make a guarded statement about the players' sexual preferences? The word "ho" is used in a sexually promiscuous context, yet their conversation inferred that they did not deem these women sexually appealing, especially when comparing their "nappy" hairstyles to the long, straight (Caucasian) do's worn by players on the competing team.

13   Look at male ballers and you'll see that many have braided hair and earrings. They wear big, baggy clothes on the court. Unlike their cheerleaders who let it all hang out, the only balls on display are being shot into baskets. Dennis Rodman dyed his hair pink and pierced his nose. Would anyone lob sexual insults at him, or doubt his masculinity?

14   Black women have spoken and written eloquently about hair and identity. Judgments are made inside and outside of the African-American community with something as simple as a hairstyle. Same with fat. The size of the pants I wear seems to say something about my sexual appeal and sexual preference. In the 70s, long hair was a way to stand out. In the 00s, hair is a way to fit in. No wonder the main character in *Hairspray* is a fat girl.

15   Athletic women are taunted about their sexuality in the same way fat women are, the same way women with short haircuts are. It cuts through their threat factor. "What if that chick is stronger than me? What if that chick can run faster, hit harder, and lift more?" Women are expected to be strong and muscular, with cut biceps and ripped abs, but for ogling purposes only. Don't use those muscles to shoot free throws. Don't use them to run marathons. Unless you're wearing a tiny tennis skirt over a thong, it's hard to be strong and look "feminine" at the same time.

16   We don't owe anyone an explanation when it comes the choices we make about appearance. Yet here we are, dieting and sweating and cutting and spritzing and waxing and sucking and shooting and plucking, hoping to look less like ourselves and more like Halle Berry or Angelina Jolie or Anna Kournikova, thinking our problems will be solved. I'll never understand why some men fear fat and strength and pixie cuts; it has nothing to do with them. Wait—maybe that's exactly the problem.

17   I appreciate beauty. I love feeling beautiful. And there are many ways for me to do that. Trust me, Sephora has no better customer. I do my hair, put on makeup, wear sexy clothes, show off my rack and my booty. Whether I'm a size 8 or a size 18 doesn't matter. It's not beauty that's the problem; it's our limited definition of beauty that's a problem. It's why Imus's insult hit so hard. With three little words, he managed to insult our looks and our sexuality, reinforcing our fears that we aren't good enough, pretty enough, or strong enough.

18   Beauty is how YOU see it. Eye of the beholder, remember?

19   That's why The Case of the Nappy-Headed Hos resonated so hard with women of all colors across this country. When I was 14, I didn't have the self-possession or confidence to properly respond to that loser boy behind the cabin. If he asked

me now, I'd tell him: "I don't want to have sex with you. And it's not because I like girls. It's because I don't like YOU. When it comes to my sexual preference, I'm strong enough for a woman, but I happen to be made for a man." ◆

CRITICAL THINKING

1. Try to picture your version of the perfect female body. What does it look like? Is your image influenced by outside forces, such as the media, your gender, or your age? How do real women you know compare to the image in your mind?
2. In your opinion, what made Don Imus's comments so unacceptable? Was it racism? Sexism? Both? Explain.
3. What role does sex appeal and the media play in defining men and women and how they are treated by society at large?
4. Who does Shanker blame for the cultural influences women experience that drive them to "dieting and sweating and cutting and spritzing and waxing and sucking and shooting and plucking"? Explain.
5. Evaluate how well Shanker supports her viewpoint in this essay. Does she provide supporting evidence? Is she biased? Does she provide a balanced perspective, or does she slant her data? Explain.
6. Shanker is the author of *The Fat Girl's Guide to Life*. Does the fact that she is a published author who defends her large size influence your opinion of her essay or her points? Why or why not?

CRITICAL WRITING

1. *Exploratory Writing:* Do you know someone who spends a lot of time on his or her appearance ("sweating and cutting and spritzing and waxing and sucking and shooting and plucking")? Do you agree with Shanker that such practices to look a certain way are inherently flawed and doomed to failure? Why or why not?
2. *Exploratory Writing:* Write an essay exploring the connections among the fashion industry, body image, and self-esteem. Does the fashion industry have a direct role in our feelings of self-worth and acceptance? Support your viewpoint with examples from the text and your own personal experience.
3. *Personal Narrative:* Write a personal narrative describing an incident in which a comment made about your appearance caused you discomfort. How old were you? What was the comment? How did it make you feel? In hindsight, what do you think motivated the comment and what did it reveal about the person who said it to you? Explain.

GROUP PROJECTS

1. With your group, gather magazine photographs of several models and analyze their body types. What common elements do you notice? How are they similar or different? How do they compare to "real" people? Based on the photographs, can you reach any conclusions about fashion models in today's culture?

2. Discuss the following question: If you could be either very beautiful or very wealthy, which would you choose? Explain the motivation behind your choice. Based on your group's multiple responses, can you reach any conclusions about the influence of beauty on men and women in today's society?

Modern Scholar

Body Image, Media, and Eating Disorders

Jennifer L. Derenne and Eugene V. Beresin*

Throughout history, body image has been determined by various factors, including politics and media. Studies reveal that for some people, especially young women, exposure to mass media (television, movies, magazines, Internet) can influence a negative body image, which may lead to disordered eating. In this scholarly article, psychiatrists Jennifer L. Derenne, M.D., and Eugene V. Beresin, M.D., attempt to explain the historical context of the problem and explore potential avenues for change.

"Every society has a way of torturing its women, whether by binding their feet or by sticking them into whalebone corsets. What contemporary American culture has come up with is designer jeans."

—Joel Yager, M.D.

1 Our nation's health has reached a point of crisis. According to the American Obesity Association, 65% of adults and 30% of children are overweight, and 30% of adults and 15% of children meet the criteria for obesity (1). Rarely playing outdoors, children spend their days chatting online or watching TV while snacking on nutritionally empty foods. The average child spends 4 hours per day watching TV, and only 1 hour per day completing homework (2). Similarly, the adult workplace has become more and more sedentary.

2 At the same time, rates of some eating disorders in women, such as anorexia nervosa and bulimia nervosa, are rising (3), and increasing numbers of men are seeking treatment as well (4). Patients are being referred at progressively younger ages (5). There is a significant dichotomy between society's idealized rail-thin figure and the more typical American body. The reasons for this are complex and likely involve the interplay of media pressure to be thin, family eating and exercise

---

*Jennifer L. Derenne; Eugene V. Beresin, *Academic Psychiatry,* May 1, 2006. References for this article available at http://ap.psychiatryonline.org/

patterns, and a relative surplus of non-nutritious food. Dietary restriction leads to a repetitive pattern of self-deprivation, which can result in bingeing, weight gain, and worsening self-image.

3   Although it is tempting to blame today's media for perpetuating and glorifying unrealistic standards of physical beauty, the truth is far more complicated. Throughout history, the dominant political climate and cultural ideals always have shaped the public's perception of the ideal female body type. However, today's culture is unique in that the media (including television, Internet, movies, and print) is a far more powerful presence than ever before. This article gives examples of changing ideals over time, explores possible explanations for the relationship between obesity rates and the prevalence of eating disorders (including anorexia nervosa, bulimia nervosa, and binge eating) and identifies possible avenues for prevention and change.

Ideal Body Type Throughout History

4 Throughout history, the standard of female beauty often has been unrealistic and difficult to attain. Those with money and higher socioeconomic status were far more likely to be able to conform to these standards. Women typically were willing to sacrifice comfort and even endure pain to achieve them.

5   In colonial times, the harsh environment and lack of comfortable surroundings required that all family members contribute to survival. Large families were preferred as children could help tend to the land and household chores. For these reasons, communities valued fertile, physically strong and able women. However, in the 19th century, ideals shifted and women with tiny waists and large bustles came to be valued. It was desirable for an upper-class man to be able to span a woman's waist with his hands (6). If women were too frail to work, plantation owners could justify the use of slaves (7). Indeed, much emphasis was placed on female fragility, which then made a woman a more attractive candidate for marriage. The ideal wealthy woman of the time was sickly and prone to headaches; the fine art of fainting was taught in finishing schools throughout the country. Women of significant financial means would go as far as having ribs removed to further decrease their waist size. Despite being painful and causing health problems, such as shortness of breath (which could lead to pneumonia) and dislocated visceral organs, corsets became the height of fashion (6).

6   Some have said that the invention of the corset was the main impetus for the feminist movement at the beginning of the 20th century (8). Women turned up their noses at complicated dresses, instead favoring pants, which were comfortable and did not restrict movement. They cut their hair short, bound their breasts, took up cigarette smoking, and fought for the right to vote. At this point, it was fashionable to be angular, thin, and boyish-looking, and manufacturers routinely featured pictures of "flappers" in their advertisements.

7   During the Second World War, ideals changed yet again. With their husbands overseas, young women went to work so that industry could thrive. In their spare time, some of them formed professional sports teams. Again, society valued

competent, strong, and physically able women. However, things changed after the war. The men came home and cultural values shifted again to emphasize traditional family and gender roles. Women took to wearing dresses and skirts. Again highlighting the importance of fertility (this time period marked the beginning of the Baby Boom era), the population favored a more curvaceous frame like that of Marilyn Monroe (9).

8   In the 1960s, major changes were in the works. Along with people of color, women were again fighting for equality both in the home and in the workplace. The advent of the birth control pill afforded increased sexual freedom (9); women burned their bras. Similar to the trends found during the suffrage movement at the beginning of the century, women of the decade idealized thin and boyish bodies like that of the emaciated supermodel Twiggy.

Current Media Influence

9 The current media culture is complicated and very confusing. Women are told that they can and should "have it all." They expect family, career, and home to be perfect, and Martha Stewart tells them how to do it. The media inundates them with mixed messages about what is sexy, making it difficult to choose a role model. The heroin chic waif made popular by Kate Moss in the early 1990s competes with the voluptuous Baywatch babe personified by Pamela Anderson and the athletic soccer stars who celebrated a World Cup victory by tearing their shirts off. Though it is highly unlikely for a rail-thin woman to have natural DD-cup size breasts, toy manufacturers set this expectation by developing and marketing the Barbie doll, whose measurements are physiologically impossible. Thankfully, Barbie's designers revamped her figure back in the late 1990s (10). However, with increased availability of plastic surgery, today's women are faced with similarly unrealistic expectations every time they open a fashion magazine.

10   In 2002, actress Jamie Lee Curtis famously posed for More magazine, both in typical "glammed up" attire and then in her sports bra and shorts. The reality is that most magazines airbrush photos and use expensive computer technology to correct blemishes and hide figure flaws. In fact, in Jamie Lee's own words, she has " . . . very big breasts and a soft, fatty little tummy . . . and . . . back fat" (11). She felt that women should know that the figures portrayed by the media are rarely real. Granted, celebrities can afford to hire personal trainers and nutritionists to assist in their weight loss endeavors. Stylists select fetching outfits and tailors wait on standby to make sure that clothes fit like second skin. Before awards ceremonies, attendees routinely fast and endure tight-fitting undergarments to flatten their stomachs for unforgiving evening gowns.

11   Celebrities are no less susceptible to eating disorders than the rest of the population. Mary-Kate Olsen was hospitalized with anorexia nervosa, and the weekly gossip magazines have speculated consistently about the health of Lindsay Lohan and Nicole Richie. Their concern for the well-being of these young women is tainted by additional articles in the same issues of their publications which criticize

singer-actress Jennifer Lopez's ample bottom and praise supermodel Heidi Klum for being "runway ready" merely 4 weeks after giving birth to her second child. Twenty-five years ago, the average fashion model was 8% thinner than the average woman. Today, that number has risen to 23% (12), likely reflecting a combination of rising obesity rates in the general population and progressively thinner ideals. Even health and fitness magazines are not above scrutiny. Articles tout the importance of moderate diet and exercise, but pages are filled with advertisements for appetite suppressants and diet supplements. The diet industry is a multibillion dollar business (13). Women are consistently given the message that they are not pretty enough or thin enough.

12   No discussion of body image and the media would be complete without referencing Becker's landmark study comparing rates of eating disorders before and after the arrival of television in Fiji in 1995 (14). Ethnic Fijians have traditionally encouraged healthy appetites and have preferred a more rotund body type, which signified wealth and the ability to care for one's family (15). Strong cultural identity is thought to be protective against eating disorders; there was only one case of anorexia nervosa reported on the island prior to 1995. However, in 1998, rates of dieting skyrocketed from 0 to 69%, and young people routinely cited the appearance of the attractive actors on shows like "Beverly Hills 90210" and "Melrose Place" as the inspiration for their weight loss (14). For the first time, inhabitants of the island began to exhibit disordered eating.

13   Television shows continue to feature impossibly thin actors in lead roles. More recently, reality shows such as "The Swan" and "Dr. 90210," which feature plastic surgery and major makeovers, have been criticized for promoting unhealthy body image. In "The Swan," young women are separated from family and friends for several weeks to undergo an intensive diet and exercise plan. Hair stylists recommend hair extensions and highlights, and plastic surgeons perform breast augmentation, facelifts, and Botox and collagen injections. The end results are showcased in a beauty pageant, where formerly "ugly ducklings" compete against each other for the title of "The Swan."

Effects on Health

14 According to a recent study, children exposed to excessive TV viewing, magazines, and movies are at higher risk of obesity. When other variables are controlled, TV exposure independently increases the odds of becoming overweight by 50% for both men and women (16). Furthermore, the type of exposure, not the amount, is correlated with negative body image. Specifically, rates of exposure to soap operas, movies, and music videos were associated with higher rates of body dissatisfaction and drive for thinness (17). Excessive media consumption also may be correlated with the rate of childhood depression. This could be a function of negative body image, or may reflect the tendency of depressed kids to spend more time in front of the TV because of diminished energy.

15   As highlighted in a recent Newsweek article, classic eating disorders such as anorexia and bulimia are being diagnosed at younger ages (some as young as eight or

nine), and with higher frequency (18). A 1994 survey found that 40% of 9-year-olds have been on a diet (19). Clinicians now believe that eating disorders, previously ascribed to dysfunctional family dynamics, are multifactorial in origin. While family dynamics are certainly important, so too are biological predisposition to anxiety and mood disorders, interpersonal effectiveness skills, and cultural expectations of beauty. The development of proanorexia (pro-ana) and probulimia (pro-mia) websites on the Internet has been particularly concerning. Here, people who have made a "life style choice" to engage in eating-disordered behavior post messages detailing their weight loss progress and provide tips, support, and encouragement for their peers. Pictures of emaciated women resembling concentration camp victims serve as "thinsperation" (20).

16   Although fewer men meet criteria for anorexia and bulimia than do women, more men are becoming concerned with shape and weight (21, 22). While some of the manifestations are similar to the disordered eating found in women, there are some important differences as well. Men too are bombarded by media pressure. Pictures of thin, muscular, and perfectly coiffed "metrosexual" models appear in men's magazines. Gay and straight men alike are shelling out significant sums of money for gym memberships, styling products, salon haircuts, manicures, and waxing treatments. Duggan and McCreary found that reading muscle and fitness magazines correlated with levels of body dissatisfaction in both gay and straight men (23). Unlike Barbie, whose shape has become more realistic in recent years, action figures have become increasingly muscular and devoid of body fat (24). In the "Adonis Complex," a phenomenon with similarities to body dysmorphic disorder and anorexia nervosa, young men become obsessed with bulk and muscle mass, which can lead to overexercise, dietary restriction, and abuse of anabolic steroids (25).

17   With media pressure to be thin and a multibillion dollar dieting industry at our disposal, higher rates of eating disorders in the population seem concerning, but are also understandable. While cultural standards of beauty are certainly not new, today's media is far more ubiquitous and powerful. However, the reasons behind the growing obesity epidemic are not entirely clear.

18   For the most part, members of society strive to lead healthy lives. In addition to preaching the cosmetic appeal of weight loss, news reports warn of the risks of obesity, including heart disease and stroke (26). Frightened and inspired, overweight individuals begin strict diet and exercise regimens. They may even lose weight. However, our society is unique in that there is a surplus of cheap, micronutrient-dense food available, which is being advertised by the same media outlets advertising thinness and warning of the risks of obesity (27). After restricting too heavily, dieters often feel deprived. They binge on the unhealthy foods seen in advertisements, gain weight, feel poorly about themselves, and perpetuate the cycle. Less than 5% of individuals who have lost 20 pounds are able to keep it off for 5 years (28). In short, dieters pin all of their hopes on overly restrictive diets that were doomed to fail from the start. This, combined with a relatively sedentary life style, is likely responsible for increasing rates of obesity and disordered-eating behavior, such as dietary restriction, bingeing, and purging.

Baby Steps Toward Change

19 Clearly, the problem is complicated and there are no easy solutions. Parents and health care providers alike have a responsibility to talk with children about media messages and healthy life styles. Parents can limit exposure to television and talk with children about the messages portrayed on TV shows and in advertising. The American Academy of Pediatrics' current guidelines suggest that children watch no more than 1 to 2 hours of quality television per day and that parents watch programs with their children so they can discuss the content together (29).

20 A strong cultural identity is thought to be protective against eating disorders, and families can use this to their advantage by teaching children about the history of their ethnic or religious group. Furthermore, families can eat dinner together on a daily basis. In addition to ensuring that all family members are getting a nutritionally balanced dinner, parents have the opportunity to inquire about children's experiences at school, and the family can brainstorm together when problems arise.

21 In addition to providing regular family meals, parents need to take responsibility for providing healthy meals and snacks spaced at regular intervals throughout the day. They also need to allow for a reasonable number of treats so that kids do not feel deprived. Clinical experience consistently shows that individuals overeat when they are hungry or emotionally stressed; skipping meals during the day can lead to overeating at night. Moreover, studies have shown that children's eating behavior is influenced by the habits modeled by their parents (30) and that parental concern about a child's weight can negatively affect a child's self-evaluation (31). Families can plan fun outdoor activities, which increase physical activity without subjecting children to shame about their physical shortcomings. Studies consistently have shown that life style changes are most effective when undertaken by the entire family (32).

22 Health care providers should be quick to address concerns about obesity but must be careful to adopt an empathic, nonshaming approach. It is important not to restrict what children eat, but to encourage a healthy amount of physical activity and a moderate, healthy diet. Parents and clinicians should discourage dieting, as it rarely works in the long term. In addition, they should try not to focus too much on appearance or weight, as perceived pressure to be thin can lead to disordered eating. Most importantly, parents, teachers, and members of the health care community can encourage children to develop strengths such as music, art, or sports to foster healthy self-esteem. It is important for children to focus on mastery of an activity rather than comparing themselves to others (33). When adults suspect mood disorders or eating problems, children should be referred promptly for diagnosis and treatment.

23 Finally, the government needs to allocate funds to produce exciting, media-driven advertising campaigns to provide information to kids and families about good nutrition, exercise, and healthy self-esteem. Messages need to be visible at school, on TV, and online. Media is a formidable opponent precisely because advertising firms have the financial resources to produce clever advertisements that convince consumers to buy their products. Advertising executives are paid hefty salaries to try to find a way into the consumer's psyche. Magazine editors need to find ways to incorporate images of average-sized adults and teenagers into their publications. In addition, they need to find ways to resist publishing advertisements featuring emaciated models. ◆

ANALYSIS AND DISCUSSION

1. The authors note that it is tempting to blame today's media for "perpetuating and glorifying unrealistic standards of physical beauty," but that the truth is far more complex. What other factors have contributed to creating social pressure to confirm to an unrealistic body shape?
2. In what ways has the ideal body type been connected to socioeconomic status, both historically and currently? Explain.
3. The authors point out that today the average fashion model is 23% thinner than the average woman. Based on the article, and your personal experience, what accounts for this sharp disparity?
4. What solutions do the authors provide to counteract the media-driven pressure to be thin? In your opinion, how realistic are their solutions?

RESEARCH AND WRITING

1. Write an essay exploring the connections among the fashion industry, body image, and self-esteem. How has the media influenced our sense of self-worth and social acceptance? Support your view with research drawn from the references provide by the authors for their article as well as outside research of your own.
2. Gather photos from several different fashion magazines and analyze the body types presented in the ads and articles. What common elements do you notice? How are they similar or different? How do they compare to "real" people? Based on the photographs, what conclusions can you draw about fashion models in today's culture?
3. Prepare a response to the authors' recommendations. Directly address how realistic their solutions are to implement in the average American family. Include any additional recommendations of your own, pointing back to the authors' research as well as outside research of your own.

CULTURE SHOCK

Get Real Ad*

Most people who suffer from eating disorders, such as anorexia nervosa or bulimia, also experience distorted self-perception. The person they see in the mirror differs drastically from their physical reality. The National Eating Disorders Association (NEDA) launched the "Get Real" awareness campaign to portray how distorted the self-image of someone suffering from an eating disorder can be.

THINKING CRITICALLY ─────────────────

1. If you were leafing through a magazine and saw this ad, would you stop to read it? Why or why not? What catches your eye? How long would you spend looking at the ad? Explain.
2. Visit the NEDA Web site at *www.nationaleatingdisorders.org* and read about eating disorders in men and women (look at the "Eating Disorder Info" pages). Who is at risk for an eating disorder? What roles do social and cultural pressures play in exacerbating eating disorders? Explain.
3. What is happening in the photo? What is the woman thinking? What does she see? What do we see? What message does the photo convey?
4. Who is the target audience for this ad? Do you think someone with an eating disorder will be persuaded to follow the advice in the ad? If not, who is likely to respond to it? Explain.

───────────────

*This print ad was created for NEDA in 2005 by Porter Novelli, a public relations firm known for health promotion campaigns.

Out-of-Body Image
*Caroline Heldman**

Every day men and women are bombarded with images of buff and beautiful bodies. Media and advertising in particular present an idealized female shape that few women actually embody. Women begin to think of their bodies as objects rather than seeing themselves as people. The result, explains Caroline Heldman, professor of politics at Occidental College in Los Angeles, is a self-objectification that impairs women's body image, mental health, motor skills, and even their sex lives.

1   On a typical day, you might see ads featuring a naked woman's body tempting viewers to buy an electronic organizer, partially exposed women's breasts being used to sell fishing line, and a woman's rear—wearing only a thong—being used to pitch a new running shoe. Meanwhile, on every newsstand, impossibly slim (and digitally airbrushed) cover "girls" adorn a slew of magazines. With each image, you're hit with a simple, subliminal message: Girls' and women's bodies are objects for others to visually consume.

2   If such images seem more ubiquitous than ever, it's because U.S. residents are now exposed to 3,000 to 5,000 advertisements a day—as many per year as those living a half century ago would have seen in a lifetime. The Internet accounts for much of this growth, and young people are particularly exposed to advertising: 70 percent of 15- to 34-year-olds use social networking technologies such as MySpace and Facebook, which allow advertisers to infiltrate previously private communication space.

3   A steady diet of exploitative, sexually provocative depictions of women feeds a poisonous trend in women's and girl's perceptions of their bodies, one that has recently been recognized by social scientists as self-objectification—viewing one's body as a sex object to be consumed by the male gaze. Like W. E. B. DuBois' famous description of the experience of black Americans, self-objectification is a state of "double consciousness...a sense of always looking at one's self through the eyes of others."

> **What would disappear from our lives if we stopped seeing ourselves as objects? Painful high heels? Body hatred? Constant dieting? Liposuction? It's hard to know.**

4   Women who self-objectify are desperate for outside validation of their appearance and present their bodies in ways that draw attention. A study I did of 71 randomly selected female students from a liberal arts college in Los Angeles, for example, found that 70 percent were medium or high self-objectifiers, meaning that they have internalized the male gaze and chronically monitor their physical appearance. Boys and men experience self-objectification as well, but at a much lower

*Caroline Heldman, *Ms. Magazine,* Spring 2008

rate—probably because, unlike women, they rarely get the message that their bodies are the primary determination of their worth.

5   Researchers have learned a lot about self-objectification since the term was coined in 1997 by University of Michigan psychology professor Barbara Fredrickson and Colorado College psychology professor Tomi-Ann Roberts. Numerous studies since then have shown that girls and women who self-objectify are more prone to depression and low self-esteem and have less faith in their own capabilities, which can lead to diminished success in life. They are more likely to engage in "habitual body monitoring"—constantly thinking about how their bodies appear to the outside world—which puts them at higher risk for eating disorders such as anorexia and bulimia.

6   Self-objectification has also been repeatedly shown to sap cognitive functioning because of all the attention devoted to body monitoring. For instance, a study by Yale psychologists asked two groups of women to take a math exam—one group in swimsuits, the other in sweaters. The swimsuit-wearers, distracted by body concerns, performed significantly worse than their peers in sweaters.

7   Several of my own surveys of college students indicate that this impaired concentration by self-objectifiers may hurt their academic performance. Those with low self-objectification reported an average GPA of 3.5, whereas those with high self-objectification reported a 3.1. While this gap may appear small, in graduate school admissions, it represents the difference between being competitive and being out of the running for the top schools.

8   Another worrisome effect of self-objectification is that it diminishes political efficacy—a personal belief that he or she can have an impact through the political process. In another survey, 33 percent of high self-objectifiers felt low political efficacy, compared to 13 percent of low self-objectifiers. Since political efficacy leads to participation in politics, having less of it means that self-objectifiers may be less likely to vote or run for office.

9   The effects of self-objectification on young girls are of such growing concern that the American Psychological Association published an investigative report on it in 2007. The APA found that girls as young as 7 years old are exposed to clothing, toys, music, magazines, and television programs that encourage them to be sexy or "hot"—teaching them to think of themselves as sex objects before their own sexual maturity. Even thong underwear is being sold in sizes for 7- to 10-year-olds. The consequence, wrote Kenyon College psychology professor Sarah Murnen in the journal *Sex Roles*, is that girls "are taught to view their bodies as 'projects' that need work before they can attract others, whereas boys are likely to learn to view their bodies as tools to use to master the environment."

10   Fredrickson, along with Michigan communications professor Kristen Harrison (both work within the university's Institute for Research on Women and Gender), recently discovered that self-objectification actually impairs girls' motor skills. Their study of 202 girls, ages 10 to 17, found that self-objectification impeded girls' ability to throw a softball, even after differences in age and prior experience were factored out. Self-objectification forced girls to split their attention between how their bodies looked and what they wanted them to do, resulting in less forceful throws and worse aim.

11   One of the more stunning effects of self-objectification is its impact on sex. One young woman I interviewed described sex as being an "out of body" experience during which she viewed herself through the eyes of her lover, and, sometimes, through the imaginary lens of a camera shooting a porn film. As a constant critic of her body, she couldn't focus on her own sexual pleasure.

12   Self-objectification can likely explain some other things that researchers are just starting to study. For instance, leading anti-sexist male activist and author Jackson Katz observes, "'Many young women now engage in sex acts with men that prioritize the man's pleasure, with little or no expectation of reciprocity.' Could this be another result of women seeing themselves as sexual objects, not agents?"

13   Disturbingly, some girls and women celebrate their object status as a form of empowerment. This is evident in a booming industry of T-shirts for women that proclaim their object status. It would be encouraging if these choices reflected the sexual agency for women that feminists have fought so hard for, but they do not. The notion of objectification as empowering is illogical, since objects are acted upon, rather than taking action themselves. The real power in such arrangements lies with boys and men, who come to feel entitled to consume women as objects—first in media, then in real life.

14   Self-objectification isn't going anywhere anytime soon. So what can we do about it? First, we can recognize how our everyday actions feed the larger beast, and realize that we are not powerless. Mass media, the primary peddler of female bodies, can be assailed with millions of little consumer swords. We can boycott companies and engage in other forms of consumer activism, such as socially conscious investments and shareholder actions. We can also contact companies directly to voice our concerns and refuse to patronize businesses that overtly depict women as sex objects.

15   An example of women's spending power, and the limits of our tolerance for objectification, can be found in the 12-percent dip in profits of clothing company Victoria's Secret, due, according to the company's CEO, to its image becoming "too sexy." Victoria's Secret was not the target of an organized boycott; rather its increasingly risqué "bra and panty show" seems to have begun alienating women, who perhaps no longer want to simply be shown as highly sexualized window dressing.

16   Another strategy to counter one's own tendency to self-objectify is to make a point of buying products, watching programs, and reading publications that promote more authentic women's empowerment. This can be difficult, of course, in a media climate in which companies are rarely wholeheartedly body-positive. For instance, Dove beauty products launched a much lauded advertising campaign that used "real women" instead of models, but then Dove's parent company, Unilever, put out hypersexual ads for Axe men's body spray that showed the fragrance driving scantily clad women into orgiastic states.

17   Locating unadulterated television and film programming is also tough. Even Lifetime and Oxygen, TV networks created specifically for women, often portray us as weak victims or sex objects and present a narrow version of thin, white "beauty." Action films that promise strong female protagonists (think of the women in *X-Men*, or Lara Croft in *Tomb Raider*) usually deliver these characters in skintight clothes, serving the visual pleasure of men.

18   ˙ A more radical, personal solution is to actively avoid media that compels us to self-objectify—which, unfortunately, is the vast majority of movies, television programs, and women's magazines. Research with college-age women indicates that the less women consume media, the less they self-objectify, particularly if they avoid fashion magazines. What would women's lives look like if they viewed their bodies as tools to master their environment, instead of projects to be worked on? What would disappear if they stopped seeing themselves as objects? Painful high heels? Body hatred? Constant dieting? Liposuction?

19   It's hard to know. Perhaps the most striking outcome of self-objectification is the difficulty women have in imagining identities and sexualities truly our own. In solidarity, we can start on this path, however confusing and difficult it may be. ◆

CRITICAL THINKING

1. Heldman notes that young girls are taught—through media, toys, images, and culture—to think of themselves as objects rather than agents. If you are female, does this observation ring true? If you are male, what messages, images, and toys encouraged the development of your own identity? Explain.

2. Heldman notes that self-objectification is a state of "double consciousness . . . a sense of always looking at one's self through the eyes of others." How do young women "self-objectify"? What does it mean to self-objectify, and why is it harmful?

3. In paragraph 4, Heldman notes that a majority of women self-objectify, because they have learned through cultural and social messages that "their bodies are the primary determination of their worth." Respond to this statement with your own viewpoint.

4. What do you think of the test administered by Yale researchers, in which two groups of women took a math test, one group fully clothed and the other in swimsuits? What other factors could have contributed to the results? What do you think would have happened if the test had also been given to young men?

5. Evaluate the suggestions Heldman provides at the end of her essay. Would you consider doing any of them? Why or why not?

CRITICAL WRITING

1. *Exploratory Writing:* Vanity and obsessive preoccupation with self-image have historically been connected to women more than men. In your opinion, do men and women approach the issue of fashion and body image differently? If so, in what ways? What social and cultural pressures influence how men and women view themselves?

2. *Exploratory Writing*: In this essay, Heldman explains how self-objectification can harm women in many different ways. Write an essay in which you address how we strive to look a certain way to conform to

social expectations. Drawing from this article and others in the chapter, write an essay in which you explore the connection between our personal sense of self and our physical appearance.

GROUP PROJECTS

1. Make a list of the most popular prime-time shows on television. After compiling the list, identify the body size of the characters on each program. How many male and female characters could be considered overweight? What is the male-to-female ratio of these characters? Discuss your findings with the rest of the class in a discussion about how actors on television promote or do not promote certain body types as more desirable than others.

2. Heldman notes that women who read fashion magazines are more likely to self-objectify and to be uncomfortable with their physiques. Each member of your group should read a different fashion magazine, and include a men's magazine such as *Maxim* or *Men's Health*. Evaluate how men and women are presented in these magazines; include physical appearance, clothing style, accessories, and how they interact with other people in the articles and ads. As a group, discuss your observations and write a short summary of your discussion. Include any conclusions your group came to regarding the influence of fashion magazines on male and female body image and the messages we send to each gender about self-worth.

The Natural Beauty Myth
*Garance Franke-Ruta**

Critics of the beauty industry argue that it attacks women's self-esteem as it raises the beauty bar impossibly high. But journalist Garance Franke-Ruta argues that the fashion industry does not oppress women, but makes beauty accessible to all, because the truth is that there is no such thing as "natural beauty." Is what we have come to recognize as "natural beauty" really the result of chemicals, surgery, and a whole lot of suffering in the name of fashion?

1 Last week, Italy's government and some of its fashion moguls announced plans to crack down on the use of ultrathin models on the catwalk. This decision follows in the wake of Madrid's recently instituted ban on underweight models at its annual fashion show. Let's not rush to celebrate.

2 Pictures of beautiful but undernourished-looking women have led, in recent months, to a round of fashion-industry bashing in the press. One anonymous wit

---

*Garance Franke-Ruta, *The Wall Street Journal,* December 15, 2006

even mocked up satirical pictures of women who looked like concentration camp victims—except that they had masses of glossy hair and wore slinky clothes. As often happens when satire meets a mass audience, lots of people thought that the doctored pictures were real—which is how, one day in November, they wound up in my inbox, courtesy of a women and media list-serv.

3   A predictable discussion followed. Curvy women were praised for their healthy-seeming fuller figures. "Self-acceptance" was praised, too. It was argued that the evil images presented to women by the fashion industry were part of the broader plan of beauty magazines to make women feel bad about themselves and thus buy products for self-improvement.

4   Such a critique, which we hear over and over today, is based on a conceptual error. The beauty industry is not the problem; it is a part of the solution. American women today are the victims of a more insidious idea, an idea that underlies the American obsession with self-esteem: the tyrannical ideal of "natural beauty."

5   Few Americans today live a "natural" life, whatever that may be. The more educated and well-to-do among us may eat organic foods and avoid chemicals as best they can, but such efforts hardly make us "natural." Our society is too complex for that. Indeed, all societies involve such a thick layering of culture over our malleable essence that it is virtually impossible to say what we might be like in a natural state.

6   What is clear is that over the past century, American women have changed their shape. Most noticeably, they have gained so much poundage that today more than half are overweight and a third are clinically obese. The sharpest spike in obesity has come since the late 1970s. There are all sorts of reasons, of course—from the rise of corn syrup as a sweetener to the increased portion sizes of our daily meals and our increasingly sedentary styles of life. And yet the doctrine of "natural beauty"—so favored by the self-esteem brigades of the 1970s and still confusing women today—asks women to accept themselves as this unnatural environment has made them.

7   What the critics of the beauty industry further fail to recognize is that the doctrine of "natural beauty"—and the desire it breeds in women to be accepted as they are or to be seen as beautiful without any effort—is a ruthless and anti-egalitarian ideal. It is far more punishing than the one that says any woman can be beautiful if she merely treats beauty as a form of discipline.

8   Only in America do we think that beauty is a purely natural attribute rather than a type of artistry requiring effort. Look at the French: They are no more beautiful as a people than we Americans, but they understand that every woman can be attractive—if not beautiful—if she chooses to be. Yes, we are given forms by nature, but how we choose to present them is a matter of our own discretion. Few people are blessed by nature and circumstance with the Golden Mean proportions that seem to be universally appreciated. Thus, in the end, it is more democratic to think of beauty or attractiveness as an attribute that one can acquire, like speaking a foreign language or cooking well. To see

Only in America do we think that beauty is a purely natural attribute, rather than a type of artistry requiring effort.

beauty as a capacity like any other—the product of educated taste and daily discipline—is to see it as something chosen: to be possessed or left aside, according to one's preference.

9   The same goes, relatedly, for maintaining a certain size. In contemporary America, becoming thin is a choice that for most people requires rigorous and sometimes painful self-discipline. But so does becoming a lawyer or a concert pianist. The celebrity press is wrongly decried for giving women false ideals. In fact, it has demystified the relationship between effort and beauty, between discipline and weight. It opens up a path for non-celebrities.

10   One celebrity glossy recently estimated that in a single year, actress Jennifer Aniston spends close to the average woman's annual salary on trainers and other aspects of a high-level work-out. Former tween-queen Britney Spears told Oprah Winfrey that she used to do between 500 and 1,000 crunches a day to perfect her on-display abs. Actress Kate Hudson told one interviewer that to lose post-pregnancy "baby weight," she worked out three hours a day until she lost her 70 pounds: It was so hard that she used to sit on the exercise cycle and cry. Entertainment figures and models are like athletes; it takes a lot of discipline and social support to look like them. Money helps, too.

11   The celebrity magazines also specialize in a genre of stories best understood as tutorials in beauty as artifice: celebrities without their make-up. Makeover shows like "What Not to Wear" and "The Biggest Loser"—even "Queer Eye for the Straight Guy"—show beauty as something created, a condition to which anyone can have access with the right education and effort. This is a meritocratic ideal, not an insistent, elitist one. The makeover shows also help to make it clear that a life of artifice is not for everyone. Once we see the effort and hours that go into making a body more appealing, we may decide not to attempt a labor-intensive presentation of the self. We may decide that other things are more important.

12   Take, for example, U.S. Navy Cmdr. Sunita L. Williams, an astronaut who recently joined the staff of the International Space Station for six months. Since entering orbit she has announced plans to cut her long chestnut tresses and donate them to charity, because all that hair was uncomfortable and hard to manage in a zero-gravity environment. Most of us live in a less exotic environment, but the essence of our choice is the same. Just as it would be difficult for anyone to be a concert pianist and a nuclear scientist at the same time, it can be a pointless distraction for women to strive to maintain the time-consuming artifices of beauty while pursuing their other goals.

13   Ms. Williams spent her time in other ways and today has access to the most majestic natural beauty of all: the vision of our globe from space. But it took a half-century of human effort and discipline to put her there. ◆

CRITICAL THINKING

1. Evaluate the author's tone in this editorial. Identify phrases and words in which the author's tone attempts to influence her readers' reception of her point of view.

2. Is the fashion industry exerting pressure on women to be thin? Consider the women featured on the covers of popular magazines for men and women, including *Marie Claire*, *Cosmopolitan*, *Vogue*, *Maxim*, and *Vibe*. Do you think such magazine covers influence how we define beauty and desirability?
3. What does "natural beauty" mean to you? Why does the author claim that natural beauty is a false concept? Do you agree?
4. What is the conceptual error (paragraph 4) underlying critiques that the fashion industry is out to make women "feel bad" about their bodies? Explain.
5. The author points out that the physique of the average American woman has clearly changed its shape, and not for the better. Does this shift in size influence our concept of natural beauty?

CRITICAL WRITING

1. *Personal Narrative:* Write an essay in which you analyze your own feelings about your self-image. What factors do you think have shaped your feelings? What elements of our culture, if any, have influenced your development of body consciousness? Explain.
2. *Research Writing:* In this essay, Franke-Ruta claims that any woman can be beautiful, but it takes work. Does she have a point? Interview at least 10 people, men and women, from different ages and backgrounds, and ask them how much work is reasonable to be considered attractive. Do people who work harder, such as Kate Hudson on the treadmill, deserve our admiration? Why or why not?
3. *Reader's Response:* This essay appeared as an editorial in the *Wall Street Journal*. Imagine that you are a newspaper editorialist. Write a response to Franke-Ruta's essay, focusing on how effective you find her argument. Support your critique with examples from your personal observations and external research if necessary.

GROUP PROJECTS

1. With your group, gather magazine photographs of several models and analyze their body types. What common elements do you notice? How are they similar or different? How do they compare to "real" people? Based on the photographs, can you reach any conclusions about fashion models in today's culture and what it means to be beautiful?
2. Select two characters from a recent film or popular television program. Write a description of each character's body type and attire. Discuss with your group the connection, if any, between the physical appearance of the characters you selected and the temperament, personality, or nature of the character. What influence, if any, do the characters, or the actors who play them, exert on the fashion world and on our cultural constructions of beauty?

How Men Really Feel About Their Bodies

*Ted Spiker**

Many women are surprised to learn that many men fret about their bodies. While rarely discussed, many men worry about what they see in the mirror but feel that it is socially inappropriate to admit it. In this essay, author and journalism professor Ted Spiker relates his own experiences with male body image. Uncomfortable in his own skin since childhood, he explains to women why body image really does matter to men.

1 Dressed only in my underwear, I'm eight years old and sitting on the pediatrician's exam table, waiting for my checkup. My mother points to the two mounds of fatty flesh between my chest and belly. She asks the doctor, "Could they be tumors?" "No," he says, "it's just fat." Since that day, my fat has absorbed more darts than the back wall of a bar.

2 At six feet two and 215 pounds, I'm not huge. I just carry my weight where women do—in my hips, butt, and thighs. And I hate it. I hate the way clothes fit. I hate that friends say I use the "big-butt defense" in basketball.

3 I'm not the only man who wishes his body looked more like Michael Jordan's and less like a vat of pudding. A recent survey showed that only 18 percent of men are happy enough with their physiques that they wouldn't change them.

4 While women get there first, they don't have a monopoly on stressing over looks.

5 *One: We have more body angst than you realize . . .*
. . . but we'll never have a serious conversation with you about it. Look at the standards we have to measure up to: If we're fat, we're labeled as beer-guzzling couch potatoes. Too thin, and we're deemed wimpy. We can have too little hair on our heads or too much on our backs. And maybe worst of all, we can be too big in the backside of our pants yet too small in the front.

> *I'm not the only man who wishes his body looked more like Michael Jordan's and less like a vat of pudding.*

6 Now add the fact that our mental struggle has two layers.

7 "A man thinks, 'Not only does it bother me that I'm fat and my hair is thinning. It bothers me that it bothers me, because I'm not supposed to feel this way,'" says Thomas Cash, Ph.D., a professor of psychology at Old Dominion University in Norfolk, Virginia. "The thinking is that it's like a woman to worry about looks."

8 *Two: Instead, we'll joke about our bodies*
We make fun of ourselves to cover up what we're really feeling—frustration, embarrassment, and anger that we're not perfect.

9 But other people's jokes sting. Mark Meador, 37, of Westerville, Ohio, returned from a trip to Disney World with photos of himself.

---

10   "Man, you look like Big Pun," Meador's friend said, referring to the obese rapper who died of a heart attack. Meador laughed off the comment, not letting on that
it hurt. That same weekend, his daughter said, "Dad, you look like you're having a
baby." Fortunately for Meador, the gentle pokes inspired him to change. He dropped
junk food, started Tae Bo, and lost more than 40 pounds.

11   *Three: We're worried about our bodies because we're competing for you—and
against you*
With more people both marrying later and getting divorced, it's a competitive environment for finding mates. And since this generation of women can support themselves, they're freer to pick a man for his cute butt. Lynne Luciano, Ph.D., who
has researched body-image issues at California State University at Dominguez Hills,
says women are tired of being objectified and have turned the tables on men. "They
don't like a man to be overly vain," she says. "He shouldn't care too much about the
way he looks, but on the other hand, he should look good."

12   At the same time, men are also shaping up because they're seeing that people
who are fit are more successful at work. "Women are very good at using their looks
for competition," Cash says. "So men think, 'I'd better clean up my act.'"

13   *Four: We're not just checking you out*
We're a visual gender. We like the way you look. A lot. But that doesn't mean we
don't compare ourselves to other men the way women compare themselves to other
women. I notice the way men look on the beach, at work, or simply walking by.
Maybe it's male competitiveness or primal instincts, but we don't just want to have
better bodies to attract you. We want better bodies to improve our position among
ourselves.

14   A scary thought that proves the point: When Luciano interviewed doctors who
perform penis enlargements, they reported that the main reason men undergo the
surgery isn't to improve their relationships, but to be more impressive in the locker
room.

15   *Five: We want to look like we're 25*
It used to be that our mythical heroes had wisdom, experience, and maturity. Think
Harrison Ford as Indiana Jones. Now our heroes are baby-faced with six-pack abs.
Think Tobey Maguire as Spider-Man.

16   "The youth movement has been cruel to men," says Luciano. "The Cary Grants
have fallen through the cracks. Today's ideal is younger, buffer, more muscular. A
lot of men in their 40s and 50s have trouble trying to emulate that." So men, like
women, are swimming against the age current. That might explain why from 1997 to
2001, the number of men who had cosmetic surgery increased 256 percent.

17   *Six: Desperation makes us do desperate things*
Delusion makes us do nothing. I can't remember the last pair of pants that fit me
well. If I buy size 38s, they fit around the waist but suffocate my hips and butt. If I
go to a 40, they're roomy where I need it but gaping in the waist.

18   Several years ago, I tried on my wife's post-pregnancy size-20 jeans to see
if they were cut differently. The jeans fit me perfectly. I wore those jeans for
six months, and I felt leaner every day I wore them. My wife asked me why I
didn't just buy a big pair of men's jeans and have a tailor alter them. My answer:
Why pay for alterations when I know that tomorrow I'm going to start an exercise

routine that will change my body shape forever? It's been my mantra for two decades.

19 *Seven: Men's body image problems can be just as dangerous as women's*
For some men, poor body image can lead to anger, anxiety, depression, sexual dysfunction, and steroid abuse. Doctors may fail to recognize eating disorders or muscle dysmorphia (the need to constantly bulk up), even though it's estimated that eating disorders affect one million men.

20 Roberto Olivardia, Ph.D., a clinical psychologist at Harvard Medical School and coauthor of *The Adonis Complex,* says secrecy reinforces the patients' sense of shame. "I've treated men who would tell people they were alcoholics, but they'd never admit they were bulimic," he says.

21 *Eight: We don't blame anyone*
(Except maybe Tiger Woods and Taco Bell.) But we'll be grateful to anyone who makes us feel good about shaping up. We know what it's like to be bombarded with images of perfect bodies. We see the men in commercials and on magazine covers, the bigger-stronger-better mentality that dominates our culture.

22 "Look at Tiger Woods. The best golfer in the world has an outstanding physique. Golfers used to be everyday men," says J. Kevin Thompson, Ph.D., professor of psychology at the University of South Florida. "Basketball players used to be skinny. They're all muscular now." ◆

CRITICAL THINKING

1. Try to imagine the "perfect" male body. What does it look like? Is your image influenced by outside forces, such as the media, your gender, or your age? How do "real men" you know compare to the image in your mind?

2. "The thinking is that it's like a woman to worry about looks." Do you agree with the author's assertion? Give examples to contradict or corroborate the statement.

3. Who is Spiker's intended audience, and what do you think he is trying to achieve in this article? Give a concrete example from the text to explain your answer.

4. When is it right to criticize others for how they look in hopes of eliciting change? Could these "gentle pokes" potentially backfire, or can they inspire a positive outcome? Find the example in Spiker's article in which criticism influenced weight loss.

5. Spiker asserts that men want to have better bodies to "improve our position among ourselves." For men, is physical perfection necessarily related to social stature? Explain.

CRITICAL WRITING

1. *Persuasive Writing:* You have probably heard the expressions "Don't judge a book by its cover" and "The clothes don't make the man." Write an essay in which you agree or disagree with these statements. Be sure to support your position with logical examples.

2. *Exploratory Writing:* Media critic George Gerbner has observed that "what we see on TV and in magazines eventually becomes our standard of reality and desire." Respond to this statement with your own opinion and experience. How has the media, especially TV and magazines, influenced your personal reality of body image? What about your expectations of what you desire in a partner?

3. *Research Writing:* According to Spiker's statistical data, "from 1997 to 2001, the number of men who had cosmetic surgery increased 256 percent." Research the most popular trends of cosmetic surgery for men along with how and why they are doing this. Find at least one male celebrity who has had cosmetic surgery and report your findings.

GROUP PROJECTS

1. Create and administer your own survey regarding the ideal male appearance. As a group, come up with a list of qualities—such as intelligence, body build, facial features, sense of humor, and physical strength—that can be ranked in order of importance. Try to come up with 8 to 12 qualities or characteristics. Distribute your poll among men and women on your campus (indicate whether the poll is given to a man or a woman). Tabulate the results and present your findings to the class. For an interesting comparison, groups may also want to distribute a similar list of female characteristics and qualities.

2. Spiker mentions modern day superheroes being "baby-faced with six-pack abs." As a group, determine the 10 most popular superheroes found on television and/or on the big screen. In a chart, compare and contrast age, size, body shape, gender, race, hair, and facial features. Discuss what might account for the similarities and/or differences.

CULTURE SHOCK

Mr. Olympia

The Mr. Olympia competition is organized by the International Federation of Bodybuilding and Fitness (IFBB). The 2011 Mr. Olympia winner was Phil Heath, pictured here.

THINKING CRITICALLY

1. What social messages do competitions such as Mr. Olympia and Mr. Universe convey to young males about the ideal male physique?
2. In your opinion, is this an ideal male body? Why or why not?
3. In what ways do advertising, the media, and professional sports influence male body image?
4. Review some popular men's magazines. How are men depicted in these magazines? Do they resemble Mr. Olympia or Mr. Universe?

Never Too Buff

*John Cloud**

We tend to assume that most men simply do not care about their appearance the way women do. But psychiatrists Harrison Pope and Katharine Phillips and psychologist Roberto Olivardia report in *The Adonis Complex* (2000) on a disturbing trend: just as many young women aspire to be supermodel thin, an increasing number of young men yearn for the steroid-boosted and buff bodies typical of today's action heroes and weightlifters. John Cloud reports on this groundbreaking research and what it might mean for boys and men in the years ahead.

1 Pop quiz: Who is more likely to be dissatisfied with the appearance of their chests, men or women? Who is more likely to be concerned about acne, your teenage son or his sister? And who is more likely to binge eat, your nephew or your niece?

2 　　If you chose the women and girls in your life, you are right only for the last question—and even then, not by the margin you might expect. About 40 percent of Americans who go on compulsive eating sprees are men. Thirty-eight percent of men want bigger pecs, while only 34 percent of women want bigger breasts. And more boys have fretted about zits than girls, going all the way back to a 1972 study.

3 　　A groundbreaking new book declares that these numbers, along with hundreds of other statistics and interviews the authors have compiled, mean something awful has happened to American men over the past few decades: They have become obsessed with their bodies. Authors Harrison Pope and Katharine Phillips, professors of psychiatry at Harvard and Brown, respectively, and Roberto Olivardia, a clinical psychologist at McLean Hospital in Belmont, Massachusetts, have a catchy name to describe this obsession, a term that will soon be doing many reps on chat shows: the *Adonis complex.*

4 　　The name, which refers to the gorgeous half man, half god of mythology, may be a little too ready for Oprah, but the theory behind it will start a wonderful debate. Based on original research involving more than a thousand men over the past 15 years, the book argues that many men desperately want to look like Adonis, because they constantly see the "ideal," steroid-boosted bodies of actors and models, and because their muscles are all they have over women today. In an age when women fly combat missions, the authors ask, "What can a modern boy or man do to distinguish himself as being 'masculine'?"

5 　　For years, of course, some men—ice skaters, body builders, George Hamilton— have fretted over aspects of their appearance. But the numbers suggest that body-image concerns have gone mainstream: nearly half of men do not like their overall appearance, in contrast to just 1 in 6 in 1972. True, men typically are fatter now, but

*John Cloud, *TIME* magazine, April 24, 2000

another study found that 46 percent of men of normal weight think about their appearance "all the time" or "frequently." And some men—probably hundreds of thousands, if you extrapolate from small surveys—say they have passed up job and even romantic opportunities because they refuse to disrupt workouts or dine on restaurant food. In other words, an increasing number of men would rather look brawny for their girlfriends than have sex with them.

6   Consider the money spent: Last year American men forked over $2 billion for gym memberships and another $2 billion for home exercise equipment. *Men's Health* ("Rock-hard abs in six weeks!" it screams every other issue) had 250,000 subscribers in 1990; now it has 1.6 million. In 1996 alone, men underwent some 700,000 cosmetic procedures.

7   At least those profits are legal. Anabolic steroids, the common name for synthetic testosterone, have led to the most dramatic changes in the male form in modern history; and more and more average men want those changes for themselves. Since steroids became widely available on the black market in the 1960s, perhaps three million American men have swallowed or injected them—mostly in the past 15 years. A 1993 survey found that 1 Georgia high school boy in every 15 admitted to having used steroids without a prescription. And the Drug Enforcement Administration reports that the percentage of all high school students who have used steroids has increased 50 percent in the past four years, from 1.8 to 2.8

The G.I. Joe of 1982 looks scrawny compared with G.I. Joe Extreme, introduced in the mid-1990s. If G.I. Joe Extreme were a real man, he would have a 55-inch chest and 27-inch biceps, which simply cannot be replicated in nature.

percent. The abuse of steroids has so alarmed the National Institute on Drug Abuse that it launched a campaign in gyms, malls, bookstores, clubs, and on the Internet to warn teenagers about the dangers. Meanwhile, teenagers in even larger numbers are buying legal but lightly regulated food supplements, some with dangerous side effects, that promise to make them bigger, leaner, or stronger.

8   As they infiltrated the bodybuilding world in the 1970s and Hollywood a decade later, steroids created bodies for mass consumption that the world had literally never seen before. Pope likes to chart the changes by looking at Mr. America winners, which he called up on the Internet in his office last week. "Look at this guy," Pope exclaimed when he clicked on the 1943 winner, Jules Bacon. "He couldn't even win a county bodybuilding contest today." Indeed, there are 16-year-olds working out at your gym who are as big as Bacon. Does that necessarily mean that today's bodybuilders—including those 16-year-olds—are 'roided? Pope is careful. "The possibility exists that rare or exceptional people, those with an unusual genetic makeup or a hormonal imbalance, could achieve the muscularity and leanness of today's big bodybuilders," he says.

9   But it is not likely. And Pope is not lobbing dumbbells from an ivory tower: he lifts weights six days a week, from 11 AM to 1 PM. (He can even mark historical occasions by his workouts: "I remember when the Challenger went down; I was doing a set of squats.") "We are being assaulted by images virtually impossible to attain

without the use of drugs," says Pope. "So what happens when you change a million-year-old equilibrium of nature?"

10   A historical loop forms: Steroids beget pro wrestlers—Hulk Hogan, for one, has admitted to taking steroids—who inspire boys to be just like them. Steroids have changed even boys' toys. Feminists have long derided Barbie for her tiny waist and big bosom. The authors of *The Adonis Complex* see a similar problem for boys in the growth of G.I. Joe. The grunt of 1982 looks scrawny compared with G.I. Joe Extreme, introduced in the mid-1990s. If he were a real man, G.I. Joe Extreme would have a 55-inch chest and 27-inch biceps, which simply cannot be replicated in nature. Pope also points out a stunning feature of the 3-year-old video game *Duke Nukem: Total Meltdown,* developed by GT Interactive Software. When Duke gets tired, he can find a bottle of steroids to get him going. "Steroids give Duke a super adrenaline rush," the game manual notes.

11   To bolster their argument, the *Adonis* authors developed a computerized test that allows subjects to "add" muscle to a typical male body. Subjects estimate their own size and then pick the size they would like to be and the size they think women want. Pope and his colleagues gave the test to college students and found that on average, the men wanted 28 pounds more muscle, and they thought women wanted them to have 30 pounds more. In fact, the women who took the test picked an ideal man only slightly more muscular than average, which goes a long way toward explaining why Leonardo DiCaprio can be a megastar in a nation that also idealizes "Stone Cold" Steve Austin.

12   But when younger boys took Pope's test, they revealed an even deeper sense of inadequacy about their bodies. More than half of the boys aged 11 to 17 chose as their physical ideal an image attainable only by using steroids: So they do. Boys are a big part of the clientele at Muscle Mania (not its real name), a weight-lifting store that *TIME* visited last week at a strip mall in a Boston suburb. A couple of teenagers came in to ask about Tribulus, one of the many over-the-counter drugs and body-building supplements the store sells—all legally.

13   "A friend of mine," one boy begins, fooling no one, "just came off a cycle of juice, and he heard that Tribulus can help you produce testosterone naturally." Patrick, 28, who runs the store and who stopped using steroids four years ago because of chest pain, tells the kid, "The s__ shuts off your nuts," meaning steroids can reduce sperm production, shrink the testicles, and cause impotence. Tribulus, Patrick says, can help restart natural testosterone production. The teen hands over $12 for 100 Tribulus Fuel pills. (Every day, Muscle Mania does $4,000 in sales of such products, with protein supplements and so-called fat burners leading the pack.)

14   Patrick says many of his teen customers, because they are short on cash, will not pay for a gym membership "until they've saved up for a cycle [of steroids]. They don't see the point without them." The saddest customers, he says, are the little boys, 12 and 13, brought in by young fathers. "The dad will say, 'How do we put some weight on this kid?' with the boy just staring at the floor. Dad is going to turn him into Hulk Hogan, even if it's against his will."

15   What would motivate someone to take steroids? Pope, Phillips, and Olivardia say the Adonis complex works in different ways for different men. "Michael," 32,

one of their research subjects, told *TIME* he had always been a short kid who got picked on. He started working out when he was about 14, and he bought muscle magazines for advice. The pictures taunted him: he sweated, but he was not getting as big as the men in the photos. Other men in his gym also made him feel bad. When he found out they were on steroids, he did two cycles himself, even though he knew they could be dangerous.

16   But not all men with body-image problems take steroids. Jim Davis, 29, a human services manager, told *TIME* he never took them, even when training for bodybuilding competitions. But Davis says he developed a form of obsessive-compulsive disorder around his workouts. He lifted weights six days a week for at least six years. He worked out even when injured. He adhered to a rigid regimen for every session, and if he changed it, he felt anxious all day. He began to be worried about clothes, and eventually he could wear only three shirts—the ones that made him look big. Yet he still felt small. "I would sit in class at college with a coat on," he says. You may have heard of this condition, called *bigorexia:* thinking your muscles are puny when they are not. Pope and his colleagues call it *muscle dysmorphia* and estimate that hundreds of thousands of men suffer from it.

17   Even though most boys and men never approach the compulsion of Michael or Jim, who eventually conquered it, they undoubtedly face more pressure now than in the past to conform to an impossible ideal. Ripped male bodies are used today to advertise everything that shapely female bodies advertise: not just fitness products but also dessert liqueurs, microwave ovens, and luxury hotels. The authors of *The Adonis Complex* want guys to rebel against those images, or at least to see them for what they are: a goal unattainable without drug use.

18   Feminists raised these issues for women years ago, and more recent books, such as *The Beauty Myth* (1991), were part of a backlash against the hourglass ideal. Now, says Phillips, "I actually think it may be harder for men than women to talk about these problems, because it's not considered masculine to worry about such things." But maybe there is a masculine alternative: Next time WWE comes on, guys, throw the TV out the window and order a large pizza. ◆

CRITICAL THINKING

1. Pope, Phillips, and Olivardia report that, in general, men would like to add 28 pounds more muscle to their frames but believe women would prefer at least 30 pounds more muscle. What, in your opinion, accounts for this perception? Does it seem reasonable?

2. Evaluate the comment made by Pope, Phillips, and Olivardia that young men are increasingly obsessed with body image, because they feel that muscle is "all they have over women today." Do you agree or disagree with this statement? Explain.

3. Analyze the author's use of statistics to support his points. Do their conclusions seem reasonable based on the data they cite? Why or why not?

4. According to the author, what cultural messages tell children that steroid use is okay? Describe some of the ways children receive these messages.

CRITICAL WRITING

1. *Analytical Writing:* Write a detailed description of your ideal male image (what you desire in a male or what you would most want to look like as a male). How does your description compare with the conclusions drawn by the psychiatrists and psychologist in the article? Did outside cultural influences direct your description? Explain.
2. *Personal Narrative:* Looking back at your experience in high school, write a narrative about the males who were considered the most buff. What qualities made these particular males more desirable and more enviable than their peers? How much of their appeal was based on their physical appearance? How much was based on something else?
3. *Persuasive Writing:* Pope, Phillips, and Olivardia comment that media pressure is connected to the emergence of men's new obsession with body image. Write an essay discussing whether this is true or not true. Support your perspective using examples from Cloud's article and your own experience.

GROUP PROJECTS

1. Have everyone in the group bring a copy of a men's magazine, such as *Details, GQ,* or *Esquire.* Different group members may want to focus on different aspects of the magazines, such as advertising, articles, fashion, or advice columns. Do the models in the magazine fit the description in Cloud's article? What do the articles suggest men should aspire to look like? How many articles on improving appearance are featured? After reviewing the magazines, discuss your findings and collaborate on an essay about how men's fashion magazines help define the ideal male.
2. Working in small groups, arrange to visit your campus gym or local health club. Split up and take notes about what kinds of men you see working out there. What patterns of behavior do you see? For example, are there more men working out with weights than doing aerobics? Write brief descriptions of the men's workout attire. Do they seem concerned with how they look? Why or why not? After your visit, get together and compare notes. Write a report on your findings and present your conclusions to the class.

► **Why I Rue My Tattoo**
Beth Janes*

► **Tattoo Me Again and Again**
Stephanie Dolgoff

The next two readings explore the aftereffects of tattooing. The process of tattooing can be traced back 5,000 years, and tattoos are as diverse as the people who wear them. In recent years, however, tattooing has gone from a subversive form of self-expression to a popular form of body art, especially among people under 30. For some of the initiated, the tattoo is a source of pride; however, for others, the tattoo causes embarrassment and regret. In "Why I Rue My Tattoo," Beth Janes explains how her impulsive attempt at body art went awry. Stephanie Dolgoff, however, observes in "Tattoo Me Again and Again" her choice of body art reflects important moments in her life. Carefully considered, tattoos are reminders of the things we care deeply about. How will this new generation of the tattooed feel in 10, 20, or 40 years? Perhaps they will be as diverse as these next two articles.

Why I Rue My Tattoo
Beth Janes

1 I got my second tattoo when I was 19. For two hours, I lay belly down, butt up, with my Levi's pulled low enough to have a good plumber look happening. Doc, the tatted-out, 50-something shop owner, hunched over my bum, his wiry gray hair dusting my skin and his buzzing, needled handpiece imprinting me with what turned out to be a permanent Rorschach inkblot. Not exactly the swirling design I initially had in mind. I wanted an image that was one part delicate, one part strong, like something you'd see on a fancy wrought-iron gate. Instead I was branded with an abstract, somewhat vulgar design with a point directed straight down my crack.

2 "Wow, it's great," I said, lying through my teeth, still gritted from the needle's sting.

3 "Hot. Really hot," Doc said. My friend Jessie, seated next to me and there for moral support, offered similar affirmations. But a little voice inside of my head said, Ugh.

---

*Beth Janes, *MSNBC,* October 4, 2007; Stephanie Dolgoff, *Self,* September, 2007.

4   It wasn't Doc's fault. He was a pro; I was the amateur, an amateur at thinking things through. I had thought I possessed that skill. It had been present a year earlier when, in the same chair, with Jessie by my side, I got my first tattoo, a good-luck ladybug southwest of my belly button.

5   Jessie and I got our first tats together to spice up our senior year at Catholic school. Three times before the appointment, I drove my 1988 Oldsmobile to the library, where I sat cross-legged in my uniform kilt, thumbing through books, looking for the perfect depiction. The spot I had chosen on my body was a bit clichéd but easily hidden from potential employers and by a wedding dress. (That was my mother's sole wish, which I granted because she was less than thrilled about the tattoo but didn't try to stop me.) When it was done, I loved it. I loved it even after someone pointed out that, thanks to the ladybug's tilt and placement, it looked as if a bug were crawling out of my underwear.

6   But when I got that second tattoo a year later, there was no research involved. I simply made a decision right before the lower-back-tattoo trend took off. To me, the tattoos, and those who sported them at the time, seemed tough—in a good way. If I got one, I thought, I would still be a nice girl, the occasional Ann Taylor shopper and A student, but I'd be drawing out the Sonic Youth–listening, beer-swigging badass I also identified with.

For every tattoo cherished, there's another that brings regret.

7   I gave Doc the picture of the design, which I had found on a friend's T-shirt. He said it wouldn't reproduce with the same detail on my skin but that he'd sketch something similar that would. My critical mistakes came after that: The final design wasn't exactly what I wanted, but I convinced myself that it looked cool enough (mistake one). Not only was I too shy to ask for other sketches (two), but I was so eager to get the tattoo that I spent 30 seconds thinking it over after seeing the drawing (three). Once I saw the stencil on my skin, I thought, it will be fine. The Ugh voice was there, but I ignored it. Perhaps the voice, likely dressed in a cashmere sweater set, was being smothered by a badass in a concert tee.

8   In the weeks after, I lied to friends about my feelings. I even tried to convince myself that I liked the tattoo, that it conveyed the tough side I was desperate to show off to the world in order to balance my good-girl side. A few months later, though, I started seeing girls everywhere (and not only the tough types that had initially inspired me) sporting lower-back tattoos. Mall rats in belly shirts, cheerleaders, sex sirens, moody emo-girls and preppy blondes all showed off ink when bending over to pick up their pom-poms/mix tapes/polo mallets. I had little in common with these girls before my tattoo, but now we were officially connected. My plan had backfired. Not only might people get the wrong idea about me, they might actually get the worst idea: that I was yet another too-trendy girl who thought tattoos were just, like, so cool. I might as well have asked for a tattoo that said "Trying too hard."

9   Somewhere along the way, though, the regret started to fade. At first it was superficial realizations: I thought, At least I didn't get an ex-boyfriend's name

or a Chinese character that instead of meaning beautiful symbolizes harlot. But then, as I graduated from college and began living on my own and flourishing in my career, I started to feel more comfortable with myself at a deeper level. I liked the person I had become and accepted all the decisions I had made along the way, including the tattoo. While at a friend's wedding, reflecting on how marriage would change her life, I began to ponder my own path and realized that I had, in fact, become a real badass. To me, that had nothing to do with listening to the right music, wearing the latest clothes or deciding to get my second tattoo—and everything to do with being fearless about my true self and accepting who I was, inside and out.

10   A decade later, I'm not embarrassed if my tattoo peeks out or friends make a joke. At my grandfather's funeral, for instance, I had to bow at the altar before giving my reading. I was wearing high-waisted pants (thank you, Marc Jacobs, for a rise of more than 8 inches) and a blouse I was certain fell beyond the safety zone. After mass, though, a cousin said, "Father Michael saw your tattoo, and he wanted me to tell you he's very disappointed." He then clapped me on the back and broke into a full belly laugh. I felt good, even honored, that the tattoo could provide joke fodder for my relatives—and that I could laugh, too.

11   When it comes to regrets, my tattoo falls somewhere between a misguided hookup and the time I drove after one too many beers. For it and all my other mistakes, I've forgiven myself—and instead of contemplating laser removal, I choose to look at the tattoo as a reminder of who I was and who I am now. Sure, I'll keep making mistakes, but I'm smart enough now to recognize and avoid those I may later come to regret. Why spend thousands of dollars erasing this bad decision when I could use the money to make good ones: traveling, helping a friend, buying more Marc Jacobs trousers? And as far as worrying about what people will think of me if they accidentally see my tattoo: If they don't also see that I'm a fun and empathetic friend, a smart woman and a kind and responsible person, then f--- 'em ; the badass in me doesn't care. ◆

 ## Tattoo Me Again and Again
Stephanie Dolgoff

1 Anyone who tells you that getting a tattoo doesn't hurt is either lying or lying. Or she may be so hopped up on Vicodin that although the process is torturous, she's too loopy to care. Or it might be like childbirth amnesia: She's so pleased with the results that she's blocked out what it feels like to have an electric needle scraped back and forth over her delicate skin. Any of those would explain why people—like me—get more than one.

2   I went the Vicodin route when I got my third and most recent tattoo six months ago, popping one pill and then later another, which I had saved from my cesarean

section a few years ago. This latest tattoo, two lush pink and plum peonies on my left inner ankle, hurt more than the C-section. Like I've never regretted having my twin girls, I've never regretted getting my tats or looked back and thought, What was I thinking? (They don't give epidurals for tattoos, after all.) That's because I knew exactly what I was thinking all three times.

> *Like I've never regretted having my twin girls, I've never regretted getting my tats or looked back and thought, What was I thinking?*

3   I got my first tattoo—a small line drawing of one of Picasso's doves—above my right shoulder blade when I was 25, right before I quit my job, packed up my life, and moved to Seville to teach English. I'd felt so embraced by the city (and by a guy named Manolo) when I'd visited a few years earlier that I was sure it was my natural home. I didn't wind up staying, but the decision was one of the best I've ever made. I learned that I could fly above life's expectations and rely on myself for all my needs if I had to. (Oh, and that Spanish men who still live with their parents—i.e., most single Spanish men—are a wee bit immature.)

4   Nine years later, I got a second dove on the small of my back, right before my husband and I became engaged. It signified the calm, soaring feeling I had after years of searching for the right partner. It had partly to do with Paul, who made me feel safe and loved, but even more to do with the fact that I'd grown into a person who knew how to include people like Paul in her life. And the third tattoo, the largest and most painful, those dual-colored peonies situated above my foot? They represent my fraternal twin girls, Sasha and Vivian, two very different flowers growing on the same vine. Now they'll always be with me, even when we're apart.

5   Each of my three tattoos represents a major emotional milestone or epiphany and serves as a bodily reminder of the freedom I felt because of my new experience or bit of knowledge. They're like signposts along the road to now, someplace I feel lucky to be. When I look at them, I can feel again the exhilaration of the life-altering shift that pointed me squarely toward personal peace and fulfillment. If I'd gotten Denzel Forever on my butt or Hello Kitty on my inner arm during a drunken moment, I might well regret it. In general, though, I'm not a big regretter. I tend to see even the dumbest decisions as learning experiences ("Google? What a stupid name for a company. No way am I investing!"), as opposed to evidence of what a fool I was when I was younger.

6   My reasons for getting my tattoos make sense to me, and that's all that matters. There are as many reasons to get a tattoo as there are images to express people's personal experiences, memories, emotions or even favorite band, if you feel that strongly about it. The best reasons have this in common: They please the person wearing the body art, not necessarily the person looking at it. One friend got a leafy cuff around her upper arm purely because it made her feel like a hot mama; another went with her best friend and got matching Japanese symbols for happiness, to give their friendship its symbolic due; still another got a C-sized battery on her hip, to remind her that she needs to stop and recharge.

7   Whatever the meaning, you're more likely to be happy with your tattoo if you have a reason—or reasons, in my case—you can live with forever, like the tattoo itself. You can't think of a permanent piece of skin art as a haircut that, once you're tired of it, you can let grow out. And even though it's possible to have a tattoo removed, the process certainly isn't easy. The few people I know who regret their tattoos say they liked them when they got them but now hate what they project to potential bosses or mothers-in-law. It's true that you never know how radically your priorities or career goals (or the names of your lovers—I'm talking to you, Angelina) will change over time. (Case in point: I know a woman who, in her 20s, covered both of her arms in colorful mermaids and ivy vines. She now works with children; the kids think her tattoos are cool, but she wears long-sleeved shirts around the parents, mostly because she doesn't want to lose clients.) But I like to think if I ever forsook writing for, say, holding public office, becoming a trophy wife for a prominent real estate magnate or even turning letters on Wheel of Fortune, I'd be so good at what I did that people would forgive my tattoos as one of the eccentricities that come with creative genius. Clearly I'm not that concerned, though—not least of all because I know many hard-driving female CEOs have secret ladybugs, hearts or lotus blossoms hidden under their posh, tailored suits. These days, Satanic pentagrams, swastikas and symbols of anarchy aside, most tattoos hardly signify rebellion.

8   Although I love my tattoos, I don't plan on getting any more, mostly because I'm running out of spots on my body that will never droop, get stretched out or grow hair—all of which would ruin even the most beautiful, well-thought-out design. After getting the peonies, I told Paul of my decision to call it quits. He said he distinctly remembered my saying that the last time. And he's probably right. So I never say never, except that I know I'll never regret my tattoos. ◆

CRITICAL THINKING

1. Janes's article sets up the audience to believe that she "rues" her tattoo; however, she changes her tone to one of acceptance in her conclusion. Does the author convince you of her acceptance, or do you think she is still trying to convince herself that she likes the tattoo?

2. How were Janes's and Dolgoff's experiences different when getting their tattoos? Do you think this could have led to why they have different attitudes about their tattoos?

3. If you have a tattoo, what image do you think it will project to "potential bosses or mothers-in-law"? If you don't have a tattoo, what have been your reasons for not getting one? Would you ever consider it? Why or why not?

4. Dolgoff argues, "If I ever forsook writing for, say, holding public office, becoming a trophy wife for a prominent real estate magnate or even turning letters on Wheel of Fortune, I'd be so good at what I did that people would forgive my tattoos as one of the eccentricities that come with

creative genius." Do you agree that her tattoos would be "forgiven" in these circumstances? Explain. Also, is getting a tattoo a form of "creative genius"? Explain.

5. In Dolgoff's article, she asserts, "These days, Satanic pentagrams, swastikas and symbols of anarchy aside, most tattoos hardly signify rebellion." Do you agree or disagree with this statement? Explain.

CRITICAL WRITING

1. *Persuasive Writing:* Write an essay in which you argue either for getting a tattoo or against getting one. Use personal experience for your reasoning, and if you already have a tattoo, explain whether you have any regrets or, if you have none, why you would do it again.

2. *Research Writing:* Research the current trend for tattoo removal. Try to find statistics on how many people are getting tattoos compared to how many people are removing them. Also explain the different processes for tattoo removal and which are most effective. Add details on any personal experiences that you may find in your research.

3. *Exploratory Writing:* Write an essay in which you explore the idea of tattoos as a form of self-expression that set you apart from others. For example, when you see someone with a tattoo, what do you think? Is this person a rebel, subversive, trendy, a "creative genius," or something else? Which prejudices are associated with tattoos in our current lifestyle, and which prejudices no long exist?

GROUP PROJECT

1. Explore the reasoning behind getting a tattoo. Is it to be a "badass" as Janes suggests, or is it to give a special memory permanence as Dolgoff suggests? Try to come up with a brainstorm list of as many reasons as you can think of. Summarize all of the reasons given by the authors and then creative a more extensive list of your own. You may wish to interview students who have tattoos and ask them to discuss their motivations for their choices in body art.

Perspectives: Restroom Designation

Mike Keefe/PoliticalCartoons.com

THINKING CRITICALLY

1. What issue is this cartoon highlighting for discussion? Explain.
2. Do you think this cartoon would appeal to both women and men? Does it make a connection to one group more than another?
3. Based on articles in this chapter, do you think this cartoon would have resonated 50 years ago? 20? Explain.

CHAPTER
2

Consumer Nation

Wanting It, Selling It

Advertising is everywhere—television, newspapers, magazines, the Internet, the sides of buses and trains, highway billboards, T-shirts, sports arenas, and even license plates. It is the driving force of our consumptive economy, accounting for $150 billion worth of commercials and print ads each year—more than the gross national product of many countries. Advertising fills a quarter of each television hour and the bulk of most newspapers and magazines. It is everywhere people are, and its appeal goes to the quick of our fantasies: happiness, material wealth, eternal youth, social acceptance, sexual fulfillment, and power. Through carefully selected images and words, advertising is the most pervasive form of persuasion in America and perhaps the single most significant manufacturer of meaning in our consumer society, and many of us are not aware of its astounding influence on our lives.

Most of us are so accustomed to advertising that we hear it without listening and see it without looking. However, if we stop to examine how it works on our subconscious, we would be amazed at how powerful and complex a psychological force it is. This chapter examines how words compel us to buy, how images feed our fantasies, how the advertising industry tempts us to part with our money, and even how they are using breakthroughs in medical science to manipulate our purchasing decisions.

We begin by taking a closer look at the connections among advertisements, media, and our consumer culture. The first two articles confirm what parents have long suspected—that Madison Avenue is after their children. Television and the Internet make it easier to target the child market. In "Which One of These Sneakers Is Me?" Douglas Rushkoff explains that advertisers have declared an all-out market assault on today's kids, surrounding them with logos, labels, and ads literally from the day they are born. Are we simply giving children more choices, or are we controlling childhood itself? Next, Peggy Orenstein questions why the marketing moguls at Disney want her little girl to be a princess—with all the frippery princesses encompass—in her essay, "Just a Little Princess?" Are America's little girls being forced to buy pink and wear tutus, or is Disney just giving children what they want and love?

In this chapter's *Modern Scholar* essay, Joseph Turow discusses the ways in which advertisers exploit rips in the American social fabric to target particular products to specific audiences in "The Daily You." Although it may seem obvious that advertisers wish to target their ads to the people who will want to use their products most, Turow questions the long-term social impact of this marketing strategy and what it might mean to American culture in general. Then *Frontline* producer Mary Carmichael explores another ethical issue in advertising as she describes how marketers are using scans of the brain to find ways to get us to buy. "Coming to a Lab Near You" describes the new world of "neuromarketing" in which advertisers collaborate with medical technology to find out what really turns us on (and off).

American's continual thirst for luxury, even in a down economy, is examined by consumer-culture critic James Twitchell in "The Allure of Luxury." Twitchell argues that while academics like to wring their hands over the materialistic excesses of society, the truth is humans have always loved nice things. We are creatures of luxury—in general, humans prefer comfort, style, and the next new thing. Such materialism is not necessarily bad either; it is all in how you look at it. His piece is followed by an essay by *Slate* editor Daniel Gross, who explores another luxury item—Starbucks Coffee—as he proposes a new economic theory based on the frequency of Starbucks coffee houses located in a given area in "Will Your Recession Be Tall, Grande, or Venti?"

This chapter's Viewpoints section focuses on advertising language. By its nature, the language of advertising is a very special one that combines words cleverly and methodically to get us to spend our money. In "With These Words, I Can Sell You Anything," word-watcher William Lutz explores how advertisers twist simple words so that they appear to promise whatever the consumer wants. In the second piece, "The Language of Advertising," advertising executive Charles A. O'Neill concedes that the language of ads can be very appealing, but that's the point. However, unless consumers are willing, no ad can force them to part with their money.

Which One of These Sneakers Is Me?
*Douglas Rushkoff**

Brand-name products target groups of consumers: sometimes large, diverse populations, such as Pepsi or Coke, or elite ones, such as Coach or Gucci. Brands depend on image—the image they promote and the image the consumer believes they will project by using the product. For teens, brands can announce membership in a particular group, value system, and personality type. Media analyst Douglas Rushkoff explains in this article that the younger generation is more consumer savvy, forcing retailers to rethink how they brand and market goods. Brands are still very important to them, but they like to think they are hip to the advertising game. But as Rushkoff explains, it is a game they cannot win.

1   I was in one of those sports "superstores" the other day, hoping to find a pair of trainers for myself. As I faced the giant wall of shoes, each model categorized by either sports affiliation, basketball star, economic class, racial heritage, or consumer niche, I noticed a young boy standing next to me, maybe 13 years old, in even greater awe of the towering selection of footwear.

2   His jaw was dropped and his eyes were glazed over—a psycho-physical response to the overwhelming sensory data in a self-contained consumer environment. It's a phenomenon known to retail architects as "Gruen Transfer," named for the gentleman who invented the shopping mall, where this mental paralysis is most commonly observed.

3   Having finished several years of research on this exact mind state, I knew to proceed with caution. I slowly made my way to the boy's side and gently asked him, "What is going through your mind right now?"

* Douglas Rushkoff, *The London Times*, April 30, 2000

4   He responded without hesitation, "I don't know which of these trainers is 'me.'" The boy proceeded to explain his dilemma. He thought of Nike as the most utilitarian and scientifically advanced shoe, but had heard something about third-world laborers and was afraid that wearing this brand might label him as too anti-Green. He then considered a skateboard shoe, Airwalk, by an "indie" manufacturer (the trainer equivalent of a micro-brewery), but had recently learned that this company was almost as big as Nike. The truly hip brands of skate shoe were too esoteric for his current profile at school—he'd look like he was "trying." This left the "retro" brands, like Puma, Converse, and Adidas, none of which he felt any real affinity for, since he wasn't even alive in the 70s, when they were truly and nonironically popular.

5   With no clear choice and, more importantly, no other way to conceive of his own identity, the boy stood there, paralyzed in the modern youth equivalent of an existential crisis. Which brand am I, anyway?

6   Believe it or not, there are dozens, perhaps hundreds of youth culture marketers who have already begun clipping out this article. They work for hip, new advertising agencies and cultural research firms who trade in the psychology of our children

Marketers spend millions developing strategies to identify children's predilections and then capitalize on their vulnerabilities.

and the anthropology of their culture. The object of their labors is to create precisely the state of confusion and vulnerability experienced by the young shopper at the shoe wall—and then turn this state to their advantage. It is a science, though not a pretty one.

7   Yes, our children are the prey and their consumer loyalty is the prize in an escalating arms race. Marketers spend millions developing strategies to identify children's predilections and then capitalize on their vulnerabilities. Young people are fooled for a while, but then develop defense mechanisms, such as media-savvy attitudes or ironic dispositions. Then marketers research these defenses, develop new countermeasures, and on it goes. The revolutionary impact of a new musical genre is co-opted and packaged by a major label before it reaches the airwaves. The ability of young people to deconstruct and neutralize the effects of one advertising technique are thwarted when they are confounded by yet another. The liberation children experience when they discover the Internet is quickly counteracted by the lure of e-commerce Web sites, which are customized to each individual user's psychological profile in order to maximize their effectiveness.

8   The battle in which our children are engaged seems to pass beneath our radar screens, in a language we don't understand. But we see the confusion and despair that results—not to mention the ever-increasing desperation with which even 3-year-olds yearn for the next Pokemon trading card. How did we get in this predicament, and is there a way out? Is it your imagination, you wonder, or have things really gotten worse?

9   Alas, things seem to have gotten worse. Ironically, this is because things had gotten so much better.

10   In olden times—back when those of us who read the newspaper grew up—
media was a one-way affair. Advertisers enjoyed a captive audience, and could quite
authoritatively provoke our angst and stoke our aspirations. Interactivity changed all
this. The remote control gave viewers the ability to break the captive spell of television programming whenever they wished, without having to get up and go all the
way up to the set. Young people proved particularly adept at "channel surfing," both
because they grew up using the new tool, and because they felt little compunction to
endure the tension-provoking narratives of storytellers who did not have their best
interests at heart. It was as if young people knew that the stuff on television was
called "programming" for a reason and developed shortened attention spans for the
purpose of keeping themselves from falling into the spell of advertisers. The remote
control allowed young people to deconstruct TV.

11   The next weapon in the child's arsenal was the video game joystick. For the
first time, viewers had control over the very pixels on their monitors. The television
image was demystified.

12   Lastly, the computer mouse and keyboard transformed the TV receiver into a
portal. Today's young people grew up in a world where a screen could as easily be
used for expressing oneself as consuming the media of others. Now the media was
up for grabs, and the ethic, from hackers to camcorder owners, was "do it yourself."

13   Of course, this revolution had to be undone. Television and Internet programmers, responding to the unpredictable viewing habits of the newly liberated, began
to call our media space an "attention economy." No matter how many channels they
had for their programming, the number of "eyeball hours" that human beings were
willing to dedicate to that programming was fixed. Not coincidentally, the channel surfing habits of our children became known as "attention deficit disorder"—a
real disease now used as an umbrella term for anyone who clicks away from programming before the marketer wants him to. We quite literally drug our children
into compliance. Likewise, as computer interfaces were made more complex and
opaque—think Windows—the do-it-yourself ethic of the Internet was undone. The
original Internet was a place to share ideas and converse with others. Children actually had to use the keyboard! Now, the Internet encourages them to click numbly
through packaged content. Web sites are designed to keep young people from using
the keyboard, except to enter in their parents' credit card information.

14   But young people had been changed by their exposure to new media. They constituted a new "psychographic," as advertisers like to call it, so new kinds of messaging had to be developed that appealed to their new sensibility.

15   Anthropologists—the same breed of scientists that used to scope out enemy
populations before military conquests—engaged in focus groups, conducted "trend-
watching" on the streets, in order to study the emotional needs and subtle behaviors
of young people. They came to understand, for example, how children had abandoned narrative structures for fear of the way stories were used to coerce them.
Children tended to construct narratives for themselves by collecting things instead,
like cards, bottlecaps called "pogs," or keychains and plush toys. They also came
to understand how young people despised advertising—especially when it did not
acknowledge their media-savvy intelligence.

16   Thus, Pokemon was born—a TV show, video game, and product line where the object is to collect as many trading cards as possible. The innovation here, among many, is the marketer's conflation of TV show and advertisement into one piece of media. The show and movies are essentially long advertisements. The storyline, such as it is, concerns a boy who must collect little monsters in order to develop his own character. Likewise, the Pokemon video game engages the player in a quest for those monsters. Finally, the card game itself (for the few children who actually play it) involves collecting better monsters—not by playing, but by buying more cards. The more cards you buy, the better you can play.

17   Kids feel the tug, but in a way they can't quite identify as advertising. Their compulsion to create a story for themselves—in a world where stories are dangerous—makes them vulnerable to this sort of attack. In marketers' terms, Pokemon is "leveraged" media, with "cross-promotion" on "complementary platforms." This is adspeak for an assault on multiple fronts.

18   Moreover, the time a child spends in the Pokemon craze amounts to a remedial lesson in how to consume. Pokemon teaches them how to want things that they can't or won't actually play with. In fact, it teaches them how to buy things they don't even want. While a child might want one particular card, he needs to purchase them in packages whose contents are not revealed. He must buy blind and repeatedly until he gets the object of his desire.

19   Worse yet, the card itself has no value—certainly not as a plaything. It is a functionless purchase, slipped into a display case, whose value lies purely in its possession. It is analogous to those children who buy action figures from their favorite TV shows and movies with no intention of ever removing them from their packaging! They are purchased for their collectible value alone. Thus, the imagination game is reduced to some fictional moment in the future where they will, presumably, be resold to another collector. Children are no longer playing. They are investing.

20   Meanwhile, older kids have attempted to opt out of aspiration altogether. The "15–24" demographic, considered by marketers the most difficult to wrangle into submission, have adopted a series of postures they hoped would make them impervious to marketing techniques. They take pride in their ability to recognize when they are being pandered to and watch TV for the sole purpose of calling out when they are being manipulated. They are armchair media theorists, who take pleasure in deconstructing and defusing the messages of their enemies.

21   But now advertisers are making commercials just for them. Soft drink advertisements satirize one another before rewarding the cynical viewer: "image is nothing," they say. The technique might best be called "wink" advertising, for its ability to engender a young person's loyalty by pretending to disarm itself. "Get it?" the ad means to ask. If you're cool, you do.

22   New magazine advertisements for jeans, such as those created by Diesel, take this even one step further. The ads juxtapose imagery that actually makes no sense—ice cream billboards in North Korea, for example. The strategy is brilliant. For a media-savvy young person to feel good about himself, he needs to feel he "gets" the joke. But what does he do with an ad where there's obviously something to get that he can't figure out? He has no choice but to admit that the brand is even cooler than he is. An ad's ability to confound its audience is the new credential for a brand's authenticity.

23   Like the boy at the wall of shoes, kids today analyze each purchase they make, painstakingly aware of how much effort has gone into seducing them. As a result, they see their choices of what to watch and what to buy as exerting some influence over the world around them. After all, their buying patterns have become the center of so much attention!

24   But however media-savvy kids get, they will always lose this particular game. For they have accepted the language of brands as their cultural currency and the stakes in their purchasing decisions as something real. For no matter how much control kids get over the media they watch, they are still utterly powerless when it comes to the manufacturing of brands. Even a consumer revolt merely reinforces one's role as a consumer, not an autonomous or creative being.

25   The more they interact with brands, the more they brand themselves. ◆

CRITICAL THINKING

1. When you were a teenager, did you have particular brands to which you were most loyal? Did this loyalty change as you got older? Why did you prefer certain brands over others? What cultural and social influences contributed to your desire for that brand?

2. What can a brand tell you about the person who uses it? Explain.

3. Look up the phrase "Gruen Transfer" on the Internet. Were you aware of this angle of marketing practice? Does it change the way you think about how products are sold to you?

4. While the boy's dilemma in Rushkoff's introduction is humorous on the surface, it is a serious situation for the teen. Why is his choice of sneaker so important to him? What expectations does he seem to connect with his choice? What could happen if he picks the wrong shoe?

5. In order to stay in business, marketers have had to rethink how they sell products to the youth market. How is the youth market changing the way marketers do business? Explain.

6. How does Rushkoff support his essay? Evaluate his use of supporting sources. Are there any gaps in his article? If so, identify areas where his essay could be stronger. If not, highlight some of the essay's particular strengths.

7. In paragraph 9, Rushkoff notes that things have gotten worse because they have gotten better. What does he mean? What is the irony of the youth consumer market?

8. Rushkoff notes in paragraph 14 that the youth generation "constituted a new 'psychographic'." What makes this generation different from previous generations of consumers? If you are a part of this generation (ages 12 to 21), explain why you think you do or do not represent a "new psychographic."

9. In his conclusion, Rushkoff predicts that even media-savvy kids will still "lose" the game. Why will they fail? Explain.

CRITICAL WRITING

1. *Exploratory Writing:* Teens and young adults covet certain brand-name clothing because they believe it promotes a particular image. What defines brand image? Is it something created by the company or by the people who use the product? How does advertising influence the social view we have of ourselves and of the brands we use? Write an essay on the connections between advertising and our cultural values of what is "in" and what is not.
2. *Interview:* Ask several people about the products they like and why they like them. Inquire about what they like about a brand and the reasons why they would not buy another brand. Ask your subjects to what degree brand factors into their decision to buy a particular product. Evaluate the results in a short essay on the purchasing habits of consumers and the importance of brands.

GROUP PROJECTS

1. In small groups, do some research on how the Internet is used as a marketing tool to sell to children. Locate Web sites for toys and games and evaluate how they market to children. What do these sites offer? How do they contribute to the desirability and sale of the product? Report your findings to the class.
2. In the past, toys modeled after a particular television program proved popular and marketable. As Rushkoff describes in the case of Pokemon, now toys are created first, and the television program and Internet Web site help market the product. Each member of your group should select a different popular cartoon to watch and research. After viewing each cartoon for a few days, research the products that are associated with the cartoon. In class, discuss how today's cartoons promote products.
3. Each member of your group should watch an hour of television aimed at children: Saturday morning programs, after-school features, Nickelodeon, or the Cartoon Network. Jot down the shows you watch and all the commercials that run during the programs. Include how much time is spent airing commercials. As a group, analyze the data. How many commercials ran during a 15-minute segment of programming? Was there a pattern to the commercials? Did any seem manipulative or compelling, and if so, how? (As an additional writing project, watch these programs with a child. Note his or her responses to the commercials. Did the child seem influenced by the ads? Explain.)

Just a Little Princess?
Peggy Orenstein*

To call the allure of princesses a passing fad among little girls is "like calling Harry Potter a book," explains author and noted feminist Peggy Orenstein in a *New York Times* commentary. The Disney media engine has been pushing princess culture since practically stumbling upon its popularity in 2001. Today, Disney sales in princess gear exceed $3 billion. Is the pitch too intense? What does it reveal about how companies market to children? What messages does it send to little girls, and what impact could it have on American culture overall? In the next essay, Orenstein describes her reaction to the princess onslaught and her helplessness to stop it from drawing in her own little girl.

1 I finally came unhinged in the dentist's office—one of those ritzy pediatric practices tricked out with comic books, DVDs and arcade games—where I'd taken my 3-year-old daughter for her first exam. Until then, I'd held my tongue. I'd smiled politely every time the supermarket-checkout clerk greeted her with "Hi, Princess," ignored the waitress at our local breakfast joint who called the funny-face pancakes she ordered her "princess meal," made no comment when the lady at Long's Drugs said, "I bet I know your favorite color" and handed her a pink balloon rather than letting her choose for herself. Maybe it was the dentist's Betty Boop inflection that got to me, but when she pointed to the exam chair and said, "Would you like to sit in my special princess throne so I can sparkle your teeth?" I lost it.

2 "Oh, for God's sake," I snapped. "Do you have a princess drill, too?"

3 She stared at me as if I were an evil stepmother.

4 "Come on!" I continued, my voice rising. "It's 2006, not 1950. This is Berkeley, California. Does every little girl really have to be a princess?"

5 My daughter, who was reaching for a Cinderella sticker, looked back and forth between us. "Why are you so mad, Mama?" she asked. "What's wrong with princesses?"

6 Diana may be dead and Masako disgraced, but here in America, we are in the midst of a royal moment. To call princesses a "trend" among girls is like calling Harry Potter a book. Sales at Disney Consumer Products, which started the craze six years ago by packaging nine of its female characters under one royal rubric, have shot up to $3 billion, globally, this year, from $300 million in 2001. There are now more than 25,000 Disney Princess items. "Princess," as some Disney execs call it, is not only the fastest-growing brand the company has ever created; they say it is on its way to becoming the largest girls' franchise on the planet.

7 Meanwhile in 2001, Mattel brought out its own "world of girl" line of princess Barbie dolls, DVDs, toys, clothing, home décor and myriad other products. At a time when Barbie sales were declining domestically, they became instant best sellers. Shortly before that, Mary Drolet, a Chicago-area mother and former Claire's

* Peggy Orenstein, *New York Times*, December 2006

and Montgomery Ward executive, opened Club Libby Lu, now a chain of mall stores based largely in the suburbs in which girls ages 4 to 12 can shop for "Princess Phones" covered in faux fur and attend "Princess-Makeover Birthday Parties." Saks bought Club Libby Lu in 2003 for $12 million and has since expanded it to 87 outlets; by 2005, with only scant local advertising, revenues hovered around the $46 million mark, a 53 percent jump from the previous year. Pink, it seems, is the new gold.

8   Even Dora the Explorer, the intrepid, dirty-kneed adventurer, has ascended to the throne: in 2004, after a two-part episode in which she turns into a "true princess," the Nickelodeon and Viacom consumer-products division released a satin-gowned "Magic Hair Fairytale Dora," with hair that grows or shortens when her crown is touched. Among other phrases the bilingual doll utters: "Vámonos! Let's go to fairy-tale land!" and "Will you brush my hair?"

9   As a feminist mother—not to mention a nostalgic product of the Grranimals era—I have been taken by surprise by the princess craze and the girlie-girl culture that has risen around it. What happened to William wanting a doll and not dressing your cat in an apron? Whither Marlo Thomas? I watch my fellow mothers, women who once swore they'd never be dependent on a man, smile indulgently at daughters who warble "So This Is Love" or insist on being called Snow White. I wonder if they'd concede so readily to sons who begged for combat fatigues and mock AK-47s.

10   More to the point, when my own girl makes her daily beeline for the dress-up corner of her preschool classroom—something I'm convinced she does largely to torture me—I worry about what playing Little Mermaid is teaching her. I've spent much of my career writing about experiences that undermine girls' well-being, warning parents that a preoccupation with body and beauty (encouraged by films, TV, magazines and, yes, toys) is perilous to their daughters' mental and physical health. Am I now supposed to shrug and forget all that? If trafficking in stereotypes doesn't matter at 3, when does it matter? At 6? Eight? Thirteen?

11   On the other hand, maybe I'm still surfing a washed-out second wave of feminism in a third-wave world. Maybe princesses are in fact a sign of progress, an indication that girls can embrace their predilection for pink without compromising strength or ambition; that, at long last, they can "have it all." Or maybe it is even less complex than that: to mangle Freud, maybe a princess is sometimes just a princess. And, as my daughter wants to know, what's wrong with that?

12   The rise of the Disney princesses reads like a fairy tale itself, with Andy Mooney, a former Nike executive, playing the part of prince, riding into the company on a metaphoric white horse in January 2000 to save a consumer-products division whose sales were dropping by as much as 30 percent a year. Both overstretched and underfocused, the division had triggered price wars by granting multiple licenses for core products (say, Winnie-the-Pooh undies) while ignoring the potential of new media. What's more, Disney films like "A Bug's Life" in 1998 had yielded few merchandising opportunities—what child wants to snuggle up with an ant?

13   It was about a month after Mooney's arrival that the magic struck. That's when he flew to Phoenix to check out his first "Disney on Ice" show. "Standing in line in the arena, I was surrounded by little girls dressed head to toe as princesses," he told

me last summer in his palatial office, then located in Burbank, and speaking in a rolling Scottish burr. "They weren't even Disney products. They were generic princess products they'd appended to a Halloween costume. And the light bulb went off. Clearly there was latent demand here. So the next morning I said to my team, 'O.K., let's establish standards and a color palette and talk to licensees and get as much product out there as we possibly can that allows these girls to do what they're doing anyway: projecting themselves into the characters from the classic movies.'"

14   Mooney picked a mix of old and new heroines to wear the Pantone pink No. 241 corona: Cinderella, Sleeping Beauty, Snow White, Ariel, Belle, Jasmine, Mulan and Pocahontas. It was the first time Disney marketed characters separately from a film's release, let alone lumped together those from different stories. To ensure the sanctity of what Mooney called their individual "mythologies," the princesses never make eye contact when they're grouped: each stares off in a slightly different direction as if unaware of the others' presence.

15   It is also worth noting that not all of the ladies are of royal extraction. Part of the genius of "Princess" is that its meaning is so broadly constructed that it actually has no meaning. Even Tinker Bell was originally a Princess, though her reign didn't last. "We'd always debate over whether she was really a part of the Princess mythology," Mooney recalled. "She really wasn't." Likewise, Mulan and Pocahontas, arguably the most resourceful of the bunch, are rarely depicted on Princess merchandise, though for a different reason. Their rustic garb has less bling potential than that of old-school heroines like Sleeping Beauty. (When Mulan does appear, she is typically in the kimonolike hanfu, which makes her miserable in the movie, rather than her liberated warrior's gear.)

16   The first Princess items, released with no marketing plan, no focus groups, no advertising, sold as if blessed by a fairy godmother. To this day, Disney conducts little market research on the Princess line, relying instead on the power of its legacy among mothers as well as the instant-read sales barometer of the theme parks and Disney Stores. "We simply gave girls what they wanted," Mooney said of the line's success, "although I don't think any of us grasped how much they wanted this. I wish I could sit here and take credit for having some grand scheme to develop this, but all we did was envision a little girl's room and think about how she could live out the princess fantasy. The counsel we gave to licensees was: What type of bedding would a princess want to sleep in? What kind of alarm clock would a princess want to wake up to? What type of television would a princess like to see? It's a rare case where you find a girl who has every aspect of her room bedecked in Princess, but if she ends up with three or four of these items, well, then you have a very healthy business."

17   Every reporter Mooney talks to asks some version of my next question: Aren't the Princesses, who are interested only in clothes, jewelry and cadging the handsome prince, somewhat retrograde role models?

18   "Look," he said, "I have friends whose son went through the Power Rangers phase who castigated themselves over what they must've done wrong. Then they talked to other parents whose kids had gone through it. The boy passes through. The girl passes through. I see girls expanding their imagination through visualizing

themselves as princesses, and then they pass through that phase and end up becoming lawyers, doctors, mothers or princesses, whatever the case may be."

19   Mooney has a point: There are no studies proving that playing princess directly damages girls' self-esteem or dampens other aspirations. On the other hand, there is evidence that young women who hold the most conventionally feminine beliefs— who avoid conflict and think they should be perpetually nice and pretty—are more likely to be depressed than others and less likely to use contraception. What's more, the 23 percent decline in girls' participation in sports and other vigorous activity between middle and high school has been linked to their sense that athletics is unfeminine. And in a survey released last October by Girls Inc., school-age girls overwhelmingly reported a paralyzing pressure to be "perfect": not only to get straight A's and be the student-body president, editor of the newspaper and captain of the swim team but also to be "kind and caring," "please everyone, be very thin and dress right." Give those girls a pumpkin and a glass slipper and they'd be in business.

20   At the grocery store one day, my daughter noticed a little girl sporting a Cinderella backpack. "There's that princess you don't like, Mama!" she shouted.

21   "Um, yeah," I said, trying not to meet the other mother's hostile gaze.

22   "Don't you like her blue dress, Mama?"

23   I had to admit, I did.

24   She thought about this. "Then don't you like her face?"

25   "Her face is all right," I said, noncommittally, though I'm not thrilled to have my Japanese-Jewish child in thrall to those Aryan features. (And what the heck are those blue things covering her ears?) "It's just, honey, Cinderella doesn't really do anything."

26   Over the next 45 minutes, we ran through that conversation, verbatim, approximately 37 million times, as my daughter pointed out Disney Princess Band-Aids, Disney Princess paper cups, Disney Princess lip balm, Disney Princess pens, Disney Princess crayons and Disney Princess notebooks—all cleverly displayed at the eye level of a 3-year-old trapped in a shopping cart—as well as a bouquet of Disney Princess balloons bobbing over the checkout line. The repetition was excessive, even for a preschooler. What was it about my answers that confounded her? What if, instead of realizing: Aha! Cinderella is a symbol of the patriarchal oppression of all women, another example of corporate mind control and power-to-the-people! my 3-year-old was thinking, Mommy doesn't want me to be a girl?

27   According to theories of gender constancy, until they're about 6 or 7, children don't realize that the sex they were born with is immutable. They believe that they have a choice: they can grow up to be either a mommy or a daddy. Some psychologists say that until permanency sets in, kids embrace whatever stereotypes our culture presents, whether it's piling on the most spangles or attacking one another with light sabers. What better way to assure that they'll always remain themselves? If that's the case, score one for Mooney. By not buying the Princess Pull-Ups, I may be inadvertently communicating that being female (to the extent that my daughter is able to understand it) is a bad thing.

28   Anyway, you have to give girls some credit. It's true that, according to Mattel, one of the most popular games young girls play is "bride," but Disney found that a groom or prince is incidental to that fantasy, a regrettable necessity at best. Although

they keep him around for the climactic kiss, he is otherwise relegated to the bottom of the toy box, which is why you don't see him prominently displayed in stores.

29   What's more, just because they wear the tulle doesn't mean they've drunk the Kool-Aid. Plenty of girls stray from the script, say, by playing basketball in their finery, or casting themselves as the powerful evil stepsister bossing around the sniveling Cinderella. I recall a headline-grabbing 2005 British study that revealed that girls enjoy torturing, decapitating and microwaving their Barbies nearly as much as they like to dress them up for dates. There is spice along with that sugar after all, though why this was news is beyond me: anyone who ever played with the doll knows there's nothing more satisfying than hacking off all her hair and holding her underwater in the bathtub. Princesses can even be a boon to exasperated parents: in our house, for instance, royalty never whines and uses the potty every single time.

30   "Playing princess is not the issue," argues Lyn Mikel Brown, an author, with Sharon Lamb, of "Packaging Girlhood: Rescuing Our Daughters From Marketers' Schemes." "The issue is 25,000 Princess products," says Brown, a professor of education and human development at Colby College. "When one thing is so dominant, then it's no longer a choice: it's a mandate, cannibal-

> *When one thing is so dominant, then it's no longer a choice: it's a mandate, cannibalizing all other forms of play.*

izing all other forms of play. There's the illusion of more choices out there for girls, but if you look around, you'll see their choices are steadily narrowing."

31   It's hard to imagine that girls' options could truly be shrinking when they dominate the honor roll and outnumber boys in college. Then again, have you taken a stroll through a children's store lately? A year ago, when we shopped for "big girl" bedding at Pottery Barn Kids, we found the "girls" side awash in flowers, hearts and hula dancers; not a soccer player or sailboat in sight. Across the no-fly zone, the "boys" territory was all about sports, trains, planes and automobiles. Meanwhile, Baby GAP's boys' onesies were emblazoned with "Big Man on Campus" and the girls' with "Social Butterfly"; guess whose matching shoes were decorated on the soles with hearts and whose sported a "No. 1" logo? And at Toys"R"Us, aisles of pink baby dolls, kitchens, shopping carts and princesses unfurl a safe distance from the "Star Wars" figures, GeoTrax and tool chests. The relentless resegregation of childhood appears to have sneaked up without any further discussion about sex roles, about what it now means to be a boy or to be a girl. Or maybe it has happened in lieu of such discussion because it's easier this way.

32   Easier, that is, unless you want to buy your daughter something that isn't pink. Girls' obsession with that color may seem like something they're born with, like the ability to breathe or talk on the phone for hours on end. But according to Jo Paoletti, an associate professor of American studies at the University of Maryland, it ain't so. When colors were first introduced to the nursery in the early part of the 20th century, pink was considered the more masculine hue, a pastel version of red. Blue, with its intimations of the Virgin Mary, constancy and faithfulness, was thought to be dainty. Why or when that switched is not clear, but as late as the 1930s a significant

percentage of adults in one national survey held to that split. Perhaps that's why so many early Disney heroines—Cinderella, Sleeping Beauty, Wendy, Alice-in-Wonderland—are swathed in varying shades of azure. (Purple, incidentally, may be the next color to swap teams: once the realm of kings and N.F.L. players, it is fast becoming the bolder girl's version of pink.)

33   It wasn't until the mid-1980s, when amplifying age and sex differences became a key strategy of children's marketing (recall the emergence of "'tween"), that pink became seemingly innate to girls, part of what defined them as female, at least for the first few years. That was also the time that the first of the generation raised during the unisex phase of feminism—ah, hither Marlo!—became parents. "The kids who grew up in the 1970s wanted sharp definitions for their own kids," Paoletti told me. "I can understand that, because the unisex thing denied everything—you couldn't be this, you couldn't be that, you had to be a neutral nothing."

34   The infatuation with the girlie girl certainly could, at least in part, be a reaction against the so-called second wave of the women's movement of the 1960s and '70s (the first wave was the fight for suffrage), which fought for reproductive rights and economic, social and legal equality. If nothing else, pink and Princess have resuscitated the fantasy of romance that that era of feminism threatened, the privileges that traditional femininity conferred on women despite its costs—doors magically opened, dinner checks picked up, Manolo Blahniks. Frippery. Fun. Why should we give up the perks of our sex until we're sure of what we'll get in exchange? Why should we give them up at all? Or maybe it's deeper than that: the freedoms feminism bestowed came with an undercurrent of fear among women themselves—flowing through "Ally McBeal," "Bridget Jones's Diary," "Sex and the City"—of losing male love, of never marrying, of not having children, of being deprived of something that felt essentially and exclusively female.

35   I mulled that over while flipping through "The Paper Bag Princess," a 1980 picture book hailed as an antidote to Disney. The heroine outwits a dragon who has kidnapped her prince, but not before the beast's fiery breath frizzles her hair and destroys her dress, forcing her to don a paper bag. The ungrateful prince rejects her, telling her to come back when she is "dressed like a real princess." She dumps him and skips off into the sunset, happily ever after, alone.

36   There you have it, "Thelma and Louise" all over again. Step out of line, and you end up solo or, worse, sailing crazily over a cliff to your doom. Alternatives like those might send you skittering right back to the castle. And I get that: the fact is, though I want my daughter to do and be whatever she wants as an adult, I still hope she'll find her Prince Charming and have babies, just as I have. I don't want her to be a fish without a bicycle; I want her to be a fish with another fish. Preferably, one who loves and respects her and also does the dishes and half the child care.

37   There had to be a middle ground between compliant and defiant, between petticoats and paper bags. I remembered a video on YouTube, an ad for a Nintendo game called Super Princess Peach. It showed a pack of girls in tiaras, gowns and elbow-length white gloves sliding down a zip line on parasols, navigating an obstacle course of tires in their stilettos, slithering on their bellies under barbed wire, then using their telekinetic powers to make a climbing wall burst into flames. "If

you can stand up to really mean people," an announcer intoned, "maybe you have what it takes to be a princess."

38   Now here were some girls who had grit as well as grace. I loved Princess Peach even as I recognized that there was no way she could run in those heels, that her peachiness did nothing to upset the apple cart of expectation: she may have been athletic, smart and strong, but she was also adorable. Maybe she's what those once-unisex, postfeminist parents are shooting for: the melding of old and new standards. And perhaps that's a good thing, the ideal solution. But what to make, then, of the young women in the Girls Inc. survey? It doesn't seem to be "having it all" that's getting to them; it's the pressure to be it all. In telling our girls they can be anything, we have inadvertently demanded that they be everything. To everyone. All the time. No wonder the report was titled "The Supergirl Dilemma."

39   The princess as superhero is not irrelevant. Some scholars I spoke with say that given its post-9/11 timing, princess mania is a response to a newly dangerous world. "Historically, princess worship has emerged during periods of uncertainty and profound social change," observes Miriam Forman-Brunell, a historian at the University of Missouri–Kansas City. Francis Hodgson Burnett's original "Little Princess" was published at a time of rapid urbanization, immigration and poverty; Shirley Temple's film version was a hit during the Great Depression. "The original folk tales themselves," Forman-Brunell says, "spring from medieval and early modern European culture that faced all kinds of economic and demographic and social upheaval—famine, war, disease, terror of wolves. Girls play savior during times of economic crisis and instability." That's a heavy burden for little shoulders. Perhaps that's why the magic wand has become an essential part of the princess get-up. In the original stories—even the Disney versions of them—it's not the girl herself who's magic; it's the fairy godmother. Now if Forman-Brunell is right, we adults have become the cursed creatures whom girls have the thaumaturgic power to transform.

40   In the 1990s, third-wave feminists rebelled against their dour big sisters, "reclaiming" sexual objectification as a woman's right—provided, of course, that it was on her own terms, that she was the one choosing to strip or wear a shirt that said "Porn Star" or make out with her best friend at a frat-house bash. They embraced words like "bitch" and "slut" as terms of affection and empowerment. That is, when used by the right people, with the right dash of playful irony. But how can you assure that? As Madonna gave way to Britney, whatever self-determination that message contained was watered down and commodified until all that was left was a gaggle of 6-year-old girls in belly-baring T-shirts (which I'm guessing they don't wear as cultural critique). It is no wonder that parents, faced with thongs for 8-year-olds and Bratz dolls' "passion for fashion," fill their daughters' closets with pink sateen; the innocence of Princess feels like a reprieve.

41   "But what does that mean?" asks Sharon Lamb, a psychology professor at Saint Michael's College. "There are other ways to express "innocence"—girls could play ladybug or caterpillar. What you're really talking about is sexual purity. And there's a trap at the end of that rainbow, because the natural progression from pale, innocent pink is not to other colors. It's to hot, sexy pink—exactly the kind of sexualization parents are trying to avoid."

42   Lamb suggested that to see for myself how "Someday My Prince Will Come" morphs into "Oops! I Did It Again," I visit Club Libby Lu, the mall shop dedicated to the "Very Important Princess." Walking into one of the newest links in the store's chain, in Natick, Mass., last summer, I had to tip my tiara to the founder, Mary Drolet: Libby Lu's design was flawless. Unlike Disney, Drolet depended on focus groups to choose the logo (a crown-topped heart) and the colors (pink, pink, purple and more pink). The displays were scaled to the size of a 10-year-old, though most of the shoppers I saw were several years younger than that. The decals on the walls and dressing rooms—"I Love Your Hair," "Hip Chick," "Spoiled"—were written in "girlfriend language." The young sales clerks at this "special secret club for super-fabulous girls" are called "club counselors" and come off like your coolest baby sitter, the one who used to let you brush her hair. The malls themselves are chosen based on a company formula called the G.P.I., or "Girl Power Index," which predicts potential sales revenues. Talk about newspeak: "Girl Power" has gone from a riot grrrrl anthem to "I Am Woman, Watch Me Shop."

43   Inside, the store was divided into several glittery "shopping zones" called "experiences": Libby's Laboratory, now called Sparkle Spa, where girls concoct their own cosmetics and bath products; Libby's Room; Ear Piercing; Pooch Parlor (where divas in training can pamper stuffed poodles, pugs and Chihuahuas); and the Style Studio, offering "Libby Du" makeover choices, including 'Tween Idol, Rock Star, Pop Star and, of course, Priceless Princess. Each look includes hairstyle, makeup, nail polish and sparkly tattoos.

44   As I browsed, I noticed a mother standing in the center of the store holding a price list for makeover birthday parties—$22.50 to $35 per child. Her name was Anne McAuliffe; her daughters—Stephanie, 4, and 7-year-old twins Rory and Sarah—were dashing giddily up and down the aisles.

45   "They've been begging to come to this store for three weeks," McAuliffe said. "I'd never heard of it. So I said they could, but they'd have to spend their own money if they bought anything." She looked around. "Some of this stuff is innocuous," she observed, then leaned toward me, eyes wide and stage-whispered: "But … a lot of it is horrible. It makes them look like little prostitutes. It's crazy. They're babies!"

46   As we debated the line between frivolous fun and JonBenét, McAuliffe's daughter Rory came dashing up, pigtails haphazard, glasses askew. "They have the best pocketbooks here," she said breathlessly, brandishing a clutch with the words "Girlie Girl" stamped on it. "Please, can I have one? It has sequins!"

47   "You see that?" McAuliffe asked, gesturing at the bag. "What am I supposed to say?" On my way out of the mall, I popped into the 'tween mecca Hot Topic, where a display of Tinker Bell items caught my eye. Tinker Bell, whose image racks up an annual $400 million in retail sales with no particular effort on Disney's part, is poised to wreak vengeance on the Princess line that once expelled her. Last winter, the first chapter book designed to introduce girls to Tink and her Pixie Hollow pals spent 18 weeks on *The New York Times* children's best-seller list. In a direct-to-DVD now under production, she will speak for the first time, voiced by the actress Brittany Murphy. Next year, Disney Fairies will be rolled out in earnest. Aimed at 6- to 9-year-old girls, the line will catch them just as they outgrow Princess. Their colors

will be lavender, green, turquoise—anything but the Princess's soon-to-be-babyish pink.

48   To appeal to that older child, Disney executives said, the Fairies will have more "attitude" and "sass" than the Princesses. What, I wondered, did that entail? I'd seen some of the Tinker Bell merchandise that Disney sells at its theme parks: T-shirts reading, "Spoiled to Perfection," "Mood Subject to Change Without Notice" and "Tinker Bell: Prettier Than a Princess." At Hot Topic, that edge was even sharper: magnets, clocks, light-switch plates and panties featured "Dark Tink," described as "the bad girl side of Miss Bell that Walt never saw."

49   Girl power, indeed.

50   A few days later, I picked my daughter up from preschool. She came tearing over in a full-skirted frock with a gold bodice, a beaded crown perched side-ways on her head. "Look, Mommy, I'm Ariel!" she crowed, referring to Disney's Little Mermaid. Then she stopped and furrowed her brow. "Mommy, do you like Ariel?"

51   I considered her for a moment. Maybe Princess is the first salvo in what will become a lifelong struggle over her body image, a Hundred Years' War of dieting, plucking, painting and perpetual dissatisfaction with the results. Or maybe it isn't. I'll never really know. In the end, it's not the Princesses that really bother me any-way. They're just a trigger for the bigger question of how, over the years, I can help my daughter with the contradictions she will inevitably face as a girl, the dissonance that is as endemic as ever to growing up female. Maybe the best I can hope for is that her generation will get a little further with the solutions than we did.

52   For now, I kneeled down on the floor and gave my daughter a hug.

53   She smiled happily. "But, Mommy?" she added. "When I grow up, I'm still going to be a fireman." ◆

CRITICAL THINKING

1. Think about your consumer habits as a child. What did you want to buy, and how did you learn about the product? What made you want the product?

2. Why does the author object so strongly to the idea of princesses and prin-cess toys? Explain.

3. How did Disney fill in the niche that little girls had created themselves? In your opinion, do you think the company went overboard? Why or why not?

4. Lyn Mikel Brown, co-author of *Packaging Girlhood: Rescuing Our Daughters from Marketers' Schemes*, notes "When one thing is so domi-nant, then it's no longer a choice: it's a mandate, cannibalizing all other forms of play." In what ways has the princess craze "cannibalized" other forms of play?

5. In addition to princesses, to what other toys and products does the author object and why?

6. How does the concept of princess conflict with the principles of feminism? Can a little girl understand both? Why or why not?
7. This article focuses on how young girls are the target of marketing gimmicks that channel them to desire certain toys and embrace certain types of play. Can the same argument be made for little boys? Explain.
8. What is the author's conclusion about the princess trend and her daughter? Does the author feel she is fighting a losing battle? What would you do in the same situation? Explain.

CRITICAL WRITING

1. *Research Writing:* Are popular toys—such as Princess gear, Bratz dolls, Lego sets, Matchbox cars—leading kids to unconsciously embrace prescribed gender roles? Visit the toy section of a department store such as Target, Walmart, or Kmart and take a look at the merchandise options. Write an essay discussing how the toys you saw could influence gender roles for children.
2. *Personal Narrative:* Write about how any toys you played with as a child did or did not influence the way you viewed yourself and the world around you.

GROUP PROJECTS

1. In small groups, research how popular culture, media, and marketing—including Internet and television—sell products to children. Locate Web sites and identify television programs that target children. How do theme parks, such as Disneyland, and merchandise, such as DVDs and books, also influence children? Report your findings to the class as part of a broader group discussion on this issue.
2. Research the Disney Princess phenomenon online and in stores—and even with children who play "princess." The author conjectures a few reasons for why princess play is popular with little girls. As a group, discuss the phenomenon and the popularity behind princess play. Why do you think it is so popular today? Do you think it can be harmful to young girls? Explain.
3. As a group, analyze several commercials airing during television programs for young children (girls as well as boys) and analyze them. How do the commercials use color, music, graphics, narration, other children, and celebrities to promote their product? What cultural assumptions do they make? How do they target little children? Do they lead children to embrace certain types of play? Explain.

Perspectives: My Things Define Me

Andy Singer/PoliticalCartoons.com

THINKING CRITICALLY

1. What is your perception of how the things you own define who you are? Are you what you own? Explain your point of view.
2. Many people agree that they desire certain things not simply for the item itself, but for how that item contributes to their image. This is especially true of things for which brands distinguish similar items, such as handbags, cars, watches, and sporting equipment. How would the items you own right now convey an image of who you "are" to others?
3. What is this cartoon trying to get viewers to think about? What is the cartoonist trying to achieve?

Modern Scholar

The Daily You
Joseph Turow*

> Advertisers do not target their campaigns to universal audiences. Rather, they target specific audiences to market specific products. Communications professor Joseph Turow explains how the Internet is being leveraged against the consumer by providing online experiences that presume to target the user but instead severely limit choices, while collecting more data in the guise of "tailoring" the online experience. Now not just ads but also news and entertainment are being customized by newly powerful media agencies on the basis of data we don't know they have collected and compiled into profiles of who we are and what we want to see. Are you, for example, a "Socially Liberal Organic Eater," "a Diabetic Individual in the Household," or "Single City Struggler"? And, if so, how does that affect what you see and do online?

1 At the start of the twenty-first century, the advertising industry is guiding one of history's most massive stealth efforts in social profiling. At this point you may hardly notice the results of this trend. You may find you're getting better or worse discounts on products than your friends. You may notice that some ads seem to follow you around the internet. Every once in a while a website may ask you if you like a particular ad you just received. Or perhaps your cell phone has told you that you will be rewarded if you eat in a nearby restaurant where, by the way, two of your friends are hanging out this very minute.

2 You may actually like some of these intrusions. You may feel that they pale before the digital power you now have. After all, your ability to create blogs, collaborate with others to distribute videos online, and say what you want on Facebook (carefully using its privacy settings) seems only to confirm what marketers and even many academics are telling us: that consumers are captains of their own new-media ships.

3 But look beneath the surface, and a different picture emerges. We're at the start of a revolution in the ways marketers and media intrude in—and shape—our lives. Every day most if not all Americans who use the internet, along with hundreds of millions of other users from all over the planet, are being quietly peeked at, poked, analyzed, and tagged as they move through the online world. Governments undoubtedly conduct a good deal of snooping, more in some parts of the world than in others. But in North America, Europe, and many other places companies that work for marketers have taken the lead in secretly slicing and dicing the actions and backgrounds of huge populations on a virtually

---

* Joseph Turow, *The Daily You* [excerpt], 2012

minute-by-minute basis. Their goal is to find out how to activate individuals' buying impulses so they can sell us stuff more efficiently than ever before. But their work has broader social and cultural consequences as well. It is destroying traditional publishing ethics by forcing media outlets to adapt their editorial content to advertisers' public-relations needs and slice-and-dice demands. And it is performing a highly controversial form of social profiling and discrimination by customizing our media content on the basis of marketing reputations we don't even know we have.

4 Consider a fictional middle class family of two parents with three children who eat out a lot in fast-food restaurants. After a while the parents receive a continual flow of fast-food restaurant coupons. Data suggest the parents, let's call them Larry and Rhonda, will consistently spend far more than the coupons' value. Additional statistical evaluations of parents' activities and discussions online and off may suggest that Larry and Rhonda and their children tend toward being overweight. The data, in turn, result in a small torrent of messages by marketers and publishers seeking to exploit these weight issues to increase attention or sales. Videos about dealing with overweight children, produced by a new type of company called content farms, begin to show up on parenting websites Rhonda frequents. When Larry goes online, he routinely receives articles about how fitness chains emphasize weight loss around the holidays. Ads for fitness firms and diet pills typically show up on the pages with those articles. One of Larry and Rhonda's sons, who is fifteen years old, is happy to find a text message on his phone that invites him to use a discount at an ice cream chain not too far from his house. One of their daughters, by contrast, is mortified when she receives texts inviting her to a diet program and an ad on her Facebook page inviting her to a clothing store for hip, oversized women. What's more, people keep sending her Twitter messages about weight loss. In the meantime, both Larry and Rhonda are getting ads from check-cashing services and payday-loan companies. And Larry notices sourly on auto sites he visits that the main articles on the home page and the ads throughout feature entry-level and used models. His bitterness only becomes more acute when he describes to his boss the down-market Web he has been seeing lately. Quite surprised, she tells him she has been to the same auto sites recently and has just the opposite impression: many of the articles are about the latest German cars, and one home-page ad even offered her a gift for test-driving one at a dealer near her home.

5 This scenario of individual and household profiling and media customization is quite possible today. Websites, advertisers, and a panoply of other companies are continuously assessing the activities, intentions, and backgrounds of virtually everyone online; even our social relationships and comments are being carefully and continuously analyzed. In broader and broader ways, computer-generated conclusions about who we are affect the media content—the streams of commercial messages, discount offers, information, news, and entertainment—each of us confronts. Over the next few decades the business logic that drives these tailored activities will transform the ways we see ourselves, those around us, and the world at large. Governments too may be able to use marketers' technology and data to influence what we see and hear.

6   From this vantage point, the rhetoric of consumer power begins to lose credibility. In its place is a rhetoric of esoteric technological and statistical knowledge that supports the practice of social discrimination through profiling. We may note its outcomes only once in a while, and we may shrug when we do because it seems trivial—just a few ads, after all. But unless we try to understand how this profiling or reputation-making process works and what it means for the long term, our children and grandchildren will bear the full brunt of its prejudicial force.

7   The best way to enter this new world is to focus on its central driving force: the advertising industry's media-buying system. Media buying involves planning and purchasing space or time for advertising on outlets as diverse as billboards, radio, websites, mobile phones, and newspapers. For decades, media buying was a backwater, a service wing of advertising agencies that was known for having the lowest-paying jobs on Madison Avenue and for filling those jobs with female liberal arts majors fresh out of college. But that has all changed. The past twenty years have seen the rise of "media agencies" that are no longer part of ad agencies, though they may both be owned by the same parent company. Along with a wide array of satellite companies that feed them technology and data, media agencies have become magnets for well-remunerated software engineers and financial statisticians of both sexes.

8   In the United States alone, media-buying agencies wield more than $170 billion of their clients' campaign funds; they use these funds to purchase space and time on media they think will advance their clients' marketing aims. But in the process they are doing much more. With the money as leverage, they are guiding the media system toward nothing less than new ways of thinking about and evaluating audience members and defining what counts as a successful attempt to reach them. Traditionally, marketers have used media such as newspapers, magazines, radio, billboards, and television to reach out to segments of the population through commercial messages. These advertisers typically learned about audience segments from survey companies that polled representative portions of the population via a variety of methods, including panel research. A less prestigious direct-marketing business has involved contacting individuals by mail or phone. Firms have rented lists of public data or purchase information that suggests who might be likely customers.

9   The emerging new world is dramatically different. The distinction between reaching out to audiences via mass media and by direct-response methods is disappearing. Advertisers in the digital space expect all media firms to deliver to them particular types of individuals—and, increasingly, *particular* individuals—by leveraging a detailed knowledge about them and their behaviors that was unheard of even a few years ago. The new advertising strategy involves drawing as specific a picture as possible of a person based in large part on measurable physical acts such as clicks, swipes, mouseovers, and even voice commands. The strategy uses new digital tracking tools like cookies and beacons as well as new organizations with names like BlueKai, Rapleaf, Invidi, and eXelate. These companies track people on websites and across websites in an effort to learn what

CULTURE SHOCK

A Portfolio of Advertisements

The following section features seven recently published magazine advertisements. Diverse in content and style, some ads use words to promote the product; others depend on emotion, name recognition, visual appeal, or association. They present a variety of sales pitches and marketing techniques. The ads are followed by questions to help you analyze how the ads work their appeal to promote their products. When studying them, consider how they target our social perception and basic desires for happiness, beauty, and success. Approach each as a consumer, an artist, a social scientist, and a critic with an eye for detail.

BOYS AND GIRLS CLUBS

1. Do you find this ad particularly compelling? Why or why not? What kind of an impact does the universal statement made by the group have on the reader? Explain.
2. What is happening in this ad? Does the photographic element make the ad more effective? If so, why?
3. If you were leafing through a magazine and saw this ad, would you stop to look at it? Why or why not?
4. What message is this ad trying to convey? To whom is it addressed? What action does it want consumers to take?

M & M'S

1. Evaluate this advertisement's use of color and texture. How does it promote the product? Would the effectiveness of this ad be the same if it were printed in black and white, such as in a newspaper? Explain.
2. What is this ad mimicking? Explain.
3. None of the text in this advertisement is "serious"; that is, the advertisers do not "speak" to the audience about the product. Evaluate the use of text in this ad. How does it complement the picture? Is anything lost by not telling the audience about the product? Why or why not?
4. Would you stop and look at this ad? Why or why not?
5. Evaluate the personification of the candy in this ad. Does this seem like an effective vehicle to promote the product? Explain.

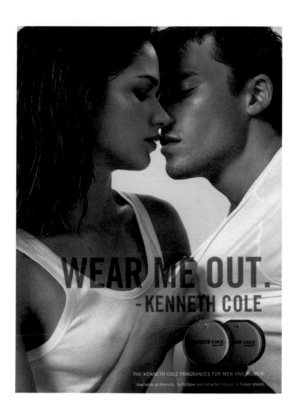

KENNETH COLE

1. What is this ad selling? How can you tell? If you had never heard of the company, Kenneth Cole, what might you guess this ad was selling? Explain.
2. How do the woman and man "sell" the fragrance?
3. Who is the target audience for this ad? How does the ad appeal to this target audience?
4. Would the impression of this ad, or its presumed effectiveness, be different if the subjects were smiling? Standing up straight? Who or why not?
5. Does this ad appeal to you? Why or why not?

HONDA

———————————

1. What makes you look at the ad? Why?
2. What does the image have to do with the product being sold? Do you find this ad confusing? Smart? Clever? Weird? Funny? Explain.
3. How does the written copy on the banana sell the product? How does the image of the banana reinforce the ad copy?
4. Who do you think is the target audience for this advertisement? How do you think a child would respond to it? A woman? A man? Explain.
5. Evaluate how symbolism serves as an unspoken form of language. How does symbolism work to sell the product in this advertisement?

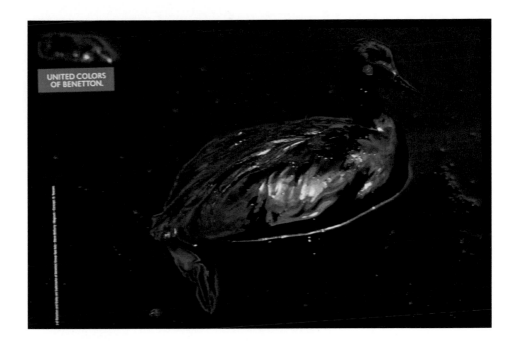

UNITED COLORS OF BENETTON ————————————————

1. What is the purpose of this ad? What is it selling?
2. How is this ad connected to the product it promotes?
3. What are your gut reactions to this ad? Do you find it disturbing? Offensive? Effective? Enlightening? Explain.
4. Evaluate the effectiveness of photographic decisions in this ad.

DOLCE & GABBANA

1. In what ways does this ad surprise you? How does it twist your assumptions?
2. What is the woman doing in this ad? Does her activity have anything to do with the product being sold?

3. If you were leafing through a magazine and saw this ad, would you stop to look at it? Would
   the ad convince you to purchase the product? Why or why not?
4. Who is this ad likely to appeal to, and why?
5. Where would you expect to see this advertisement?

Calvin Klein Jeans

introducing Body

starring Eva Mendes
and Jamie Dornan
Photographed by Steven Klein
in Palm Springs 2009

calvinklein.com

LONDON 170 Regent Street, Westfield
KENT Bluewater Shopping Centre
MANCHESTER Trafford Centre

CALVIN KLEIN

1. How does the model "sell" the product in this ad? Explain.
2. Would this ad be as effective if the model were not topless? What if she were posed differently?
3. Who is the target audience for this advertisement? Where would you expect to see it?
4. Who is Eva Mendes? Does her endorsement of the product (by wearing it in the ad) influence your decision to purchase it? Why or why not?
5. What, if anything, would you change about this advertisement? If you would keep it exactly the same, explain why you would not change it.

they do, what they care about, and who their friends are. Firms that exchange the information often do ensure that the targets' names and postal addresses remain anonymous—but not before they add specific demographic data and lifestyle information. For example:

10 • Rapleaf is a firm that claims on its website to help marketers "customize your customers' experience." To do that, it gleans data from individual users of blogs, internet forums, and social networks. It uses ad exchanges to sell the ability to reach those people. Rapleaf says it has "data on 900+ million records, 400+ million consumers, [and] 52+ billion friend connections." Advertisers are particularly aware of the firm's ability to predict the reliability of individuals (for example, the likelihood they will pay their mortgage) based on Rapleaf's research on the trustworthiness of the people in those individuals' social networks.

11 • A company called Next Jump runs employee discount and reward programs for about one-third of U.S. corporate employees. It gets personal information about all of them from the human relations departments of the companies and supplements that information with transactional data from the manufacturers it deals with as well as from credit companies. Armed with this combination of information, Next jump can predict what people want and what they will pay for. It also generates a "UserRank" score for every employee based on how many purchases a person has made and how much he or she has spent. That score plays an important role in determining which employee gets what product e-mail offers and at what price.

12 • A firm called The Daily Me already sells an ad and news personalization technology to online periodicals. If a *Boston Globe* reader who reads a lot of soccer sports news visits a *Dallas Morning News* site, the Daily Me's technology tells the *Dallas Morning News* to serve him soccer stories. Moreover, when an ad is served along with the story, its text and photos are instantly configured so as to include soccer terms and photos as part of the advertising pitch. A basketball fan receiving an ad for the same product will get language and photos that call out to people with hoop interests.

13 These specific operations may not be in business a few years from now. In the new media-buying environment companies come and go amid furious competition. The logic propelling them and more established firms forward, though, is consistent: the future belongs to marketers and media firms—*publishers,* in current terminology—that learn how to find and keep the most valuable customers by surrounding them with the most persuasive media materials. Special online advertising exchanges, owned by Google, Yahoo!, Microsoft, Interpublic, and other major players, allow publishers to auction and media agencies to "buy" individuals with particular characteristics, often in real time. That is, it is now possible to buy the right to deliver an ad to a person with specific characteristics at the precise moment that that person loads a Web page. In fact, through an activity called cookie matching, which I discuss in detail later, an advertiser can actually bid for the right to reach an individual whom the advertiser knows from previous contacts and is

now tracking around the Web. Moreover, the technology keeps changing. Because consumers delete Web cookies and marketers find cookies difficult to use with mobile devices, technology companies have developed methods to "fingerprint" devices permanently and allow for persistent personalization across many media platforms.

14   The significance of tailored commercial messages and offers goes far beyond whether or not the targeted persons buy the products. Advertisements and discounts are status signals: they alert people as to their social position. If you consistently get ads for low-priced cars, regional vacations, fast-food restaurants, and other products that reflect a lower-class status, your sense of the world's opportunities may be narrower than that of someone who is feted with ads for national or international trips and luxury products. Moreover, if like Larry and Rhonda you happen to know that your colleague is receiving more ads for the luxury products than you are, and more and better discounts to boot, you may worry that you are falling behind in society's estimation of your worth.

15   In fact, the ads may signal your opportunities actually *are* narrowed if marketers and publishers decide that the data points—profiles—about you across the internet position you in a segment of the population that is relatively less desirable to marketers because of income, age, past-purchase behavior, geographical location, or other reasons. Turning individual profiles into individual evaluations is what happens when a profile becomes a reputation. Today individual marketers still make most of the decisions about which particular persons matter to them, and about how much they matter. But that is beginning to change as certain publishers and data providers—Rapleaf and Next Jump, for example—allow their calculations of value to help advertisers make targeting decisions. In the future, these calculations of our marketing value, both broadly and for particular products, may become routine parts of the information exchanged about people throughout the media system.

16   The tailoring of news and entertainment is less advanced, but it is clearly under way. Technologies developed for personalized advertising and coupons point to possibilities for targeting individuals with personalized news and entertainment. Not only is this already happening, the logic of doing that is becoming more urgent to advertisers and publishers. Advertisers operate on the assumption that, on the internet as in traditional media, commercial messages that parade as soft (or "human interest") news and entertainment are more persuasive than straightforward ads. Publishers know this too, and in the heat of a terrible economic downturn even the most traditional ones have begun to compromise long-standing professional norms about the separation of advertising and editorial matter. And in fact many of the new online publishers—companies, such as Demand Media, that turn out thousands of text and video pieces a day—never really bought into the old-world ideas about editorial integrity anyway. What this means is that we are entering a world of intensively customized content, a world in which publishers and even marketers will package personalized advertisements with soft news or entertainment that is tailored to fit both the selling needs of the ads and the reputation of the particular individual.

17   The rise of digital profiling and personalization has spawned a new industrial jargon that reflects potentially grave social divisions and privacy issues. Marketers

divide people into *targets* and *waste*. They also use words like *anonymous* and *personal* in unrecognizable ways that distort and drain them of their traditional meanings. If a company can follow your behavior in the digital environment—an environment that potentially includes your mobile phone and television set—its claim that you are "anonymous" is meaningless. That is particularly true when firms intermittently add off-line information such as shopping patterns and the value of your house to their online data and then simply strip the name and address to make it "anonymous." It matters little if your name is John Smith, Yesh Mispar, or 3211466. The persistence of information about you will lead firms to act based on what they know, share, and care about you, whether you know it is happening or not.

18   All these developments may sound more than a little unsettling; *creeped out* is a phrase people often use when they learn about them. National surveys I have conducted over the past decade consistently suggest that although people know companies are using their data and do worry about it, their understanding of exactly how the data are being used is severely lacking. That of course shouldn't be surprising. People today lead busy, even harried, lives. Keeping up with the complex and changing particulars of data mining is simply not something most of us have the time or ability to do. There are many great things about the new media environment. But when companies track people without their knowledge, sell their data without letting them know what they are doing or securing their permission, and then use those data to decide which of those people are targets or waste, we have a serious social problem. The precise implications of this problem are not yet clear. If it's allowed to persist, and people begin to realize how the advertising industry segregates them from and pits them against others in the ads they get, the discounts they receive, the TV-viewing suggestions and news stories they confront, and even the offers they receive in the supermarket, they may begin to suffer the effects of discrimination. They will likely learn to distrust the companies that have put them in this situation, and they may well be incensed at the government that has not helped to prevent it. A comparison to the Financial industry is apt. Here was an industry engaged in a whole spectrum of arcane practices that were not at all transparent to consumers or regulators but that had serious negative impact on our lives. It would be deeply unfortunate if the advertising system followed the same trajectory.

19   Despite valiant efforts on the part of advocacy groups and some federal and state officials, neither government rulings nor industry self-regulation has set policies that will address these issues before they become major sources of widespread social distress. Part of the reason for the lack of action may be that neither citizens nor politicians recognize how deeply embedded in American life these privacy-breaching and social-profiling activities are. Few individuals outside advertising know about the power of the new media-buying system: its capacity to determine not only what media firms do but how we see ourselves and others. They don't know that that system is working to attach marketing labels to us based on the clicks we make, the conversations we have, and the friendships we enjoy on websites, mobile devices, iPads, supermarket carts, and even television sets. They don't know that the new system is forcing many media firms to sell their souls for ad money while they serve us commercial messages, discounts, and, increasingly, news and entertainment based on our marketing labels. They don't realize that the wide sharing

of data suggests that in the future marketers and media firms may find it useful to place us into personalized "reputation silos" that surround us with worldviews and rewards based on labels marketers have created reflecting our value to them. Without this knowledge, it is hard to even begin to have broad-based serious discussions about what society and industry should do about this sobering new world: into the twenty-first century the media-buying system's strategy of social discrimination will increasingly define how we as individuals relate to society—not only how much we pay but what we see and when and how we see it. ◆

ANALYSIS AND DISCUSSION

1. What are the broader cultural and social consequences of social profiled marketing tactics? How can they harm consumers?
2. Turow posits that in a few decades, the business logic used by online data mining will "transform the way we see ourselves, those around us, and the world at large." How can the ads you see every day influence the way you view yourself and the people around you? Explain.
3. Turow uses the example of a typical American family that uses the Internet. How does this example help support the points he raises in his essay? Is it an effective way to explain to his audience what data mining could do/is doing? Explain.
4. How does packaging individuals or groups of people make them "useful targets" for advertisers? Can you think of examples of how advertisers package people or groups of people?
5. Evaluate Turow's tone in this essay. What phrases or words reveal his tone? Who is his audience? How does this tone connect to his intended audience?
6. Turow notes that data mining should "creep out" people who think that they are in control of technology, or even know about it, but think it won't have an impact on them. Why does he feel this way? Are you creeped out? Why or why not?

RESEARCH AND WRITING

1. Go to your school's library and assess the ads that you see. Try to see if you can influence the ads you view by typing in certain words, such as "colleges" and "college loans" or "child care" and "children's clothing." Applying some of the information you learned from Turow's essay, discuss the ways online ads are targeted to specific audiences. Do you think they help contribute to the fragmenting of American culture? Explain your viewpoint.
2. Turow once commented that "new approaches to marketing make it increasingly worthwhile for ... media companies to separate audiences into different worlds according to distinctions that ad people feel make the audiences feel secure and comfortable." What types of ads appeal to you and why? Do you feel that online advertisements that actively target you as

part of a particular segment of society work more effectively on you as a consumer? Explain your perspective in a well-considered essay. Cite specific ads in your response to support your view.

3. *Exploratory Writing:* Turow notes that based on their Internet use, two people may receive very different ad pitches and discount offers from the same company, because data mining has classified them as different types of consumers. Write an essay in which you explore the connections among product targeting, audience packaging, and social diversification.

GROUP PROJECTS

1. Turow describes some of the ways advertisers target audiences by exploiting Internet data. You and the members of your group are members of an advertising agency developing a campaign for a new cologne. First, determine to whom you will market this new product and then create an advertising strategy for the product. What will your online ads look like? If you use commercials, when will they air and during what programs? Explain the rationale for your campaign to the class, referring to some of the points Turow makes in his article about product targeting.

2. Each member of your group should spend an hour on line visiting various Web sites, including Facebook, news sites, and various online retailers. Record all the ads you see. With your group, try to determine the ways in which each ad uses product targeting.

Coming to a Lab Near You
*Mary Carmichael**

Consumers are growing increasingly savvy to and more cynical about marketers' claims. With so many similar brands selling similar products, the "persuasion industries" of marketing and advertising are researching and refining methods to reinforce the emotional attachments between Americans and the brands they buy. One tool in their arsenal may be the emerging field of neuromarketing, in which functional magnetic resonance imaging equipment—called fMRI—is being used to watch how our brains respond to brands, advertising appeals, and products. Is using such technology ethical? And is there anything we can do about it?

1 For an ad campaign that started a revolution in marketing, the Pepsi Challenge TV spots of the 1970s and '80s were almost absurdly simple. Little more than a series of blind taste tests, these ads showed people being asked to choose between Pepsi and Coke without knowing which one they were consuming. Not surprisingly, given the sponsor, Pepsi was usually the winner.

---

* Mary Carmichael, "The Persuaders," *Frontline,* November 2004

2   But 30 years after the commercials debuted, neuroscientist Read Montague was still thinking about them. Something didn't make sense. If people preferred the taste of Pepsi, the drink should have dominated the market. It didn't. So in the summer of 2003, Montague gave himself a "Pepsi Challenge" of a different sort: to figure out why people would buy a product they didn't particularly like.

3   What he found was the first data from an entirely new field: neuromarketing, the study of the brain's responses to ads, brands, and the rest of the messages littering the cultural landscape. Montague had his subjects take the Pepsi Challenge while he watched their neural activity with a functional MRI machine, which tracks blood flow to different regions of the brain. Without knowing what they were drinking, about half of them said they preferred Pepsi. But once Montague told them which samples were Coke, three-fourths said that drink tasted better, and their brain activity changed too. Coke "lit up" the medial prefrontal cortex—a part of the brain that controls higher thinking. Montague's hunch was that the brain was recalling images and ideas from commercials, and the brand was overriding the actual quality of the product. For years, in the face of failed brands and laughably bad ad campaigns, marketers had argued that they could influence consumers' choices. Now, there appeared to be solid neurological proof. Montague published his findings in the October 2004 issue of *Neuron*, and a cottage industry was born.

4   Neuromarketing, in one form or another, is now one of the hottest new tools of its trade. At the most basic levels, companies are starting to sift through the piles of psychological literature that have been steadily growing since the 1990s' boom in brain-imaging technology. Surprisingly few businesses have kept tabs on the studies—until now. "Most marketers don't take a single class in psychology. A lot of the current communications projects we see are based on research from the '70s," says Justine Meaux, a scientist at Atlanta's BrightHouse Neurostrategies Group, one of the first and largest neurosciences consulting firms. "Especially in these early years, it's about teaching people the basics. What we end up doing is educating people about some false assumptions about how the brain works."

5   Getting an update on research is one thing; for decades, marketers have relied on behavioral studies for guidance. But some companies are taking the practice several steps further, commissioning their own fMRI studies à la Montague's test. In a study of men's reactions to cars, Daimler-Chrysler has found that sportier models activate the brain's reward centers—the same areas that light up in response to alcohol and drugs—as well as activating the area in the brain that recognizes faces, which may explain people's tendency to anthropomorphize their cars. Steven Quartz, a scientist at Stanford University, is currently conducting similar research on movie trailers. And in the age of poll-taking and smear campaigns, political advertising is also getting in on the game. Researchers at the University of California, Los Angeles have found that Republicans and Democrats react differently to campaign ads showing images of the Sept. 11th terrorist attacks. Those ads cause the part of the brain associated with fear to light up more vividly in Democrats than in Republicans.

6   That last piece of research is particularly worrisome to anti-marketing activists, some of whom are already mobilizing against the nascent field of neuromarketing. Gary Ruskin of Commercial Alert, a non-profit that argues for strict regulations on advertising, says that "a year ago almost nobody had heard of neuromarketing

except for Forbes readers." Now, he says, it's everywhere, and over the past year he has waged a campaign against the practice, lobbying Congress and the American Psychological Association (APA) and threatening lawsuits against BrightHouse and other practitioners. Even though he admits the research is still "in the very preliminary stages," he says it could eventually lead to complete corporate manipulation of consumers—or citizens, with governments using brain scans to create more effective propaganda.

7   Ruskin might be consoled by the fact that many neuromarketers still don't know how to apply their findings. Increased activity in the brain doesn't necessarily mean increased preference for a product. And, says Meaux, no amount of neuromarketing research can transform otherwise rational people into consumption-driven zombies. "Of course we're all influenced by the messages around us," she says. "That doesn't take away free choice." As for Ruskin, she says tersely, "there is no grounds for what he is accusing." So far, the regulatory boards agree with her: the government has decided not to investigate BrightHouse and the APA's most recent ethics statement said nothing about neuromarketing. Says Ruskin: "It was a total defeat for us."

8   With Commercial Alert's campaign thwarted for now, BrightHouse is moving forward. In January, the company plans to start publishing a neuroscience newsletter aimed at businesses. And although it "doesn't conduct fMRI studies except in the rarest of cases," it is getting ready to publish the results of a particularly tantalizing set of tests. While neuroscientist Montague's "Pepsi Challenge" suggests that branding appears to make a difference in consumer preference, BrightHouse's research promises to show exactly how much emotional impact that branding can have. Marketers have long known that some brands have a seemingly magic appeal; they can elicit strong devotion, with buyers saying they identify with the brand as an extension of their personalities. The BrightHouse research is expected to show exactly which products those are. "This is really just the first step," says Meaux, who points out that no one has discovered a "buy button" in the brain. But with more and more companies peering into the minds of their consumers, could that be far off? ◆

CRITICAL THINKING

1. What did researchers discover about the connection between brands and the brain when they used fMRI to assess the "Pepsi Challenge"? Explain.
2. Does the discovery that parts of the brain "light up" instinctively in response to certain advertising stimuli make you feel less in control of your buying decisions? Why or why not?
3. Why are consumer protection organizations concerned that fMRI and neuromarketing will be used unethically by marketing companies?
4. A larger question concerning the use of fMRI is whether it is ethical to use equipment designed to heal patients and advance medicine for the purpose of finding new ways to neurologically influence our purchasing decisions. In your opinion, if such technology is available, should it be used by anyone, for any reason, or should such equipment be restricted to its intended purpose—medicine and medical research?

CRITICAL WRITING

1. *Exploratory Writing:* Carmichael describes how a panel of experts is reviewing the use of fMRI beyond medical applications. If you were a member of this panel of experts, explain why you would or would not bar this type of science.

2. *Personal Narrative:* Have you ever experienced an intense desire to purchase a particular brand of product, such as a handbag, sneaker, or article of clothing, without understanding exactly why you wanted that product/brand so much? Explore your feelings about the item, why you want/wanted it, and how you felt after you purchased it (if you did indeed buy it). What connection exists between our emotions and what we decide to buy?

3. *Research Writing:* Research the field of neuromarketing and write a paper in which you explore the future applications of this new field. How might advertising change as a result of neuromarketing? Explain.

GROUP PROJECTS

1. Watch the program "The Persuaders" produced by PBS at http://www .pbs.org/wgbh/pages/frontline/shows/persuaders. Select one portion of the program to focus on, and then prepare a report for the class summarizing the information conveyed in the program. If possible, make connections between the points raised in the program, with real-world examples.

2. Create your own "Pepsi Challenge" in which your group creates an "identity" for two bottled waters (drawn from the same tap). Create a campaign around each, and have friends and family take the challenge to see which water they prefer. Are there any correlations you can make between the Pepsi Challenge described in the article and the water experiment you conducted with your group? Explain.

The Allure of Luxury
James B. Twitchell*

Although media and academic critics question the methods of advertising agencies and lament the sacrifice of values in the name of consumerism, professor James B. Twitchell openly embraces the media-driven world of advertising. In the next piece, Twitchell explores the joys of luxury and challenges the academic criticism that condemns our material instincts as shallow and self-centered. He realizes that his viewpoint may not be popular, but it is honest. Because the truth is, we love nice stuff. Is that so wrong?

* James Twitchell, *The Wilson Quarterly,* Winter 2007

> *At length I recollected the thoughtless saying of a great princess who, on being informed that the country had no bread, replied, "Let them eat cake."*
>
> —Jean-Jacques Rousseau, *Confessions*

1 Well, okay, so Marie Antoinette never said, "Let them eat cake." When Rousseau wrote those words, Marie was just 11 years old and living in Austria. But Americans used to like the story that, when the French queen was told by an official that the people were angry because they had no bread, she responded, *"Qu'ils mangent de la brioche."* We liked to imagine her saying it with a snarl and a curled lip. She was a luxury bimbo whose out-of-control spending grated on the poor and unfortunate French people. We fought a revolution to separate ourselves from exactly that kind of uppercrustiness. She got her just "desserts."

2 But that was 200 years ago. Now cake is one of *our* favorite foods, part of the fifth food group, totally unnecessary luxury consumption. We're not talking about a few crumbs, but the real stuff. Brioche by the loaf. Not for nothing has Marie become a favorite subject for current infotainment. Novelists, historians, biographers, and even hip young filmmaker Sofia Coppola are telling her story, not because we want her reviled but because we want to be like her.

3 And we're doing a pretty good job. Luxury spending in the United States has been growing more than four times as fast as overall spending, and the rest of the West is not far behind. You might think that modern wannabe Maries are grayhairs with poodles. Not so. This spending is being done by younger and younger consumers. Take a walk up Fifth Avenue, and then, at 58th, cross over and continue up Madison. You'll see who is swarming through the stores with names we all recognize: Louis Vuitton, Gucci, Prada, Dior, Coach. . . . Or cruise Worth Avenue or Rodeo Drive, and you'll see the same furious down-marketing and up-crusting. This is the Twinkiefication of deluxe.

4 You don't have to go to these streets of dreams to see who's on a sugar high. Take a tour of your local Costco or Sam's Club discount warehouse and you'll see the same stuff, only a day old and about to become stale, being consumed by a slightly older crowd. Observe the parking lot, where shiny new imported sedans and SUVs are parked beside aging subcompacts. Or spend an hour watching the Home Shopping Network, a televised flea market for impulse buyers. Its call centers now have some 23,000 incoming phone lines capable of handling up to 20,000 calls a minute. The network no longer sells cubic zirconia rings. It sells Gucci handbags.

5 We've developed a powerful desire to associate with recognized objects of little intrinsic but high positional value, which is why Martha Stewart, our faux Marie, is down at Kmart introducing her Silver Label goods, why a courtier the likes of Michael Graves is designing toasters for Target (pronounced by wits, with an ironic French flair, tar-ZHAY), why the Duke of Polo, Ralph Lauren, is marketing house paint, and why suave Cole Porter–brand furniture is appearing on the floor at Ethan Allen stores.

6 Look around, and you will see that almost every category of consumables has cake at the top. This is true not just for expensive products such as town cars and McMansions, but for everyday objects. In bottled water, for instance, there is Evian,

advertised as if it were a liqueur. In coffee, there's Starbucks; in ice cream, Häagen-Dazs; in sneakers, Nike; in wine, Château Margaux; in cigars, Arturo Fuente Hemingway, and well,

> *[Now] the duchess's precious things are within your grimy reach. From her point of view, she might just as well take 'em to the dump.*

you know the rest. Having a few TVs around the house is fine, but what you really need is a home entertainment center worthy of Versailles, with a JBL Ultra Synthesis One audio system, a Vidikron Vision One front projector, a Stewart Ultramatte 150 screen, a Pioneer DV-09 DVD player, and an AMX ViewPoint remote control. Hungry for chow with your entertainment? Celebrity chef Wolfgang Puck has his own line of TV dinner entrées.

7   Ironically, what this poaching of deluxe by the middle class has done is make things impossible for the truly rich. Ponder this: A generation ago, the Duke and Duchess of Windsor surrounded themselves with the world's finest goods—from jewelry to bed linens to flatware. The duchess, the twice-divorced American Wallis Simpson, would never be queen, but that didn't prevent her from carrying off a passable imitation of Marie. In the Windsor household, the coasters were Cartier and the placemats were Porthault, and the pooches ate from silver-plated Tiffany bowls.

8   When Sotheby's auctioned more than 40,000 items from the Windsors' Paris home in 1997, the remnants of their royal life went out for bid. Most of the items listed in the Sotheby's catalog are still being made, either in the same form or in an updated version. In other words, the duchess's precious things are within your grimy reach. From her point of view, she might just as well take 'em to the dump.

9   • Chanel faux-pearl earrings given to the duchess by the duke can be picked up for about $360 at Chanel stores.

10   • The duchess's Cartier love bracelet in 18-karat gold with screw closure, which was presented by the president of Cartier to the Windsors and other "great lovers" in 1970 (among the other recipients: Elizabeth Taylor and Richard Burton, Sophia Loren and Carlo Ponti), is yours for $3,625 at Cartier boutiques.

11   • T. Anthony luggage, the Windsors' favorite (they owned 118 such trunks), is still being manufactured and can be bought in Manhattan.

12   • Hand-embroidered Porthault linens are stocked at your local mall.

13   • The Windsors' stationery from the Mrs. John L. Strong company, complete with hand-engraved monogrammed pieces on pure cotton paper, can be yours for $80 to $750, depending on the ornamentation.

14   • The duke's velvet slippers can be purchased for $188 at Brooks Brothers, which owns the London company that made them. Instead of an E for "Edward" below the embroidered crown, the slippers have a BB.

15   • Okay, okay, you'll never own as many scarves and gloves as the duchess did, but Hermes and Balenciaga sell exactly the same ones she wore for upward of $300 a pop.

16   Here's the takeaway: There is very little cake a rich person once gorged on that a middle-class person can't get on his plate. You name it; I can taste it. So I can't afford a casita on Bermuda, but I can get in on a time-share for a weekend. No, I can't

own a stretch limo, but I can rent one by the hour. Maybe Venice is out this year, but I'll go to the Venetian in Vegas instead. I can't afford an Armani suit, but what about these eyeglasses with Giorgio's name plastered on them? Commodore Vanderbilt said that if you have to ask how much a yacht costs, you can't afford one, but check out my stateroom on my chartered Majestic Princess. True, I don't have my own Gulfstream V jet, but I can upgrade to first class on Delta with the miles I "earn" by using my American Express card. Is that my own Lexus out front? Or is it on lease from a used car dealer? You'll never know.

17   Lux populi may be the end of deluxe. "Real" luxury used to be for the "happy few," but in the world of the supra-12,000 Dow Jones industrial average, there are only the minted many. "Sudden Wealth Syndrome," as the *Los Angeles Times* has called it, is not just for dot.com innovators or contestants on *Who Wants to Be a Millionaire,* but for a generation that is inheriting its wealth through the steady attrition of the Generation Who Fought the War. The "wealth effect," as former Federal Reserve chairman Alan Greenspan termed it, drives more and more money to chase after goods whose production can hardly be called beneficial and cannot now even be called positional.

18   There's a story, perhaps apocryphal, that when Tom Ford, chief designer for Gucci in the 1990s, was passing through the Newark airport (what the hell was he doing there?!), he saw one of his swanky T-shirts on the tummy of a portly prole. He immediately canceled the clothing line. Too late. Perhaps the social construction of luxury as a material category has already been deconstructed into banality.

19   The very unreachableness of old luxe made it safe, like an old name, old blood, old land, an old coat of arms, or old service to the crown. Primogeniture, the cautious passage and consolidation of wealth to the firstborn male, made the anxiety of exclusion from luxe somehow bearable. After all, you knew your place from the moment of birth and had plenty of time to make your peace. If you drew the short straw, not to worry. A comfortable life as a vicar would await you. Or the officer corps.

20   The application of steam, then electricity, to the engines of production brought a new market to status objects, an industrial market made up of people who essentially bought their way into having a bloodline. These were the people who so disturbed economist Thorstein Veblen, and from them this new generation of consumer has descended. First the industrial rich, then the inherited rich, and now the incidentally rich, the accidentally rich, the golden-parachute rich, the buyout rich, the lottery rich.

21   Call them yuppies, yippies, bobos, nobrows, or whatever, the consumers of the new luxury have a sense of entitlement that transcends social class, a conviction that the finest things are their birthright. Never mind that they may have been born into a family whose ancestral estate is a tract house in the suburbs, near the mall, not paid for, and whose family crest was downloaded from the Internet. Ditto the signet ring design. Language reflects this hijacking. Words such as *gourmet, premium, boutique, chic, accessory,* and *classic* have loosened from their elite moorings and now describe such top-of-category items as popcorn, hamburgers, discount brokers, shampoo, scarves, ice cream, and trailer parks. "Luxury for all" is an oxymoron, all right, the aspirational goal of modern culture, and the death knell of the real thing.

22   These new *customers* for luxury are younger than *clients* of the old luxe used to
be, there are far more of them, they make their money much sooner, and they are far
more flexible in financing and fickle in choice. They do not stay put. When Richie
Rich starts buying tulips by the ton, Nouveau Riche is right there behind him picking them up by the pound.

23   In a sense, the filthy rich have only two genuine luxury items left: time and
philanthropy. As the old paradox goes, the rich share the luxury of too much time
on their hands with the very people on whom they often bestow their philanthropy.
Who knows, maybe poverty will become the new luxury, as the philosophes predicted. Wonder Bread becomes the new cake. Once you've ripped out all the old
patinaed hardware, once you've traded in the Bentley for a rusted-out Chevy, once
you've carted all the polo pony shirts to Goodwill, once you've given the Pollock to
the Met, once you've taken your last trip up Everest and into the Amazon, there's not
much left to do to separate yourself but give the rest of the damned stuff away. Competitive philanthropy has its allure. Why do you think there are more than 20 universities with multibillion-dollar pledge campaigns? Those bobos sure as hell can't do
it. Little wonder that Warren Buffett dumped his load rather casually on top of a pile
amassed by another modern baron, almost as if to say, "Top that." Now that's a show
stopper. Even The Donald can't trump that. ◆

CRITICAL THINKING

1. Why is materialism so criticized yet obviously so wholeheartedly embraced by American society? If we are basically lovers of luxury, why are
   we so quick to condemn advertising and consumerism?
2. What is luxury to you? Is there a point when it seems excessive? If so,
   what is your luxury threshold, and why?
3. Twitchell refers to Marie Antoinette in his opening paragraphs. Why does
   he choose her to demonstrate the American thirst for luxury? Explain.
4. Evaluate Twitchell's tone and style in this piece. What can you surmise
   from his tone and use of language? Does it make him more or less credible? Explain.
5. Twitchell lists a number of items belonging to the Windsors that were
   auctioned at Sotheby's. He observes that if the Duchess were alive today,
   she would probably "take 'em to the dump." Why would she do this?
   What happens when luxury is accessible to "the populi"?
6. How does Twitchell's opinion expressed in this essay differ from others
   in this section in his attitude toward advertising? Are they likely to be
   swayed by his argument? Why or why not?
7. According to Twitchell, why is luxury so important to Americans? What
   is the connection between desire and social status? In what ways is luxury
   "socially constructed"? Explain.
8. How well does Twitchell support his argument? Evaluate his use of supporting evidence. How well does he convince his readers that his position
   is reasonable and correct? Explain.

CRITICAL WRITING

1. *Exploratory Writing:* Twitchell wonders in his conclusion whether poverty will become the next luxury. Respond to his question with your own opinion.
2. *Personal Narrative:* Write a brief narrative about a time you experienced a decadent spending situation—either for yourself or with someone else. What motivated your spending? How did you feel after it?

GROUP PROJECTS

1. With your group, make a list of standard appliances, equipment, and possessions that people have in their homes—refrigerators, microwave ovens, pocketbooks, personal planners, fans, coffeemakers, DVD players, computers, VCRs, televisions, stereos (include components), iPods, blow-dryers, scooters, and so on. Make a list of at least 25 to 30 items. After the group has created a list, separately rank each item as a necessary, desirable, or luxury item. For example, you may decide a refrigerator is a necessary item but list an air conditioner as a luxury item. Do not look at how other members of your group rank the items until you are all finished. Compare your list with others in your group. Do the lists match, or are there some surprising discrepancies? Discuss the similarities and differences among your lists.
2. Examine the collection of ads included in this chapter. Select one and identify the consumer group it targets. Develop a profile of a typical consumer of the product the ad promotes, the sort of people who are likely to purchase the product, and their motivations for owning it.

Will Your Recession Be Tall, Grande, or Venti?
*Daniel Gross**

How could coffee, that morning staple on which so many of us depend, also be linked to the health of our economy? While financial gurus argue over the deciding factors of our current recession and the direction it will take, business columnist Daniel Gross has already figured it out. The problem, he explains, is Starbucks. In this next editorial, Gross illustrates the correlation between having too many Starbucks and having a financial crisis. Perhaps economists should be counting the number of baristas when they judge the direction the economy will take.

1 Remember Thomas Friedman's McDonald's theory of international relations? The thinking was that if two countries had evolved into prosperous, mass-consumer societies, with middle classes able to afford Big Macs, they would generally find peaceful means of adjudicating disputes. They'd sit down over a Happy Meal to

* Daniel Gross, *Slate* Magazine, October 20, 2008

resolve issues rather than use mortars. The recent unpleasantries between Israel and Lebanon, which both have McDonald's operations, put paid to that reasoning. But the Golden Arches theory of realpolitik was good while it lasted.

2   In the same spirit, I propose the Starbucks theory of international economics. The higher the concentration of expensive, nautically themed, faux-Italian-branded Frappuccino joints in a country's financial capital, the more likely the country is to have suffered catastrophic financial losses.

> *"We haven't heard much about bailouts in Central America, where Starbucks has no presence."*

3   It may sound doppio, but work with me. This recent crisis has its roots in the unhappy coupling of a frenzied nationwide real-estate market centered in California, Las Vegas, and Florida, and a nationwide credit mania centered in New York. If you could pick one brand name that personified these twin bubbles, it was Starbucks. The Seattle-based coffee chain followed new housing developments into the suburbs and exurbs, where its outlets became pit stops for real-estate brokers and their clients. It also carpet-bombed the business districts of large cities, especially the financial centers, with nearly 200 in Manhattan alone. Starbucks' frothy treats provided the fuel for the boom, the caffeine that enabled deal jockeys to stay up all hours putting together offering papers for CDOs, and helped mortgage brokers work overtime processing dubious loan documents. Starbucks strategically located many of its outlets on the ground floors of big investment banks. (The one around the corner from the former Bear Stearns headquarters has already closed.)

4   Like American financial capitalism, Starbucks, fueled by the capital markets, took a great idea too far (quality coffee for Starbucks, securitization for Wall Street) and diluted the experience unnecessarily (subprime food such as egg-and-sausage sandwiches for Starbucks, subprime loans for Wall Street). Like so many sadder-but-wiser Miami condo developers, Starbucks operated on a "build it and they will come" philosophy. Like many of the humiliated Wall Street firms, the coffee company let algorithms and number-crunching get the better of sound judgment: If the waiting time at one Starbucks was over a certain number of minutes, Starbucks reasoned that an opposite corner could sustain a new outlet. Like the housing market, Starbucks peaked in the spring of 2006 and has since fallen precipitously.

5   America's financial crisis has gone global in the past month. European and Asian governments, which until recently were rejoicing over America's financial downfall, have had to nationalize banks and expand depositors' insurance. Why? Many of their banks feasted on American subprime debt and took shoddy risk-management cues from their American cousins. Indeed, the countries whose financial sectors were most connected to the U.S.-dominated global financial system, the ones whose financial institutions plunged into CDOs, credit-default swaps, and the whole catalog of horribles have suffered the most.

6   What does this have to do with the price of coffee? Well, when you start poking around Starbucks' international store locator, some interesting patterns

emerge. At first blush, there's a pretty close correlation between a country having a significant Starbucks presence, especially in its financial capital, and major financial cock-ups, from Australia (big blowups in finance, hedge funds, and asset management companies; 23 stores) to the United Kingdom (nationalization of its largest banks). In many ways, London in recent years has been a more concentrated version of New York—the wellspring of many toxic innovations, a hedge-fund haven. It sports 256 Starbucks. In Spain, which is now grappling with the bursting of a speculative coastal real-estate bubble (sound familiar?), the financial capital, Madrid, has 48 outlets. In crazy Dubai, 48 Starbucks outlets serve a population of 1.4 million. And so on: South Korea, which is bailing outs its banks big time, has 253; Paris, the locus of several embarrassing debacles, has 35.

7   But there are many spots on the globe where it's tough to find a Starbucks. And these are precisely the places where banks are surviving, in large part because they have not financially integrated with banks in the Starbucks economies. In the entire continent of Africa, whose banks don't stray too far, I count just three (in Egypt). We haven't heard much about bailouts in Central America, where Starbucks has no presence. South America's banks may be buckling, but they haven't broken. Argentina, formerly a financial basket case and now a pocket of relative strength, has just one store. Brazil, with a population of nearly 200 million, has a mere 14. Italy hasn't suffered any major bank failures in part because its banking sector isn't very active on the international scene. The number of Starbucks there? Zero. And the small countries of Northern Europe, whose banking systems have been largely spared, are largely Starbucks-free. (There are two in Denmark, three in the Netherlands, and none in the Scandinavian trio of Sweden, Finland, and Norway.)

8   My tentative theory: Having a significant Starbucks presence is a pretty significant indicator of the degree of connectedness to the form of highly caffeinated, free-spending capitalism that got us into this mess. It's also a sign of a culture's willingness to abandon traditional norms and ways of doing business (virtually all the countries in which Starbucks has established beachheads have their own venerable coffee-house traditions) in favor of fast-moving American ones. The fact that the company or its local licensee felt there was room for dozens of outlets where consumers would pony up lots of euros, liras, and rials for expensive drinks is also a pretty good indicator that excessive financial optimism had entered the bloodstream.

9   This theory isn't foolproof. Some places that have relatively high concentrations of Starbucks, such as Santiago, Chile (27), have been safe havens. Russia, which has just six, has blown up. But it's close enough. And so, if you're looking for potential trouble spots, forget about the *Financial Times* or the Bloomberg terminal. Just look at the user-friendly Starbucks store locator. The next potential trouble spot? I just returned from a week in Istanbul, Turkey, a booming financial capital increasingly tied to the fortunes of Western Europe. It has a storied coffee culture, yet I gave up counting the number of Starbucks stores occupying prime real estate. It turns out there are 67 of them. Watch out, Turkey. ◆

CRITICAL THINKING

1. What is the tone of Gross's article? Is it serious, tongue-in-cheek, sarcastic, angry, harsh, or something else? Give at least one example from the text to support your opinion.
2. Does Gross convince you of his "Starbucks theory of international economics"? What do you find convincing or not convincing?
3. In the last paragraph of this article, Gross gives a warning to Turkey. What is the warning?
4. Gross uses interesting vocabulary in his article to support his points. Find unfamiliar words, uncommon vocabulary, or the use of slang and acronyms in his article. Why do you think he chose to use those precise words?
5. What image does Starbucks have? How does this image tie in with the economic health of an area?

CRITICAL WRITING

1. *Expository Writing Compare/Contrast:* Read Daniel Gross's article "Obscure Economic Indicator: Keeneland Thoroughbred Sales: What the Price of Racehorses Signals about the Health of the World Economy" posted on the December 2, 2005, edition of *Slate* in which Gross states, "When the world's economy catches a sniffle, the horseflesh market starts wheezing." Compare the correlation between elite racehorses and the economy to the number of Starbucks and the economy. Explain which article makes the better argument. Can you think of other minutiae of American life that might reveal the health of the economy?
2. *Exploratory Writing:* Consider the thesis of this article: "Having a significant Starbucks presence is a pretty significant indicator of the degree of connectedness to the form of highly caffeinated, free-spending capitalism that got us into this mess." Explore other indicators besides Starbucks that prove we are a consumer-driven nation.

GROUP PROJECTS

1. Look up Thomas Friedman's "McDonald's Theory," described in his book *The Lexus and the Olive Tree,* and then summarize this theory in your own words. As a group, discuss Friedman's theory and its strengths and weaknesses.
2. Research the history of the Starbucks franchise—how it started, how it grew, where it is today, and then predict where it will be in the future. Report the key points of your discussion to the class as part of a larger discussion on how consumer culture is tied to the health of the economy.

▶ **With These Words, I Can Sell You Anything**
*William Lutz**

▶ **The Language of Advertising**
Charles A. O'Neill

Words such as *help* and *virtually* and phrases such as *new and improved* and *acts fast* seem like innocuous weaponry in the arsenal of advertising. But not to William Lutz, who analyzes how such words are used in ads and how they misrepresent, mislead, and deceive consumers. In this essay, he alerts us to the special power of "weasel words," those familiar and sneaky little critters that "appear to say one thing when in fact they say the opposite, or nothing at all." The real danger, Lutz argues, is how such language debases reality and the values of the consumer. Marketing executive Charles A. O'Neill, however, disputes Lutz's criticism of advertising doublespeak. Although admitting to some of the craftiness of his profession, O'Neill defends the huckster's language—both verbal and visual—against claims that it distorts reality. Examining some familiar television commercials and magazine ads, he explains why the language may be charming and seductive but far from brainwashing.

With These Words, I Can Sell You Anything
William Lutz

1 One problem advertisers have when they try to convince you that the product they are pushing is really different from other, similar products is that their claims are subject to some laws. Not a lot of laws, but there are some designed to prevent fraudulent or untruthful claims in advertising. Even during the happy years of nonregulation under Ronald Reagan, the FTC did crack down on the more blatant abuses in advertising claims. Generally speaking, advertisers have to be careful in what they say in their ads, in the claims they make for the products they advertise. Parity claims are safe because they are legal and supported by a number of court decisions. But beyond parity claims there are weasel words.

2 Advertisers use weasel words to appear to be making a claim for a product, when in fact they are making no claim at all. Weasel words get their name from the way weasels eat the eggs they find in the nests of other animals. A weasel will make a small hole in the egg, suck out the insides, then place the egg back in the nest. Only when the egg is examined closely is it found to be hollow. That's the way it is with weasel words in advertising: Examine weasel words closely and you'll find that they're as hollow as any egg sucked by a weasel. Weasel words appear to say one thing when in fact they say the opposite, or nothing at all.

---

* William Lutz, *Doublespeak* (excerpt), 1990; Charles A. O'Neill, original essay, updated 2011

"Help"—The Number One Weasel Word

3   The biggest weasel word used in advertising doublespeak is "help." Now "help" only means to aid or assist, nothing more. It does not mean to conquer, stop, eliminate, end, solve, heal, cure, or anything else. But once the ad says "help," it can say just about anything after that because "help" qualifies everything coming after it. The trick is that the claim that comes after the weasel word is usually so strong and so dramatic that you forget the word "help" and concentrate only on the dramatic claim. You read into the ad a message that the ad does not contain. More importantly, the advertiser is not responsible for the claim that you read into the ad, even though the advertiser wrote the ad so you would read that claim into it.

4   The next time you see an ad for a cold medicine that promises that it "helps relieve cold symptoms fast," don't rush out to buy it. Ask yourself what this claim is really saying. Remember, "helps" means only that the medicine will aid or assist. What will it aid or assist in doing? Why, "relieve" your cold "symptoms." "Relieve" only means to ease, alleviate, or mitigate, not to stop, end, or cure. Nor does the claim say how much relieving this medicine will do. Nowhere does this ad claim it will cure anything. In fact, the ad doesn't even claim it will do anything at all. The ad only claims that it will aid in relieving (not curing) your cold symptoms, which are probably a runny nose, watery eyes, and a headache. In other words, this medicine probably contains a standard decongestant and some aspirin. By the way, what does "fast" mean? Ten minutes, one hour, one day? What is fast to one person can be very slow to another. "Fast" is another weasel word.

5   Ad claims using "help" are among the most popular ads. One says, "Helps keep you young looking," but then a lot of things will help keep you young looking, including exercise, rest, good nutrition, and a facelift. More importantly, this ad doesn't say the product will keep you young, only "young looking." Someone may look young to one person and old to another.

6   A toothpaste ad says, "Helps prevent cavities," but it doesn't say it will actually prevent cavities. Brushing your teeth regularly, avoiding sugars in foods, and flossing daily will also help prevent cavities. A liquid cleaner ad says, "Helps keep your home germ free," but it doesn't say it actually kills germs, nor does it even specify which germs it might kill.

7   "Help" is such a useful weasel word that it is often combined with other action-verb weasel words such as "fight" and "control." Consider the claim, "Helps control dandruff symptoms with regular use." What does it really say? It will assist in controlling (not eliminating, stopping, ending, or curing) the symptoms of dandruff, not the cause of dandruff nor the dandruff itself. What are the symptoms of dandruff? The ad deliberately leaves that undefined, but assume that the symptoms referred to in the ad are the flaking and itching commonly associated with dandruff. But just shampooing with any shampoo will temporarily eliminate these symptoms, so this shampoo isn't any different from any other. Finally, in order to benefit from this product, you must use it regularly. What is "regular use"—daily, weekly, hourly? Using another shampoo "regularly" will have the same effect. Nowhere does this advertising claim say this particular shampoo stops, eliminates, or cures dandruff. In fact, this claim says nothing at all, thanks to all the weasel words.

8   Look at ads in magazines and newspapers, listen to ads on radio and television, and you'll find the word "help" in ads for all kinds of products. How often do you read or hear such phrases as "helps stop . . . ," "helps overcome . . . ," "helps eliminate . . . ," "helps you feel . . . ," or "helps you look . . . "? If you start looking for this weasel word in advertising, you'll be amazed at how often it occurs. Analyze the claims in the ads using "help," and you will discover that these ads are really saying nothing.

9   There are plenty of other weasel words used in advertising. In fact, there are so many that to list them all would fill the rest of this book. But, in order to identify the doublespeak of advertising and understand the real meaning of an ad, you have to be aware of the most popular weasel words in advertising today.

Virtually Spotless

10 One of the most powerful weasel words is "virtually," a word so innocent that most people don't pay any attention to it when it is used in an advertising claim. But watch out. "Virtually" is used in advertising claims that appear to make specific, definite promises when there is no promise. After all, what does "virtually" mean? It means "in essence of effect, although not in fact." Look at that definition again. "Virtually" means "not in fact." It does not mean "almost" or "just about the same as," or anything else. And before you dismiss all this concern over such a small word, remember that small words can have big consequences.

11 In 1971 a federal court rendered its decision on a case brought by a woman who became pregnant while taking birth control pills. She sued the manufacturer, Eli Lilly and Company, for breach of warranty. The woman lost her case. Basing its ruling on a statement in the pamphlet accompanying the pills, which stated that, "When taken as directed, the tablets offer virtually 100% protection," the court ruled that there was no warranty, expressed or implied, that the pills were absolutely effective. In its ruling, the court pointed out that, according to Webster's Third New International Dictionary, "virtually" means "almost entirely" and clearly does not mean "absolute" (Whittington v. Eli Lilly and Company, 333 F. Supp. 98). In other words, the Eli Lilly company was really saying that its birth control pill, even when taken as directed, did not in fact provide 100 percent protection against pregnancy. But Eli Lilly didn't want to put it that way, because then many women might not have bought Lilly's birth control pills.

12 The next time you see the ad that says that this dishwasher detergent "leaves dishes virtually spotless," just remember how advertisers twist the meaning of the weasel word "virtually." You can have lots of spots on your dishes after using this detergent, and the ad claim will still be true, because what this claim really means is that this detergent does not in fact leave your dishes spotless. Whenever you see or hear an ad claim that uses the word "virtually," just translate that claim into its real meaning. So the television set that is "virtually trouble free" becomes the television set that is not in fact trouble free, the "virtually foolproof operation" of any appliance becomes an operation that is in fact not foolproof, and the product that "virtually never needs service" becomes the product that is not in fact service free.

New and Improved

13 If "new" is the most frequently used word on a product package, "improved" is the second most frequent. In fact, the two words are almost always used together. It seems just about everything sold these days is "new and improved." The next time you're in the supermarket, try counting the number of times you see these words on products. But you'd better do it while you're walking down just one aisle, otherwise you'll need a calculator to keep track of your counting.

14 Just what do these words mean? The use of the word "new" is restricted by regulations, so an advertiser can't just use the word on a product or in an ad without meeting certain requirements. For example, a product is considered new for about six months during a national advertising campaign. If the product is being advertised only in a limited test market area, the word can be used longer, and in some instances has been used for as long as two years.

15 What makes a product "new"? Some products have been around for a long time, yet every once in a while you discover that they are being advertised as "new." Well, an advertiser can call a product new if there has been "a material functional change" in the product. What is "a material functional change," you ask? Good question. In fact it's such a good question it's being asked all the time. It's up to the manufacturer to prove that the product has undergone such a change. And if the manufacturer isn't challenged on the claim, then there's no one to stop it. Moreover, the change does not have to be an improvement in the product. One manufacturer added an artificial lemon scent to a cleaning product and called it "new and improved," even though the product did not clean any better than without the lemon scent. The manufacturer defended the use of the word "new" on the grounds that the artificial scent changed the chemical formula of the product and therefore constituted "a material functional change."

Advertisers use weasel words to appear to be making a claim for a product when in fact they are making no claim at all.

16 Which brings up the word "improved." When used in advertising, "improved" does not mean "made better." It only means "changed" or "different from before." So, if the detergent maker puts a plastic pour spout on the box of detergent, the product has been "improved," and away we go with a whole new advertising campaign. Or, if the cereal maker adds more fruit or a different kind of fruit to the cereal, there's an improved product. Now you know why manufacturers are constantly making little changes in their products. Whole new advertising campaigns, designed to convince you that the product has been changed for the better, are based on small changes in superficial aspects of a product. The next time you see an ad for an "improved" product, ask yourself what was wrong with the old one. Ask yourself just how "improved" the product is. Finally, you might check to see whether the "improved" version costs more than the unimproved one. After all, someone has to pay for the millions of dollars spent advertising the improved product.

17 Of course, advertisers really like to run ads that claim a product is "new and improved." While what constitutes a "new" product may be subject to some

regulation, "improved" is a subjective judgment. A manufacturer changes the shape of its stick deodorant, but the shape doesn't improve the function of the deodorant. That is, changing the shape doesn't affect the deodorizing ability of the deodorant, so the manufacturer calls it "improved." Another manufacturer adds ammonia to its liquid cleaner and calls it "new and improved." Since adding ammonia does affect the cleaning ability of the product, there has been a "material functional change" in the product, and the manufacturer can now call its cleaner "new," and "improved" as well. Now the weasel words "new and improved" are plastered all over the package and are the basis for a multimillion-dollar ad campaign. But after six months, the word "new" will have to go, until someone can dream up another change in the product. Perhaps it will be adding color to the liquid, or changing the shape of the package, or maybe adding a new, dripless pour spout, or perhaps a _____. The "improvements" are endless, and so are the new advertising claims and campaigns.

18   "New" is just too useful and powerful a word in advertising for advertisers to pass it up easily. So they use weasel words that say "new" without really saying it. One of their favorites is "introducing," as in, "Introducing improved Tide," or "Introducing the stain remover." The first is simply saying, here's our improved soap; the second, here's our new advertising campaign for our detergent. Another favorite is "now," as in, "Now there's Sinex," which simply means that Sinex is available. Then there are phrases like "Today's Chevrolet," "Presenting Dristan," and "A fresh way to start the day." The list is really endless because advertisers are always finding new ways to say "new" without really saying it. If there is a second edition of this book, I'll just call it the "new and improved" edition. Wouldn't you really rather have a "new and improved" edition of this book rather than a "second" edition?

Acts Fast

19   "Acts" and "works" are two popular weasel words in advertising, because they bring action to the product and to the advertising claim. When you see the ad for the cough syrup that "Acts on the cough control center," ask yourself what this cough syrup is claiming to do. Well, it's just claiming to "act," to do something, to perform an action. What is it that the cough syrup does? The ad doesn't say. It only claims to perform an action or do something on your "cough control center." By the way, what and where is your "cough control center"? I don't remember learning about that part of the body in human biology class.

20   Ads that use such phrases as "acts fast," "acts against," "acts to prevent," and the like are saying essentially nothing, because "act" is a word empty of any specific meaning. The ads are always careful not to specify exactly what "act" the product performs. Just because a brand of aspirin claims to "act fast" for headache relief doesn't mean this aspirin is any better than any other aspirin. What is the "act" that this aspirin performs? You're never told. Maybe it just dissolves quickly. Since aspirin is a parity product, all aspirin is the same and therefore functions the same.

Works Like Anything Else

21 If you don't find the word "acts" in an ad, you will probably find the weasel word "works." In fact, the two words are almost interchangeable in advertising. Watch out for ads that say a product "works against," "works like," "works for," or "works longer." As with "acts," "works" is the same meaningless verb used to make you think that this product really does something, and maybe even something special or unique. But "works," like "acts," is basically a word empty of any specific meaning.

Like Magic

22 Whenever advertisers want you to stop thinking about the product and to start thinking about something bigger, better, or more attractive than the product, they use that very popular weasel word, "like." The word "like" is the advertiser's equivalent of a magician's use of misdirection. "Like" gets you to ignore the product and concentrate on the claim the advertiser is making about it. "For skin like peaches and cream" claims the ad for a skin cream. What is this ad really claiming? It doesn't say this cream will give you peaches-and-cream skin. There is no verb in this claim, so it doesn't even mention using the product. How is skin ever like "peaches and cream"? Remember, ads must be read literally and exactly, according to the dictionary definition of words. (Remember "virtually" in the Eli Lilly case.) The ad is making absolutely no promise or claim whatsoever for this skin cream. If you think this cream will give you soft, smooth, youthful-looking skin, you are the one who has read that meaning into the ad.

23 The wine that claims "It's like taking a trip to France" wants you to think about a romantic evening in Paris as you walk along the boulevard after a wonderful meal in an intimate little bistro. Of course, you don't really believe that a wine can take you to France, but the goal of the ad is to get you to think pleasant, romantic thoughts about France and not about how the wine tastes or how expensive it may be. That little word "like" has taken you away from crushed grapes into a world of your own imaginative making. Who knows, maybe the next time you buy wine, you'll think those pleasant thoughts when you see this brand of wine, and you'll buy it. Or, maybe you weren't even thinking about buying wine at all, but now you just might pick up a bottle the next time you're shopping. Ah, the power of "like" in advertising.

24 How about the most famous "like" claim of all, "Winston tastes good like a cigarette should"? Ignoring the grammatical error here, you might want to know what this claim is saying. Whether a cigarette tastes good or bad is a subjective judgment because what tastes good to one person may well taste horrible to another. Not everyone likes fried snails, even if they are called escargot. (*De gustibus non est disputandum*, which was probably the Roman rule for advertising as well as for defending the games in the Colosseum.) There are many people who say all cigarettes taste terrible, other people who say only some cigarettes taste all right, and still others who say all cigarettes taste good. Who's right? Everyone, because taste is a matter of personal judgment. Moreover, note the use of the conditional, "should." The complete claim is, "Winston tastes good like a cigarette should taste." But should

cigarettes taste good? Again, this is a matter of personal judgment and probably depends most on one's experiences with smoking. So, the Winston ad is simply saying that Winston cigarettes are just like any other cigarette: Some people like them and some people don't. On that statement, R. J. Reynolds conducted a very successful multimillion-dollar advertising campaign that helped keep Winston the number two–selling cigarette in the United States, close behind number one, Marlboro.

Can't It Be Up to the Claim?

25 Analyzing ads for doublespeak requires that you pay attention to every word in the ad and determine what each word really means. Advertisers try to wrap their claims in language that sounds concrete, specific, and objective, when in fact the language of advertising is anything but. Your job is to read carefully and listen critically so that when the announcer says that "Crest can be of significant value . . . " you know immediately that this claim says absolutely nothing. Where is the doublespeak in this ad? Start with the second word.

26   Once again, you have to look at what words really mean, not what you think they mean or what the advertiser wants you to think they mean. The ad for Crest only says that using Crest "can be" of "significant value." What really throws you off in this ad is the brilliant use of "significant." It draws your attention to the word "value" and makes you forget that the ad only claims that Crest "can be." The ad doesn't say that Crest is of value, only that it is "able" or "possible" to be of value, because that's all that "can" means.

27   It's so easy to miss the importance of those little words, "can be." Almost as easy as missing the importance of the words "up to" in an ad. These words are very popular in sale ads. You know, the ones that say, "Up to 50 percent off!" Now, what does that claim mean? Not much, because the store or manufacturer has to reduce the price of only a few items by 50 percent. Everything else can be reduced a lot less, or not even reduced. Moreover, don't you want to know 50 percent off of what? Is it 50 percent off the "manufacturer's suggested list price," which is the highest possible price? Was the price artificially inflated and then reduced? In other ads, "up to" expresses an ideal situation. The medicine that works "up to ten times faster," the battery that lasts "up to twice as long," and the soap that gets you "up to twice as clean"—all are based on ideal situations for using those products, situations in which you can be sure you will never find yourself.

Unfinished Words

28 Unfinished words are a kind of "up to" claim in advertising. The claim that a battery lasts "up to twice as long" usually doesn't finish the comparison—twice as long as what? A birthday candle? A tank of gas? A cheap battery made in a country not noted for its technological achievements? The implication is that the battery lasts twice as long as batteries made by other battery makers, or twice as long as earlier model batteries made by the advertiser, but the ad doesn't really make these claims. You read these claims into the ad, aided by the visual images the advertiser so carefully provides.

29   Unfinished words depend on you to finish them, to provide the words the advertisers so thoughtfully left out of the ad. Pall Mall cigarettes were once advertised as "A longer, finer, and milder smoke." The question is, longer, finer, and milder than what? The aspirin that claims it contains "Twice as much of the pain reliever doctors recommend most" doesn't tell you what pain reliever it contains twice as much of. (By the way, it's aspirin. That's right; it just contains twice the amount of aspirin. And how much is twice the amount? Twice of what amount?) Panadol boasts that "nobody reduces fever faster," but, since Panadol is a parity product, this claim simply means that Panadol isn't any better than any other product in its parity class. "You can be sure if it's Westinghouse," you're told, but just exactly what it is you can be sure of is never mentioned. "Magnavox gives you more" doesn't tell you what you get more of. More value? More television? More than they gave you before? It sounds nice, but it means nothing, until you fill in the claim with your own words, the words the advertisers didn't use. Since each of us fills in the claim differently, the ad and the product can become all things to all people, and not promise a single thing.

30   Unfinished words abound in advertising, because they appear to promise so much. More importantly, they can be joined with powerful visual images on television to appear to be making significant promises about a product's effectiveness without really making any promises. In a television ad, the aspirin product that claims fast relief can show a person with a headache taking the product and then, in what appears to be a matter of minutes, claiming complete relief. This visual image is far more powerful than any claim made in unfinished words. Indeed, the visual image completes the unfinished words for you, filling in with pictures what the words leave out. And you thought that ads didn't affect you. What brand of aspirin do you use?

31   Some years ago, Ford's advertisements proclaimed "Ford LTD—700 percent quieter." Now, what do you think Ford was claiming with these unfinished words? What was the Ford LTD quieter than? A Cadillac? A Mercedes Benz? A BMW? Well, when the FTC asked Ford to substantiate this unfinished claim, Ford replied that it meant that the inside of the LTD was 700 percent quieter than the outside. How did you finish those unfinished words when you first read them? Did you even come close to Ford's meaning?

Combining Weasel Words

32 A lot of ads don't fall neatly into one category or another, because they use a variety of different devices and words. Different weasel words are often combined to make an ad claim. The claim, "Coffee-Mate gives coffee more body, more flavor," uses unfinished words ("more" than what?) and also uses words that have no specific meaning ("body" and "flavor"). Along with "taste" (remember the Winston ad and its claim to taste good), "body" and "flavor" mean nothing, because their meaning is entirely subjective. To you, "body" in coffee might mean thick, black, almost bitter coffee, while I might take it to mean a light brown, delicate coffee. Now, if you think you understood that last sentence, read it again, because it said nothing

of objective value; it was filled with weasel words of no specific meaning: "thick," "black," "bitter," "light brown," and "delicate." Each of those words has no specific, objective meaning, because each of us can interpret them differently.

33   Try this slogan: "Looks, smells, tastes like ground-roast coffee." So, are you now going to buy Taster's Choice instant coffee because of this ad? "Looks," "smells," and "tastes" are all words with no specific meaning and depend on your interpretation of them for any meaning. Then there's that great weasel word "like," which simply suggests a comparison but does not make the actual connection between the product and the quality. Besides, do you know what "ground-roast" coffee is? I don't, but it sure sounds good. So, out of seven words in this ad, four are definite weasel words, two are quite meaningless, and only one has any clear meaning.

34   Remember the Anacin ad—"Twice as much of the pain reliever doctors recommend most"? There's a whole lot of weaseling going on in this ad. First, what's the pain reliever they're talking about in this ad? Aspirin, of course. In fact, any time you see or hear an ad using those words "pain reliever," you can automatically substitute the word "aspirin" for them. (Makers of acetaminophen and ibuprofen pain relievers are careful in their advertising to identify their products as nonaspirin products.) So, now we know that Anacin has aspirin in it. Moreover, we know that Anacin has twice as much aspirin in it, but we don't know twice as much as what. Does it have twice as much aspirin as an ordinary aspirin tablet? If so, what is an ordinary aspirin tablet, and how much aspirin does it contain? Twice as much as Excedrin or Bufferin? Twice as much as a chocolate chip cookie? Remember those unfinished words and how they lead you on without saying anything.

35   Finally, what about those doctors who are doing all that recommending? Who are they? How many of them are there? What kind of doctors are they? What are their qualifications? Who asked them about recommending pain relievers? What other pain relievers did they recommend? And there are a whole lot more questions about this "poll" of doctors to which I'd like to know the answers, but you get the point. Sometimes, when I call my doctor, she tells me to take two aspirin and call her office in the morning. Is that where Anacin got this ad?

Read the Label, or the Brochure

36   Weasel words aren't just found on television, on the radio, or in newspaper and magazine ads. Just about any language associated with a product will contain the doublespeak of advertising. Remember the Eli Lilly case and the doublespeak on the information sheet that came with the birth control pills. Here's another example.

37   Estée Lauder cosmetics company announced a new product called "Night Repair." A small brochure distributed with the product stated that "Night Repair was scientifically formulated in Estée Lauder's U.S. laboratories as part of the Swiss Age-Controlling Skincare Program. Although only nature controls the aging process, this program helps control the signs of aging and encourages skin to look and feel younger." You might want to read these two sentences again, because they sound great but say nothing.

38   First, note that the product was "scientifically formulated" in the company's laboratories. What does that mean? What constitutes a scientific formulation? You wouldn't expect the company to say that the product was casually, mechanically, or carelessly formulated, or just thrown together one day when the people in the white coats didn't have anything better to do. But the word "scientifically" lends an air of precision and promise that just isn't there.

39   It is the second sentence, however, that's really weasely, both syntactically and semantically. The only factual part of this sentence is the introductory dependent clause—"only nature controls the aging process." Thus, the only fact in the ad is relegated to a dependent clause, a clause dependent on the main clause, which contains no factual or definite information at all and indeed purports to contradict the independent clause. The new "skin care program" (notice it's not a skin cream but a "program") does not claim to stop or even retard the aging process. What, then, does Advanced Night Repair, at a price of over $85 for a 1-ounce bottle, do? According to this brochure, nothing. It only "helps," and the brochure does not say how much it helps. Moreover, it only "helps control," and then it only helps control the "signs of aging," not the aging itself. Also, it "encourages" skin not to be younger but only to "look and feel" younger. The brochure does not say younger than what. Of the sixteen words in the main clause of this second sentence, nine are weasel words. So, before you spend all that money for Night Repair, or any other cosmetic product, read the words carefully and then decide if you're getting what you think you're paying for.

Other Tricks of the Trade

40 Advertisers' use of doublespeak is endless. The best way advertisers can make something out of nothing is through words. Although there are a lot of visual images used on television and in magazines and newspapers, every advertiser wants to create that memorable line that will stick in the public consciousness. I am sure pure joy reigned in one advertising agency when a study found that children who were asked to spell the word "relief" promptly and proudly responded "r-o-l-a-i-d-s."

41   The variations, combinations, and permutations of doublespeak used in advertising go on and on, running from the use of rhetorical questions ("Wouldn't you really rather have a Buick?" "If you can't trust Prestone, who can you trust?") to flattering you with compliments ("The lady has taste." "We think a cigar smoker is someone special." "You've come a long way, Baby."). You know, of course, how you're supposed to answer those questions, and you know that those compliments are just leading up to the sales pitches for the products. Before you dismiss such tricks of the trade as obvious, however, just remember that all of these statements and questions were part of very successful advertising campaigns.

42   A more subtle approach is the ad that proclaims a supposedly unique quality for a product, a quality that really isn't unique. "If it doesn't say Goodyear, it can't be polyglas." Sounds good, doesn't it? Polyglas is available only from Goodyear because Goodyear copyrighted that trade name. Any other tire manufacturer could make exactly the same tire but could not call it "polyglas," because that would be

copyright infringement. "Polyglas" is simply Goodyear's name for its fiberglass-reinforced tire.

43   Since we like to think of ourselves as living in a technologically advanced country, science and technology have a great appeal in selling products. Advertisers are quick to use scientific doublespeak to push their products. There are all kinds of elixirs, additives, scientific potions, and mysterious mixtures added to all kinds of products. Gasoline contains "HTA," "F-130," "Platformate," and other chemical-sounding additives, but nowhere does an advertisement give any real information about the additive. Shampoo, deodorant, mouthwash, cold medicine, sleeping pills, and any number of other products all seem to contain some special chemical ingredient that allows them to work wonders. "Certs contains a sparkling drop of Retsyn." So what? What's "Retsyn"? What's it do? What's so special about it? When they don't have a secret ingredient in their product, advertisers still find a way to claim scientific validity. There's "Sinarest. Created by a research scientist who actually gets sinus headaches." Sounds nice, but what kind of research does this scientist do? How do you know if she is any kind of expert on sinus medicine? Besides, this ad doesn't tell you a thing about the medicine itself and what it does.

Advertising Doublespeak Quick Quiz

The following is a list of statements from some recent ads. Test your awareness of advertising doublespeak by figuring out what each of these ads really says:

DOMINO'S PIZZA: "The pizza delivery experts."
TUMS: "Fast, effective heartburn relief."
SCOPE: "Get close with Scope."
CASCADE: "For virtually spotless dishes, nothing beats Cascade."
ADVIL: "The pain reliever for fast, strong pain relief."
DUNKIN DONUTS: "America runs on Dunkin."
SUDAFED: "Fast sinus relief that won't put you fast asleep."
TYLENOL: "Stop. Think. Tylenol."
MCDONALD'S: "I'm lovin' it."
MILLER LITE BEER: "Tastes great. Less filling."
PHILLIP'S MILK OF MAGNESIA: "Phillip's. The comfortable way."
KRAFT MACARONI AND CHEESE: "It's the cheesiest."
CRACKER BARREL: "Judged to be the best."
L'OREAL: "Because you're worth it."
BURGER KING: "Have it your way."
JC PENNEY: "It's all inside."
SARA LEE: "Nobody doesn't like Sara Lee."
TOYOTA: "Moving forward."
TACO BELL: "Think outside the bun."
MICROSOFT: "Where do you want to go today?"

The World of Advertising

44 In the world of advertising, people wear "dentures," not false teeth; they suffer from "occasional irregularity," not constipation; they need deodorants for their "nervous wetness," not for sweat; they use "bathroom tissue," not toilet paper; and they don't dye their hair, they "tint" or "rinse" it. Advertisements offer "real counterfeit diamonds" without the slightest hint of embarrassment, or boast of goods made out of "genuine imitation leather" or "virgin vinyl."

45 In the world of advertising, the girdle becomes a "body shaper," "form persuader," "control garment," "controller," "outerwear enhancer," "body garment," or "anti-gravity panties," and is sold with such trade names as "The Instead," "The Free Spirit," and "The Body Briefer."

46 A study some years ago found the following words to be among the most popular used in U.S. television advertisements: "new," "improved," "better," "extra," "fresh," "clean," "beautiful," "free," "good," "great," and "light." At the same time, the following words were found to be among the most frequent on British television: "new," "good-better-best," "free," "fresh," "delicious," "full," "sure," "clean," "wonderful," and "special." While these words may occur most frequently in ads, and while ads may be filled with weasel words, you have to watch out for all the words used in advertising, not just the words mentioned here.

47 Every word in an ad is there for a reason; no word is wasted. Your job is to figure out exactly what each word is doing in an ad—what each word really means, not what the advertiser wants you to think it means. Remember, the ad is trying to get you to buy a product, so it will put the product in the best possible light, using any device, trick, or means legally allowed. Your only defense against advertising (besides taking up permanent residence on the moon) is to develop and use a strong critical reading, listening, and looking ability. Always ask yourself what the ad is really saying. When you see ads on television, don't be misled by the pictures, the visual images. What does the ad say about the product? What does the ad not say? What information is missing from the ad? Only by becoming an active, critical consumer of the doublespeak of advertising will you ever be able to cut through the doublespeak and discover what the ad is really saying. ◆

 # The Language of Advertising

Charles A. O'Neill

1 We all recognize the value of advertising, but on some level we can't quite fully embrace it as a "normal" part of our experience. At best, we view it as distracting. At worst, we view it as a pernicious threat to our health, wealth, and social values.

2 How does advertising work? Why is it so powerful? Why does it raise such concern? What case can be made for and against the advertising business? In order to understand advertising, you must accept that it is not about truth, virtue, love, or positive social values. It is about selling a product.

3   But this simple fact does not explain the unique power of advertising. Whatever the product or creative strategy, advertisements derive their power from a purposeful, directed combination of images. Images can take the form of words, sounds, or visuals, used individually or together. The combination of images is the language of advertising, a language unlike any other.

4   Everyone who grows up in the Western world soon learns that advertising language is different from other languages. We may have forgotten the sponsors, but we certainly know that these popular slogans "sound like ads."

> "The Real Thing" (Coca Cola)
> "The Ultimate Driving Machine" (BMW)
> "Intel Inside" (Intel)
> "Just Do It" (Nike)
> "Have it your way" (Burger King)

Edited and Purposeful

5 At heart, advertising is nothing more than the delivery system for salesmanship, something woven into the fabric of our society. There is nothing a consumer can do to hide from sales messages. This is not limited to what we think of as advertising media. We encounter it face-to-face, too.

6   For example: When you stop at a fast food restaurant for a cup of breakfast coffee, the young man or woman who takes your order will more than likely try to "upsell" you—No what you ordered, but something else. The manager of one such restaurant left a laminated card on the counter following an early morning motivational session for his crew. The card shows clerks how to promoting items the customers did not know they wanted—i.e., a scripted sales track laced with words designed to make the customer feel *hungrier*. Simply order coffee, for example, and they might offer you "*piping hot, fresh pancakes to go with your coffee*" or the opportunity to "*top off your breakfast with something sweet. Maybe some yummy Blueberry biscuits with a dollop of sweet Vermont butter? They're my favorite.*"

7   Here perfectly ordinary language is carefully enlisted in the service of sales. Even a small increase in business for a national fast food chain generates hundreds of millions of dollars of new revenue, in this case created by a few clever words delivered with a sparkling smile. Like sales scripts, advertising slogans may seem casual, but in fact they are carefully engineered with a clear purpose: to trigger a specific response.

8   If you listen to the radio, you have undoubtedly heard an ad for "Kars4Kids." The first verse is sung by a child; and the second verse is the same as the first, but a man sings it. Both are accompanied by a strumming guitar.

> *1-877-kars for kids*
> *k-a-r-s kars for kids*
> *1-877-kars for kids*
> *donate your car today*

9   This is followed by the reassurance that Kars4Kids is a registered charity, and donors may be able to claim the value of their car as a tax deduction. It's not a

particularly artful ad, but it does attract attention, and it works, principally through mind numbing repetition. Never mind that some listeners have found it profoundly disturbing.

In a comment on a Topix forum titled, "The most irritating radio commercial of all time" a poster from Houston said, "I couldn't stop it from playing in my head . . . I just wanted to take a power drill to my temple to drill out the awful repetition!"

10   Vexing though it may be, repetition is a reliable tool in advertising. According to Answers.Com "the average person needs to hear something twenty times before they truly learn it." So once you have heard about Kars4Kids a 21st time, it has been filed away in your neocortex. What else could an advertiser possibly hope to achieve? On its website, "Joy for Our Youth," parent of Kars4Kids, reports 2009 contributions of $23 Million.

Rich and Arresting

11   Repetition works, but the all-time favorite advertising device is sex. Why? Because the desire to be sexually attractive is our most powerful instinct. Flip through any popular magazine, and you will find ads that are unabashedly, unapologetically sexual. Victoria's Secret, Calvin Klein, and every other clothing and fragrance marketer uses sex to sell. Popular media is a veritable playground of titillation, abounding with images of barely clothed men and women in poses suggesting that if only you would wear one of our little padded brassieres or cologne, a world a sexual adventure will reveal itself to you.

12   Every successful ad uses a creative strategy based on an idea intended to attract and hold the attention of the consumer. This may include a photo of a pretty girl, strong creative execution or a straightforward list of product features, or as we've seen, even mind-numbing repetition. Soft drink and fast-food companies are famous for their "Slice of life" ads. Coke or Pepsi are often staged in Fourth of July parades or family events, the archetype being a scene of tots frolicking with puppies in the sunlit foreground while their youthful parents play touch football. On the porch, Grandma and Pops are seen smiling as they wait for all of this affection to transform itself in a climax of warmth, harmony, and joy. The intent is to seduced us into feeling that if we drank the right combination of sugar, preservatives, caramel coloring, and secret ingredients, we'd join the crowd that—in the words of Coca-Cola's ad from 1971—would help "teach the world to sing in perfect harmony."

Involving

13   Now that they have our attention, advertisers present information intended to show us that their product fills a need and differs from the competition. It is the copywriter's responsibility to express, exploit, and intensify product differences where they exist.

14   When product differences do not exist, the writer must glamorize superficial differences—for example, the packaging. As long as the ad gets our attention, the "action" is mostly in the words and visuals. But as we read or watch an ad, we

become more involved. The action starts to take place in us. Our imagination is set in motion, and our individual fears and aspirations, quirks, and insecurities come into play. Consider, again, the running battle among soft drinks. The cola wars have spawned many "look-alike" advertisements, because the product features and consumer benefits are generic, applying to all products in the category. Substitute one cola brand name for another, and the messages are often identical, right down to the way the cans are photographed. This strategy relies on mass saturation and exposure for impact.

15   Another device is the use of famous personalities as product spokespeople or models. Although ad writers didn't invent the human tendency to admire famous people, once we have seen a celebrity in an ad, we associate the product with that person. "Britney Spears drinks milk. She's a hottie. I want to be a hottie, too! 'Hey Mom, Got Milk?'" Celine Dion pitches her own perfume; Sharon Stone sells Christal watches. The logic is faulty, but we fall under the spell just the same. Advertising works, not because Britney is a nutritionist, Celine an expert perfumer-diva or Sharon a horologist, but because we participate in it. The ads bring the words, sounds, and pictures. We bring the chemistry.

A Simple Language

16 Advertising language differs from other types of language in its simplicity. To determine how the text of a typical advertisement rates on a "simplicity index" in comparison with text in a magazine article, for example, try this exercise: Clip a typical story from the publication you read. Calculate the number of words in an average sentence. Count the number of words of three or more syllables in a typical 100-word passage, omitting words that are capitalized or hyphenated or verbs made into three syllables words by the addition of –ed or –es. Add the two figures (average number of words per sentence and the number of three-syllable words per 100 words), then multiply the result by .4. According to Robert Gunning the result is the approximate grade level required to understand the content. He developed this formula, the "Fog Index," to determine the comparative ease with which any given piece of written communication can be read.

17   Let's apply the Fog Index to the lyrics in the Kars4Kids ad.

> *1-877-kars for kids*
> *k-a-r-s kars for kids*
> *1-877-kars for kids*
> *donate your car today*

Counting each digit in the phone number as a word, the average sentence in this ad is 6.25 words. There *are no three-syllable words.*

> 6.25 words per sentence
> 0 three syllable words/100
> -----
> 6.25
> X4 =
> **2.5**

According to Gunning's scale, the language of the Kars4Kids commercial is so simple that even Geico's cavemen—and children half way through the second grade—could understand it.

18   Why do advertisers favor simple language? The answer lies with the consumer: People of every age are subject to an overwhelming number of commercial messages each day. As a practical matter, we would not notice many of these messages if engaging content or eloquence were counted among their virtues. Today's consumer cannot take the time to focus on anything for long. Every aspect of modern life runs at an accelerated pace. Voice mail, smart phones, tweets, Facebook updates, text messages—the world is always switched-on, feeding our hunger for more information, now. Time generally, and TV-commercial time in particular, is experienced in increasingly smaller segments. Fifteen-second commercials are no longer unusual.

19   Advertising language is simple; in the engineering process, difficult words or images—which in other forms of communication may be used to lend color or shades of meaning—are replaced by simple words or images less vulnerable to misinterpretation.

Who Is Responsible?

20 Some critics view the advertising business as a cranky, unwelcome child of the free enterprise system. In reality, advertising mirrors the fears, quirks, and aspirations of the society that creates it (and is, in turn, sold by it). This fact alone exposes advertising to parody and ridicule. The overall level of acceptance and respect for advertising is also influenced by the varied quality of the ads themselves. Some ads are deliberately designed to provoke controversy. But this is only one of the many charges frequently levied against advertising. Others include:

1. Advertising encourages unhealthy habits.
2. Advertising feeds on human weaknesses and exaggerates the importance of material things, encouraging "impure" emotions and vanities.
3. Advertising sells daydreams—distracting, purposeless visions of lifestyles beyond the reach of most people exposed to advertising.
4. Advertising warps our vision of reality, implanting groundless fears and insecurities.
5. Advertising downgrades the intelligence of the public.
6. Advertising debases English.
7. Advertising perpetuates racial and sexual stereotypes.

21 What can be said in advertising's defense? First, it's only a reflection of society. What about the charge that advertising debases the intelligence of the public? Those who support this particular criticism would do well to ask themselves another question: Exactly how intelligent is the public? Sadly, evidence abounds that "the public" at large is not particularly intelligent, after all. Johnny can't read. Susie can't write. And the entire family spends the night in front of the television, watching one mindless reality show after another. Ads are effective because they sell products. They would not succeed if they did not reflect the values and motivations of the real world. Advertising both reflects and shapes our perception of reality. Consider prominent

brand names and the impressions they create: Absolut is cool. Mercedes represents quality. BMW is the ultimate driving machine. Our sense of what these brand names stand for has as much to do with advertising as with the objective "truth."

22   That said, advertising shapes our perception of the world as surely as architecture shapes our impression of a city. It is part of our environment. Good, responsible advertising can serve as a positive influence for change, and encourage product innovation, while generating profits. Of course, the problem is that the obverse is also true: Advertising, like any form of mass communication, can be a force for both "good" and "bad." It can just as readily reinforce or encourage irresponsible behavior, ageism, sexism, ethnocentrism, racism, homophobia—you name it—as it can encourage support for diversity and social progress. People living in society create advertising. Society isn't perfect.

23   Perhaps, by learning how advertising works, we can become better equipped to sort out content from hype, product values from emotions, and salesmanship from propaganda. No one is forcing you to buy yummy biscuits just because they're the server's favorite. No one is holding you hostage until you call 1-877-kars for kids and give away your grandfather's car in exchange for a tax deduction and a vacation voucher. You must listen. You must read. And finally you must think—all by yourself. ◆

CRITICAL THINKING

1. O'Neill says that advertisers create in consumers a sense of need for products. Do you think it is ethical for advertisers to create such a sense when their products are "generic" and do not differ from the competition? Consider ads for gasoline, beer, and coffee.

2. O'Neill anticipates potential objections to his defense of advertising. What are some of these objections? What does he say in defense of advertising? Which set of arguments do you find stronger?

3. O'Neill describes several ways that advertising language differs from other kinds of language. Briefly list the ways he mentions. Can you think of any other characteristics of advertising language that set it apart?

4. Symbols are important elements in the language of advertising. Can you think of some specific symbols from the advertising world that you associate with your own life? Are they effective symbols for selling? Explain your answer.

5. Why do people buy products sold by famous people? What is the appeal of a product endorsed by a celebrity?

6. William Lutz teaches English and writes books about the misuse of language. Charles O'Neill is a professional advertiser. How do their views about advertising reflect their occupations? Which side of the argument do you agree with?

7. How effective do you think O'Neill's introductory paragraphs are? How well does he hook the reader? What particular audience might he be appealing to early on? What attitude toward advertising is established in the introduction?

8. A "weasel word" is a word so hollow it has no meaning. Consider your own reaction to weasel words when you hear them. Try to identify as many weasel words as you can. What are the words, and what do consumers think they mean?

9. Consider Lutz's argument that advertisers are trying to "trick" consumers with their false promises and claims. How much are our expectations of product performance influenced by the claims and slogans of advertising? How do you think O'Neill would respond to Lutz's accusation?

CRITICAL WRITING

1. *Exploratory Writing:* In his essay, O'Neill makes several generalizations that characterize the language of advertising. Think about ads that you have recently seen or read and make a list of your own generalizations about the language of advertising. Refer to some specific advertisements in your response.

2. *Persuasive Writing:* O'Neill believes that advertising language "mirrors the fears, quirks, and aspirations of the society that creates it." Do you agree or disagree with this statement? Explain your perspective in a brief essay, and support your response with examples.

3. *Analytical Writing:* Choose a brand-name product that you use regularly, or to which you have particular loyalty, and identify one or more of its competitors. Examine some advertisements for each brand. Write a short paper explaining what makes you prefer your brand to the others.

GROUP PROJECTS

1. Review Lutz's "Doublespeak Quick Quiz." Choose five items and analyze them, using dictionary meanings to explain what the ads are really saying.

2. With your group, think of some recent advertising campaigns that created controversy (Abercrombie & Fitch, Dove's "Real Beauty," PETA, Dolce & Gabbana, or Snickers). What made them controversial? How did this affect sales?

3. O'Neill notes that sometimes advertisers use symbols to engage their audience. With your group, create a list of brand symbols or logos, their corresponding products, and what lifestyle we associate with the logo or symbol. Are some logos more popular or prestigious? Explain.

4. Working in a group, develop a slogan and advertising campaign for one of the following products: sneakers, soda, a candy bar, or jeans. How would you apply the principles of advertising language to market your product? After completing your marketing plan, "sell" your product to the class. If time permits, explain the reasoning behind your selling technique.

CHAPTER
3

Generation Recession
The Challenges We Face

Today's college graduates face challenges more difficult than the struggles faced by their parents at the same time in their lives. As we emerge from a prolonged recession, prospects still look bleak for many job seekers. College tuition rates are at their highest, the housing market is at a historic low, and a credit crisis still threatens to bankrupt nations around the globe. The group of young people who are heirs to this mess are often referred to as, in the words of *Village Voice* executive editor Laura Conaway, "Generation Debt." The economic situation many "twixters" face is in itself controversial. On the one hand, today's twentysomethings point out that student loans, credit card debt, employment instability, lack of affordable health care, and financial irresponsibility have melded into a foreboding landscape that they have unwillingly inherited. On the other hand, some parents and elders argue that today's youth has come to expect too many handouts, does not know real struggle, and is unwilling to sacrifice.

It's a classic generational argument, but statistics seem to be pointing to a disturbing fact—that today's twentysomethings are the first generation to be less successful than their parents. More students face high debt upon graduation. More are returning home after college, unable to find a job or pay for an apartment, let alone buy a home or start a family—the hallmarks of adult life. Many feel abandoned by government, which has effectively silenced them in political arenas. This chapter takes a look at the financial crisis many young Americans—indeed, all Americans—are dealing with today.

The chapter begins with an excerpt from the book, *Generation Debt*, by Anya Kamenetz. Writing as a member of the "postmillennials," Kamenetz describes an economic scene in which today's twentysomethings are up to their ears in debt with little hope of digging their way out. Tamara Draut describes how credit card companies target college students who have no way of paying off the debt they are so freely given in "Strapped." An essay by Lev Grossman follows, "Grow Up? Not So Fast." It describes how "twixters"—young adults caught between adolescence and full adulthood—are dealing with a new social landscape, and coping by carving out a new life-phase between adolescence and adulthood.

The next two essays focus on changes in attitude connected to economic changes experienced over the last five years. First, Sharon Jayson explores how "Generation Recession" is versatile and flexible—and above all realistic in their expectations for the future. Growing up in a time of excess, this "end of Disneyland" presents a new landscape for today's young people. Then Tali Sharot writes about the science of optimism. Humans, it seems, are hardwired to believe that things will work out in their favor. In "Major Delusions," Sharot wonders if graduating students are being given the wrong message at peppy graduation ceremonies. Is it fair to encourage students "to soar like eagles" when financial meltdowns, rampant unemployment, and political unrest threaten to keep them firmly on the ground? The answer may surprise you.

A broader view of the social attitudes toward debt comes next in this chapter's Modern Scholar essay. Award-winning author Margaret Atwood explores the role debt has played in great novels and how literature reflects social attitudes of debt in "Debtor's Prism."

The chapter's Viewpoints takes a look at the growing trend of college graduates moving back to the parental nest after graduation. Known as "boomerang kids," they leave home only to return, unable to financially survive on their own. First, Ryan

Healy, himself a twentysomething, urges his peers to go home and rely on parents for a bit longer in order to save money and pay down debt. Florinda Vasquez, writing from the perspective of a parent, wonders why parents aren't really being consulted in this decision. Should parents expect their kids to return home for a while after college?

Generation Debt
*Anya Kamenetz**

Many young Americans report that they are trapped by low-end jobs with low wages, few opportunities, high taxes, and huge student loans. Many fear that they are facing a lifetime of recycled debt. Sometime over the last 20 years, something happened: The cost of a college education skyrocketed. It became acceptable to carry large debt. People stopped expecting to work in one company for their entire career and started hopping around in search of a better deal. Unable to get on solid financial footing, college graduates started putting off marriage plans and moved back in with their parents. In this excerpt from the book with the same title, Anya Kamenetz explores some of the challenges her generation faces in an economic landscape vastly different from that of her parents' only a generation before.

1 The simplest definition of a "generation" is those people who pass through a specific stage of life at the same time. We tend to think of human life stages as natural demarcations of growth, like the rings on a tree. Yet social and economic structures also determine the divisions between infancy and old age. Since 1960, when historian Philippe Aries published the book *Centuries of Childhood*, scholars have been writing about how childhood was "discovered" for sentimental and moralistic reasons in eighteenth- and nineteenth-century Europe. Before this historical turning point, infants were often farmed out to indifferent wet nurses, and seven-year-olds herded sheep.

2 Likewise, for most of human history, sexual maturity occurred just a year or two before marriage, and adolescence, as we know it, didn't exist. As Thomas Hine chronicles in *The Rise and Fall of the American Teenager,* when the United States was industrializing in the nineteenth century, people thirteen and up were the backbone of the semiskilled workforce. Teenagers came to America alone as immigrants. They ran weaving machines, dug mines, herded cattle, picked cotton, and fought wars. If they weren't slaves or indentured servants, they contributed their earnings to their families of origin until they got married and started families of their own.

3 American psychologist G. Stanley Hall popularized the term "adolescent" in 1904, as the rise of compulsory schooling and the move away from an agricultural economy began to lengthen the expected period of youthful preparation. It wasn't until the Great Depression, though, that teenagers' economic life assumed the limits it has today. Hine points out that Roosevelt's New Deal was explicitly designed to take jobs away from young people and give them to heads of households. Teenagers

---

* Anya Kamenetz, *Generation Debt,* 2007

were thus compelled to enroll in high school in much larger numbers than ever before. Young people's secondary economic role has persisted ever since. The affluence and restiveness of postwar America gave new cultural prominence in the 1950s to the modern version of teenhood, a distinct stage of life, a subculture, and a commercial market, funded ultimately by parents. The accepted age of independence for the middle class and above was pushed forward to twenty-one.

4   Now the postmillennial years are bringing in an entirely new life stage: "emerging adulthood," a term coined by developmental psychologist Jeffrey Jensen Arnett in a 2000 article. The Research Network on Transitions to Adulthood at the University of Pennsylvania is a group of a dozen or so experts in various fields: sociologists, policy experts, developmental psychologists, and economists. Their 2005 book, *On the Frontier of Adulthood*, explores emerging adulthood in depth.

"A new period of life is emerging in which young people are no longer adolescents but not yet adults . . . It is simply not possible for most young people to achieve economic and psychological autonomy as early as it was half a century ago."

5   "More youth are extending education, living at home longer, and moving haltingly, or stopping altogether, along the stepping stones of adulthood," writes Frank F. Furstenberg, chair of the network. "A new period of life is emerging in which young people are no longer adolescents but not yet adults . . . .It is simply not possible for most young people to achieve economic and psychological autonomy as early as it was half a century ago." The underlying reason, once again, is an economic shift, this time to a labor market that rewards only the highly educated with livable and growing wages.

6   In 2002, there were 68 million people in the United States aged eighteen to thirty-four. The social and economic upheaval of the past three decades, not to mention that of the past five years, affects us in complex ways. We have all come of age as part of Generation Debt.

7   The Penn researchers use five milestones of maturity: leaving home, finishing school, becoming financially independent, getting married, and having a child. By this definition, only 46 percent of women and 31 percent of men were grown up by age thirty in 2000, compared to 77 percent of women and 65 percent of men of the same age in 1960.

8   "I went from being a child to being a mother," says "Doris," now in her fifties. "I was married at twenty. By thirty I had four children and was divorced." Doris completed college and a master's degree while keeping house and raising her children, then supported her family as a medical physicist.

9   Doris's youngest daughter, "Miriam," graduated from Southern Connecticut State University in 2000, after six years of work and school, with $20,000 in student loans and $5,000 in credit card debt. Now, at twenty-nine, she is living in Madison, Wisconsin, and training to be a commodities broker, a job she could have pursued with only a high school diploma. Her mother, who bought her first house with her husband in her early twenties, helped Miriam pay off her credit cards and gave her the down payment on the condo she lives in. Miriam earns $28,000 a year and just

manages the minimum payments on her loans. She is single. She hasn't passed the five milestones of adulthood; she is barely out to the driveway.

10   Young people are falling behind first of all because of money. College tuition has grown faster than inflation for three decades, and faster than family income for the past fifteen years. Federal aid has lagged behind. An unprecedented explosion of borrowing has made up the difference between what colleges charge and what families can afford. Between 1995 and 2005, the annual volume of federal student loans tripled, to $85 billion in new loans in 2005. Two-thirds of four-year students are graduating with loan debt, an average of up to $23,000 in 2004 and growing every year. Three out of four college students have credit cards, too, carrying an average unpaid balance of $2,169 in 2005. Nearly a quarter of all students, according to a 2004 survey, are actually putting their tuition directly on plastic.

11   Even as the price has risen, more young people than ever aspire to college. Over 90 percent of high school graduates of all backgrounds say in national surveys that they hope to go on to college. Yet the inadequacy of aid shoots down their hopes.

12   As a direct consequence of the decline in public investment in education at every level, young people today are actually less educated than their parents. The nationwide high school graduation level peaked in 1970 at 77 percent. It was around 67 percent in 2004. According to a recent study cited in the 2004 book *Double the Numbers*, by Richard Kazis, Joel Vargas, and Nancy Hoffman, of every 100 younger people who begin their freshman year of high school, just 38 eventually enroll in college, and only 18 graduate within 150 percent of the allotted time—six years for a bachelor's degree or three years for an associates' degree. Only 24.4 percent of the adult population has a B.A., according to the 2000 Census, and those twenty-five to thirty-four years old are a little less likely to have one than forty-five-to-fifty-four-year-olds. Sociologists call non-college youth "the forgotten majority."

13   Statistically, the typical college student is a striving young adult; nearly half are twenty-four or older. She (56 percent are women) is spending several years in chronic exhaustion splitting her days between a nearly full-time, low-wage job, and part-time classes at a community college or four-year public university. She uses her credit cards to make ends meet—for books, meals, and clothes—and barely manages the minimum payments. Overloaded and falling behind, she is likely to drop out for a semester or for good. Almost one in three Americans in his or her twenties is a college dropout, compared with one in five in the late 1960s.

14   What happens to the three out of four young people who don't get a four-year degree? They are much more likely to remain in the working class than previous generations. Youths eighteen to twenty-four are the most likely to hold minimum-wage jobs, giving them a poverty rate of 30 percent in 2000, according to the U.S. Census; that's the highest of any age group. For those aged twenty-five to thirty-four, the poverty rate is 15 percent, compared with 10 percent for older working adults.

15   As policy analyst Heather McGhee, formerly of the think tank Demos, points out, when the Boomers were entering the workforce in 1970, the nations' largest private employer was General Motors. They paid an average wage of $17.50 an hour in today's dollars. The largest employer in the postindustrial economy is Wal-Mart. Their average wage? Eight dollars an hour. The service-driven economy is also a youth-driven economy, burning young people's energy and potential over a deep-fat

fryer. McDonald's is the nation's largest youth employer; workers under twenty-four make up nearly half of the food services, department store, and grocery store workforce nationwide. The working world has always been tough for those starting out, but today's economy relies on a new element—a "youth class." The entire labor market is downgrading toward what was once entry level.

16   . . . For better-off, college-educated sons and daughters, it's the same song, different verse. An astonishing 44 percent of dependent students from families making over $100,000 a year borrowed money for school in 2002. Credit card debt is higher for the middle class than for the poor. Unable to find good jobs with a bachelor's degree, young people are swelling graduate school classes, only to join the ranks of the unemployed or underemployed, after all.

17   The middle class has been shrinking for two decades. On a family-by-family basis, this means that many people my age who grew up in comfort and security are experiencing a startling decline in their standard of living. Median annual earnings for male workers twenty-five to thirty-four sank nearly 20 percent in constant dollars between 1971 and 2002. We start out in the working world with large monthly debt payments but without health insurance, pension benefits, or dependable jobs. It is impossible to predict whether we will be able to make up these deficits with higher earnings later on, but the evidence suggests that most of us will not.

18   In the 1960s the phrase "midlife crisis" captured the malaise of educated middle-class man confronting his mortality and an unfulfilling job or family life. Today "quarterlife crisis" has entered the lexicon for a generation whose unbelievably expensive educations didn't guarantee them success, a sense of purpose, or even a livable income.

19   When we talk about economics, we are also talking about ambition, responsibility, trust, and family. The new economic realities are distorting the life paths and relationships of the young. We are spending more time moving in and out of school, finding and losing jobs. Some of us move back home, and we put off marriage, children, and home buying. The older generation's response to these changes has been a chorus of disapproval and dismay.

20   The scholars of the Research Network on Transitions to Adulthood, relying on hard data, make the point that economic factors far outweigh psychological ones in explaining what has happened to young adults. "The current changing timetable of adulthood has given rise to a host of questions about whether current generations of young people are more dependent on their parents, less interested in growing up, and more wary of making commitments," they write. Our generation's delay in entering adulthood is often interpreted as a reflection of the narrowed generation gap.

21   In the 1980s, President Ronald Reagan began to dismantle the welfare state and put to rest the liberal dream of ending poverty on a large scale in America. His rhetorical ace was the Cadillac driving, government-cheating "welfare queen." Creating this infamous bogeywoman blamed the poor for their own problems and made taking away their means of support into the morally right thing to do.

22   The lazy, irresponsible, possibly sociopathic "twixter" is this decade's welfare queen, an insidious image obscuring public perception of a real inequity. If you look at where public resources are directed—toward the already wealthy, toward building prisons and expanding the military, away from education and jobs programs—it is easy to see a prejudice against young people as a class.

23   This is not to say that the phenomenon of emerging adulthood in and of itself is exclusively bad. It's a fact of history, like the so-called discoveries of childhood and adolescence before it. This change in the way we experience the life cycle brings upsides and downsides that we may not realize for decades to come. My friends and I overwhelmingly relish the time that we have, as postmillennial young adults, to try out prospective jobs, travel, volunteer, study, and form strong friendships before settling down into career and family responsibilities. Young women, especially, tend to appreciate the way their options have widened, and the chance that medical science gives us to possibly delay motherhood into our thirties and forties. The more money and education you start out with, the better this time of uncertainty starts to look. The problems arise because our society does not recognize this new state of life, and is instead withdrawing resources from young people. Therefore, the majority of us face obstacles that make it harder to see the bright side of emerging adulthood.

24   In the past few decades, the trend in the United States has been toward smaller families and looser kinship ties. The bonds of kinship in our national family are weakening too. It's not too dramatic to say that the nation is abandoning its children. In everything from national budget deficits to the rise of household debt to cuts in student aid and public funds for education, Americans are living in the present at the expense of the future. ◆

CRITICAL THINKING

1. What is the purpose of Kamenetz's recounting of the history of childhood and how childhood has been viewed over the centuries? What point is she trying to support by providing us with this background?

2. Kamenetz observes that the New Deal was largely responsible for our expectations of teenhood today. What factor does she identify as responsible for another shift that marks young adulthood?

3. What are the "five milestones of maturity"? Where are you on the timeline? Have you followed a linear timeline, or have you hopped around, reaching some milestones out of order? At what age would you expect to reach all five milestones? Explain.

4. What reasons does Kamenetz give for why young people are "falling behind"? Explain.

5. What is the "the forgotten majority"? Why are they forgotten? What does this segment of people represent now and in the future? Explain.

6. In paragraph 13 Kamenetz describes the typical college student. Summarize the characteristics she cites, and then describe how you and your friends compare.

7. What is the author's opinion of low-wage and/or service-driven employment? What does she imply happens to young workers who do not earn college degrees?

8. Do you think young people in their twenties are viewed as this decade's "welfare queens"? What comparison is Kamenetz making? Do you agree? Explain.

CRITICAL WRITING

1. *Persuasive Writing:* Sociologist Frank F. Furstenberg notes, "A new period of life is emerging in which young people are no longer adolescents but not yet adults. . . . It is simply not possible for most young people to achieve economic and psychological autonomy as early as it was half a century ago." Write an essay in which you either agree or disagree with his assessment, using examples from the essay, personal experience, and outside research.

2. *Research Writing:* How might one of the Baby Boomers Kamenetz refers to in this essay respond to her arguments? Highlight key points in the essay, and interview at least three people over 50 about the differences between the lives/expectations of twentysomethings today and those of 30 years ago.

3. *Research Writing:* Kamenetz asserts that America is living in the present at the expense of the future. Research the history and future of Social Security and other forms of federal financial support, including student financial aid. Then respond to Kamenetz's argument with your own view, supported by your research.

GROUP PROJECTS

1. Kamenetz observes that young adulthood is emerging as a "new" distinct phase of life, similar to the recognition of childhood and adolescence in centuries before. "This change in the way we experience the life cycle brings upsides and downsides that we may not realize for decades to come." As a group, discuss this phase of life. If you are beginning or are in the middle of it, what are your expectations from this phase of your life? What challenges do you face, and what benefits might you expect? If you are past young adulthood, compare your experience with the trend now emerging. Then, project what average young adulthood might look like in America 20 years from now.

2. Outline the financial reasons Kamenetz cites for why postmillennial youth is "generation debt." Discuss her reasoning and add more of your own. After discussing the topic with your group, share your views with the class as part of a broader discussion on the issue. Present solutions or strategies to mediate the challenges young adults face in an uncertain economy.

Strapped
Tamara Draut*

Most graduates 20 years ago expected to leave college with some student-loan debt along with their newly earned diplomas. But many of today's graduates carry an additional burden—credit card debt. It used be "no job, no credit." The big credit card companies have

---

* Tamara Draut, *Strapped: Why America's 20- and 30-Somethings Can't Get Ahead,* 2007

erased this policy in favor of ensnaring young consumers by offering students sizable credit lines. The result is that many students are up to their ears in credit card debt long before they have a job. This next excerpt from Tamara Draut's book *Strapped* explains why it is harder than ever for young adults to get ahead. Rather than preparing students to succeed, college campuses are promoting products that practically ensure that they never will.

1   It starts with a free T-shirt. If you've strolled through a college campus lately, chances are you've witnessed the phenomenon known as *tabling*. It used to be tabling was the province solely of student campus groups, with table after table offering pamphlets and sign-up sheets for everything from the ultimate Frisbee team to the Young Democrats or Young Republicans. But in the last ten years, tabling has been co-opted by capitalism, particularly by the industry one young adult referred to as "those credit card pushers."

2   At colleges across America, especially at state universities, credit card companies have taken a page out of the student organizations' playbook and table alongside the best of them. But the card companies have a leg up on the student groups: swag, and lots of it. In exchange for filling out a credit card application, students can get free stuff ranging from T-shirts to mugs and pizzas. The tables are staffed not by marketing representatives from the company but by college students trying to earn an extra buck themselves. On college campuses, credit card companies not only find profitable customers, but cash-strapped minions to do their shilling for them.

3   But what about the colleges themselves? Where are they in this picture? Far too often, they're in on the profit mongering. This is especially true of big state universities. The University of Tennessee, for example, accepted $16 million from First USA (now Chase) in exchange for exclusive marketing rights on campus, and hundreds of other schools receive money for every new application filled out by students. According to Robert Manning, author of *Credit Card Nation*, these types of deals yield the 300 largest universities about $1 billion year.

4   The marketing onslaught has paid off: in 2002, the average college senior had six credit cards and an average balance of just over $3,200. Many college students are in deeper trouble. One in five students has credit card debt of $3,000 to $7,000. Not surprisingly, student credit card debt increases with each successive year and more than doubles from freshman to senior year.

5   Recently, some states have closed their open-door policies regarding on-campus credit card marketers. In 2003, West Virginia passed legislation requiring all the public colleges in the state to regulate credit card marketing on campus. Some schools in the state banned the practice outright, whereas West Virginia University simply put an end to swag—at least swag without permission granted by the university. According to a General Accounting Office report in 2001, at least twenty-four states had introduced legislation to restrict credit card marketing on campus, but so far only Arkansas, Louisiana, New York, and West Virginia have actually passed such legislation. Where state legislatures have failed to ban the practice, many individual schools have taken the initiative. In 1998, the University of Minnesota banned credit cards companies from campus. Smaller, private liberal arts colleges have been more effective at patrolling card marketing on campus. Enforcement is easier on small campuses, and there's less incentive for these elite schools to raise money through

deals with the card companies, because they tend to have fat endowments and a steady stream of very high tuition monies filling their coffers.

6   But the card companies are nothing if not persistent. Even if they're forbidden to table on campus, they have other crafty methods to reach students. Some colleges make it really easy by selling the card companies their students' information. A report by the Maryland Public Interest Group found that Towson University sells its student list to MBNA—although after the publication of the report, it told the authors they would stop this practice in mid 2004. If a college bans a company outright, the friendly campus bookstore will usually help out the card mongers by agreeing to stuff its bags with credit card offers.

7   About a quarter of students report using their credit cards to pay for tuition and books. What about the other three quarters? Certainly their credit card debt represents in part what we tend to think of as frivolous debt. Visa and Mastercard have no doubt funded a great many pizzas, kegs, and spring breaks.

8   The problem is that after graduation, the need for credit often morphs into a whole new category: survival debt. Making the transition from college grad to full-fledged working adult takes more than a good résumé. For young twentysomethings who can't turn to Mom and Dad for start-up money, launching their adult lives often entails going further into credit card debt. And with substantial debt already built up from college, young adults can get caught off guard and tangled in a debt spiral they most likely never saw coming.

9   Of course, it's not only college grads who are using credit cards as a private safety net. In fact, the ubiquity of credit cards among under-34ers makes it hard to categorize young debtors. They're college-educated, non-college-educated, males, female, black, Hispanic, and white. They're receptionists, project managers, teachers, and health care workers. During the 1990s, credit card debt among those under age 34 grew by 47 percent. But that doesn't mean that young adults don't take debt seriously or that it isn't a major stress in their lives. This generation regards credit card debt as a necessary evil.

10   Every three years, the Federal Reserve collects information specifically on household credit card debt as part of its Survey of Consumer Finances, with 2004 being the latest data available. To compare credit card debt between Gen-Xers and the late Baby Boomers, we can use survey findings from 1989, when the 25- to 34-year-old population was made up of Baby Boomers, and 2004, when it was made up of Gen-Xers. My analysis of the data indeed confirms that Gen-Xers are more indebted than Baby Boomers were at the same age. In 2004, 25- to 34-year-olds averaged $4,358 in credit card debt—47 percent higher than it was for Baby Boomers in 1989.

11   Keep in mind that these numbers are based on self-reported amounts, not actual credit card statements. For many reasons, people tend to underreport their credit card debt. For example, in 2004, the average household credit card debt reported in the survey was just over $5,219. But aggregate data on outstanding credit card debt reported by the credit card industry puts the average household debt at $12,000. New survey research conducted by Demos of low- to middle-class households found that the average indebted under 34-er had just over $8,000 in credit card debt in 2005. According to these households, the most common reasons cited for their credit card debt were car repairs, loss of a job, and home repairs. Forty-five percent of under

34-ers reported using credit cards in the last year to pay for basic living expenses, such as rent, mortgage payments, groceries, and utilities. Not exactly the stuff of the young debtor stereotype.

12   The rise in credit card debt, coupled with the surge in student loan debt, is the main reason why today's young adults are spending much more on debt payments than the previous generation. On average those aged 25 to 34 years spent nearly 25 cents out of every dollar of income on debt payments in 2001, according to the Federal Reserve's data. That's more than double what Baby Boomers of the same age spent on debt payments in 1989. The fact that young adults are already spending a quarter of their income on debt is particularly worrisome, because most in the 25-to-34 age group aren't homeowners. So that 25 cents is going to non-mortgage debt: primarily student loans, car loans, and credit cards.

13   The soaring debt among young adults is landing more of this generation in the throes of bankruptcy. By 2001, nearly 12 out of every 1,000 young adults aged 25 to 34 were filing for bankruptcy, a 19 percent increase since 1991. Young adults now have the second highest rate of bankruptcy, just after those aged 35 to 44.

As being young and single has become practically synonymous with being in debt, it's no surprise that when young people finally find love, they also find more debt.

14   As being young and single has become practically synonymous with being in debt, it's no surprise that when young people finally find love, they also find more debt. While the economic benefits of living together or getting married are still pretty good—especially in expensive cities—today's young couples aren't getting quite the economic benefits that previous generations enjoyed when they combined incomes. Why? Because in addition to joining together in matrimony, young couples today are joining together in debt servitude.

15   Despite being broke and in credit card debt, many of the young adults I spoke with actually managed to put some money into a savings account. Most young adults want to build up an emergency fund and save for retirement. Unfortunately, it isn't until they hit their thirties that they are able to do both.

16   Young adults aren't alone in struggling to save money. Over the last twenty years, our nation's personal saving rate has plummeted from about 8 percent through the 1980s and early 1990s to zero in 2005—its lowest point since the Great Depression. There is growing concern that Americans now live by the rule "If you have it, spend it." Most social critics hold up the Greatest Generation, those who came of age during the Great Depression, as the moral pinnacle of scrimping and saving. The Baby Boomers took a lot of flak during the 1980s for their spending habits. Remember yuppies? The Baby Boomers seemed to have invented conspicuous consumption. And now that the Baby Boomers have reached the age where they control the commentary on all things social, political and economic—they've taken to criticizing the younger generation for its spending habits.

17   If today's young adults can be accused of wanting it all too soon, the "it" isn't riches, gadgets, or luxury cars. The elusive "it" that today's twentysomethings are after is financial independence, and then, hopefully, financial security. All the buzz

about young bucks making millions in stock options and entrepreneurial start-ups simply distracted attention from a bigger story. The 1990s ushered in the Era of Debt. While the popular media made it look as though riches had landed at our feet, the real new economy meant that obtaining a middle-class lifestyle now required a large credit line and five-figure student debt.

18   Without bold thinking and the courage to uphold our nation's most sacred values, a whole generation of young adults will come of age in an America that doesn't reward hard work, family values, or collective responsibilities. The grim economic reality and choked opportunity facing young adults didn't have to happen. And it doesn't have to continue. ◆

CRITICAL THINKING

1. In her introduction, Draut describes the practice of tabling and its role in connecting new students to their first credit card. What is your own experience with tabling? Were you approached on campus and offered a card? Did you get one, or do you know someone who did? Explain.

2. Some students are given credit cards by their parents "for emergencies." Do you think this is a good idea? If you have such an arrangement, have you ever used your card for something other than an emergency? What constituted an "emergency"?

3. Draut observes that "This generation regards credit card debt as a necessary evil." Do you agree? What is your personal view of credit card debt? Is it simply a way of life? Can you survive in this world without credit cards and the debt that comes with them? Explain.

4. What is Draut's argument in this essay? What is her objective? Evaluate her use of examples to support her view.

5. How did the spending habits of the Baby Boomers and Generation Xers contribute to our current consumption habits? Explain.

CRITICAL WRITING

1. *Expository Writing:* What, if anything, can the younger generation learn from the older generation about debt? Speak to a few people older than you about their views of debt, including student loans, credit card debt, and car loans. What is their view of debt? Does it differ from your view? Explain.

2. *Research Writing:* Draut notes that most social critics hold up the "Greatest Generation," those who came of age during the Great Depression. Research the social impact of the Great Depression. What are the merits of thrift? What role does it play in our social consciousness? Is it as important today as it was 50 years ago? As America once again faces the most challenging economic climate since the Great Depression, how might your generation measure up?

3. *Personal Narrative:* Write about a time when you had to make a personal choice that involved incurring debt. Describe the circumstances and your feelings about the incident.

GROUP PROJECTS

1. Draut's conclusion observes that "bold thinking" is needed to help the current generation reclaim its right to financial security and the American dream. As a group, outline the things you feel represent the American dream. After completing your list, discuss as a group or as a class the challenges you face in reaching that dream.

2. Several writers in this chapter cite government and corporate policies that have contributed to the current generation's debt crisis. As a group, discuss ways that students can turn the tide of the "Era of Debt." Include grassroots efforts, political policy, and campus initiatives in your discussion.

Grow Up? Not So Fast
*Lev Grossman**

When does adulthood begin? In terms of starting a family and being financially solvent, what was once a milestone reached in the 20s is more likely to be reached in the 30s. In this next article, author Lev Grossman looks at the new generation of twentysomethings, which he calls "twixters," because they are "betwixt and between" in that they are putting off becoming adults by living with their parents. Twixters tend to take 5 or more years to graduate college, put off marriage and children, and wander from city to city and from job to job. Rather than representing a passing trend, their numbers are growing. Is this a new life stage to look forward to after graduation?

1 Michele, Ellen, Nathan, Corinne, Marcus and Jennie are friends. All of them live in Chicago. They go out three nights a week, sometimes more. Each of them has had several jobs since college; Ellen is on her 17th, counting internships, since 1996. They don't own homes. They change apartments frequently. None of them are married, none have children. All of them are from 24 to 28 years old.

2 Thirty years ago, people like Michele, Ellen, Nathan, Corinne, Marcus and Jennie didn't exist, statistically speaking. Back then, the median age for an American woman to get married was 21. She had her first child at 22. Now it all takes longer. It's 25 for the wedding and 25 for baby. It appears to take young people longer to graduate from college, settle into careers and buy their first homes. What are they waiting for? Who are these permanent adolescents, these twentysomething Peter Pans? And why can't they grow up?

3 Everybody knows a few of them—full-grown men and women who still live with their parents, who dress and talk and party as they did in their teens, hopping from job to job and date to date, having fun but seemingly going nowhere. Ten years ago, we might have called them Generation X, or slackers, but those labels don't

---

* Lev Grossman, *Time Magazine,* January 16, 2005

quite fit anymore. This isn't just a trend, a temporary fad or a generational hiccup. This is a much larger phenomenon, of a different kind and a different order.

4   Social scientists are starting to realize that a permanent shift has taken place in the way we live our lives. In the past, people moved from childhood to adolescence and from adolescence to adulthood, but today there is a new, intermediate phase along the way. The years from 18 until 25 and even beyond have become a distinct and separate life stage, a strange, transitional never-never land between adolescence and adulthood in which people stall for a few extra years, putting off the iron cage of adult responsibility that constantly threatens to crash down on them. They're betwixt and between. You could call them twixters.

> *Social scientists are starting to realize that a permanent shift has taken place in the way we live our lives. In the past, people moved from childhood to adolescence and from adolescence to adulthood, but today there is a new, intermediate phase along the way.*

5   Where did the twixters come from? And what's taking them so long to get where they're going? Some of the sociologists, psychologists and demographers who study this new life stage see it as a good thing. The twixters aren't lazy, the argument goes, they're reaping the fruit of decades of American affluence and social liberation. This new period is a chance for young people to savor the pleasures of irresponsibility, search their souls and choose their life paths. But more historically and economically minded scholars see it differently. They are worried that twixters aren't growing up because they can't. Those researchers fear that whatever cultural machinery used to turn kids into grownups has broken down, that society no longer provides young people with the moral backbone and the financial wherewithal to take their rightful places in the adult world. Could growing up be harder than it used to be?

6   The sociologists, psychologists, economists and others who study this age group have many names for this new phase of life—"youthhood," "adultescence"—and they call people in their 20s "kidults" and "boomerang kids," none of which have quite stuck. Terri Apter, a psychologist at the University of Cambridge in England and the author of *The Myth of Maturity*, calls them "thresholders."

7   Apter became interested in the phenomenon in 1994, when she noticed her students struggling and flailing more than usual after college. Parents were baffled when their expensively educated, otherwise well-adjusted 23-year-old children wound up sobbing in their old bedrooms, paralyzed by indecision. "Legally, they're adults, but they're on the threshold, the doorway to adulthood, and they're not going through it," Apter says. The percentage of 26-year-olds living with their parents has nearly doubled since 1970, from 11% to 20%, according to Bob Schoeni, a professor of economics and public policy at the University of Michigan.

8   Jeffrey Arnett, a developmental psychologist at the University of Maryland, favors "emerging adulthood" to describe this new demographic group, and the term is the title of his new book on the subject. His theme is that the twixters are misunderstood. It's too easy to write them off as overgrown children, he argues. Rather, he suggests, they're doing important work to get themselves ready for adulthood. "This is the one time of their lives when they're not responsible for anyone else or

to anyone else," Arnett says. "So they have this wonderful freedom to really focus on their own lives and work on becoming the kind of person they want to be." In his view, what looks like incessant, hedonistic play is the twixters' way of trying on jobs and partners and personalities and making sure that when they do settle down, they do it the right way, their way. It's not that they don't take adulthood seriously; they take it so seriously, they're spending years carefully choosing the right path into it.

9   But is that all there is to it? Take a giant step backward, look at the history and the context that led up to the rise of the twixters, and you start to wonder, Is it that they don't want to grow up, or is it that the rest of society won't let them?

School Daze

10 Matt Swann is 27. He took 6 1/2 years to graduate from the University of Georgia. When he finally finished, he had a brand-spanking-new degree in cognitive science, which he describes as a wide-ranging interdisciplinary field that covers cognition, problem solving, artificial intelligence, linguistics, psychology, philosophy and anthropology. All of which is pretty cool, but its value in today's job market is not clear. "Before the '90s maybe, it seemed like a smart guy could do a lot of things," Swann says. "Kids used to go to college to get educated. That's what I did, which I think now was a bit naïve. Being smart after college doesn't really mean anything. 'Oh, good, you're smart. Unfortunately your productivity's s___, so we're going to have to fire you.'"

11   College is the institution most of us entrust to watch over the transition to adulthood, but somewhere along the line that transition has slowed to a crawl. In a *Time* poll of people ages 18 to 29, only 32% of those who attended college left school by age 21. In fact, the average college student takes five years to finish. The era of the four-year college degree is all but over.

12   Swann graduated in 2002 as a newly minted cognitive scientist, but the job he finally got a few months later was as a waiter in Atlanta. He waited tables for the next year and a half. It proved to be a blessing in disguise. Swann says he learned more real-world skills working in restaurants than he ever did in school. "It taught me how to deal with people. What you learn as a waiter is how to treat people fairly, especially when they're in a bad situation." That's especially valuable in his current job as an insurance-claims examiner.

13   There are several lessons about twixters to be learned from Swann's tale. One is that most colleges are seriously out of step with the real world in getting students ready to become workers in the postcollege world. Vocational schools like DeVry and Strayer, which focus on teaching practical skills, are seeing a mini-boom. Their enrollment grew 48% from 1996 to 2000. More traditional schools are scrambling to give their courses a practical spin. In the fall, Hendrix College in Conway, Ark., will introduce a program called the Odyssey project, which the school says will encourage students to "think outside the book" in areas like "professional and leadership development" and "service to the world." Dozens of other schools have set up similar initiatives.

14   As colleges struggle to get their students ready for real-world jobs, they are charging more for what they deliver. The resulting debt is a major factor in keeping twixters from moving on and growing up. Thirty years ago, most financial aid came

in the form of grants, but now the emphasis is on lending, not on giving. Recent college graduates owe 85% more in student loans than their counterparts of a decade ago, according to the Center for Economic and Policy Research. In *Time*'s poll, 66% of those surveyed owed more than $10,000 when they graduated, and 5% owed more than $100,000. (And this says nothing about the credit-card companies that bombard freshmen with offers for cards that students then cheerfully abuse. Demos, a public-policy group, says credit-card debt for Americans 18 to 24 more than doubled from 1992 to 2001.) The longer it takes to pay off those loans, the longer it takes twixters to achieve the financial independence that's crucial to attaining an adult identity, not to mention the means to get out of their parents' house.

15   Meanwhile, those expensive, time-sucking college diplomas have become worth less than ever. So many more people go to college now—a 53% increase since 1970—that the value of a degree on the job market has been diluted. The advantage in wages for college-degree holders hasn't risen significantly since the late 1990s, according to the Bureau of Labor Statistics. To compensate, a lot of twixters go back to school for graduate and professional degrees. Swann, for example, is planning to head back to business school to better his chances in the insurance game. But piling on extra degrees costs precious time and money and pushes adulthood even further into the future.

Work in Progress

16   Kate Galantha, 29, spent seven years working her way through college, transferring three times. After she finally graduated from Columbia College in Chicago (major: undeclared) in 2001, she moved to Portland, Ore., and went to work as a nanny and as an assistant to a wedding photographer. A year later she jumped back to Chicago, where she got a job in a flower shop. It was a full-time position with real benefits, but she soon burned out and headed for the territories, a.k.a. Madison, Wis. "I was really busy but not accomplishing anything," she says. "I didn't want to stay just for a job."

17   She had no job offers in Madison, and the only person she knew there was her older sister, but she had nothing tying her to Chicago (her boyfriend had moved to Europe) and she needed a change. The risk paid off. She got a position as an assistant at a photo studio, and she loves it. "I decided it was more important to figure out what to do and to be in a new environment," Galantha says. "It's exciting, and I'm in a place where I can accomplish everything. But starting over is the worst."

18   Galantha's frenetic hopping from school to school, job to job and city to city may look like aimless wandering. (She has moved six times since 1999. Her father calls her and her sister gypsies.) But *Emerging Adulthood*'s Arnett—and Galantha— see it differently. To them, the period from 18 to 25 is a kind of sandbox, a chance to build castles and knock them down, experiment with different careers, knowing that none of it really counts. After all, this is a world of overwhelming choice: there are 40 kinds of coffee beans at Whole Foods Market, 205 channels on DirecTV, 15 million personal ads on Match.com and 800,000 jobs on Monster.com. Can you blame Galantha for wanting to try them all? She doesn't want to play just the hand she has been dealt. She wants to look through the whole deck. "My problem is I'm really overstimulated by everything," Galantha says. "I feel there's too much

information out there at all times. There are too many doors, too many people, too much competition."

19   Twixters expect to jump laterally from job to job and place to place until they find what they're looking for. The stable, quasi-parental bond between employer and employee is a thing of the past, and neither feels much obligation to make the relationship permanent. "They're well aware of the fact that they will not work for the same company for the rest of their life," says Bill Frey, a demographer with the Brookings Institution, a think tank based in Washington. "They don't think long-term about health care or Social Security. They're concerned about their careers and immediate gratification."

20   Twixters expect a lot more from a job than a paycheck. Maybe it's a reaction to the greed-is-good 1980s or to the whatever-is-whatever apathy of the early 1990s. More likely, it's the way they were raised, by parents who came of age in the 1960s as the first generation determined to follow its bliss, who want their children to change the world the way they did. Maybe it has to do with advances in medicine. Twixters can reasonably expect to live into their 80s and beyond, so their working lives will be extended accordingly, and when they choose a career, they know they'll be there for a while. But whatever the cause, twixters are looking for a sense of purpose and importance in their work, something that will add meaning to their lives, and many don't want to rest until they find it. "They're not just looking for a job," Arnett says. "They want something that's more like a calling, that's going to be an expression of their identity." Hedonistic nomads, the twixters may seem, but there's a serious core of idealism in them.

21   Still, self-actualization is a luxury not everybody can afford, and looking at middle- and upper-class twixters gives only part of the picture. Twixters change jobs often, but they don't all do it for the same reasons, and one twixter's playful experimentation is another's desperate hustling. James Côté is a sociologist at the University of Western Ontario and the author of several books about twixters, including *Generation on Hold* and *Arrested Adulthood*. He believes that the economic bedrock that used to support adolescents on their journey into adulthood has shifted alarmingly. "What we're looking at really began with the collapse of the youth labor market, dating back to the late '70s and early '80s, which made it more difficult for people to get a foothold in terms of financial independence," Côté says. "You need a college degree now just to be where blue-collar people the same age were 20 or 30 years ago, and if you don't have it, then you're way behind." In other words, it's not that twixters don't want to become adults. They just can't afford to.

22   One way society defines an adult is as a person who is financially independent, with a family and a home. But families and homes cost money, and people in their late teens and early 20s don't make as much as they used to. The current crop of twixters grew up in the 1990s, when the dotcom boom made Internet millions seem just a business proposal away, but in reality they're worse off than the generation that preceded them. Annual earnings among men 25 to 34 with full-time jobs dropped 17% from 1971 to 2002, according to the National Center for Education Statistics. Timothy Smeeding, a professor of economics at Syracuse University, found that only half of Americans in their mid 20s earn enough to support a family, and in *Time*'s poll only half of those ages 18 to 29 consider themselves financially

independent. Michigan's Schoeni says Americans ages 25 and 26 get an average of $2,323 a year in financial support from their parents.

23   The transition to adulthood gets tougher the lower you go on the economic and educational ladder. Sheldon Danziger, a public-policy professor at the University of Michigan, found that for male workers ages 25 to 29 with only a high school diploma, the average wage declined 11% from 1975 to 2002. "When I graduated from high school, my classmates who didn't want to go to college could go to the Goodyear plant and buy a house and support a wife and family," says Steve Hamilton of Cornell University's Youth and Work Program. "That doesn't happen anymore." Instead, high school grads are more likely to end up in retail jobs with low pay and minimal benefits, if any. From this end of the social pyramid, Arnett's vision of emerging adulthood as a playground of self-discovery seems a little rosy. The rules have changed, and not in the twixters' favor.

Weddings Can Wait

24   With everything else that's going on—careers to be found, debts to be paid, bars to be hopped—love is somewhat secondary in the lives of the twixters. But that doesn't mean they're cynical about it. Au contraire: among our friends from Chicago—Michele, Ellen, Nathan, Corinne, Marcus and Jennie—all six say they are not ready for marriage yet but do want it someday, preferably with kids. Naturally, all that is comfortably situated in the eternally receding future. Thirty is no longer the looming deadline it once was. In fact, five of the Chicago six see marriage as a decidedly post-30 milestone.

25   "It's a long way down the road," says Marcus Jones, 28, a comedian who works at Banana Republic by day. "I'm too self-involved. I don't want to bring that into a relationship now." He expects to get married in his mid to late 30s. "My wife is currently a sophomore in high school," he jokes.

26   "I want to get married but not soon," says Jennie Jiang, 26, a sixth-grade teacher. "I'm enjoying myself. There's a lot I want to do by myself still."

27   "I have my career, and I'm too young," says Michele Steele, 26, a TV producer. "It's commitment and sacrifice, and I think it's a hindrance. Lo and behold, people have come to the conclusion that it's not much fun to get married and have kids right out of college."

28   That attitude is new, but it didn't come out of nowhere. Certainly, the spectacle of the previous generation's mass divorces has something to do with the healthy skepticism shown by the twixters. They will spend a few years looking before they leap, thank you very much. "I fantasize more about sharing a place with someone than about my wedding day," says Galantha, whose parents split when she was 18. "I haven't seen a lot of good marriages."

29   But if twixters are getting married later, they are missing out on some of the social-support networks that come with having families of their own. To make up for it, they have a special gift for friendship, documented in books like Sasha Cagen's *Quirkyalone* and Ethan Watters' *Urban Tribes*, which asks the not entirely rhetorical question, Are friends the new family? They throw cocktail parties and dinner parties. They hold poker nights. They form book groups. They stay in touch constantly and

in real time, through social-networking technologies like cell phones, instant messaging, text messaging and online communities like Friendster. They're also close to their parents. *Time*'s poll showed that almost half of Americans ages 18 to 29 talk to their parents every day.

30   Marrying late also means that twixters tend to have more sexual partners than previous generations. The situation is analogous to their promiscuous job-hopping behavior—like Goldilocks, they want to find the one that's just right—but it can give them a cynical, promiscuous vibe too. Arnett is worried that if anything, twixters are too romantic. In their universe, romance is totally detached from pragmatic concerns and societal pressures, so when twixters finally do marry, they're going to do it for Love with a capital L and no other reason. "Everybody wants to find their soul mate now," Arnett says, "whereas I think, for my parents' generation—I'm 47—they looked at it much more practically. I think a lot of people are going to end up being disappointed with the person that's snoring next to them by the time they've been married for a few years and they realize it doesn't work that way."

Twixter Culture

31 When it comes to social change, pop culture is the most sensitive of seismometers, and it was faster to pick up on the twixters than the cloistered social scientists. Look at the Broadway musical *Avenue Q,* in which puppets dramatize the vagaries of life after graduation. ("I wish I could go back to college," a character sings. "Life was so simple back then.") Look at that little TV show called *Friends,* about six people who put off marriage well into their 30s. Even twice-married Britney Spears fits the profile. For a succinct, albeit cheesy summation of the twixter predicament, you couldn't do much better than her 2001 hit "I'm Not a Girl, Not Yet a Woman."

32   The producing duo Edward Zwick and Marshall Herskovitz, who created the legendarily zeitgeisty TV series "Thirtysomething" and "My So-Called Life," now have a pilot with ABC called "1/4life," about a houseful of people in their mid-20s who can't seem to settle down. "When you talk about this period of transition being extended, it's not what people intended to do," Herskovitz says, "but it's a result of the world not being particularly welcoming when they come into it. Lots of people have a difficult time dealing with it, and they try to stay kids as long as they can because they don't know how to make sense of all this. We're interested in this process of finding courage and one's self."

33   As for movies, a lot of twixters cite *Garden State* as one that really nails their predicament. "I feel like my generation is waiting longer and longer to get married," says Zach Braff, 29, who wrote, directed and starred in the film about a twentysomething actor who comes home for the first time in nine years. "In the past, people got married and got a job and had kids, but now there's a new 10 years that people are using to try and find out what kind of life they want to lead. For a lot of people, the weight of all the possibility is overwhelming."

34   Pop culture may reflect the changes in our lives, but it also plays its part in shaping them. Marketers have picked up on the fact that twixters on their personal voyages of discovery tend to buy lots of stuff along the way. "They are the optimum market to be going after for consumer electronics, Game Boys, flat-screen TVs, iPods, couture

fashion, exotic vacations and so forth," says David Morrison, president of Twenty-something, Inc., a marketing consultancy based in Philadelphia. "Most of their needs are taken care of by Mom and Dad, so their income is largely discretionary. [Many twentysomethings] are living at home, but if you look, you'll see flat-screen TVs in their bedrooms and brand-new cars in the driveway." Some twixters may want to grow up, but corporations and advertisers have a real stake in keeping them in a tractable, exploitable, pre-adult state—living at home, spending their money on toys.

Living with Peter Pan

35 Maybe the twixters are in denial about growing up, but the rest of society is equally in denial about the twixters. Nobody wants to admit they're here to stay, but that's where all the evidence points. Tom Smith, director of the General Social Survey, a large sociological data-gathering project run by the National Opinion Research Center, found that most people believe that the transition to adulthood should be completed by the age of 26, on average, and he thinks that number is only going up. "In another 10 or 20 years, we're not going to be talking about this as a delay. We're going to be talking about this as a normal trajectory," Smith says. "And we're going to think about those people getting married at 18 and forming families at 19 or 20 as an odd historical pattern."

36   There may even be a biological basis to all this. The human brain continues to grow and change into the early 20s, according to Abigail Baird, who runs the Laboratory for Adolescent Studies at Dartmouth. "We as a society deem an individual at the age of 18 ready for adult responsibility," Baird points out. "Yet recent evidence suggests that our neuropsychological development is many years from being complete. There's no reason to think 18 is a magic number." How can the twixters be expected to settle down when their gray matter hasn't?

37   A new life stage is a major change, and the rest of society will have to change to make room for it. One response to this very new phenomenon is extremely old-fashioned: medieval-style apprenticeship programs that give high school graduates a cheaper and more practical alternative to college. In 1996 Jack Smith, then CEO of General Motors, started Automotive Youth Educational Systems (AYES), a program that puts high school kids in shops alongside seasoned car mechanics. More than 7,800 students have tried it, and 98% of them have ended up working at the business where they apprenticed. "I knew this was my best way to get into a dealership," says Chris Rolando, 20, an AYES graduate who works at one in Detroit. "My friends are still at pizza-place jobs and have no idea what to do for a living. I just bought my own house and have a career."

38   But success stories like Rolando's are rare. Child welfare, the juvenile-justice system, special-education and support programs for young mothers usually cut off at age 18, and most kids in foster care get kicked out at 18 with virtually no safety net. "Age limits are like the time limits for welfare recipients," says Frank Furstenberg, a sociologist who heads a research consortium called the MacArthur Network on Transitions to Adulthood. "They're pushing people off the rolls, but they're not necessarily able to transition into supportive services or connections to other systems." And programs for the poor aren't the only ones that need to grow up with the times.

Only 54% of respondents in the *Time* poll were insured through their employers. That's a reality that affects all levels of society, and policymakers need to strengthen that safety net.

39   Most of the problems that twixters face are hard to see, and that makes it harder to help them. Twixters may look as if they have been overindulged, but they could use some judicious support. Apter's research at Cambridge suggests that the more parents sympathize with their twixter children, the more parents take time to discuss their twixters' life goals, the more aid and shelter they offer them, the easier the transition becomes. "Young people know that their material life will not be better than their parents'," Apter says. "They don't expect a safer life than their parents had. They don't expect more secure employment or finances. They have to put in a lot of work just to remain O.K." Tough love may look like the answer, but it's not what twixters need.

40   The real heavy lifting may ultimately have to happen on the level of the culture itself. There was a time when people looked forward to taking on the mantle of adulthood. That time is past. Now our culture trains young people to fear it. "I don't ever want a lawn," says Swann. "I don't ever want to drive two hours to get to work. I do not want to be a parent. I mean, hell, why would I? There's so much fun to be had while you're young." He does have a point. Twixters have all the privileges of grownups now but only some of the responsibilities. From the point of view of the twixters, upstairs in their childhood bedrooms, snuggled up under their Star Wars comforters, it can look all downhill.

41   If twixters are ever going to grow up, they need the means to do it—and they will have to want to. There are joys and satisfactions that come with assuming adult responsibility, though you won't see them on *The Real World*. To go to the movies or turn on the TV is to see a world where life ends at 30; these days, every movie is *Logan's Run*. There are few road maps in the popular culture—and to most twixters, this is the only culture—to get twixters where they need to go. If those who are 30 and older want the rest of the world to grow up, they'll have to show the twixters that it's worth their while. "I went to a Poster Children concert, and there were 40-year-olds still rocking," says Jennie Jiang. "It gave me hope." ◆

CRITICAL THINKING

1. Grossman asserts, "Everybody knows a few of them—full-grown men and women who still live with their parents, who dress and talk and party as they did in their teens, hopping from job to job and date to date, having fun but seemingly going nowhere." Do you know anyone who fits this description? Explain what you know about these people. If you don't know anyone like this, discuss why Grossman is incorrect in his assertion.

2. Grossman states that our current culture trains young people to fear becoming adults. Do you agree or disagree? Explain using concrete examples.

3. According to researcher Abigail Baird, 18 is not the magic number for adulthood, as the human brain continues to grow and change into the early 20s. With this in mind, should the official age of adulthood be changed from 18 to 21? Even older? Explain.

4. This article mentions many possible reasons for the new "twixter" phenomenon. Skim through the article and find as many reasons as you can. Which ones seem the most plausible to you? Can you add any more of your own?
5. Grossman looks at how an undergraduate degree tends not to be practically useful for this new generation but is a necessity nonetheless. What specific points does Grossman make about the value of college? Do you agree or disagree with his view?
6. Do you like the term "twixter"? What other terms have been used for this new demographic group? Which do you prefer? Explain your preference.

CRITICAL WRITING

1. *Personal Narrative:* Try to predict where you will be in 10 years and the journey you will take to get there. Will you be a twixter? Think about what your goals are for the future and how you will accomplish them.
2. *Exploratory Writing:* What do think has contributed to this so-called intermediate phase between adolescence and adulthood?

GROUP PROJECTS

1. As a group, create 10 survey questions to ask 50 or so 18- to 28-year-olds to find out if they fit the "twixter" model. Synthesize your data and share your results with the class.
2. In Grossman's article, the audience is told, "Corporations and advertisers have a real stake in keeping [twixters] in a tractable, exploitable, pre-adult state—living at home, spending their money on toys." Look through magazines, online advertisements, and television advertisements geared toward the 18- to 28-year-old set to find six examples to confirm Grossman's statement. Share these advertisements in a PowerPoint presentation to the entire class.
3. Watch Zach Braff's film *Garden State* with your group and discuss whether this movie is indeed one that really nails the predicament of being a twixter. Explore how the movie does or does not exemplify this new demographic.

Recession Generation?
Sharon Jayson*

Although today's graduating class may be one of the first generations to do less well than their parents, that might not be as bad as it sounds. Perhaps expectations were set too high, and the savings rate too low? In this next essay, Sharon Jayson explores how many young people are coping in a down economy, as they build their own American Dream, part two.

* Sharon Jayson, *USA Today,* June 23, 2009

1   At age 26, Angela Trilli doesn't think she's one of those so-called materialistic Millennials she has heard about—young people who are absorbed with themselves and their consumption. She says she's a saver, not a spender, but unlike many of her peers who didn't have much to lose in this struggling economy, she says she lost $15,000—about half of the savings she built up since childhood. "It's a very insecure world out there," says Trilli, of Kendall Park, N.J., who works in marketing for a non-profit. "It was a little shocking to the system. You think things are going in a certain way, but you can't expect that things are always going to be the same."

2   The Millennial generation, or Gen Y, ranges from people in their 20s to those still in grade school. But what they all have in common is the knowledge that the recession has in some way shattered the world they thought they knew. And, depending upon how long the downturn lasts, historians, economists and psychologists say it could shape Millennials' values and attitudes in much the same way the Depression shaped the attitudes of those growing up in the 1930s.

3   "I call it the end of Disney World," says Michael Bradley, an adolescent psychologist in suburban Philadelphia. But now, young people are reordering their values. "It is their version of the American Dream," he says. "They talk more about having autonomy and freedom, and in so doing, not being as enslaved to material goals that they perceived their parents being caught up in. They do talk about life happiness not based on economic success or achievement as much."

4   Although many surveys have tried to gauge the economy's effect on Americans, few have focused on Millennials. But one survey in February by the New York City-based marketing and advertising agency JWT (formerly J. Walter Thompson) focused on the recession's effect on this group. The survey of 1,065 Americans 18 and older, including 243 ages 18-29, suggests 60% feel their generation is being dealt an unfair blow because of the recession. But some see opportunity, as well. For example, 44% say they might be able to afford a house now that home prices have plummeted; 25% say that if they have trouble finding a job, they'll just start their own business.

5   The virtues of simple living now coming into vogue especially strike a chord with Millennials, whom pollster John Zogby describes as more socially conscious, environmentally aware and demanding as consumers than previous generations. "I don't go shopping as often, even though I like to," says Gabriella Ring, 16, of Oak Park, Mich., who will be a high school junior in the fall. "I go when there's end-of-season clearance sales and when I really need something. I used to want to go all the time."

6   Experts differ on whether such restraint will continue when the economy turns around, but they agree that these are formative years. "This is the time where a lot of their attitudes are set. The long-term is still in question, but it has the potential to have a big impact and change the views that they'll have throughout their lives," says economist Richard Curtin, who directs consumer surveys at the University of Michigan in Ann Arbor. "They'll be more oriented toward economic security and relationships, more toward savings and less toward spending."

7   James Burroughs, an associate professor of commerce who studies consumer culture at the University of Virginia in Charlottesville, says he has seen a shift in student attitudes in his classes since the downturn. "While students were going to

consume less, there was also a psychological shift," he says. "It wasn't necessarily that they weren't going to consume, but they were giving a lot more thought to consumption."

8   Anthony Durr, 21, of Columbus, Ohio, says the recession has influenced how he views money, especially since his grandmothers, both raised during the Depression, are preaching caution. "Their generation—they were all about saving money. They understood the value of every single dollar," says Durr, who will be a senior this fall at Case Western Reserve University in Cleveland. "I would like to believe that with my generation, it's going to definitely come to that point. Even if you're very successful with your company, there's always that chance of losing your job, and then what?"

9   Already, young people are envisioning their futures, and it's not necessarily what they had in mind before the economy tanked. "I just think we're having to get used to living a little less luxurious than we grew up," says Dan Appel, 21, a psychology student at Montgomery County Community College in Blue Bell, Pa. "We'll have to realize we need to settle for slightly less than our parents had when they were first entering the job market."

10   Francesca Saracino, 19, of Grosse Pointe Woods, Mich., says the economy seems to be setting her life course. Not only did her father get laid off in May after taking a pay cut last November, but Saracino had to delay plans to transfer to Michigan State University for her sophomore year of college. She has been living at home and commuting to Wayne State University in Detroit. And she's not sure what to major in because she's concerned about what careers will produce jobs. "The recession does have a lot of impact on my future," she says.

11   Laurisa Rodrigues, 18, also believes the recession will have longer-term effects on her financial future. She just graduated from high school in Pueblo, Colo., and will be a freshman this fall at the University of Puget Sound in Tacoma, Wash. "A lot of us have seen our parents live paycheck to paycheck, and we don't want that for us," she says. "Our generation is learning, but I don't think we're learning quite as fast as we should. Once we get jobs and get settled, I know I'm going to be a little tighter with my money, so I don't have to live paycheck to paycheck."

12   Although experts consider Millennials overall an optimistic bunch, the down economy has made many cynical, saying they have less confidence in traditional approaches to saving money. "I think my generation feels a lot less financially secure. I feel like I need to be more creative and pay more attention to how I use and manage my money," says Mike Woodward, 23, of Fredericksburg, Va. "Growing up, I felt like if you have a job and contribute to a retirement plan and save here and there, you'll be OK. That was the mind-set of many people my age from seeing their parents. But now . . . I have to have a different way to do things."

13   Woodward, a 2008 bioengineering graduate of Stanford University in Palo Alto, Calif., is living with his parents and preparing to launch a non-profit this summer to train the homeless, the unemployed and non-violent offenders in construction to help rebuild New Orleans. He had planned to go to medical school, but the recession piqued his interest in the economy. "I think people are going to shift what they go after because they have to—not necessarily on their own accord. 'I can't have what I wanted, so I'm going to more or less settle,'" he says. "However, I think that sparks

creativity. We will have people who are going to rise to the occasion and look for creative solutions."

14   Although more entrepreneurs may emerge from the down economy, psychologist Bradley says there are potential emotional repercussions, particularly among younger Millennials, if the downturn lasts longer than expected and the impact is more severe. "A kid who is actually losing his house is going to be traumatized much more than a neighbor who watches this happen. It's more of a fear response, and that could lead to the Depression-era reaction in the generation down the road. They might be more survival-oriented."

15   Economic uncertainty can create greater materialism, according to research co-written by psychologist Tim Kasser of Knox College in Galesburg, Ill., and published last year in the journal Motivation and Emotion. "Most people, when they go through economic recession, may become more frugal," he says, but they "respond to moments of psychological insecurity by becoming more materialistic."

16   A smaller strand of research, he adds, "suggests that during times of insecurity and trauma, there is an opportunity for changing one's values. If they use that trauma as a way to re-evaluate their lives, to think about what's really important, there is evidence that people will care less about money and possessions than they did before."

17   Historians note that the economy became more dependent on consumption after the Depression and World War II and fueled the dictum that each succeeding generation would be financially better off than the previous one—something most experts say isn't likely for the Millennials. Lizabeth Cohen, a history professor at Harvard University, is among those with a wait-and-see attitude about whether any values change will happen.

18   But Jim Cullen, author of the 2003 book *The American Dream: A Short History of an Idea That Shaped a Nation*, says he expects long-term attitudinal changes prompted by what he calls "structural changes in the global economy." "Jobs will be less secure. Our way of life is going to become more expensive. We will be paying more for the things we've had all along," he says. "We will see recovery, but in some sense, I feel like the hard work of changing our values has barely begun. I don't think people have any idea about what they're really going to have to do."

19   But Trilli, like many others, hasn't given up on her dream: "I want to own a restaurant one day, and I still think I can." ◆

CRITICAL THINKING

1. Has the economic recession changed your social view of employment? Of success? Explain.

2. Are you a member of the Millennial generation? If so, do you think that the economic downturn will have a permanent impact on the way you view the world and your financial outlook? Why or why not? If you are a member of another generation, discuss what impact, if any, the recession has had on your worldview.

3. Jayson notes that experts feel that if the economy continues to perform poorly, the generation coming of age today and over the next few years

will have a different "value system" than the one their parents had. What is the value system they mean? How will a new value system be created, and what might it look like?

4. This essay uses many quotes from members of the Millennial generation. How does Jayson's use of quoted material support her article? Do you think her use of quotes is balanced? Is anyone missing? Explain.

5. This essay is titled "Recession Generation?" What does the title mean? How might members of this generation react to this description of their age group?

6. What are some of the positive aspects of growing up in a period of economic instability? Explain.

CRITICAL WRITING

1. *Personal Narrative:* Explore your personal value system and how it has been shaped, for better or worse, by your life experiences growing up in both an up and a down economy. Has your value system changed at all as a result of economic challenge? For example, have you personally experienced any of the things mentioned in this article? Or have you emerged largely unscathed by recession? Explain.

2. *Expository Writing:* Write an essay in which you explore the long-term social implications of a down economy. Include possible positive and negative trends in your exploration.

3. *Research and Analysis:* It is a common practice for each generation to be critical of the ones preceding and following it, and to hold their value system as the best one. How do you view the generation that came of age before you? How do you think they view your generation? If possible, speak to several people of different generations (20s, 40s, 60s) and ask them for their views. Assess differences in values in your essay.

GROUP PROJECTS

1. As a group, discuss whether each of you is optimistic or pessimistic about your financial future. What role does your current major play in this view?

2. Occupy Wall Street expanded to many cities and college campuses. Explore the history of this movement and how the ideals of the movement might be influenced by generational viewpoints. As a group, discuss how different generations may bring different expectations of economic prosperity and government responsibility.

3. The terms "generation debt" and "recession generation" have been used to describe postmillennial youth. Are these accurate titles for this generation? Do they carry any negative connotations that might influence the self-esteem of this group? Discuss these phrases as a group and explain why they are, or are not, appropriate to use.

Major Delusions
Tali Sharot[†]

Every May and June, graduating students gather together to participate in the ritual of commencement, where degrees are conferred, awards handed out, and speeches promising a bright future are shared. Most of these speeches rehash the same theme—that the graduates gathered on this special day have bright futures in front of them. In this next essay, however, Tali Sharot, a research fellow at the Wellcome Trust Centre for Neuroimaging at University College London, wonders about the appropriateness of such hopeful speeches, which may set unrealistic expectations in the hearts of new graduates. Are such speeches just too optimistic?

1   This month American college seniors will don caps and gowns. As they await receipt of their diplomas, they will absorb lessons handed to them by the accomplished men and women who deliver commencement speeches. More often than not the speakers will be outliers: rare individuals who made it against all odds. More often than not their message will be "dreams come true . . . take chances . . . if you try hard enough you will succeed."

2   "Don't know that you can't fly, and you will soar like an eagle," Earl E. Bakken, founder of the medical technology company Medtronic, told the University of Hawaii's class of 2004. "You have to trust that the dots will somehow connect in your future," Steven P. Jobs told Stanford's 2005 graduates.

3   But in an era of unemployment, financial meltdowns, political unrest and natural disasters, is this message of optimism helpful?

4   By and large, the answer is yes. Although the graduates are unlikely to be as fortunate as their commencement speakers, evidence from the science of optimism indicates that believing in their optimistic message will nonetheless be a good thing.

5   We now know that underestimating the obstacles life has in store lowers stress and anxiety, leading to better health and well-being. This is one reason optimists recover faster from illnesses and live longer. Believing a goal is attainable motivates us to get closer to our dreams. Because of the power of optimism, enhancing graduates' faith in the American dream by presenting them with rare examples as proof may be just what the doctor ordered. Their hopes may not be fully realized, but they will be more successful, healthier and happier if they hold on to positively biased expectations.

6   Surveys show that students expect to receive more job offers and higher salaries upon graduation than they wind up getting. They anticipate being married till death do them part, though they are acutely aware that statistics say there's a good chance they won't be. They underestimate their likelihood of suffering from cancer, heart

---

[†] Tali Sharot, *The New York Times*, May 14, 2011

attack and other misfortunes and overestimate their likelihood of acquiring wealth and professional success. The list goes on and on.

7   It's not just the young who embrace positive delusions. Whether you are 9 or 90, male or female, of African or European descent, you are likely to have an optimism bias. In fact, 80 percent of the world does. (Many believe optimism is unique to Americans; studies show the rest of the world is just as optimistic.)

8   In fact, the people who accurately predict the likelihood of coming events tend to be mildly depressed. The rest of us systematically fail when interpreting the crystal ball.

9   For many years, scientists were puzzled by the existence of this unshakable optimism. It did not make sense. How is it that people remain optimistic even though information challenging those predictions is abundantly available? It turns out it is not commencement speeches or self-help books that make us hopeful. Recently, with the development of non-invasive brain imaging techniques, we have gathered evidence that suggests our brains are hard-wired to be unrealistically optimistic. When we learn what the future may hold, our neurons efficiently encode unexpectedly good information, but fail to incorporate information that is unexpectedly bad.

10   That's why when we listen to Oprah Winfrey's rags-to-riches story our brain takes note and concludes that we too may become immensely rich and powerful one day; but when told the likelihood of being unemployed is almost 1 in 10 or of suffering from cancer is over 1 in 3 we take no notice.

11   Such optimistic illusions, with all of their advantages, unfortunately come at a price. Underestimating risk makes us less likely to practice safe sex, save for retirement, buy insurance or undergo medical screenings. In some cases, relatively minor biases can even lead to global disaster. Take the financial crisis of 2008. Each investor, homeowner, banker or economic regulator expected slightly better profits than were realistically warranted. On its own, each bias would not have created huge losses. Yet when combined in one market they produced a giant financial bubble that did just that.

12   As the Duke economists Manju Puri and David T. Robinson suggest, optimism is like red wine: a glass a day is good for you, but a bottle a day can be hazardous. The optimal solution then? Believe you will live a long healthy life, but go for frequent medical screenings. Aspire to write the next "Harry Potter" series, but have a safety net in place too.

13   At a time when the economic crisis is deepened by revolutions and tsunamis, cautious optimism may be the most useful message to communicate to graduates—believe you can fly, with a parachute attached, and you will soar like an eagle. ◆

CRITICAL THINKING

1. What is "optimism bias"? Explain.
2. What are the benefits of underestimating the challenges we face? Conversely, what are the pitfalls of feeling too optimistic about the future?
3. Sharot explains that almost 80 percent of the world's population is inclined toward optimism. Why would such belief be helpful to the human condition? What would the world be like if we were all realists, or even pessimists?

4. Many graduating students realize that they face a tough job market. How can the science of optimism help them deal with the current economic climate?
5. In an essay appearing earlier in this chapter, Lev Grossman notes that today's twixters have a rather sunny attitude, despite the economic downturn. Connect Grossman's observations to points Sharot makes in this essay. Why might it be crucial to the overall survival of this generation to be optimistic even in times of trouble?

CRITICAL WRITING

1. *Personal Narrative:* Think back to an experience in which you faced a personal challenge, such as a sports competition, completion of a very tough course or a difficult project, admission to a particular college, or an application for a job. How did you feel about your odds for success? What steps did you take to help improve your chances? What role, if any, do you think your attitude played in the entire situation? What was the outcome?
2. *Research and Analysis:* Look up several commencement speeches online and analyze their optimism quotient. What do the speakers say is possible? What implied promises do the speakers make? How are the speeches similar, and in what ways are they different? Explain.
3. *Creative Writing:* You have been selected to serve a speaker at this year's commencement. Write your own speech for the graduating class. What would you say and why?

GROUP PROJECTS

1. In this essay, Sharot notes that as a rule, humans are hard-wired to be optimistic. Working as a group, interview at least 20 senior students and ask them about their feelings about the future following graduation. Ask them to focus on their personal future, rather than that of the graduating class as a whole. Are students individually optimistic? Or pessimistic? Realistic? Discuss the results as a group, connecting your findings to points raised in this essay.
2. As a group, research the phenomenon of "optimism bias" and "the science of optimism" online. Then, discuss how optimism, especially among young people, can influence the future. What role will optimism play for the next generation? How might it influence the direction of government, education, science, and medicine? Explain.

Modern Scholar

Debtor's Prism
*Margaret Atwood**

Since ancient times, the notion of debt has been deeply interwoven into our culture, literature, and social structure. With the global markets in turmoil, Margaret Atwood looks at the history and meaning of being in hock. This next essay, adapted from acclaimed writer Margaret Atwood's novel *Payback*, describes the history and psychology of debt, its notable role in literature, and what we might learn from these as we face uncertain economic times.

1 Without memory, there is no debt. Put another way: Without story, there is no debt.

2   The story of debt reached a historic moment this week. An outsized bubble of interlocking debt burst, leading to the downfalls of prominent companies. Loans by and to the government, financial institutions, and consumers collided on an epic scale. Still, the idea of what we owe one another is an ancient theme, and this is just the latest chapter in a long cultural history.

3   A story is a string of actions occurring over time—one damn thing after another, as we glibly say in creative writing classes—and debt happens as a result of actions occurring over time. Therefore, any debt involves a plot line: how you got into debt, what you did, said, and thought while you were in there, and then—depending on whether the ending is to be happy or sad—how you got out of debt, or else how you got further and further into it until you became overwhelmed by it and sank from view.

4   The hidden metaphors are revealing: We get "into" debt, as if into a prison, swamp, or well, or possibly a bed; we get "out" of it, as if coming into the open air or climbing out of a hole. If we are "overwhelmed" by debt, the image is possibly that of a foundering ship, with the sea and the waves pouring inexorably in on top of us as we flail and choke. All of this sounds dramatic, with much physical activity: jumping in, leaping or clambering out, thrashing around, drowning. Metaphorically, the debt plot line is a far cry from the glum actuality, in which the debtor sits at a desk fiddling around with numbers on a screen, or shuffles past-due bills in the hope that they will go away, or paces the room wondering how he can possibly extricate himself from the fiscal molasses.

5   In our minds—as reflected in our language—debt is a mental or spiritual non-place, like the Hell described by Christopher Marlowe's Mephistopheles when

---

* Margaret Atwood, *The Wall Street Journal,* September 20, 2008

Faust asks him why he's not in Hell but right there in the same room as Faust. "Why, this is Hell, nor am I out of it," says Mephistopheles. He carries Hell around with him like a private climate: He's in it and it's in him. Substitute "debt" and you can see that, in the way we talk about it, debt is the same kind of placeless place. "Why, this is Debt, nor am I out of it," the beleaguered debtor might similarly declaim.

6   Which makes the whole idea of debt—especially massive and hopeless debt—sound brave and noble and interesting rather than merely squalid and gives it a larger-than-life tragic air. Could it be that some people get into debt because, like speeding on a motorbike, it adds an adrenalin hit to their otherwise humdrum lives? When the bailiffs are knocking at the door and the lights go off because you didn't pay the water bill and the bank's threatening to foreclose, at least you can't complain of ennui.

7   Debt can constitute one such story-of-my-life. Eric Berne's 1964 bestselling book on transactional analysis, *Games People Play,* lists five "life games"—patterns of behavior that can occupy an individual's entire lifespan, often destructively, but with hidden psychological benefits or payoffs that keep the games going. Needless to say, each game requires more than one player—some players being consciously complicit, others being unwitting dupes. "Alcoholic," "Now I've Got You, You Son of a Bitch," "Kick Me," and "See What You Made Me Do" are Berne's titles for four of these life games. The fifth one is called "Debtor."

8   Mr. Berne says, "'Debtor' is more than a game. In America it tends to become a script, a plan for a whole lifetime, just as it does in some of the jungles of Africa and New Guinea. There the relatives of a young man buy him a bride at an enormous price, putting him in their debt for years to come." In North America, says Mr. Berne, "the big expense is not a bride but a house, and the enormous debt is a mortgage; the role of the relatives is taken by the bank. Paying off the mortgage gives the individual a purpose in life." Indeed, I can remember a time from my own childhood—was it the 1940s?—when it was considered cute to have a framed petit-point embroidered motto hanging in the bathroom that said "God Bless Our Mortgaged Home." During this period, people would have mortgage-burning parties at which they would, in fact, burn the mortgage papers in the barbecue or fireplace once they'd paid the mortgage off.

9   I pause here to add that "mortgage" means "dead pledge"—"mort" from the French for "dead," "gage" for "pledge," like the part in medieval romances where the knight throws down his glove, thus challenging another knight to a duel—the glove or gage being the pledge that the guy will actually show up on time to get his head bashed in, and the accepting of the gage being a reciprocal pledge. Which should make you think twice about engagement rings, since they too are a gage or pledge—what actually are you pledging when you present such a ring to your one true love?

10   So "paying off the mortgage" is what happens when people play the life game of "Debtor" nicely. But what if they don't play nicely? Not-nice play involves cheating, as every child knows. But it's not always true that cheaters never prosper, and every child knows that, too: Sometimes they do prosper, in the playground and elsewhere.

11   Debt can have another kind of entertainment value when it becomes a motif, not in a real-life plot line, but in a fictional one. How this kind of debt plot unfolds and changes over time, as social conditions, class relations, financial climates, and literary fashions change; but debts themselves have been present in stories for a very long time.

12   I'd like to begin by interrogating a familiar character—a character so familiar that he's made it out of the fiction in which he stars into another kind of stardom: that of television and billboard advertising. That character is Ebenezer Scrooge, from Charles Dickens's *A Christmas Carol*. Even if you haven't read the book or seen the play or the several movies made about Scrooge, you'd probably recognize him if you met him on the street. "Give like Santa, save like Scrooge," as some ads have said, and we then have a lovable, twinkly old codger telling us about some great penny-pinching bargain or other.

13   But, wanting to have it both ways, the ads conflate two Scrooges: the reformed Scrooge, who signals the advent of grace and the salvation of his soul by going on a giant spend-o-rama, and the Scrooge we see at the beginning of the book—a miser so extreme that he doesn't even spend any of his money-hoard on himself—not on nice food, or heat, or warm outfits—not anything. Scrooge's abstemious gruel-eating lifestyle might have been applauded as a sign of godliness back in the days of the early bread-and-water saintly ascetic hermits, who lived in caves and said Bah! Humbug! to all comers. But this is not the case with mean old Ebenezer Scrooge, whose first name chimes with "squeezer" as well as with "geezer," whose last name is a combination of "screw" and "gouge," and whose author disapproves mightily of his ways:

14   Oh! But he was a tight-fisted hand at the grindstone, Scrooge! A squeezing, wrenching, grasping, scraping, clutching, covetous old sinner! Hard and sharp as flint, from which no steel had ever struck out generous fire; secret and self-contained and solitary as an oyster. The cold within him froze his old features, nipped his pointed nose, shrivelled his cheek, stiffened his gait; made his eyes red, his thin lips blue; and spoke out shrewdly in his grating voice.

15   That Scrooge has—consciously or not—made a pact with the Devil is signaled to us more than once. Not only is he credited with the evil eye, that traditional mark of sold-to-the-Devil witches, but he's also accused of worshipping a golden idol; and when, during his night of visions, he skips forward to his own future, the only comment he can overhear being made about himself in his former place of business is " . . . old Scratch has got his own at last, hey?" Old Scratch is of course the Devil, and if Scrooge himself isn't fully aware of the pact he's made, his author most certainly is.

16   But it's an odd pact. The Devil may get Scrooge, but Scrooge himself gets nothing except money, and he does nothing with it except sit on it. Scrooge has some interesting literary ancestors. Pact-makers with the Devil didn't start out as misers—quite the reverse. Christopher Marlowe's late-16th-century Doctor Faustus sells his body and soul to Mephistopheles with a loan document signed in blood, collection due in 24 years, but he doesn't do it cheaply. He has a magnificent wish list, which contains just about everything you can read about today in luxury magazines for gentlemen. Faust wants to travel; he wants to be very, very rich; he wants

knowledge; he wants power; he wants to get back at his enemies; and he wants sex with a facsimile of Helen of Troy.

17   Marlowe's Doctor Faustus isn't mean and grasping and covetous. He doesn't want money just to have it—he wants to dispense it on his other wishes. He's got friends who enjoy his company, he's a big spender who shares his wealth around, he likes food and drink and fun parties and playing practical jokes, and he uses his power to rescue at least one human being from death. In fact, he behaves like Scrooge, after Scrooge has been redeemed—the Scrooge who buys huge turkeys, giggles a lot, plays practical jokes on his poor clerk, Bob Cratchit, goes to his nephew's Christmas party and joins in the parlor games, and saves Bob's crippled offspring, Tiny Tim, leading us to wonder if Scrooge didn't inherit a latent gene for bon-vivantery from his distant ancestor Doctor Faustus—a gene that was just waiting to be epigenetically switched on.

18   The ghost of Scrooge's former business partner, Marley, displaying the principles of post-mortem-heart weighing worthy of the Ancient Egyptians and also of medieval Christianity, has to pay after death for Marley's sins during life. None of these sins involved a dalliance with Helen of Troy; all of them came from the relentless business practices typical both of Scrooge and of unbridled 19th-century capitalism. Marley totes a long chain made of "cash-boxes, keys, padlocks, ledgers, deeds, and heavy purses wrought in steel." He is fettered, he tells Scrooge, by the chain he forged in life—yet another example of the imagery of bondage and slavery so often associated with debt, except that now the chain is worn by the creditor. Indulging in grinding, usurious financial practices is a spiritual sin as well as a material one, for it requires a cold indifference to the needs and sufferings of others and imprisons the sinner within himself.

19   Scrooge is set free from his own heavy chain of cash boxes at the end of the book, when, instead of sitting on his pile of money, he begins to spend it. True, he spends it on others, thus displaying that most treasured of Dickensian body parts, an open heart; but the main point is that he does spend it. The saintly thing in earlier times would have been for him to have given the whole packet away, donned sackcloth, and taken up the begging bowl. But Dickens has nothing against Scrooge's being rich: in fact, there are quite a few delightful rich men in his work, beginning with Mr. Pickwick. It's not whether you have it; it's not even how you get it, exactly: the post-ghost Scrooge, for instance, doesn't give up his business, though whether it remained in part a moneylending business we aren't told. No, it's what you do with your riches that really counts.

20   Scrooge's big sin was to freeze his money; for money, as all students of it recognize, is of use only when it's moving, since it derives its value entirely from whatever it can translate itself into. Thus the Scrooges of this world who refuse to change their money into anything else are gumming up the works: currency is called "currency" because it must flow. Scrooge's happy ending is therefore entirely in keeping with the cherished core beliefs of capitalism. His life pattern is worthy of Andrew Carnegie—make a bundle by squeezing and grinding, then go in for philanthropy. We love him in part because, true to the laws of wish-fulfillment, which always involve a free lunch or a get-out-of-jail-free card, he embodies both sides of the equation—the greedy getting and the gleeful spending—and comes out of it just fine.

21   But we don't have enough cash. Or so we keep telling ourselves. And that's why you lied to the charity worker at your door and said, "I gave at the office." You want it both ways. Just like Scrooge.

22   I began by talking about debt as a story-of-my-life plot line, which is the approach Eric Berne takes in describing the variants of the life game of "Debtor."

23   But debt also exists as a real game—an old English parlor game. In fact, it's one of the games witnessed by the invisible Scrooge at his nephew's Christmas party. By no accident on the part of Dickens—for everything Scrooge is shown by the spirits must have an application to his own wicked life—this game is "Forfeits."

24   "Forfeits" has many variants, but here are the rules for perhaps the oldest and most complete form of it that we know about. The players sit in a circle, and one of them is selected to be the judge. Each player—including the judge—contributes a personal article. Behind the judge's back, one of these articles is selected and held up. The following verse is recited:

25   Heavy, heavy hangs over thy head.

26   What shall I do to redeem thee?

27   The judge—not knowing whose article it is—names some stunt or other that the owner of the article then has to perform. Much merriment is had at the absurdities that follow.

28   There's nothing we human beings can imagine, including debt, that can't be turned into a game—something done for entertainment. And, in reverse, there are no games, however frivolous, that cannot also be played very seriously and sometimes very unpleasantly. You'll know this yourself if you've ever played social bridge with a gang of white-haired, ruthless ace-trumpers or watched any news items about cheerleaders' mothers trying to assassinate their daughters' rivals. Halfway between tiddlywinks and the Battle of Waterloo—between kids' games and war games—fall hockey and football and their ilk, in which the fans shouting "Kill!" are only partly joking. But when the play turns nasty in dead earnest, the game becomes what Eric Berne calls a "hard game." In hard games the stakes are high, the play is dirty, and the outcome may well be a puddle of gore on the floor. ◆

ANALYSIS AND DISCUSSION

1. Is philanthropy an important part of life? Do you give to charity? Explain which charities you would give to if you had the funds.

2. Describe the organization of Atwood's essay. It has been referred to as a "meditation." Would you agree? Explain.

3. Try to calculate how much debt you will owe in 5 to 10 years. What plan of action would you need in order to pay down this debt?

4. Atwood asserts, "But it's not always true that cheaters never prosper, and every child knows that, too: Sometimes they do prosper, in the playground and elsewhere." From personal experience, have you known cheaters to prosper? Explain.

5. "Scrooge's happy ending is therefore entirely in keeping with the cherished core beliefs of capitalism." What are the core beliefs of capitalism?

6. As a class or in large subgroups, play the game Forfeits. Review Atwood's article for instructions on how to play, or search online for a description of the game. Learn more about the game online, what it might have meant to Victorians, and what we might learn from it today.

RESEARCH AND WRITING

1. In this essay, Atwood analyzes how the concept of moneylending or debt plays out in *A Christmas Carol* by Dickens and in *Doctor Faustus* by Christopher Marlowe. For this writing assignment, find a work of literature with debt, moneylending, or business dealings as one of its themes. After reading the novel, poem, or play, analyze how the work describes these concepts and how they alter the characters' lives. (Some works to consider: *The Merchant of Venice*, by William Shakespeare; *Middlemarch,* by George Eliot; *Robinson Crusoe*, by Daniel Defoe; Geoffrey Chaucer's *Shipman's Tale*; and "The Debt," by Paul Laurence Dunbar.)
2. The title of this article is "Debtor's Prism," which is a play on "debtor's prison." Learn what the debtor's prison was used for throughout history, and then explore whether a modern form of the debtor's prison exists for yours and future generations.
3. Atwood suggests that her readers should "think twice about engagement rings, since they too are a gage or pledge—what actually are you pledging when you present such a ring to your one true love?" Review what Atwood means by "gage" or "pledge" when it comes to debt, and discuss whether marriage is also a form of debt, and if one should think twice about presenting an engagement ring to another based on Atwood's analogy.

Perspectives: Who Pays for Debt?

Mike Keefe/PoliticalCartoons.com

THINKING CRITICALLY

1. What issue does this cartoon raise? Explain.
2. What does the woman in the picture mean? To whom is she speaking?
3. Would this cartoon be understandable, or funny, if it appeared 20 years ago? Thirty years ago? Why or why not?

 **VIEWPOINTS**

▶ **Twentysomething: Be Responsible, Go Back Home After College**
Ryan Healy*

▶ **The Responsible Child?**
Florinda Vasquez

College grads are spreading their wings—only to fly right back home. "Failure to Launch" no longer carries the stigma it once did. In fact, according to the 2007 U.S. Census, 55 percent of men and 48 percent of women ages 18 to 24 live with their parents. The next two essays, which first appeared as blog entries, discuss different views of the "boomerang kid" phenomenon. On the one hand, moving back home makes good financial sense, if you can tolerate returning to the same place where curfews were once imposed and you have to mind your manners. On the other, parents may resent this intrusion on their newly gained freedom. Having an adult child at home is very different than housing a teenager, and some parents resent the presumption that their homes are hotels to crash in. As more and more kids return home, it is clear that some thoughtful discussion is needed on both sides.

 ## Twentysomething: Be Responsible, Go Back Home After College
Ryan Healy

1 According to Monster.com, 60 percent of college graduates move home with mom and dad after graduation and the trend is on the rise. The statistic holds true with my friends from the class of 2006. More than half moved back to the suburbs to start adult life, much the same way they ended high school life—with their parents. A lot of people say generation Y needs to grow up and take some personal responsibility and that we have been coddled by our helicopter parents.

2 But when you look closely, it is glaringly apparent that moving back in with parents is one of the most responsible things a new college grad can do. By sucking it up at home for a year or two, young people give themselves the opportunity to take

> *When you look closely, it is glaringly apparent that moving back in with parents is one of the most responsible things a new college grad can do. By sucking it up at home for a year or two, young people give themselves the opportunity to take control.*

* Ryan Healy, Employee Evolution blog [www.employeerevolution.com], September 4, 2007. Florinda Vasquez, The 3 R's: Reading, 'Riting, and Randomness blog [www.3rsblog.com], September 6, 2007

control of their career, take control of their finances and transition from the care-free college fantasy world to the real-world of work, marriage, kids, mortgages and car payments.

Take Control of Your Career

3 To live comfortably in a big city like New York, students are forced to take a high-paying, but less than satisfying job. Often, top graduates end up working for the best-paying investment bank or law firm. I'm sure you could find a small minority of conservative students who had dreams of becoming an I-banker since middle school, but for the most part, these jobs are going to the top tier students who are trying to make a quick buck before they retire at 30 (or so they say).

4   By moving home after graduation, you have little or no rent, which allows for more freedom when searching for a job. There is no need to sell out to an investment bank if your real goal is to work with underprivileged children. Depending on where your parents are located, you are probably missing out on the big city night life and social scene, but you have lots of opportunities to find the perfect job, regardless of pay. If ditching the social scene for career sake doesn't demonstrate responsibility and independence, I don't know what does.

Take Control of Your Finances

5 Real wages today are lower than they were for the past two generations of workers. Couple that fact with today's insane housing costs and an increase in contract workers not receiving benefits, just getting by on forty or fifty thousand a year in a major city is nearly impossible. Attempting to save any reasonable amount of money the first few years is a joke.

6   However, moving home with Mom and Dad will immediately save you about $700 a month in housing costs. At least there is some extra cash flow. In two years, you can save up enough to move out on your own without worrying about going into credit card debt for basic necessities, like fixing your car or buying groceries.

Take an Appropriate Adjustment Period between College and the Real World

7 People really do struggle adjusting from college to the real world. A good friend of mine just fulfilled her life-long dream of moving to New York. She still loves the city, but she is overwhelmed and doesn't exactly like her day job. Sure, many people go through this tough transition period, and chances are she will eventually enjoy it, but the transition from child to adult is different and oftentimes more difficult for today's youth.

8   "This period is not a transition, but an actual life stage," according to Jeffrey Arnett, associate professor at University of Missouri and author of *Emerging Adulthood: A Theory of Development from the Late Teens through Early Twenties*. Arnett describes the period between college and adulthood as "a self-focused stage where people have the freedom to focus on their own development." Notice he calls this period a stage in development and not just a transition between two stages.

9   So why do we still try to go from adolescent to adult in a matter of weeks or months? Moving home for awhile enables an appropriate and productive transition. Rather than focus on rent, bills and kids, emerging adults living at home with their parents have the ability to focus on the most important aspects of emerging adult life: figuring out who they are and what career is right for them.

The "Responsible" Child?
Florinda Vasquez

1   I know times have changed, and it's a lot harder for young adults to get started on their "real" lives these days. The late-night phone calls and long-distance online counseling of my son the insomniac—who actually does seem to be making a decent transition to the post-college, living-on-his-own, working-adult world—have reminded me of this lately. Even so, I have some major disagreements with this post blogger Ryan Healy, suggesting that it's a "responsible" decision to move back home after college.

2   I sent the link to my son for his take and to help gauge my own reaction. This is a snippet of our discussion via IM:

> **me:** Don't read this unless you have a few minutes, but speaking as a parent, I'm glad you're "irresponsible"
> **C:** only took a minute to read
>   the points they make are kind of valid, but you could make the same argument for staying in the same city you went to school at
> **me:** or living at home while in college, and THEN moving out
> **C:** yeah
>   but you need to have experience living on your own
> **me:** and once you have it, why move back home if you don't really have to? and where's "home" if your parents live in different places?
> **C:** there is a financial benefit
>   but that's about it
> **me:** I can see that, but yeah. that's about it . . . especially if you've had that taste of being on your own already
> **C:** yeah
> **me:** it's hard on EVERYONE to go back
> **C:** yeah, I know
>   in a vacuum it doesn't look bad

3   I guess it's hard to argue the benefits for a recent graduate, especially if everything reverts to pre-college status and parents are picking up the tab for everything. And if the grad takes advantage of that—in the "good" way—by working hard and saving up that money during this time period, he or she will be much better positioned financially for a more desirable lifestyle when the time to move out finally arrives. A friend of mine actually did this; she stayed in her parents' home until she'd

been out of college about eight years, but when she did move out, it was into a house she bought on her own.

4 I actually think that being able to go away to college, living on or near campus, is a great opportunity. It's a taste of independence—being responsible for your own time management, for one thing, along with making lots of other choices—but it's also still sheltered, since most college kids aren't quite as "on their own" as they like to think they are. Directly and indirectly, most are still getting a substantial amount of support from parents during this time. But having had that taste of independence can mean giving it up when returning to the family home—and as a parent, I think to some extent that's entirely appropriate. Unless the recent grad is paying rent and other housing expenses to the parent, and doing his or her own laundry, errands, cleaning, etc.—that is, approximating living on one's own as closely as possible under the circumstances—I'm inclined to think "my house, my rules" applies, especially if there's also some amount of "my support" involved. And I'd suggest that rather than going away and coming back, one might ultimately arrive at the same place by attending a local university and living at home, preparing for a transition to independence after graduation. (I did this, and believe me, everyone was ready to move on after five years of it.)

5 For generations, it's been traditional for young adults to have to work their way up in the world; it's a formative experience intellectually, emotionally, and materially. Maybe I'm a traditionalist, but I see a lot of value to this. Depending on where you live and what you do, though, it can be harder to get on that footing and take longer to move forward—and I think that going back to the family home signals a reluctance to take on those challenges, as well as a sense of entitlement to a particular lifestyle that these young adults grew up with and don't want to sacrifice.

6 I gather that a lot of parents don't want them to have to sacrifice it, either. My take on the job of parenthood is that the goal is raising functional adults, and thereby ultimately working yourself out of a job—but I know that not all parents agree, and some have a hard time letting go appropriately. I'm not talking about kicking the baby birds out of the nest, mind you, and I don't think any parent wants to become truly unnecessary to his or her child, but I think we do more for them by helping them prepare to fly. (Teaching someone to fish vs. giving them a fish, you know . . .) I'm not sure letting them back into the nest really does help. I tend to think that moving back home after college has a lot more advantages for the child than the parents—but if the parents aren't ready to let go, I guess they get some benefit, too. If the parent is encouraging the child to return home, I wonder if that speaks more to the parent's needs than what's best for the young-adult child in the long run.

7 As I say, I'm probably a traditionalist, and my viewpoint is in line with my own experiences. I think those experiences were a good basis on which to raise my own child, though, and am glad to see him following that more traditional route; I hope that his upbringing has prepared him to make a good go of it. And considering that he was pretty anxious to get started on his own and not head back to stay with either of his parents after graduation, I guess he might be a bit of a traditionalist himself. ◆

CRITICAL THINKING

1. Florinda Vasquez observes of college graduates returning home, "it's hard on EVERYONE to go back." Describe not only how the college graduate is affected by moving back home, but also how others in the family are affected.

2. Both Healy and Vasquez use the word "transition" to describe the time between graduating from college and becoming independent; however, Healy also tries to explain this as a "stage." What is Healy's purpose in calling the phenomenon "a stage"? In your opinion, is this phenomenon simply a transitional period, or a stage of life, or both? Explain.

3. Vasquez shares that a friend of hers stayed in her parents' home until she'd been out of college about 8 years. If adult children do move back home, what is the appropriate time span to live with one's parents? Eight years? Something else? How do you determine the appropriate length of time?

4. Healy reports, "A lot of people say generation Y needs to grow up and take some personal responsibility and that we have been coddled by our helicopter parents." What are "helicopter parents" and how might they have contributed to the trend of kids coming home after graduation?

5. Vasquez asserts that the purpose of being a parent is "raising functional adults, and thereby ultimately working yourself out of a job." What else does she say about parenthood? Do you agree or disagree? What is the purpose of being a parent?

6. If an adult child does need to rely on his/her parents through the transition to full independence, which of the following paths, as Vasquez points out, is the best route to take: going away and coming back or attending a local university and living at home? In your opinion, which is the best solution and why?

CRITICAL WRITING

1. *Persuasive Writing:* Write your own blog entry. Convince other college students to either move back home after college or take off on their own. Provide concrete reasons to support your position.

2. *Technical Writing:* Write a contract agreement between a college graduate returning home and his or her parents. Consider in your contract issues such as rent, chores, grocery and telephone expenses, visitors, curfews, and other responsibilities in the home. In other words, what are the expectations of the child and what are the expectations of the parents?

3. *Analytical Writing:* Analyze the passage from Healy's article, "People really do struggle adjusting from college to the real world. A good friend of mine just fulfilled her life-long dream of moving to New York. She still loves the city, but she is overwhelmed and doesn't exactly like her day job. Sure, many people go through this tough transition period, and chances are she will eventually enjoy it, but the transition from child

to adult is different and oftentimes more difficult for today's youth." Is Healy's example of his friend effective enough to get his point across? What exactly is the "struggle" his friend is going through? Analyze the specific words Healy uses to explain himself. Follow your analysis with your own opinion of whether "the transition from child to adult is different and oftentimes more difficult for today's youth."

GROUP PROJECTS

1. With your group, make up a set of 10 survey questions asking other college students whether they plan on moving back home after school, and what that may entail, or if they plan on making it on their own, and what that may entail. Give your survey to 20 peers, and share your data with the rest of the class.

2. Crunch the numbers: As a group, agree on a city to live in after graduation. Research how much it will cost to live in that city on a monthly basis. To get you started, decide on a typical living establishment for twentysomethings, then look up the average amount of rent paid; in addition, find out how much is needed for utilities, groceries, transportation, insurance, entertainment, and other necessities. If first and last month's rent and a security deposit are needed to rent an apartment, include that in your discussion.

That's Entertainment?

Amusing Ourselves

In just a generation, our sources for entertainment have drastically changed. Cell phones, e-books, video games, the Internet, and cable TV either did not exist or were still nascent technologies only a generation ago. Today, young children read e-books, ask their parents to download video game apps to play on cell phones, and cannot imagine a world in which you can't "Google" for information. More than ever, we live in a media-drenched world. Critics warn that we make the wrong people "celebrities" as we glorify bad behavior, endorse violence-laden video games and music with our pocketbooks, and dismiss harmful stereotypes as harmless amusement. This chapter questions some of the ways we entertain ourselves in a world where anyone can be famous—if they create a sex video that rocks the Internet.

Just over 40 years ago, artist Andy Warhol commented, "In the future, everyone will be world-famous for fifteen minutes." With the advent of reality television, YouTube, MySpace, and Facebook, it would appear that the future is now. Warhol recognized that any person could be famous if he or she leveraged the media and did something of interest, however fleeting, for the masses. But while Warhol may have implied that everyone may have a moment of glory, he recognized the disposable nature of celebrity.

Although there are legitimate celebrities who have earned our respect through talent, many more maintain their notoriety not for their achievements but for making poor judgments in their personal lives. Celebrity antics even appear on the front pages of major metropolitan newspapers, rather than on the gossip pages in the entertainment section.

The first three essays in this chapter explore our expectations of celebrity, and the impact our obsession has on our culture overall. First, author Joseph Epstein, provides a topical overview in "The Culture of Celebrity." His essay is followed by an editorial—"Death to Film Critics! Hail to the CelebCult!"—from acclaimed film critic Roger Ebert, in which Ebert wonders what happens when we make icons out of people known only for their foolishness. The review of the construction of celebrity in our society continues with an essay by Rebecca Traister, "Return of the Brainless Hussies." Traister describes how pop culture seems to glorify women who make foolish choices, to the point that some young women may think that in order to be popular and liked, they may also need to play down their intelligence.

The next two essays explore the darker side of entertainment. In this chapter's Modern Scholar essay, "The Role of Violent Video Game Content in Adolescent Development: Boys' Perspectives," psychiatrists Cheryl Olsen, Lawrence Kutner, and Dorothy Warner discuss how video games, embraced by young minds as harmless amusement, can warp minds and make players insensitive to violence. Continuing this investigation into the influence of media on behavior, Luke Bobo describes the troubling trend of exploiting women in rap music, both in the lyrics and on the screen in "Rap Artists' Use of Women."

Although e-books may be replacing paper tomes gathering dust on bookshelves, it appears that reading itself is alive and well, as two highly popular book series featuring young women have been made into equally successful movies. Noah Berlatsky writes about how many critics and "grown ups" prefer one character to another. In

"'Twilight' vs. 'Hunger Games,'" Berlatsky wonders what differences exist between the two heroines that make adults so clearly prefer one character over another.

Preceding the Viewpoints section is a piece by Dana Vachon on the popularity of the reality program *Jersey Shore*. Vachon explains in "Poof!" that the popularity of *Jersey Shore* is connected to more than our mere voyeuristic desire to watch members of the third state in the Union behave badly. Rather, the program reflects the financial status of society, and how we view ourselves and our friends in a time of economic recession.

This chapter's Viewpoints section explores the role of reality TV in our culture. Why do we love reality TV? Is it a guilty pleasure? Are some voyeuristic programs preying on young people who just want to be famous? Do we build people up merely to make fun of them on the air? Are such programs ethical? On the one hand, there may be something sordid about watching people air their dirty laundry in public. On the other, reality program participants willingly exchange their privacy for time in front of the camera. And some people, as in the case of the final segment in this section, sell their rights to live and die on camera.

The Culture of Celebrity
*Joseph Epstein**

What do Paris Hilton, Nicole Richie, and Tara Reid all have in common? In this next essay, author Joseph Epstein explores the distinctions between fame and celebrity, demonstrating that they are not mutually inclusive. The American pop-culture engine places the desire for celebrity at the forefront. We want to know every nuance of their lives, especially their embarrassments, mistakes, and failures. We wish we could be like them, while making fun of them. Many celebrities are known only for being known, rather than for their achievements. As Epstein explains, we now reserve our praise and attention for famous airheads.

1   Celebrity at this moment in America is epidemic, and it's spreading fast, sometimes seeming as if nearly everyone has got it. Television provides celebrity dance contests, celebrities take part in reality shows, perfumes carry the names not merely of designers but of actors and singers. Without celebrities, whole sections of *The New York Times* and the *Washington Post* would have to close down. So pervasive has celebrity become in contemporary American life that one now begins to hear a good deal about a phenomenon known as the Culture of Celebrity.

2   The word "culture" no longer, I suspect, stands in most people's minds for whole congeries of institutions, relations, kinship patterns, linguistic forms, and the rest for which the early anthropologists meant it to stand. Words, unlike disciplined soldiers, refuse to remain in place and take orders. They insist on being unruly, and slither and slide around, picking up all sorts of slippery and even goofy meanings.

---

* Joseph Epstein, *The Weekly Standard,* October 17, 2005

An icon, as we shall see, doesn't stay a small picture of a religious personage but usually turns out nowadays to be someone with spectacular grosses. "The language," as Flaubert once protested in his attempt to tell his mistress Louise Colet how much he loved her, "is inept."

3   Today, when people glibly refer to "the corporate culture," "the culture of poverty," "the culture of journalism," "the culture of the intelligence community"—and "community" has, of course, itself become another of those hopelessly baggy-pants words, so that one hears talk even of "the homeless community"—what I think is meant by "culture" is the general emotional atmosphere and institutional character surrounding the word to which "culture" is attached. Thus, corporate culture is thought to breed selfishness practiced at the Machiavellian level; the culture of poverty, hopelessness and despair; the culture of journalism, a taste for the sensational combined with a short attention span; the culture of the intelligence community, covering-one's-own-behind viperishness; and so on. "*Culture*" used in this way is also brought in to explain unpleasant or at least dreary behavior. "The culture of NASA has to be changed," is a sample of its current usage. The comedian Flip Wilson, after saying something outrageous, would revert to the refrain line, "The debbil made me do it." So, today, when admitting to unethical or otherwise wretched behavior, people often say, "The culture made me do it."

4   As for "celebrity," the standard definition is no longer the dictionary one but rather closer to the one that Daniel Boorstin gave in his book *The Image: Or What Happened to the American Dream:* "The celebrity," Boorstin wrote, "is a person who is well-known for his well-knownness," which is improved in its frequently misquoted form as "a celebrity is someone famous for being famous." The other standard quotation on this subject is Andy Warhol's "In the future, everyone will be world-famous for fifteen minutes," which also frequently turns up in an improved misquotation as "everyone will have his fifteen minutes of fame."

5   But to say that a celebrity is someone well-known for being well-known, though clever enough, doesn't quite cover it. Not that there is a shortage of such people who seem to be known only for their well-knownness. What do a couple named Sid and Mercedes Bass do, except appear in bold-face in *The New York Times* "Sunday Styles" section and other such venues (as we now call them) of equally shimmering insignificance, often standing next to Ahmet and Mica Ertegun, also well-known for being well-known? Many moons ago, journalists used to refer to royalty as "face cards"; today celebrities are perhaps best thought of as bold faces, for as such do their names often appear in the press (and in a *New York Times* column with that very name, "Bold Face").

6   The distinction between celebrity and fame is one most dictionaries tend to fudge. I suspect everyone has, or prefers to make, his own. The one I like derives not from Aristotle, who didn't have to trouble with celebrities, but from the career of Ted Williams. A sportswriter once said that he, Williams, wished to be famous but had no interest in being a celebrity. What Ted Williams wanted to be famous for was his hitting. He wanted everyone who cared about baseball to know that he was— as he believed and may well have been—the greatest pure hitter who ever lived. What he didn't want to do was to take on any of the effort off the baseball field involved in making this known. As an active player, Williams gave no interviews, signed no

baseballs or photographs, chose not to be obliging in any way to journalists or fans. A rebarbative character, not to mention often a slightly menacing s.o.b., Williams, if you had asked him, would have said that it was enough that he was the last man to hit .400; he did it on the field, and therefore didn't have to sell himself off the field. As for his duty to his fans, he didn't see that he had any.

7   Whether Ted Williams was right or wrong to feel as he did is of less interest than the distinction his example provides, which suggests that fame is something one earns—through talent or achievement of one kind or another—while celebrity is something one cultivates or, possibly, has thrust upon one. The two are not, of course, entirely exclusive. One can be immensely talented and full of achievement and yet wish to broadcast one's fame further through the careful cultivation of celebrity; and one can have the thinnest of achievements and be talentless and yet be made to seem otherwise through the mechanics and dynamics of celebrity creation, in our day a whole mini (or maybe not so mini) industry of its own.

> *One can become a celebrity with scarcely any pretense to talent or overachievement whatsoever. Much modern celebrity seems the result of careful promotion or great good luck or something besides talent and achievement.*

8   Or, another possibility, one can become a celebrity with scarcely any pretense to talent or achievement whatsoever. Much modern celebrity seems the result of careful promotion or great good luck or something besides talent and achievement: Mr. Donald Trump, Ms. Paris Hilton, Mr. Regis Philbin, take a bow. The ultimate celebrity of our time may have been John F. Kennedy Jr., notable only for being his parents' very handsome son—both his birth and good looks factors beyond his control—and, alas, known for nothing else whatsoever now, except for the sad, dying-young-Adonis end to his life.

9   Fame, then, at least as I prefer to think of it, is based on true achievement; celebrity on the broadcasting of that achievement, or the inventing of something that, if not scrutinized too closely, might pass for achievement. Celebrity suggests ephemerality, while fame has a chance of lasting, a shot at reaching the happy shores of posterity.

10   Oliver Goldsmith, in his poem "The Deserted Village," refers to "good fame," which implies that there is also a bad or false fame. Bad fame is sometimes thought to be fame in the present, or fame on earth, while good fame is that bestowed by posterity—those happy shores again. (Which doesn't eliminate the desire of most of us, at least nowadays, to have our fame here and hereafter, too.) Not false but wretched fame is covered by the word "infamy"—"Infamy, infamy, infamy," remarked the English wit Frank Muir, "they all have it in for me"—while the lower, or pejorative, order of celebrity is covered by the word "notoriety," also frequently misused to mean noteworthiness.

11   Leo Braudy's magnificent book on the history of fame, *The Frenzy of Renown*, illustrates how the means of broadcasting fame have changed over the centuries: from having one's head engraved on coins, to purchasing statuary of oneself, to (for the really high rollers—Alexander the Great, the Caesar boys) naming cities or even months after oneself, to commissioning painted portraits, to writing books or having

books written about one, and so on into our day of the publicity or press agent, the media blitz, the public relations expert, and the egomaniacal blogger. One of the most successful of public-relations experts, Ben Sonnenberg Sr., used to say that he saw it as his job to construct very high pedestals for very small men.

12   Which leads one to a very proper suspicion of celebrity. As George Orwell said about saints, so it seems only sensible to say about celebrities: They should all be judged guilty until proven innocent. Guilty of what, precisely? I'd say of the fraudulence (however minor) of inflating their brilliance, accomplishments, worth, of passing themselves off as something they aren't, or at least are not quite. If fraudulence is the crime, publicity is the means by which the caper is brought off.

13   Is the current heightened interest in the celebrated sufficient to form a culture— a culture of a kind worthy of study? The anthropologist Alfred Kroeber defined culture, in part, as embodying "values which may be formulated (overtly as mores) or felt (implicitly as in folkways) by the society carrying the culture, and which it is part of the business of the anthropologist to characterize and define." What are the values of celebrity culture? They are the values, almost exclusively, of publicity. Did they spell one's name right? What was the size and composition of the audience? Did you check the receipts? Was the timing right? Publicity is concerned solely with effects and does not investigate causes or intrinsic value too closely. For example, a few years ago a book of mine called *Snobbery: The American Version* received what I thought was a too greatly mixed review in *The New York Times Book Review*. I remarked on my disappointment to the publicity man at my publisher's, who promptly told me not to worry: It was a full-page review, on page 11, right-hand side. That, he said, "is very good real estate," which was quite as important as, perhaps more important than, the reviewer's actual words and final judgment. Better to be tepidly considered on page 11 than extravagantly praised on page 27, left-hand side. Real estate, man, it's the name of the game.

14   We must have new names, Marcel Proust presciently noted—in fashion, in medicine, in art, there must always be new names. It's a very smart remark, and the fields Proust chose seem smart, too, at least for his time. (Now there must also be new names, at a minimum, among movie stars and athletes and politicians.) Implicit in Proust's remark is the notion that if the names don't really exist, if the quality isn't there to sustain them, it doesn't matter; new names we shall have in any case. And every sophisticated society somehow, more or less implicitly, contrives to supply them.

15   I happen to think that we haven't had a major poet writing in English since perhaps the death of W. H. Auden or, to lower the bar a little, Philip Larkin. But new names are put forth nevertheless—high among them in recent years has been that of Seamus Heaney—because, after all, what kind of a time could we be living in if we didn't have a major poet? And besides there are all those prizes that, year after year, must be given out, even if so many of the recipients don't seem quite worthy of them.

16   Considered as a culture, celebrity does have its institutions. We now have an elaborate celebrity-creating machinery well in place—all those short-attention-span television shows (*Entertainment Tonight, Access Hollywood, Lifestyles of the Rich and Famous*); all those magazines (beginning with *People* and far from ending with the *National Enquirer*). We have high-priced celebrity-mongers—Barbara Walters,

Diane Sawyer, Jay Leno, David Letterman, Oprah—who not only live off others' celebrity but also, through their publicity-making power, confer it and have in time become very considerable celebrities each in his or her own right.

17   Without the taste for celebrity, they would have to close down the whole Style section of every newspaper in the country. Then there is the celebrity profile (in *Vanity Fair, Esquire, Gentlemen's Quarterly*; these are nowadays usually orchestrated by a press agent, with all touchy questions declared out-of-bounds), or the television talk-show interview with a star, which is beyond parody. Well, almost beyond: Martin Short in his parody of a talk-show host remarked to the actor Kiefer Sutherland, "You're Canadian, aren't you? What's that all about?"

18   Yet we still seem never to have enough celebrities, so we drag in so-called "It Girls" (Paris Hilton, Gisele Bunchen, other supermodels), tired television hacks (Regis Philbin, Ed McMahon), back-achingly boring but somehow sacrosanct news anchors (Walter Cronkite, Tom Brokaw). Toss in what I think of as the lower-class punditi, who await calls from various television news and chat shows to demonstrate their locked-in political views and meager expertise on major and cable stations alike: Pat Buchanan, Eleanor Clift, Mark Shields, Robert Novak, Michael Beschloss, and the rest. Ah, if only Lenny Bruce were alive today, he could do a scorchingly cruel bit about Dr. Joyce Brothers sitting by the phone wondering why Jerry Springer never calls.

19   Many of our current-day celebrities float upon "hype," which is really a publicist's gas used to pump up and set aloft something that doesn't really quite exist. Hype has also given us a new breakdown, or hierarchical categorization, of celebrities. Until twenty-five or so years ago great celebrities were called "stars," a term first used in the movies and entertainment and then taken up by sports, politics, and other fields. Stars proving a bit drab, "superstars" were called in to play, this term beginning in sports but fairly quickly branching outward. Apparently too many superstars were about, so the trope was switched from astronomy to religion, and we now have "icons." All this takes Proust's original observation a step further: the need for new names to call the new names.

20   This new ranking—stars, superstars, icons—helps us believe that we live in interesting times. One of the things celebrities do for us is suggest that in their lives they are fulfilling our fantasies. Modern celebrities, along with their fame, tend to be wealthy or, if not themselves beautiful, able to acquire beautiful lovers. Their celebrity makes them, in the view of many, worthy of worship. "So long as man remains free," Dostoyevsky writes in the Grand Inquisitor section of *The Brothers Karamazov,* "he strives for nothing so incessantly and painfully as to find someone to worship." If contemporary celebrities are the best thing on offer as living gods for us to worship, this is not good news.

21   But the worshipping of celebrities by the public tends to be thin, and not uncommonly it is nicely mixed with loathing. We also, after all, at least partially, like to see our celebrities as frail, ready at all times to crash and burn. Cary Grant once warned the then-young director Peter Bogdanovich, who was at the time living with Cybill Sheppard, to stop telling people he was in love. "And above all," Grant warned, "stop telling them you're happy." When Bogdanovich asked why, Cary

Grant answered, "Because they're not in love and they're not happy…. Just remember, Peter, people do not like beautiful people."

22   Grant's assertion is borne out by our grocery press, the *National Enquirer,* the *Star,* the *Globe,* and other variants of the English gutter press. All these tabloids could as easily travel under the generic title of the *National Schadenfreude,* for more than half the stories they contain come under the category of "See How the Mighty Have Fallen": Oh, my, I see where that bright young television sitcom star, on a drug binge again, had to be taken to a hospital in an ambulance! To think that the handsome movie star has been cheating on his wife all these years—snakes loose in the Garden of Eden, evidently! Did you note that the powerful senator's drinking has caused him to embarrass himself yet again in public? I see where that immensely successful Hollywood couple turn out to have had a child who died of anorexia! Who'd've thought?

23   How pleasing to learn that our own simpler, less moneyed, unglamorous lives are, in the end, much to be preferred to those of these beautiful, rich, and powerful people, whose vast publicity has diverted us for so long and whose fall proves even more diverting now. "As would become a lifelong habit for most of us," Thomas McGuane writes in a recent short story in the *New Yorker* called "Ice," "we longed to witness spectacular achievement and mortifying failure. Neither of these things, we were discreetly certain, would ever come to us; we would instead be granted the frictionless lives of the meek."

24   Along with trying to avoid falling victim to schadenfreude, celebrities, if they are clever, do well to regulate the amount of publicity they allow to cluster around them. And not celebrities alone. Edith Wharton, having published too many stories and essays in a great single rush in various magazines during a concentrated period, feared, as she put it, the danger of becoming "a magazine bore." Celebrities, in the same way, are in danger of becoming publicity bores, though few among them seem to sense it. Because of improperly rationed publicity, along with a substantial helping of self-importance, the comedian Bill Cosby will never again be funny. The actress Elizabeth McGovern said of Sean Penn that he "is brilliant, brilliant at being the kind of reluctant celebrity." At the level of high culture, Saul Bellow used to work this bit quite well on the literary front, making every interview (and there have been hundreds of them) feel as if given only with the greatest reluctance, if not under actual duress. Others are brilliant at regulating their publicity. Johnny Carson was very intelligent about carefully husbanding his celebrity, choosing not to come out of retirement, except at exactly the right time or when the perfect occasion presented itself. Apparently it never did. Given the universally generous obituary tributes he received, dying now looks, for him, to have been an excellent career move.

25   Careful readers will have noticed that I referred above to "the actress Elizabeth McGovern" and felt no need to write anything before or after the name Sean Penn. True celebrities need nothing said of them in apposition, fore or aft. The greatest celebrities are those who don't even require their full names mentioned: Marilyn, Johnny, Liz, Liza, Oprah, Michael (could be Jordan or Jackson—context usually clears this up fairly quickly), Kobe, Martha (Stewart, not Washington), Britney, Shaq, J-Lo, Frank (Sinatra, not Perdue), O. J., and, with the quickest recognition and shortest name of all—trumpets here, please—W.

26   One has the impression that being a celebrity was easier at any earlier time than it is now, when celebrity-creating institutions, from paparazzi to gutter-press exposés to television talk-shows, weren't as intense, as full-court press, as they are today. In the *Times Literary Supplement,* a reviewer of a biography of Margot Fonteyn noted that Miss Fonteyn "was a star from a more respectful age of celebrity, when keeping one's distance was still possible." My own candidate for the perfect celebrity in the twentieth century would be Noël Coward, a man in whom talent combined with elegance to give off the glow of glamour—and also a man who would have known how to fend off anyone wishing to investigate his private life. Today, instead of elegant celebrities, we have celebrity criminal trials: Michael Jackson, Kobe Bryant, Martha Stewart, Robert Blake, Winona Ryder, and O. J. Simpson. Schadenfreude is in the saddle again.

27   American society in the twenty-first century, received opinion has it, values only two things: money and celebrity. Whether or not this is true, vast quantities of money, we know, will buy celebrity. The very rich—John D. Rockefeller and powerful people of his era—used to pay press agents to keep their names out of the papers. But today one of the things money buys is a place at the table beside the celebrated, with the celebrities generally delighted to accommodate, there to share some of the glaring light. An example is Mort Zuckerman, who made an early fortune in real estate, has bought magazines and newspapers, and is now himself among the punditi, offering his largely unexceptional political views on the McLaughlin Group and other television chat shows. Which is merely another way of saying that, whether or not celebrity in and of itself constitutes a culture, it has certainly penetrated and permeated much of American culture generally.

28   Such has been the reach of celebrity culture in our time that it has long ago entered into academic life. The celebrity professor has been on the scene for more than three decades. As long ago as 1962, in fact, I recall hearing that Oscar Cargill, in those days a name of some note in the English Department of NYU, had tried to lure the then-young Robert Brustein, a professor of theater and the drama critic for the New Republic, away from Columbia. Cargill had said to Brustein, "I'm not going to bulls—t you, Bob, we're looking for a star, and you're it." Brustein apparently wasn't looking to be placed in a new constellation, and remained at Columbia, at least for a while longer, before moving on to Yale and thence to Harvard.

29   The academic star, who is really the academic celebrity, is now a fairly common figure in what the world, that ignorant ninny, reckons the Great American Universities. Richard Rorty is such a star; so is Henry Louis Gates Jr. (who as "Skip" even has some celebrity nickname-recognition); and, at a slightly lower level, there are Marjorie Garber, Eve Sedgwick, Stanley Fish, and perhaps now Stephen Greenblatt. Stanley Fish doesn't even seem to mind that much of his celebrity is owed to his being portrayed in novels by David Lodge as an indefatigable, grubby little operator (though Lodge claims to admire Fish's happy vulgarity). Professors Garber and Sedgwick seem to have acquired their celebrity through the outrageousness of the topics they've chosen to write about.

30   By measure of pure celebrity, Cornel West is, at the moment, the star of all academic stars, a man called by *Newsweek* "an eloquent prophet with attitude." (A bit difficult, I think, to imagine *Newsweek* or any other publication writing something

similar of Lionel Trilling, Walter Jackson Bate, Marjorie Hope Nicolson, or John Hope Franklin.) He records rap CDs and appears at benefits with movie stars and famous athletes. When the president of Harvard spoke critically to West about his work not constituting serious scholarship (as if that had anything to do with anything), it made front-page news in *The New York Times*. When West left Harvard in indignation, he was instantly welcomed by Princeton. If West had been a few kilowatts more the celebrity than he is, he might have been able to arrange for the firing of the president of the university, the way certain superstars in the National Basketball Association—Magic Johnson, Isiah Thomas, Larry Bird, Michael Jordan—were able, if it pleased them, to have their coaches fired.

31   Genuine scholarship, power of ratiocination glowing brightly in the classroom, is distinctly not what makes an academic celebrity or, if you prefer, superstar. What makes an academic celebrity, for the most part, is exposure, which is ultimately publicity. Exposure can mean appearing in the right extra-academic magazines or journals: the *New York Review of Books*, the *London Review of Books,* the *Atlantic Monthly*; *Harper's* and the *New Republic* possibly qualify, as do occasional cameo performances on the op-ed pages of *The New York Times* or the *Washington Post*. Having one's face pop up on the right television and radio programs—PBS and NPR certainly, and enough of the right kinds of appearances on C-SPAN—does not hurt. A commercially successful, much-discussed book helps hugely.

32   So does strong public alignment with the correct political causes. Harvey Mansfield, the political philosopher at Harvard, is a secondary academic celebrity of sorts, but not much in demand, owing to his conservatism; Shelby Steele, a black professor of English who has been critical of various aspects of African-American politics, was always overlooked during the days when universities knocked themselves out to get black professors. Both men have been judged politically incorrect. The underlying and overarching point is, to become an academic celebrity you have to promote yourself outside the academy, but in careful and subtle ways.

33   One might have assumed that the culture of celebrity was chiefly about show business and the outer edges of the arts, occasionally touching on the academy (there cannot be more than twenty or so academic superstars). But it has also much altered intellectual life generally. The past ten years or so have seen the advent of the "public intellectual." There are good reasons to feel uncomfortable with that adjective "public," which drains away much of the traditional meaning of intellectual. An intellectual is someone who is excited by and lives off and in ideas. An intellectual has traditionally been a person unaffiliated, which is to say someone unbeholden to anything but the power of his or her ideas. Intellectuals used to be freelance, until fifty or so years ago, when jobs in the universities and in journalism began to open up to some among them.

34   Far from being devoted to ideas for their own sake, the intellectual equivalent of art for art's sake, the so-called public intellectual of our day is usually someone who comments on what is in the news, in the hope of affecting policy, or events, or opinion in line with his own political position or orientation. He isn't necessarily an intellectual at all, but merely someone who has read a few books, mastered a style, a jargon, and a maven's authoritative tone, and has a clearly demarcated political line.

35   But even when the public intellectual isn't purely tied to the news, or isn't thoroughly political, what he or she really is, or ought to be called, is a "publicity intellectual." In Richard A. Posner's interesting book *Public Intellectuals,* intellectuals are in one place ranked by the number of media mentions they or their work have garnered, which, if I am correct about publicity being at the heart of the enterprise of the public intellectual, may be crude but is not foolish. Not knowledge, it turns out, but publicity is power.

36   The most celebrated intellectuals of our day have been those most skillful at gaining publicity for their writing and their pronouncements. Take, as a case very much in point, Susan Sontag. When Susan Sontag died at the end of last year, her obituary was front-page news in *The New York Times,* and on the inside of the paper, it ran to a full page with five photographs, most of them carefully posed—a variety, it does not seem unfair to call it, of intellectual cheesecake. Will the current prime ministers of England and France when they peg out receive equal space or pictorial coverage? Unlikely, I think. Why did Ms. Sontag, who was, let it be said, in many ways the pure type of the old intellectual—unattached to any institution, earning her living (apart from MacArthur Foundation and other grants) entirely from her ideas as she put them in writing—why did she attract the attention she did?

37   I don't believe Susan Sontag's celebrity finally had much to do with the power or cogency of her ideas. Her most noteworthy idea was not so much an idea at all but a description of a style, a kind of reverse or antistyle, that went by the name of Camp and that was gay in its impulse. Might it have been her politics? Yes, politics had a lot to do with it, even though when she expressed herself on political subjects, she frequently got things mightily askew: During the Vietnam war she said that "the white race is the cancer of human history." As late as the 1980s, much too late for anyone in the know, she called communism "fascism with a friendly face" (what do you suppose she found so friendly about it?). To cheer up the besieged people of Sarajevo, she brought them a production of Samuel Beckett's *Waiting for Godot.* She announced in the *New Yorker* that the killing of 3,000 innocent people on 9/11 was an act that America had brought on itself. As for the writing that originally brought her celebrity, she later came to apologize for *Against Interpretation,* her most influential single book. I do not know any people who claim to have derived keen pleasure from her fiction. If all this is roughly so, why, then, do you suppose that Susan Sontag was easily the single most celebrated—the greatest celebrity—intellectual of our time?

38   With the ordinary female professor's face and body, I don't think Ms. Sontag would quite have achieved the same celebrity. Her attractiveness as a young woman had a great deal to do with the extent of her celebrity; and she and her publisher took that (early) physical attractiveness all the way out. From reading Carl Rollyson and Lisa Paddock's biography *Susan Sontag: The Making of an Icon,* one gets a sense of how carefully and relentlessly she was promoted by her publisher, Roger Straus. I do not mean to say that Sontag was unintelligent, or talentless, but Straus, through having her always dramatically photographed, by sending angry letters to the editors of journals where she was ill-reviewed, by bringing out her books with the most careful accompanying orchestration, promoted this often difficult and unrewarding writer into something close to a household name with a face that was ready, so to say, to be Warholed. That Sontag spent her last years with Annie Leibowitz, herself the most

successful magazine photographer of our day, seems somehow the most natural thing in the world. Even in the realm of the intellect, celebrities are not born but made, usually very carefully made—as was, indubitably, the celebrity of Susan Sontag.

39   One of the major themes in Leo Braudy's *The Frenzy of Renown* is the fame and celebrity of artists, and above all, writers. To sketch in a few bare strokes the richly complex story Braudy tells, writers went from serving power (in Rome) to serving God (in early Christendom) to serving patrons (in the eighteenth century) to serving themselves, with a careful eye cocked toward both the contemporary public and posterity (under Romanticism), to serving mammon, to a state of interesting confusion, which is where we are today, with celebrity affecting literature in more and more significant ways.

40   Writers are supposed to be aristocrats of the spirit, not promoters, hustlers, salesmen for their own work. Securing a larger audience for their work was not thought to be their problem. "Fit audience, though few," in John Milton's phrase, was all right, so long as the few were the most artistically alert, or aesthetically fittest. Picture Lord Byron, Count Tolstoy, or Charles Baudelaire at a lectern at Barnes & Noble, C-SPAN camera turned on, flogging (wonderful word!) his own most recent books. Not possible!

41   Some superior writers have been very careful caretakers of their careers. In a letter to one of his philosophy professors at Harvard, T. S. Eliot wrote that there were two ways to achieve literary celebrity in London: One was to appear often in a variety of publications; the other to appear seldom but always to make certain to dazzle when one did. Eliot, of course, chose the latter, and it worked smashingly. But he was still counting on gaining his reputation through his actual writing. Now good work alone doesn't quite seem to make it; the publicity catapults need to be hauled into place, the walls of indifference stormed. Some writers have decided to steer shy from publicity altogether: Thomas Pynchon for one, J. D. Salinger for another (if he is actually still writing or yet considers himself a writer). But actively seeking publicity was thought for a writer, somehow, vulgar—at least it was until the last few decades.

42   Edmund Wilson, the famous American literary critic, used to answer requests with a postcard that read:

43   Edmund Wilson regrets that it is impossible for him to: Read manuscripts, Write articles or books to order, Make statements for publicity purposes, Do any kind of editorial work, Judge literary contests, Give interviews, Conduct educational courses, Deliver lectures, Give talks or make speeches, Take part in writers congresses, Answer questionnaires, Contribute or take part in symposiums or "panels" of any kind, Contribute manuscripts for sale, Donate copies of his books to Libraries, Autograph books for strangers, Allow his name to be used on letterheads, Supply personal information about himself, Supply photographs of himself, Supply opinions on literary or other subjects.

44   A fairly impressive list, I'd say. When I was young, Edmund Wilson supplied for me the model of how a literary man ought to carry himself. One of the things I personally found most impressive about his list is that everything Edmund Wilson clearly states he will not do, Joseph Epstein has now done, and more than once, and,

like the young woman in the Häagen-Dazs commercial sitting on her couch with an empty carton of ice cream, is likely to do again and again.

45   I tell myself that I do these various things in the effort to acquire more readers. After all, one of the reasons I write, apart from pleasure in working out the aesthetic problems and moral questions presented by my subjects and in my stories, is to find the best readers. I also want to sell books, to make a few shekels, to please my publisher, to continue to be published in the future in a proper way. Having a high threshold for praise, I also don't in the least mind meeting strangers who tell me that they take some delight in my writing. But, more than all this, I have now come to think that writing away quietly, producing (the hope is) good work, isn't any longer quite sufficient in a culture dominated by the boisterous spirit of celebrity. In an increasingly noisy cultural scene, with many voices and media competing for attention, one feels—perhaps incorrectly but nonetheless insistently—the need to make one's own small stir, however pathetic. So, on occasion, I have gone about tooting my own little paper horn, doing book tours, submitting to the comically pompous self-importance of interviews, and doing so many of the other things that Edmund Wilson didn't think twice about refusing to do.

46   "You're slightly famous, aren't you, Grandpa?" my then eight-year-old granddaughter once said to me. "I am slightly famous, Annabelle," I replied, "except no one quite knows who I am." This hasn't changed much over the years. But of course seeking celebrity in our culture is a mug's game, one you cannot finally hope to win. The only large, lumpy kind of big-time celebrity available, outside movie celebrity, is to be had through appearing fairly regularly on television. I had the merest inkling of this fame when I was walking along one sunny morning in downtown Baltimore, and a red Mazda convertible screeched to a halt, the driver lowered his window, pointed a long index finger at me, hesitated, and finally, the shock of recognition lighting up his face, yelled, "C-SPAN!"

47   I was recently asked, through email, to write a short piece for a high price for a volume about the city of Chicago. When I agreed to do it, the editor of the volume, who is (I take it) young, told me how very pleased she was to have someone as distinguished as I among the volume's contributors. But she did have just one request. Before making things final, she wondered if she might see a sample of my writing. More than forty years in the business, I thought, echoing the character played by Zero Mostel in *The Producers,* and I'm still wearing the celebrity equivalent of a cardboard belt.

48   "Every time I think I'm famous," Virgil Thomson said, "I have only to go out into the world." So it is, and so ought it probably to remain for writers, musicians, and visual artists who prefer to consider themselves serious. The comedian Richard Pryor once said that he would deem himself famous when people recognized him, as they recognized Bob Hope and Muhammad Ali, by his captionless caricature. That is certainly one clear criterion for celebrity. But the best criterion I've yet come across holds that you are celebrated, indeed famous, only when a crazy person imagines he is you. It's especially pleasing that the penetrating and prolific author of this remark happens to go by the name of Anonymous. ◆

CRITICAL THINKING

1. Who are your favorite celebrities, and why are they your favorites? What are they known for?
2. What is the "culture of celebrity"? Is this term an oxymoron? In what ways has the American media engine created this culture, and how is it sustained?
3. If you could be famous, what would you want to be famous for? Would you also want to be a "celebrity"? Try to be as honest and thoughtful in your answer as possible.
4. According to Epstein, what is the distinction between being famous and being a celebrity? What example does he use to illustrate his point?
5. Should movie stars pay a price for their fame, such as enduring the paparazzi and fan adoration, or should they be seen as merely practicing a profession and be able to live in privacy? Explain your answer.
6. In *The Brothers Karamazov,* Dostoevsky writes, "So long as man remains free, he strives for nothing so incessantly and painfully as to find someone to worship." Do you agree with this statement? Do you think we worship celebrities? Explain.

CRITICAL WRITING

1. *Research and Persuasive Writing:* Choose three well-known celebrities, research their backgrounds, scrutinize their accomplishments, and make a case for or against their fame or celebrity by showing that they are "with scarcely any pretense to talent or achievement whatsoever," that their career seems to be "the result of careful promotion or great good luck," or that their fame has been earned through true talent or achievement.
2. *Speech Writing:* Twenty years from now, you will receive an award for a great accomplishment in your field of study. Write the acceptance speech to go along with receiving this award. Think about what type of award you would want to be presented with and what you did to receive it.
3. *Persuasive Writing:* Agree or disagree with this statement from the article: "American society in the twenty-first century, received opinion has it, values only two things: money and celebrity." Make sure to use concrete examples and details to illustrate your point.

GROUP PROJECTS

1. As a group, review a copy each of *The New York Times* and the *Washington Post,* and count how many times celebrities are mentioned in these "highbrow" newspapers. Which celebrities make the most news, and why?
2. Epstein's article mentions many celebrity names. As a group, write down why each person mentioned is famous. If there are some people mentioned in the article that you have not heard of before, look them up online to see who they are and why they are famous.

3. Decide on two authors whom you would characterize as having turned "celebrity" after becoming famous for their literature. Read articles on the authors and watch videotapes of interviews, book signings, lectures, and so on, and analyze how, why, and when they reached celebrity status.

Death to Film Critics! Hail to the CelebCult!
Roger Ebert*

Years ago, to determine the methane and carbon-monoxide levels in underground mines, miners would use a canary to test the air. If the canary stopped singing, the miners knew to get out before they all died. Today, the expression "canary in a coal mine" is used to describe a harbinger of danger. In this next editorial, Roger Ebert compares the firing of newspaper film critics to the canary in the coal mine. He laments the loss of true objective analysis in favor of giving the masses "mindless drivel" that sells newspapers and does little to advance our society as a whole. Film critics, he explains, are told to promote the celebrity engine instead of honestly evaluating the merits of the films they review. The result is that the cult of celebrity is ruining our culture overall.

1 A newspaper film critic is like a canary in a coal mine. When one croaks, get the hell out. The lengthening toll of former film critics acts as a poster child for the self-destruction of American newspapers, which once hoped to be more like *The New York Times* and now yearn to become more like the *National Enquirer*. We used to be the town crier. Now we are the neighborhood gossip.

2 The crowning blow came this week when the once-magisterial Associated Press imposed a 500-word limit on all of its entertainment writers. The 500-word limit applies to reviews, interviews, news stories, trend pieces and "thinkers." Oh, it can be done. But with "Synecdoche, New York?"

3 Worse, the AP wants its writers on the entertainment beat to focus more on the kind of brief celebrity items its clients apparently hunger for. The AP, long considered obligatory to the task of running a North American newspaper, has been hit with some cancellations lately, and no doubt has been informed what its customers want: affairs, divorces, addiction, disease, success, failure, death watches, tirades, arrests, hissy fits, scandals, who has been "seen with" somebody, who has been "spotted with" somebody, and "top ten" lists of the above. (Celebs "seen with" desire to be seen, celebs "spotted with" do not desire to be seen.)

4 The CelebCult virus is eating our culture alive, and newspapers voluntarily expose themselves to it. It teaches shabby values to young people, festers unwholesome curiosity, violates privacy, and is indifferent to meaningful achievement. One of the TV celeb shows has announced it will cover the Obama family as "a Hollywood story." I want to smash something against a wall.

* Roger Ebert, *Chicago-Sun Times,* November 26, 2008

5   In *Toots,* a new documentary about the legendary Manhattan saloon keeper Toots Shor, there is a shot so startling I had to reverse the DVD to see it again. After dinner, Joe DiMaggio and Marilyn Monroe leave the restaurant, give their ticket to a valet, wait on the curb until their

> *The CelebCult virus is eating our culture alive, and newspapers voluntarily expose themselves to it. It teaches shabby values to young people, festers unwholesome curiosity, violates privacy, and is indifferent to meaningful achievement.*

car arrives, tip the valet and then Joe opens the car door for Marilyn, walks around, gets in, and drives them away. This was in the 1950s. Brad Pitt and Angelina Jolie have not been able to do that once in their adult lifetimes. Celebrities do not use limousines because of vanity. They use them as a protection against cannibalism.

6   As the CelebCult triumphs, major newspapers have been firing experienced film critics. They want to devote less of their space to considered prose and more to ignorant gawking. What they require doesn't need to be paid for out of their payrolls. Why does the biggest story about *Twilight* involve its *fans?* Do we need interviews with 16-year-old girls about Robert Pattinson? When was the last time *they* read a paper? Isn't the movie obviously about sexual abstinence and the teen fascination with doomy, Goth death flirtation?

7   The age of film critics has come and gone. While the big papers on the coasts always had them (Bosley Crowther at *The New York Times,* Charles Champlin at the *Los Angeles Times*), many other major dailies had rotating bylines anybody might be writing under ("Kate Cameron" at the *New York Daily News,* "Mae Tinay" at the *Chicago Tribune*—get it?). Judith Crist changed everything at the *New York Herald-Tribune* when she panned *Cleopatra* (1963) and was banned from 20th Century-Fox screenings. There was a big fuss, and suddenly every paper hungered for a "real" movie critic. The Film Generation was upon us.

8   In the coverage of new directors and the rediscovery of classic films, no paper was more influential than the weekly *Village Voice,* with such as Andrew Sarris and Jonas Mekas. Earlier this year the *Voice* fired Dennis Lim and Nathan Lee, and recently fired all the local movie critics in its national chain, to be replaced, *Variety*'s Anne Thompson reported, by syndicating their critics on the two coasts, the *Voice*'s J. Hoberman and the *L.A. Weekly*'s Scott Foundas. Serious writers, yes, but....

9   Meanwhile, the *Detroit Free-Press* has decided it needs no film critic at all. Michael Wilmington is gone from the *Chicago Tribune,* Jack Mathews and Jami Bernard from the *New York Daily News,* Kevin Thomas from the *Los Angeles Times*—and the internationally-respected film critic of the *Chicago Reader,* Jonathan Rosenbaum, has retired, accepted a buy-out, will write for his blog, or something. I still see him at all the screenings. My shining hero remains Stanley Kauffmann of the *New Republic,* as incisive and penetrating as ever at 92. I don't give him points for his age, which anyone can attain simply by living long enough, but for his criticism. Study any review and try to find a wrong or unnecessary word. There is your man for an intelligent 500-word review.

10   Why do we need critics? A good friend of mine in a very big city was once told by his editor that the critic should "reflect the taste of the readers." My friend said, "Does that mean the food critic should love McDonald's?" The editor: "Absolutely." I don't believe readers buy a newspaper to read variations on the Ed McMahon line, "You are correct, sir!" A newspaper film critic should encourage critical thinking, introduce new developments, consider the local scene, look beyond the weekend fanboy specials, be a weatherman on social trends, bring in a larger context, teach, inform, amuse, inspire, be heartened, be outraged.

11   At one time all newspapers by definition did those things on every page. Now they are lascivious gossips, covering invented beats. On *one single day* recently, I was informed that Tom and Katie's daughter Suri "won't wear pants" and shares matching designer sunglasses with her mom. No, wait, they're not matching, they're only both wearing sunglasses. Eloping to Mexico: Heidi and Spencer. Britney is feeling old. Amy is in the hospital. George called Hugh in the middle of the night to accuse him of waging a campaign to take away the title of "sexiest man alive." Pete discussed naming his son Bronx Mowgli. Ann's jaw was wired shut. Karolina's belly button is missing. Madonna and A-Rod might, or might not, spend Thanksgiving together. Some of Valentino's makeup rubbed off on Sarah Jessica. Miley and Justin went out to lunch. Justin and Jessica took their dogs for a walk.

12   Perhaps fearing the challenge of reading a newspaper will prove daunting, papers are using increasing portions of their shrinking news holes in providing guides to reading themselves. Before the *Chicago Tribune*'s new design started self-correcting (i.e., rolling itself back), I fully expected a box at the top of a page steering me to a story lower on the same page.

13   The celebrity culture is infantilizing us. We are being trained not to think. It is not about the disappearance of film critics. We are the canaries. It is about the death of an intelligent and curious readership, interested in significant things and able to think critically. It is about the failure of our educational system. It is not about dumbing-down. It is about snuffing out.

14   The news is still big. It's the newspapers that got small. ◆

CRITICAL THINKING   ————————————————————

1. What does Ebert mean when he says that newspaper film critics "used to be the town crier," but now they are "the neighborhood gossip"? Explain.

2. What issue is Ebert raising in his editorial? What is his argument, and how persuasive is his case? What does he hope his readers will do as a result of reading his editorial?

3. According to Ebert, what do the newspapers believe its customers want to read about? Do you agree with the newspaper's assessment of its readership? What do you want to read about?

4. What is the "CelebCult" virus? How has it impacted newspapers and film critics and the general public? Who feeds the virus?

5. Who is Roger Ebert? What is he known for? What risks does he assume, if any, in speaking out this way against the culture of celebrity?

CRITICAL WRITING

1. *Expository Writing:* In this essay, Roger Ebert warns that celebrity culture is "infantilizing us" and training us "not to think." Write your own editorial exploring this claim.
2. *Analytical Writing:* What claims does Ebert make in this editorial? Make a list of his claims, and evaluate how he supports each. Write a response to his editorial directly addressing his claims, commenting on the strengths and weaknesses of his argument.

GROUP PROJECTS

1. Test Ebert's claims about the vacuous nature of celebrity gossip. Get several copies of your local newspaper, and review the headlines and sections. Which sections are larger? Which stories lead? What information does the newspaper feel its readers care about most, based on the headlines and bylines it prints? Discuss your analysis as a group.
2. Research the work of some of the film critics Ebert cites, including Stanley Kauffmann. Then, read some film reviews in your local paper. Based on what you read, discuss the similarities and differences between how career film critics write and the reviews published in many papers today. Select a recent film and watch it as a group. Discuss the film's merits, and prepare your own review of it, employing either the style of past film critics or the 500-word gossipy review style promoted by today's papers.

Perspectives: Bloody Paparazzi

www.CartoonStock.com

THINKING CRITICALLY

1. What is happening in this cartoon? What contemporary social issue does it highlight?
2. What stereotypes does the cartoon use to convey its point? What do the people look like?
3. Review the words in the cartoon and what they mean. What is the cartoonist saying about the paparazzi? About celebrities?

Return of the Brainless Hussies

*Rebecca Traister**

It appears that many of America's most famous young women are known not only for their beauty but also for their lack of intelligence. From *American Idol* Kellie Pickler to Paris Hilton to an army of jiggly video stars, vapid females seem to be everywhere these days. Are young women playing to the stereotype that they are more attractive and likable when they play dumb? Why are we glorifying female stupidity by honoring this trait in our most publicized celebrities? In this next essay, Rebecca Traister wonders, have we really gone this far backward, Baby?

1 During the last week of April 2006, Ellen DeGeneres welcomed Paris Hilton and her four Chihuahuas to her daytime talk show, ostensibly for a special episode about dogs. Once the host had the hotel heiress sitting down, however, she pressed her on a non-canine issue, asking whether she was hurt by Pink's video for "Stupid Girls," which mocks Hilton and her shopping-zombie peers for their essentially somnambulant behavior, and which two weeks earlier, DeGeneres had praised on her show. "I haven't even seen it yet," said the hotel heiress, in her flat monotone. "But I think…it's just a form of flattery."

2   Any thinking person who has seen Pink's video, in which she sends up Jessica Simpson's "These Boots Were Made for Walking" video by humping a soapy car, imitates an Olsen twin in Montana-size sunglasses and Wyoming-size handbag walking straight into the plate-glass door of a boutique, and savagely mocks Hilton's appearance in a dingy night-vision sex tape, would not confuse the clip with any known form of flattery. Especially if that thinking person heard the "Stupid Girls" lyrics, which go, in part: "They travel in packs of two or three/ With their itsy-bitsy doggies and their teeny-weeny tees/ Where, oh where, have the smart people gone?"

3   But Hilton is not a thinking person. Or, if she is, she hasn't let on. For the purposes of the American public, she is chief Stupid Girl, unembarrassed to admit that she doesn't know what Wal-Mart is, to testify that she isn't aware that London is in the United Kingdom, or to get the name of her own video game wrong; Hilton is so vacant that her behavior recently inspired a new Page Six epithet: "celebutard." When DeGeneres pressed her on whether she felt any responsibility as a role model to young girls, Hilton averred: "I think I definitely am a role model. I work very hard. I came from a name, but I've done my own thing." DeGeneres neglected to point out that doing one's own thing in the face of terrible privilege is not the same as being a role model, especially when one's own thing involves trademarking the phrase "That's hot."

4   Listening to Hilton try to have a conversation, the wind whistling between her eardrums, makes it hard to ignore claims of cultural critics who have noticed an alarming new vogue for feminine vapidity. In addition to Pink's sharp-toothed

* Rebecca Traister, *Salon,* May 19, 2006

treatise, the recent *American Idol* ascension of blond malapropism-spewing Kellie Pickler prompted a spate of stories about how playing dumb seems a sure way to get embraced by the American public. And Oprah recently summoned Pink, Naomi Wolf, *Female Chauvinist Pigs* author Ariel Levy and others for an episode called "Stupid Girls," which she kicked off by ominously announcing that culture is "devaluing an entire generation of young girls" by celebrating women as jiggly video stars, boobie-flashing twits, half-clad clotheshorses, and label-whoring anorexics. To hear media watchdogs tell it, dumbness—authentic or put on—is rampant in pop-culture products being consumed by kids; it gets transmitted through their downy skin and into their bloodstreams through the books and magazines they read, the television they watch, the trends they analyze like stock reports, and the celebrities they aspire to be.

5   In an effort to find out exactly what signals teens could be picking up, I spent a couple of weeks as immersed in girl pop culture as an old-fogy 30-year-old can get—reading sudsy high school novels and teen magazines, surfing MySpace, and watching MTV reality shows—waiting to see if I'd be overtaken with the urge to don giant sunglasses and pretend not to understand math. I found myself pleasantly surprised at some of the teen media I encountered—surprised enough to consider that the criticism we've been hearing may be vastly overblown by grown-ups who've forgotten the air-popped diversions of their own youth. But I was dismayed enough by the rest of it to acknowledge that the adults crying "fire" have a troubling point. Some of the images currently being retailed to teens illuminate both how far young women have come, and how easy it still is to cling to, recycle, and sell outmoded yet comfortable images of unthreatening femininity.

6   More problematic than teen literature is the craze for celebrity. Of all the evidence out there about the propagation of stupid-girl culture, it's most convincing to hear Pink talk about it. Her lyrics on the subject raise good questions: "Whatever happened to the dreams of a girl president?/ She's dancing in the video next to 50 Cent." In *Entertainment Weekly*, Pink pointed out that she doesn't actually think the women she goes after are truly stupid. "They've dumbed themselves down to be cute," she said. "I just feel like one image is being force-fed down people's throats. There's a lot of smart women. There's a lot of smart girls. Who is representing them?"

7   It's an excellent question. We have never been more soaked in celebrity culture. And yet, which celebrities hold teens in their thrall? There are women like Nicole Richie, who even venerable columnist Liz Smith took time to bemoan, "became a 'star' as soon as her weight dropped to scary skinny, [and who is] famous for being thin." There's Lohan, who may or may not be a good actress, but whose craft has come second to carousing and the development of her handbag collection. Even the Olsen twins, kajillionaires whose business acumen was widely touted when they were preteens, seemed to shrivel when they hit their 18th birthday. Now, their reputations as precocious entrepreneurs are shadowed by their profiles as consumptive, shabby-chic munchkins: little, dim, and more famous than ever.

8   The video clips that played behind Winfrey's dirge for the emancipated female at the start of her show amplified concerns about the dearth of female role models: There were Lohan, Richie and Jessica Simpson, "Video Vixen" Karrine Steffans,

a "rose ceremony" from desper-
ate-mate-foraging spectacle *The
Bachelor*, along with anachronistic shots of senescent stars
like Madonna and J. Lo showing
off their attenuated limbs and
bubblicious booty, respectively.
In a taped interview for *Oprah*,

Pink told Oprah that she and her friends could name only three celebrity women her age and under who were known for being bright; they were Natalie Portman, Reese Witherspoon, and Angelina Jolie.

a worked-up Wolf said, "What's beaming at young teenage girls is unfortunately an
image of celebrity perfection which is pretty mindless."

9   Pink told Oprah that she and her friends could name only three celebrity women
her age and under who were known for being bright; they were Natalie Portman,
Reese Witherspoon, and Angelina Jolie. There are a few other young favorites who
could have qualified for the list: Maggie Gyllenhaal, Alicia Keys, and Pink herself,
who was recently reported to be reading Maya Angelou's I Know Why the Caged
Bird Sings and Levy's Female Chauvinist Pigs, and whose bristling ditty "Dear
Mr. President" is smart enough to be getting banned in high schools across the country. But basically, the pickings are slim.

10   And while vacuous pink-fleshed icons of privilege would seem to hold sway
mostly on white-girl culture, the picture isn't much brighter on African-American
radar, where celebrity and material aspiration is embodied by mute, bling-laden,
gyrating "video girls," the most famous of whom is Karrine Steffans. Steffans'
recent tell-all, *Confessions of a Video Vixen,* earned her a place on Oprah's couch,
where she cried about the way she had been objectified by the rappers she danced
for and slept with. But her book isn't being read as a cautionary tale; it's become a
cult hit with young readers who refer to it as "Superhead," the nickname Steffans
earned in her years as a dancer, presumably by administering super head to a variety
of famous men. Days after she appeared on *Oprah*, it was reported in the *New York
Post* that Steffans would be moving on to porn.

11   If there were anywhere I would have expected to find an airhead ethos come
alive, it would have been in the crop of teen magazines I'd always considered
beauty-obsessed gateway drugs to full-blown fashion addiction. A stack of these
volumes, with their citrus typeface and cotton-candy cover lines, seemed to promise
unthreatening vapidity inside, right down to Pink herself on the cover of *Seventeen*,
next to the thunder-stealing headline: "I'm a stupid girl every other day." Inside,
the magazines confirmed some of my suspicions with expensive fashion spreads,
headlines that read, "So You Want to Be Sienna Miller," and the occasional, lame
deployment of teenage patois, like "for realz." But to my surprise, the same issue
of (recently defunct) *ElleGirl* that printed those words also featured book reviews
under the headline "Word: Reading Comprehension Is Sexy." *CosmoGirl* interviewed *Napoleon Dynamite* star Jon Heder, who advised, "Guys love smart girls, so
don't act dumber than you are," and published love advice from *Saturday Night Live*
eggheads Tina Fey and Amy Poehler.

12   Most startling were the "Real Life" pages over at *Seventeen*, one of which explained threats to American privacy. "After 9/11, Congress passed the USA Patriot
Act, which lets the Feds look at your private medical and financial records," read

the text. "Plus, it just came out that the National Security Agency has been eaves-dropping on people's phone calls since 2002—without warrants!" A later section on "anti-American feelings" explained that "The US is very wealthy compared with other nations and has a lot more resources and weapons. Many people . . . feel we use this power to help our own interests—like they believe we invaded Iraq to get cheaper oil—and that we don't respect or care about their way of life."

13   So it's not Susan Sontag. But it's a hell of a lot closer than the "plaids are in for fall" pap I remember reading as a 12- or 13-year-old (17-year-olds do not read *Seventeen*). Yes, teen magazines are riddled with images of richly swaddled urchins who look a couple of PowerBars short of a healthy Body Mass Index. But the editorial content presented a serious progression. The reason that the late magazine *Sassy* is so revered by women my age is because it treated its readers like human beings with interests: in their own health, in music, books, movies, politics. Now, it seems, *Sassy*'s mainstream sisters have begun treating young women with a similar regard.

14   My attempt at honest immersion in teenage-girl land necessarily stalled on-line, specifically on MySpace. I spent hours in the maze of profiles and messages; I saw dishabille Lolitas beckoning to Web-savvy Humbert Humberts, suggestively Sapphic images on the home pages of girls who claimed to be 15 and 16, several teens who listed *The South Beach Diet* as their favorite book. But I also visited pages of 17- and 18-year-olds decorated with teddy bears and pictures of horses. Teen women use [Facebook] to post enunciations of their devotion to field hockey, feminism, God, and Kanye West. [Facebook] is a country unto itself. Finding the evidence for any argument you'd like to make about American teens is possible: A search mechanism will dredge up any predilection or bad habit or nickname. Reading public expressions that would only recently have been private—cringey blogs chronicling breakups and bad grades, extensive online exchanges about girls cashing in their "v-cards" and plotting to get wine coolers for sleepovers—will confuse anyone who ever thought of a diary as something that had a lock and key, or who threaded a phone cord up the stairs and down the hall and under a door so that they could trade whispered secrets with friends, far out of earshot.

15   But my perplexity at the "Hiya! LOL! XO!" genre of communication was based in a lack of context for what I was watching, context I didn't lack when I turned on my television and found *My Super Sweet Sixteen*. A reality show on MTV, the program chronicles the celebratory excesses of 15-year-old girls (and boys) who persuade their parents to shower them with adulation and automobiles as they make the profound passage between teenager and incrementally older teenager. Watching this orgy of consumption on a couple of occasions, before beginning this story, is the closest I have come to fearing that the end of the world is near. These kids get carried into their parties on litters; they get dropped from helicopters; invitations are handed out by manservants.

16   *Super Sweet's* sister show is *Tiara Girls,* which follows beauty pageant contestants. The pageant circuit, on the opposite side of the culture war divide from some of the lavish, celebrity-studded events featured on *My Super Sweet Sixteen,* is no less materialistic. Contestants discuss the amount of money they spend on dresses; they hire pageant coaches; and whatever the current line on pageantry is, there is no focus on the female intellect. In one episode, an aspiring Miss Louisiana Queen

of Hope prepared for the interview segment with a little quizzing from her coach. What, asked the coach, is the vice president's name? "Wait," the contestant said, stalling. "His name's Kennedy, right?" It's a knee-slapper that apparently never gets old; the *Tiara Girls* season finale has been advertised by a clip of another pageant entrant flubbing the name of the commander in chief himself, then grumping to the camera: "It's a beauty pageant; what does it matter who the president is?" In one episode, a contestant's father ordered her to stop doing her homework to prepare for competition. "But I want to do my homework," the young woman said hopelessly to the camera.

17   *Sweet Sixteen* and *Tiara Girls* are transmitting aggressively mixed signals to their viewers. On one hand, they're car wrecks that mock their subjects in strict accordance with the basest class and cultural assumptions out there. The hyper-affluent party throwers on *Sweet Sixteen* come across as empty-headed, entitled brats, while the mostly lower-class beauty contestants appear simultaneously thick and shallow. But the degradation of the subjects is the backbeat to the melody being broadcast to kids: This is what you are supposed to look like; this is what you do look like; these are our expectations of you; if you fulfill them, you too can be on television.

18   Both shows demonstrate the complicity of parents in their kids' exploitation. If it long ago ceased to astound me that any kid could survive seeing their own avarice and vapidity broadcast on national television, the question remains: Why on earth would their parents participate? But on *Super Sweet Sixteen* and *Tiara Girls,* parents seem to be seeking the same cable-television spotlight that must motivate their children to self-exposure, without any concern that a nation (let alone their neighbors) will get to see them pushing their daughters to get collagen lip injections, or enabling their offspring's insatiable greed by never setting limits and getting them two cars.

19   When describing what's problematic in trashy teen fiction, Wolf wrote of the good old days, when the fictional younger generation's role was to poke holes in their parents' social artifice and find their own paths. Today, Wolf complained, teenage heroines "try on adult values and customs as though they were going to wear them forever. The narrative offer the perks of the adult world not as escapist fantasy but in a creepily photorealistic way."

20   The tension between adolescent and adult has always been a tricky mix of imitation and rejection. Vexing her elders, adopting ill-advised role models, and cleaving to habits that will most aggravate her parents is basically the job description of a teenager. But we're in a period when adult and teenage worlds seem to be meshing, making Wolf's implied wish—that teenagers would crumple up and jettison parental mores—a complicated proposition. Adults push children to learn and socialize earlier than ever; we rush them with Baby Einstein videos, obsess over their achievements, and wail over their failures. We treat them as mini-me's at the same time that we infantilize them, fretting over just about every message that's been transmitted to them from the moment they are expelled from the womb, except for the ones we set for them by example.

21   Adults have made careless consumption the crowning American pursuit. We have invented and happily consume magalogs full of luxury items. Teenagers didn't create Paris Hilton. In fact, they wouldn't have any idea who she was if adults hadn't

elevated her from a dull table-dancing heiress by circulating a porn tape and giving her a reality show. Teenage girls don't write the *Gossip Girl* books; 35-year-old Cecily von Ziegesar does. And consider the cabal of studio heads, publicists, club owners, photographers, designers, and magazine publishers who have colluded to make Lindsay Lohan famous, drunk, and ubiquitous so that she can sell their magazines, movies, and handbags to teens who might rightly get the impression that they should live like her. Eliot Spitzer, of all people, recently accused the grown-ups over at Lohan's record company of goosing her popularity by bribing radio stations and MTV to play her music. It's all in the name of legitimate American enterprise, sure. But how can we be surprised when the kids we are hustling take our cues and mimic even our most corrupt behaviors?

22   And how about the fact that it's not just teens photo realistically aping the adults, but adults who are aping their own teens? The Alcotts and Austens and Brontës that Wolf recalls with deserved reverence would have blanched had they encountered the slice of the maternal population currently striving to look and dress like their daughters. Which is more alarming—reading about Lohan drinking too much and collapsing from "exhaustion," or reading about her mother, Dina, sponging off her daughter's success and cavorting with her beyond every velvet rope? It's fair to ask, as Pink does, how many girls long to mimic Lohan. But it's also reasonable to wonder whether any of their mothers long to live like Dina?

23   The current wave of flaky-chic is no more potent than other historical iterations of American worship of the dumb blonde, which has venerable roots with Marilyn Monroe and Judy Holliday. Teens (and adults, for that matter) have never fallen for celebrity heroes based on their great calculus grades. But that particular mold of femininity was one of the constructs from which women's liberation was supposed to deliver us. What does it mean that in 2004, Jessica Simpson got famous for being flummoxed by a can of Chicken of the Sea tuna on *Newlyweds,* and that in 2006, Kellie Pickler became a star by asking, "What's a ballsy?" For one thing, it means that the same young women who had hung on Simpson's every word about staying a virgin till marriage and who were calling in their votes for Pickler were also getting the message that it's funny and attractive to be an idiot.

24   *MTV News* producer Jim Fraenkel told the *New York Post*'s Farrah Weinstein in a piece about Pickler that he "wouldn't necessarily say that she's so savvy she's tapped into the idea that America loves a stupid girl, so much as that she may think of herself as Jessica Simpson was." But aren't both realizations pretty much the same thing? And aren't they both an embarrassing sign that we haven't come very far at all, baby?

25   Yes, they are. But modern women, like generations of men before them, now have many areas in which to hunt for role models. They receive instructions that directly contradict the Pickler-Simpson Principle of Sexy Vacancy every day: achieve, go to school, work, make money, compete. Retro visions of stupid appeal are answered by fresh acknowledgment of energetic female sexuality that is far more open—if dangerously commodified in its own way, critics argue—than ever before. None of it is in perfect balance; women are punished for their progress all the time, in media and politics and in classrooms. Adolescent girls still have no female president to look up to, and too few artists and tycoons and athletes and activists. But

there is no denying the past half-century's earth-shaking and positive shifts in the gender terrain. As has been widely reported (with varying degrees of rancor) women now make up more than half the country's collegiate student body.

26   But these new, varied, and wildly threatening options help to explain and undergird a rejuvenated craze for dumb chic. Perhaps, as social progress propels women slowly but undeniably forward into public spheres of influence, baser human impulses—erotic desire, capitalist greed—dig in, summoning and then clinging to a dusty daydream of the fast-fading ideal woman of yesteryear.

27   Working on this story, I received an e-mail from a Harvard graduate student who told me that while he'd dated only smart girls, he "liked the 'idea' of dating a dumb girl." The fantasy, the student explained, "is almost certainly formed for us by the media representations of . . . celebrities [like Hilton, Lohan, and Simpson]. Blonde dumb girls are sexy. And won't talk back. Add in various shades of male ego/guaranteed superiority notions, and you've pretty much got it." In a world in which male superiority is no longer guaranteed, it becomes a lascivious desire that can be gratified, performatively if need be, by willing women. As Pink trills, mockingly, "Maybe if I act like that/ that guy will call me back."

28   But it's time to put that transactional model for romance out of its misery, and make room in the pop firmament for examples that sound more like Pink's self-assessment: "I'm so glad that I'll never fit in/ That will never be me/ Outcasts and girls with ambition/ That's what I wanna see." ◆

CRITICAL THINKING

1. Who were the female celebrities from your childhood? Who were they in your teen years? Ask your parents or older adults this same question. How do female celebrities from the past compare with the young women we focus our cameras on today? Are they different or fundamentally the same?

2. According to Traister, why do the women she mentions—such as Jessica Simpson, the Olsen twins, and Paris Hilton—get so much attention from the press and the general public? How have they made female stupidity desirable? Have you noticed this phenomenon yourself? Does it represent an aberration or a trend? Explain.

3. Traister observes that programs such as *My Super Sweet Sixteen* not only glorify the worst of human behavior but also encourage youth to covet the very things the show seems to mock. Do you agree?

4. Why are people so willing to allow themselves to be exploited on reality television? According to Traister, what motivates youth and their parents to broadcast the most intimate details of their lives?

5. What mixed signals are teens getting from media today? What messages are conveyed to young women? What messages are conveyed to young men? Is media constructing reality or merely reflecting it? Explain.

6. What culpability do adults have in the creation of the "cult of celebrity"? Explain.

CRITICAL WRITING

1. *Research and Analysis:* What issue does the singer Pink raise in her song "Stupid Girls"? Review the lyrics in the song and write a short essay responding to her points with your own perspective.
2. *Expository Writing:* Traister quotes an e-mail she received from a Harvard graduate student who expresses a personal yearning to date "a dumb girl." What reasons does he give? What qualities do you look for in a significant other, and how many of these qualities are driven by social norms and media-constructed ideals? Explain.
3. *Personal Narrative:* Have you ever aspired to be on a reality program? If so, why? What program would you want to be on? What would your expectations be during the program and after it? Would you expect to be a celebrity? Why or why not?

GROUP PROJECTS

1. As a group, discuss this statement: "America loves a stupid girl." In what ways is this statement true or untrue? Identify women in popular culture who represent both intelligent and unintelligent females. What are each known for? Why are they famous?
2. Watch Pink's video "Stupid Girls" online. Identify the women she holds up for ridicule and the personalities to which she objects. As a group, answer her question: "Where have all the smart girls gone?"
3. Plan a follow-up program for Ellen DeGeneres on the issue of the glorification of "stupid women" in the media. Who would you have on her show and why? What issues would you address? Share your program with the class.

Modern Scholar

The Role of Violent Video Game Content in Adolescent Development: Boys' Perspectives

Cheryl Olsen, Lawrence Kutner, and Dorothy Warner*

The last reading focused on the entertainment industry's influence on teen girls. The next essay addressed the popular pastime of video games—a diversion that statistically is used more by young males (60/40 male/female ratio). The argument that violent video games create violent kids is almost as old as video games when parents wondered if shooting at amorphous blobs on an Atari screen could make kids more aggressive. Today, violent games

---

*Cheryl Olsen, Lawrence Kutner, and Dorothy Warner, *Journal of Adolescent Research*, January 1, 2008

may involve role-playing, graphic blood and gore, and ruthless murder of clearly human men, women, and children. Some titles even allow for rape and torture. But do these games incite violence in young men? Do they indeed inure teens from feeling remorse, sympathy, and empathy? Psychiatrists Cheryl Olsen, Lawrence Kutner, and Dorothy Warner set out to study this issue and why these games are so appealing to adolescent boys, as they consider the boys' point of view. The online version of this article, with full annotations, can be found at: http://jar.sagepub.com/cgi/content/abstract/23/1/55

1 Numerous policies have been proposed at the local, state, and national level to restrict youth access to violent video and computer games. Although studies are cited to support policies, there is no published research on how children perceive the uses and influence of violent interactive games. The authors conduct focus groups with 42 boys ages 12 to 14. Boys use games to experience fantasies of power and fame, to explore and master what they perceive as exciting and realistic environments (but distinct from real life), to work through angry feelings or relieve stress, and as social tools. Boys did not believe they had been harmed by violent games but were concerned that younger children might imitate game behavior (especially swearing).

2 Young adolescents have increasing access to electronic interactive games on game consoles, handheld players, computers, the Internet, and cellular phones. National surveys of American youth ages 8 to 18 by the Kaiser Family Foundation (Roberts, Foehr, & Rideout, 2005) found that in 2005, 49% of children had a game console in their bedroom (up from 45% in 1999), 31% had a computer (up from 21% in 1999), and 20% had Internet access (up from 10% in 1999). European surveys also show that new media, including electronic games, are part of children's everyday life (Roe, 2000).

3 The widespread prevalence of this type of play across most industrialized nations makes it normative (Warner & Raiter, 2005). However, many parents, clinicians, researchers, and policy makers are concerned that electronic games, especially those featuring violent content, may be harmful to youth. Researchers have fiercely debated the applicability of the literature on effects of violent video game content to real-world behaviors (Vastag, 2004). To further our understanding of the ways in which video game play, risky behavior, and healthy development may be related, it is useful to consider the perspectives of adolescents themselves.

Prevalence of Video Game Play

4 Almost all boys and most girls play video and computer games, including games with violent content. A Kaiser Family Foundation survey (Roberts et al., 2005) found that 77% of boys in Grades 7 to 12 had played a game in the *Grand Theft Auto* series (Rockstar Entertainment), and nearly half (49%) had played a game in the popular *Madden NFL* series (Electronic Arts). In a recent study of middle school students' media habits (Olson et al., 2007), 94% reported having played computer or video games during the preceding 6 months. Of those who played electronic games, one third of boys and 11% of girls said they played nearly every day; 49% had

played at least one Mature-rated title (intended for players age 17 and older) "a lot" in the previous 6 months. Data collected in the late 1990s in 10 European countries and Israel found that children ages 6 to 16 averaged more than a half hour per day on electronic video and computer games (Beentjes, Koolstra, Marseille, & van der Voort, 2001).

Concerns About Effects of Violent Game Content

5 Researchers, clinicians, and policy makers have expressed concern that the violence children see in video and computer games could carry over into the real world as aggressive behavior or thoughts, desensitization to violence, and decreased empathy (Funk, 2005). They fear that the greater immersion and interactivity of video games, compared to passive media such as television, could blur players' perceptions of the boundaries between fantasy and reality (American Psychological Association, 2005; Calvert & Tan, 1994). Furthermore, repeated acting out of "aggressive scripts" within violent game scenarios might lead to automatic aggressive responses to perceived provocations in the real world (Funk, 2005). Some reviews of research assert that existing data support a large and consistent effect of violent games on aggressive thoughts, feelings, and behaviors (Anderson, 2004). Other reviews conclude that any harmful effects of interactive games are small or evidence is mixed and that more study is needed (Bensley & van Eenwyk, 2001; Browne & Hamilton-Giachritsis, 2005; Sherry, 2001).

6 Academics and policy makers in the United States (Anderson, 2004) and, most recently, in Germany (Dobson, 2006) have cited anecdotal reports linking violent video games to highly publicized violent crimes such as school shootings. However, these reports often neglect other known contributors to violence. For example, the attorney for Lee Malvo, the adolescent charged with a series of fatal sniper shootings in the Washington, D.C., area in 2002, cited his exposure to violent video games in his defense. Yet the young man had a history of parental abandonment, poverty, animal torture, and violent attacks with weapons (Liptak, 2003; Miller, 2003).

7 After the Columbine High School murders, the U.S. Secret Service reviewed a quarter century of school-based attacks. The report did not single out violent media use as a contributor to school shootings (Vossekuil, Fein, Reddy, Borum, & Modzeleski, 2002). Furthermore, although the majority of adolescent boys now play violent video games, juvenile violent crime (including murder) has steadily declined in the United States; arrest rates are down 49% from their 1994 peak, reaching their lowest level since at least 1980 (Snyder, 2006).

8 More study is needed on the possibility that video games and other media with violent content could have less visible but still significant harmful effects on children's behavior. For example, certain types or amounts of video game play could affect emotions, cognition, perceptions, and behaviors in ways that promote bullying and victimization (Olson, 2004).

9 The many well-established risk factors for aggressive or violent behavior include individual characteristics, such as neurological damage, insecure attachment, and parental neglect or abuse, as well as exposure to social problems, such as poverty and neighborhood violence. These risk factors are complicated and interwoven

over time such that it is impossible to identify one specific cause of aggressive or violent behavior. Evidence of harm from media with violent content is less clear-cut (U.S. Department of Health and Human Services, 2001).

10   However, even if effects are small, exposure to violence through electronic media is one risk factor that could potentially be modified. It is therefore important to understand which types of media content, including various video game genres, have potential to negatively affect arousal, cognition, emotions, and behavior. Equally important, we must look for differing effects among subgroups of children, such as those who have aggressive temperaments or exposure to family or neighborhood violence (Browne & Hamilton-Giachritsis, 2005), and consider factors related to play patterns and settings, including game preferences and time spent playing, which might serve as markers for behavioral or emotional problems.

Electronic Game Play and Healthy Development

11 Although most research on video games has emphasized harm, some surveys of adolescents have found links between interactive game play and social and emotional well-being (Colwell & Kato, 2003; Durkin & Barber, 2002). Researchers have theorized that video games—perhaps including those with violent content—may have benefits for adolescents (Gelfond & Salonius-Pasternak, 2005; Goldstein, 2000; Griffiths, 2003; Kirsh, 2003; McNamee, 2000; Sherry, 2001). As adolescents explore different roles and social situations, including the inevitable conflicts with peers and parents, they create, break, and negotiate rules. By providing adolescents with situations not typically experienced in the real world, video game play may facilitate exploration of rules and consequences (Scarlett, Naudeau, Salonius-Pasternak, & Ponte, 2004). Violent games are also a safe place to experiment with emotions and roles that may be unacceptable in daily life (Jansz, 2005). Interviews with adolescents and young adults suggest that many view violent video games as incorporating realistic situations and consequences (Malliet, 2006).

12   Some researchers posit that older children and adolescents understand that violent video game play is simply a form of play; they distinguish fantasy aggression and violence from real-world behavior that includes intent to harm a real victim (Goldstein, 2001; Malliet, 2006). According to catharsis theory, playing violent video games could provide a safe outlet for aggressive and angry feelings (Griffiths, 2000). Others have criticized this idea, citing a lack of empirical support in television studies (Dill & Dill, 1998; Huesmann & Taylor, 2003). Research on elementary-age boys found that aggressive motoric activity (e.g., throwing a ball at a drawing of a frowning face) could reduce levels of fantasy aggression (Murray & Feshbach, 1978). Unlike television, video games allow player-directed acting out of aggressive fantasies, and new game controllers allow an increasing amount of physical interaction. The potential link between violent video games and catharsis merits further exploration.

13   Video game play may serve particular needs of adolescent boys with regard to aggression and socialization. In this period of development, boys use rough-and-tumble play to explore aggression, establishing peer status by focusing on

dominance rather than causing physical harm to participants (Pellegrini, 2003; Pellegrini & Smith, 1998). It is possible that adolescent boys achieve some of these goals through their video game play. Rather than encouraging aggressive or violent behavior, video game play may help adolescent boys consider issues of war, violence, and death (Gelfond & Salonius-Pasternak, 2005). As with physical activity play, some adolescents may engage with video games in a dysfunctional manner.

Adolescents' Perspectives on Video Game Play

14 Our understanding of these complex relations, as well as any policy or legislation that may be implemented, should be informed by adolescents' own perspectives on their video game play. This includes recognizing the personal, social, and emotional goals boys have for game play; their perceptions of game characters and actions; and the context of game play (Sherry, 2001; Williams, 2005). To date, no published studies have examined young adolescents' descriptions of why they play video games, what leads them to choose games with violent content, and how they perceive the influence of games on themselves and their peers. To begin addressing this gap, we conducted focus groups with young adolescent boys.

15 We chose to focus on young adolescents for several reasons. They may be more vulnerable to the influence of violent content during this stage of cognitive, emotional, social, and neurological development (Kirsh, 2003). They are more likely to engage in risky behavior, especially with peers, and less able to assess the consequences of those behaviors (Gardner & Steinberg, 2005). The potential effects of game violence on aggressive behavior is a central concern, and the prevalence of externalizing problems tends to peak in mid-adolescence (Steinberg & Morris, 2001). Finally, on a practical level, their activities are less subject to adult oversight than those of younger children.

16 The current study was limited to boys. Boys are more likely than girls to play video games in general and action or combat games in particular; they are also far more likely to play games in the presence of multiple peers (Olson et al., 2007). Physically aggressive behavior is more common among boys than girls (Loeber & Hay, 1997). Also, research has shown considerable gender differences in the perception and expression of aggression (Galen & Underwood, 1997).

17 We addressed the following research questions:

1. What do boys identify as the reasons they play violent video games? What attracts boys to particular games, or game characters? Can electronic games be fun without violent content?
2. How do boys view the role of video games in social relationships?
3. What influence do boys believe violent video games have on their thoughts, feelings, and behaviors and those of their peers? How do they believe violent games might affect younger children?

18 Because these issues have been little explored, we also paid close attention to unanticipated themes that arose spontaneously in boys' discussions.

Method

Participants

19 We recruited 42 seventh- and eighth-grade boys ages 12 to 14. Two sets of focus groups were conducted using similar protocols: concurrent groups (in separate rooms) of 21 parents and sons, held in a suburban office building, and boys-only groups with 21 additional participants, held at three Boston-area clubs serving disadvantaged urban youth. For the parent/son groups, participants were recruited via an e-mail broadcast to more than 2,500 employees of the Partners HealthCare System, as well as flyers posted in local businesses and near schools. For the boys-only groups, the youth clubs posted flyers for groups to be held at their facilities. (Additional findings from the parent/son groups are presented in a companion article titled "Parents' and Sons' Perspectives on Video Game Play: A Qualitative Study.")

20 Respondents were screened by telephone. To qualify, boys had to report playing video or computer games at least 2 hours per week. We also required experience with two or more games from a list of eight bestselling violent games rated either "Teen" (ages 13 and older) or "Mature" (m; ages 17 and older) by the Entertainment Software Rating Board. Games were selected based on three criteria: availability on the industry-leading PlayStation 2 console (at minimum), the popularity of the game (based on sales data), and the presence of violent content (shooting, fighting, and/ or blood). The Teen-rated titles used were *Def Jam Vendetta*, *Soul Caliber II*, and *Tekken Tag Tournament*. The Mature-rated games were *Mortal Kombat: Deadly Alliance*, *Grand Theft Auto 3*, *Grand Theft Auto: Vice City*, *Metal Gear Solid 2: Sons of Liberty*, and *Resident Evil: Code Veronica X*.

21 Potential participants were told that the groups would discuss adolescent video game play but were not informed of the specific emphasis. Video games were defined as games played on game consoles, computers, or handheld devices. The Partners HealthCare System/Massachusetts General Hospital human research committee approved the protocol and procedures. Participants came from 15 communities in the greater Boston area and represented a diverse mix of socioeconomic and racial/ethnic backgrounds. Each boy received $50 for his participation.

Procedure

22 We held eight focus groups with 42 boys, half concurrent with parent groups (conducted in a separate room) and half with boys only. Groups averaged four to five participants and lasted 75 to 90 minutes. Boys gave written assent to participate, and a parent or guardian gave written consent. We made audio recordings of all focus groups with the permission of the participants.

23 A senior researcher and a research assistant moderated each group, working from a written list of research questions recast in open-ended, conversational language; standardized probe questions were used to elicit details (Stewart & Shamdasani, 1990). Moderators also asked follow-up questions about themes introduced by participants. To stimulate conversation and provide a visual reference, printed color images from the eight video games were displayed on the table. Although all of the games contain violence, only nonviolent screenshots were presented so that boys were not exposed to additional or novel violent content. To start the group

discussion, each boy was asked to select a game screenshot from the table and to describe what he liked about his chosen game. After each boy had shared his opinions, this process was repeated; the group then moved on to a broader discussion of issues related to video games.

24   Boys were asked the following:

- What do you like about (name of video game)? What is your favorite part? What do you like to do?
- Are there any characters in this game that you especially like? What is it about this character that you like?
- What makes a video game good enough to play more than once? What makes a game exciting for you?
- Notice that all of the games we have talked about have violence in them: fighting or shooting or blood. Do you think these make a game more fun?
- Can a game be fun without violence? [*If yes*] What game do you have in mind? [*If no, or not sure*] Can you think of any fun game that does not have violence?
- Some people think that games with fighting, shooting, or blood can affect the way kids behave. Do you think games like these can make kids act or think any different? Do you think you would be different if you had never played any violent games?
- How do you feel while you are playing a violent game, and how do you feel afterward? Give me an example (e.g., a game played yesterday). How did you feel before versus after?
- Some kids play video games by themselves, some kids play video games with other people, and there are some kids who do both. What do you do? What do you like about playing alone versus playing with other people? Do you ever play with other people on the Web?
- Have you ever made a new friend playing video games? Do you ever feel that playing video games keeps you from being with other people/gets in the way of friendships? [Groups held at youth clubs spent more time on social questions.]
- If you have a little brother or sister, are there games you would not want him or her to play? Why? Are there games that you think kids your age should not play?

Data Analysis

25 The principal investigator and co-investigator (who were the primary group moderators), the research coordinator, and another researcher reviewed full print transcripts of group audio recordings prepared by a research assistant. We identified and coded responses to the research questions and made marginal notes on recurring themes in these responses as well as issues that emerged independently. We periodically conducted reliability checks during this process to ensure consistency in interpretation and coding terminology among reviewers (Krueger, 1998; Miles & Huberman, 1994). After completing the initial analyses, reviewers discussed their findings and compiled a document that included each other's notes, so that data analyses were both independent and collaborative. This process incorporated the recommendations suggested by Marshall and Rossman (1998) to establish and maintain

credibility, transferability, dependability, and confirmability via discussions with other researchers.

Results

26 The following results and illustrative comments are organized by research question, concluding with unexpected themes or topics that were not related to our a priori* questions.

The Appeal of Violent Video Games

27 Our analyses suggest that boys are attracted to video and computer game play, and especially to violent games, for five clusters of reasons: (a) fantasies of power and fame; (b) challenge, exploration, and mastery; (c) emotional regulation, especially coping with anger and stress; (d) sociability (cooperation, competition, and status seeking); and (e) learning new skills (particularly in the case of sports games).

28 ***Games and fantasies of power.*** Boys talked about playing games with violent content as a way to express their fantasies of power and glory. Some boys described aspects of main characters' skills, personalities, or appearance as something with which they identify outside of the game. For example:

> "What I like about [*Grand Theft Auto*] *Vice City* is, I like Tommy Vercetti because he never gives up and he never quits or anything. And it's played by Ray Liotta; he's one of my favorite actors." (Boy 8)

29 Boys also imagined what they would do if suddenly blessed with the abilities of a favorite game character. These descriptions included references to conflicts or problems they encountered in their lives:

> "If I could be powerful like Jin, when somebody's getting bullied or something, and they can't defend themselves, I'd go help them out." (Boy 33)

> "I wish I could be stronger, so if someone's afraid of me—not that I want them to be afraid of me—but they won't try to start something with me. And I want to be famous." (Boy 39)

> "If I were Sub-Zero, I would go to school, I would freeze my teacher and the principal, and all the other teachers. So the students could do whatever they want. They could run in the hallways!" (Boy 33)

30 However, boys were also aware that game actions would have very different consequences in the real world. When asked what he would do if he woke up tomorrow as Mitsurugi from *Tekken*, one participant (Boy 4) said, "I don't know, because if I took the sword out in public, then I'd get arrested!" Other boys made similar comments about *Grand Theft Auto* games:

---

* *a priori* means "from the earlier"

"I'm kind of scared to do that stuff. If I shoot somebody and they die, then I'll go to jail for a long time, so I don't want to do that." (Boy 34)

"The whole thug thing seems kind of cool, but in real life, I wouldn't really want to have that life. In here, you don't mind just getting out of your car and killing somebody, because you're not going to get in trouble for it. You can just turn off the game system and you're done." (Boy 10)

31   Some boys mentioned special powers or weapons that they enjoyed using in the game; for example, Boy 14 said, "The swords in *Mortal Kombat* are fun to use; they look cool." These references did not include an indication of identification or imitation outside of the game.

32 *Games and exploration, challenge and mastery.*   To lead into the topic of violent games, boys were asked what made a game fun to play more than once. Many mentioned challenge, action, excitement, and the more in-depth development of characters:

"I like adventure games because you don't only play for 20 minutes and then beat it. I like a game that takes time and focus-ness [*sic*] to do it." (Boy 23)

"And then you can do a whole different storyline and beat it again. Also, you could go exploring." (Boy 27)

33   When asked whether violence makes a game more fun, many boys agreed:

"It's stuff that you can't do in real life, like kill people. So you could just, like, go crazy with the games." (Boy 34)

34   Others described games with violent content as having more action or challenges:

"I like sports games a lot, and when I do play a violent game, it's fun too, because I like the action and stuff. I think there's a little more action in violence games [*sic*] than there is in nonviolence games." (Boy 24)

"I think a game could have no violence at all and still be really good, because I like the realism and the challenge and stuff." (Boy 26)

35   Most boys felt that some types of games could be fun without violence. They cited sports games, racing games, or older games such as *Pac-Man,* pinball, or online checkers. They especially liked games with realistic sounds or actions, such as choosing draft picks as a coach in *Madden NFL.*

36 *Games and anger.*   Many boys described using violent games to cope with feelings of anger or frustration. This type of play served as an outlet for emotional expression or as a form of distraction. For example:

"Getting wrapped up in a violent game, it's good. 'Cause if you mad, when you come home, you can take your anger out on the people in the game." (Boy 32)

"If I had a bad day at school, I'll play a violent video game and it just relieves all my stress." (Boy 12)

"Last week, I missed one homework and my teacher yelled at me . . . . When I went home, I started playing *Vice City* and I did a cheat code to get a tank and I ran over everybody. And I smashed a lot of cars and blew them up . . . . I was mad, and I turned happy afterwards." (Boy 34)

37 One boy described coping with a real-life conflict by role-playing it in the game:

"Say some kid wants to fight you, and he talks trash about you. When you go home and play, you're like, 'This is the kid that I hate,' and you beat him up and stuff." (Boy 39)

38 When asked if playing the game might help him avoid a fight, the boy said:

"Maybe. 'Cause if I don't play a game or if I don't do nothing, it gets me even angrier, real mad. If I play a game, it's, 'All right, I beat him.' Then, it feels like I really did something and I'm done, man." (Boy 39)

39 ***Games as social tools.***   For many boys, video games are a focus of social activities and discussions:

"Usually me and my friends, when we're over at each others' houses, and they have a good game [we'll play it]. They're like, 'Oh, I'll kill you in *Madden 2005*.' It's fun to beat them." (Boy 15)

"If I didn't play video games—it's kind of a topic of conversation, and so I don't know what I'd talk about. 'Cause I talk about video games a lot." (Boy 4)

40 Several boys noted that talking about video game play helped them structure initial conversations with potential or new friends:

"You say, 'Do you own a system, a game system?' If he says yes, then, 'What kind? PS2, Gamecube, Xbox?' Like that." (Boy 28)

41 A number of boys mentioned playing games over the Internet, sometimes teaming up with players from different cities or countries to play against other virtual teams:

"[Playing games over the Web] makes me friends, like that you don't even know; all I know is by computer. Never met them. . . . You talk to them [on the headset] as you play, like 'Oh, go this way and I'll go that way.'" (Boy 30)

Boys' Perceptions of the Influence of Video Games

42 When asked about the influence of electronic games, boys mentioned potential positive and negative effects. Positive effects were organized around game genres, whereas negative effects were organized around specific types of content.

43 ***Role-playing and realistic sports games.***   Boys' references to video games' positive influences focused on two game genres: role-playing and sports:

"With role-playing games, you have to think of every possibility. Like, 'That chest over there . . . walk over there and maybe there is something over there.' It helps you think, what would you want to do, how would you get further. So it also helps you in life [in the future], by thinking, 'Okay, what could help the business?' " (Boy 20)

44   Many boys said they were inspired by games to take up new sports or learn new moves. They tried to imitate physical activities they saw in the games they played. Some said that playing sports games could improve their real-life coordination and timing:

"You see them do amazing plays, and then if you were to go outside and try them, and keep practicing that, you could get better so sometime later on in life, you could possibly do that." (Boy 9)

"Like in basketball, if you see them do a fancy crossover, whatever, you want to learn how to do the same thing . . . . With this game I have called *Street Hoops,* I figured out how to do some of the moves. Still working on it." (Boy 18)

"I play *Aggressive Inline,* a roller-blading game. [My little brother and I] get in trouble 'cause we start jumping on the couches, imitating the people in the game. Then, my mom tells us to go outside and roller-blade, and we try to imitate the tricks. I think that's how we get better and better, 'cause we actually want to be one of the people in the game." (Boy 21)

45 ***Games with violent content.***   Only a few boys said that playing video games with violent content could affect their peers' or their own behavior. When pressed, they could not offer examples from their lives; the risk was theoretical. For example:

[Moderator: Do you think that playing a lot of games like this makes kids think, act, or talk differently?]

"Yeah, definitely. 'Cause you might not want to fight a lot, and then when you play one of these games, you might want to fight more, so you might get in trouble a lot more." (Boy 19)

[Has that ever happened to you?]

"No, not really." (Boy 19)

[Has anybody you know gotten into trouble because they play a lot of violent games?] "No, not really." (Boy 19)

[But you just figure it's logical, or . . . ?]

"Yeah, it could happen." (Boy 19)

[Moderator: Do you think playing violent games makes you any more violent?]

"Depends, if you're like really, really into games." (Boy 40)

[What about you personally?]

"Me? No, I'm not. I have no urge to pick up guns and shoot people." (Boy 40)

46   Boys repeatedly made distinctions between the game world and real life. Their distinctions focused less on the realism of visual images, and more on whether actions or situations were realistic:

> "I think the really violent games like *Vice City* where you can just go around killing anybody, that's pretty much less realistic. The environment, the people are real, but not the actions." (Boy 26)

> "I like the gore [in *Mortal Kombat*]. . . . The special moves that kill them, and how they finish the moves. They made the graphics good." (Boy 35)

> [Moderator: Good like realistic, fun?]

> "It's not realistic; it's fancy and fun." (Boy 35)

47   Several boys thought violent games could actually increase understanding of the real world and of consequences to actions. For example:

> "If you've never seen someone get hurt or something, like you see in a video game, then you probably wouldn't know that that could happen." (Boy 1)

48   Many boys felt that the influence of a game with violent content would depend on the cognitive maturity of the player. They focused on the ways in which violent content could harm others and seemed to consider themselves immune. They expressed a great deal of concern about exposing younger siblings to inappropriate content:

> "Before people start playing the [violent] game, they need to know what happens if you ever did something illegal that you're not supposed to do. Because if you don't know the consequences of your actions, you can just go out, start shooting people and you'll go to jail for life, and that's not a good thing." (Boy 17)

> "In M [rated games], there's a lot of swearing, a lot of killing, and a lot of things that I don't want [my younger brother] knowing." (Boy 41)

49   Boys were not worried about exposure to gore but about salient behaviors that could be easily imitated in the real world, especially swearing:

> "Little kids, they don't know the basic meanings of life. So once they see that [bad behavior in games], they're going to think, 'Oh, that's how life goes. You can swear and go around hitting people and stuff.'" (Boy 23)

> "I don't like my little brother or sisters to watch me play *Vice City* because they might swear at other people 'cause of the attitude, how they do in *Vice City*. They always give people attitude and take swears at other people. That could make my family look bad, like my mom isn't raising us regular." (Boy 24)

> "Well, if he was younger than 8, then I wouldn't let him play. But maybe 8, I'd probably let him play, but I'd probably lower down the volume so he wouldn't hear the swears." (Boy 38)

50 ***Games with sexual content.*** Boys also had concerns about protecting younger children from sexual content in games:

> "In *Grand Theft Auto,* when you're driving around, you could see girls that you could pick up, like hookers. So I think children under 13 or 14 should not be buying it." (Boy 28)

> [Moderator: So why do you think it's more okay for someone your age to play that?] "'Cause I'm mature, and I already know what that [sex] is, and I learned it in class." (Boy 28)

51   Interestingly, there was one game that several boys felt that they were too young to play, perhaps because of its salience to key issues in their stage of development:

> [Moderator: Is there anything you think you shouldn't be allowed to play at your age?]

> "Well . . . sort of like *The Sims.*" (Boy 34)

> "Yeah, *Sims,* because they go to, like . . ." (Boy 31)

> "They go to, like, people and like . . ." (Boy 34)

> "Kiss." (Boy 31)

52   These two boys agreed with a third that seeing kissing in a game was okay at age 15.

Discussion

53 Much of the current debate on youth and media has focused, perhaps excessively, on potential harms and limiting use (Christakis & Zimmerman, 2006). This study adds balance by highlighting some developmentally appropriate uses of electronic games.

54   The boys we spoke with were articulate about their attitudes and behavior regarding video games. Boys from a range of racial/ethnic and socioeconomic backgrounds used games in similar ways and raised similar themes. Boys use violent games specifically (a) as a means to express fantasies of power and glory, (b) to explore and master what they perceived as exciting and realistic environments, and (c) as a tool to work out their feelings of anger and stress. Games—especially violent or sports games—are also social tools that allow boys to compete with and/or work cooperatively with peers. Boys gain status among peers by owning or mastering these popular games. This supports the idea that video game play with violent content may serve a function similar to rough-and-tumble play for young adolescent boys.

55   Most boys did not believe that they were negatively influenced by violent games. All boys believed that they knew the difference between behaviors that are rewarded in games and behaviors in real life. They clearly distinguished between antisocial or violent behaviors that were unlikely to occur in their lives (e.g., using powerful weapons and stealing cars) and those that were likely to occur (e.g., swearing and intimidation). In distinguishing between real life and the game world, they

focused on actions rather than realism of graphic depictions. These results are consistent with Malliet's (2006) study of perceptions of video game realism among 32 Belgian older teens and young adults; he found that players made nuanced distinctions between the context of the game world and the context of reality.

56   Our findings are also consistent with a "third person effect": the common belief that other people are more susceptible to the influence of media messages. In a telephone survey, sixth- and seventh-grade youth felt that same-age peers and younger children were more likely to be affected by violent video games (Scharrer & Leone, 2006).

57   Boys thought that violent video games might have a negative effect on younger siblings, who might be less able to distinguish between fantasy and reality and might inappropriately carry over attitudes or behaviors (especially swearing) from the game into daily life. This concern aligns with research showing that children under 9 may indeed confuse media images with reality (Villani, Olson, & Jellinek, 2005).

58   One unexpected finding was that for some boys, playing realistic sports games influenced the amount and variety of their physical activity. The use of electronic games to encourage exercise merits further study. A British study of college undergraduates found a relationship between sports video game play and knowledge of and interest in particular sports, though this was far more likely among men than women (Crawford, 2005).

59   Given the role of video game play in starting and maintaining friendships, there is potential for games to help socially awkward children gain acceptance and self-esteem. A number of boys, including those from less advantaged neighborhoods, enjoyed playing games with friends and strangers over the Internet. Industry surveys suggest that game play among adolescents is a social activity (Boyer, 2006). Studies of adults and older adolescents have found that social interaction is a primary motivator for video game play, especially for men (Jansz & Tanis, 2007; Lucas & Sherry, 2004). Given that most new game consoles as well as computers allow Web-based play, socializing over the Internet will continue to increase.

60   Another positive influence of video games reported by boys, particularly for role-playing games, was the motivation and encouragement to think creatively to solve problems. This use of games may be reassuring for parents and clinicians.

61   Boys' use of violent games to regulate their emotions, and perhaps to substitute fantasy fights for real-life ones, is a particularly interesting finding. In a survey of 1,254 children ages 12 to 14 (Olson et al., 2007), 45% of boys who played video games agreed that one reason they did so was "it helps me get my anger out"; one in four boys strongly agreed. Also, 62% of boys agreed (23% strongly) that electronic game play "helps me relax." Boys and girls who regularly played Mature-rated games were significantly more likely to use games to cope with anger.

62   Boys' use of games to channel anger and to relieve stress may lend support to catharsis theory. Other qualitative data suggest that adolescents may use violent media content, such as heavy metal music, to purge anger and calm themselves (Arnett, 1996). There are also research reports from Europe suggesting that adolescents use computer games and music to cope with negative moods (Flammer & Schaffner, 2003). Further study is needed to determine whether using violent games for emotional regulation is healthy or potentially harmful, including effects on subgroups of children, such as those with depression or other psychosocial problems.

63   A qualitative study comparing 17 elementary-school students to 51 college students (Funk, Chan, Brouwer, & Curtiss, 2006), focusing on perceived gains and losses from video game play, had some findings consistent with the current study. The authors concluded that younger children experienced psychological gains such as enjoyable immersion in game characters, excitement, and pride in game mastery and successful competition with peers. (However, these children also reported finding in-game dangers overly intense at times.) By contrast, young adults focused on use of games to manage moods, including relief of stress and boredom, and adding pleasurable excitement to life. Our young adolescent sample appears to fall between these two groups, experiencing some psychological benefits in common with both younger children and adults.

64   Results of a qualitative study such as this cannot be generalized to all boys and should not be overinterpreted. However, they do suggest areas for further exploration through more targeted qualitative studies, large surveys, or observational studies, as well as content for pilot educational or behavioral interventions to promote game benefits and reduce potential harms. Studies of children at different ages could also help to inform our understanding of the ways in which video game play may influence—or be influenced by—aspects of social, emotional, and cognitive development.

65   This study could also serve as a useful comparison for future qualitative research with young adolescent girls. It is not known how girls may perceive game violence differently from boys, whether girls use violent games for similar social and emotional purposes, or whether encouraging play of sports or dance games might promote physical activity among girls. A survey of college students found that women did not share men's social and competitive motivations for game play (Lucas & Sherry, 2004).

66   We do know that violent game play is not the sole province of boys. The survey by Olson et al. (2007) noted above found that 20% of female game players reported frequent use of at least one title in the Mature-rated *Grand Theft Auto* series; it was second only to *The Sims* in popularity among girls. A substantial number of girls also used games to cope with anger (29%) and other emotions. Recent studies of massively multiplayer online role-playing games challenge the assumption that women are not interested in violent games (Yee, 2008). Female players reported that the male-oriented culture of game players, not the death-dealing content, deters women from greater participation. The situation may be different for today's young girls, as they grow up with access to a proliferation of game genres and technologies. ◆

ANALYSIS AND DISCUSSION

1. Did you play video games when you were a teenager? Do you still play them now? If so, what were/are your favorite games and why? How realistic were/are the graphics in these games? Was/is aggression a part of the entertainment of these games? Explain.

2. The authors note that violent video games appeal to boys for a variety of reasons. What five "clusters" of reasons do the authors cite?

3. One boy mentions that seeing graphic violence could be beneficial because if one has never seen it, they will now understand it better. Respond to this observation with your own viewpoint.
4. Evaluate the authors' use of quoted material taken from their study. How do they use this material?
5. After reading this article, summarize your viewpoint that violent video games are—or are not—harmful for teen boys to play.
6. Identify the positive and negative aspects of violent game play for boys, based on the information provided in this research study.

RESEARCH AND WRITING

1. What is catharsis theory? How does it apply to video games? Research this theory and explain why violent video games could help reduce violence in teens, if the theory applied in the case of video content.
2. Working in a small group, research different types of violent video games rated "M" for mature content. Based on your research, what themes seem to be most popular?
3. Write an evaluation of this study identifying any gaps you feel the researchers might have missed. What questions could they have added or changed? Do you think any of their questions were too leading? How could their questions have skewed their results? Conversely, if you feel this study did not have any gaps, prepare a recommendation for what the researchers should study next, related to this topic, and why.

Rap Artists' Use of Women
*Luke Bobo**

Since the advent of MTV, teens have had to listen to their parents criticize music videos. Parental concerns over the scanty clothing, sexually charged lyrics, and various physical gyrations by dancers and musicians often fall on deaf ears. But what if such videos really *are* harmful? In this next essay, a Christian youth ministry leader wonders about the harmful effects of rap music in what it teaches young women about themselves, and what messages it conveys to young men about how to treat women. Is the way we present women as scantily clad objects in the entertainment industry harmful to women overall?

It's Not Neutral!

1 Nearly every parent has engaged in conversations with their teenager only to discover that their adolescent was all wise and all knowing. I have had several such conversations with my lovely 17-year-old daughter about rap music and the overt and cloaked

---

* Luke Bobo, *Ransom Fellowship,* 2009

messages communicated. On one occasion I recall talking with my daughter about the many messages conveyed by some rap music videos. In particular, I asked her the following question, "Doesn't it seem odd that the male rappers are fully dressed and the women are barely dressed?" My daughter responded, "Oh Dad, you are always preaching. You're old fashioned and reading too much into these videos!" My overlooked point was that these rap music videos are not neutral. They communicate cogently clear and subtle messages. Namely, many of the rap music videos tend to objectify or de-humanize women. Of course, my daughter's assessment of me is all too common for parents: Dad is stupid and doesn't know a thing.

Rap Music Videos

2 View many rap music videos and it is blatantly obvious that women are 'used' for the mere delight of the male rapper and his friends (and male viewer-ship). Put simply, it is painfully clear that women are mere sex objects; and this is predominately true of gangsta rap music videos. Consider TI King's rap music video that dramatizes the song "Why You Wanna." In this video TI and his boys are reclining on the beach: fully clothed. TI and his friends are scanning the beach (as predators it appears) and spot many ladies wearing bikinis while the camera focuses on and follows every move of the female's rear anatomy. Other rap music videos features barely dressed women gyrating their back sides up against the males' groin area while the rapper is spitting (rapping) the b-word and 'ho' (whore) liberally and unabashedly. Scenes like this are all too common in rap videos: fully clothed male rapper and scantily-clad women. Some of the lyrics are explicitly sexual or raw. For instance, parents should do an Internet search for the lyrics to Dem Franchize Boyz' Lean Wit It, Rock Wit It. For many rappers—like Dem Franchize Boyz—women are only useful for performing some sexual trick or favor (e.g., oral sex).

It's the American Way

3 However, we should not be surprised that these rappers denigrate women since we live in a sex-saturated culture; a culture that has reduced women to a commodity or 'object' for years. I echo St. Louis Post-Dispatch newspaper columnist Sylvester Brown's question, "Which came first: rappers as a misogynistic influence or misogyny's influence on rappers?" While I think any form of woman exploitation is deplorable, I think Brown's question is a relevant and thoughtful one. I would have to say that our culture's obsession with using women precedes the advent of rap music. Consider these few examples. In 1970 (nine years before the first rap song aired and ten years before MTV made its official debut) boxing ring card girls donned the string bikini to announce the rounds. What's this all about—a nearly naked female in a context where two men are beating each other to a pulp? Muscle car magazines also use women who are scantily clad. Marketers have used women and sex as 'tools' for years to push alcohol sales. Twenty four years ago, rock videos featured scantily clad women. For years, *Sports Illustrated* has published its coveted Swimsuit Issue. Lisa Bennett commenting on the 2002 issue said, ". . . I almost didn't open

it because I knew exactly what would be inside. Lots of leggy, busty supermodels in beside-the-point teeny bikinis. But I am glad I did, because this year's issue serves as a catalog of sexism, objectification. . ."

4   Many fashion magazines feature an overwhelmingly number of barely clothed females. Prominent on these pages is an abundance of slender well-groomed legs and cleavage. Today women are barely clothed at some restaurants (I am thinking of Hooters for example). National Football League (NFL) cheerleaders are barely clothed (and it appears they are wearing less and less fabric each year). And today a woman's sex appeal sells everything from cars to toothpaste to tans to burgers. A few years ago Hardees aired a commercial in which a very attractive white woman was riding a mechanical bull while holding a large burger. This seems innocent enough but the woman was making obvious suggestive sexual gestures while riding the bull and eating the burger. Now, I would admit that this young lady demonstrated superb hand-eye coordination but the commercial left me asking Hardees: what are you selling—the female bull rider or the burger? While we should not pardon rappers from degrading women, the painful reality is we have all seen instances of women being exploited for some type of 'gain' for years.

5   Let's face it: rappers are unfortunately continuing a long legacy of objectifying women in America. We simply live in a time where objectifying women thrives. Why? Because we live in a postmodern era where many Americans have lost all notions of shame, discretion, decency, and guilt. Those who live and play by this postmodern worldview reject any claims to objective truth. So, in our pluralistic and relativistic culture, one should be allowed to do anything he or she darn well pleases with no fear of retribution or flack. Welcome to the time in which everyone does what is right in his own sight!

Unfortunate Consequences

6   Sadly, I remember something my former secretary said to me about some Hispanic men's assessment of American women. She had spent time in Mexico on a mission's trip and she said that many Hispanic men consider American women to be 'easy.' This should not come as a surprise considering the way our media portrays women on TV, the movie screen, and in magazines. An example can be found at your local grocer. As you pay for your groceries, just gaze at the magazine racks. Many of these magazines portray women as mere sex objects; as 'bait' for buying the magazine.

7   Tragically, the image of black women has also suffered tremendous damage due to rap music videos. Consider these words from Kimberly Allers, writing for *Essence Magazine*, ". . . Lil Jon and Nelly, hang their careers on lyrics that often demean women and videos that border on pornography—with half-naked sisters who gyrate, pop it and generally drop it like it's hot. Together they [rappers and re-cord-label executives] are fashioning a legacy that does immeasurable damage to the global perception of Black women because these images are broadcast worldwide. Welcome to the new hustle."

8   Some African American women have publicly voiced their displeasure with rappers who exploit women. Oprah has publicly said she will not invite rappers who

degrade women on to her show. And rappers such as Ice Cube, 50 Cent, and Ludacris have in turn criticized Oprah for not being black enough. Diane Weathers writes, "I'm mad at an industry that shamelessly peddles music videos with images of us as gangsters, players or pimps surrounded by half-naked women eager to please." Quite frankly, I am surprised that more African-American women have not publicly voiced their disdain over the rap culture's obsession with objectifying women.

Laden with Contradictions

9 There are a plethora of contractions with rappers who degrade women and women who like their lyrics. First, the late gangsta rapper icon Tupac and today's Kanye West have rapped lovingly and respectfully about their mothers. Consider these tender and admirable lyrics from Kanye West's song "Hey Mama" (from his CD, Late Registration):

10   I wanna tell the whole world about a friend of mine

  This little light of mine and I'm finna let it shine

  I'm finna take yall back to them better times

  I'm finna talk about my mama if yall don't mind

  I was three years old, when you and I moved to the Chi

  Late December, harsh winter gave me a cold

  You fixed me up something that was good for my soul

  Famous homemade chicken soup, can I have another bowl?

  You work late nights just to keep on the lights

  Mommy got me training wheels so I could keep on my bike

  And you would give anything in this world

11   Kanye serenades and honors his mother who was a struggling single mother in Chicago yet [songs] on the same CD degrade women. Don't rappers see the blaring contradiction here?

12   Young African American women scream themselves into a tizzy in the presence of rap artists. They are enamored with the celebrity status of male rap artists yet they see images of black women being exploited on their TV screens. What gives here? Has the brain checked out because the rap artist is a celebrity? Why are black women and white women buying rap music and singing along with rappers who are obviously degrading them?

Redemptive Response

13 How should we respond to this perennial issue of women being objectified or used? Let me suggest [a few] ideas.

14   First, we need to say and acknowledge that some women are physically attractive. We should admire and celebrate their beauty. Amen! On the other hand, we should also teach our girls that beauty is not to be flaunted or idolized; rather, beauty is to be appreciated and regarded as a gift.

15   Second, it is imperative that women model modesty before their daughters in particular and young women in general. Paul encourages ladies to dress modestly in 1 Tim 2:8-10. The Greek word (*aidos*) for modesty ". . . indicates a sense of shame, a shrinking from trespassing the boundaries of propriety . . ." So, by modest, Paul means that women dress tastefully and not provocatively. Therefore, fashions that are immoral or indecent should be avoided. But like Peter (see 1 Peter 3:1ff), Paul reminds us that our focus should not be on one's outside adorning but rather the adorning of the heart or cultivating one's spiritual beauty (the matters of the heart). In other words, God finds virtues such as patience, honesty, faithfulness, self-control, and kindness as 'sexy.'

16   We need to commend and celebrate modesty and not treat those who dress modestly as geeks or freaks. However, a woman "…must not look decidedly old-fashioned, awkward. It must be borne in mind that a proud heart is sometimes concealed behind a mask of pretended modesty. That too is sin. Extremes must be carefully avoided." While I say this, I also know that finding clothes that are modest will be a bit difficult for our daughters.

17   Third, pastors and teachers need to help our communities recover a biblical view of sexuality. The common view of sexuality preached by our culture is expressed in this interview with Christina Aquilera (CA) in the magazine *Seventeen*:

18   **17:**   How have you changed since "Dirrty"?

      CA: When you're 21, you just want to go out and have a good time. You want to explore new things. I have expressed myself—and always will express myself—sexually through my art in some way or another. I think it's important as a female to feel empowered in your sexuality and to embrace it, rather than try to live out society's ideal of what a woman should think about her sexuality—and conform to those ideals.

19   Women need to teach their daughters that they are not required to express their sexuality by wearing tight, short; cleavage baring clothing. A man or woman's sexuality is to be enjoyed and shared graciously in the confines of a monogamous heterosexual marriage between husband and wife; one's sexuality is not something to be paraded.

20   Fourth, men can counter rappers' treatment of women by treating all women as human beings made in God's image. That is, as men we must treat all women not as 'things that satisfy our needs' but rather we are called to treat them with the utmost dignity and respect.

21   Fifth, we must be courageous to speak the truth in love about the negative lyrics that depict women as men's 'play toys.' This means perhaps writing letters seasoned with salt to the editorial staff of magazines and newspapers, and to TV programming executives that promote the de-humanization of women. This also means educating our kids not to consume music and their music videos mindlessly but rather to mindfully critique them.

One Final Word to Parents

22 All this to say that we need not fear our kids listening to rap music or looking at rap music videos. Some parents think that banning their kids from listening to rap music or from looking at rap music videos is somehow protecting. Is this really possible? If we make a big ado about listening to rap music or looking at rap music videos, it seems to me that this will only stoke the curiosity of our kids to do it behind our backs. Furthermore, rap music is so influential in our culture, it is nearly impossible to 'protect' our kids from the exposure to rap music. I hear rap music at the St. Louis Cardinals ballpark; in elevators; in clothing stores; and at my daughter's high school father-daughter dance and athletic events. Other parents think that listening to rap music will not undo years of biblical instruction. Think about your adolescent period. When you listened to less than parent-approved-music, did your value system collapse? Let me suggest that whether you listen to rap music or look at rap music videos with your kids, this is not a time to overreact. This musical art form yet provides us parents an excellent opportunity to engage with our kids and to hone their discernment skills (despite their opinions about us). ◆

CRITICAL THINKING

1. What do you need to know about rap music in order to understand the point of this essay and the music genre it describes? Explain.
2. What response does Luke Bobo's daughter give him when he questions her about rap music and rap music videos? What response would you give him if he posed the same questions to you?
3. Luke Bobo is an evangelical Christian who teaches at a Christian university. In your view, does his religious position influence his view of rap music? Or does religious position matter to his argument?
4. Evaluate Bobo's five-point solution to the problem of rap music's treatment of women.
5. Who does Bobo blame for the exploitation of women in music and in media? Explain using several examples from the essay.
6. What contradiction does Bobo cite that appears in music lyrics by some rap artists? Why does this contradiction confuse him? What might account for this contradiction?

CRITICAL WRITING

1. *Personal Narrative:* Do you think that music can influence behavior? Write about a time when music influenced the way you behaved. Describe the incident and your behavior and why the medium influenced you the way it did.
2. *Persuasive Writing:* Luke Bobo cites several examples of rap videos and rap music lyrics that exploit women. Write an essay expressing your own viewpoint on this issue. Can lyrics and images be harmful? Or are they

just in fun or maybe to shock but not to be taken seriously, as his daughter suggests? Explain.

3. *Expository Writing:* Luke Bobo claims that men from other countries assume American women are "easy" because of how American media presents women. Compare the images of females on rap music covers and videos to real women. What images of women are they promoting? Assume you are a foreign visitor to the United States who has never seen a music video or listened to rap music. What might you assume about the cultural attitude toward American women based on what you see and hear? Explain.

GROUP PROJECTS

1. How could some rap lyrics damage how men view/treat women and how young women view themselves? Look up the lyrics of some popular rap songs and, as a group, analyze them for their social and cultural messages.
2. Luke Bobo provides five suggestions to help "solve" the problem of the issue of the objectification of women in rap music. Discuss each suggestion, examining its possible limitations, feasibility, and perspective.

'Twilight' vs. 'Hunger Games': Why Do So Many Grown-Ups Hate Bella?
Noah Berlatsky*

After a parade of predominantly male film heroes, cinema has embraced a series of female characters drawn from the pages of popular fiction: Lisbeth Salander from the Millennium Trilogy, Bella Swan from the Twilight series, and Katniss Everdeen from the Hunger Games. Introduction to the latter two heroines began, for many girls, as they curled up with the books on which the movies were later based. The books also proved popular for many adults. In this next essay, Noah Berlatsky wonders why so few adults, especially film critics, care for the character of Bella. Is Bella simply a dated archetype to whom adults cannot relate? And what might this dislike of a fictional character reveal about our feelings about strong female role models?

1   If Bella fought Katniss, who would win?

2   This isn't a Superman-vs.-Hulk stumper or anything; if you have even a passing acquaintance with Stephanie Meyer's *Twilight* or Suzanne Collins' *The Hunger Games,* you know that, unless Edward or Jacob came to her rescue as they are wont to do, Bella is going to get stomped. Bella's main distinguishing characteristic is her

---

*Noah Berlatsky, *The Atlantic,* November 15, 2011

clumsiness; she can't get out of gym class without getting injured, much less survive a fight. Over the course of the series' four books, I'm pretty sure Bella never kills, or even injures, anyone. When she does resort to violence, it's always ineffectual and comical, as when she hits Jacob and injures her fist. Katniss, on the other hand, is an extremely competent hunter and archer, a born survivor who is deadly when cornered. Through the *Hunger Games* series, she racks up a body count that would impress *Dirty Harry*. Thumb-fingered Bella wouldn't stand a chance.

3   Critics have expressed the Katniss-would-beat-the-tar-out-of-Bella dynamic in various ways. Tina Jordan at EW.com says that "compared to Katniss, Bella is simply the more passive character." Meghan Lewitt here at *The Atlantic* compared the "swoony Bella" to the "tough-as-nails Katniss," and enthusiastically welcomes the latter as a return to heroines like Nancy Drew and Buffy: "the tomboys and the rule-breakers, resourceful, whip-smart girls who were doing it for themselves with minimal parental supervision." Alyssa Rosenberg laments, "Bella's overriding passivity," while Yvonne Zip at *Christian Science Monitor* enthuses that "Katniss is too much of a fighter to go serenely to her death." Bella, on the other hand, is stereotypically girly, and as Melinda Beasi argues, even women and feminists (especially women and feminists?) are nervous about being "associated with anything 'girly.'" Thus the appeal of Katniss, who is a badass. Because whether it's in a fist fight or in the hearts of critics, butch beats girly every time.

4   The relative discomfort with Bella, then, can be seen as reflecting a larger discomfort with femininity. That discomfort is prevalent not just among men, but (as Melinda Beasi says) among women as well. In fact, feminists have long struggled with how to think about and value femininity. Second-wave feminists (to generalize wildly) tended to be down on the feminine; they saw frills and pink and bows and childishness (or even, in the case of radicals like Shulamith Firestone, pregnancy itself) as part of the patriarchy's effort to infantilize and denigrate women. Third-wave feminists, on the other hand, have been (in general) more interested in reclaiming the feminine. For writers like Julia Serrano in *Whipping Girl,* the negative association with femininity is just another way through which the patriarchy devalues women.

5   Comparing *Twilight* and *The Hunger Games,* it's easy to see why second-wave feminists, and adults in general, find a girly teen so much less attractive than a tomboyish one. Bella is, as the critics say, passive, hapless, and an utter mess. Not only is she physically inept, but she has no particular talents or even distinguishing characteristics other than her desperation for romance. Katniss sees everyone she loves die one by one and still manages to fight on. Bella's boyfriend dumps her and she spends most of an entire book in a deep, infuriating depression. She wants wants WANTS sex, rides motorcycles and jumps off cliffs maybe for the adrenaline rush but also maybe just because the boy she's interested in jumps off cliffs and rides motorcycles. She gets knocked up and refuses to abort. She won't go to college. And she decides to become one of the living dead. She's emotional, out-of-control, mopey, makes horrible decisions, and is generally the nightmare troubled teen: a girly girl who rides her aimlessness and hormones straight to damnation.

6   And then there's Katniss: an extremely competent, tomboyish young woman who is athletic, focused, responsible, and able to take care of herself. She's not especially interested in boys and doesn't have sex, or even really think about sex for almost the entire series. She's also politically engaged, especially as the story moves on. She is, in other words, the ideal second-wave feminist daughter; smart, fierce, independent, and sexually restrained.

7   And yet, for all the critical accolades…is masculinity really categorically better and more feminist than femininity? Would we really rather have our 17-year-old daughters kill dozens than have them carry a baby to term? Certainly, there are aspects of *The Hunger Games* that make the butch ideal seem problematic at the very least. The series is organized around a bloodthirsty yearly ritual, in which children are thrown into a high-tech arena and forced to battle to the death. The analogy with reality TV is obvious—and if the *Hunger Games* competition is reality TV, that makes the readers part of the audience, enjoying the adrenalin rush of watching the wee ones kill one another.

8   The book, of course, never acknowledges the parallel. It can't explicitly embrace violence—which means that Katniss can't embrace violence either. As Laura Miller points out in a smart review at *Salon,* "In some ways, Katniss is more passive than Bella, allowed to have all kinds of goodies [nice clothes, political power] but only if she demonstrates her virtue by not really wanting them in the first place." Bella, like any good girly girl, is in touch with her desires—she wants to marry and screw Edward, not necessarily in that order, and she spends the series trying to do just that. Katniss, on the other hand, spends *The Hunger Games* unleashing mayhem on behalf of other people—the evil government, the maybe-evil rebels, the readers. To be masculine, she has to be strong, but to want to be strong is to be bad. Power and desire have to separate. Katniss has the first only because she doesn't have the second; Bella's got the second only because she doesn't have the first.

9   At the end of *Twilight*, Bella actually does get power. She turns into a vampire who has the physical and magical wherewithal to save her entire family from death—not to mention flatten Katniss with a flick of her perfect pale sparkly wrist. Katniss, conversely, finds that what she desired all along was domestic bliss with her nice-guy suitor and a bunch of kids running around the cottage. Explaining why she chose Peeta for her husband rather than the more swaggering Gale, Katniss says, "what I need to survive is not Gale's fire, kindled with rage and hatred. I have plenty of fire myself. What I need is the dandelion in the spring." When you're butch, you want your lover to give you flowers. When you're a girly girl like Bella, you want a lover who will give you the ability to run down and slaughter wild animals with your bare hands.

10   I don't know that Bella and Katniss would necessarily like each other much if they met. But I think they might understand each other's desires and each other's strength. In any case, I doubt they'd fight. Masculinity and femininity isn't a duel to the death. The many tween fans of both books know that, even if adult critics occasionally get confused. ◆

CRITICAL THINKING

1. How does Berlatsky compare the characters of Bella and Katniss? Is he fair and balanced in his comparison?
2. What does Berlatsky mean as he descries the power quandary each character faces as we judge them: "Power and desire have to separate. Katniss has the first only because she doesn't have the second; Bella's got the second only because she doesn't have the first."
3. Berlatsky observes that "for writers like Julia Serrano in *Whipping Girl,* the negative association with femininity is just another way through which the patriarchy devalues women." In what ways could associating femininity with negative connotations devalue women as a whole? Explain.
4. In this essay, Berlatsky wonders if our discomfort with Bella's character is really a larger discomfort with femininity. What is "femininity" and how do we define it? Why does it have a bad rap? Or does it? Explain.
5. Based on this essay, who do you think Berlatsky prefers—Katniss or Bella?
6. What influences our perception of "likable" female characters? Are Katniss and Bella likeable? Do we need to "like" a character in order to root for her success in the story? Why or why not?

CRITICAL WRITING

1. *Research and Analysis:* In this essay, Berlatsky describes two very different types of female characters. Consider movies you have seen in the past and list examples of other Hollywood female main characters in dramatic roles. Discuss the role and the importance of this type of character and what is gained by promoting it in media. What is lost? Explain.
2. *Research and Analysis:* Watch both of the films Berlatsky describes making careful notes on the female lead roles (Watch the first movie of *Twilight*). What are we told about each? How is each girl dressed? How does she interact with the other characters? What impact does she have on the action of the film? Then, respond to the observation that Berlatsky makes in the final paragraph: "I don't know that Bella and Katniss would necessarily like each other much if they met. But I think they might understand each other's desires and each other's strength." What are the strengths of each character?
3. *Research and Analysis:* Find a female character in another movie who is "masculine" as opposed to "feminine." Describe the desirable and undesirable qualities the film attaches to this character.

GROUP PROJECTS

1. Berlatsky wonders, "Would we really rather have our 17-year-old daughters kill dozens than have them carry a baby to term?" With your group, discuss this statement and what society seems to expect from young women coming of age. What about of young men?

2. Survey a group of students as to which character they prefer—Bella or Katniss—asking each person to explain his or her preference. Discuss your results and connect them back to points Berlatsky makes about our comfort, or discomfort, of "the feminine" in today's culture.

Poof!
Dana Vachon[*]

America's obsession with real people behaving badly is nothing new. Every week, people across the country tune in to watch the latest antics of fighting housewives, beauty pageant wannabes, and pushy brides driving their friends over the brink. Interestingly, the economy influences our preferences for reality programing. Five years ago, when students could still get a credit card without a level-3 security check, we gravitated toward shows that glorified excess—programs such as *My Super Sweet 16* and *The Hills*. Today, however, we prefer to watch regular people from New Jersey booze it up. In this next article, Dana Vachon explores obsession with "guidos" behaving badly. If *The Hills* defined the boom; *Jersey Shore* is today's bust.

1   America's first television stars emerged just after World War II. First among these were professional wrestlers, and greatest among them was Gorgeous George. A golden-tressed brutalizer, Gorgeous enjoyed mirrors and Chanel No. 5. He entered the ring to "Pomp and Circumstance," bathed in purple light, a valet, Jeffries, carrying "GG" monogrammed towels on a silver tray. He was vain, absurd—and essential. Because, after 16 years of Depression and destruction, he showed Americans how to adjust to the postwar world, its eerily unprecedented prosperity. How to become newer, "better" people. He eased the transition from wartime savagery to peacetime consumerism by joining both in a performance piece for which George Raymond Wagner, his creator, was by 1949 making $70,000 a year.

2   American television has long stood in for American education. TV "shows" us how to live, how to survive in an office and a family, how to train our dogs and cook our food. How to successfully date, marry, and disarm nuclear devices. Cultural Gospel holds that *Jersey Shore* became a hit as a triumph of vulgarity. This is wrong. *Jersey Shore's* success has rather to do with the offering of lessons in remedial humanity and is best understood in juxtaposition to the MTV franchise it eclipsed.

3   In times of prosperity we are encouraged to consume our way toward better selves, a process that helps fuel the prosperity already fueling it until, as we say, the bubble bursts. During the credit boom, *The Hills*, with its young, beautiful cast, informed national aspiration with images of glossy life in Los Angeles, the cradle of simulation. "I got an apartment with my good friend Heidi. I'm going to fashion school. And I scored an interview for a killer internship with *Teen Vogue*. This is

my chance to make it all happen in the one city where they say dreams come true," Lauren Conrad, Everygirl, told us before the pilot's title-sequence even began. The camera then went close on her veal-calf face as she drove a German car toward Hollywood, the show's theme song, Natasha Bedingfield's "Unwritten," evoking Fitzgerald: "Reaching for something in the distance, so close you almost taste it."

4   The song's opening lyric is, "I am unwritten, can't read my mind, I'm unde-fined" and might have better described the moment at hand and madness to come were it not edited out. As the aughts' prosperity approached maximum falseness, *The Hills* evinced the dehumanizing effects of hyperstriving with a story line that veered toward blackmail and a sex tape. Characters grew increasingly paranoid, isolated, schizophrenically camera-conscious. By the time Lauren Conrad left the show, episode titles were evoking Nashian game-theory scenarios: "It's On, Bitch," "Mess With Me, I Mess With You," and, most tenderly, "I'm Done With You." Her farewell episode saw her at Hollywood's Beso with on-off love Brody Jenner, Cold War Olympic spawn, noting a shared smallness of the ears. "You shouldn't trust people with small cars," said Conrad. "Why?" said Jenner. "Cause they lie a lot," she told him, and when he asked whether that was really a saying, said she'd just made it up. Their romance had long since tired.

5   After the '08 crash, the empty promises of false prosperity became dark les-sons in reality; *The Hills* no longer offered valuable lifestyle instruction but rather became a failed era's gross artifact. A final season was shot without Conrad. In it, her great antagonist, Heidi Montag, nearly died after a plastic surgeon's overhaul of her entire face. ("I had too much Demerol, like Michael Jackson did.") Producers mined self-mutilation for pathetic tension, following Heidi home to Crested Butte, Colo., where her L.L. Bean-pretty mother cried when she walked in the door, then asked what she had done. What followed is readable as dark poetry of the American postwar experience:

6   *I got a slight eyebrow lift*
And that's why I have these staples in my head
I had my nose redone
I had my own fat injected into my cheeks
I had my ears pinned back
I had injections in my lips
I had my chin shaved-down
I had my breasts redone
And my back shaped
And then I had a little bit
Of inner and outer lipo done
You have to realize that
I've been through so much pain.

7   The decreasingly young dreamer had ceased to resemble the viewer quite as fully as she had ceased to resemble herself. But most had long-since lost interest.

8   We were watching *Jersey Shore,* filled with the sort of people we'd deny ever knowing pre-Madoff (lifeworn bikini models, drivers of Clinton-era Hondas, Ronnie Magro) but couldn't get enough of post-. The cast, having apparently sat out the prosperity, were powerfully able to show the rest of us how to go on living now that it was over. Critics called them shallow, vain, depraved. They were all these things. But it was their miraculously intact humanity that most affected us; "I am the Kim Kardashian of Staten Island, baby," said Angelina Pivarnick, carrying trashbags as luggage, demonstrating self-esteem divorced from wealth; "I can never go out without my hair extensions," said Sammi "Sweetheart" Giancola, the show's great beauty, camera close on said hair-extensions, subverting the very artifice of glamour on which *The Hills* existed. She was adolescent, needy, took forever to get ready; "If you're not a guido," she warned, "You can get the fuck out of my face." Lucky for Ronnie Magro, soon deeply in love. And for all of his Neanderthalisms, he experienced sex with Sammi not as some air-brushed cliché pushed from the offices of *Teen Vogue* or Vivid Video (have they yet merged?) but an awesome human wonder to be met with childlike awe. "Yeah," he said of their consummation. "We smooshed."

9   Beneath their tans and gel, the cast of *Jersey Shore* showed us how to be good to ourselves and one another. Mainly they fought for, not with each other; "We stood together as a family," reflected DJ Pauly D in the finale, invoking civilization's very core. And in watching we recovered something of the past. We left the wreckage of the false and paranoid era and like stroke victims relearned to be alive on the planet.

10   Those still paying attention to the post-plastic Heidi Montag, a plasma victim of the cathode cult founded by George Raymond Wagner 63 years ago, wondered why a pretty young girl would do that to herself. They shouldn't have; Colorado's prodigal daughter was maimed in the line of national duty, seeking a better self. Which is what the *Jersey Shore* cast have discovered, for better or worse. We loved them largely because they were unknown, but in loving them we made them known and so, potentially, unlovable. The culture eats its young, then goes to yoga. It ought to be interesting to see them as celebrities, if only for a little while. ◆

CRITICAL THINKING

1. Vachon observes that *The Hills* represented American culture before "the bubble burst." What did *The Hills* depict? How did it illustrate a moment in American culture? Explain.
2. According to Vachon, what accounts for the popularity of *Jersey Shore*? How does it compare with *The Hills*?
3. If you have watched *Jersey Shore*, respond to Vachon's hypothesis as to what has made this program so successful. If you have never seen the show, view it online and summarize your impression of it.
4. Many critics of reality programing observe that it can run the gamut of quality to trash. In your opinion, where do the programs *The Hills* and *Jersey Shore* fall? Cite some other reality programs in your response for comparison.
5. In what ways does reality television reflect the financial and social time of the culture in which it airs? Explain.

CRITICAL WRITING

1. *Compare and Contrast*: Compare *Jersey Shore* with *The Hills*. In what ways are the programs similar? In what ways are they different? What fundamental differences, if any, do you notice between the two programs?
2. *Exploratory Writing*: Is your life more like *The Hills* or more like *Jersey Shore*? Explain using examples. If you wish, you could include that your life has, or had, elements of both.

GROUP PROJECTS

1. Prepare a questionnaire that seeks to find just what people would like to watch on reality programs. Do they want competition? Simple voyeurism? Conflict? Participants' systematic elimination from the program? Is there an ideal formula?
2. Discuss the popularity of reality programming in American culture. Print a copy of the week's programming, such as from TV Guide, and identify as many reality programs as you can. What percentage does reality programming comprise overall? What trends, if any, can you determine about what reality programming might look like in the next three to five years? As a group, describe these trends and then share how they connect to cultural trends now at work in the United States.

VIEWPOINTS

▶ **The Case for Reality TV**
*Michael Hirschorn**

▶ **Reality TV: Should We Really Watch?**
*Elizabeth Larkin**

Although reality television programs are fodder for critics, there is no denying their popularity. Far from a passing fad, there are more reality television programs than ever before. Several programs have emerged as constant hits, including *Project Runway, The Biggest Loser, The Apprentice*, and *American Idol*. Others track the daily lives of people known only for having money or behaving badly, as in the case of *The Real Housewives* series on Bravo. First, Michael Hirschorn notes that the critics can tut-tut all they want, but reality shows rule television for a simple reason: The best of them are far more compelling than the worn-out sitcoms and crime dramas the networks keep churning out. Elizabeth Larkin challenges that watching reality programming, especially the kind that holds up people for ridicule, is morally suspect. Just because something is entertaining, she counters, doesn't mean we should watch it.

---

*Michael Hirschorn, *The Atlantic,* May 2007; Elizabeth Larkin, About.com, 2004

The Case for Reality TV
Michael Hirschorn

1   This past January, I had the pleasure of serving as official spear-catcher for a *CBS Evening News* report on the increasing levels of humiliation on *American Idol* and other reality-TV shows, including some on my channel, VH1. The segment featured snippets of our shows *I Love New York* (a dating competition with an urban vibe) and *Celebrity Fit Club* (which tracks the efforts of overweight singers and actors to get back in shape, and, by extension, reignite their careers). "VH1, among other things, showcases faded celebrities who are fat," said the CBS correspondent Richard Schlesinger.

2   In between shots of me fake-working at my computer and fake-chatting with the amiable Schlesinger while fake-strolling down our corporate-looking hallway, I took my best shot at defending the alleged horrors of *AI* and *Celebrity Fit Club*. But it was clear that *CBS News* was set on bemoaning what it saw as yet another outrage against the culture. The central complaint, per Katie Couric's intro to the report, was that more people had watched *American Idol* the previous week than watched the State of the Union address on all the broadcast networks combined. When the segment ended, Couric signed off with an extravagant eye roll. "We're doing our part here at *CBS News*," she seemed to be saying, "but the barbarians are massing at the gates, people." A line had been drawn in the sand, as if the news were now akin to an evening at the Met.

3   Is there an easier position to take in polite society than to patronize reality TV? Even television programmers see the genre as a kind of visual Hamburger Helper: cheap filler that saves them money they can use elsewhere for more worthy programming. Reality shows cost anywhere from a quarter to half as much to produce as scripted shows. The money saved on *Extreme Makeover: Home Edition*, the logic goes, allows ABC to pay for additional gruesome medical emergencies and exploding ferries on *Grey's Anatomy*. NBC's crappy *Fear Factor* pays for the classy *Heroes*.

4   As befits a form driven largely by speed and cost considerations, reality TV is not often formally daring. Fifteen years after MTV's *The Real World* set the template for contemporary reality TV by placing seven strangers in a downtown Manhattan loft, reality television has developed its own visual shorthand: short doses of documentary footage interspersed with testimonials (often called OTFs, for "on-the-fly" interviews) in which the participants describe, ex post facto, what they were thinking during the action you are watching.

5   The current boom may be a product of the changing economics of the television business, but reality TV is also the liveliest genre on the set right now. It has engaged hot-button cultural issues—class, sex, race—that respectable television, including the august *CBS Evening News*, rarely touches. And it has addressed a visceral need for a different kind of television at a time when the Web has made more traditionally produced video seem as stagey as Molière.

6   Reality TV may be an awkward admixture of documentary (with its connotations of thousands of hours of footage patiently gathered, redacted by monk-like figures into the purest expression of truth possible in 90 to 120 minutes) and scripted

(with its auteurs and Emmys and noble overtones of craft). But this kludge also happens to have allowed reality shows to skim the best elements of scripted TV and documentaries while eschewing the problems of each. Reality shows steal the story structure and pacing of scripted television but leave behind the canned plots and characters. They have the visceral impact of documentary reportage without the self-importance and general lugubriousness. Where documentaries must construct their narratives from found matter, reality TV can place real people in artificial surroundings designed for maximum emotional impact.

7   Scripted television is supposedly showing new ambition these days, particularly in the hour-long drama form. *Studio 60 on the Sunset Strip* was going to bring the chatty intelligence of *The West Wing* back to prime time. *Lost* was going to challenge network audiences like never before, with complex plots, dozens of recurring characters, and movie-level production values. Shows are bigger now: On *24* this season, a nuclear bomb exploded. But network prime-time television remains dominated by variants on the police procedural (*Law & Order, CSI, Criminal Minds*), in which a stock group of characters (ethnically, sexually, and generationally diverse) grapples with endless versions of the same dilemma. The episodes have all the ritual predictability of Japanese Noh theater: Crimes are solved, lessons are learned, order is restored.

8   Reality shows have leaped into this imaginative void. Discovery's *Deadliest Catch*, which began its third season in April, is an oddly transfixing series about... crab fishermen in the Bering Sea. As a straightforward documentary, *Catch* would have been worthy fodder, but the producers have made it riveting by formatting the whole season as a sporting event, with crab tallies for each of the half dozen or so boats and a race-against-the-clock urgency that, for all its contrivance, gives structure and meaning to the fishermen's efforts.

9   Narrative vibrancy is not the only thing that electrifies these shows. Reality TV presents some of the most vital political debate in America, particularly about class and race. Fox's *Nanny 911* and ABC's *Supernanny* each offer object lessons on the hazards of parenting in an age of instant gratification and endless digital diversion. ABC's *Extreme Makeover: Home Edition* features intensely emotional tales of people who have fallen through the cracks of Bush-era America—often blue-collar families ravaged by disease, health-care costs, insurance loopholes, layoffs, and so forth. My channel's *The (White) Rapper Show* turned into a running debate among the aspiring white MC's over cultural authenticity—whether it is more properly bestowed by class or race.

10   Class realities are plumbed to remarkable effect on *The Real Housewives of Orange County*, a "docu soap" that completed its second season on Bravo this spring. The show is inspired by a trio of suburban dramas: The O. C., *Desperate Housewives*, and the 1999 movie *American Beauty*. Lacking the visual panache, or the budgets, of its scripted forebears, *Real Housewives* nonetheless goes deeper, charting the spiritual decay of life in gated communities, where financial anxieties, fraying families, and fear of aging leave inhabitants grasping for meaning and happiness as they steer their Escalades across Southern California's perfectly buffed, featureless landscape. *Crash*, the 2006 Oscar winner, trafficked in similar white California dread, but with all the nuance of a two-by-four to the face.

11   In *Real Housewives*, businessman Lou Knickerbocker stages a photo shoot to promote his new "highly oxygenated" water, variously called "Aqua Air" and "O. C. Energy Drink" ("We have patented technology that produces water from air"). The models are attractive-ish teen and twenty something girls: Lou's daughter Lindsey, by ex-wife Tammy; a few other daughters of O. C. housewives; and a newcomer whom Lou apparently found waitressing at a local restaurant.

12   Lou and Tammy made piles of money—it's not clear how—but their finances seem to have fractured along with their marriage. The photo shoot, therefore, is throwing off more than the normal amount of flop sweat. Lou apparently has personally selected the girls, which means he has declined to showcase his other daughter, Megan, because of her tattoos and lack of physical fitness. Lou believes the "Aqua Air Angels" should embody the Aqua Air ideal, which is why they can't drink or smoke and must have grade-point averages higher than 3.5. "This is a photo shoot," he barks after a fight breaks out between one of the girls and the waitress, "not a gang bang, for chrissakes."

13   The detail is what puts the scene over: Lou's lip-smacking focus on the girls, the girls' bland acquiescence. "That's it, baby, smile," Lou urges his daughter. "Show those teeth," says Tammy. A similar scenario on *Desperate Housewives* could never have been quite this preposterous, quite this blandly amoral. The characters would have been scripted with softening, redeeming qualities, or been rendered comically evil. Lou would've gotten his comeuppance, like Wallace Shawn's money-siphoning literary agent in that series. Here, the apparent willingness of the young women and at least some of the parents to indulge Lou's bottom-of-the-barrel scheming outlines, in a few short brushstrokes, a community's shared value system.

14   Value systems are smashed into each other, like atoms in an accelerator, on ABC's *Wife Swap*, where the producers find the most extreme pairings possible: lesbian mommies with bigots, godless cosmopolites with Bible thumpers. On one February show, a Pentacostal family, the Hoovers, was paired with the family of a former pastor, Tony Meeks, who has turned from God to follow his rock-and-roll dreams (mom Tish rocks out as well). "I feel by being there," Kristin Hoover said, "I was able to remind Tony that God still loves him and is not finished with him." The episode took seriously the Hoovers' commitment to homeschooling and their rejection of contemporary culture (a rejection not taken to the extreme of declining an invitation to appear on reality TV). Compare this with the tokenism of "born-again Christian" Harriet Hayes on NBC's dramedy *Studio 60 on the Sunset Strip*. Harriet's but a cipher, a rhetorical backboard against which ex-boyfriend Matt Albie can thwack his heathen wisecracks.

15   The competitions and elimination shows are latter-day Milgram experiments that place real people in artificial situations to see what happens. *The Apprentice* is Darwinism set loose inside an entrepreneurial Habitrail. Post-9/11, *Survivor* became less a fantasy and more a metaphor for an imagined post-apocalyptic future. What happens on these shows might be a Technicolor version of how we behave in real life, but so is most fiction. Creative endeavors—written, scripted, or produced— should be measured not by how literally they replicate actual life but by how effectively they render emotional truths. The best moments found on reality TV are unscriptable, or beyond the grasp of most scriptwriters. It's no coincidence that 2006's

best scripted dramas—*The Wire*, HBO's multi-season epic of inner-city Baltimore; and *Children of Men*, Alfonso Cuarón's futuristic thriller—were studies in meticulously crafted "realness," deploying naturalistic dialogue, decentered and chaotic action, stutter-step pacing, and a reporter's eye for the telling detail. *The Wire*'s season and Cuarón's movie both ended on semi-resolved novelistic notes, scorning the tendency in current television and cinema toward easy narrative closure. Watching them only threw into higher relief the inability of so much other scripted product to get beyond stock characterizations and pat narrative.

16   For all the snobbism in the doc community, reality TV has actually contributed to the recent boom in documentary filmmaking. The most successful docs of recent vintage have broken through in part by drawing heavily from reality television's bag of tricks, dropping the form's canonical insistence on pure observation. In *Fahrenheit 9/11*, Michael Moore brings an Army recruiter with him to confront legislators and urge them to enlist their children in the Iraq War effort. In *Bowling for Columbine*, Moore takes children who were shot at Columbine to a Kmart, where they ask for a refund on the bullets that are still lodged in their bodies. Of course, Moore's never been a doc purist. *TV Nation*, his short-lived 1994 television series, prefigured a long line of gonzo reality, from *Joe Millionaire* to *Punk'd*. Having the Serbian ambassador sing along to the *Barney* theme song ("I love you, you love me") while statistics about the number of Bosnians killed during the breakup of Yugoslavia appeared on the screen was not only ur-reality; it was ur-Borat. And speaking of talking animals, *March of the Penguins* turned stunning footage of mating and migrating penguins into an utterly contrived Antarctic version of *Love Story*.

17   The resistance to reality TV ultimately comes down to snobbery, usually of the generational variety. People under 30, in my experience, tend to embrace this programming; they're happy to be entertained, never mind the purity of conception. As an unapologetic producer of reality shows, I'm obviously biased, but I also know that any genre that provokes such howls of protest is doing something interesting. Try the crab. ◆

 Reality TV: Should We Really Watch?
Elizabeth Larkin

1   Media both in America and around the world seem to have "discovered" that so-called reality shows are very profitable, resulting in a growing string of such shows in recent years. Although not all are successful, many do achieve significant popularity and cultural prominence. That does not mean, however, that they are good for society or that they should be aired.

2   The first thing to keep in mind is that "reality TV" is nothing new—one of the most popular examples of this sort of entertainment is also one of the oldest, *Candid Camera*. Originally created by Allen Funt, it showcased hidden video of people in all manner of unusual and strange situations and was popular for many years. Even game shows, long a standard on television, are a sort of reality TV.

3   Today's programming, including a new version of *Candid Camera* produced by Funt's son, goes quite a bit further. The primary basis for many of these shows (but not all) seems to be to put people in painful, embarrassing, and humiliating situations for the rest of us to watch—and, presumably, laugh at and be entertained by.

4   These reality TV shows wouldn't be made if we didn't watch them, so why do we watch them? Either we find them entertaining or we find them so shocking that we are simply unable to turn away. I'm not sure that the latter is an entirely defensible reason for supporting such programming; turning away is as easy as hitting a button on the remote control. The former, however, is a bit more interesting.

Humiliation as Entertainment

5 What we are looking at here is, I think, an extension of *Schadenfreude*, a German word used to describes people's delight and entertainment at the failings and problems of others. If you laugh at someone slipping on the ice, that's Schadenfreude. If you take pleasure in the downfall of a company you dislike, that is also Schadenfreude. The latter example is certainly understandable, but I don't think that's what we're seeing here. After all, we don't know the people on reality shows.

6   So what causes us to derive entertainment from the suffering of others? Certainly there may be catharsis involved, but that is also achieved through fiction—we don't need to see a real person suffer in order to have a cathartic experience. Perhaps we are simply happy that these things aren't happening to us, but that seems more reasonable when we see something accidental and spontaneous rather than something deliberately staged for our amusement.

7   That people do suffer on some reality TV shows is beyond question—the very existence of reality programming may be threatened by the increase in lawsuits by people who have been injured and/or traumatized by the stunts these shows have staged. One of the reasons such programming is attractive is that it can be much cheaper than traditional shows, but that may change as insurance premiums for reality TV begin to reflect higher to insurers.

8   There is never any attempt to justify these shows as enriching or worthwhile in any way, though certainly not every program needs to be educational or highbrow. Nevertheless, it **does** raise the question as to why they are made. Perhaps a clue about what is going on lies in the aforementioned lawsuits. According to Barry B. Langberg, a Los Angeles lawyer who represents one couple:

9   Something like this is done for no other reason than to embarrass people or humiliate them or scare them. The producers don't care about human feelings. They don't care about being decent. They only care about money.

10   Comments from various reality TV producers often fail to demonstrate much sympathy or concern with what their subjects experience—what we are seeing is a great callousness towards other human beings who are treated as means towards achieving financial and commercial success, regardless of the consequences for them. Injuries, humiliation, suffering, and higher insurance rates are all just the "cost of doing business" and a requirement for being edgier.

Where's the Reality?

11 One of the attractions of reality television is the supposed "reality" of it—unscripted and unplanned situations and reactions. One of the ethical problems of reality television is the fact that it isn't nearly as "real" as it pretends to be. At least in dramatic shows one can expect the audience to understand that what they see on the screen doesn't necessarily reflect the reality of the actors' lives; the same, however, cannot be said for heavily edited and contrived scenes on sees on reality shows.

12 There is now a growing concern about how reality television shows can help perpetuate racial stereotypes. In many shows a similar black female character has been featured—all different women, but very similar character traits. It's gone so far that Africana.com has trademarked the expression The Evil Black Woman to describe this sort of individual: brazen, aggressive, pointing fingers, and always lecturing others on how to behave.

13 MSNBC has reported on the matter, noting that after so many "reality" programs, we can discern a pattern of "characters" that isn't very far different from the stock characters found in fictional programming. There's the sweet and naive person from a small town looking to make it big while still retaining small-town values. There's the party girl/guy who's always looking for a good time and who shocks those around them. There's the aforementioned Evil Black Woman with an Attitude, or sometimes Black Man with an Attitude—and the list goes on.

14 MSNBC quotes Todd Boyd, critical-studies professor at the University of Southern California's School of Cinema-Television as saying "We know all these shows are edited and manipulated to create images that look real and sort of exist in real time. But really what we have is a construction…. The whole enterprise of reality television relies on stereotypes. It relies on common stock, easily identifiable images."

15 Why do these stock characters exist, even in so-called "reality" television that it supposed to be unscripted and unplanned? Because that's the nature of entertainment. Drama is more readily propelled by the use of stock characters, because the less you have to think about who a person really is, the more quickly the show can get to things like the plot (such as it may be). Sex and race are especially useful for stock characterizations, because they can pull from a long and rich history of social stereotypes.

16 This is especially problematic when so few minorities appear in programming, whether reality or dramatic, because those few individuals end up being representatives of their entire group. A single angry white man is just an angry white man, while an angry black man is an indication of how all black men "really" are. MSNBC explains:

17 "Indeed, the [Sista with an Attitude] feeds off preconceived notions of African American women. After all, she's an archetype as old as D. W. Griffith, first found in the earliest of movies where slave women were depicted as ornery and cantankerous, uppity Negresses who couldn't be trusted to remember their place. Think Hattie McDaniel in *Gone With the Wind*, bossing and fussing as she yanked and tugged on Miss Scarlett's corset strings. Or Sapphire Stevens on the much-pilloried *Amos N' Andy,* serving up confrontation on a platter, extra-spicy, don't hold the sass. Or Florence, the mouthy maid on *The Jeffersons.*

18   How do stock characters appear in "unscripted" reality shows? First, the people themselves contribute to the creation of these characters because they know, even if unconsciously, that certain behavior is more likely to get them air time. Second, the shows editors contribute mightily to the creation of these characters, because they completely validate just that motivation. A black woman sitting around smiling isn't perceived to be as entertaining as a black woman pointing her finger at a white man and angrily telling him what to do.

19   An especially good (or egregious) example of this can be found in Manigault-Stallworth, a star of Donald Trump's *The Apprentice*. She has been called "the most hated woman on television" because of the behavior and attitude people see her with. But how much of her on-screen persona is real and how much is a creation of the shows editors? Quite a lot of the latter, according to Manigault-Stallworth in an e-mail quoted by MSNBC:

20   What you see on the show is a gross misrepresentation of who I am. For instance they never show me smiling, it's just not consistent with the negative portrayal of me that they want to present. Last week they portrayed me as lazy and pretending to be hurt to get out of working, when in fact I had a concussion due to my serious injury on the set and spent nearly…10 hours in the emergency room. It's all in the editing!

21   Reality television shows are not documentaries. People are not put into situations simply to see how they react—the situations are heavily contrived, they are altered in order to make things interesting, and large amounts of footage are heavily edited into what the show's producers think will result in the best entertainment value for viewers. Entertainment, of course, often comes from conflict—so conflict will be created where none exists. If the show cannot incite conflict during the filming, it can be created in how pieces of footage are stitched together. It's all in what they choose to reveal to you—or not reveal, as the case may be.

Moral Responsibility

22   If a production company creates a show with the explicit intention of trying to make money from the humiliation and suffering which they themselves create for unsuspecting people, then that seems to me to be immoral and unconscionable. I simply cannot think of any excuse for such actions—pointing out that others are willing to watch such events does not relieve them of the responsibility for having orchestrated the events and willed the reactions in the first place. The mere fact that they **want** others to experience humiliation, embarrassment, and/or suffering (and simply in order to increase earnings) is itself unethical; actually going forward with it is even worse.

23   What of the responsibility of the reality TV advertisers? Their funding makes such programming possible, and therefore they must shoulder part of the blame as well. An ethical position would be to refuse to underwrite any programming, no matter how popular, if it is designed to deliberately cause others humiliation, embarrassment, or suffering. It's immoral to do such things for fun (especially on a regular basis), so it's certainly immoral to do it for money or to pay to have it done.

24   What of the responsibility of contestants? In shows which accost unsuspecting people on the street, there isn't really any. Many, however, have contestants who volunteer and sign releases—so aren't they getting what they deserve? Not necessarily. Releases don't necessarily explain everything that will happen, and some are pressured to sign new releases part way through a show in order to have a chance at winning—if they don't, all they have endured up to that point will have been for nothing. Regardless, the producers' desire to cause humiliation and suffering in others for profit remains immoral, even if someone volunteers to be the object of humiliation in exchange for money.

25   Finally, what about the reality TV viewers? If you watch such shows, **why**? If you find that you are entertained by the suffering and humiliation of others, that's a problem. Perhaps an occasional instance wouldn't merit comment, but a weekly schedule of such pleasure is another matter entirely.

26   I suspect that people's ability and willingness to take pleasure in such things may stem from the increasing separation we experience from others around us. The more distant we are from each other as individuals, the more readily we can objectify each other and fail to experience sympathy and empathy when others around us suffer. The fact that we are witnessing events not in front of us but rather on television, where everything has an unreal and fictional air about it, probably aids in this process as well.

27   I'm not saying that you shouldn't watch reality TV programming, but the motivations behind being a viewer are ethically suspect. Instead of passively accepting whatever media companies try to feed you, it would be better to take some time to reflect on **why** such programming is made and **why** you feel attracted to it. Perhaps you will find that your motivations themselves are not so attractive. ◆

CRITICAL THINKING

1. Do you watch reality TV programs? If so, which ones? What inspires you to watch these programs? What is their appeal?
2. If you could be a contestant on a reality television program, which one would you go on, and why?
3. Why does Larkin believe watching reality programs is unethical, or at the very least, morally questionable? Do all reality television programs exploit their participants in one way or another? Does the fact that people on reality programs agree to be followed on camera make this acceptable? Why or why not?
4. Hirschorn notes that most respectable television critics automatically debunk the role of reality TV in our culture and the quality and appeal of subject matter. In your opinion, what accounts for this disparity between the critics and the viewing public?
5. According to Hirschorn, in what ways does reality TV fill the void left by traditional programming? Do you agree or disagree with his assessment?

CRITICAL WRITING

1. *Expository Writing:* Write a short essay addressing the ways that reality television programs do or do not represent actual reality. Refer to current programs in your essay to support your points.
2. *Research Writing:* Visit the *NewsHour* Web site, at http://www.pbs.org/newshour/forum/july00/reality.html, on the popularity of reality programming, featuring Robert Thompson, head of the Center for the Study of Popular Television at Syracuse University, and Frank Farley, a past president of the American Psychological Association and professor at Temple University. Read the questions and responses posted at the Web site, and respond to them with your own viewpoint. Note that the Web site was first posted in 2000. How has reality television changed since then?

GROUP PROJECTS

1. With your group, compile a list of reality programs and their contestant profiles. (You may have to look up these programs online to see the most recent contestant roster.) What programs were the most successful? Did they appeal to a broad, multicultural audience? Discuss your list and observations in class as part of a wider discussion on diversity and reality TV programs.
2. Develop your own reality TV program plot. Include the show's premise, its objective and goal, why people would want to watch it, and who would be a typical contestant. Outline the program and present it to the class. The class should vote on which program it finds the most engaging.

CHAPTER

5

The Social Animal

Connecting in a Digital World

The attention and appeal of celebrity culture make many of us long for notoriety in our own lives, even if it may be only within our own social circle. Andy Warhol's famous quip, cited in the introduction to the last chapter, was rephrased for our times by the Scottish artist Momus, who noted, "On the Web, everyone will be famous to fifteen people." Momus was referring to the current practice of social networking, blogging, and self-broadcasting on YouTube.

Human beings have always been a social species. From the tribes and clans of the past to the cliques and clubs of the present, we naturally gravitate to each other and seek a sense of belonging and inclusion. The next group of essays examines our desire to connect with others, while maintaining our own sense of self and unique identity.

Although few of us will be as famous as Ashton Kutcher, an actor known for his tweets to fans, many of us do enjoy the attention we may earn from posting something witty online. We all crave some recognition. We like the "likes." But are we giving too much away when we post information on blogs and social networking pages such as Facebook? Are we making spectacles of ourselves, parading online the most intimate details of our lives? Lakshmi Chaudhry wonders what the wave of online narcissism means to the culture as a whole in "Mirror, Mirror, on the Web." Christine Rosen continues this line of inquiry in "Virtual Friendship and the New Narcissism," in which she ponders whether social networking sites have raised the bar on our level of self-absorption to new levels. We must be popular if we have over 350 Facebook friends, right? Robin Dunbar explains that while some people would like to think they have hundreds of "friends" online, our brains really only have the capacity to handle about 150 different relationships at any one time. In "You Gotta Have (150) Friends," Dunbar demonstrates what happens when we exceed the magic number of 150.

This chapter's Modern Scholar essay is by social media researcher danah boyd, who explores the impact of the constant barrage of content—Tweets, posts, blogs, texts, e-mails—on our ability to really tune in to the world around us. Her article, "Streams of Content, Limited Attention" describes the delicate balance between feeling connected and overwhelmed.

The next two essays take a closer look how we work at creating just the right online persona. First, Stuart Wolpert explores the nuances of constructing the self in his essay "Crafting Your Image for Your 1,000 Friends on Facebook." Then Peggy Orenstein explores the ironies of Tweeting one day while enjoying a moment in the park, in which she pauses to carefully consider how to phrase the experience so her friends realize how thoughtful and reflective she is in "I Tweet, Therefore I Am."

The chapter concludes with two pieces examining the troubling trend of bullying online and off. First, in "Privacy Strikes Back," academic and legal expert Jeffrey Rosen provides some suggestions on how to stop cyber-bullies. Then, Nick Gillespie in "Stop Panicking about Bullies" argues that childhood is safer than ever before and that today's parents just need to worry about something. Although he admits that some mean kids may use Twitter to taunt the peers, the demand to legislate the issue is overblown.

Mirror, Mirror, on the Web
*Lakshmi Chaudhry**

Mirror, mirror, on the wall, who's the fairest of them all? Maybe the over 33 million MySpace users or the 900 million registrants on Facebook. The Web has become a place where we are all beautiful, witty, talented, and popular, especially if we are describing ourselves. But why do we need to be the center of attention and admired by so many? Lakshmi Chaudhry explores this new generation of fame seekers who are recreating Narcissus' pool and shows that we haven't learned anything from his cautionary tale.

1 "Everyone, in the back of his mind, wants to be a star," says YouTube co-founder Chad Hurley, explaining the dizzying success of the online mecca of amateur video in *Wired* magazine. And thanks to YouTube, Facebook, LiveJournal and other bastions of the retooled Web 2.0, every Jane, Joe or Jamila can indeed be a star, be it as wannabe comics, citizen journalists, lip-syncing geeks, military bloggers, aspiring porn stars or even rodent-eating freaks.

2 We live in the era of micro-celebrity, which offers endless opportunities to celebrate that most special person in your life, i.e., you—who not coincidentally was also *Time* magazine's widely derided Person of the Year for 2006. An honor once reserved for world leaders, pop icons and high-profile CEOs belonged to "you," the ordinary netizen with the time, energy and passion to "make a movie starring my pet iguana . . . mash up 50 Cent's vocals with Queen's instrumentals . . . blog about my state of mind or the state of the nation or the steak-frites at the new bistro down the street."

3 The editors at *Time* touted this "revolution" in the headiest prose: "It's a story about community and collaboration on a scale never seen before. It's about the cosmic compendium of knowledge on Wikipedia and the million-channel people's network YouTube and the online metropolis [Facebook]. It's about the many wresting power from the few and helping one another for nothing and how that will not only change the world, but also change the way the world changes."

4 This is the stuff of progressive fantasy: change, community, collaboration. And it echoes our cherished hope that a medium by, of and for the people will create a more democratic world. So it's easy to miss the editorial sleight of hand that slips from the "I" to the "we," substitutes individual self-expression for collective action and conflates popular attention with social consciousness.

5 For all the talk about coming together, the Web's greatest successes have capitalized on our need to feel significant and admired and, above all, to be seen. The latest iteration of digital democracy has indeed brought with it a new democracy of fame, but in doing so it has left us ever more in the thrall of celebrity, except now we have a better shot at being worshiped ourselves. As MySpace luminary Christine

* Lakshmi Chaudhry, *The Nation*, January 11, 2007

Dolce told the *New York Post*, "My favorite comment is when people say that I'm their idol. That girls look up to me."

6   So we upload our wackiest videos to YouTube, blog every sordid detail of our personal lives so as to insure at least fifty inbound links, add 200 new "friends" a day to our [Facebook] page . . . , all the time hoping that one day all our efforts at self-promotion will merit—at the very least—our very own Wikipedia entry.

7   In *The Frenzy of Renown*, written in 1986, Leo Braudy documented the long and intimate relationship between mass media and fame. The more plentiful, accessible and immediate the ways of gathering and distributing information have become, he wrote, the more ways there are to be known: "In the past that medium was usually literature, theater, or public monuments. With the Renaissance came painting and engraved portraits, and the modern age has added photography, radio, movies, and television. As each new medium of fame appears, the human image it conveys is intensified and the number of individuals celebrated expands." It's no surprise then that the Internet, which offers vastly greater immediacy and accessibility than its top-down predecessors, should further flatten the landscape of celebrity.

8   The democratization of fame, however, comes at a significant price. "Through the technology of image reproduction and information reproduction, our relation to the increasing number of faces we see every day becomes more and more transitory, and 'famous' seems as devalued a term as 'tragic,'" Braudy wrote. And the easier it is to become known, the less we have to do to earn that honor. In ancient Greece, when fame was inextricably linked to posterity, an Alexander had to make his mark on history to insure that his praises would be sung by generations to come. The invention of the camera in the nineteenth century introduced the modern notion of fame linked inextricably to a new type of professional: the journalist. Aspiring celebrities turned increasingly to achievements that would bring them immediate acclaim, preferably in the next day's newspaper, and with the rise of television, on the evening news.

9   The broadcast media's voracious appetite for spectacle insured that notoriety and fame soon became subsumed by an all-encompassing notion of celebrity, where simply being on TV became the ultimate stamp of recognition. At the same time, advertisers sought to redefine fame in terms of buying rather than doing, fusing the American Dream of material success with the public's hunger for stars in programs such as *Lifestyles of the Rich and Famous*.

10   But the advent of cyber-fame is remarkable in that it is divorced from any significant achievement—farting to the tune of "Jingle Bells," for example, can get you on VH1. While a number of online celebrities are rightly known for doing something (a blogger like Markos Moulitsas, say), and still others have leveraged their virtual success to build lucrative careers (as with the punk-rock group Fall Out Boy), it is no longer necessary to do either in order to be "famous."

11   Fame is now reduced to its most basic ingredient: public attention. And the attention doesn't have to be positive either, as in the case of the man in Belfast who bit the head off a mouse for a YouTube video. "In our own time merely being looked at carries all the necessary ennoblement," Braudy wrote twenty years ago, words that ring truer than ever today.

12   Celebrity has become a commodity in itself, detached from and more valuable than wealth or achievement. Even rich New York socialites feel the need for their own blog,

SocialiteRank.com, to get in on the action. The advice for aspiring celebutantes may be tongue-in-cheek—"To become a relevant socialite, you are virtually required to have your name in the press"—but no less true in this age of Paris Hilton wannabes.

13   Fame is no longer a perk of success but a necessary ingredient, whether as a socialite, chef, scholar or skateboarder. "For a great many people it is no longer enough to be very good at what you do. One also has to be a public figure, noticed and celebrated, and preferably televised," writes Hal Niedzviecki in his book *Hello, I'm Special.* When it is more important to be seen than to be talented, it is hardly surprising that the less gifted among us are willing to fart our way into the spotlight.

> *Fame is now reduced to its most basic ingredient: public attention . . . Fame is no longer a perk of success but a necessary ingredient, whether as a socialite, chef, scholar or skateboarder.*

14   The fantasy of fame is not new, but what is unprecedented is the primacy of the desire, especially among young people. "I wanna be famous because I would love it more than anything. . . . Sometimes I'll cry at night wishing and praying for a better life to be famous . . . To be like the others someday too! Because i know that I can do it!" declares Britney Jo, writing on iWannaBeFamous.com.

15   She is hardly unusual. A 2000 Interprise poll revealed that 50 percent of kids under 12 believe that becoming famous is part of the American Dream. It's a dream increasingly shared by the rest of the world, as revealed in a recent survey of British children between 5 and 10, who most frequently picked being famous as the "very best thing in the world." The views of these young children are no different from American college freshmen, who, according to a 2004 survey, most want to be an "actor or entertainer." Our preoccupation with fame is at least partly explained by our immersion in a media-saturated world that constantly tells us, as Braudy described it, "we should [be famous] if we possibly can, because it is the best, perhaps the only, way to be." Less obvious, however, is how our celebrity culture has fueled, and been fueled by, a significant generational shift in levels of narcissism in the United States.

16   In the 1950s, only 12 percent of teenagers between 12 and 14 agreed with the statement, "I am an important person." By the late 1980s, the number had reached an astounding 80 percent, an upward trajectory that shows no sign of reversing. Preliminary findings from a joint study conducted by Jean Twenge, Keith Campbell and three other researchers revealed that an average college student in 2006 scored higher than 65 percent of the students in 1987 on the standard Narcissism Personality Inventory test, which includes statements such as "I am a special person," "I find it easy to manipulate people" and "If I were on the Titanic, I would deserve to be on the first lifeboat." In her recent book *Generation Me*, Twenge applies that overarching label to everyone born between 1970 and 2000.

17   According to Twenge and her colleagues, the spike in narcissism is linked to an overall increase in individualism, which has been fostered by a number of factors, including greater geographical mobility, breakdown of traditional communities and, more important, "the self-focus that blossomed in the 1970s [and] became mundane and commonplace over the next two decades." In schools, at home and in popular culture, children

over the past thirty-odd years have been inculcated with the same set of messages: You're special; love yourself; follow your dreams; you can be anything you want to be.

18   These mantras, in turn, have been woven into an all-pervasive commercial narrative used to hawk everything from movie tickets to sneakers. Just do it, baby, but make sure you buy that pair of Nikes first. The idea that every self is important has been redefined to suit the needs of a cultural marketplace that devalues genuine community and selfhood in favor of "success." In this context, "feeling good about myself" becomes the best possible reason to staple one's stomach, buy that shiny new car, or strip for a Girls Gone Wild video. The corollary of individualism becomes narcissism, an inflated evaluation of self-worth devoid of any real sense of "self" or "worth."

19   Since a key component of narcissism is the need to be admired and to be the center of attention, Generation Me's attraction to fame is inevitable. "You teach kids they're special. And then they watch TV, the impression they get is that everyone should be rich and famous. Then they hear, 'You can be anything you want.' So they're like, 'Well, I want to be rich and famous,'" says Twenge. Or if not rich and famous, at least to be "seen"—something the rest of us plebeians can now aspire to in the brave new media world. "To be noticed, to be wanted, to be loved, to walk into a place and have others care about what you're doing, even what you had for lunch that day: that's what people want, in my opinion," *Big Brother* contestant Kaysar Ridha told *The New York Times*, thus affirming a recent finding by Drew Pinsky and Mark Young that reality TV stars are far more narcissistic than actors, comedians or musicians—perhaps because they reflect more closely the reason the rest of us are obsessed more than ever with "making it."

20   Not only do Americans increasingly want to be famous, but they also believe they will be famous, more so than any previous generation. A Harris poll found that 44 percent of those between the ages of 18 and 24 believed it was at least somewhat likely that they would be famous for a short period. Those in their late twenties were even more optimistic: Six in ten expected that they would be well-known, if only briefly, sometime in their lives. The rosy predictions of our destiny, however, contain within them the darker conviction that a life led outside the spotlight would be without value. "People want the kind of attention that celebrities receive more than anything else," says Niedzviecki. "People want the recognition, the validation, the sense of having a place in the culture [because] we no longer know where we belong, what we're about or what we should be about."

21   Without any meaningful standard by which to measure our worth, we turn to the public eye for affirmation. "It's really the sense that Hey, I exist in this world, and that is important. That I matter," Niedzviecki says. Our "normal" lives therefore seem impoverished and less significant compared with the media world, which increasingly represents all that is grand and worthwhile, and therefore more "real."

22   No wonder then that 16-year-old Rachel, Britney Jo's fellow aspirant to fame on iWannaBeFamous.com, rambles in desperation, "I figured out that I am tired of just dreaming about doing something, I am sick of looking for a "regular" job . . . I feel life slipping by, and that 'something is missing' feeling begins to dominate me all day and night, I can't even watch the Academy Awards ceremony without crying . . . that is how I know . . . that is me. . . . I have to be . . . in the movies!!!"

23   The evolution of the Internet has both mirrored and shaped the intense focus on self that is the hallmark of the post-boomer generation. "If you aren't posting, you don't exist. People say, 'I post, therefore I am,'" Rishad Tobaccowala, CEO of Denuo, a new media consultancy, told *Wired*, inadvertently capturing the essence of the Web, which is driven by our hunger for self-expression. Blogs, amateur videos, personal profiles, even interactive features such as Amazon.com's reviews offer ways to satisfy our need to be in the public eye.

24   But the virtual persona we project online is a carefully edited version of ourselves, as "authentic" as a character on reality TV. People on reality TV "are ultra–self-aware versions of the ordinary, über-facsimiles of themselves in the same way that online personals are recreations of self constantly tweaked for maximum response and effect," writes Niedzviecki in his book.

25   Self-expression glides effortlessly into self-promotion as we shape our online selves—be it on a Facebook profile, LiveJournal blog or a YouTube video—to insure the greatest attention. Nothing beats good old-fashioned publicity even in the brave new world of digital media. So it should come as no shock that the oh-so-authentic LonelyGirl15 should turn out to be a PR stunt or that the most popular person on MySpace is the mostly naked Tila Tequila, the proud purveyor of "skank pop" who can boast of 1,626,097 friends, a clothing line, a record deal and making the cover of *Maxim UK* and *Stuff* magazines. YouTube has become the virtual equivalent of Los Angeles, the destination de rigueur for millions of celebrity aspirants, all hoping they will be the next Amanda Congdon, the videoblogger now with a gig on ABCNews.com, or the Spiridellis brothers, who landed venture capital funding because of their wildly popular video "This Land."

26   Beginning with the dot-com boom in the 1990s through to its present iteration as Web 2.0, the cultural power of the Internet has been fueled by the modern-day Cinderella fantasy of "making it." With their obsessive focus on A-list bloggers, upstart twentysomething CEOs and an assortment of weirdos and creeps, the media continually reframe the Internet as yet another shot at the glittering prize of celebrity. "We see the same slow channeling of the idea that your main goal in life is to reach as many people as possible all over the world with your product. And your product is you," says Niedzviecki. "As long as that's true, it's very hard to see how the Internet is going to change that." As long as more democratic media merely signify a greater democracy of fame—e.g., look how that indie musician landed a contract with that major label—we will remain enslaved by the same narrative of success that sustains corporate America.

27   In our eagerness to embrace the Web as a panacea for various political ills, progressives often forget that the Internet is merely a medium like any other, and the social impact of its various features—interactivity, real-time publishing, easy access, cheap mass distribution—will be determined by the people who use them. There is no doubt that these technologies have facilitated greater activism, and new forms of it, both on- and offline. But we confuse the Web's promise of increased visibility with real change. Political actions often enter the ether of the media world only to be incorporated into narratives of individual achievement. And the more successful among us end up as bold-faced names, leached dry of the ideas and values they

represent—yet another face in the cluttered landscape of celebrity, with fortunes that follow the usual trajectory of media attention: First you're hot, and then you're not.

28   "It's all about you. Me. And all the various forms of the First Person Singular," writes cranky media veteran Brian Williams in his contribution to *Time*'s year-end package. "Americans have decided the most important person in their lives is … them, and our culture is now built upon that idea." So, have we turned into a nation of egoists, uninterested in anything that falls outside our narrow frame of self-reference?

29   As Jean Twenge points out, individualism doesn't necessarily preclude a social conscience or desire to do good. "But [Generation Me] articulates it as 'I want to make a difference,'" she says. "The outcome is still good, but it does put the self in the center." Stephen Duncombe, on the other hand, author of the new book *Dream: Re-imagining Progressive Politics in an Age of Fantasy*, argues that rather than dismiss our yearning for individual recognition, progressives need to create real-world alternatives that offer such validation. For example, in place of vast anonymous rallies that aim to declare strength in numbers, he suggests that liberal activism should be built around small groups. "The size of these groups is critical. They are intimate affairs, small enough for each participant to have an active role in shaping the group's direction and voice," he writes. "In these 'affinity groups,' as they are called, every person is recognized: in short, they exist."

30   Such efforts, however, would have to contend with GenMe's aversion to collective action. "The baby boomers were self-focused in a different way. Whether it was self-examination like EST or social protest, they did everything in groups. This new generation is allergic to groups," Twenge says. And as Duncombe admits, activism is a tough sell for a nation weaned on the I-driven fantasy of celebrity that serves as "an escape from democracy with its attendant demands for responsibility and participation."

31   There is a happier alternative. If these corporate technologies of self-promotion work as well as promised, they may finally render fame meaningless. If everyone is onstage, there will be no one left in the audience. And maybe then we rock stars can finally turn our attention to life down here on earth. Or it may be life on earth that finally jolts us out of our admiring reverie in the mirrored hall of fame. We forget that this growing self-involvement is a luxury afforded to a generation that has not experienced a wide-scale war or economic depression. If and when the good times come to an end, so may our obsession with fame. "There are a lot of things on the horizon that could shake us out of the way we are now. And some of them are pretty ugly," Niedzviecki says. "You won't be able to say that my [Facebook] page is more important than my real life. . . . When you're a corpse, it doesn't matter how many virtual friends you have." Think global war, widespread unemployment, climate change. But then again, how cool would it be to vlog your life in the new Ice Age—kind of like starring in your very own *Day After Tomorrow*. LOL. ◆

CRITICAL THINKING

1. Who is Narcissus? How does his story connect to the points Chaudhry makes in her essay? Explain.

2. Think of some examples of when "it is more important to be seen than to be talented."

3. What is your personal definition of the American Dream? Does it include becoming famous? Explain.
4. As a child, were you told "You're special; love yourself; follow your dreams; you can be anything you want to be"? Explain the outcome of being given (or not being given) this message.
5. Do you agree or disagree with this statement: "Life led outside the spotlight would be without value"? Explain your answer.
6. What is Chaudhry's tone in this essay? How does she feel about social networking sites and the people who use them?
7. How does Chaudhry define "Generation Me"? Are you a member of this generation? What is she saying about social trends for this generation? Explain.

CRITICAL WRITING

1. *Personal Narrative:* Do you want to be rich and famous? Discuss where you see yourself 5 years, 10 years, and 20 years from now.
2. *Research Writing:* In the distant past, the medium to becoming well-known "was usually literature, theater, or public monuments." Research a famous person from history (before 1900) and show how his or her popularity grew and which media were used to expand this popularity.
3. *Personal Narrative:* Take a standard Narcissism Personality Inventory test, which can be located online at various sites, such as www.4degreez.com. Evaluate your score. Are you narcissistic? What does it mean to be narcissistic? How does your score compare to your online social activities? What are the advantages and disadvantages of being narcissistic?

GROUP PROJECTS

1. In this article, Chaudhry states, "So we upload our wackiest videos to YouTube, blog every sordid detail of our personal lives so as to insure at least fifty inbound links, add 200 new 'friends' a day to our [Facebook] page..., all the time hoping that one day all our efforts at self-promotion will merit—at the very least—our very own Wikipedia entry." Have each member of your group discuss how many videos you have collectively placed on YouTube, how many times you have blogged personal details, how many online friends you have, if you have a Wikipedia entry, and your other online exploits.
2. As a group, discuss some of the challenges and benefits a "me first" mentality can have on a generation. If social networking, reality television, blogging, and vlogging are defining elements of your generation, how might these trends be viewed historically in the future? What will social critics identify as unique and transformational about this phenomenon? After discussing the issue as a group, write a short essay exploring the impact the media Chaudhry describes in this essay will have on society and history.

Virtual Friendship and the New Narcissism
*Christine Rosen**

How is a Facebook page like a self-portrait? What do they reveal about subjects and how they view themselves? More than simply connecting us with each other, social networking sites allow us to present a persona to the world—publicly sharing who we know, what we think, what we do, and even what we own. In this slightly abridged essay, sociologist and writer Christine Rosen wonders whether social networking sites raise the bar on our level of self-absorption and desire to be famous.

1 For centuries, the rich and the powerful documented their existence and their status through painted portraits. A marker of wealth and a bid for immortality, portraits offer intriguing hints about the daily life of their subjects—professions, ambitions, attitudes, and, most importantly, social standing. Such portraits, as German art historian Hans Belting has argued, can be understood as "painted anthropology," with much to teach us, both intentionally and unintentionally, about the culture in which they were created.

2 Self-portraits can be especially instructive. By showing the artist both as he sees his true self and as he wishes to be seen, self-portraits can at once expose and obscure, clarify and distort. They offer opportunities for both self-expression and self-seeking. They can display egotism and modesty, self-aggrandizement and self-mockery.

3 Today, our self-portraits are democratic and digital; they are crafted from pixels rather than paints. On social networking websites like MySpace and Facebook, our modern self-portraits feature background music, carefully manipulated photographs, stream-of-consciousness musings, and lists of our hobbies and friends. They are interactive, inviting viewers not merely to look at, but also to respond to, the life portrayed online. We create them to find friendship, love, and that ambiguous modern thing called *connection*. Like painters constantly retouching their work, we alter, update, and tweak our online self-portraits; but as digital objects they are far more ephemeral than oil on canvas. Vital statistics, glimpses of bare flesh, lists of favorite bands and favorite poems all clamor for our attention—and it is the timeless human desire for attention that emerges as the dominant theme of these vast virtual galleries.

> *Today, our self-portraits are democratic and digital; they are crafted from pixels rather than paints . . . Like painters constantly retouching their work, we alter, update, and tweak our online self-portraits; but as digital objects they are far more ephemeral than oil on canvas.*

* Christine Rosen, *The New Atlantis,* Summer 2007

4   Although social networking sites are in their infancy, we are seeing their impact culturally: in language (where *to friend* is now a verb), in politics (where it is de rigueur for presidential aspirants to catalogue their virtues on Facebook), and on college campuses (where not using Facebook can be a social handicap). But we are only beginning to come to grips with the consequences of our use of these sites: for friendship, and for our notions of privacy, authenticity, community, and identity.

Making Connections

5 The earliest online social networks were arguably the Bulletin Board Systems of the 1980s that let users post public messages, send and receive private messages, play games, and exchange software. Some of those BBS's, like The WELL (Whole Earth 'Lectronic Link) that technologist Larry Brilliant and futurist Stewart Brand started in 1985, made the transition to the World Wide Web in the mid-1990s. (Now owned by Salon.com, The WELL boasts that it was "the primordial ooze where the online community movement was born.") Other websites for community and connection emerged in the 1990s, including Classmates.com (1995), where users register by high school and year of graduation; Company of Friends, a business-oriented site founded in 1997; and Epinions, founded in 1999 to allow users to give their opinions about various consumer products.

6   A new generation of social networking websites appeared in 2002 with the launch of Friendster, whose founder, Jonathan Abrams, admitted that his main motivation for creating the site was to meet attractive women. Unlike previous online communities, which brought together anonymous strangers with shared interests, Friendster used a model of social networking known as the "Circle of Friends" (developed by British computer scientist Jonathan Bishop), in which users invited friends and acquaintances—that is, people they already know and like—to join their network.

7   Friendster was an immediate success, with millions of registered users by mid-2003. But technological glitches and poor management at the company allowed a new social networking site, MySpace, launched in 2003, quickly to surpass it. Originally started by musicians, MySpace has become a major venue for sharing music as well as videos and photos. It became the behemoth of online social networking, with over 100 million registered users. [Then, MySpace was eclipsed by Facebook in February 2009.]

8   The best-known social networking site today is Facebook, launched in 2004. Originally restricted to college students, Facebook—which takes its name from the small photo albums that colleges once gave to incoming freshmen and faculty to help them cope with meeting so many new people—soon extended membership to high schoolers and is now open to anyone. Still, it is most popular among college students and recent college graduates, many of whom use the site as their primary method of communicating with one another. Millions of college students check their Facebook pages several times every day and spend hours sending and receiving messages, making appointments, getting updates on their friends' activities, and learning about people they might recently have met or heard about.

9   There are dozens of other social networking sites, including Orkut, Bebo, and Yahoo 360°. Niche social networking sites are also flourishing: there are sites offering forums and fellowship for photographers, music lovers, and sports fans. There

are professional networking sites, such as LinkedIn, that keep people connected with present and former colleagues and other business acquaintances.

10   Despite the increasingly diverse range of social networking sites, the most popular sites share certain features. On Facebook, for example, the process of setting up one's online identity is relatively simple: Provide your name, address, e-mail address, and a few other pieces of information, and you're up and running and ready to create your online persona. You can post your name, age, where you live, and other personal details such as your zodiac sign, religion, sexual orientation, and relationship status. MySpace users can also blog on their pages. A user "friends" people—that is, invites them by e-mail to appear on the user's "Friend Space," where they are listed, linked, and ranked. Below the Friends space is a Comments section where friends can post notes. MySpace allows users to personalize their pages by uploading images and music and videos; indeed, one of the defining features of most MySpace pages is the ubiquity of visual and audio clutter. With silly, hyper flashing graphics in neon colors and clip-art style images of kittens and cartoons, MySpace pages often resemble an over-decorated high school yearbook.

11   By contrast, Facebook limits what its users can do to their profiles. Besides general personal information, Facebook users have a "Wall" where people can leave them brief notes, as well as a Messages feature that functions like an in-house Facebook e-mail account. You list your friends on Facebook as well, but in general, unlike MySpace friends, which are often complete strangers (or spammers), Facebook friends tend to be part of one's offline social circle. (This might change, however, now that Facebook has opened its site to anyone rather than restricting it to college and high school students.) Facebook (and MySpace) allow users to form groups based on mutual interests. Facebook users can also send "pokes" to friends; these little digital nudges are meant to let someone know you are thinking about him or her. But they can also be interpreted as not-so-subtle come-ons; one Facebook group with over 200,000 members is called "Enough with the Poking, Let's Just Have Sex."

Won't You Be My Digital Neighbor?

12 According to a survey recently conducted by the Pew Internet and American Life Project, more than half of all Americans between the ages of twelve and seventeen use some online social networking site. Indeed, media coverage of social networking sites usually describes them as vast teenage playgrounds—or wastelands, depending on one's perspective. Central to this narrative is a nearly unbridgeable generational divide, with tech-savvy youngsters redefining friendship while their doddering elders look on with bafflement and increasing anxiety. This seems anecdotally correct; I can't count how many times I have mentioned social networking websites to someone over the age of forty and received the reply, "Oh yes, I've heard about that MyFace! All the kids are doing that these days. Very interesting!"

13   Numerous articles have chronicled adults' attempts to navigate the world of social networking, such as the recent *New York Times* essay in which columnist Michelle Slatalla described the incredible embarrassment she caused her teenage daughter when she joined Facebook: "everyone in the whole world thinks its super creepy when adults have facebooks," her daughter instant-messaged her. "unfriend

paige right now. im serious. . . . i will be soo mad if you dont unfriend paige right now actually." In fact, social networking sites are not only for the young. More than half of the visitors to Facebook claim to be over the age of 35. What's more, the proliferation of niche social networking sites, including those aimed at adults, suggests that it is not only teenagers who will nurture relationships in virtual space for the foreseeable future.

The New Taxonomy of Friendship

14 There is a Spanish proverb that warns, "Life without a friend is death without a witness." In the world of online social networking, the warning might be simpler: "Life without hundreds of online 'friends' is virtual death." On these sites, friendship is the stated raison d'être. "A place for friends," is the slogan of MySpace. Facebook is a "social utility that connects people with friends." Orkut describes itself as "an online community that connects people through a network of trusted friends."

15 But "friendship" in these virtual spaces is thoroughly different from real-world friendship. In its traditional sense, friendship is a relationship which, broadly speaking, involves the sharing of mutual interests, reciprocity, trust, and the revelation of intimate details over time and within specific social (and cultural) contexts. Because friendship depends on mutual revelations that are concealed from the rest of the world, it can only flourish within the boundaries of privacy; the idea of public friendship is an oxymoron.

16 The hypertext link called "friendship" on social networking sites is very different: public, fluid, and promiscuous, yet oddly bureaucratized. Friendship on these sites focuses a great deal on collecting, managing, and ranking the people you know. Everything about Facebook, for example, is designed to encourage users to gather as many friends as possible, as though friendship were philately. If you are so unfortunate as to have but one online friend, for example, your page reads: "You have 1 friends," along with a stretch of sad empty space where dozens of thumbnail photos of your acquaintances should appear.

17 The structure of social networking sites also encourages the bureaucratization of friendship. Each site has its own terminology, but among the words that users employ most often is "managing." The Pew survey mentioned earlier found that "teens say social networking sites help them manage their friendships." There is something Orwellian about the management-speak on social networking sites: "Change My Top Friends," "View All of My Friends" and, for those times when our inner Stalins sense the need for a virtual purge, "Edit Friends." With a few mouse clicks one can elevate or downgrade (or entirely eliminate) a relationship.

18 To be sure, we all rank our friends, albeit in unspoken and intuitive ways. One friend might be a good companion for outings to movies or concerts; another might be someone with whom you socialize in professional settings; another might be the kind of person for whom you would drop everything if he needed help. But social networking sites allow us to rank our friends publicly. And not only can we publicize our own preferences in people, but we can also peruse the favorites among our other acquaintances. We can learn all about the friends of our friends—often without having ever met them in person.

Status-Seekers

19 Of course, it would be foolish to suggest that people are incapable of making distinctions between social networking "friends" and friends they see in the flesh. The use of the word "friend" on social networking sites is a dilution and a debasement, and surely no one with hundreds of Facebook "friends" is so confused as to believe those are all real friendships. The impulse to collect as many "friends" as possible is not an expression of the human need for companionship, but of a different need no less profound and pressing: the need for status. Unlike the painted portraits that members of the middle class in a bygone era would commission to signal their elite status once they rose in society, social networking websites allow us to create status—not merely to commemorate the achievement of it. There is a reason that most of the profiles of famous people are fakes, often created by fans: Celebrities don't need legions of friends to prove their importance. It's the rest of the population, seeking a form of parochial celebrity, that does.

20 But status-seeking has an ever-present partner: anxiety. Unlike a portrait, which, once finished and framed, hung tamely on the wall signaling one's status, maintaining status on MySpace or Facebook requires constant vigilance. As one 24-year-old wrote in a *New York Times* essay, "I am obsessed with testimonials and solicit them incessantly. They are the ultimate social currency, public declarations of the intimacy status of a relationship. . . . Every profile is a carefully planned media campaign."

21 The sites themselves were designed to encourage this. Describing the work of B. J. Fogg of Stanford University, who studies "persuasion strategies" used by social networking sites to increase participation, *The New Scientist* noted, "The secret is to tie the acquisition of friends, compliments and status—spoils that humans will work hard for—to activities that enhance the site." As Fogg told the magazine, "You offer someone a context for gaining status, and they are going to work for that status." Network theorist Albert-László Barabási notes that online connection follows the rule of "preferential attachment"—that is, "when choosing between two pages, one with twice as many links as the other, about twice as many people link to the more connected page." As a result, "while our individual choices are highly unpredictable, as a group we follow strict patterns." Our lemming-like pursuit of online status via the collection of hundreds of "friends" clearly follows this rule.

22 What, in the end, does this pursuit of virtual status mean for community and friendship? Writing in the 1980s in *Habits of the Heart*, sociologist Robert Bellah and his colleagues documented the movement away from close-knit, traditional communities to "lifestyle enclaves," which were defined largely by "leisure and consumption." Perhaps today we have moved beyond lifestyle enclaves and into "personality enclaves" or "identity enclaves"—discrete virtual places in which we can be different (and sometimes contradictory) people, with different groups of like-minded, though ever-shifting, friends.

Beyond Networking

23 This past spring, Len Harmon, the director of the Fischer Policy and Cultural Institute at Nichols College in Dudley, Massachusetts, offered a new course about

social networking. Nichols is a small school whose students come largely from Connecticut and Massachusetts; many of them are the first members of their families to attend college. "I noticed a lot of issues involved with social networking sites," Harmon told me when I asked him why he created the class. How have these sites been useful to Nichols students? "It has relieved some of the stress of transitions for them," he said. "When abrupt departures occur—their family moves or they have to leave friends behind—they can cope by keeping in touch more easily."

24   So perhaps we should praise social networking websites for streamlining friendship the way e-mail streamlined correspondence. In the nineteenth century, Emerson observed that "friendship requires more time than poor busy men can usually command." Now, technology has given us the freedom to tap into our network of friends when it is convenient for us. "It's a way of maintaining a friendship without having to make any effort whatsoever," as a recent graduate of Harvard explained to the *New Yorker*. And that ease admittedly makes it possible to stay in contact with a wider circle of offline acquaintances than might have been possible in the era before Facebook. Friends you haven't heard from in years, old buddies from elementary school, people you might have (should have?) fallen out of touch with—it is now easier than ever to reconnect to those people.

25   But what kind of connections are these? In his excellent book *Friendship: An Exposé*, Joseph Epstein praises the telephone and e-mail as technologies that have greatly facilitated friendship. He writes, "Proust once said he didn't much care for the analogy of a book to a friend. He thought a book was better than a friend, because you could shut it—and be shut of it—when you wished, which one can't always do with a friend." With e-mail and caller ID, Epstein enthuses, you can. But social networking sites (which Epstein says "speak to the vast loneliness in the world") have a different effect: they discourage "being shut of" people. On the contrary, they encourage users to check in frequently, "poke" friends, and post comments on others' pages. They favor interaction of greater quantity but less quality.

26   This constant connectivity concerns Len Harmon. "There is a sense of, 'if I'm not online or constantly texting or posting, then I'm missing something,'" he said of his students. "This is where I find the generational impact the greatest—not the use of the technology, but the overuse of the technology." It is unclear how the regular use of these sites will affect behavior over the long run—especially the behavior of children and young adults who are growing up with these tools. Almost no research has explored how virtual socializing affects children's development. What does a child weaned on Club Penguin learn about social interaction? How is an adolescent who spends her evenings managing her MySpace page different from a teenager who spends her night gossiping on the telephone to friends? Given that "people want to live their lives online," as the founder of one social networking site recently told *Fast Company* magazine, and they are beginning to do so at ever-younger ages, these questions are worth exploring.

27   The few studies that have emerged do not inspire confidence. Researcher Rob Nyland at Brigham Young University recently surveyed 184 users of social networking sites and found that heavy users "feel less socially involved with the community around them." He also found that "as individuals use social networking more for entertainment, their level of social involvement decreases." Another recent

study conducted by communications professor Qingwen Dong and colleagues at the University of the Pacific found that "those who engaged in romantic communication over MySpace tend to have low levels of both emotional intelligence and self-esteem."

28   The implications of the narcissistic and exhibitionistic tendencies of social networkers also cry out for further consideration. There are opportunity costs when we spend so much time carefully grooming ourselves online. Given how much time we already devote to entertaining ourselves with technology, it is at least worth asking if the time we spend on social networking sites is well spent. In investing so much energy into improving how we present ourselves online, are we missing chances to genuinely improve ourselves?

29   We should also take note of the trend toward giving up face-to-face for virtual contact—and, in some cases, a preference for the latter. Today, many of our cultural, social, and political interactions take place through eminently convenient technological surrogates—Why go to the bank if you can use the ATM? Why browse in a bookstore when you can simply peruse the personalized selections Amazon.com has made for you? In the same vein, social networking sites are often convenient surrogates for offline friendship and community. In this context it is worth considering an observation that Stanley Milgram made in 1974, regarding his experiments with obedience: "The social psychology of this century reveals a major lesson," he wrote. "Often it is not so much the kind of person a man is as the kind of situation in which he finds himself that determines how he will act." To an increasing degree, we find and form our friendships and communities in the virtual world as well as the real world. These virtual networks greatly expand our opportunities to meet others, but they might also result in our valuing less the capacity for genuine connection. As the young woman writing in the *Times* admitted, "I consistently trade actual human contact for the more reliable high of smiles on MySpace, winks on Match.com, and pokes on Facebook." That she finds these online relationships more reliable is telling: it shows a desire to avoid the vulnerability and uncertainty that true friendship entails. Real intimacy requires risk—the risk of disapproval, of heartache, of being thought a fool. Social networking websites may make relationships more reliable, but whether those relationships can be humanly satisfying remains to be seen. ◆

CRITICAL THINKING

1. This essay makes the bold statement: "Public friendship is an oxymoron." From your point of view, discuss what the meaning of friendship is and whether social networking sites are using the term "friend" properly.

2. Rosen compares online networking pages to "self-portraits." Explore this concept in more depth. In what ways is this true? If you have a personal page, discuss what that page says about you and in what ways it is indeed a "self-portrait." How are painted portraits and Web sites similar? How are they different?

3. What does Rosen mean when she uses the term "Orwellian" and the phrase "our inner Stalins" when referring to social networking sites? To what or whom is she referring, and how do these references connect to her point?

4. What does Rosen think of online networking sites? Identify areas in her essay in which she reveals her viewpoint.
5. The author comments, "Tech-savvy youngsters [are] redefining friendship while their doddering elders look on with bafflement and increasing anxiety." Do you find this to be true? How do your older family members view social networking sites? Do any of them have MySpace or Facebook sites? Why or why not?

CRITICAL WRITING

1. *Expository Writing:* Write an essay exploring the consequences of social networking sites on the future of friendship and community.
2. *Analytical Writing:* This article gives the evolution of social networking sites. Outline this evolution, showing how these sites have evolved from "the primordial ooze" of the 1980s to the newest site being planned by Microsoft.

GROUP PROJECTS

1. Each member of your group should track all of their online correspondence—received and sent—for a period of one week. This should include e-mail, IM, text messaging, and posting on social networking sites. Keep track of how much time you spend online. Discuss your personal results with the group. Discuss as a group how the Internet both enhances and complicates life, and whether it is indeed changing our personal relationships with each other and our personal view of ourselves, for better or for worse.
2. Rosen notes that social networking sites promote self-centeredness, thereby reducing our ability to cope with emotions, and that they cheapen what it means to be a friend. Interview at least 10 people of different age groups regarding how they use social networking sites. Create simple questions, but make them broad enough to allow for the expression of detailed viewpoints and options. Discuss the interviews as a group, and write a short essay evaluating the role of social networking on the lives of people today. Based on your surveys, can you predict the role social networking will have in our lives in the next decade?

You Gotta Have (150) Friends
*Robin Dunbar**

Can social networking sites fulfill the need to connect with others in the same way face-to-face relationships do? Can they really be as meaningful as our in-person interactions with others? In this next essay, anthropologist Robin Dunbar, professor of evolutionary biology,

---

* Robin Dunbar, *The New York Times,* December 25, 2010

explains that they can, to a certain extent. Social networking sites allow us to broadcast to (and thereby connect with) a large group of people. But the number of people we can truly handle, offline and on, is capped—at about 150. Dunbar is best known for formulating "Dunbar's number," a measurement of the "cognitive limit to the number of individuals with whom any one person can maintain stable relationships." Which of course begs the question, what's the point of having more than 150 "friends" on Facebook?

1   More than anything since the invention of the postal service, Facebook has revolutionized how we relate to one another. But the revolution hasn't come in quite the way that the people behind it and other social networking sites assume.

2   These sites may have allowed us to amass thousands of "friends," but they have not yet devised a way to cut through the clunky, old-fashioned nature of relationships themselves. Our circle of actual friends remains stubbornly small, limited not by technology but by human nature. What Facebook has done, though, is provide us a way to maintain those circles in a fractured, dynamic world.

3   Social networking and other digital media have long promised to open up wonderful new vistas, all from the comfort of our own homes. The limitations of face-to-face interaction that have, until now, bound us to our small individual worlds—the handful of people we meet in our everyday lives—would be overcome.

4   The critical component in social networking is the removal of time as a constraint. In the real world, according to research by myself and others, we devote 40 percent of our limited social time each week to the five most important people we know, who represent just 3 percent of our social world and a trivially small proportion of all the people alive today. Since the time invested in a relationship determines its quality, having more than five best friends is impossible when we interact face to face, one person at a time.

5   Instant messaging and social networking claim to solve that problem by allowing us to talk to as many people as we like, all at the same time. Like the proverbial lighthouse blinking on the horizon, our messages fan out into the dark night to every passing ship within reach of an Internet connection. We can broadcast, literally, to the world.

6   I use the word "broadcast" because, despite Facebook's promise, that is the fundamental flaw in the logic of the social-networking revolution. The developers at Facebook overlooked one of the crucial components in the complicated business of how we create relationships: our minds.

7   Put simply, our minds are not designed to allow us to have more than a very limited number of people in our social world. The emotional and psychological investments that a close relationship requires are considerable, and the emotional capital we have available is limited.

8   Indeed, no matter what Facebook allows us to do, I have found that most of us can maintain only around 150 meaningful relationships, online and off—what has become known as Dunbar's number. Yes, you can "friend" 500, 1,000, even 5,000 people with your Facebook page, but all save the core 150 are mere voyeurs

looking into your daily life—a fact incorporated into the new social networking site Path, which limits the number of friends you can have to 50.

9   What's more, contrary to all the hype and hope, the people in our electronic social worlds are, for most of us, the same people in our offline social worlds. In fact, the average number of friends on Facebook is 120 to 130, just short enough of Dunbar's number to allow room for grandparents and babies, people too old or too young to have acquired the digital habit.

10   This isn't to say that Facebook and its imitators aren't performing an important, even revolutionary, task—namely, to keep us in touch with our existing friends.

11   Until relatively recently, almost everyone on earth lived in small, rural, densely interconnected communities, where our 150 friends all knew one another, and everyone's 150 friends list was everyone else's.

12   But the social and economic mobility of the past century has worn away at that interconnectedness. As we move around the country and across continents, we collect disparate pockets of friends, so that our list of 150 consists of a half-dozen subsets of people who barely know of one another's existence, let alone interact.

13   Our ancestors knew the same people their entire lives; as we move around, though, we can lose touch with even our closest friends. Emotional closeness declines by around 15 percent a year in the absence of face-to-face contact, so that in five years someone can go from being an intimate acquaintance to the most distant outer layer of your 150 friends.

14   Facebook and other social networking sites allow us to keep up with friendships that would otherwise rapidly wither away. And they do something else that's probably more important, if much less obvious: they allow us to reintegrate our networks so that, rather than having several disconnected subsets of friends, we can rebuild, albeit virtually, the kind of old rural communities where everyone knew everyone else. Welcome to the electronic village. ◆

CRITICAL THINKING

1. The author's research indicates that we devote 40 percent of our social time each week to the five most important people we know. First, think about how many people you would define as the "most important people" in your life and then determine how much time per week you actually spend with those people. Does it seem to be about 40 percent of your social time? Does the author's research reflect your lifestyle and experiences? Explain.

2. What is "Dunbar's number"? How many friends do you have on Facebook (or another social networking site)? Does it fit with "Dunbar's number"?

3. Consider the author's words: "The emotional and psychological investments that a close relationship requires are considerable, and the emotional capital we have available is limited." Explain what you think the author means here. Have any of your own friendships required emotional and psychological investment? Explain.

4. What point is Dunbar making in the final sentence of his article?
5. If the number of friends—online and offline—we can handle is about 150, is there any point to having more than that on a social networking site? Why or why not?
6. Do you have any personal examples of long-distance friendships? Dunbar asserts, "Emotional closeness declines by around 15 percent a year in the absence of face-to-face contact." Do you find this assertion to be true according to your own examples of long-distance friendship?

CRITICAL WRITING

1. *Research and Analysis:* Watch the film *The Social Network* and do research on the beginnings of Facebook. Then write an essay arguing whether Robin Dunbar is correct in stating: "Facebook has revolutionized how we relate to one another. But the revolution hasn't come in quite the way that the people behind it and other social networking sites assume."
2. *Exploratory Writing:* According to a blog post by Path's founder Dave Morin, "Path allows you to capture your life's most personal moments and share them with the 50 close friends and family in your life who matter most. Because your personal network is limited to your closest friends and family, you can always trust that you can post any moment, no matter how personal. Path is a place where you can be yourself." Analyze Morin's comments and argue which site is better for college students, Path or Facebook, and state whether you think Path will take over Facebook in the future.

GROUP PROJECTS

1. In the article, Dunbar states that we can only maintain around 150 meaningful relationships, online and off. With your group, discuss what the word "maintain" really means. What would your definition of "maintaining a friendship" be? Do you agree that it is impossible to "maintain" more than 150 friends? After exploring the meaning of the word and the limitations of friendship with your group, share the highlights of your discussion with the class.
2. Each member of your group should share how many "friends" they have on Facebook, MySpace, Twitter, or other social networking site. (If a group member does not participate in social networking, he or she can estimate how many friends they have offline. Each group member should explain what their number means to them. Why do they have the friends they do? Does each member know all of his or her friends? Does one member have many more "friends" than the others?

Modern Scholar

Streams of Content: Limited Attention
danah boyd*

For much of history, information was something that was given to us—controlled by govern-ments, companies, and other groups in power who decided what we needed to know, and when we would know it. Until recently, most consumers of information received news at the same time, filtered by the outlets conveying the information itself. Today, however, informa-tion can hit us from multiple avenues, both official and unofficial, complimented by video and as-it happens updates. In this next essay, danah boyd, a professor of media, culture, and communications, explains how the Internet is changing the way we consume information and how we interact with content and with each other.

1 In his seminal pop-book, Mihaly Csikszentmihalyi argued that people are happiest when they can reach a state of "flow." He talks about performers and athletes who are in the height of their profession, the experience they feel as time passes by and everything just clicks. People reach a state where attention appears focused and, simultaneously, not in need of focus at the same time. The world is aligned and everything just feels right.

2 Consider what it means to be "in flow" in an information landscape defined by networked media, and you will see where Web 2.0 is taking us. The goal is not to be a passive consumer of information or to simply tune in when the time is right, but rather to live in a world where information is everywhere. To be peripherally aware of information as it flows by, grabbing it at the right moment when it is most rel-evant, valuable, entertaining, or insightful. Living with, in, and around information. Most of that information is social information, but some of it is entertainment infor-mation or news information or productive information. Being in flow with informa-tion is different than Csikszentmihalyi's sense, as it's not about perfect attention, but it is about a sense of alignment, of being aligned with information.

3 As of late, we've been talking a lot about content streams, streams of informa-tion. This metaphor is powerful. The idea is that you're living inside the stream: add-ing to it, consuming it, redirecting it. The stream metaphor is about reaching flow. It's also about restructuring the ways in which information flows in modern society.

4 Those who are most enamored with services like Twitter talk passionately about feeling as though they are living and breathing with the world around them, peripherally aware and in-tune, adding content to the stream and grabbing it when

* danah boyd, *UX Magazine,* February 5, 2010

appropriate. This state is delicate, plagued by information overload and weighed down by frustrating tools.

5   For the longest time, we have focused on sites of information as a destination, of accessing information as a process, of producing information as a task. What happens when all of this changes? While things are certainly clunky at best, this is the promise land of the technologies we're creating. This is all happening because of how our information society is changing. But before we talk more about flow, we need to step back and talk about shifts in the media landscape.

From Broadcast to Networked

6   For the last few centuries, we have been living in an era of broadcast media, but we have been switching to an era of networked media. This fundamentally alters the structure by which information flows.

7   Those who believe in broadcast structures recognize the efficiency of a single, centralized source. There's some nostalgia here. The image is clear: 1950s nightly news, everyone tuning in to receive the same message at the same time. There are the newspapers, the radio stations, magazines—all telling the same newsy story. Centralized sources of information are powerful because they control the means of distribution. There is also the town gossip, the church, and the pub. These too were centralized channels for disseminating information.

8   Broadcast media structures take one critical thing for granted: attention. There is an assumption that everyone will tune in and give their attention to the broadcast entity, even though that was never true in the first place. As TV channels and publishing brands proliferated, we've seen that attention can easily be fragmented. Over the last few decades, increasing numbers of entities have been fighting for a smaller and smaller portion of the pie. Even gossip rags started competing for attention.

9   The opportunities for media creation have been rising for decades, but the Internet provided new mechanisms through which people could make their own content available. From blogging to social network sites to media sharing sites to sites that provide social streams, we are seeing countless ways in which a motivated individual can make their personal content available. There were always folks willing to share their story but the Internet gave them a pulpit on which to stand.

10   Internet technologies are fundamentally dismantling and reworking the structures of distribution. Distribution is a process by which content creators find channels through which they can disseminate their creation. In effect, they're pushing out the content. Sure, people have to be there to receive it, but the idea is that there are limited channels for distribution and thus getting access to this limited resource is hard. That is no longer the case.

11   As networked technologies proliferate around the world, we can assume that there is a channel of distribution available to everyone and between everyone. In theory, anyone could get content to anyone else. With the barriers to distribution collapsing, what matters is not the act of distribution, but the act of consumption. Thus, the power is no longer in the hands of those who control the channels of distribution, but those who control the limited resource of attention. This is precisely why YOU were *Time* magazine's the Person of the Year in 2006. Your attention is precious and

valuable. It's no longer about push; it's about pull. And the "Law of Two Feet" is now culturally pervasive.

12   While we're dismantling traditional structures of distribution, we're also building out new forms of information dissemination. Content is no longer being hocked, but links are. People throughout the network are using the attention they receive to traffic in pointers to other content, serving as content mediators. Numerous people have become experts as information networkers.

13   To many people, this seems like old news. Isn't that the whole point of Web 2.0? Isn't that what we've been living? Sure, of course. But now that we're seeing Web 2.0 go mainstream, we're seeing all sorts of folks get into the game. What they're doing often looks different than what early adopters were doing. And the business folks are all trying to turn the Internet into a new broadcast channel (don't worry, they're failing). But we need to talk about these shifts so we can talk about what innovation needs to happen. If folks are going to try to get in-flow with information, we need to understand how information flows differently today. Let me highlight four challenges, points where technological hope and reality collide.

Four Core Issues

14 **1) Democratization.** Switching from a model of distribution to a model of attention is disruptive, but it is not inherently democratizing. This is a mistake we often make when talking about this shift. We may be democratizing certain types of access, but we're not democratizing attention. Just because we're moving towards a state where anyone has the ability to get information into the stream does not mean that attention will be divided equally. Opening up access to the structures of distribution is not democratizing when distribution is no longer the organizing function.

15   Some people might immediately think, "Ah, but it's a meritocracy. People will give their attention to what is best!" This too is mistaken logic. What people give their attention to depends on a whole set of factors that have nothing to do with what's best. At the most basic level, consider the role of language. People will pay attention to content that is in their language, even if they can get access to content in any language. This means Chinese language content will soon get more attention than English content, let alone Dutch or Hebrew content.

16 **2) Stimulation.** People consume content that stimulates their mind and senses. That which angers, excites, energizes, entertains, or otherwise creates an emotional response. This is not always the "best" or most informative content, but that which triggers a reaction.

17   This isn't inherently a good thing. Consider the food equivalent. Our bodies are programmed to consume fat and sugars because they're rare in nature. Thus, when they come around, we should grab them. In the same way, we're biologically programmed to be attentive to things that stimulate: content that is gross, violent, or sexual and that gossip which is humiliating, embarrassing, or offensive. If we're not careful, we're going to develop the psychological equivalent of obesity. We'll find ourselves consuming content that is least beneficial for ourselves or society as a whole.

18   We are addicted to gossip for a reason. We want to know what's happening because such information brings us closer to people. When we know something about someone, there's a sense of connection. But the information ecology we live in today has twisted this whole thing upside down. Just because I can follow the details of Angelina Jolie's life doesn't mean she knows I exist. This is what scholars talk about as parasocial relations. With Facebook, you can turn your closest friends into celebrities, characters you gawk at and obsess over without actually gaining the benefits of social intimacy and bonding.

19   Stimulation creates cognitive connections. But it is possible for there to be too much stimulation. We don't want a disconnected, numb society, nor a society of unequal social connections. So driving towards greater and more intense stimulation may not be what we want.

20   Of course, there's money here and people will try to manipulate this dynamic for their own purposes. There are folks who put out highly stimulating content or spread gossip to get attention. And often they succeed, creating a pretty unhealthy cycle. So we have to start asking ourselves what balance looks like and how we can move towards an environment where there are incentives for consuming healthy content that benefit individuals and society as a whole. Or, at the very least, how not to feed the trolls.

21   **3) Homophily.** In a networked world, people connect to people like themselves. What flows across the network flows through edges of similarity. The ability to connect to others like us allows us to flow information across space and time in impressively new ways, but there's also a downside.

22   Prejudice, intolerance, bigotry, and power are all baked into our networks. In a world of networked media, it's easy to not get access to views from people who think from a different perspective. Information can and does flow in ways that create and reinforce social divides. Democratic philosophy depends on shared informational structures, but the combination of self-segmentation and networked information flow means that we lose the common rhetorical ground through which we can converse.

23   Throughout my studies of social media, I have been astonished by the people who think that XYZ site is for people like them. I interviewed gay men who thought Friendster was a gay dating site because all they saw were other gay men. I interviewed teens who believed that everyone on MySpace was Christian because all of the profiles they saw contained biblical quotes. We all live in our own worlds with people who share our values and, with networked media, it's often hard to see beyond that.

24   Ironically, the one place where I'm finding people are being forced to think outside their box is the Trending Topics on Twitter. Consider a topic that trended a while ago: #thingsdarkiessay. Started in South Africa, this topic is fundamentally about language and cultural diversity but, when read in a U.S.-context, it reads as fundamentally racist. Boy did this blow up, forcing a lot of folks to think about language and cultural differences. Why? Because Trending Topics brings a topic that gained traction in a segment of the network to broader awareness, often out of context. Unfortunately, it's hard to get meaningful dialogue going once a Trending Topic triggers reactions.

25   In an era of networked media, we need to recognize that networks are homophilous and operate accordingly. Technology does not inherently disintegrate social divisions. In fact, more often then not, in reinforces them. Only a small percentage of people are inclined to seek out opinions and ideas from cultures other than their own. These people are and should be highly valued in society, but just because people can be what Ethan Zuckerman calls "xenophiles" doesn't mean they will be.

26   **4) Power.** When we think about centralized sources of information distribution, it's easy to understand that power is at stake. But networked structures of consumption are also configured by power and we cannot forget that or assume that access alone is power. Power is about being able to command attention, influence others' attention, and otherwise traffic in information. We give power to people when we give them our attention and people gain power when they bridge between different worlds and determine what information can and will flow across the network.

27   In a networked culture, there is also power in being the person spreading the content. When my colleagues and I were examining retweets in Twitter, we saw something fascinating: a tension between citationality and attribution. In short, should you give credit to the author of the content or acknowledge the person through whom you learned of the information? Instinctually, many might believe that the author is the most important person to credit. But, few ideas are truly the product of just one individual. So why not credit the messenger who is helping the content flow? We found that reasonable people disagreed about what was best.

28   In a broadcast model, those who control the distribution channels often profit more than the creators. Think: Clear Channel, record labels, TV producers, etc. Unfortunately, there's an assumption that if we get rid of limitations to the means of distribution, the power will revert to the creators. This is not what's happening. Distribution today is making people aware that they can come and get something, but those who get access to people's attention are still a small, privileged few.

29   Instead, what we're seeing [is] a new type of information broker emerge. These folks get credit for their structural position. While the monetary benefits are indirect, countless consulting gigs have arisen for folks based on their power as information brokers. The old controllers of information are losing their stature (and are not happy about it). What's emerging is not inherently the power of the creators, but the power of the modern-day information brokers.

Making It Work

30 As our information ecosystem evolves, we will see some radical changes take place. First, I believe that information spaces will get more niche. We will see evidence of this in the ways people direct their attention, and also in what new enterprises are succeeding. Successful businesses will not be everything to everyone; that's the broadcast mentality. Instead, they will play a meaningful role to a cohort of committed consumers who give their attention to them because of their relevance.

31   To be relevant today requires understanding context, popularity, and reputation. In the broadcast era, we assumed the disseminator organized information because they were a destination. In a networked era, there will be no destination, but rather

a network of content and people. We cannot assume that content will be organized around topics or that people will want to consume content organized as such. We're already seeing this in streams-based media consumption. When consuming information through social media tools, people consume social gossip alongside productive content, news alongside status updates. Right now, it's one big mess. But the key is not going to be to create distinct destinations organized around topics, but to find ways in which content can be surfaced in context, regardless of where it resides.

32   Making content work in a networked era is going to be about living in the streams, consuming and producing alongside "customers." Consuming to understand, producing to be relevant. Content creators are not going to get to dictate the cultural norms just because they can make their content available; they are still accountable to those who are trafficking content.

33   We need technological innovations. For example, tools that allow people to more easily contextualize relevant content regardless of where they are and what they are doing and tools that allow people to slice and dice content so as to not reach information overload. This is not simply about aggregating or curating content to create personalized destination sites. Frankly, I don't think this will work. Instead, the tools that consumers need are those that allow them to get into flow, that allow them to live inside information structures wherever they are, whatever they're doing. The tools that allow them to easily grab what they need and stay peripherally aware without feeling overwhelmed.

34   Finally, we need to rethink our business plans. I doubt this cultural shift will be paid for by better advertising models. Advertising is based on capturing attention, typically by interrupting the broadcast message or by being inserted into the content itself. Trying to reach information flow is not about being interrupted. Advertising does work when it's part of the flow itself. Ads are great when they provide a desirable answer to a search query or when they appear at the moment of purchase. But when the information being shared is social in nature, advertising is fundamentally a disruption.

35   Figuring out how to monetize sociality is a problem, and not one that's new to the Internet. Think about how we monetize sociality in physical spaces. Typically, it involves second-order consumption of calories. Venues provide a space for social interaction to occur and we are expected to consume to pay rent. Restaurants, bars, cafes . . . they all survive on this model. But we have yet to find the digital equivalent of alcohol.

36   As we continue to move from a broadcast model of information to a networked one, we will continue to see reworking of the information landscape. Some of what is unfolding is exciting, some is terrifying. The key is not [to] be all utopian or dystopian about it, but to recognize what changes and what stays the same. The future of Web 2.0 is about information flow and if you want to help people, help them reach that state. ◆

ANALYSIS AND DISCUSSION

1. What is "flow"? What happens when true flow occurs? How does the concept of flow connect to the Internet and how we use information?
2. What does boyd mean when she states that with the Internet, we are "living inside the stream"?

3. What is the difference between broadcast media and networked media? What are the primary attributes of each?

4. How does the advancement of networked media over broadcast media represent a significant power shift for both producers of content and consumers of content? Explain.

5. Summarize boyd's primary points. What is her argument?

6. In what ways is our use of Internet media an act of consumption? Explain.

7. Boyd warns that if we are not careful, we are going to "develop the psychological equivalent of obesity." What does she mean? Explain.

8. In what ways does advertising impede flow? Why does boyd feel that in order to advance the effective and useful consumption of information, advertising will not be part of the solution?

RESEARCH AND WRITING

1. How does information flow differently today than it did ten years ago? Research trends in media and write an essay comparing how people obtained information—news, commerce, connections with friends—a decade ago with how they receive information today.

2. How do you "consume" information? Track your media-driven activities—including cell phone usage, texts, traditional paper media, and online actions for two days. Describe how you did, or did not, become part of the "stream."

3. What reasons does boyd give for why access to more content is not necessarily more democratizing? How can it act counter to creating equal access to information? In a short essay, agree or disagree with her position that the popularity of certain types of content does not mean that information is being consumed equally, or to any social benefit.

4. After reading boyd's essay, write an essay in which you explore the future of information content in the next ten years. How will our access to information, content, and media material change? Refer to points boyd makes in her essay, as well as from your own online experiences.

Perspectives: The Evolution of Communication

Mike Keefe/PoliticalCartoons.com

THINKING CRITICALLY

1. What is the cartoonist saying about communication today? Explain.
2. According to the cartoon, at what moment is communication at its peak? How can you tell?
3. What opinion does the cartoonist seem to have for online media? Explain.

Crafting Your Image for Your 1,000 Friends on Facebook

Stuart Wolpert *

Identities can be changed, and are being changed, at a rapid rate on the Internet. Users of Facebook and MySpace can become anyone they want to be at the click of a mouse. But are there downfalls to showing the cyberworld a "you" that isn't necessarily "you"? Or can people finally become who they really want to be and fulfill their own destinies? In this article, author Stuart Wolpert reports on the growing trend of image adjusting and the rise of the public profile.

1 Students are creating idealized versions of themselves on social networking websites—Facebook and MySpace are the most popular—and using these sites to explore their emerging identities, UCLA psychologists report. Parents often understand very little about this phenomenon, they say.

2 "People can use these sites to explore who they are by posting particular images, pictures or text," said UCLA psychology graduate student Adriana Manago, a researcher with the Children's Digital Media Center, Los Angeles (CDMCLA), and lead author of a study that appears in a special November–December issue of the *Journal of Applied Developmental Psychology* devoted to the developmental implications of online social networking. "You can manifest your ideal self. You can manifest who you want to be and then try to grow into that.

These websites intensify the ability to present yourself in a positive light and explore different aspects of your personality and how you present yourself.

3 "We're always engaging in self-presentation; we're always trying to put our best foot forward," Manago added. "Social networking sites take this to a whole new level. You can change what you look like, you can Photoshop your face, you can select only the pictures that show you in a perfect lighting. These websites intensify the ability to present yourself in a positive light and explore different aspects of your personality and how you present yourself. You can try on different things, possible identities, and explore in a way that is common for emerging adulthood. It becomes psychologically real. People put up something that they would like to become—not completely different from who they are but maybe a little different—and the more it gets reflected off of others, the more it may be integrated into their sense of self as they share words and photos with so many people."

* Stuart Wolpert, *UCLA Newsroom,* November 18, 2008

4   "People are living life online," said Manago's co-author Patricia Green-field, a UCLA distinguished professor of psychology, director of the CDMCLA and co-editor of the journal's special issue. "Social networking sites are a tool for self-development."

5   The websites allow users to open free accounts and to communicate with other users, who number in the tens of millions on Facebook and MySpace. Participants can select "friends" and share photos, videos and information about themselves—such as whether they are currently in a relationship—with these friends. Many college students have 1,000 or more friends on Facebook or MySpace. Identity, romantic relations and sexuality all get played out on these social networking sites, the researchers said.

6   "All of these things are what teenagers always do," Greenfield said, "but the social networking sites give them much more power to do it in a more extreme way. In the arena of identity formation, this makes people more individualistic and more narcissistic; people sculpt themselves with their profiles. In the arena of peer relations, I worry that the meaning of 'friends' has been so altered that real friends are not going to be recognized as such. How many of your 1,000 'friends' do you see in person? How many are just distant acquaintances? How many have you never met?"

7   "Instead of connecting with friends with whom you have close ties for the sake of the exchange itself, people interact with their 'friends' as a performance, as if on a stage before an audience of people on the network," Manago said.

8   "These social networking sites have a virtual audience, and people perform in front of their audience," said Michael Graham, a former UCLA undergraduate psychology student who worked on this study with Greenfield and Manago for his honors thesis. "You're a little detached from them. It's an opportunity to try different things out and see what kind of comments you get.

9   "Sometimes people put forth things they want to become, and sometimes people put forth things that they're not sure about how other people will respond," he added. "They feel comfortable doing that. If they put something forward that gets rave reviews from people, it can alter the way they view their own identity. Through this experimentation, people can get surprised by how the molding goes."

10   Is this exploration of identity through these websites psychologically healthy?

11   "Every medium has its strengths and weaknesses, its psychological costs and benefits," said Greenfield, an expert in developmental psychology and media effects. "Costs may be the devaluing of real friendships and the reduction of face-to-face interaction. There are more relationships, but also more superficial relationships. Empathy and other human qualities may get reduced because of less face-to-face contact. On the other hand, new college students can make contact with their future roommates and easily stay in touch with high school friends, easing the social transition to college, or from one setting to another."

12   "I hate to be an older person decrying the relationships that young people form and their communication tools, but I do wonder about them," said Kaveri Subrahmanyam, associate director of the CDMCLA, professor of psychology at California State University, Los Angeles, and senior editor of the special journal issue. "Having 1,000 friends seems to be like collecting accessories."

13   Middle school is too young to be using Facebook or MySpace, Subrahmanyam believes, but by ninth grade, she considers the websites to be appropriate. She recommends that parents speak with their children, starting at about age 10, concerning what they do online and with whom they are interacting. Subrahmanyam notes that some of parents' greatest online fears—that their children will be harassed by predators or receive other unwanted or inappropriate Internet contact—have been decreasing, although parents may not know this.

14   In her own study in the journal, Subrahmanyam and colleagues Stephanie Reich of the University of California, Irvine, Natalia Waechter of the Austrian Institute for Youth Research and Guadalupe Espinoza, a UCLA psychology graduate student, report that, for the most part, college students are interacting with "people they see in their offline, or physical, lives."

15   "Young people are not going online to interact with strangers or for purposes removed from their offline lives," she said. "Mostly they seem to be using these social networking sites to extend and strengthen their offline concerns and relationships."

16   Research shows that adolescents who have discussed online safety with their parents and teachers are less likely to have a meeting with anyone they met online, Subrahmanyam noted.

17   "The best thing that parents can do is to have a rough idea of what their teens do online and have discussions with them about being safe online," she said.

18   What does having 1,000 friends do to your relationships with your true friends?

19   "Relationships now may be more fleeting and more distant," Manago said. "People are relating to others trying to promote themselves and seeing how you compare with them. We found a lot of social comparisons, and people are comparing themselves against these idealized self-presentations.

20   "Women feel pressure to look beautiful and sexy, yet innocent, which can hurt their self-esteem" she said. "Now you are part of the media; your MySpace profile page is coming up next to Victoria's Secret models. It can be discouraging to feel like you cannot live up to the flawless images you see."

21   "You're relating to people you don't really have a relationship with," Greenfield said. "People have a lot of diffuse, weak ties that are used for informational purposes; it's not friendship. You may never see them. For a large number of people, these are relationships with strangers. When you have this many people in your network, it becomes a performance for an audience. You are promoting yourself. The line between the commercial and the self is blurring.

22   "The personal becomes public, which devalues close relationships when you display so much for everyone to see," Greenfield added.

23   "Who we are is reflected by the people we associate with," Manago said. "If I can show that all these people like me, it may promote the idea that I am popular or that I associate with certain desirable cliques."

24   Not much remains private.

25   "You can be at a party or any public place, and someone can take a picture of you that appears on Facebook the next day," Manago said.

26   However, Graham said, the social networking sites can also strengthen relationships. He also said many people have "second-tier friends that they may have met

once but would not have stayed in touch with if not for the MySpace or Facebook networks."

27   The study by Manago, Greenfield and Graham, along with co-author Goldie Salimkhan, a former UCLA psychology undergraduate major, was based on small focus groups with a total of 11 women and 12 men, all UCLA students who use MySpace frequently.

28   One male student in the study said of MySpace, "It's just a way to promote yourself to society and show everyone, 'I'm moving up in the world, I've grown. I've changed a lot since high school.'"

29   How honestly do people present themselves on these sites?

30   Another male student in a focus group said, "One of my friends from high school, I saw her profile and I was like, 'Whoa, she's changed so much from high school,' and I see her this summer and I'm like, 'No, she's exactly the same!' Her MySpace is just a whole other level."

31   "Just at the age where peers are so important, that's where social networking—which is all about peers—is very attractive," Greenfield said. "Just at the age where you're exploring identity and developing an identity, that's where this powerful tool for exploring identity is very appealing. These sites are perfectly suited for the expanded identity exploration characteristic of emerging adults."

32   Another study in the special issue of the journal, conducted by Larry Rosen of California State University, Dominguez Hills, and colleagues Nancy Cheever and Mark Carrier, shows that parents have high estimates of the dangers of social networking but very low rates of monitoring and of setting limits on their children.

33   Rosen and his colleagues found that a parenting style that is marked by rational discussion, monitoring of children, setting limits and giving reasons for the limits is associated with less risky online behavior by children.

34   Greenfield advises parents of adolescents not to give their child a computer with Internet access in his or her bedroom.

35   "But even with a computer in a family room, complete monitoring is impossible," she said. "Children have so much independence that parents have to instill a compass inside them. Seeing what they are doing on the computer and discussing it with them is a good way to instill that compass."

36   In an additional study in the journal that highlights the beneficial nature of Facebook "friends," Charles Steinfield, Nicole B. Ellison and Cliff Lampe of Michigan State University examine the relationship between Facebook use and social capital, a concept that describes the benefits one receives from one's social relationships. They focus on "bridging social capital," which refers to the benefits of a large, heterogeneous network—precisely the kind of network these sites can support.

37   Their article argues that there is a direct connection between students' social capital and their use of Facebook, and using data over a two-year period, they found that Facebook use appears to precede students' gains in bridging social capital.

38   They also found that Facebook use appears to be particularly beneficial for students with lower self-esteem, as it helps them overcome the barriers they would otherwise face in building a large network that can provide access to information and opportunity.

39   "Young people do seem to be aware of the differences between their close friends and casual acquaintances on Facebook," Steinfield said. "Our data suggest that students are not substituting their online friends for their offline friends via Facebook; they appear to be using the service to extend and keep up with their network." ◆

CRITICAL THINKING

1. Is your own online identity an "idealized version" of yourself? Explain. If you do not have an online identity, explain why not.
2. According to Wolpert, when putting an image online of what someone hopes to become, that person may achieve a self-fulfilling prophecy. Explain how this could happen.
3. Do you agree that people who have an online identity are performing "as if on a stage before an audience of people on the network"? Give examples of how someone could be "performing" instead of just relaying information.
4. Are online profiles this generation's answer to voyeurism and exhibitionism?

CRITICAL WRITING

1. *Expository Writing:* Define "friend." Are online and offline friends the same entities, or do you view them separately? Some questions to consider: if you met one of your online friends offline, and you discovered that their "identity" was quite skewed from what you had been led to believe, would you still view this person as a friend? If an online friend suddenly disappeared, would you grieve? In other words, write an essay defining what makes someone a "friend." Use examples of online and offline friends.
2. *Persuasive Writing:* Take a side. Are online identities beneficial or detrimental to overall psychological health? Write an essay in which you persuade someone to have an online identity or else try to persuade someone to give up the process.

GROUP PROJECTS

1. With your group, create a fictional identity, either on MySpace or Facebook. Be as creative as you want. Throughout the semester, check on your "character" and see how many people ask to become friends with you. Carry on these friendships. Report back at the end of the semester with why you think your person was popular or ignored.
2. As a group, find three Facebook or MySpace users whom everyone in the group knows personally or has had offline contact with. Compare the offline persona of each person with his or her online identity. Is there a discrepancy in image? Explain the differences if any and explain how their online identities exemplify their offline identities.

I Tweet, Therefore I Am
*Peggy Orenstein**

Most people agree that social networking sites have allowed users to connect with people in a way they never could before. The social networking site Twitter allows people to share, almost instantly, moments in time (as long as we can summarize these moments into 140 characters or fewer). What do our online postings reveal about us and how we view ourselves? More than simply connecting us, social networking sites allow us to present a persona to the world—publicly sharing who we know, what we think, what we do, and even who we wish to be. In this next essay, author and essayist Peggy Orenstein wonders whether social networking sites are helping her share poignant moments with her friends or are distracting her from living fully in the moment. Or a little of both?

1   On a recent lazy Saturday morning, my daughter and I lolled on a blanket in our front yard, snacking on apricots, listening to a download of E.B. White reading "The Trumpet of the Swan." Her legs sprawled across mine; the grass tickled our ankles. It was the quintessential summer moment, and a year ago, I would have been fully present for it. But instead, a part of my consciousness had split off and was observing the scene from the outside: this was, I realized excitedly, the perfect opportunity for a tweet.

2   I came late to Twitter. I might have skipped the phenomenon altogether, but I have a book coming out this winter, and publishers, scrambling to promote 360,000-character tomes in a 140-character world, push authors to rally their "tweeps" to the cause. Leaving aside the question of whether that actually boosts sales, I felt pressure to produce. I quickly mastered the Twitterati's unnatural self-consciousness: processing my experience instantaneously, packaging life as I lived it. I learned to be "on" all the time, whether standing behind that woman at the supermarket who sneaked three extra items into the express check-out lane (you know who you are) or despairing over human rights abuses against women in Guatemala.

3   Each Twitter post seemed a tacit referendum on who I am, or at least who I believe myself to be. The grocery-store episode telegraphed that I was tuned in to the Seinfeldian absurdities of life; my concern about women's victimization, however sincere, signaled that I also have a soul. Together they suggest someone who is at once cynical and compassionate, petty yet deep. Which, in the end, I'd say, is pretty accurate.

4   Distilling my personality provided surprising focus, making me feel stripped to my essence. It forced me, for instance, to pinpoint the dominant feeling as I sat outside with my daughter listening to E.B. White. Was it my joy at being a mother? Nostalgia for my own childhood summers? The pleasures of listening to the author's quirky, underinflected voice? Each put a different spin on the occasion, of who I was within it. Yet the final decision ("Listening to E.B. White's 'Trumpet of the Swan'

---

* Peggy Orenstein, *New York Times,* July 30, 2010

with Daisy. Slow and sweet.") was not really about my own impressions: it was about how I imagined—and wanted—others to react to them. That gave me pause. How much, I began to wonder, was I shaping my Twitter feed, and how much was Twitter shaping me?

5   Back in the 1950s, the sociologist Erving Goffman famously argued that all of life is performance: we act out a role in every interaction, adapting it based on the nature of the relationship or context at hand. Twitter has extended that metaphor to include aspects of our experience that used to be considered off-set: eating pizza in bed, reading a book in the tub, thinking a thought anywhere, flossing. Effectively, it makes the greasepaint permanent, blurring the lines not only between public and private but also between the authentic and contrived self. If all the world was once a stage, it has now become a reality TV show: we mere players are not just aware of the camera; we mug for it.

6   The expansion of our digital universe—Second Life, Facebook, MySpace, Twitter—has shifted not only how we spend our time but also how we construct identity. For her coming book, "Alone Together," Sherry Turkle, a professor at M.I.T., interviewed more than 400 children and parents about their use of social media and cellphones. Among young people especially she found that the self was increasingly becoming externally manufactured rather than internally developed: a series of profiles to be sculptured and refined in response to public opinion. "On Twitter or Facebook you're trying to express something real about who you are," she explained. "But because you're also creating something for others' consumption, you find yourself imagining and playing to your audience more and more. So those moments in which you're supposed to be showing your true self become a performance. Your psychology becomes a performance." Referring to "The Lonely Crowd," the landmark description of the transformation of the American character from inner- to outer-directed, Turkle added, "Twitter is outer-directedness cubed."

7   The fun of Twitter and, I suspect, its draw for millions of people, is its infinite potential for connection, as well as its opportunity for self-expression. I enjoy those things myself. But when every thought is externalized, what becomes of insight? When we reflexively post each feeling, what becomes of reflection? When friends become fans, what happens to intimacy? The risk of the performance culture, of the packaged self, is that it erodes the very relationships it purports to create, and alienates us from our own humanity. Consider the fate of empathy: in an analysis of 72 studies performed on nearly 14,000 college students between 1979 and 2009, researchers at the Institute for Social Research at the University of Michigan found a drop in that trait, with the sharpest decline occurring since 2000. Social media may not have instigated that trend, but by encouraging self-promotion over self-awareness, they may well be accelerating it.

8   None of this makes me want to cancel my Twitter account. It's too late for that anyway: I'm already hooked. Besides, I appreciate good writing whatever the form: some "tweeple" are as deft as haiku masters at their craft. I am experimenting with the art of the well-placed "hashtag" myself (the symbol that adds your post on a particular topic, like #ShirleySherrod, to a stream. You can also use them whimsically, as in, "I am pretending not to be afraid of the humongous spider on the bed. #lieswetellourchildren").

9   At the same time, I am trying to gain some perspective on the perpetual performer's self-consciousness. That involves trying to sort out the line between person and persona, the public and private self. It also means that the next time I find myself lying on the grass, stringing daisy chains and listening to E. B. White, I will resist the urge to trumpet about the swan. ◆

CRITICAL THINKING

1. Do you use Twitter? If so, how often do you tweet, and what do you tweet about? If not, explain why you chose not to participate in this social medium.
2. When you post something online, do you think carefully about what you are about to post and how it might sound to others? Do you consider, as Orenstein does, how people will think about you and react to your post? Or do you shoot from the hip, writing whatever comes to mind? Explain.
3. What does Orenstein mean when she refers to the "packaged self"? How do we "package" ourselves online? What does this mean for our communication with others?
4. Evaluate Orenstein's style of writing in the first person narrative. How does this style allow her to reach her audience?

CRITICAL WRITING

1. *Exploratory Writing:* Write an essay exploring the consequences of social networking sites such as Twitter on the future of friendship and community.
2. *Exploratory Writing:* Orenstein admits that when she tweets, she isn't necessarily conveying the truth of a moment as she lives it. She is, rather, creating tweets for how she imagines, and wants, people to react to what she says. What does this reveal about her tweeting? Write a short essay exploring the connection between what we tweet and the "self-portraits" we create for our friends through our words.
3. *Personal Narrative:* Orenstein observes that she spends more time than she cares to admit constructing the right tweet. It you use Twitter, deconstruct one of your latest tweets. What did it say? How long did it take to write, and what thought did you put into it, and why? What were you trying to share with your friends, and what did you hope they would think of your message?

GROUP PROJECT

1. In your opinion, do Twitter and other social networking sites interfere with our ability to truly engage in the present? Do they distract us from our "live" moments, or do they allow us to live these moments more fully and with more engagement with others? Discuss this issue with your group.

► **Privacy Strikes Back**
Jeffrey Rosen*

► **Stop Panicking About the Bullies**
Nick Gillespie

Like any space where people gather, the virtual world is not immune to the problems we face in real life. The problems just shift and bring new challenges. The issue of cyberbullying has received a great deal of press, especially in the light of several suicides that seemed to have online connections. It used to be that kids could find respite in the safe haven of their own homes, but bullying seems to have taken on a whole new dimension online. Cyberbullies can text and call cell phones, post cruel messages on Facebook pages, set up cameras to capture video, and even set up fake pages to haunt their victims. In the past, with schoolyard bullying, everyone knew who the bullies were; but on the Internet, bullies can remain faceless and do far more damage. This chapter's *Viewpoints* takes a closer look at the problem of cyberbullying. What happens when there is no place to escape the taunting? Can anything be done to stop it? Or do we need to take a step back and put the issue into better perspective? Are we making a mountain out of a molehill? Jeffrey Rosen and Nick Gillespie share their views on the issue.

 # Privacy Strikes Back
Jeffrey Rosen

1 In the era of Facebook and YouTube, it's often said that privacy is dead. The recent suicide of Tyler Clementi seemed only to reinforce this conclusion. Clementi, an 18-year-old Rutgers student, killed himself after his roommate secretly webcast his dorm-room intimacies and publicized the livestream on Twitter. ("I went into molly's room and turned on my webcam. I saw him making out with a dude. Yay.") Indeed, the entire tragedy was transmitted via social media: On September 22, Clementi posted a note on his Facebook page: "Jumping off the gw bridge sorry."

2 Clementi's death was only one of several recent cases involving extreme invasions of privacy that were made possible by the ubiquity of webcams and online social networks. In Pennsylvania, a school district gave free MacBook laptops to students and then allegedly used the built-in webcams to spy on some students at home. At Duke University, a former student named Karen Owen composed a mock thesis detailing her sexual encounters with 13 athletes, complete with a PowerPoint slideshow

* Jeffrey Rosen, *The New Republic*, November 11, 2010; Nick Gillespie, *The Wall Street Journal*, March 31, 2012, WSJ Online on April 2, 2012

of names, photographs, and graphic descriptions of their performances. Owen e-mailed her narrative to a few friends, who forwarded it to their friends, after which it went viral and was published by the snarky sports website *Deadspin.* The media swiftly latched onto Clementi's death, in particular, as evidence that personal surveillance technologies have spun so far out of control that nothing can reign them in.

3   What is fascinating about these cases, however, is how quickly a legal response emerged. Within days, New Jersey prosecutors announced that Clementi's roommate, Dharun Ravi, and a friend had been charged with criminal invasion of privacy, carrying a potential jail sentence of up to five years. The Pennsylvania school district paid more than $600,000 to settle two lawsuits. And Karen Owen and *Deadspin* could be sued for invasion of privacy as well.

4   The responses to the first two cases are the good news. They show that even in the age of Facebook, there is legal recourse available for the most offensive incursions on our private lives. But the Duke case is more complicated, because it suggests that remedies for invasions of privacy can also threaten free speech. With our understandable desire to protect privacy online, do we risk going too far?

5   One country that the United States should *not* use as a model in balancing privacy and free expression is Argentina. Last year, an Argentinian judge held Google and Yahoo liable for causing "moral harm" and violating the privacy of Virginia Da Cunha, a pop star, actress, and lead singer of a band called the Virgin Pancakes. The judge ordered Google and Yahoo to pay 50,000 pesos each in damages simply because their search results had included pictures of Da Cunha that were linked to erotic content. The ruling was overturned on appeal in August, but there are at least 130 similar cases pending in Argentina to force search engines to remove or block offensive content, according to *The New York Times.* In the United States, search engines are protected by the Communications Decency Act, which immunizes Internet service providers from being held liable for content posted by third parties. But, as liability against search engines expands abroad, it will seriously curtail free speech: Yahoo says that the only way to comply with injunctions is to block all sites that refer to a particular plaintiff.

6   In the United States, courts and legislatures have generally struck a better balance by limiting liability for invasions of privacy to egregious cases of sexual surveillance. Under New Jersey law, for example, it's a crime if someone "photographs, films, videotapes, records, or otherwise reproduces in any manner, the image of another person whose intimate parts are exposed or who is engaged in an act of sexual penetration or sexual contact, without that person's consent and under circumstances in which a reasonable person would not expect to be observed." That's what Tyler Clementi's roommate, Dharun Ravi, did with his webcam, although he certainly didn't intend the suicide that followed. Rutgers students may be debating whether the five-year jail sentence that Ravi faces is too harsh, but there's widespread agreement that he deserves to be punished. Similarly, the Pennsylvania school district that used a webcam on a school-issued MacBook to spy on a student in his bedroom quickly settled the lawsuits. Everyone agrees that secretly filming students in various states of undress at home isn't a reasonable way of locating lost or stolen laptops.

7   Sexual surveillance cases become trickier—and potentially a greater threat to free expression—when they involve written descriptions of intimate activities, as in

the Duke case. Most state courts consider it a civil offense to publish details about someone's private life if the material would be highly offensive to a reasonable person and is not of legitimate concern to the public. Because details of their sexual performances would certainly qualify under that standard, the Duke athletes could plausibly sue both Karen Owen and *Deadspin* for invading their privacy. Judges might disagree, however, about whether Owen's e-mail distribution to a few friends should qualify as a form of publication and whether *Deadspin* was the first platform to make the material widely available—both requirements for liability. It's hard to say whether Owen should be held liable, since she didn't intend to circulate her narrative to a mass audience, but the mere threat of lawsuits could deter less careless authors from publishing explicit memoirs in the future.

8   The Duke case in many ways resembles the lawsuits sparked by Jessica Cutler, a former staffer for Ohio Republican Senator Mike DeWine who blogged as the Washingtonienne. In 2004, Cutler chronicled her sexual experiences with six men whom she identified by their initials, including details of their performances and proclivities. One of the men, Robert Steinbuch, a fellow DeWine staffer, sued Cutler—as well as Hyperion, which published Cutler's tell-all book—for invasion of privacy. In 2006, a district judge in D.C. refused to dismiss the lawsuit against Cutler, who went bankrupt, and, after the U.S. Court of Appeals for the Eighth Circuit refused to dismiss the lawsuit against Hyperion two years later, the publisher settled with Steinbuch. I asked Steinbuch, now a law professor at the University of Arkansas, whether he was glad he brought the lawsuits. "Absolutely," he told me. "What these courts did was wonderful, and absolutely it was a vindication, although it was a long time coming."

9   The outrage over the Clementi suicide, and the attendant anxieties about protecting our private lives from the march of technology, comes just as the Supreme Court is considering two important privacy cases that could expand liability for invasions of privacy beyond sexual surveillance—and seriously threaten free speech in the process. The Court recently heard a case involving an invasion of privacy suit against the Westboro Baptist Church, which picketed the funerals of American soldiers with offensive signs, such as "GOD HATES THE U.S.A." (The church views the deaths of soldiers as God's punishment of the United States for tolerating homosexuality.) A lower court properly dismissed the suit on the grounds that the privacy rights of the soldier's family were trumped by the free-speech rights of the protesters, who were kept about 1,000 feet away from the funeral—so far away that the family wasn't aware of them until after the ceremony. If the Supreme Court disagrees, it would become too easy for people who are offended by protests—either online or off—to sue for invasion of privacy, even when they're not being stalked or threatened.

10   In another case, the Supreme Court will decide whether a California law that restricts violent video games violates the First Amendment. The law provides civil penalties of up to $1,000 for selling or renting video games to minors if the games depict "killing, maiming, dismembering, or sexually assaulting an image of a human being" in a manner that appeals to the minors' "deviant or morbid interest." It makes sense to try to limit the access of minors to depictions of extreme violence, but the issue is complicated by the obvious threats to free speech. The dangers of giving governments the power to ban violent video games or videos were foreshadowed

in a recent Italian case where three Google executives were convicted of breaking Italian privacy laws after a video of a disabled boy being bullied was posted on Google. Italian prosecutors successfully argued that the boy's privacy was violated and that Google should have taken the videos down more quickly. Once the category of videos that can be banned expands beyond the narrow category of sexual voyeurism, governments have too much discretion to censor any videos that someone finds offensive.

11   At a time of rapid technological change, citizens are understandably concerned about whether the law is moving fast enough to keep up with new devices capable of recording or publicizing private activities. But the law will always have to react to incursions after the fact, prohibiting only the most shocking invasions while tolerating the rest. As it turns out, the balance between privacy and free speech that the United States has struck in the past is a sensible model for the future. People should be able to sue for invasions of privacy when they're victimized by extreme sexual surveillance, but almost nothing else. That's a bright line that the rest of the world has been reluctant to embrace; now it's up to the Supreme Court to preserve it. ◆

Stop Panicking About Bullies
Nick Gillespie

1   "When I was younger," a remarkably self-assured, soft-spoken 15-year-old kid named Aaron tells the camera, "I suffered from bullying because of my lips—as you can see, they're kind of unusually large. So I would kind of get [called] 'Fish Lips'—things like that a lot—and my glasses too, I got those at an early age. That contributed. And the fact that my last name is Cheese didn't really help with the matter either. I would get [called] 'Cheeseburger,' 'Cheese Guy'—things like that, that weren't really very flattering. Just kind of making fun of my name—I'm a pretty sensitive kid, so I would have to fight back the tears when I was being called names."

2   It's hard not to be impressed with—and not to like—young Aaron Cheese. He is one of the kids featured in the new Cartoon Network special "Stop Bullying: Speak Up," which premiered last week and is available online. I myself am a former geekish, bespectacled child whose lips were a bit too full, and my first name (as other kids quickly discovered) rhymes with two of the most-popular slang terms for male genitalia, so I also identified with Mr. Cheese. My younger years were filled with precisely the sort of schoolyard taunts that he recounts; they led ultimately to at least one fistfight and a lot of sour moods on my part.

3   As the parent now of two school-age boys, I also worry that my own kids will have to deal with such ugly and destructive behavior. And I welcome the commonsense anti-bullying strategies relayed in "Stop Bullying": Talk to your friends, your parents and your teachers. Recognize that you're not the problem. Don't be a silent witness to bullying.

4   But is America really in the midst of a "bullying crisis," as so many now claim? I don't see it. I also suspect that our fears about the ubiquity of bullying are just the

latest in a long line of well-intentioned yet hyperbolic alarms about how awful it is to be a kid today.

5   I have no interest in defending the bullies who dominate sandboxes, extort lunch money and use Twitter to taunt their classmates. But there is no growing crisis. Childhood and adolescence in America have never been less brutal. Even as the country's overprotective parents whip themselves up into a moral panic about kid-on-kid cruelty, the numbers don't point to any explosion of abuse. As for the rising wave of laws and regulations designed to combat meanness among students, they are likely to lump together minor slights with major offenses. The anti-bullying movement is already conflating serious cases of gay-bashing and vicious harassment with things like . . . a kid named Cheese having a tough time in grade school.

6   How did we get here? We live in an age of helicopter parents so pushy and overbearing that Colorado Springs banned its annual Easter-egg hunt on account of adults jumping the starter's gun and scooping up treat-filled plastic eggs on behalf of their winsome kids. The Department of Education in New York City—once known as the town too tough for Al Capone—is seeking to ban such words as "dinosaurs," "Halloween" and "dancing" from citywide tests on the grounds that they could "evoke unpleasant emotions in the students," it was reported this week. (Leave aside for the moment that perhaps the whole point of tests is to "evoke unpleasant emotions.")

7   And it's not only shrinking-violet city boys and girls who are being treated as delicate flowers. Early versions of new labor restrictions still being hashed out in Congress would have barred children under 16 from operating power-driven farm equipment and kept anyone under 18 from working at agricultural co-ops and stockyards (the latest version would let kids keep running machines on their parents' spreads). What was once taken for granted—working the family farm, October tests with jack-o-lantern-themed questions, hunting your own Easter eggs—is being threatened by paternalism run amok.

8   Now that schools are peanut-free, latex-free and soda-free, parents, administrators and teachers have got to worry about something. Since most kids now have access to cable TV, the Internet, unlimited talk and texting, college and a world of opportunities that was unimaginable even 20 years ago, it seems that adults have responded by becoming ever more overprotective and thin-skinned.

9   Kids might be fatter than they used to be, but by most standards they are safer and better-behaved than they were when I was growing up in the 1970s and '80s. Infant and adolescent mortality, accidents, sex and drug use—all are down from their levels of a few decades ago. Acceptance of homosexuality is up, especially among younger Americans. But given today's rhetoric about bullying, you could be forgiven for thinking that kids today are not simply reading and watching grim, postapocalyptic fantasies like "The Hunger Games" but actually inhabiting such terrifying terrain, a world where "Lord of the Flies" meets "Mad Max 2: The Road Warrior," presided over by Voldemort. Even President Barack Obama has placed his stamp of approval on this view of modern childhood. Introducing the Cartoon Network documentary, he solemnly intones: "I care about this issue deeply, not just as the president, but as a dad. ... We've all got more to do. Everyone has to take action against bullying."

10   The state of New Jersey was well ahead of the president. Last year, in response to the suicide of the 18-year-old gay Rutgers student Tyler Clementi, the state legislature

passed "The Anti-Bullying Bill of Rights." The law is widely regarded as the nation's toughest on these matters. It has been called both a "resounding success" by Steve Goldstein, head of the gay-rights group Garden State Equality, and a "bureaucratic nightmare" by James O'Neill, the interim school superintendent of the township of Roxbury. In Congress, New Jersey Sen. Frank Lautenberg and Rep. Rush Holt have introduced the federal Tyler Clementi Higher Education Anti-Harassment Act.

11   The Foundation for Individual Rights in Education has called the Lautenberg-Holt proposal a threat to free speech because its "definition of harassment is vague, subjective and at odds with Supreme Court precedent." Should it become law, it might well empower colleges to stop some instances of bullying, but it would also cause many of them to be sued for repressing speech. In New Jersey, a school anti-bullying coordinator told the Star-Ledger that "The Anti-Bullying Bill of Rights" has "added a layer of paperwork that actually inhibits us" in dealing with problems. In surveying the effects of the law, the Star-Ledger reports that while it is "widely used and has helped some kids," it has imposed costs of up to $80,000 per school district for training alone and uses about 200 hours per month of staff time in each district, with some educators saying that the additional effort is taking staff "away from things such as substance-abuse prevention and college and career counseling."

12   One thing seems certain: The focus on bullying will lead to more lawsuits against schools and bullies, many of which will stretch the limits of empathy and patience. Consider, for instance, the current case of 19-year-old Eric Giray, who is suing New York's tony Calhoun School and a former classmate for $1.5 million over abuse that allegedly took place in 2004. Such cases can only become more common.

13   Which isn't to say that there aren't kids who face terrible cases of bullying. The immensely powerful and highly acclaimed documentary "Bully," whose makers hope to create a nationwide movement against the "bullying crisis," opens in selected theaters this weekend. The film follows the harrowing experiences of a handful of victims of harassment, including two who killed themselves in desperation. It is, above all, a damning indictment of ineffectual and indifferent school officials. No viewer can watch the abuse endured by kids such as Alex, a 13-year-old social misfit in Sioux City, Iowa, or Kelby, a 14-year-old lesbian in small-town Oklahoma, without feeling angry and motivated to change youth culture and the school officials who turn a blind eye.

14   But is bullying—which the stopbullying.gov website of the Department of Health and Human Services defines as "teasing," "name-calling," "taunting," "leaving someone out on purpose," "telling other children not to be friends with someone," "spreading rumors about someone," "hitting/kicking/pinching," "spitting" and "making mean or rude hand gestures"—really a growing problem in America?

15   Despite the rare and tragic cases that rightly command our attention and outrage, the data show that things are, in fact, getting better for kids. When it comes to school violence, the numbers are particularly encouraging. According to the National Center for Education Statistics, between 1995 and 2009, the percentage of students who reported "being afraid of attack or harm at school" declined to 4% from 12%. Over the same period, the victimization rate per 1,000 students declined fivefold.

16   When it comes to bullying numbers, long-term trends are less clear. The makers of "Bully" say that "over 13 million American kids will be bullied this year," and estimates of the percentage of students who are bullied in a given year range from 20% to 70%. NCES changed the way it tabulated bullying incidents in 2005 and cautions against using earlier data. Its biennial reports find that 28% of students ages 12–18 reported being bullied in 2005; that percentage rose to 32% in 2007, before dropping back to 28% in 2009 (the most recent year for which data are available). Such numbers strongly suggest that there is no epidemic afoot (though one wonders if the new anti-bullying laws and media campaigns might lead to more reports going forward).

17   The most common bullying behaviors reported include being "made fun of, called names, or insulted" (reported by about 19% of victims in 2009) and being made the "subject of rumors" (16%). Nine percent of victims reported being "pushed, shoved, tripped, or spit on," and 6% reported being "threatened with harm." Though it may not be surprising that bullying mostly happens during the school day, it is stunning to learn that the most common locations for bullying are inside classrooms, in hallways and stairwells, and on playgrounds—areas ostensibly patrolled by teachers and administrators.

18   None of this is to be celebrated, of course, but it hardly paints a picture of contemporary American childhood as an unrestrained Hobbesian nightmare. Before more of our schools' money, time and personnel are diverted away from education in the name of this supposed crisis, we should make an effort to distinguish between the serious abuse suffered by the kids in "Bully" and the sort of lower-level harassment with which the Aaron Cheeses of the world have to deal.

19   In fact, Mr. Cheese, now a sophomore in high school with hopes of becoming a lawyer, provides a model in dealing with the sort of jerks who will always, unfortunately, be a presence in our schools. At the end of "Stop Bullying," he tells younger kids, "Just talk to somebody and I promise to you, it's going to get better." For Aaron, it plainly has: "It has been turned around actually. I am a generally liked guy. My last name has become something that's a little more liked. I have a friend named Mac and so together we are Mac and Cheese. That's cool."

20   Indeed, it is cool. And if we take a deep breath, we will realize that there are many more Aaron Cheeses walking the halls of today's schools than there are bullies. Our problem isn't a world where bullies are allowed to run rampant; it's a world where kids like Aaron are convinced that they are powerless victims. ◆

CRITICAL THINKING ──────────────

1. In his essay, Jeffrey Rosen connects issues of bullying with issues of privacy. Is privacy indeed a "right"? What are the limitations of our privacy rights?

2. Rosen provides an example of a student who created a fake recounting of her exploits with various members of her school's athletic teams, which was then posted online for everyone to see. Was her action a violation of the athlete's privacy? Was her privacy violated? Would this be a different issue if *she* later committed suicide because of the misunderstanding?

3. Why does Nick Gillespie feel that the issue of bullying is blown out of proportion? Agree or disagree with his viewpoint in a short response to his article.

4. Gillespie describes both traditional and cyberbullying. What is the difference between the two? Or are they essentially the same thing?

5. What are "helicopter parents"? What role do they play in the issue of bullying? Explain.

6. Rosen recounts the case of Tyler Clementi, who committed suicide after he was videoed kissing another male student. Was the Clementi suicide a case of bullying, or a case of invasion of privacy? Or both? Explain.

CRITICAL WRITING

1. *Personal Narrative:* Have you ever been cyberbullied or know someone who has? Conversely, have you ever cyberbullied someone else? Describe your experience.

2. *Exploratory Writing:* Write an essay describing your views on personal freedom and the Internet. How does personal freedom connect to privacy rights? To the issue of cyberbullying? Explain.

3. *Research Writing:* Since Tyler Clementi's death, several other cyber- and traditional bullying cases have been blamed for teen suicides, including Massachusetts high school student Phoebe Prince. Research this issue online and include information on how different schools and states are addressing the issue of bullying.

GROUP PROJECTS

1. As a group, research the anti-bullying laws cropping up in most states. Does your state have a law against cyberbullying? Against bullying in general? Report your results to the class as part of a broader discussion on the issue.

2. The Ohio State Bar Foundation's 2009 Fellows Class sponsored a statewide student video challenge, B4USend, to teach students the lawful and social consequences of cyberbullying and sexting. The winning entry was turned into a public service announcement (PSA). With your group, create your own PSA on the issue of cyberbullying. As you create your campaign, consider points made in this section as well as from your own experiences online and in school.

Perspectives on Gender

Bridging the Gap

We have witnessed enormous changes in the social and professional lives of men and women over the past century. Traditional ways of defining others and ourselves along gender lines have been irrevocably altered. Only 100 years ago, the full financial responsibility of a family was squarely on the shoulders of men. Women could not vote and had limited legal resources at their disposal. Sex was something that happened within the confines of marriage. Women were expected to remain at home, relegated to housework and childrearing. Men were expected to be the disciplinarians of family life, with limited involvement in the daily lives of their children. Now, women may pursue many different career options and lifestyles. Men are not expected to be the sole breadwinner for the family, and men and women together often share financial responsibilities. Sexual mores have relaxed, and both men and women enjoy greater freedoms socially, professionally, and intellectually than they ever have before.

Most college-age men and women were born after the Sexual Revolution of the 1960s and the feminist movement of the 1970s, but these movements have largely shaped the way men and women interact, view each other, evaluate opportunity, and envision the future. Although much has changed, and we have moved toward greater gender equality, vestiges of gender bias remain—for both sexes. The essays in this section examine how society has changed its expectations of gender and how these changes have affected men and women as they continue to define themselves and their relationships with each other and society as a whole.

The first two readings examine how subtle gender bias is woven into the very fabric of our culture, and comes out in unexpected, but disconcerting ways. In "My Most Attractive Adversary," Madeleine Begun Kane, a former lawyer, describes how expressions of understated sexism, such as physical compliments paid by men to women in professional settings, belittle women and reinforce dated notions about women in the workforce. Glenn Sacks and Richard Smaglick question the way men are portrayed by the popular media and especially in commercials in "Advertisers: Men Are Not Idiots." Why is it acceptable, they wonder, to make men look so stupid in ads?

Next, Hanna Rosin explores the new social phenomenon of "women at the top." In 2010, more women were in the workforce in the United States than ever before. More, in fact, than men. And in higher education, more women graduated with a four-year degree, no small feat considering many women never considered going to college only 50 years ago. In "The End of Men?" Hanna Rosin wonders what this shift means for our society as a whole and, more specifically, what it means for men. Then, Scott Russell Sanders challenges some widely held assumptions that men enjoy power and privilege in "The Men We Carry in Our Minds," as he describes the role of men in his childhood and how these men shaped his view of what it means to be male.

Balancing these two perspectives, linguist and social scientist Steven Pinker discusses the differences between men and women and how biological variations may influence career choice and career advancement in "The Science of Difference," this section's Modern Scholar essay.

Reforming traditional gender roles has taken decades of social change. Only 50 years ago, many people, including women, agreed that a woman's role was in the home, or, if she worked, her role was to support men. In "Feminism in a Mad World," Aviva Dove-Viebahn describes how the women in the popular television drama *Mad Men* give us a unique and compelling window to our not so distant past. The women of *Mad Men*, she explains, show us how far we have come, and where we need to go.

The chapter's Viewpoints section takes a closer look at men and women in sports. It has been over 35 years since Title IX became law, ensuring equal opportunity for women in education and in sports. Since then, we have witnessed a fourfold increase in women's participation in intercollegiate athletics. But while Title IX paved the way for many women to become professional female athletes, critics argue that revisions to the act are unfair to men. Student Brittney Johnson argues that Title IX is interfering with popular men's sports. Her position is countered by sports writer Joe Gisondi, who says Title IX is still needed. The section ends with an editorial by *Sports Illustrated* columnist E. M. Swift, who argues that the need for Title IX has passed in his essay "Gender Inequality."

My Most Attractive Adversary
*Madeleine Begun Kane**

Women may seem to have made tremendous progress professionally and academically, but they are held back by indirect sexist comments and attitudes. They are caught in a catch-22. If they react against these seemingly small slights, they appear to be overreacting or too sensitive. But to let them pass may signal that such comments are somehow acceptable. In the next essay, humorist and self-described "recovering lawyer" Madeleine Begun Kane holds that subtle sexism maintains gender differences.

1 "Our Portia has come up with an excellent solution." A trial judge said this about me several years ago in open court, when I was still a full-time litigator. I've never forgotten it. Not because it was a compliment to be compared to so formidable a lawyer as Shakespeare's Portia, although I think he meant it as a compliment. But what I really remember is my discomfort at being singled out as a woman in what, even today, remains a predominantly male world.

2 Despite our progress in the battle against workplace discrimination, the fact of being a female is almost always an issue. It may not be blatant, but it usually lurks just below the surface. We are not lawyers, executives, and managers. We are female lawyers, female executives, and

> *Men often use physical compliments to call attention to the fact that we are different . . . It's a clever technique, because any response other than a gracious "thank you" seems like a petty overreaction.*

---

* Madeleine Begun Kane, *Women's Village*, 2002

female managers. Just when we are lulled into believing otherwise, something happens to remind us, and those around us, of our gender in subtle yet unsettling ways.

3   Men often use physical compliments to call attention to the fact that we are different. References to "my lovely opponent" or "my most attractive adversary" remain remarkably common. It's a clever technique, because any response other than a gracious "thank you" seems like a petty overreaction.

4   Consequently, unless the remark is obviously offensive, as in references to certain unmentionable body parts, a simple nod or "thank you" is usually the prudent response. Of course if you're feeling less cautious, you may want to return the compliment. Done with a slight note of irony, this can be an effective way to get your point across. But saying, "You look very handsome yourself, Your Honor," is probably not a good idea.

5   Concern for the tender female sensibility rivals compliments in the subtle sexism department. I've experienced this most often during business meetings—high-powered meetings where a lone female is surrounded by her peers and superiors. At some point during the meeting the inevitable will happen. One of the men will use an expletive—a minor one in all likelihood. The expedient course is to ignore it. She is a woman of the world. She has heard and possibly used such language—and even worse.

6   But is she allowed to ignore it? Of course not! That would be too easy. The curser inevitably turns to the lone female (who until this moment has somehow managed not to blush) and apologizes. This singles her out as a delicate female who doesn't quite belong and needs to be protected. This also reminds everyone that the rest of the group would be ever so much more comfortable, at ease, and free to be themselves, if only a woman hadn't invaded their turf.

7   This has happened to me more times than I care to recall. And I still don't know the proper response. Should I ignore both the profanity and the apology? Is it best to graciously accept the apology, as if one were appropriate? Or should I say what I'm always tempted to say: "That's all right, I swear like a sailor, too."

8   Most women, myself included, overlook these subtle forms of sexism. I'm troubled by this, and I worry that by being silent, I'm giving up an opportunity to educate. For while some men use these tactics deliberately, others don't even know they're being offensive. Nevertheless, I usually smile discreetly and give a gracious nod. And wonder if I'm doing the right thing, or if I'm mistaking cowardice for discretion. ◆

CRITICAL THINKING

1. Do we have certain ingrained gender expectations when it comes to occupations? For example, do we expect men to be mechanics or lawyers or firefighters and women to be teachers or nurses or secretaries? Are these expectations changing, or are they still common assumptions?

2. Kane opens her essay with a story about how she was called "Portia" by a judge. Who is Portia? Why is Kane uncomfortable with what she believes to be a compliment by the judge? Explain.

3. Kane objected to compliments, such as "my lovely opponent" and "my most attractive adversary," made by male professionals. How do such compliments undermine her role as a lawyer and a professional? Do you think the men intended to slight her? Why or why not?

4. What profession do you hope to pursue? Is your profession a male- or female-dominated one, or is it balanced with both sexes? Do you think that gender will ever be an issue in your chosen profession?

5. In paragraphs 5 and 6, Kane describes a business meeting in which a man apologizes to a woman for his offensive language. Why does she object to such apologies? What assumptions do men make in offering such an apology?

6. Kane observes that it is difficult for women to openly object to sexist compliments, because to do so could backfire on them. How could their objections work against them? Explain.

7. Why does Kane worry about remaining silent against subtle sexism? What could happen if she doesn't remain silent? What would you do?

CRITICAL WRITING

1. *Research and Analysis:* In paragraph 2, Kane states that women are not "lawyers, executives, and managers." Instead, they are "female lawyers, female executives, and female managers." Interview a woman who holds a professional position in law, medicine, or business and ask her about this observation and whether she feels that the word "female" floats in front of her professional title, unspoken but still lurking "just below the surface." Summarize your interview and analyze the discussion.

2. *Personal Narrative:* Write about a time when you felt awkward because of your gender. Describe the situation, the experience, and why you felt uncomfortable. With a critical eye, analyze the situation and think about how social expectations of gender may have contributed to your feelings of discomfort.

GROUP PROJECTS

1. Kane argues that gender bias "lurks just below the surface," reminding women that they are women in what traditionally have been male professions. When does referencing gender cross a line into sexism? Is it sexist to refer to a woman as a "lady doctor" or a man as a "male nurse"? Are such references as common as Kane maintains? As a group, make a list of professions and their titles. Include old titles and their newer ones (for example, "mailman" and "postal carrier"). Has renaming the titles of these professions decreased sexism in the workplace?

2. In paragraph 7, Kane laments that she has experienced the apology-for-swearing scenario at many business meetings. As a group, consider her situation and develop a few comebacks she could use if she faced the situation again. Share your comebacks with the class.

Advertisers: Men Are Not Idiots

*Glenn Sacks and Richard Smaglick**

> The first essay in this section addressed the ways sexism can be subtly disguised in the professional world. This next essay addresses how television—especially advertising—can promote equally damaging sexism, in this case, against men. Because television reaches a broad and diverse audience, it can influence culture and social opinion. As a conduit for social persuasion, could television harm one group of people as much as it may help another? In the next editorial, Glenn Sacks and Richard Smaglick question the depiction of men as lazy, incompetent, insensitive, or simply stupid in commercials. Although such depictions may seem funny, stereotypical "male bashing," they argue, hurts men and society as a whole.

1   The way the advertising industry portrays men has drawn increasing scrutiny in both the trade press and the mainstream media. Defenders of the status quo—in which men are depicted as irresponsible fathers and lazy, foolish husbands—are starting to feel outnumbered. It's an understandable feeling. The evidence is clear: "Man as idiot" isn't going over very well these days.

2   Defenders of the advertising status quo generally put forth the following arguments: Males are "privileged" and "it's men's turn," so it's OK to portray them this way, and that men simply don't care how they're portrayed. Both of these arguments are highly questionable.

3   Young males certainly aren't privileged. The vast majority of learning-disabled students are boys, and boys are four times as likely as girls to receive diagnoses of attention-deficit hyperactivity disorder. Girls get better grades than boys and are much more likely than boys to graduate high school and enter college. According to the National Center for Education Statistics, women earn 60% of all bachelor's degrees and 60% of all master's degrees.

4   That adult men are "privileged" over women is also questionable. Yes, men do make up the majority of CEOs, politicians and powerbrokers. They also make up the majority of the homeless, the imprisoned, suicide victims and those who die young.

Negative Depiction

5   How fathers are portrayed matters. Fatherlessness is one of the greatest threats our children face. Syndicated columnist Leonard Pitts Jr. recently said: "Twenty-eight percent of American kids . . . are growing up in fatherless homes, heir to all the struggle and dysfunction that condition portends. . . . Who can deny those [are] appalling numbers[?]" Among the many ills of fatherlessness are much higher rates of teen drug abuse, crime, pregnancy and school dropouts.

6   While the advertising industry's negative depiction of fathers certainly isn't the cause of fatherlessness, it is part of the problem. In a TV culture like ours, the fact

---

* Glenn Sacks and Richard Smaglick, *Advertising Age,* April 14, 2008

that the only fathers one can see on TV are buffoonish (at best) does influence young people's perceptions of fathers.

7   For young men, it makes it less likely they'll aspire to be fathers, see their own value as fathers or, as Mr. Pitts explains, want to do the "hard but crucial work of being Dad." For young women, it means they'll be more likely to be misled into thinking that their children's fathers aren't important, that divorce or separation from them is no big deal, or that they should, as is the increasing trend, simply dispense with dad altogether and have children on their own.

8   Is it true that men really don't care how they're portrayed? Evidence strongly suggests otherwise. According to Leo Burnett Worldwide's 2005 "Man Study," four out of five men believe media portrayals of men are inaccurate. The study found that men care more about the way they are viewed than was generally believed.

9   When Kate Santich of the Orlando Sentinel did a feature on "men-as-idiots" advertising, she says she was "astounded" at the amount of mail she received, almost all of it critical of the way men are portrayed in ads. In a *Washington Times* article, advertising-industry journalist Todd Wasserman described getting a similar reaction to a recent article he wrote on anti-male ads.

10   This sentiment was reflected in the popularity of the highly publicized campaigns launched against advertising that is hostile to males. Several thousand protesters participated in a campaign against Verizon's anti-father ad "Homework" and a campaign against Arnold Worldwide.

Get on Her Good Side

11   Campaigns have drawn widespread support from women, who generally do not like to see their sons, husbands and fathers put down. As Rose Cameron, senior VP-planning director and "man expert" at Leo Burnett, says: "One of the great markers [society] looks to about the intelligence of a woman is her choice of husband. So if advertisers position men as idiots in the husband scenario, then you're commenting on her smarts. Women have told us, 'If you want to get on my good side, you do not show my husband as the idiot.'"

12   We have three suggestions for the advertising industry:

1. Create more ads that are father-positive. Some recent examples include AT&T's touching father-daughter ad "Monkey"; First Choice Holidays' "Slow-Motion Hugs"; and Ford's father-son ad "We Know."
2. As we consider whether it's wise to make men the butt of every joke, we should also consider the joke itself. Many see the 1960s as the golden age of advertising. Those who crafted the ads of that era created work of superb quality, seldom if ever resorting to the contempt, shame and aggressive ridicule of today's ads.
3. When an ad does need to poke fun at somebody, stop automatically defaulting to men as fools. Is bashing men really a good way to sell products?

13   The ad world has learned, for the most part, to respect womanhood. Given the rising level of media, ad-industry and public disgust toward anti-male ads, it's clear that good, respectful humor is a much healthier approach to advertising. ◆

CRITICAL THINKING

1. Think about the ways men and women are portrayed on television commercials. Are there certain gender-based stereotypes that seem common? What makes a male character interesting and engaging? What makes a female character noteworthy and interesting? Are the criteria different?

2. Evaluate how the authors support the thesis of their essay. First, identify their thesis. Then, analyze each supporting element they use to prove their point. Do the authors allow for alternative points of view? Do they try to see multiple sides of the issue? Explain.

3. Consider the contrast between male characters in ads and men in real life. Do male characters in commercials mirror men in the real world? Do the characters in commercials influence your perception of men in general?

4. This editorial notes that two reasons why men are ridiculed in commercials is because they are, overall, still privileged and that it is "their turn" to be mocked. Respond to these reasons with your own viewpoint, in which you either agree or disagree with this reasoning.

5. Some critics have observed that the portrayal of women as generally unintelligent in commercials would never be acceptable if the tables were turned. Respond to this view in your own words. Support your response with examples from the essay and your television viewing experience.

CRITICAL WRITING

1. *Research and Analysis:* Using online video resources research a few commercials, including the ones cited in this essay, that depict men as "idiots." Summarize your impressions of each commercial and why you feel that they do, or do not, demean men.

2. *Exploratory Writing:* Write about a male or female television character that you particularly enjoy watching. Explain why you chose this character and what made him or her so appealing to you. Do you see this character as a role model or simply entertaining? Explain.

3. *Exploratory Writing:* Consider the ways the advertising industry influences our cultural perspectives of gender and identity. Write an essay exploring the influence, however slight, television commercials have had on your own perceptions of gender. If you wish, interview other students for their opinions on this issue, and address some of their points in your essay.

GROUP PROJECTS

1. Working as a group, visit some online sites that archive television commercials and watch ads from several marketing areas—from cars to beer to cleaning products. Provide a brief explanation of each ad and describe what sort of character the men and women in the ads are. Are they smart? Stupid. Clueless? Who is the target audience of each ad, and how does this play into the depiction of the character? Share your list with the class. Did other groups categorize characters differently? Discuss this.

2. Consider Glenn Sacks and Richard Smaglick's ideas in the context of our broader culture. Do you agree that commercials present men as inept or stupid because that is what our society thinks is funny? Because it is "their turn"? Working as a group, prove or disprove this idea using movies, television, popular music, and print media such as advertisements as examples.

The End of Men?
*Hanna Rosin**

In 2010, women became the majority of the workforce for the first time in U.S. history. For every two men who will get a college degree in 2013, three women will do the same. For years, women's progress has been cast as a struggle for equality. But what if equality isn't the end point? Could modern, postindustrial society be simply better suited to women? What happens to men and their roles? To traditional family structures? In this next abridged essay, Hanna Rosin reports on the unprecedented role reversal that is now under way—and its possible cultural consequences.

1 In the 1970s the biologist Ronald Ericsson came up with a way to separate sperm carrying the male-producing Y chromosome from those carrying the X. He sent the two kinds of sperm swimming down a glass tube through ever-thicker albumin barriers. The sperm with the X chromosome had a larger head and a longer tail, and so, he figured, they would get bogged down in the viscous liquid. The sperm with the Y chromosome were leaner and faster and could swim down to the bottom of the tube more efficiently. Ericsson had grown up on a ranch in South Dakota, where he'd developed an Old West, cowboy swagger. The process, he said, was like "cutting out cattle at the gate." The cattle left flailing behind the gate were of course the X's, which seemed to please him.

2 In the late 1970s, Ericsson leased the method to clinics around the U.S., calling it the first scientifically proven method for choosing the sex of a child. Instead of a lab coat, he wore cowboy boots and a cowboy hat, and doled out his version of cowboy poetry. In 1979, he loaned out his ranch as the backdrop for the iconic "Marlboro Country" ads because he believed in the campaign's central image—"a guy riding on his horse along the river, no bureaucrats, no lawyers," he recalled when I spoke to him this spring. "He's the boss."

3 Feminists of the era did not take kindly to Ericsson and his Marlboro Man veneer. To them, the lab cowboy and his sperminator portended a dystopia of mass-produced boys. "You have to be concerned about the future of all women," Roberta Steinbacher, a nun-turned-social-psychologist, said in a 1984 *People* profile of

* Hanna Rosin, *The Atlantic*, July/August 2010

Ericsson. "There's no question that there exists a universal preference for sons." Steinbacher went on to complain about women becoming locked in as "second-class citizens" while men continued to dominate positions of control and influence.

4   Ericsson, now 74, laughed when I read him these quotes from his old antagonist. Seldom has it been so easy to prove a dire prediction wrong. In the '90s, when Ericsson looked into the numbers for the two dozen or so clinics that use his process, he discovered, to his surprise, that couples were requesting more girls than boys. In some clinics, Ericsson has said, the ratio is now as high as 2 to 1. Polling data on American sex preference is sparse, and does not show a clear preference for girls. But the picture from the doctor's office unambiguously does. A newer method for sperm selection, called MicroSort, is currently completing Food and Drug Administration clinical trials. The girl requests for that method run at about 75 percent.

5   Even more unsettling for Ericsson, it has become clear that in choosing the sex of the next generation, he is no longer the boss. "It's the women who are driving all the decisions," he says—a change the MicroSort spokespeople I met with also mentioned. At first, Ericsson says, women who called his clinics would apologize and shyly explain that they already had two boys. "Now they just call and [say] outright, 'I want a girl.'

6   *Why wouldn't you choose a girl?* That such a statement should be so casually uttered by an old cowboy like Ericsson—or by anyone, for that matter—is monumental. For nearly as long as civilization has existed, patriarchy—enforced through the rights of the firstborn son—has been the organizing principle, with few exceptions. Men in ancient Greece tied off their left testicle in an effort to produce male heirs; women have killed themselves (or been killed) for failing to bear sons. In her iconic 1949 book, *The Second Sex*, the French feminist Simone de Beauvoir suggested that women so detested their own "feminine condition" that they regarded their newborn daughters with irritation and disgust. Now the centuries-old preference for sons is eroding—or even reversing. "Women of our generation want daughters precisely because we like who we are," breezes one woman in *Cookie* magazine. Even Ericsson . . . can sigh and mark the passing of an era. "Did male dominance exist? Of course it existed. But it seems to be gone now. And the era of the firstborn son is totally gone."

7   Ericsson's extended family is as good an illustration of the rapidly shifting landscape as any other. His 26-year-old granddaughter—"tall, slender, brighter than hell, with a take-no-prisoners personality"—is a biochemist and works on genetic sequencing. His niece studied civil engineering at the University of Southern California. His grandsons, he says, are bright and handsome, but in school "their eyes glaze over. I have to tell 'em: 'Just don't screw up and crash your pickup truck and get some girl pregnant and ruin your life.'" Recently Ericsson joked with the old boys at his elementary-school reunion that he was going to have a sex-change operation. "Women live longer than men. They do better in this economy. More of 'em graduate from college. They go into space and do everything men do, and sometimes they do it a whole lot better. I mean, hell, get out of the way—these females are going to leave us males in the dust."

8   Man has been the dominant sex since, well, the dawn of mankind. But for the first time in human history, that is changing—and with shocking speed. Cultural and

economic changes always reinforce each other. And the global economy is evolving in a way that is eroding the historical preference for male children, worldwide. Over several centuries, South Korea, for instance, constructed one of the most rigid patriarchal societies in the world. Many wives who failed to produce male heirs were abused and treated as domestic servants; some families prayed to spirits to kill off girl children. Then, in the 1970s and '80s, the government embraced an industrial revolution and encouraged women to enter the labor force. Women moved to the city and went to college. They advanced rapidly, from industrial jobs to clerical jobs to professional work. The traditional order began to crumble soon after. In 1990, the country's laws were revised so that women could keep custody of their children after a divorce and inherit property. In 2005, the court ruled that women could register children under their own names. As recently as 1985, about half of all women in a national survey said they "must have a son." That percentage fell slowly until 1991 and then plummeted to just over 15 percent by 2003. Male preference in South Korea "is over," says Monica Das Gupta, a demographer and Asia expert at the World Bank. "It happened so fast. It's hard to believe it, but it is." The same shift is now beginning in other rapidly industrializing countries such as India and China.

9   Up to a point, the reasons behind this shift are obvious. As thinking and communicating have come to eclipse physical strength and stamina as the keys to economic success, those societies that take advantage of the talents of all their adults, not just half of them, have pulled away from the rest. And because geopolitics and global culture are, ultimately, Darwinian, other societies either follow suit or end up marginalized. In 2006, the Organization for Economic Cooperation and Development devised the Gender, Institutions and Development Database, which measures the economic and political power of women in 162 countries. With few exceptions, the greater the power of women, the greater the country's economic success. Aid agencies have started to recognize this relationship and have pushed to institute political quotas in about 100 countries, essentially forcing women into power in an effort to improve those countries' fortunes.

10   In feminist circles, these social, political, and economic changes are always cast as a slow, arduous form of catch-up in a continuing struggle for female equality. But in the U.S., the world's most advanced economy, something much more remarkable seems to be happening. American parents are beginning to choose to have girls over boys. As they imagine the pride of watching a child grow and develop and succeed as an adult, it is more often a girl that they see in their mind's eye.

11   What if the modern, postindustrial economy is simply more congenial to women than to men? For a long time, evolutionary psychologists have claimed that we are all imprinted with adaptive imperatives from a distant past: men are faster and stronger and hardwired to fight for scarce resources, and that shows up now as a drive to win on Wall Street; women are programmed to find good providers and to care for their offspring, and that is manifested in more-nurturing and more-flexible behavior, ordaining them to domesticity. This kind of thinking frames our sense of the natural order. But what if men and women were fulfilling not biological imperatives but social roles, based on what was more efficient throughout a long era of human history? What if that era has now come to an end? More to the point, what if the economics of the new era are better suited to women?

12   Once you open your eyes to this possibility, the evidence is all around you. It can be found, most immediately, in the wreckage of the Great Recession, in which three-quarters of the 8 million jobs lost were lost by men. The worst-hit industries were overwhelmingly male and deeply identified with macho: construction, manufacturing, high finance. Some of these jobs will come back, but the overall pattern of dislocation is neither temporary nor random. The recession merely revealed—and accelerated—a profound economic shift that has been going on for at least 30 years, and in some respects even longer.

13   Earlier this year, for the first time in American history, the balance of the workforce tipped toward women, who now hold a majority of the nation's jobs. The working class, which has long defined our notions of masculinity, is slowly turning into a matriarchy, with men increasingly absent from the home and women making all the decisions. Women dominate today's colleges and professional schools—for every two men who will receive a B.A. this year, three women will do the same. Of the 15 job categories projected to grow the most in the next decade in the U.S., all but two are occupied primarily by women. Indeed, the U.S. economy is in some ways becoming a kind of traveling sisterhood: upper-class women leave home and enter the workforce, creating domestic jobs for other women to fill.

14   The postindustrial economy is indifferent to men's size and strength. The attributes that are most valuable today—social intelligence, open communication, the ability to sit still and focus—are, at a minimum, not predominantly male. In fact, the opposite may be true. Women in poor parts of India are learning English faster than men to meet the demands of new global call centers. Women own more than 40 percent of private businesses in China, where a red Ferrari is the new status symbol for female entrepreneurs. Iceland elected Prime Minister Johanna Sigurdardottir, the world's first openly lesbian head of state, who campaigned explicitly against the male elite she claimed had destroyed the nation's banking system, and who vowed to end the "age of testosterone."

15   Yes, the U.S. still has a wage gap, one that can be convincingly explained—at least in part—by discrimination. Yes, women still do most of the child care. And yes, the upper reaches of society are still dominated by men. But given the power of the forces pushing at the economy, this setup feels like the last gasp of a dying age rather than the permanent establishment. Dozens of college women I interviewed for this story assumed that they very well might be the ones working while their husbands stayed at home, either looking for work or minding the children. Guys, one senior remarked to me, "are the new ball and chain." It may be happening slowly and unevenly, but it's unmistakably happening: in the long view, the modern economy is becoming a place where women hold the cards.

16   Men dominate just two of the 15 job categories projected to grow the most over the next decade: janitor and computer engineer. Women have everything else—nursing, home health assistance, child care, food preparation. Many of the new jobs, says Heather Boushey of the Center for American Progress, "replace the things that women used to do in the home for free." None is especially high-paying. But the steady accumulation of these jobs adds up to an economy that, for the working class, has become more amenable to women than to men.

17   The list of growing jobs is heavy on nurturing professions, in which women, ironically, seem to benefit from old stereotypes and habits. Theoretically, there is no reason men should not be qualified. But they have proved remarkably unable to adapt. Over the course of the past century, feminism has pushed women to do things once considered against their nature—first enter the workforce as singles, then continue to work while married, then work even with small children at home. Many professions that started out as the province of men are now filled mostly with women— secretary and teacher come to mind. Yet I'm not aware of any that have gone the opposite way. Nursing schools have tried hard to recruit men in the past few years, with minimal success. Teaching schools, eager to recruit male role models, are having a similarly hard time. The range of acceptable masculine roles has changed comparatively little, and has perhaps even narrowed as men have shied away from some careers women have entered. As Jessica Grose wrote in *Slate*, men seem "fixed in cultural aspic." And with each passing day, they lag further behind.

18   As we recover from the Great Recession, some traditionally male jobs will return—men are almost always harder-hit than women in economic downturns because construction and manufacturing are more cyclical than service industries—but that won't change the long-term trend. When we look back on this period, argues Jamie Ladge, a business professor at Northeastern University, we will see it as a "turning point for women in the workforce."

19   The economic and cultural power shift from men to women would be hugely significant even if it never extended beyond working-class America. But women are also starting to dominate middle management, and a surprising number of professional careers as well. According to the Bureau of Labor Statistics, women now hold 51.4 percent of managerial and professional jobs—up from 26.1 percent in 1980. They make up 54 percent of all accountants and hold about half of all banking and insurance jobs. About a third of America's physicians are now women, as are 45 percent of associates in law firms—and both those percentages are rising fast. A white-collar economy values raw intellectual horsepower, which men and women have in equal amounts. It also requires communication skills and social intelligence, areas in which women, according to many studies, have a slight edge. Perhaps most important—for better or worse—it increasingly requires formal education credentials, which women are more prone to acquire, particularly early in adulthood. Just about the only professions in which women still make up a relatively small minority of newly minted workers are engineering and those calling on a hard-science background, and even in those areas, women have made strong gains since the 1970s.

20   Office work has been steadily adapting to women—and in turn being reshaped by them—for 30 years or more. Joel Garreau picks up on this phenomenon in his 1991 book, *Edge City*, which explores the rise of suburbs that are home to giant swaths of office space along with the usual houses and malls. Companies began moving out of the city in search not only of lower rent but also of the "best educated, most conscientious, most stable workers." They found their brightest prospects among "underemployed females living in middle-class communities on the fringe of the old urban areas."

21   Near the top of the jobs pyramid, of course, the upward march of women stalls. Prominent female CEOs, past and present, are so rare that they count as minor celebrities, and most of us can tick off their names just from occasionally reading the business pages: Meg Whitman at eBay, Carly Fiorina at Hewlett-Packard, Anne Mulcahy and Ursula Burns at Xerox, Indra Nooyi at PepsiCo; the accomplishment is considered so extraordinary that Whitman and Fiorina are using it as the basis for political campaigns. Only 3 percent of Fortune 500 CEOs are women, and the number has never risen much above that.

22   But even the way this issue is now framed reveals that men's hold on power in elite circles may be loosening. In business circles, the lack of women at the top is described as a "brain drain" and a crisis of "talent retention." And while female CEOs may be rare in America's largest companies, they are highly prized: last year, they out-earned their male counterparts by 43 percent, on average, and received bigger raises.

23   "Women are knocking on the door of leadership at the very moment when their talents are especially well matched with the requirements of the day," writes David Gergen in the introduction to *Enlightened Power: How Women Are Transforming the Practice of Leadership.* What are these talents? Once it was thought that leaders should be aggressive and competitive, and that men are naturally more of both. But psychological research has complicated this picture. In lab studies that simulate negotiations, men and women are just about equally assertive and competitive, with slight variations. Men tend to assert themselves in a controlling manner, while women tend to take into account the rights of others, but both styles are equally effective, write the psychologists Alice Eagly and Linda Carli, in their 2007 book, *Through the Labyrinth.*

24   Over the years, researchers have sometimes exaggerated these differences and described the particular talents of women in crude gender stereotypes: women as more empathetic, as better consensus-seekers and better lateral thinkers; women as bringing a superior moral sensibility to bear on a cutthroat business world. In the '90s, this field of feminist business theory seemed to be forcing the point. But after the latest financial crisis, these ideas have more resonance. Researchers have started looking into the relationship between testosterone and excessive risk, and wondering if groups of men, in some basic hormonal way, spur each other to make reckless decisions. The picture emerging is a mirror image of the traditional gender map: men and markets on the side of the irrational and overemotional, and women on the side of the cool and levelheaded.

25   It could be that women boost corporate performance, or it could be that better-performing firms have the luxury of recruiting and keeping high-potential women. But the association is clear: innovative, successful firms are the ones that promote women. The same Columbia-Maryland study ranked America's industries by the proportion of firms that employed female executives, and the bottom of the list reads like the ghosts of the economy past: shipbuilding, real estate, coal, steelworks, machinery.

26   It is fabulous to see girls and young women poised for success in the coming years. But allowing generations of boys to grow up feeling rootless and obsolete is not a recipe for a peaceful future. Men have few natural support groups and little

access to social welfare; the men's-rights groups that do exist in the U.S. are taking on an angry, anti-woman edge. Marriages fall apart or never happen at all, and children are raised with no fathers. Far from being celebrated, women's rising power is perceived as a threat.

27   What would a society in which women are on top look like? We already have an inkling. This is the first time that the cohort of Americans ages 30 to 44 has more college-educated women than college-educated men, and the effects are upsetting the traditional Cleaver-family dynamics. In 1970, women contributed 2 to 6 percent of the family income. Now the typical working wife brings home 42.2 percent, and four in 10 mothers—many of them single mothers—are the primary breadwinners in their families. The whole question of whether mothers should work is moot, argues Heather Boushey of the Center for American Progress, "because they just do. This idealized family—he works, she stays home—hardly exists anymore."

28   The terms of marriage have changed radically since 1970. Typically, women's income has been the main factor in determining whether a family moves up the class ladder or stays stagnant. And increasing numbers of women—unable to find men with a similar income and education—are forgoing marriage altogether. In 1970, 84 percent of women ages 30 to 44 were married; now 60 percent are. In 2007, among American women without a high-school diploma, 43 percent were married. And yet, for all the hand-wringing over the lonely spinster, the real loser in society—the only one to have made just slight financial gains since the 1970s—is the single man, whether poor or rich, college-educated or not. Hens rejoice; it's the bachelor party that's over.

29   The sociologist Kathryn Edin spent five years talking with low-income mothers in the inner suburbs of Philadelphia. Many of these neighborhoods, she found, had turned into matriarchies, with women making all the decisions and dictating what the men should and should not do. "I think something feminists have missed," Edin told me, "is how much power women have" when they're not bound by marriage. The women, she explained, "make every important decision"—whether to have a baby, how to raise it, where to live. "It's definitely 'my way or the highway,'" she said. "Thirty years ago, cultural norms were such that the fathers might have said, 'Great, catch me if you can.' Now they are desperate to father, but they are pessimistic about whether they can meet her expectations." The women don't want them as husbands, and they have no steady income to provide.

30   Over the years, researchers have proposed different theories to explain the erosion of marriage in the lower classes: the rise of welfare, or the disappearance of work and thus of marriageable men. But Edin thinks the most compelling theory is that marriage has disappeared because women are setting the terms—and setting them too high for the men around them to reach. "I want that white-picket-fence dream," one woman told Edin, and the men she knew just didn't measure up, so she had become her own one-woman mother/father/nurturer/provider. The whole country's future could look much as the present does for many lower-class African Americans: the mothers pull themselves up, but the men don't follow. First-generation college-educated white women may join their black counterparts in a new kind of middle class, where marriage is increasingly rare.

31   In fact, the more women dominate, the more they behave, fittingly, like the dominant sex. Rates of violence committed by middle-aged women have skyrocketed since

the 1980s, and no one knows why. In Roman Polanski's *The Ghost Writer*, the traditional political wife is rewritten as a cold-blooded killer at the heart of an evil conspiracy. In her recent video *Telephone*, Lady Gaga, with her infallible radar for the cultural edge, rewrites *Thelma and Louise* as a story not about elusive female empowerment but about sheer, ruthless power. Instead of killing themselves, she and her girlfriend (played by Beyoncé) kill a bad boyfriend and random others in a homicidal spree and then escape in their yellow pickup truck, Gaga bragging, "We did it, Honey B."

32 The Marlboro Man, meanwhile, master of wild beast and wild country, seems too far-fetched and preposterous even for advertising. His modern equivalents are the stunted men in the Dodge Charger ad that ran during this year's Super Bowl in February. Of all the days in the year, one might think, Super Bowl Sunday should be the one most dedicated to the cinematic celebration of macho. The men in Super Bowl ads should be throwing balls and racing motorcycles and doing whatever it is men imagine they could do all day if only women were not around to restrain them.

33 Instead, four men stare into the camera, unsmiling, not moving except for tiny blinks and sways. They look like they've been tranquilized, like they can barely hold themselves up against the breeze. Their lips do not move, but a voice-over explains their predicament—how they've been beaten silent by the demands of tedious employers and enviro-fascists and women. Especially women. "I will put the seat down, I will separate the recycling, I will carry your lip balm." This last one—lip balm—is expressed with the mildest spit of emotion, the only hint of the suppressed rage against the dominatrix. Then the commercial abruptly cuts to the fantasy, a Dodge Charger vrooming toward the camera punctuated by bold all caps: MAN'S LAST STAND. But the motto is unconvincing. After that display of muteness and passivity, you can only imagine a woman—one with shiny lips—steering the beast. ◆

CRITICAL THINKING

1. What concerns did Ronald Ericsson's research and method raise? Why did these concerns turn out to be largely unfounded?
2. How does the story of Ronald Ericsson's work set up the rest of Rosin's essay? How does it frame the issue Rosin is raising?
3. Rosin points out that for most of human history, cultures have preferred having boys to girls. What reasons does she provide for the shift in many cultures to now prefer having girls? How well does she support her argument and with what data?
4. According to Rosin, why are women dominating in the workplace? How is this competitive edge connected to the recession? Is it likely to continue for the next decade? Beyond? Explain.
5. Why haven't men embraced the highly employable "nurturing professions"? What reasons does Rosin give? What reasons, if any, can you offer based on your knowledge of American culture? Explain.
6. What are some of the drawbacks of having women dominate the workforce? How are men being affected by this cultural shift?
7. How has marriage been impacted by the shift of women dominating the employment and educational landscape? Explain.

CRITICAL WRITING

1. *Compare and Contrast:* How do the points Rosin raises in her essay connect to points made by essays in Chapter 8 on the decline of marriage? Analyze and discuss the possible cause/effect connections between this essay and an essay from Chapter 8.
2. *Expository Writing:* Write an essay in which you consider your own sense of cultural conditioning. Do you feel your behavior has been conditioned by sex-role expectations? In what ways? Is there a difference between the "real" you and the person you present to the world? If there is a difference, is it the result of cultural pressure? Explain.
3. *Research and Analysis:* Who is the Marlboro Man? What did he represent? Write an essay tracing male or female stereotypes over the last 40 years. How have these stereotypes influenced our view of what it means to be male or female? Of our perception of what jobs are suitable for men and for women?

GROUP PROJECTS

1. Rosin observes that men, in general, have failed to embrace the "nurturing professions" including teaching, nursing, and secretarial roles. As a group, develop a list of questions designed to elicit student opinion on perceptions of gender and employment in the twenty-first century. What influence, if any, do perceptions of gender have on our employment expectations of men and women? What are "men's jobs" and "women's jobs"? What stigma is connected to a woman having a traditionally male job, such as in construction work, or a man having a female one, such as in nursing? Discuss your results with the class as part of a broader discussion on perceptions of contemporary gender roles.
2. Consider the connections between our employment status and how young women and men view themselves and each other. If a man doesn't have a job, is he less datable? What about a woman? What impact does employment status have on self-esteem? Connect your discussion back to points Rosin makes about the gender shift that appears to be happening in the United States.
3. Is it harder to grow up male or female in America today? Discuss which gender faces the greatest and most daunting challenges and why. Offer suggestions to help ease the gender-related challenges college-age men and women face in today's culture. Discuss your group's points as part of a larger class dialogue on men and women in today's society.

Perspectives: Unspoken Communication

Zits © 2008 Zits Partnership/Distributed by King Features Syndicate

THINKING CRITICALLY

1. What is this cartoon saying about how men and women communicate with the same sex?
2. If a third panel were added with a young man meeting a young woman, what do you think the observations of each would be? Create your own third panel to this cartoon.
3. Do you believe that the point made in this cartoon is true? Why or why not?

The Men We Carry in Our Minds
Scott Russell Sanders*

Statistically, men still tend to hold more positions of power and wealth than women do. Many women feel that simply being born male automatically confers status and power or, at the very least, makes life easier. This cultural assumption, however, may only apply to a very small segment of the male population. Is it fair to stereotype men this way? Writer Scott Russell Sanders grew up in rural Tennessee and Ohio, where men aged early from lives of punishing physical labor or died young in military service. When he got to college, Sanders was baffled when the daughters of lawyers, bankers, and physicians accused him and his sex of "having cornered the world's pleasures." In this essay, Sanders explores the differences between the men and women in his life and how male power is often dependent on class and social influence.

1 "This must be a hard time for women," I say to my friend Anneke. "They have so many paths to choose from, and so many voices calling them."

2 "I think it's a lot harder for men," she replies.

3 "How do you figure that?"

4 "The women I know feel excited, innocent, like crusaders in a just cause. The men I know are eaten up with guilt."

5 "Women feel such pressure to be everything, do everything," I say. "Career, kids, art, politics. Have their babies and get back to the office a week later. It's as if they're trying to overcome a million years' worth of evolution in one lifetime."

6 "But we help one another. And we have this deep-down sense that we're in the right—we've been held back, passed over, used—while men feel they're in the wrong. Men are the ones who've been discredited, who have to search their souls."

7 I search my soul. I discover guilty feelings aplenty—toward the poor, Native Americans, the whales, an endless list of debts. But toward women I feel something more confused, a snarl of shame, envy, wary, tenderness, and amazement. This muddle troubles me. To hide my unease I say, "You're right, it's tough being a man these days."

8 "Don't laugh," Anneke frowns at me. "I wouldn't be a man for anything. It's much easier being the victim. All the victim has to do is break free. The persecutor has to live with his past."

9 How deep is that past? I find myself wondering. How much of an inheritance do I have to throw off?

10 When I was a boy growing up on the back roads of Tennessee and Ohio, the men I knew labored with their bodies. They were marginal farmers, just scraping by, or welders, steelworkers, carpenters; they swept floors, dug ditches, mined coal, or drove trucks, their forearms ropy with muscle; they trained horses, stoked furnaces, made tires, stood on assembly lines wrestling parts onto cars and refrigerators. They

---

* Scott Russell Sanders, *The Paradise of Bombs,* 1984

got up before light, worked all day long, whatever the weather, and when they came home at night, they looked as though somebody had been whipping them. In the evenings and on

The fathers of my friends always seemed older than the mothers. Men wore out sooner. Only women lived into old age.

weekends, they worked on their own places, tilling gardens that were lumpy with clay, fixing broken-down cars, hammering on houses that were always too drafty, too leaky, too small. The bodies of the men I knew were twisted and maimed in ways visible and invisible. The nails of their hands were black and split, the hands tattooed with scars. Some had lost fingers. Heavy lifting had given many of them finicky backs and guts weak from hernias. Racing against conveyor belts had given them ulcers. Their ankles and knees ached from years of standing on concrete. Anyone who had worked for long around machines was hard of hearing. They squinted, and the skin of their faces was creased like the leather of old work gloves. There were times, studying them, when I dreaded growing up. Most of them coughed, from dust or cigarettes, and most of them drank cheap wine or whiskey, so their eyes looked bloodshot and bruised. The fathers of my friends always seemed older than the mothers. Men wore out sooner. Only women lived into old age.

11   As a boy I also knew another sort of man, who did not sweat and break down like mules. They were soldiers, and so far as I could tell, they scarcely worked at all. But when the shooting started, many of them would die. This was what soldiers were for, just like a hammer was for driving nails. Warriors and toilers: those seemed, in my boyhood vision, to be the chief destinies for men. They weren't the only destinies, as I learned from having a few male teachers, from reading books, and from watching television. But the men on television—the politicians, the astronauts, the generals, the savvy lawyers, the philosophical doctors, the bosses who gave orders to both soldiers and laborers—seemed as remote and unreal to me as the figures in Renaissance tapestries. I could no more imagine growing up to become one of these cool, potent creatures than I could imagine becoming a prince.

12   A nearer and more hopeful example was that of my father, who had escaped from a red dirt farm to a tire factory, and from the assembly line to the front office. Eventually, he dressed in a white shirt and tie. He carried himself as if he had been born to work with his mind. But his body, remembering the earlier years of slogging work, began to give out on him in his fifties, and it quit on him entirely before he turned 65.

13   A scholarship enabled me not only to attend college, a rare enough feat in my circle, but even to study in a university meant for the children of the rich. Here I met for the first time young men who had assumed from birth that they would lead lives of comfort and power. And for the first time, I met women who told me that men were guilty of having kept all the joys and privileges of the earth for themselves. I was baffled. What privileges? What joys? I thought about the maimed, dismal lives of most of the men back home. What had they stolen from their wives and daughters? The right to go five days a week, 12 months a year, for 30 or 40 years to a steel mill or a coal mine? The right to drop bombs and die in war? The right to feel every leak in the roof, every gap in the fence, every cough in the engine as a wound they

must mend? The right to feel, when the layoff comes or the plant shuts down, not only afraid but ashamed?

14   I was slow to understand the deep grievances of women. This was because, as a boy, I had envied them. Before college, the only people I had ever known who were interested in art or music or literature, the only ones who read books, the only ones who ever seemed to enjoy a sense of ease and grace were the mothers and daughters. Like the menfolk, they fretted about money, they scrimped and made do. But when the pay stopped coming in, they were not the ones who had failed. Nor did they have to go to war, and that seemed to me a blessed fact. By comparison with the narrow, ironclad days of fathers, there was an expansiveness, I thought, in the days of mothers. They went to see neighbors, to shop in town, to run errands at school, at the library, at church. No doubt, had I looked harder at their lives, I would have envied them less. It was not my fate to become a woman, so it was easier for me to see the graces. I didn't see then what a prison a house could be, since houses seemed to be brighter, handsomer places than any factory. I did not realize—because such things were never spoken of—how often women suffered from men's bullying. Even then I could see how exhausting it was for a mother to cater all day to the needs of young children. But if I had been asked, as a boy, to choose between tending a baby and tending a machine, I think I would have chosen the baby. (Having now tended both, I know I would choose the baby.)

15   So I was baffled when the women at college accused me and my sex of having cornered the world's pleasures. I think something like my bafflement has been felt by other boys (and by girls as well) who grew up in dirt-poor farm country, in mining country, in black ghettoes, in Hispanic barrios, in the shadows of factories, in Third World nations—any place where the fate of men is just as grim and bleak as the fate of women.

16   When the women I met at college thought about the joys and privileges of men, they did not carry in their minds the sort of men I had known in my childhood. They thought of their fathers, who were bankers, physicians, architects, stockholders, the big wheels of the big cities. They were never laid off, never short of cash at month's end, never lined up for welfare. These fathers made decisions that mattered. They ran the world.

17   The daughters of such men wanted to share in this power, this glory. So did I. They yearned for a say over their future, for jobs worthy of their abilities, for the right to live at peace, unmolested, whole. Yes, I thought, yes, yes. The difference between me and these daughters was that they saw me, because of my sex, as destined from birth to become like their fathers and, therefore, as an enemy to their desires. But I knew better. I wasn't an enemy, in fact or in feeling. I was an ally. If I had known then how to tell them so, would they have believed me? Would they now? ◆

CRITICAL THINKING

1. Consider the stereotypical view that being male automatically grants one power, status, and privilege. Then think about three men you know well, such as a father, brother, or friend. Do their everyday life experiences bear out this generalization?

2. In paragraph 7, Sanders states he has feelings of guilt toward a number of minority groups or social causes, but his feelings toward women are more complicated. What do you think might be the reasons for his feelings? Can you identify with this perspective?

3. Do you think Sanders feels women, not men, are the privileged class? Explain.

4. How do you think women from the different socioeconomic groups Sandcrs mentions in his essay would respond to his ideas? For example, how would the educated daughters of the lawyers and bankers respond? How about the women from Sanders's hometown?

5. What are the occupations and obligations of the men mentioned in the article? What socioeconomic segment of society is Sanders describing? What does this suggest about the relationship between gender and class?

6. Sanders relates his argument entirely in the first person, using personal anecdotes to illustrate his point. How does this approach influence the reader? Would this essay be different if he told it from a third-person point of view? Explain.

7. In paragraph 8, Sanders's friend Anneke says she "wouldn't be a man for anything. It's much easier being the victim." What does Anneke mean by this statement? Do you agree with her view? Why or why not?

8. What effect do Anneke's comments have on Sanders's audience? Why do you think he quotes her? How do her comments support his argument?

CRITICAL WRITING

1. *Exploratory Writing:* Write an essay in which you consider your own sense of cultural conditioning. Do you think your behavior has been conditioned by sex-role expectations? In what ways? Is there a difference between the "real" you and the person you present to the world? If there is a difference, is it the result of cultural conditioning?

2. *Analytical Writing:* What does it mean to be a man today? Write an essay explaining what you think it means to be male in today's society. How do men factor into current social, intellectual, political, economic, and religious equations? What opportunities are available—or not available—to men? Do you think it is easier or better to be male in American culture? Female? Explain.

GROUP PROJECT

1. With your group, try to define the terms "masculine" and "feminine." You might include library research on the origins of the words or research their changing implications over the years. Develop your own definition for each word, and then discuss with the rest of the class how you arrived at your definitions.

Modern Scholar

The Science of Difference
Steven Pinker*

During a speech he made in January 2005 at a National Bureau of Economics Research Conference on diversifying the science and engineering workforce, former Harvard University President Lawrence H. Summers commented that biological factors could be the reason why there were more men than women in high-end science and engineering positions. His comments sparked a great deal of controversy, especially among female academics, who challenged his viewpoint as sexist. Several months later, Summers resigned from his position as president of Harvard. In this next essay, Harvard professor and Summers-supporter Steven Pinker defends the idea that men and women are biologically, and perhaps intellectually, different and that we should admit this fact.

1   When I was an undergraduate in the early 1970s, I was assigned a classic paper, published in *Scientific American*, that began: "There is an experiment in psychology that you can perform easily in your home. . . . Buy two presents for your wife, choosing things . . . she will find equally attractive." Just ten years after those words were written, the author's blithe assumption that his readers were male struck me as comically archaic. By the early '70s, women in science were no longer an oddity or a joke but a given. Today, in my own field, the study of language development in children, a majority of the scientists are women. Even in scientific fields with a higher proportion of men, the contributions of women are so indispensable that any talk of turning back the clock would be morally heinous and scientifically ruinous.

2   Yet to hear the reaction to [former] Harvard President Lawrence Summers's remarks at a conference on gender imbalances in science, in which he raised the possibility of innate sex differences, one might guess that he had proposed exactly that. Nancy Hopkins, the eminent MIT biologist and advocate for women in science, stormed out of the room to avoid, she said, passing out from shock. An engineering dean called his remarks "an intellectual tsunami," and, with equal tastelessness, a *Boston Globe* columnist compared him to people who utter racial epithets or wear swastikas. Alumnae threatened to withhold donations, and the National Organization of Women called for his resignation. Summers was raked in a letter signed by more than 100 Harvard faculty members and shamed into issuing serial apologies.

3   Summers did not, of course, say that women are "natively inferior," that "they just can't cut it," that they suffer "an inherent cognitive deficit in the sciences," or that men have "a monopoly on basic math ability," as many academics and

* Steven Pinker, *The New Republic Online*, February 7, 2005

journalists assumed. Only a madman could believe such things. Summers's analysis of why there might be fewer women in mathematics and science is commonplace among economists who study gender disparities in employment, though it is rarely mentioned in the press or in academia when it comes to discussions of the gender gap in science and engineering. The fact that women make up only 20 percent of the workforce in science, engineering, and technology development has at least three possible (and not mutually exclusive) explanations. One is the persistence of discrimination, discouragement, and other barriers. In popular discussions of gender imbalances in the workforce, this is the explanation most mentioned. Although no one can deny that women in science still face these injustices, there are reasons to doubt they are the only explanation. A second possibility is that gender disparities can arise in the absence of discrimination as long as men and women differ, on average, in their mixture of talents, temperaments, and interests—whether this difference is the result of biology, socialization, or an interaction of the two. A third explanation is that child rearing, still disproportionately shouldered by women, does not easily coexist with professions that demand Herculean commitments of time. These considerations speak against the reflex of attributing every gender disparity to gender discrimination and call for research aimed at evaluating the explanations.

4   The analysis should have been unexceptionable. Anyone who has fled a cluster of men at a party debating the fine points of flat-screen televisions can appreciate that fewer women than men might choose engineering, even in the absence of arbitrary barriers. (As one female social scientist noted in *Science Magazine*, "Reinventing the curriculum will not make me more interested in learning how my dishwasher works.") To what degree these and other differences originate in biology must be determined by research, not fatwa. History tells us that how much we want to believe a proposition is not a reliable guide as to whether it is true.

5   Nor is a better understanding of the causes of gender disparities inconsequential. Overestimating the extent of sex discrimination is not without costs. Unprejudiced people of both sexes who are responsible for hiring and promotion decisions may be falsely charged with sexism. Young women may be pressured into choosing lines of work they don't enjoy. Some proposed cures may do more harm than good; for example, gender quotas for grants could put deserving grantees under a cloud of suspicion, and forcing women onto all university committees would drag them from their labs into endless meetings. An exclusive focus on overt discrimination also diverts attention from policies that penalize women inadvertently because of the fact that, as the legal theorist Susan Estrich has put it, "Waiting for the connection between gender and parenting to be broken is waiting for Godot." A tenure clock that conflicts with women's biological clocks, and family-unfriendly demands like evening seminars and weekend retreats, are obvious examples. The regrettably low proportion of women who received tenured job offers from Harvard during Summers's presidency may be an unintended consequence of his policy of granting tenure to scholars early in their careers, when women are more likely to be bearing the full burdens of parenthood.

6   Conservative columnists had a field day pointing to the Harvard hullabaloo as a sign of runaway political correctness at elite universities. Indeed, the quality of discussion among the nation's leading scholars and pundits is not a pretty sight.

Summers's critics repeatedly mangled his suggestion that innate differences might be one cause of gender disparities (a suggestion that he drew partly from a literature review in my book, *The Blank Slate*) into the claim that they must be the only

The belief, still popular among some academics (particularly outside the biological sciences), that children are born unisex and are molded into male and female roles by their parents and society is becoming less credible.

cause. And they converted his suggestion that the statistical distributions of men's and women's abilities are not identical to the claim that all men are talented and all women are not—as if someone heard that women typically live longer than men and concluded that every woman lives longer than every man. Just as depressing is an apparent unfamiliarity with the rationale behind political equality, as when Hopkins sarcastically remarked that, if Summers were right, Harvard should amend its admissions policy, presumably to accept fewer women. This is a classic confusion between the factual claim that men and women are not indistinguishable and the moral claim that we ought to judge people by their individual merits rather than the statistics of their group.

7   Many of Summers's critics believe that talk of innate gender differences is a relic of Victorian pseudoscience, such as the old theory that cogitation harms women by diverting blood from their ovaries to their brains. In fact, much of the scientific literature has reported numerous statistical differences between men and women. As I noted in *The Blank Slate*, for instance, men are, on average, better at mental rotation and mathematical word problems; women are better at remembering locations and at mathematical calculation. Women match shapes more quickly, are better at reading faces, are better spellers, retrieve words more fluently, and have a better memory for verbal material. Men take greater risks and place a higher premium on status; women are more solicitous to their children.

8   Of course, just because men and women are different does not mean that the differences are triggered by genes. People develop their talents and personalities in response to their social milieu, which can change rapidly. So some of today's sex differences in cognition could be as culturally determined as sex differences in hair and clothing. But the belief, still popular among some academics (particularly outside the biological sciences), that children are born unisex and are molded into male and female roles by their parents and society is becoming less credible. Many sex differences are universal across cultures (the twentieth-century belief in sex-reversed tribes is as specious as the nineteenth-century belief in blood-deprived ovaries), and some are found in other primates. Men's and women's brains vary in numerous ways, including the receptors for sex hormones.

9   Variations in these hormones, especially before birth, can exaggerate or minimize the typical male and female patterns in cognition and personality. Boys with defective genitals who are surgically feminized and raised as girls have been known to report feeling like they are trapped in the wrong body and to show characteristically male attitudes and interests. And a meta-analysis of 172 studies by psychologists Hugh Lytton and David Romney in 1991 found virtually no consistent difference in the way contemporary Americans socialize their sons and daughters.

Regardless of whether it explains the gender disparity in science, the idea that some sex differences have biological roots cannot be dismissed as Neanderthal ignorance.

10   Since most sex differences are small and many favor women, they don't necessarily give an advantage to men in school or on the job. But Summers invoked yet another difference that may be more consequential. In many traits, men show greater variance than women and are disproportionately found at both the low and high ends of the distribution. Boys are more likely to be learning disabled or retarded but also more likely to reach the top percentiles in assessments of mathematical ability, even though boys and girls are similar in the bulk of the bell curve. The pattern is readily explained by evolutionary biology. Since a male can have more offspring than a female—but also has a greater chance of being childless (the victims of other males who impregnate the available females)—natural selection favors a slightly more conservative and reliable baby-building process for females and a slightly more ambitious and error-prone process for males. That is because the advantage of an exceptional daughter (who still can have only as many children as a female can bear and nurse in a lifetime) would be canceled out by her unexceptional sisters, whereas an exceptional son, who might sire several dozen grandchildren, can more than make up for his dull, childless brothers. One doesn't have to accept the evolutionary explanation to appreciate how greater male variability could explain, in part, why more men end up with extreme levels of achievement.

11   What are we to make of the breakdown of standards of intellectual discourse in this affair—the statistical innumeracy, the confusion of fairness with sameness, the refusal to glance at the scientific literature? It is not a disease of tenured radicals; comparable lapses can be found among the political right (just look at its treatment of evolution). Instead, we may be seeing the operation of a fascinating bit of human psychology.

12   The psychologist Philip Tetlock has argued that the mentality of taboo—the belief that certain ideas are so dangerous that it is sinful even to think them—is not a quirk of Polynesian culture or religious superstition but is ingrained into our moral sense. In 2000, he reported asking university students their opinions of unpopular but defensible proposals, such as allowing people to buy and sell organs or auctioning adoption licenses to the highest-bidding parents. He found that most of his respondents did not even try to refute the proposals but expressed shock and outrage at having been asked to entertain them. They refused to consider positive arguments for the proposals and sought to cleanse themselves by volunteering for campaigns to oppose them. Sound familiar?

13   The psychology of taboo is not completely irrational. In maintaining our most precious relationships, it is not enough to say and do the right thing. We have to show that our heart is in the right place and that we don't weigh the costs and benefits of selling out those who trust us. If someone offers to buy your child or your spouse or your vote, the appropriate response is not to think it over or to ask how much. The appropriate response is to refuse even to consider the possibility. Anything less emphatic would betray the awful truth that you don't understand what it means to be a genuine parent or spouse or citizen. (The logic of taboo underlies the horrific fascination of plots whose protagonists are agonized by unthinkable thoughts, such as *Indecent Proposal* and *Sophie's Choice*.) Sacred and tabooed beliefs also work as membership badges in coalitions. To believe something with a

perfect faith, to be incapable of apostasy, is a sign of fidelity to the group and loyalty to the cause. Unfortunately, the psychology of taboo is incompatible with the ideal of scholarship, which is that any idea is worth thinking about, if only to determine whether it is wrong.

14 At some point in the history of the modern women's movement, the belief that men and women are psychologically indistinguishable became sacred. The reasons are understandable: Women really had been held back by bogus claims of essential differences. Now anyone who so much as raises the question of innate sex differences is seen as "not getting it" when it comes to equality between the sexes. The tragedy is that this mentality of taboo needlessly puts a laudable cause on a collision course with the findings of science and the spirit of free inquiry. ◆

ANALYSIS AND DISCUSSION

1. How does Pinker's introduction frame the rest of his essay? Does his example reinforce the points he makes about women in science? How does it help position Pinker and his viewpoint on the issue? Explain.
2. What reasons does Pinker offer for why women are underrepresented in science, engineering, and technology fields?
3. As a college student, do you feel that your gender, and the expectations placed upon it, influence your future career choices? Will this impact how far you go in your career? Explain.
4. What does Pinker say about sex differences? Do you agree or disagree with his viewpoint?
5. What is the "psychology of taboo"? How does it apply to Summers's remarks? Given this underlying dynamic, what are we able to say about our beliefs and our ability to pursue meaningful debate? Explain.
6. Summarize Pinker's position in this essay. Does he think Summers was right?

RESEARCH AND WRITING

1. Research the controversy that stemmed from Lawrence Summers's comments at the NBER Conference (Wikipedia has a good list of resources on the Lawrence Summers article) and write an essay about your perspective on the issue. Be sure to read the transcript of his actual speech. Were his comments taken out of context? Were they inappropriate, especially in the light of where he was speaking? Explain.
2. Pinker comments, "The belief, still popular among some academics . . . , that children are born unisex and are molded into male and female roles by their parents and society is becoming less credible." Write an essay in which you consider your own sense of cultural conditioning. Do you feel your behavior has been conditioned by sex-role expectations? If so, in what ways? Is there a difference between the "real" you and the person you present to the world? If there is a difference, is it the result of cultural pressure related to gender-based expectations of behavior? Explain.

3. What role, if any, does biology play in our lives as men and women? Make a list of commonly assumed sex differences (e.g., boys like to play with trucks, girls like to play with dolls). After you have compiled your list, weigh in on whether these conventions hold scientific merit or are socially constructed perceptions.

Feminism in a Mad World

Aviva Dove-Viebahn*

One of the most successful television dramas of 2010 was the program *Mad Men*, now in its sixth season. Airing on the AMC cable network, *Mad Men* has received critical acclaim for its historical authenticity and visual style, as well as its accurate reflection of social mores of the 1960s. Highlighting a pivotal moment in the emergence of feminism, much of the program's drama circulates around the tenuous and clearly sexist interactions between the male and female characters on the show. In this next essay, Aviva Dove-Viebahn explains how *Mad Men*'s women remind us how much has changed in 40 years.

1 Imagine it's the early 1960s and you're an up-and-coming copywriter for a large advertising firm. You're talented, smart and ambitious, and you have your life laid out before you, glittering with promise. You're also gregarious, so you ask for a raise. But your boss says no, adding icily, "You have an office and a job that a lot of full-grown men would kill for. Stop asking for things."

2 Thus chastised, you realize you've forgotten one important thing: You're a woman. In fact, all the other copywriters are men, and it's a miracle you managed to make it this far up the slippery corporate ladder. Conventional wisdom suggests that you should quit while you are ahead.

3 Luckily for fans of the hourlong TV drama *Mad Men*, Peggy Olson—the copywriter in the above scenario—is anything but conventional. She begins her tenure at fictional ad agency Sterling Cooper as secretary to hotshot creative director Don Draper (Jon Hamm). But Peggy, played by Elizabeth Moss, quickly proves she can do more than type and fetch coffee when she revolutionizes the tired, male-centered copy on a new lipstick account with the succinct pronouncement, "I don't think anyone wants to be one of a hundred colors in a box."

4 This assertion not only epitomizes Peggy, who refuses to conform to the life roles stereotypically assigned to women in the 1950s and 1960s (and to which we're often still assigned!)—mother, housewife, slut, working girl—but also holds up an instructive mirror to women's continued trials and tribulations in today's workplace. Peggy isn't a bombshell beauty, a domestic goddess, or a single-minded career woman. She's just a hardworking person finding her place in the world one step at

---

* Aviva Dove-Viebahn, *Ms. Magazine*, Summer 2010

a time. Her journey of coming into her own is one of the most gratifying aspects of what is a rewardingly complex show.

5   Set in the tumultuous 1960s and exploring the lives of philandering ad men, discontented housewives and sexualized secretaries, *Mad Men* may not immediately leap to mind as a great exemplar of feminist television. And yet, since the show emerged as the sleeper hit of 2007, going on to win the Emmy for Outstanding Television Drama two years running, it's been a hot topic on the feminist blogosphere and around water coolers everywhere, alternately lauded for its strong female characters and criticized for its nostalgic rendering of the halcyon days of sanctioned workplace misogyny.

6   It's true that *Mad Men* doesn't shy away from the fast-paced, chauvinistic world of 1960s advertising and all that comes with it: the unchecked sexual harassment of pretty secretaries by male executives; housewives with little to do other than raise the children and serve as eye-candy at business dinners; uncensored racism, homophobia and anti-Semitism; and an old-boys-club atmosphere, complete with office drinking, smoking and philandering. But amidst all this homosocial revelry, *Mad Men* gives us a cadre of women characters who, like Peggy, are multifaceted and prodigiously fleshed-out—a rare treat for a television drama, a genre in which women are often given short-shrift in favor of the male protagonist.

7   Created by Matthew Weiner, a former executive producer and writer for *The Sopranos, Mad Men* boasts a writers' room with a strong female presence (last season, 7 out of 9 writers were women, though recent turnover in the writers' room has since rendered the ratio more or less even). Perhaps this behind-the-scenes balance has something to do with the show's subtle and intricate narrative, which provides a perfect backdrop for its women characters to straddle the line between the housewives, secretaries and career girls that 1960s norms constrain them to be, and the independent, smart and socially responsible women they actually are.

8   Alongside Peggy, the lives of the other major women characters on the show—the confident and sexually liberated office manager, Joan Harris (Christina Hendricks), and Don Draper's wife, Betty (January Jones)—provide a surprising analogy to the tensions of the feminist movement today: They are positioned between empowerment and compromise, career and family, political and personal, and self-acceptance and attempts to meet standards of beauty.

9   Viewers of the show, especially feminist ones, may be particularly sensitive to these tensions; after all, it's hard to ignore that in the day-to-day battle of the sexes at Sterling Cooper, men still win out time and again. *Mad Men*'s women characters may be getting ahead, but its men figuratively get away with murder and rarely experience the consequences of their misdeeds, whether those are adultery, discrimination, cheating, back-stabbing or even rape. While Weiner insists that, "The treatment of women on *Mad Men* is the point. . . . My show is saying 'This is not right,'" one has to wonder where to draw the line between believably portraying the sexual harassment and patronizing attitude women faced daily and a wistful rendering of the glory days of cocky, can-do-no-wrong ad men and their eager-to-please secretaries and wives.

10   But getting caught up in this line of questioning is to miss the point. Far from being mere accessories, the women on the show represent most strongly the hopeful possibilities of great change. Even if *Mad Men*'s chauvinism and its implicit glorification of masculinist office shenanigans are difficult to swallow, its skillfully meandering narrative not only reveals 1960s misogyny but tells us something about ourselves—how far we've come, but also how far we have left to go.

11   For example, long-suffering Betty Draper divides her time between taking care of her children and waiting for her husband to return home for dinner. The fascination with Betty lies in her transformation from a naïve housewife in season one and a conflicted woman-on-the-verge in season two to a character who displays a clear and lingering discontentment with her life by the end of season three and finally decides to do something about it, demanding a divorce from Don with newfound confidence. Betty most clearly exemplifies the caged, uncertain dependency that led another Betty (Friedan, that is) to consider the plight of the "happy housewife heroine" in her 1963 book, *The Feminine Mystique*. It's probably not a coincidence that *Mad Men*'s third season, in which Betty truly begins to come into her own, is set in 1963.

12   Betty's hesitant understanding of her own potential is instructive of the ways patriarchal culture confined women of her generation, but her journey of self-discovery is more passive than deliberate. Peggy, however, is a clear and outspoken proto-feminist, even if she doesn't know it yet. At first, her male co-workers find her ambition entertaining, a veritable party trick; one even jokes that hearing her come up with a good idea for ad copy is like "watching a dog play the piano." In season two, when Peggy nervously asks agency partner Roger Sterling (John Slattery) for her own office, he concedes, but is more amused than impressed by her chutzpah. "It's cute," Roger says, smirking. "There are 30 men out there who didn't have the balls to ask me."

13   Peggy's burgeoning self-confidence in the face of Roger's teasing is one thing, but by the third season finale, when Don, Roger and several of their colleagues leave Sterling Cooper to start a new agency, it's a far greater rush to watch her confidently refuse Don's brusque insistence that she join them, declaring, "You just assume I'll do whatever you say. Just follow you like some nervous poodle. . . . Everyone thinks you do all my work. Even you. I don't want to make a career out of being there so you can kick me when you fail."

14   Peggy only relents when Don later apologizes, admitting that her ambition reminds him of his own youthful sense of purpose and acknowledging her value as a professional equal: "I don't know if I can do it without you. Will you help me?" And season three's ultimate reversal? While preparing to set up their new agency, Roger, displaying his typical expectation that women will automatically serve his every whim, asks Peggy to bring him coffee. "No," she responds without hesitation and continues working; it's a moment in which it's nearly impossible as a viewer not to erupt in a cheer.

15   The decisive reversal at the end *of Mad Men*'s third season sets the stage for some defining moments for the show's women, but it's still up in the air whether

season four will follow through. Hopefully it will build on this burgeoning sense of equality—or, more accurately, a burgeoning-if-reluctant acceptance by its male characters that their female counterparts have worthwhile feelings and valuable opinions of their own—and will continue to offer a trenchant reminder of feminism's necessity and the consequences of denying women a voice. But will we ever see and hear explicit references to feminism on the show? Well, since last season was set in 1963, we know that the women's movement is just around the corner for *Mad Men*'s characters . . . and for us. ◆

CRITICAL THINKING

1. Who is Peggy Olson? What does she represent? What makes her remarkable on the show Mad Men?
2. As Dove-Viebahn explains, *Mad Men* focuses on the social changes taking place in the early 1960s as seen through the eyes of the men and women who are all connected in some way to the Sterling Cooper ad agency. In what ways does the program provide a mirror to our current social landscape? Or is it a completely different world from the one we know today? Explain.
3. If you have watched the program *Mad Men*, what do you think of it? How does it represent male and female relationships in the 1960s? If you had a choice, would you want to live in the world of Mad Men? Why or why not?
4. Dove-Viebahn wrote this article in 2010, when *Mad Men* was in its third season. She wonders if the season will "follow through" on some "defining moments" for the show's women. What happens to Peggy? To Betty? How does what happens to them reflect the time in which the program is set?
5. Why is it so pivotal that Peggy refuses to get Don Draper coffee? Would this situation happen today? Why or why not?

CRITICAL WRITING

1. *Exploratory Writing:* Does the program *Mad Men* and the social history of the early 1960s that it highlights tell us something about the current sexual and cultural challenges that we have today? Write an essay exploring how the program's storyline, and the issues it raises, is relevant today.
2. *Analytical Writing:* Watch several consecutive episodes of *Mad Men*. Then prepare a character analysis on one of the main characters. What sort of person is the character? What does he or she care about? What drives him or her? How does he or she reflect the social mores of the time? How would the character you chose fit into society today—both inside an office and outside of it? Explain.

GROUP PROJECTS

1. *Mad Men* has won accolades for its accurate depiction of life in the 1960s. Each member of your group should watch several episodes of the first season of *Mad Men*. Then, meet to discuss how the show depicts a particular moment in history with a focus on the gender differences that are illuminated as part of the action. Was anything particularly surprising? Discuss your impressions with the group and then, individually, prepare of summary of your discussion.

2. Dove-Viebahn points out that part of Peggy's success is that she understands that ads targeting women should actually appeal to women. Most ads in the 1960s were created by men. Locate some ads from the 1960s (a good source to start with is www.advertisingarchives.co.uk/). Analyze the ads for gender differences. Do the ads seem to be created from male point of view? Discuss with your group.

CULTURE SHOCK

The *Onion* is a parody newspaper published weekly in print and online, featuring satirical "news" articles on national and international topics. The *Onion*'s articles "comment on current events, both real and imagined." The publication also parodies a traditional newspaper in appearance, editorial voice, and features that include letters, editorials, man-on-the-street interviews, and stock quotes.

Annika Sorenstam Has Another Remarkable Year For A Lady

December 1, 2005 | Issue 41 • 48

WEST PALM BEACH, FL—Annika Sorenstam, the absolutely adorable doll of golf's lighter, gentler side and a true lady who has absolutely charmed ladies' golf fans since joining the always-heartwarming Ladies' Professional Golf Association Tour in 1994, capped off another sensational ten-victory year and became the first lady in history to win two straight ADT Championships For Ladies.

Miss Sorenstam, hitting from the ladies' tee throughout the tournament, finished with a 6-under 282 for a two-stroke ladies' victory, just barely holding off little ladies Soo-Yun Kang, Michele Redman, and Lisolette Neumann. "I thought I had a chance to catch up to her, but there was no stopping that lady today," Neumann said. "All you can do is lower your eyes demurely, curtsy, and say 'Congratulations, ma'am,' in a meek tone of voice befitting a lady."

Sweeping all the major lady-awards for a fifth year and moving within 22 ladies' wins of the all-time ladies' record, Miss Sorenstam is carving out her place in ladies' history alongside legendary golfers such as Nancy Lopez and Kathy Whitworth, both also ladies.

Miss Sorenstam, who took up the sport of ladies' golf when she was just a little lady at 12 years old, has been a feminine golfing inspiration to a whole new generation of ladies, including young lady Michelle Wie and ladies' tour rookie, Paula Creamer, whose play proves her a lady despite her brief, unladylike tiff with Miss Sorenstam over an eighteenth-hole drop in the ladies' first round of the ADT Championship.

As the lady champion, Miss Sorenstam is expected to reap her proportional rewards. In addition to her career earnings of over $2.5 million—a fraction of Tiger Woods' $40 million-plus once thought unimaginable—male golf insiders expect Miss Sorenstam to receive attention from sponsors, such as ladies-wear companies, ladies' hygiene product manufacturers, and other markets of which regular golfers are ignorant or only dimly aware.

"She has proven that the ladies can play golf just like men, if not, of course, actually with men," Professional Golf Association Tour Executive Vice President Edward L. Moorhouse said of Miss Sorenstam, who in 2003 became the first lady to play on the real PGA Tour since true ladies' lady Babe Didrikson Zaharias, the grande dame [big lady] of golf, did so in 1945. "This lady golfer truly deserves our admiration in the form of the highest honor men can grant her: the honorary title First Lady of Golf."

Of course, Sorenstam's honors will include a polite and proper phone call from Laura Bush, the first lady of the United

continued

States, who will offer not only her congratulations but those of her husband George, the leader of the free world.

"You're welcome to drop by the big tour and play a round or two with the men any time you like, little lady," Moorhouse added. "As long as it's not a big event or someplace like Augusta, that bastion of golf tradition where ladies are not allowed."

THINKING CRITICALLY

1. How does this article use satire to make a point? What point is the article making?
2. What words are repeated in this article? What titles are used for men and women? Note that the names of men and women are not referred to in the same way in the article. How does this difference connect back to the point the article is making?
3. If you saw this article and did not know that the *Onion* is a satire, would you take the contents of the article seriously? Why or why not?

In 1972, Title IX ensured equal opportunity in education—including sports programs. It is important to remember that less than 40 years ago, many women were barred from playing sports in college. In fact, many women were barred from attending college. In 1971, only 18 percent of women completed four-year degrees. Now, women represent the majority of college graduates, largely because Title IX ensured that they were presented with equal opportunity, including equal opportunity in sports. The result was a boom in women's athletics. Today, young women can set their sights on a college basketball scholarship just as much as young men can. The question at hand, now that the playing field has been leveled, is, do we still need Title IX? This section's Viewpoints takes a look at Title IX, what it protects, and whether it is needed anymore.

The first piece is an editorial from a student newspaper in which the author argues that in aspiring to provide equal access to sports programs, Boise State would have to add some women's sports in order to add a men's baseball team to the school. She argues that Title IX is outdated and is preventing viable and popular (men's) sports programs from reaching their true potential. Her position is countered by sports journalist Joe Gisondi, who explains why Title IX is still necessary, reflecting on what it has accomplished, and what is protects. Finally, *Sports Illustrated* columnist E. M. Swift brings the argument full circle as he explains why he thinks the time for Title IX has passed.

 Lose Title IX Please, Boise State Wants Baseball

Brittney Johnson

1   The Arbiter asked readers if Boise State should add some women's sports to fulfill its Title IX arrangement so the university could add baseball as a varsity sanctioned sport.

2   Sixty eight percent of Arbiter readers supported the idea.

* Brittney Johnson, *The Arbiter Online*, February 1, 2011; Joe Gisondi, *Sports Field Guide*, February 2011; E. M. Swift, *SI.com (Sports Illustrated)*, October 10, 2006

3   Adding women's sports should not be a roadblock for Boise State to add a base-ball team. Title IX, which is highly outdated, has in its bylaws that a University must offer the same number of scholarships for female student athletes as it does male student athletes. At Boise State, there are about 80 male scholarships directed spe-cifically to football. What single women's sport fills 80 scholarships?

4   Football is the reason Boise State has three more women's sports than it does men's. Title IX is what holds back the Broncos from bringing a highly popular, fan attracting, and major moneymaking sport.

5   The state of Idaho is a hot bed for successful collegiate baseball with NAIA powerhouse Lewis Clark State College attracting pro prospects along with fellow NAIA competitor College of Idaho. College of Southern Idaho, a junior college, also brings in baseball studs. For powerhouse baseball players who have come through high school in Idaho, they are left with few options and if they crave Division I play, they go outside the state.

6   Adding baseball would be extremely valuable to high school athletes in Idaho and give players the option of a Division I education and competition. Boise State is moving to the Mountain West Conference, which is known for the superb baseball programs that rank in the elite among the nation. Recruiting would not be a chal-lenge for Boise State.

7   Title IX, while progressive when installed, is now extremely regressive for up-start universities such as Boise State. Title IX needs to be looked at and changed to fit the new era of collegiate athletics. A positive change, while still keeping equality, would be to make a new rule to have equal number of athletic programs instead of equal number of scholarships. This would give universities an opportunity to expand its athletics programs without being held back by the outdated scholarship rule. ◆

 Title IX Needed Now More Than Ever
Joe Gisondi

1 A writer for Boise State's Arbiter, one of the better college newspapers in the coun-try, is taking a regressive stance on gender equity, essentially saying that Title IX is antiquated.

2   To be fair, this writer is a student journalist trying to learn her craft. However, the column fell flat because this reporter clearly did not do the requisite research nor did she interview those who coach any of the 10 women's sports on campus. Instead, this sports columnist echoed what many other misinformed fans are saying—that Title IX is toxic for college athletics.

3   People continue to fight against gender equity, believing it is unreasonable to abide by the Education Amendments' main purpose: "No person in the United States shall, on the basis of sex, be excluded from participation in, be denied the benefits of, or be subjected to discrimination under any education program or activ-ity receiving federal financial assistance."

4   The Arbiter's columnist implies that Title IX is outdated because the system is working smoothly. But nothing could further from the truth. In reality, gender ≠

equity in college athletics. Nearly 40 years after Title IX was passed into law, the battles are still being waged in the courts, university offices, and playing fields. Too many administrators, fans and parents continue to block access for female athletes. Let me count some of the ways.

5 1. At Quinnipiac, males have been offered about twice as many athletic opportunities than females even though women make up a larger percentage of the student body. In addition, Quinnipiac tried cutting its women's volleyball program, replacing it with competitive cheerleading, which has more participants, in order to balance its inequity. In addition, the school counted its women's distance runners three times—as participants for cross country, indoor track and outdoor track, making it seem that the school had significantly more women athletes. Last summer, a federal judge ruled against the school, saying cheerleading is not suitable replacement for volleyball. Since then, Quinnipiac added a women's rugby program and retained its volleyball squad.

6 2. At Ramona High in California, the girls softball team had to practice and play at a beat-up field with no real backstop at the nearby middle school while players had to change into uniforms at a dirty public restroom frequented by numerous homeless people. The boys, meanwhile, had a top-notch facility on the high school campus. So players and parents sued. Without Title IX, these girls would still be playing on a dangerously poor field and in an unsafe location.

7 3. A federal judge prevented Delaware State from folding its equestrian team in order to add competitive cheer. In addition, the university must add women's sports teams to abide by Title IX.

8 4. At Bemidji State, male athletes earn 63 percent of all athletic opportunities, which is why the Minnesota university just announced that it would cut indoor and outdoor men's track. As always, opponents will blame Title IX instead of focusing on mismanagement that allowed this inequity.

9 5. The University of Delaware is also cutting men's programs—cross country and indoor track. Of course, the school blamed Title IX, citing it 12 times in its announcement. But cross country and track are inexpensive sports, especially compared to the costs related to the school's 103-member football team. Cross country's budget = $20,000. Football at Delaware, meanwhile, loses a great deal of money and lacks fan interest. Fewer than 9,000 fans attended a football playoff game last fall.

10 6. A judge ordered Lincoln Land Community College in Illinois to construct a practice field, build two bullpens for pitchers, improve the scoreboard and press box facilities, and give softball players equal access to the school's five batting cages. In other words, the school must treat the softball team the same as the baseball team.

11 7. At Slippery Rock University, school officials failed to comply with an earlier ruling that was supposed to improve facilities for softball, field hockey, lacrosse and soccer. So the courts intervened once more.

12 8. Public school systems in New York, Chicago and Houston have been violating gender equity requirements by offering far more opportunities to boys than girls. In Chicago, the participation gap between the two genders might be as high as 33 percent, says the National Women's Law Center. That means nearly

a third more boys compete than girls even though more than half the school system's students are female. In New York, the discrepancy is about 8 percent. The number is about 12 percent in Houston. "These school are just the tip of the iceberg," says Marcia Greenberger, co-president of the NWLC. Nationally, about 41 percent of all prep athletes are females, or an estimated 3.1 million. About 4.4 million high school boys compete.

13   9. Other local school districts that might not be in compliance—Columbus, Ohio; Deer Valley, Ariz.; Irvine, Calif.; Oldham County, Ky.; Clark County, Nev.; Worcester, Mass.; Wake Forest, N.C.; and Sioux Falls, S.D. School officials have typically decided to cut boys' sports instead of adding more girls' teams, which fuels the hatred many have for Title IX. At the NCAA level, male participation has decreased by 6 percent at the collegiate level since 1981 whereas women's numbers have increased by 34 percent. Wrestling, tennis, and men's gymnastics have been hit hardest.

14   10. California's Cuesta College cut its women's tennis program in 2009 after the state sent a late budget requiring considerable cuts. At the time, the college did not have a Title IX compliance director, a requirement. Meanwhile, no men's teams were cut.

15   As you can see, young women still must fight to get the same opportunities that men receive.

16   Football is actually the culprit here, not Title IX. Football is considerably more expensive than any other sport, losing money in most instances. An NCAA report revealed that only 19 of 119 Football Bowl Subdivision teams earned a net profit in 2006. These same Division I schools lost, on average, $7.265 million. So why not scale back scholarships and limit rosters? The NCAA allows way too many slots for college football—85 scholarships for Division I, which is 32 more than play for an NFL team. Allowing 85 for football is far more burdensome than Title IX. How about reducing the number to 60, 50, maybe even 45? That would open anywhere from 42 to 25 slots, enough to reach equity and to add another men's team, such as wrestling, swimming, soccer, or, yes, baseball.

17   Targeting Title IX is way too easy (and way too wrong). Instead, let's look at options that can offer equal opportunities for men and women across all sports, a road that begins and ends with college football. Actually, that road begins with tenacious journalists and ends with an informed public. ◆

  Gender Inequality

E. M. Swift

1   *No person in the United States shall, on the basis of sex, be excluded from participation in, be denied the benefits of, or be subject to discrimination under any educational programs or activity receiving federal financial assistance.*

—From the preamble to Title IX of the Education Amendments of 1972

2   Thus is it clearly stated: You can't be excluded from participating in a sport because of your sex. Yet this important law is flaunted every year, every season. Only today, the victims are men, not the women that Title IX was originally enacted to protect.

3   The most recent, egregious example of male sex discrimination in intercollegiate sports occurred at James Madison University in Harrisonburg, VA, where the visitor's board voted to eliminate 10 of the university's 28 sports teams: seven men's teams (archery, cross-country, gymnastics, indoor track, outdoor track, swimming and wrestling) and three women's teams (archery, fencing, gymnastics).

4   If you are a member of the James Madison men's cross-country team, next year you will be "excluded from participation in" your sport on the basis of your sex. It's as simple as that. You have no team. I recommend that you file a lawsuit. Because the James Madison women's cross-country team will continue to compete.

5   Why? In this instance, it isn't about money. The James Madison Board enacted the cuts to comply with Title IX, at least as it is interpreted by the Department of Education, which hews to the misguided concept of "proportionality": that if 61 percent of a student population is female, then 61 percent of the student athletes must be female, too. Never mind if a majority of those women have no interest in competing in intercollegiate sports, do not feel discriminated against, are not discriminated against and stand to gain absolutely nothing from the elimination of men's sports teams. Numbers are numbers.

6   "With so many teams, we faced an insurmountable challenge coming into compliance with Title IX," said Joseph Damico, rector of the JMU Board of Visitors. "Fundamentally, that is why the Board voted today for this plan." That is the evil of quotas—and "proportionality" is a quota by another name. JMU fielded 15 women's sports and 13 men's sports before the vote to eliminate the 10 sports—not exactly the ratio one would expect of an institution out of compliance with Title IX. A majority of its student athletes (50.7 percent) were women.

7   Problem was, the overall enrollment of the school is 61 percent female. By the standard of "proportionality"—a word that isn't used in the original Title IX amendment—the James Madison sports program was out of whack. Next year it'll be in whack: 61 percent of the athletes will be female, 39 percent male.

8   That's whacked out and it needs to be stopped. Why not racial proportionality in sports, too? Isn't that what civil rights is all about? Sixty-seven percent

> *Title IX was needed in 1972. And it worked brilliantly. But the world has changed.*

white, 14 percent African American, 13 percent Hispanic, 6 percent Asian American—let's count noses, colors and genders, take to the field and fight, team, fight!

9   Look, Title IX was needed in 1972. And it worked brilliantly. But the world has changed. I was a junior in college when it was passed. Now my son is a senior in college. A generation has elapsed, and women's sports are here to stay. Thank God and Title IX. But because of Title IX's unintended consequences, in 2006 the law is causing more harm than good. Women's sports are no longer on life support. They are vibrant, popular, well-funded and growing. They can be taken off the endangered-species list.

10   Meanwhile, the percentage of women attending college relative to men continues to increase—enrollment nationally is approximately 57 percent women to 43 percent men today. If "proportionality" continues to be adhered to by school administrators, the number of men's collegiate sports programs will continue to shrink.

11   That wasn't the idea behind Title IX. It was designed to create, not eliminate, opportunity. But since its enactment, more than 170 men's wrestling teams have disappeared. Eighty men's tennis teams, 45 track teams and 106 men's gymnastics teams have been axed.

12   UCLA's men's swimming team, which boasted 22 Olympic medals, is gone, along with some 30 other men's swimming and diving programs. Forty schools have dropped football. Walk-on male athletes in all sports are routinely turned away to keep rosters at a minimum so the male/female ratios in college sports programs don't get thrown off.

13   It's social engineering, and it's wrong. If you believe that being on a team, practicing, and learning discipline through sports is beneficial to the development of the individual, as I do, then as a society, we are poorer every time a school eliminates any athletic program—male or female. School administrators don't enforce gender proportionality for chemistry, economics or English-lit classes. Why should they try to engineer gender ratios in sports?

14   There is a wealth of data that show that young males, as a whole, are more inclined toward athletic competition than young females. That doesn't mean the female athletes are any less committed or driven than men. It means that— surprise!—men and women are different, creatures of Mars and Venus, and that a higher percentage of men like, and perhaps need, to compete. They crave being on teams, even if they don't start. It adds to their self-esteem and channels their energy in a constructive fashion. While many women's collegiate teams must actively recruit participants in order to fill their rosters, men's teams turn away walk-ons in droves.

15   Over a 15-year period between 1980 and 1994, the National Center for Educational Statistics polled high school seniors and found that 20 percent of males were more interested in participating in sports than females, and more than twice as many exercised vigorously on a daily basis.

16   In collegiate intramural sports, whose numbers are largely determined on the basis of interest, 78 percent of participants are male, 22 percent female. Put another way, most guys have a more difficult time adapting to life without sports than most girls do.

17   Yet there are some 580 more women's teams at NCAA schools today than men's teams, a disparity that is likely to continue to grow. Faced with budgetary cuts last summer, the board at Rutgers University elected to eliminate six teams, five of which were men's: lightweight and heavyweight crew, tennis, swimming and diving, and fencing. "The minute you start cuts, you have to meet the proportionality test," said Athletic Director Robert E. Mulcahy III.

18   Shame on the proportionality test. Shame on the budgetary cuts. And shame on administrators at Rutgers and James Madison for allowing Title IX to become a dirty word to advocates of men's sports such as wrestling, cross-country and track. The law was never intended to be a zero-sum game, the right hand welcoming a female athlete as the left hand shoves a male out the door.

19   After word reached members of the James Madison cross-country team that the men's team would be eliminated in '07 while the women's team would continue, runners on both squads shared a tearful four-hour bus ride home from a meet in Pennsylvania. "Fourteen guys and 19 girls, all crying together," Jennifer Chapman, a senior on the women's team, told *The New York Times*. "How is that supposed to have been Title IX's intent?" ◆

CRITICAL THINKING

1. Joe Gisondi responds to Brittney Johnson's editorial with 10 reasons as to why Title IX is still necessary. Who makes the more compelling argument, and why?
2. Should men's and women's programs receive equal financial support and provide students with equal opportunity to participate? To receive scholarships to finance their schooling? Why or why not?
3. Based on what you have read in this section, is a law still necessary to ensure that women are provided with equal access to athletic participation and athletic scholarships? Is Title IX outdated? Does it focus on the wrong issues?
4. What is "proportionality"? Do you think that athletic programs should be based on proportionality? Why or why not?
5. Swift argues that Title IX is no longer needed. Analyze his argument and respond to it in your own words. What might happen if it were repealed?

CRITICAL WRITING

1. *Research Writing:* Research the history of Title IX. Why was it passed and what does it protect or guarantee? Arrange an interview with a coach or coaches in your athletic department to discuss the impact of Title IX— both positive and negative—on the history of athletic activity at your school over the past 30 years.
2. *Expository Writing:* Write an essay exploring how the world would be different if Title IX had *not* passed in 1972. If you think your life is different because of this act, write about what impact it had on you.
3. *Persuasive Writing:* Select an author from this section and write a response to their editorial in which you directly address their argument and provide your own viewpoint to either counter or support it.

GROUP PROJECTS

1. Each member of your group should visit several sports-related Web sites, such as ESPN.com and SI.com, and locate some current articles on women in sports. Are the stories about female athletes parallel to the reporting on male athletes? Are men and women judged on similar or different criteria? If photographs accompany the articles, are the photos similar in style and content (action shots, etc.). Discuss your findings as a group. Do we view

women's sports differently than men's sports? Do we take them equally seriously? If not, what could this mean for college athletic programs influenced by Title IX?

2. Swift argues that Title IX is no longer needed. Each member of your group should interview 5 to 10 students on the issue. Ask students what they know about Title IX and whether they think it is a necessary law and why. Be prepared to explain what Title IX is (your group should create a definition and agree to its accuracy). Review the responses as a group. Discuss current opinion on this act and whether the time has come for reform.

Race and Racism

Can We Be Color-Blind?

As a nation of immigrants, the United States comprises many races, ethnic traditions, religions, and languages. Under a common political and legal system, we agree that we have the right to life, liberty, and the pursuit of happiness. Many of us take pride in our cultural differences. And, in theory, we Americans embrace the principles of the Declaration of Independence: that we are all created equal, despite our differences. But the social reality demonstrates that differences can pose challenges to the very fabric of American culture. Racism is one of these challenges.

Racism is the conviction that people of a particular race or ethnicity possess traits that distinguish them as superior or inferior to another racial or ethnic group. The roots of racism are disturbingly deep in American history, extending all the way back to the early seventeenth century and the Puritan settlers' blatant mistreatment of Native Americans. Considered uncivilized savages, and wrongfully named "Indians," indigenous tribes were stripped of their land, their power, and their way of life by white European immigrants. Over the following centuries, every new immigrant group to arrive on American soil—Irish, Italian, Polish, German, Mexican, Chinese—experienced some form of racism and racial profiling, usually at the hands of the groups that came before them. But as America became more ethnically blended, prejudice against some groups decreased and even disappeared.

The candidacy of Barack Obama for the highest office in the land raised new questions about racism in America. His campaign itself raised many questions—foremost, could people cast color-blind votes? The answer, of course, was "yes." Some people viewed Obama's election as proof that Americans had overcome institutionalized racism. But in April 2012, the shooting death of Trayvon Martin at the hands of George Zimmerman brought racial tensions back to the fore, with many minority groups accusing Zimmerman of shooting 16-year-old Martin for "walking while black." The incident demonstrated that race and racism are still very raw issues in the United States, even as Obama enters his second presidential race. In this chapter, we will look at a few of the lingering issues of racial equality.

Alan Jenkins begins the discussion with an examination of the connections of race to inequality, stereotypes, and poverty. His essay, "Inequality, Race, and Remedy," briefly reviews the history of racism and describes current challenges for removing racial barriers. Jenkins charges that until Americans can honestly admit that racism still runs rampant in this country, we cannot begin to remedy it. His essay is followed by this chapter's Modern Scholar piece, "Why Should We Care About Racial Inequality?" by Glenn Loury, director of the Institute on Race and Social Division at Boston University. In this essay, Loury explains why he changed his view that affirmative action was no longer necessary. Although it might be comforting to say that we have moved beyond race, he says, to do so denies "social reality." His position would likely meet with disagreement from the next author, Amitai Etzioni, who describes how racial identification holds us back as a nation in "Leaving Race Behind." The expanding Hispanic population, he explains, represents an opportunity for us to dismantle institutionalized racism in America. Then Hua Hsu connects the election of Barack Obama to our writing of a new chapter for race in America in "The End of White America?" Hsu believes that Obama's election is a signal that racism is on the decline. Does this presidency represent a rebalancing of power? Is it time for us to rethink race entirely?

Despite the desire of many people to believe that race "is over," the United States is still quite divided. The next essay explores how we tend to congregate with people with whom we share social, cultural, and, yes, racial ties. David Brooks wonders if racism can ever really be erased. In "People Like Us," he hazards to state that no matter how much lip service people publicly pay to diversity, they still tend to gather with people who look, act, and believe "basically like themselves."

The remaining articles, including the chapter's Viewpoints section, address the issue of racial profiling. Racial profiling occurs when an individual is considered more likely to engage in criminal behaviors based on race alone. For years, many black men and women have cited instances when they were pulled over merely because they were "driving while black." Black teens, especially young males, face daily discrimination in cities across the country, a phenomenon described by Nicholas K. Peart in "Why Is the N.Y.P.D. After Me?" More than ever, people who appear to be of Middle Eastern descent find themselves eyed with distrust. It is not uncommon for one airline passenger to report that another is acting "suspiciously" merely because the accused passenger "looks like a terrorist"—someone who could be from the Middle East. The Viewpoints section features two articles by young Muslim American women with very different points of view. How does one fight against the injustice of being viewed as a criminal based on how he or she looks? Is there any way to stop racial profiling? Or can it be a useful tool in the fight against terrorism? The viewpoints of each woman raise provocative arguments for these troubling times.

Inequality, Race, and Remedy
Alan Jenkins *

It would be hopeful to believe that race is no longer a factor in poverty and that we can be a color-blind society. But America still has a legacy to overcome—and to achieve. In this next essay, Alan Jenkins, executive director of the Opportunity Agenda, an organization dedicated to expanding opportunity in America, explains why we cannot ignore the past if we are to create a more hopeful future. The truth is, he explains, racial barriers still exist, and to overcome them, we must admit that. Can we ever become a color-blind society?

1   Our nation, at its best, pursues the ideal that what we look like and where we come from should not determine the benefits, burdens, or responsibilities that we bear in our society. Because we believe that all people are created equal in terms of rights, dignity, and the potential to achieve great things, we see inequality based on race, gender, and other social characteristics as not only unfortunate but unjust. The value of equality, democratic voice, physical and economic security, social mobility, a shared sense of responsibility for one another, and a chance to start over after misfortune or missteps—what many Americans call *redemption*—are the moral pillars of the American ideal of opportunity.

---

* Alan Jenkins, *The American Prospect*, April 22, 2007

2   Many Americans of goodwill who want to reduce poverty believe that race is no longer relevant to understanding the problem or to fashioning solutions for it. This view often reflects compassion as well as pragmatism. But we cannot solve the problem of poverty—or, indeed, be the country that we aspire to be—unless we honestly unravel the complex and continuing connection between poverty and race.

3   Since our country's inception, race-based barriers have hindered the fulfillment of our shared values, and many of these barriers persist today. Experience shows, moreover, that reductions in poverty do not reliably reduce racial inequality, nor do they inevitably reach low-income people of color. Rising economic tides do not reliably lift all boats.

4   In 2000, after a decade of remarkable economic prosperity, the poverty rate among African Americans and Latinos taken together was still 2.6 times greater than that for white Americans. This disparity was stunning, yet it was the smallest difference in poverty rates between whites and others in more than three decades. And from 2001 to 2003, as the economy slowed, poverty rates for most communities of color increased more dramatically than they did for whites, widening the racial poverty gap. From 2004 to 2005, while the overall number of poor Americans declined by almost one million, to 37 million, poverty rates for most communities of color actually increased. Reductions in poverty do not inevitably close racial poverty gaps, nor do they reach all ethnic communities equally.

5   Poor people of color are also increasingly more likely than whites to find themselves living in high-poverty neighborhoods with limited resources and limited options. An analysis by the Opportunity Agenda and the Poverty and Race Research Action Council found that while the percentage of Americans of all races living in high-poverty neighborhoods (those with 30 percent or more residents living in poverty) declined between 1960 and 2000, the racial gap grew considerably. Low-income Latino families were three times as likely as low-income white families to live in these neighborhoods in 1960, but 5.7 times as likely in 2000. Low-income blacks were 3.8 times more likely than poor whites to live in high-poverty neighborhoods in 1960, but 7.3 times more likely in 2000.

6   These numbers are troubling, not because living among poor people is somehow harmful in itself, but because concentrated high-poverty communities are far more likely to be cut off from quality schools, housing, health care, affordable consumer credit, and other pathways out of poverty. And African Americans and Latinos are increasingly more likely than whites to live in those communities. Today, low-income blacks are more than three times as likely as poor whites to be in "deep poverty"— meaning below half the poverty line—while poor Latinos are more than twice as likely.

The Persistence of Discrimination

7 Modern and historical forces combine to keep many communities of color disconnected from networks of economic opportunity and upward mobility. Among those forces is persistent racial discrimination that, while subtler than in past decades, continues to deny opportunity to millions of Americans. Decent employment and housing are milestones on the road out of poverty. Yet these are areas in which racial discrimination stubbornly persists. While the open hostility and "Whites Only"

signs of the Jim Crow era have largely disappeared, research shows that identically qualified candidates for jobs and housing enjoy significantly different opportunities depending on their race.

8   In one study, researchers submitted identical résumés by mail for more than 1,300 job openings in Boston and Chicago, giving each "applicant" either a distinctively "white-sounding" or "black-sounding" name—for instance, "Brendan Baker" versus "Jamal Jones." Résumés with white-sounding names were 50 percent more likely than those with black-sounding names to receive callbacks from employers. Similar research in California found that Asian American and, especially, Arab American résumés received the least-favorable treatment compared to other groups. In recent studies in Milwaukee and New York City, meanwhile, live "tester pairs" with comparable qualifications but of differing races tested not only the effect of race on job prospects but also the impact of an apparent criminal record. In Milwaukee, whites reporting a criminal record were more likely to receive a callback from employers than were blacks without a criminal record. In New York, Latinos and African Americans without criminal records received fewer callbacks than did similarly situated whites and at rates comparable to whites with a criminal record.

9   Similar patterns hamper the access of people of color to quality housing near good schools and jobs. Research by the U.S. Department of Housing and Urban Development (HUD) shows that people of color receive less information from real estate agents, are shown fewer units, and are frequently steered away from predominantly white neighborhoods. In addition to identifying barriers facing African Americans and Latinos, this research found significant levels of discrimination against Asian Americans and that Native American renters may face the highest discrimination rates (up to 29 percent) of all.

10   This kind of discrimination is largely invisible to its victims, who do not know that they have received inaccurate information or been steered away from desirable neighborhoods and jobs. But its influence on the perpetuation of poverty is nonetheless powerful.

The Present Legacy of Past Discrimination

11   These modern discriminatory practices often combine with historical patterns. In New Orleans, for example, as in many other cities, low-income African Americans were intentionally concentrated in segregated, low-

Since our country's inception, race-based barriers have hindered the fulfillment of our shared values, and many of these barriers persist today.

lying neighborhoods and public-housing developments at least into the 1960s. In 2005, when Hurricane Katrina struck and the levees broke, black neighborhoods were most at risk of devastation. And when HUD announced that it would close habitable public-housing developments in New Orleans rather than clean and reopen them, it was African Americans who were primarily prevented from returning home and rebuilding. This and other failures to rebuild and invest have exacerbated poverty—already at high levels—among these New Orleanians.

12   In the case of Native Americans, a quarter of whom are poor, our government continues to play a more flagrant role in thwarting pathways out of poverty. Unlike other racial and ethnic groups, most Native Americans are members of sovereign tribal nations with a recognized status under our Constitution. High levels of Native American poverty derive not only from a history of wars, forced relocations, and broken treaties by the United States, but also from ongoing breaches of trust—like our government's failure to account for tens of billions of dollars that it was obligated to hold in trust for Native American individuals and families. After more than a decade of litigation, and multiple findings of governmental wrongdoing, the United States is trying to settle these cases for a tiny fraction of what it owes.

13   The trust-fund cases, of course, are just the latest in a string of broken promises by our government. But focusing as they do on dollars and cents, they offer an important window into the economic status that Native American communities and tribes might enjoy today if the U.S. government lived up to its legal and moral obligations.

14   Meanwhile, the growing diversity spurred by new immigrant communities adds to the complexity of contemporary poverty. Asian American communities, for example, are culturally, linguistically, and geographically diverse, and they span a particularly broad socioeconomic spectrum.

15   Census figures from 2000 show that while one third of Asian American families have annual incomes of $75,000 or more, one fifth have incomes of less than $25,000. While the Asian American poverty rate mirrored that of the country as a whole, Southeast Asian communities reflected far higher levels. Hmong men experienced the highest poverty level (40.3 percent) of any racial group in the nation.

Race and Public Attitudes

16 Americans' complex attitudes and emotions about race are crucial to understanding the public discourse about poverty and the public's will to address it. Researchers such as Martin Gilens and Herman Gray have repeatedly found that the mainstream media depict poor people as people of color—primarily African Americans—at rates far higher than their actual representation in the population. And that depiction, the research finds, interacts with societal biases to erode support for antipoverty programs that could reach all poor people.

17   Gilens found, for instance, that while blacks represented only 29 percent of poor Americans at the time he did his research, 65 percent of poor Americans shown on television news were black. In a more detailed analysis of TV newsmagazines in particular, Gilens found a generally unflattering framing of the poor, but the presentation of poor African Americans was more negative still. The most "sympathetic" subgroups of the poor—such as the working poor and the elderly—were underrepresented on these shows, while unemployed working-age adults were overrepresented. And those disparities were greater for African Americans than for others, creating an even more unflattering (and inaccurate) picture of the black poor.

18   Gray similarly found that poor African Americans were depicted as especially dysfunctional and undeserving of assistance, with an emphasis on violence, poor choices, and dependency. As Gray notes, "The black underclass appears as a menace and a

source of social disorganization in news accounts of black urban crime, gang violence, drug use, teenage pregnancy, riots, homelessness, and general aimlessness. In news accounts, poor blacks (and Hispanics) signify a social menace that must be contained."

19   Research also shows that Americans are more likely to blame the plight of poverty on poor people themselves, and less likely to support antipoverty efforts, when they perceive that the people needing help are black. These racial effects are especially pronounced when the poor person in the story is a black single mother. In one study, more than twice the number of respondents supported individual solutions (like the one that says poor people "should get a job") over societal solutions (such as increased education or social services) when the single mother was black.

20   This research should not be surprising. Ronald Reagan, among others, effectively used the "racialized" mental image of the African American "welfare queen" to undermine support for antipoverty efforts. And the media face of welfare recipients has long been a black one, despite the fact that African Americans have represented a minority of the welfare population. But this research also makes clear that unpacking and disputing racial stereotypes is important to rebuilding a shared sense of responsibility for reducing poverty in all of our communities.

Removing Racial Barriers

21 We cannot hope to address poverty in a meaningful or lasting way without addressing race-based barriers to opportunity. The most effective solutions will take on these challenges together.

22   That means, for example, job-training programs that prepare low-income workers for a globalized economy, combined with antidiscrimination enforcement that ensures equal access to those programs and the jobs to which they lead. Similarly, strengthening the right to organize is important in helping low-wage workers to move out of poverty, but it must be combined with civil-rights efforts that root out the racial exclusion that has sometimes infected union locals. And it means combining comprehensive immigration reform that offers newcomers a pathway to citizenship with living wages and labor protections that root out exploitation and discourage racial hierarchy.

23   Another crucial step is reducing financial barriers to college by increasing the share of need-based grants over student loans and better coordinating private-sector scholarship aid—for example, funds for federal Pell Grants should be at least double current levels. But colleges should also retain the flexibility to consider racial and socioeconomic background as two factors among many, in order to promote a diverse student body (as well as diverse workers and leaders once these students graduate). And Congress should pass the DREAM Act, which would clear the path to a college degree and legal immigration status for many undocumented students who've shown academic promise and the desire to contribute to our country.

24   Lack of access to affordable, quality health care is a major stress on low-income families, contributing to half of the nation's personal bankruptcies. Guaranteed health care for all is critical, and it must be combined with protections against poor quality and unequal access that, research shows, affect people of color irrespective of their insurance status.

25   Finally, we must begin planning for opportunity in the way we design metropolitan regions, transportation systems, housing, hospitals, and schools. That means, for example, creating incentives for mixed-income neighborhoods that are well publicized and truly open to people of all races and backgrounds.

26   A particularly promising approach involves requiring an "opportunity impact statement" when public funds are to be used for development projects. The statement would explain, for example, whether a new highway will connect low-income communities to good jobs and schools or serve only affluent communities. It would detail where and how job opportunities would flow from the project, and whether different communities would share the burden of environmental and other effects (rather than having the project reinforce traditional patterns of inequality). It would measure not only a project's expected effect on poverty but on opportunity for all.

27   When we think about race and poverty in terms of the shared values and linked fate of our people, our approach to politics as well as policy begins to change. Instead of balancing a list of constituencies and identity groups, our task becomes one of moving forward together as a diverse but cohesive society, addressing through unity the forces that have historically divided us. ◆

CRITICAL THINKING

1. Jenkins opens his essay with the comment, "Our nation, at its best, pursues the ideal that what we look like and where we come from should not determine the benefits, burdens, or responsibilities that we bear in our society." What are the ideals of America? Do we believe in equality for all, at least in theory? If so, how well do we, as a society, promote the values of equality? Explain.

2. What are the connections between race and poverty in the United States? Why does Jenkins feel it is important to address these connections in order to promote a more color-blind society? Explain.

3. Jenkins observes that while "Jim Crow" signs barring African Americans from employment have disappeared, employment racism still persists. In what ways does employment racism perpetuate the cycle of poverty?

4. In addition to employment inequalities, what other forms of racism are rampant in America? Can you think of any other examples in addition to the ones Jenkins cites?

5. What external forces can influence race and perceptions of race? How can perceptions drive racism in the United States?

6. What steps does Jenkins offer to help remedy racial inequalities and remove racial barriers?

CRITICAL WRITING

1. *Research and Writing:* Jenkins describes how "attitudes and emotions about race" are often media-driven. Write an essay exploring how race is presented in the media. In your response, cite several examples of how

various races are presented and how these representations can influence public opinions in general.

2. *Research and Persuasive Writing:* Visit the ACLU's Web site on racial inequality at http://www.aclu.org and review its information about race and race relations. What are the most pressing issues concerning race and racial inequality today? Select an issue on the Web site and research it in greater depth. Write a short essay summarizing the issue, your position, and your thoughts about it.

3. *Expository Writing:* What is your own perception of race? Do you think you enjoy certain benefits or encounter certain obstacles because of your race? Explain.

GROUP PROJECTS

1. In this essay, Jenkins offers some suggestions for working toward a more color-blind society. With your group acting as a "think tank," evaluate each of his suggestions for plausibility, implementation strategies, and outcome.

2. Jenkins charges that the media, especially television, contributes to racism by presenting groups of people differently. With the help of *TV Guide* or another television guide, make a list of programs on prime-time—from 8:00 to 11:00 PM—network television, and describe the characters in terms of race and ethnicity. For example, are African Americans more likely to be portrayed as dysfunctional or poor? Based on your review of the prime-time lineup, discuss how television may contribute to racial stereotypes. Alternatively, if your data reveal little or no racism, make a note of that as well. Share the results of your group discussion with the class.

Modern Scholar

Why Should We Care About Racial Inequality?
*Glenn Loury**

Most of us have seen the little boxes on forms that ask us to define our racial background. Beyond mere data collection, this information can be used to help ensure racial diversity in areas of education and employment. The practice of factoring race and gender in hiring or admissions decisions is called "affirmative action." Advocates for the practice say that it

---

* Glenn Loury, *Presentation at the Markkula Seminar on Affirmative Action,* 1998

balances historical inequalities connected to race and gender. Critics claim that it creates different standards of quality for different racial backgrounds, and unfairly works against those who are not members of minority groups. In this next essay, Glenn Loury, a professor of social sciences and economics at Brown University, explains why we still must care about racial inequality, and maintain practices to alleviate and correct them.

1 Early in my career, with a Ph.D. from MIT and a limitless future ahead of me in academia, I was one of those people who could be heard complaining that my reputation was being besmirched by affirmative action policies. After all, I got tenure at Northwestern University three years out of graduate school with a flurry of technical articles published in the best economic journals. I didn't want anybody thinking I was an affirmative action professor. I could do the differential equations and the functional analysis with the best of them.

2 I was also one of the people to stress that it was the better-off among the designated minority groups who would reap the benefits from affirmative action. Although the moral impetus for doing something about racial inequality derives substantially from the suffering of the worst-off people in the minority group—the ghetto poor—affirmative action was dispensing benefits that could only be accessed by those who had already solved the problem of moving from the margin into the mainstream of society. Those were the people who already owned businesses that might benefit from a contract set-aside, the people who could succeed were they to achieve admission to a top-flight state university. So, based on my analysis of the costs and benefits of this particular remedy for racial injustice, I found myself in the camp of affirmative action's opponents.

3 But in the wake of what has become a well-organized and concerted campaign to wipe out "racial preferences" wherever they "rear their ugly heads," I began to see that there was something missing in my understanding. Consider the campaign's rhetoric. One of the advocates likes to point to a typical application form and proclaim that Americans should not have to check off those "disgusting little boxes" to identify their race. This is a language one can fall in love with. It has a certain self-justifying tone about it: "America is a country where individuals—not groups—have rights, a country where we succeed or fail on the basis of our merit."

4 As I've watched the righteous campaign to rid ourselves of disgusting little boxes spread across the nation, I've noticed a certain narrative account emerging from it. It goes like this: We had racism; we had Jim Crow segregation. But we also had the civil rights movement. Martin Luther King stood before the Lincoln Memorial in 1963 and cried out that he had a dream that one day his children would live in a country where they would be judged not by the color of their skin but by the content of their character. Now we are approaching being such a country, but for those who insist upon irrationally continuing to define themselves in terms of race. What does a person's race have to do with any assessment of justice?

5 As I listen to that line, I have to object. The campaign against affirmative action as it has developed is dangerous, in my judgment, because within it lies the implication that any question of social or public justice that is formulated in racial terms is prima facie illegitimate.

6   One can oppose affirmative action and still believe that the racial composition of a student body is a relevant factor among many for a university to consider in the construction of its educational mission. One can critique particular policy instruments without rejecting the notion that racial justice is an appropriate goal.

7   The key issue is not whether the instrument is colorblind. One could use colorblind instruments to pursue racial goals and color-conscious instruments to pursue goals that are not necessarily racially defined. For example, let's say a governor needs to appoint judges to the courts. He might say, "I need to have a diverse group of appointees both for my own political protection and in the long-term interest of maintaining the legitimacy of the administration of justice in this jurisdiction. If I appoint all white men, I'm going to do damage not only to my own reputation but also to the institution of the court itself because I'm going to create a situation in which people do not feel that the institution fairly represents them. I have a responsibility as the governor to ensure that does not happen."

8   Maintaining the legitimacy of the institution of the court is not a racial goal. That's something everybody has a stake in. And yet in order to do it, the governor might have to peek into those disgusting little boxes to see whether his list of possible appointees contains a sufficient number of women and minorities.

9   On the other hand, a federal anti-drug policy concentrating on arresting street-level traffickers and putting them away for a long time is a colorblind policy, but it has racial consequences. Such policies have led to the incarceration of young people of color in vastly disproportionate numbers, young people who to some degree are engaged in the illicit traffic precisely because they are at the margin of society and their alternative opportunities are scant.

10   As a result of this and similar policies, out of the 1.8 million people under lock and key on any given day in this country, 900,000 are African Americans. If we focus on the color-blindness of the instrument, we fail to pay attention to the larger question: Aren't we prosecuting a public policy in the criminal justice area that has to be examined because of the cost it is imposing on a particular community?

11   I don't want to put too much stress on the criminal justice example because I understand that it is arguable. There are people who will disagree with my sense that our anti-drug policy is unjust. But I think one has to accept the logical claim that this colorblind instrument raises questions of justice that have as a part of their formulation the racial dimension of the policy's effects.

12   I want to insist on this distinction because you can slide very quickly from a forceful critique of policy instruments into a stand that denies the legitimacy of any discussion of public issues formulated in racial terms.

13   There are plenty of examples: Suppose many universities make a commitment to hiring an African American economist of the highest merit and quality, and suppose there are relatively few African American economists of the highest merit and quality. The consequence is going to be that the price of quality African American economists is going to get bid up. They will get better offers; they will get summer research stipends; they will get the corner office.

14   You can pass a law that everybody has to be paid the same salary, but that doesn't keep me from getting seven offers and my white colleague from getting one.

He and I may be the same quality, but if the universities want to have a meritorious African American faculty member, I'm going to enjoy a better market.

15   I don't necessarily deserve this result because my ancestors were enslaved; that's not the point. My circumstances are an inescapable logical consequence of the structure of the situation. Unfortunately, many people who are unhappy with that outcome have begun to object to what's generating the outcome: the desire of universities to have qualified black faculty. What begins as an argument against a practice—hiring at the level of an individual college—becomes an argument against a goal—wanting to have some minority presence on the school's top-flight social science faculty.

16   What is wrong with the goal? To answer that question, opponents are forced to argue that the color of university economics professors doesn't matter. They're forced to deny the common sense observation that it is desirable for universities with African American students to have some African Americans represented on their faculties.

17   In other words, they're compelled to make ahistorical arguments that deny our social reality in order to protect a claim about treatment. They have made the administrative practice the site of the moral discussion, but the moral question doesn't just reside there.

18   What happens if young people of color see the world through a racial lens? What happens if the descendants of slaves have not forgotten that they're black? When we send a young black man to prison boot camp, and we say, "Straighten up your life," what happens if he finds that a more compelling narrative when it's delivered by somebody he knows has walked the same streets he has?

19   Consider the cold, hard reality of growing up in one of these communities where every third person goes off to the penitentiary, where gangs and violence and drugs are everywhere. You can walk proud and tall wearing your colors in your 'hood, but you put on a suit, go downtown, and try to get a job, and nobody will give you the time of day. That's where these young men are coming from.

20   And then we have intellectuals sitting back and saying, "What does race matter?"—saying in effect, "Those kids should just get over it. They should stop seeing the world in racial terms." Well, that is a wishful irrelevancy. It hasn't got anything to do with the reality of those kids. It's an abstraction put against the concrete history that generated the racial division in our society in the first place.

21   This is not special pleading for a minority student to get a seat at Berkeley that a white student has earned because the white student's SAT scores are 1500 and the minority student's are only 1200. This is an effort to keep our eye on the ball: The question of social justice in our society cannot be meaningfully formulated without entering into the ambiguous and morally complicated morass of race.

22   There are some who would deny that racial justice is a meaningful category. They would say, "There's justice, and there's non-justice." I reject that argument. This is not a principled rejection; it's historically contingent. It's a rejection based upon the specific facts of our society and the way in which people see themselves.

23   In America, people identify and define themselves in racial terms—and it's not only the minorities who do so. For example, white men intermarry with Asian women at a rate 10 times higher than they intermarry with African American women. I'm not saying the men or the women are racist, but the figures do show something

about the preference for intimate association across racial lines at the place where it really counts—where people make lifetime commitments to bind themselves together and build families together.

24   Take the case of adoption. To prospective parents, the price of a healthy white baby is $40,000 as revealed by what people are willing to pay the lawyers and social workers who arrange the adoptions. The price of a healthy black baby seems to be $6,000 to $7,000 by the same economic criteria.

25   Many black babies languish unadopted while white families travel across great oceans and thousands of miles to adopt infants from other countries. Again, I'm not saying the white families are racist. There are blacks who don't want black babies adopted by whites; I know that. What I'm saying is that the phenomenon of disparity in intimate association is a reflection of the depth of racial separation in our society.

26   You can see it on a less intimate level, as well, in *Still the Promised City*, a study by UCLA sociologist Roger Waldinger. Waldinger noticed that immigrants from all over the world were occupying the bottom occupational niches in relatively low-skill trades and low-paid factory work in New York City, and he asked, "Why can't poor blacks get those jobs?"

27   Were the employers racist? No, it was much more complicated than that. It had to do with the fact that people get jobs in the low-wage sector of manufacturing in New York by belonging to a network of referral: The employer relies on incumbent employees to bring him new workers.

28   Those networks turn out to have an ethnic coloration. Often, they stretch back to the old country. The migrant who has already settled in finds a job for the cousin or the friend of the family who has just immigrated. This is not about skills; it's not about merit. Basically, anybody who shows up every day is meritorious in this kind of work. This phenomenon is about connection.

29   In contrast, New York inner city blacks, who walk with a certain gait and listen to a certain kind of music and talk in a certain way, tend to be stigmatized. They tend to be associated with the drugs and violence that are prevalent in their neighbor-hoods although the majority of them are just trying to find work like anybody else.

30   The fact that they are locked out of work is not a conspiracy. It's not some evil we can point to as we would to a Southern segregationist governor and say, "If you get out of the schoolhouse door, everything will be fine." It's a complex residue of a historically evolved system of racial segregation and stigma.

31   How can we talk about justice and equality in American society without any reference to this reality? That's not colorblindness; that's just blindness.

32   We must be prepared to define and map the social landscape, in part, in racial terms. History and contemporary social reality compel that. When we do, we will find that sometimes instruments of public action formulated in racial terms are use-ful and their benefits outweigh their costs as we pursue justice ideals that can be defended with the best universalist philosophy. Sometimes we will find that public purposes pursued by racially defined instruments—such as affirmative action—are not a good idea. That's a call we'll have to make.

33   But the one thing that, as serious people, we mustn't do is suppose that we're talking about the real question of racial justice when we limit ourselves

to a disavowal of those disgusting little boxes. That is weak intellectually and unforgivable morally. ◆

ANALYSIS AND DISCUSSION

1. Loury begins his discussion by reflecting on how he used to feel about affirmative action. Why does he feel that something was missing from his understanding? What changes his perception of affirmative action?
2. What are the "disgusting little boxes" Loury refers to in his essay? Who calls them this? Under what circumstances does he feel that the boxes are necessary? Explain.
3. Why does Loury believe that the campaign against affirmative action is "dangerous"?
4. When it comes to getting jobs, Loury notes that in New York City, "inner city blacks, who walk with a certain gait and listen to a certain kind of music and talk in a certain way, tend to be stigmatized." Why are they stigmatized? How might a critic of affirmative action respond to this argument?
5. Loury notes that those who argue that affirmative action is no longer necessary are denying "social reality." Respond to his position with your own point of view, referring to specific issues he raises.
6. Have you ever felt discriminated against because of your race? Have you ever found yourself making stereotypical assumptions of others based on their ethnicity, even inadvertently? Explain.
7. Loury argues, "How can we talk about justice and equality in American society without any reference to this reality? That's not colorblindness; that's just blindness." Can justice and equality exist without considering race? Alternatively, what happens when decisions of justice and equality are made only when considering the influence of race?

RESEARCH AND WRITING

1. List as many forms as you can think of that require people to denote race—come up with at least 10 different occurrences. Then explain why these forms need to contain this information. Are the "disgusting little boxes" necessary information on the form? Why or why not?
2. Research affirmative action and what it seeks to protect. What are the arguments against it? In support of it? After researching the issue, write a position paper in which you present your own view, addressing some of the concerns Loury raises in his article.
3. Do you feel that you have ever been excluded from fair consideration for school admission, employment, membership in an organization, or an athletic team or event because of your race, color, gender, or religious or sexual orientation? What were the circumstances? What, if anything, do you feel should have been done to ensure fair consideration for your candidacy?

Leaving Race Behind
*Amitai Etzioni**

Caucasian, Black, Asian, Hispanic, Native American—official forms ask us to indicate our race. In this next essay, author and sociology professor Amitai Etzioni explains why he hesitates to mark any specific race. Counter to what Glenn Loury defends in the previous essay, Etzioni explains why he feels this information is unnecessary, and even dangerous. Etzioni also questions why race matters to the government, saying that the time has come to stop asking this question on forms. Has the time come to leave race behind?

1   Some years ago the United States government asked me what my race was. I was reluctant to respond because my 50 years of practicing sociology—and some powerful personal experiences—have underscored for me what we all know to one degree or another, that racial divisions bedevil America, just as they do many other societies across the world. Not wanting to encourage these divisions, I refused to check off one of the specific racial options on the U.S. Census form and instead marked a box labeled "Other." I later found out that the federal government did not accept such an attempt to deemphasize race, by me or by some 6.75 million other Americans who tried it. Instead the government assigned me to a racial category, one it chose for me. Learning this made me conjure up what I admit is a far-fetched association. I was in this place once before.

2   When I was a Jewish child in Nazi Germany in the early 1930s, many Jews who saw themselves as good Germans wanted to "pass" as Aryans. But the Nazi regime would have none of it. Never mind, they told these Jews, we determine who is Jewish and who is not. A similar practice prevailed in the Old South, where if you had one drop of African blood you were a Negro, disregarding all other facts and considerations, including how you saw yourself.

3   You might suppose that in the years since my little Census-form protest the growing enlightenment about race in our society would have been accompanied by a loosening of racial categories by our government. But in recent years the United States government has acted in a deliberate way to make it even more difficult for individuals to move beyond racial boxes and for American society as a whole to move beyond race.

4   Why the government perpetuates racialization and what might be done to diminish the role of race in our lives are topics that have become especially timely as Hispanics begin to take a more important role demographically, having displaced African-Americans as the largest American minority. How Hispanics view themselves and how they are viewed by others are among the most important factors affecting whether or not we can end race as a major social divide in America.

5   Treating people differently according to their race is as un-American as a hereditary aristocracy and as American as slavery. The American ethos was formed

* Amitai Etzioni, *The American Scholar*, September 1, 2006

by people who left the social stratification of the Old World to live in a freer, more fluid society. They sought to be defined by what they accomplished, not by what they were born with. As Arthur M. Schlesinger Jr. puts it in his book *The Disuniting of America*, one of the great vir-

Treating people differently according to their race is as un-American as a hereditary aristocracy and as American as slavery. The national ideal says that all Americans should be able to complete as equals, whatever their background.

tues of America is that it defines individuals by where they are going rather than by where they have been. Achievement matters, not origin. The national ideal says that all Americans should be able to compete as equals, whatever their background. American society has been divided along racial lines since its earliest days.

6   Racial characterizations have trumped the achievement ideal; people born into a non-white race, whatever their accomplishments, have been unable to change their racial status. Worse, race has often been their most defining characteristic, affecting most, if not all, aspects of their being.

7   As a result, we have been caught, at least since the onset of the civil rights movement, in ambivalence. On the one hand, we continue to dream of the day when all Americans will be treated equally, whatever their race; we rail against—and sometimes punish—those who discriminate according to race in hiring, housing, and social life. At the same time, we have ensconced in law many claims based on race: requirements that a given proportion of public subsidies, loans, job training, educational assistance, and admission slots at choice colleges be set aside for people of color. Many Americans, including African-Americans, are uneasy about what some people consider reverse discrimination. Courts have limited its scope; politicians have made hay by opposing it; and some of its beneficiaries feel that their successes are hollow, because they are unsure whether their gains reflect hard-won achievements or special favors. There must be a better way to deal with past and current injustice. And the rapid changes in American demographics call for a reexamination of the place of race in America.

Enter the Hispanic

8 We have grown accustomed to thinking about America in black and white and might well have continued to do so for decades to come except that Hispanics complicate this simplistic scheme: they do not fit into the old racial categories. Some Hispanics appear to many Americans to be black (for example, quite a few Cuban-Americans), others as white (especially immigrants from Argentina and Chile), and the appearance of still others is hard for many people to pigeonhole. Anyone seeing the lineup of baseball players honored as Major League Baseball's "Latino Legends Team" would find that the players vary from those who are as fair-skinned as Roger Clemens to those who are as dark-skinned as Jackie Robinson. More important by far, survey after survey shows that most Hispanics object to being classified as either black or white. A national survey conducted in 2002 indicated that 76 percent of Hispanics say the standard racial categories used by the U.S. Census do not address

their preferences. The last thing most of those surveyed desire is to be treated as yet another race—as "brown" Americans.

9   Hispanics would have forced the question of how we define one another even if they were just another group of immigrants among the many that have made America what it is. But Hispanics are not just one more group of immigrants. Not only have Hispanic numbers surpassed those of black Americans, who until 2003 made up America's largest minority group, Hispanics have been reliably projected to grow much faster than African-Americans or any other American group. Thus, according to the Census, in 1990 blacks constituted 12 percent of the population and Hispanics 9 percent. By 2000, Hispanics caught up with blacks, amounting to 12.5 percent of the population compared to 12.3 percent for blacks. By 2050, Hispanics are projected to be 24.3 percent of the American population, compared to 14.7 percent for blacks. In many cities, from Miami to Los Angeles, in which African-Americans have been the largest minority group, Hispanics' numbers are increasingly felt. While once Hispanics were concentrated in the areas bordering Mexico, their numbers are now growing in places like Denver, St. Paul, and even New England.

10   Immigration fuels the growth of Hispanics relative to the growth of African-Americans, because Latin-American immigration, legal and illegal, continues at an explosive pace, while immigration from Africa is minuscule. Hispanics also have more children than African-Americans. During the most recent year for which data are available, 2003 to 2004, one of every two people added to America's population was Hispanic. And while black Americans have long been politically mobilized and active, Hispanics are just beginning to make their weight felt in American politics.

11   The rapid growth in the number, visibility, and power of Hispanics will largely determine the future of race in America, a point highlighted by Clara E. Rodriguez in her book *Changing Race: Latinos, the Census, and the History of Ethnicity in the U.S.* If Hispanics are to be viewed as brown or black (and some on the left aspire to color them), and above all if Hispanics develop the sense of disenfranchisement and alienation that many African-Americans have acquired (often for very good reasons), then America's immutable racial categories will only deepen.

12   If, on the other hand, most Hispanics continue to see themselves as members of one or more ethnic groups, then race in America might be pushed to the margins. Racial categories have historically set us apart; ethnic categories are part of the mosaic that makes up America. It has been much easier for an individual to assimilate from an ethnic perspective than from a racial one. Race is considered a biological attribute, a part of your being that cannot be dropped or modified. Ethnic origin, in contrast, is where you came from. All Americans have one hyphen or another attached to their ethnic status: we're Polish-, or German-, or Anglo-, or Italian-Americans. Adding Cuban-Americans or Mexican-Americans to this collage would create more comfortable categories of a comparable sort.

The Race Trap

13 Many people take it for granted that genes determine race, just as genes determine gender. And we also tend to believe that racial categories are easy to discern (though we all know of exceptions).

14   One way to show how contrived racial divisions actually are is to recall that practically all of the DNA in all human beings is the same. Our differences are truly skin deep. Moreover, the notion that most of us are of one race or another has little basis in science. The Human Genome Project informs us not only that 99.9 percent of genetic material is shared by all humans, but also that variation in the remaining 0.1 percent is greater within racial groups than across them. That is, not only are 99.9 percent of the genes of a black person the same as those of a white person, but the genes of a particular black person may be more similar to the genes of a white person than they are to another black person.

15   This point was driven home to college students in a sociology class at Penn State in April 2005. Following their professor's suggestion, the students took DNA tests that had surprising results. A student who identified himself as "a proud black man" found that only 52 percent of his ancestry traced back to Africa, while the other 48 percent was European. Another student who said she takes flak from black friends for having a white boyfriend found that her ancestry was 58 percent European and only 42 percent African. These two students are not alone: an estimated one-third of the African-American population has European ancestry.

16   Which people make up a distinct race and which are considered dark-skinned constantly changes as social prejudices change. Jewish-, Slavic-, Irish-, and Polish-Americans were considered distinct races in the mid-19th and early 20th centuries—and dark races at that, as chronicled in great detail in Matthew Frye Jacobson's book *Whiteness of a Different Color: European Immigrants and the Alchemy of Race* and in a well-documented book by Noel Ignatiev, *How the Irish Became White*. Ignatiev found that in the 1850s, Irish people were considered non-white in America and were frequently referred to as "niggers turned inside out." (Blacks were sometimes called "smoked Irish.")

17   The capriciousness of racial classifications is further highlighted by the way the U.S. Census, the most authoritative and widely used source of social classifications, divides Americans into races. When I ask my students how many races they think there are in America, they typically count four: white, black, Asian, and Native American. The Census says there are 15 racial categories: white, African-American, American Indian/Alaska Native, Asian Indian, Chinese, Filipino, Japanese, Korean, Vietnamese, "other Asian," Native Hawaiian, Guamanian/Chamorro, Samoan, and "other Pacific Islander," and as of 2000, one more for those who feel they are of some other race. (Hispanic is not on this list because the Census treats Hispanic as an ethnicity and asks about it on a separate question, but immediately following that question, the Census asks, "So what is your race, anyhow?")

18   The arbitrary nature of these classifications is demonstrated by the Census Bureau itself, which can change the race of millions of Americans by the stroke of a pen. The Census changed the race of Indian- and Pakistani-Americans from white in 1970 to Asian in 1980. In 1930 the Census made Mexicans into a different race but then withdrew this category. Similarly, Hindu made a brief appearance as a race in the 1930 and 1940 Censuses but was subsequently withdrawn.

19   Anthropologists have found that some tribes do not see colors the way many of us do; for instance, they do not "see" a difference between brown and yellow. Members of these tribes are not color-blind, but some differences found in nature (in the

color spectrum) simply don't register with them, just as young American children are unaware of racial differences until someone introduces them to these distinctions. We draw a line between white and black, but people's skin colors have many shades. It is our social prejudices that lead us to make sharp racial categories.

20   I am not one of those postmodernists who, influenced by Nietzsche and Foucault, claim that there are no epistemological truths, that all facts are a matter of social construction. I disagree with Nietzsche's description of truth as "a mobile army of metaphors, metonyms, and anthropomorphisms—in short a sum of human relations, which have been enhanced, transposed, and embellished poetically and rhetorically and which after long use seem firm, canonical, and obligatory to a people." However, there is no doubt that social construction plays a significant role in the way we "see" racial differences, although our views may in turn be affected by other factors that are less subject to construction; for example, historical differences.

21   Most important is the significance we attribute to race and the interpretations we impose on it. When we are told only that a person is, say, Asian-American, we often jump to a whole list of conclusions regarding that person's looks, intelligence, work ethic, and character; we make the same sort of jumps for Native Americans, blacks, and other races. Many things follow from these knee-jerk characterizations: whether we will fear or like this person, whether we will wish to have him or her as a neighbor or as a spouse for one of our children—all on the basis of race. In short, we load on to race a great deal of social importance that is not a reflection of the "objective" biological differences that exist. To paraphrase the UNESCO Constitution, racial divisions are made in the minds of men and women, and that is where they will have to be ended.

Defining the Hispanic

22 If racial categories have long been settled, the social characterization of the Hispanic is up for grabs. We still don't know whether Hispanics will be defined as a brown race—and align themselves with those in the United States who are, or who see themselves, as marginalized or victimized—or if they will be viewed as a conglomerate of ethnic groups, of Mexican-Americans, Cuban-Americans, Dominican-Americans, and so forth, who will fit snugly into the social mosaic.

23   The term "Hispanic" was first used in the Census in 1980. Before that, Mexican-Americans and Cuban-Americans were classified as white (except when a Census interviewer identified an individual as a member of a different racial group). Until 1980, Hispanics were part of the great American panorama of ethnic groups. Then the Census combined these groups into a distinct category unlike any other. It was as if the federal government were to one day lump together Spanish-, Italian-, and Greek-Americans into a group called "Southern European" and begin issuing statistics on how their income, educational achievements, number of offspring, and so on compare to those of Northern Europeans.

24   And as we've seen, those who define themselves as Hispanic are asked to declare a race. In the 1980 Census, the options included, aside from the usual menu of races, that ambiguous category "Other." There were 6.75 million Americans, including me, who chose this option in 1980. Most revealing: 40 percent of Hispanics

chose this option. (Note that they—and I—chose this category despite the nature of the word "Other," which suggests the idea of "not being one of us." Had the category been accorded a less loaded label, say "wish not to be identified with any one group," it seems likely that many millions more would have chosen this box.)

25   To have millions of Americans choose to identify themselves as "Other" created a political backlash, because Census statistics are used both to allocate public funds to benefit minority groups and to assess their political strength. Some African-American groups, especially, feared that if African-Americans chose "Other" instead of marking the "African-American" box, they would lose public allotments and political heft.

26   But never underestimate our government. The Census Bureau has used a statistical procedure to assign racial categories to those millions of us who sought to butt out of this divisive classification scheme. Federal regulations outlined by the Office of Management and Budget, a White House agency, ruled that the Census must "impute" a specific race to those who do not choose one. For several key public-policy purposes, a good deal of social and economic data must be aggregated into five racial groups: white, black, Asian, American Indian or Alaska Native, and native Hawaiian or other Pacific Islander. How does the government pick a race for a person who checked the "Other" box? They turn to the answers for other Census questions: for example, income, neighborhood, education level, or last name. The resulting profiles of the U.S. population (referred to as the "age-race modified profile") are then used by government agencies in allotting public funds and for other official and public purposes.

27   But the Census isn't alone in oversimplifying the data. Increasingly, other entities, including the media, have treated Hispanics as a race rather than an ethnic group. This occurs implicitly when those who generate social data—such as government agencies or social scientists—break down the data into four categories: white, black, Asian, and Hispanic, which is comparable to listing apples, oranges, bananas, and yams. In their profile of jail inmates, the Bureau of Justice Statistics lists inmates' origins as "white, black, Hispanic, American Indian/Alaska Native, Asian/Pacific Islander, and more than one race." *The New York Times* ran a front-page story in September 2005 in which it compared the first names used by whites, blacks, Asians, and Hispanics. Replace the word *Hispanics* with the name of another ethnic group, say Jews, and the unwitting racial implication of this classification will stand out.

28   Still other studies include Hispanics when they explicitly refer to racial groups. For example, a 2001 paper by Sean Reardon and John T. Yun examines what they call "racial balkanization among suburban schools," where there is increased segregation among black, Hispanic, and Asian students. A 2005 *Seattle Times* story uses racial terminology when it reports "Latinos have the fewest numbers among racial groups in master's-of-business programs nationwide, with about 5,000 enrolling annually." Similarly, the *San Diego Union Tribune* states: "A brawl between Latino and black students resulted in a lockdown of the school and revealed tensions between the two largest racial groups on campus."

29   A handful of others go a step further and refer to Hispanics as a "brown race." For example, following the recent Los Angeles mayoral election, the *Houston Chronicle* informed us that "Villaraigosa's broad-based support has analysts

wondering whether it is evidence of an emerging black–brown coalition." And National Public Radio reported: "There is no black and brown alliance at a South Central Los Angeles high school."

30　　One way or another, all of these references push us in the wrong direction— toward racializing Hispanics and deepening social divisions. America would be best served if we moved in the opposite direction.

A New Taxonomy

31　Thus far, workers at the U.S. Census Bureau, following the White House's instructions, seem determined to prevent any deemphasis of race. They are testing iterations of the wording for the relevant questions in the 2010 Census—but all of these possibilities continue to require people to identify themselves by race. Moreover, Census bureaucrats will continue to impute race to those who refuse to do so themselves, ignoring the ever-growing number of people, especially Hispanics, who do not fit into this scheme.

32　　Imagine if instead the federal government classified people by their country (or countries) of origin. For some governmental purposes, it might suffice to use large categories, such as Africa (which would exclude other so-called black groups, such as Haitians and West Indians that are now included in references to "black" Americans), Asia, Europe, Central America, and South America (the last two categories would not, of course, include Spain). For other purposes, a more detailed breakdown might work better—using regions such as the Middle East and Southeast Asia, for example—and if still more detail was desired, specific countries could be used, as we do for identifying ethnic groups (Irish, Polish, Cuban, Mexican, Japanese, Ethiopian, and so on). Kenneth Prewitt, a former director of the U.S. Census Bureau, has suggested the use of ethnic categories. As we have seen, ethnic origins carry some implications for who we are, but these implications decline in importance over time. Above all, they do not define us in some immutable way, as racial categories do. A category called something like "wish not to be identified with any particular group" should be included for those who do not want to be characterized, even by ethnicity, or for others who view themselves as having a varied and combined heritage.

33　　The classification of Americans who are second-generation and beyond highlights the importance of the no-particular-group category. Although a fourth-generation Italian-American might still wish to be identified as Italian, he might not, particularly if he has grandparents or parents who are, say, Greek, Korean, and Native American. Forcing such a person to classify himself as a member of one ethnic group conceals the significance of the most important American development in social matters: out-marriage. Out-marriage rates for all groups other than African-Americans are so high that most of us will soon be tied to Americans of a large variety of backgrounds by the closest possible social tie, the familial one. Approximately 30 percent of third-generation Hispanics and 40 percent of third-generation Asians marry people of a different racial or ethnic origin. Altogether, the proportion of marriages among people of different racial or ethnic origins has increased by 72 percent since 1970. The trend suggests more of this in the future. Even if your spouse is of the same background, chances are high that the spouse of a sibling or cousin will represent a different part of the American collage. At holidays and other family events, from birthdays to funerals, we will increasingly be in close connection with "Others." Before too long most Americans will be "Tiger Woods" Americans, whose parental heritage is black, Native American, Chinese, Caucasian, and Thai. Now is the time for our social categories to reflect this trend—and its capacity for building a sense of one community—rather than conceal it.

Where Do We Go from Here?

34 Changing the way we divide up society will not magically resolve our differences or abolish racial prejudices. Nor does a movement toward a color-blind nation mean that we should stop working for a more just America. A combination of three major approaches that deal with economic and legal change could allow us to greatly downgrade the importance of race as a social criterion and still advance social justice. These approaches include reparations, class-based social programs, and fighting discrimination on an individual basis.

35 To make amends for the grave injustice that has been done to African-Americans by slavery and racial prejudice, as well as to bring to a close claims based on past injustices—and the sense of victimhood and entitlement that often accompanies these claims—major reparations are called for. One possible plan might allot a trillion dollars in education, training, and housing vouchers to African-Americans over a period of 20 years. (The same sort of plan might be devised for Native Americans.)

36 Such reparations cannot make full compensation for the sins of slavery, of course. But nothing can. Even so, if Jews could accept restitution from Germany and move on (Germany and Israel now have normal international relations, and the Jewish community in Germany is rapidly growing), could not a similar reconciliation between black and white Americans follow reparations? A precedent in our own history is the payment of reparations to Japanese-Americans because of their internment in World War II. In 1988, the U.S. government issued a formal apology in the Civil Liberties Act and awarded $20,000 to each living person who had been interned. About 80,000 claims were awarded, totaling $1.6 billion.

37 Part of the deal should be that once reparations are made for the sins against African-Americans in the past, black people could no longer claim special entitlements or privileges on the basis of their race. Reparations thus would end affirmative action and minority set-asides as we have known them.

38 At the same time, Americans who are disadvantaged for any reason not of their own doing—the handicapped; those who grew up in parts of the country, such as Appalachia, in which the economy has long been lagging; those whose jobs were sent overseas who are too old to be retrained—would be given extra aid in applying for college admissions and scholarships, housing allowances, small-business loans, and other social benefits. The basis for such aid would be socioeconomic status, not race. The child of a black billionaire would no longer be entitled to special consideration in college admissions, for instance, but the child of a poor white worker who lost his job to outsourcing and could not find new employment would be.

39 Social scientists differ in their estimates of the extent to which differences in opportunity and upward mobility between blacks and whites are due to racial prejudice

and the extent to which they are due to economic class differences. But most scholars who have studied the matter agree that economic factors are stronger than racial ones, possibly accounting for as much as 80 percent of the differences we observe. A vivid example: In recent years, Wake County in North Carolina made sure that its public school classes were composed of students of different economic backgrounds, disregarding racial and ethnic differences. The results of this economic integration overshadowed previous attempts to improve achievement via racial integration. While a decade ago, only 40 percent of blacks in grades three through eight scored at grade level, in the spring of 2005, 80 percent did so.

40   Class differences affect not only educational achievement, health, and job selection but also how people are regarded or stereotyped. Fifty years ago, a study conducted at Howard University showed that although adjectives used to describe whites and blacks were quite different, that variance was greatly reduced when class was held constant. People described upper-class whites and upper-class blacks in a remarkably similar fashion, as intelligent and ambitious. People also described lower-class whites and lower-class blacks in a similar way, as dirty and ignorant. The author concluded that "stereotypes vary more as a function of class than of race."

41   If race-based discrimination were a thing of the past, and black Americans were no longer subjected to it, then my argument that reparations can lead to closure would be easier to sustain. Strong evidence shows, however, that discrimination remains very much with us. A 1990 Urban Institute study found that when two people of different races applied for the same job, one in eight times the white was offered the job and an equally qualified African-American was not. Another Urban Institute study, released in 1999, found that racial minorities received less time and information from loan officers and were quoted higher interest rates than whites in most of the cities where tests were conducted.

42   The victims of current racial discrimination should be fully entitled to remedies in court and through such federal agencies as the Equal Employment Opportunity Commission. These cases should be dealt with on an individual basis or in a class-action suit where evidence exists to support one. Those who sense discrimination should be required to prove it. It shouldn't be assumed that because a given workplace has more people of race *x* than race *y*, discrimination must exist.

A Vision of the Future

43 In the end, it comes down to what Americans envision for our future together: either an open society, in which everyone is equally respected (an elusive goal but perhaps closer at hand than we realize), or an even more racialized nation, in which "people of color" are arrayed in perpetual conflict with white people. The first possibility is a vision of America as a community in which people work out their differences and make up for past injustices in a peaceful and fair manner; the other is one in which charges of prejudice and discrimination are mixed with real injustices, and in which a frustrated sense of victimhood and entitlement on the one hand is met with guilt and rejection on the other.

44   A good part of what is at stake is all too real: the distribution of assets, income, and power, which reparations, class-based reforms, and the courts should be able

to sort out. But don't overlook the importance of symbols, attitudes, and feelings, which can't be changed legislatively. One place to start is with a debate over the official ways in which we classify ourselves and the ways we gather social data, because these classifications and data are used as a mirror in which we see ourselves reflected.

45   Let us begin with a fairly modest request of the powers that be: Give us a chance. Don't make me define my children and myself in racial terms; don't "impute" a race to me or to any of the millions of Americans who feel as I do. Allow us to describe ourselves simply as Americans. I bet my 50 years as a sociologist that we will all be better for it. ◆

CRITICAL THINKING

1. Why does Etzioni decline to indicate his race? What point does he make by recounting his personal experiences?
2. Is it possible to be considered one race by the U.S. government but to see yourself as a different race? Explain.
3. Do you think the government and other institutions should change the "race" category to "ethnicity"? Should there be no section on race or ethnicity at all? Would this make the process of gathering information easier or more confusing?
4. How do you think Glenn Loury from the previous essay would respond to Etzioni's argument that the time has come to stop using checkboxes on forms that require information on race?
5. Is Hispanic a "race"? Why would the government want to know racial information? What issues connected to race are unique to this population?
6. What is the "race trap"? Why is it harmful? Explain.
7. The author suggests that government aid be distributed according to socioeconomic status not race: "The child of a black billionaire would no longer be entitled to special consideration in college admissions, for instance, but the child of a poor white worker who lost his job to outsourcing and could not find new employment would be." Do you agree with basing aid on socioeconomic status instead of race? How might this change the racial divide in the United States?
8. According to Etzioni, what unique opportunity do we now have to think "beyond race"? How are Hispanics connected to this opportunity? Explain.

CRITICAL WRITING

1. *Persuasive Writing:* Write a letter to the U.S. government suggesting how race should be considered, or not, on documents, censuses, and other forms. Give concrete examples and detailed support for your point of view.
2. *Personal Narrative:* Etzioni recounts a personal experience in which race made him acutely aware of how disclosing this information can be abused. Describe how important or unimportant race has been in your life thus far.

Write about a defining moment that changed or influenced your view of yourself, or someone in your family, connected to your ethnicity.
3. *Exploratory Writing:* Explain this paradox from the article: "Treating people differently according to their race is as un-American as a hereditary aristocracy and as American as slavery."

GROUP PROJECTS

1. As a group, research DNA testing for race and ethnicity. How much does it cost, what steps are involved, and what types of results are given? How accurate are the results? Would you consider doing genetic testing? Explain your reasoning.
2. Etzioni notes that racial information has a history of causing more harm than good. Discuss as a group the ways that racial information on government forms could be abused and whether the time has come to eliminate this question from forms, no matter what good intentions, such as affirmative action, may be behind it.

Perspectives:
History Marches On

Barry Deutsch/LeftyCartoons.com

THINKING CRITICALLY

1. What issue is this cartoon raising? What connections exist between immigration and racism?
2. What is "nativism"?
3. What is the history behind each of the first three panels (1780, 1850, and 1920)? What happened after these immigrant groups entered the United States? What might one infer will happen following the "Now" panel, based on the history highlighted by the previous three panels?

The End of White America?
Hua Hsu*

> The election of Barack Obama to the nation's highest office in 2008 was hailed by many as a "new beginning" for America. With every new beginning, there is an end of something that came before. The next article explores what it means to be "white" or "black" or "multiethnic" in the United States today. Has the time come to stop checking off little boxes identifying our ethnic background? Should racial information matter? Music critic and writer Hua Hsu conjectures that the election of Barack Obama symbolizes the beginning of a "post-racial" society. The fact that the majority of Americans voted for him represents a gradual erosion of "whiteness" as the touchstone of what it means to be American. If the end of white America is a cultural and demographic inevitability, what will the new mainstream look like—and how will white Americans fit into it? Will a more ethnically diverse America be less racially divided—or more so?

1   "Civilization's going to pieces," he remarks. He is in polite company, gathered with friends around a bottle of wine in the late-afternoon sun, chatting and gossiping. "I've gotten to be a terrible pessimist about things. Have you read *The Rise of the Colored Empires* by this man Goddard?" They hadn't. "Well, it's a fine book, and everybody ought to read it. The idea is if we don't look out the white race will be— will be utterly submerged. It's all scientific stuff; it's been proved."

2   He is Tom Buchanan, a character in F. Scott Fitzgerald's *The Great Gatsby*, a book that nearly everyone who passes through the American education system is compelled to read at least once. Although Gatsby doesn't gloss as a book on racial anxiety—it's too busy exploring a different set of anxieties entirely—Buchanan was hardly alone in feeling besieged. The book by "this man Goddard" had a real-world analogue: Lothrop Stoddard's *The Rising Tide of Color Against White World-Supremacy*, published in 1920, five years before *Gatsby*. Nine decades later, Stoddard's polemic remains oddly engrossing. He refers to World War I as the "White Civil War" and laments the "cycle of ruin" that may result if the "white world" continues its infighting. The book features a series of foldout maps depicting the distribution of "color" throughout the world and warns, "Colored migration is a universal peril, menacing every part of the white world."

3   As briefs for racial supremacy go, *The Rising Tide of Color* is eerily serene. Its tone is scholarly and gentlemanly, its hatred rationalized and, in Buchanan's term, "scientific." And the book was hardly a fringe phenomenon. It was published by Scribner, also Fitzgerald's publisher, and Stoddard, who received a doctorate in history from Harvard, was a member of many professional academic associations. It was precisely the kind of book that a 1920s man of Buchanan's profile—wealthy, Ivy League–educated, at once pretentious and intellectually insecure—might have been expected to bring up in casual conversation.

---

* Hua Hsu, *The Atlantic*, February/March 2009 (*Essay has been abridged for space and may be read online in its entirety.*)

4   As white men of comfort and privilege living in an age of limited social mobility, of course, Stoddard and the Buchanans in his audience had nothing literal
to fear. Their sense of dread hovered somewhere above the concerns of everyday
life. It was linked less to any immediate danger to their class's political and cultural
power than to the perceived fraying of the fixed, monolithic identity of whiteness
that sewed together the fortunes of the fair-skinned.

5   From the hysteria over Eastern European immigration to the vibrant cultural
miscegenation of the Harlem Renaissance, it is easy to see how this imagined worldwide white kinship might have seemed imperiled in the 1920s. There's no better
example of the era's insecurities than the 1923 Supreme Court case *United States
v. Bhagat Singh Thind*, in which an Indian-American veteran of World War I sought
to become a naturalized citizen by proving that he was Caucasian. The Court considered new anthropological studies that expanded the definition of the Caucasian
race to include Indians, and the justices even agreed that traces of "Aryan blood"
coursed through Thind's body. But these technicalities availed him little. The Court
determined that Thind was not white "in accordance with the understanding of the
common man" and therefore could be excluded from the "statutory category" of
whiteness. Put another way: Thind was white, in that he was Caucasian and even
Aryan. But he was not white in the way Stoddard or Buchanan were white.

6   The '20s debate over the definition of whiteness—a legal category? a commonsense understanding? a worldwide civilization?—took place in a society gripped by
an acute sense of racial paranoia, and it is easy to regard these episodes as evidence
of how far we have come. But consider that these anxieties surfaced when whiteness was synonymous with the American mainstream, when threats to its status were
largely imaginary. What happens once this is no longer the case—when the fears of
Lothrop Stoddard and Tom Buchanan are realized, and white people actually become an American minority?

7   Whether you describe it as the dawning of a post-racial age or just the end of
white America, we're approaching a profound demographic tipping point. According to an August 2008 report by the U.S. Census Bureau, those groups currently
categorized as racial minorities—blacks and Hispanics, East Asians and South
Asians—will account for a majority of the U.S. population by the year 2042. Among
Americans under the age of 18, this shift is projected to take place in 2023, which
means that every child born in the United States from here on out will belong to the
first post-white generation.

8   Obviously, steadily ascending rates of interracial marriage complicate this picture, pointing toward what Michael Lind has described as the "beiging" of America.
And it's possible that "beige Americans" will self-identify as "white" in sufficient
numbers to push the tipping point further into the future than the Census Bureau
projects. But even if they do, whiteness will be a label adopted out of convenience
and even indifference, rather than aspiration and necessity. For an earlier generation
of minorities and immigrants, to be recognized as a "white American," whether you
were an Italian or a Pole or a Hungarian, was to enter the mainstream of American
life; to be recognized as something else, as the Thind case suggests, was to be permanently excluded. As Bill Imada, head of the IW Group, a prominent Asian American communications and marketing company, puts it: "I think in the 1920s, 1930s,

and 1940s, [for] anyone who immigrated, the aspiration was to blend in and be as American as possible so that white America wouldn't be intimidated by them. They wanted to imitate white America as much as possible: learn English, go to church, go to the same schools."

9   Today, the picture is far more complex. To take the most obvious example, whiteness is no longer a precondition for entry into the highest levels of public office. The son of Indian immigrants doesn't have to become "white" in order to be elected governor of Louisiana. A half-Kenyan, half-Kansan politician can self-identify as black and be elected president of the United States.

10   As a purely demographic matter, then, the "white America" that Lothrop Stoddard believed in so fervently may cease to exist in 2040, 2050, or 2060, or later still. But where the culture is concerned, it's already all but finished. Instead of the long-standing model of assimilation toward a common center, the culture is being remade in the image of white America's multiethnic, multicolored heirs.

11   For some, the disappearance of this centrifugal core heralds a future rich with promise. In 1998, President Bill Clinton, in a now-famous address to students at Portland State University, remarked:

12   Today, largely because of immigration, there is no majority race in Hawaii or Houston or New York City. Within five years, there will be no majority race in our largest state, California. In a little more than 50 years, there will be no majority race in the United States. No other nation in history has gone through demographic change of this magnitude in so short a time . . . [These immigrants] are energizing our culture and broadening our vision of the world. They are renewing our most basic values and reminding us all of what it truly means to be American.

13   Not everyone was so enthused. Clinton's remarks caught the attention of another anxious Buchanan—Pat Buchanan, the conservative thinker. Revisiting the president's speech in his 2001 book, *The Death of the West*, Buchanan wrote: "Mr. Clinton assured us that it will be a better America when we are all minorities and realize true 'diversity.' Well, those students [at Portland State] are going to find out, for they will spend their golden years in a Third World America."

14   Today, the arrival of what Buchanan derided as "Third World America" is all but inevitable. What will the new mainstream of America look like, and what ideas or values might it rally around? What will it mean to be white after "whiteness" no longer defines the mainstream? Will anyone mourn the end of white America? Will anyone try to preserve it?

15   Another moment from *The Great Gatsby*: as Fitzgerald's narrator and Gatsby drive across the Queensboro Bridge into Manhattan, a car passes them, and Nick Carraway notices that it is a limousine "driven by a white chauffeur, in which sat three modish negroes, two bucks and a girl." The novelty of this topsy-turvy arrangement inspires Carraway to laugh aloud and think to himself, "Anything can happen now that we've slid over this bridge, anything at all. . . ."

16   For a contemporary embodiment of the upheaval that this scene portended, consider Sean Combs, a hip-hop mogul and one of the most famous African Americans on the planet. Combs grew up during hip-hop's late-1970s rise, and he belongs to

the first generation that could safely make a living working in the industry—as a plucky young promoter and record-label intern in the late 1980s and early 1990s, and as a fashion designer, artist, and music executive worth hundreds of millions of dollars a brief decade later.

17   In the late 1990s, Combs made a fascinating gesture toward New York's high society. He announced his arrival into the circles of the rich and powerful not by crashing their parties, but by inviting them into his own spectacularly over-the-top world. Combs began to stage elaborate annual parties in the Hamptons, not far from where Fitzgerald's novel takes place. These "white parties"—attendees are required to wear white—quickly became legendary for their opulence (in 2004, Combs showcased a 1776 copy of the Declaration of Independence) as well as for the cultures-colliding quality of Hamptons elites paying their respects to someone so comfortably nouveau riche. Prospective business partners angled to get close to him and praised him as a guru of the lucrative "urban" market, while grateful partygoers hailed him as a modern-day Gatsby.

18   "Have I read *The Great Gatsby*?" Combs said to a London newspaper in 2001. "I am the Great Gatsby."

19   Yet whereas Gatsby felt pressure to hide his status as an arriviste, Combs celebrated his position as an outsider–insider—someone who appropriates elements of the culture he seeks to join without attempting to assimilate outright. In a sense, Combs was imitating the old WASP establishment; in another sense, he was subtly provoking it, by over-enunciating its formality and never letting his guests forget that there was something slightly off about his presence. There's a silent power to throwing parties where the best-dressed man in the room is also the one whose public profile once consisted primarily of dancing in the background of Biggie Smalls videos. ("No one would ever expect a young black man to be coming to a party with the Declaration of Independence, but I got it, and it's coming with me," Combs joked at his 2004 party, as he made the rounds with the document, promising not to spill champagne on it.)

20   In this regard, Combs is both a product and a hero of the new cultural mainstream, which prizes diversity above all else, and whose ultimate goal is some vague notion of racial transcendence, rather than subversion or assimilation. Although Combs's vision is far from representative—not many hip-hop stars vacation in St. Tropez with a parasol-toting manservant shading their every step—his industry lies at the heart of this new mainstream. Over the past 30 years, few changes in American culture have been as significant as the rise of hip-hop. The genre has radically reshaped the way we listen to and consume music, first by opposing the pop mainstream and then by becoming it. From its constant sampling of past styles and eras—old records, fashions, slang, anything—to its mythologization of the self-made black antihero, hip-hop is more than a musical genre: it's a philosophy, a political statement, a way of approaching and remaking culture. It's a lingua franca not just among kids in America, but also among young people worldwide. And its economic impact extends beyond the music industry, to fashion, advertising, and film. (Consider the producer Russell Simmons—the ur-Combs and a music, fashion, and television mogul—or the rapper 50 Cent, who has parlayed his rags-to-riches story line into extracurricular successes that include a clothing line; book, video game,

and film deals; and a startlingly lucrative partnership with the makers of Vitamin Water.)

21   But hip-hop's deepest impact is symbolic. During popular music's rise in the 20th century, white artists and producers consistently "mainstreamed" African American innovations. Hip-hop's ascension has been different. Eminem notwithstanding, hip-hop never suffered through anything like an Elvis Presley moment, in which a white artist made a musical form safe for white America. This is no dig at Elvis—the constrictive racial logic of the 1950s demanded the erasure of rock and roll's black roots, and if it hadn't been him, it would have been someone else. But hip-hop—the sound of the post–civil-rights, post-soul generation—found a global audience on its own terms.

22   Today, hip-hop's colonization of the global imagination, from fashion runways in Europe to dance competitions in Asia, is Disneyesque. This transformation has bred an unprecedented cultural confidence in its black originators. Whiteness is no longer a threat or an ideal: it's kitsch to be appropriated, whether with gestures like Combs's "white parties" or the trickle-down epidemic of collared shirts and cuff links currently afflicting rappers. And an expansive multiculturalism is replacing the us-against-the-world bunker mentality that lent a thrilling edge to hip-hop's mid-1990s rise.

23   Peter Rosenberg, a self-proclaimed "nerdy Jewish kid" and radio personality on New York's Hot 97 FM—and a living example of how hip-hop has created new identities for its listeners that don't fall neatly along lines of black and white—shares another example: "I interviewed [the St. Louis rapper] Nelly this morning, and he said it's now very cool and in to have multicultural friends. Like you're not really considered hip or 'you've made it' if you're rolling with all the same people."

24   Just as Tiger Woods forever changed the country-club culture of golf, and Will Smith confounded stereotypes about the ideal Hollywood leading man, hip-hop's rise is helping redefine the American mainstream, which no longer aspires toward a single iconic image of style or class. Successful network-television shows like *Lost, Heroes*, and *Grey's Anatomy* feature wildly diverse casts, and an entire genre of half-hour comedy, from *The Colbert Report* to *The Office*, seems dedicated to having fun with the persona of the clueless white male. The youth market is following the same pattern: consider the Cheetah Girls, a multicultural, multiplatinum, multiplatform trio of teenyboppers who recently starred in their third movie, or Dora the Explorer, the precocious, bilingual 7-year-old Latina adventurer who is arguably the most successful animated character on children's television today. In a recent address to the Association of Hispanic Advertising Agencies, Brown Johnson, the Nickelodeon executive who has overseen Dora's rise, explained the importance of creating a character who does not conform to "the white, middle-class mold." When Johnson pointed out that Dora's wares were outselling Barbie's in France, the crowd hooted in delight.

25   Pop culture today rallies around an ethic of multicultural inclusion that seems to value every identity—except whiteness. "It's become harder for the blond-haired, blue-eyed commercial actor," remarks Rochelle Newman-Carrasco, of the Hispanic marketing firm Enlace. "You read casting notices, and they like to cast people with brown hair because they could be Hispanic. The language of casting notices is pretty

shocking because it's so specific: 'Brown hair, brown eyes, could look Hispanic.' Or, as one notice put it: 'Ethnically ambiguous.'"

26   "I think white people feel like they're under siege right now—like it's not okay to be white right now, especially if you're a white male," laughs Bill Imada, of the IW Group. Imada and Newman-Carrasco are part of a movement within advertising, marketing, and communications firms to reimagine the profile of the typical American consumer. (Tellingly, every person I spoke with from these industries knew the Census Bureau's projections by heart.)

27   "There's a lot of fear and a lot of resentment," Newman-Carrasco observes, describing the flak she caught after writing an article for a trade publication on the need for more-diverse hiring practices. "I got a response from a friend—he's, like, a 60-something white male, and he's been involved with multicultural recruiting," she recalls. "And he said, 'I really feel like the hunted. It's a hard time to be a white man in America right now, because I feel like I'm being lumped in with all white males in America, and I've tried to do stuff, but it's a tough time.'"

28   "I always tell the white men in the room, 'We need you,'" Imada says. "We cannot talk about diversity and inclusion and engagement without you at the table. It's okay to be white!

29   "But people are stressed out about it. 'We used to be in control! We're losing control!'"

30   If they're right—if white America is indeed "losing control," and if the future will belong to people who can successfully navigate a post-racial, multicultural landscape—then it's no surprise that many white Americans are eager to divest themselves of their whiteness entirely.

31   "I get it: as a straight white male, I'm the worst thing on Earth," Christian Lander says. Lander is a Canadian-born, Los Angeles–based satirist who in January 2008 started a blog called "Stuff White People Like" (stuffwhitepeoplelike.com), which pokes fun at the manners and mores of a specific species of young, hip, upwardly mobile whites. (He has written more than 100 entries about whites' passion for things like bottled water, "the idea of soccer," and "being the only white person around.") At its best, Lander's site—which formed the basis for a recently published book of the same name (reviewed in the October 2008 *Atlantic*)—is a cunningly precise distillation of the identity crisis plaguing well-meaning, well-off white kids in a post-white world.

32   Lander's "white people" are products of a very specific historical moment, raised by well-meaning Baby Boomers to reject the old ideal of white American gentility and to embrace diversity and fluidity instead. ("It's strange that we are the kids of Baby Boomers, right? How the hell do you rebel against that? Like, your parents will march against the World Trade Organization next to you. They'll have bigger white dreadlocks than you. What do you do?") But his lighthearted anthropology suggests that the multicultural harmony they were raised to worship has bred a kind of self-denial.

33   Matt Wray, a sociologist at Temple University who is a fan of Lander's humor, has observed that many of his white students are plagued by a racial-identity crisis: "They don't care about socioeconomics; they care about culture. And to be white is to be culturally broke. The classic thing white students say when you ask them to talk

about who they are is, 'I don't have a culture.' They might be privileged, they might
be loaded socioeconomically, but they feel bankrupt when it comes to culture … They
feel disadvantaged, and they feel marginalized. They don't have a culture that's cool
or oppositional." Wray says that this feeling of being culturally bereft often prevents
students from recognizing what it means to be a child of privilege—a strange irony
that the first wave of whiteness-studies scholars, in the 1990s, failed to anticipate.

34   "The best defense is to be constantly pulling the rug out from underneath yourself," Wray remarks, describing the way self-aware whites contend with their complicated identity. "Beat people to the punch. You're forced as a white person into a
sense of ironic detachment. Irony is what fuels a lot of white subcultures. You also
see things like Burning Man, when a lot of white people are going into the desert
and trying to invent something that is entirely new and not a form of racial mimicry.
That's its own kind of flight from whiteness. We're going through a period where
whites are really trying to figure out: Who are we?"

35   The "flight from whiteness" of urban, college-educated, liberal whites isn't the
only attempt to answer this question. You can flee into whiteness as well. This can
mean pursuing the authenticity of an imagined past: think of the deliberately white-
bread world of Mormon America, where the '50s never ended, or the anachronistic
WASP entitlement flaunted in books like last year's *A Privileged Life: Celebrating
WASP Style,* a handsome coffee-table book compiled by Susanna Salk, depicting a
world of seersucker blazers, whale pants, and deck shoes. (What the book celebrates
is the "inability to be outdone," and the "self-confidence and security that comes
with it," Salk tells me. "That's why I call it 'privilege.' It's this privilege of time,
of heritage, of being in a place longer than anybody else.") But these enclaves of
preserved-in-amber whiteness are likely to be less important to the American future
than the construction of whiteness as a somewhat pissed-off minority culture.

36   As with the unexpected success of the apocalyptic *Left Behind* novels, or the Jeff
Foxworthy–organized Blue Collar Comedy Tour, the rise of country music and auto racing took place well off the American elite's radar screen. (None of Christian Lander's
white people would be caught dead at a NASCAR race.) These phenomena reflected a
growing sense of cultural solidarity among lower-middle-class whites—a solidarity defined by a yearning for American "authenticity," a folksy realness that rejects the global,
the urban, and the effete in favor of nostalgia for "the way things used to be."

37   Like other forms of identity politics, white solidarity comes complete with its
own folk heroes, conspiracy theories (Barack Obama is a secret Muslim! The U.S.
is going to merge with Canada and Mexico!), and laundry lists of injustices. The targets and scapegoats vary—from multiculturalism and affirmative action to a loss of
moral values, from immigration to an economy that no longer guarantees the American worker a fair chance—and so do the political programs they inspire. But the core
grievance, in each case, has to do with cultural and socioeconomic dislocation—the
sense that the system that used to guarantee the white working class some stability
has gone off-kilter.

38   Wray is one of the founders of what has been called "white-trash studies," a field
conceived as a response to the perceived elite-liberal marginalization of the white
working class. He argues that the economic downturn of the 1970s was the precondition for the formation of an "oppositional" and "defiant" white-working-class

sensibility—think of the rugged, anti-everything individualism of 1977's *Smokey and the Bandit*. But those anxieties took their shape from the aftershocks of the identity-based movements of the 1960s. "I think that the political space that the civil-rights movement opens up in the mid-1950s and '60s is the transformative thing," Wray observes. "Following the black-power movement, all of the other minority groups that followed took up various forms of activism, including brown power and yellow power and red power. Of course the problem is, if you try and have a 'white power' movement, it doesn't sound good."

39   The result is a racial pride that dares not speak its name, and that defines itself through cultural cues instead—a suspicion of intellectual elites and city dwellers, a preference for folksiness and plainness of speech (whether real or feigned), and the association of a working-class white minority with "the real America." (In the Scots-Irish belt that runs from Arkansas up through West Virginia, the most common ethnic label offered to census takers is "American.") Arguably, this white identity politics helped swing the 2000 and 2004 elections, serving as the powerful counter-punch to urban white liberals, and the McCain–Palin campaign relied on it almost to the point of absurdity (as when a McCain surrogate dismissed Northern Virginia as somehow not part of "the real Virginia") as a bulwark against the threatening multiculturalism of Barack Obama. Their strategy failed, of course, but it's possible to imagine white identity politics growing more potent and more forthright in its racial identifications in the future, as "the real America" becomes an ever-smaller portion of, well, the real America, and as the soon-to-be white minority's sense of being besieged and disdained by a multicultural majority grows apace.

40   At the moment, we can call this the triumph of multiculturalism, or post-racialism. But just as whiteness has no inherent meaning—it is a vessel we fill with our hopes and anxieties—these terms may prove equally empty in the long run. Does

> **But just as whiteness has no inherent meaning—it is a vessel we fill with our hope and anxieties—these terms may prove equally empty in the long run.**

being post-racial mean that we are past race completely, or merely that race is no longer essential to how we identify ourselves? Karl Carter, of Atlanta's youth-oriented GTM, Inc. (Guerrilla Tactics Media), suggests that marketers and advertisers would be better off focusing on matrices like "lifestyle" or "culture" rather than race or ethnicity. "You'll have crazy in-depth studies of the white consumer or the Latino consumer," he complains. "But how do skaters feel? How do hip-hoppers feel?"

41   The logic of online social networking points in a similar direction. The New York University sociologist Dalton Conley has written of a "network nation," in which applications like Facebook and MySpace create "crosscutting social groups" and new, flexible identities that only vaguely overlap with racial identities. Perhaps this is where the future of identity after whiteness lies—in a dramatic departure from the racial logic that has defined American culture from the very beginning. What Conley, Carter, and others are describing isn't merely the displacement of whiteness from our cultural center; they're describing a social structure that treats race as just one of a seemingly infinite number of possible self-identifications.

42   The problem of the 20th century, W. E. B. Du Bois famously predicted, would be the problem of the color line. Will this continue to be the case in the 21st century, when a black president will govern a country whose social networks increasingly cut across every conceivable line of identification? The ruling of *United States v. Bhagat Singh Thind* no longer holds weight, but its echoes have been inescapable: we aspire to be post-racial, but we still live within the structures of privilege, injustice, and racial categorization that we inherited from an older order. We can talk about defining ourselves by lifestyle rather than skin color, but our lifestyle choices are still racially coded. We know, more or less, that race is a fiction that often does more harm than good, and yet it is something we cling to without fully understanding why—as a social and legal fact, a vague sense of belonging and place that we make solid through culture and speech.

43   But maybe this is merely how it used to be—maybe this is already an outdated way of looking at things. "You have a lot of young adults going into a more diverse world," Carter remarks. For the young Americans born in the 1980s and 1990s, culture is something to be taken apart and remade in their own image. "We came along in a generation that didn't have to follow that path of race," he goes on. "We saw something different." This moment was not the end of white America; it was not the end of anything. It was a bridge, and we crossed it. ◆

CRITICAL THINKING

1. Why does Hua reference *The Great Gatsby* in his introduction to his essay? What connections exist between the story and the points he raises about race and racism?
2. Hua conjectures that we are entering a "post-racial age." What does this term mean, and what does it say about the society we lived in before this "new" age? Explain.
3. Review Bill Clinton's comment (paragraph 12 of Hua's essay) on the end of "majority race" and why this is a good thing for America.
4. Hua notes that Pat Buchanan warned that the arrival of "Third World America" is all but inevitable. What does this term imply? How does it incite fear and promote racism? What response would be appropriate to such a claim?
5. Hua notes that Sean Combs has identified himself as the Great Gatsby. What does he mean? How does his lifestyle compare to Jake Gatsby? What visible connections has he made between himself and the character in Fitzgerald's novel? What happens to Gatsby?
6. The author mentions W. E. B. Du Bois. Who was Du Bois? What is his connection to the points the author seeks to make in his essay?

CRITICAL WRITING

1. *Research Writing:* Read *The Great Gatsby* and research the book by Stoddard Lothrop, *The Rising Tide of Color Against White World-Supremacy*, published in 1920. What did "white race" mean? What did it mean to Stoddard in 1920, and how has this definition changed (or not changed) today?

2. *Expository Writing:* Answer the question Hua poses at the end of his essay: "The problem of the 20th century, W. E. B. Du Bois famously predicted, would be the problem of the color line. Will this continue to be the case in the 21st century, when a black president will govern a country whose social networks increasingly cut across every conceivable line of identification?"
3. *Exploratory Writing:* Do you think we will be more ethnically and racially melded as a nation in the next century? Write an essay postulating what race might mean 100 years from now. What about 200 years from now?
4. *Personal Narrative:* Examine your own racial and/or ethnic background. Write about whether this background has contributed to your perception of yourself and how you relate to others.

GROUP PROJECTS

1. With your group, construct a demographic picture of the future, say, in 100 years. Try to conjecture what the face of the nation will look like. Are there still checkboxes asking for one's race on job applications? What will the typical family look like? Will people still wonder what a person's ethnic background is? Share your vision, and the reasoning behind it, with the rest of the class.
2. As a group, discuss what "traditional American" and "American mainstream society" mean. How would you define these terms for a foreign visitor? Discuss this question as a group, and develop a definition. Share your group's definition with the rest of the class.
3. Hua identifies several famous people, namely Tiger Woods and Sean Combs, in his essay for their contributions to a post-racial society. As a group, identify the people he cites, and any other well-known figures who have contributed to a post-racial culture, and discuss how these individuals have contributed to our cultural identity and how we think—or don't think—about race.

People Like Us
*David Brooks**

From the hallowed halls of academia to the boardrooms of Fortune 500 companies, the concept of racial and social diversity is an important factor in efforts to create a balanced, equal society. But despite efforts to promote diversity, all too often we witness "self-segregation." As David Brooks explains in this next essay, although we tend to pay lip service to ideals of diversity, we really prefer to associate with "people like us." Is the melting pot merely a myth?

* David Brooks, *The Atlantic,* September 2003

1   Maybe it's time to admit the obvious. We don't really care about diversity all that much in America, even though we talk about it a great deal. Maybe somewhere in this country there is a truly diverse neighborhood in which a black Pentecostal minister lives next to a white anti-globalization activist, who lives next to an Asian short-order cook, who lives next to a professional golfer, who lives next to a postmodern-literature professor and a cardiovascular surgeon. But I have never been to or heard of that neighborhood. Instead, what I have seen all around the country is people making strenuous efforts to group themselves with people who are basically like themselves.

2   Human beings are capable of drawing amazingly subtle social distinctions and then shaping their lives around them. In the Washington, D.C., area, Democratic lawyers tend to live in suburban Maryland, and Republican lawyers tend to live in suburban Virginia. If you asked a Democratic lawyer to move from her $750,000 house in Bethesda, Maryland, to a $750,000 house in Great Falls, Virginia, she'd look at you as if you had just asked her to buy a pickup truck with a gun rack and to shove chewing tobacco in her kid's mouth. In Manhattan the owner of a $3 million SoHo loft would feel out of place moving into a $3 million Fifth Avenue apartment. A West Hollywood interior decorator would feel dislocated if you asked him to move to Orange County. In Georgia a barista from Athens would probably not fit in serving coffee in Americus.

3   It is a common complaint that every place is starting to look the same. But in the information age, the late writer James Chapin once told me, every place becomes more like itself. People are less often tied down to factories and mills, and they can search for places to live on the basis of cultural affinity. Once they find a town in which people share their values, they flock there and reinforce whatever was distinctive about the town in the first place. Once Boulder, Colorado, became known as congenial to politically progressive mountain bikers, half the politically progressive mountain bikers in the country (it seems) moved there; they made the place so culturally pure that it has become practically a parody of itself.

4   But people love it. Make no mistake—we are increasing our happiness by segmenting off so rigorously. We are finding places where we are comfortable and where we feel we can flourish. But the choices we make toward that end lead to the very opposite of diversity. The United States might be a diverse nation when considered as a whole, but block by block and institution by institution, it is a relatively homogeneous nation.

5   When we use the word "diversity" today, we usually mean racial integration. But even here our good intentions seem to have run into the brick wall of human nature. Over the past generation, reformers have tried heroically, and in many cases successfully, to end housing discrimination. But recent patterns aren't encouraging: according to an analysis of the 2000 census data, the 1990s saw only a slight increase in the racial integration of neighborhoods in the United States. The number of middle-class and upper–middle-class African-American families is rising, but for whatever reasons—racism, psychological comfort—these families tend to congregate in predominantly black neighborhoods.

6   In fact, evidence suggests that some neighborhoods become more segregated over time. New suburbs in Arizona and Nevada, for example, start out reasonably well

integrated. These neighborhoods don't yet have reputations, so people choose their houses for other, mostly economic reasons. But as neighborhoods age, they develop personalities (that's where the Asians live, and that's where the Hispanics live), and segmentation occurs. It could be that in a few years, the new suburbs in the Southwest will be nearly as segregated as the established ones in the Northeast and the Midwest.

7   Even though race and ethnicity run deep in American society, we should in theory be able to find areas that are at least culturally diverse. But here, too, people show few signs of being truly interested in building diverse communities. If you run a retail company and you're thinking of opening new stores, you can choose among dozens of consulting firms that are quite effective at locating your potential customers. They can do this because people with similar tastes and preferences tend to congregate by ZIP code.

8   The most famous of these precision marketing firms is Claritas, which breaks down the U.S. population into 62 psycho-demographic clusters, based on such factors as how much money people make, what they like to read and watch, and what products they have bought in the past. For example, the "suburban sprawl" cluster is composed of young families making about $41,000 a year and living in fast-growing places such as Burnsville, Minnesota, and Bensalem, Pennsylvania. These people are almost twice as likely as other Americans to have three-way calling. They are two and a half times as likely to buy Light n' Lively Kid Yogurt. Members of the "towns and gowns" cluster are recent college graduates in places such as Berkeley, California, and Gainesville, Florida. They are big consumers of Dove Bars and Saturday Night Live. They tend to drive small foreign cars and to read *Rolling Stone* and *Scientific American.*

9   Looking through the market research, one can sometimes be amazed by how efficiently people cluster—and by how predictable we all are. If you wanted to sell imported wine, obviously you would have to find places where rich people live. But did you know that the 16 counties with the greatest proportion of

> *Even though race and ethnicity run deep in American society, we should in theory be able to find areas that are at least culturally diverse. But here, too, people show few signs of being truly interested in building diverse communities.*

imported-wine drinkers are all in the same three metropolitan areas (New York, San Francisco, and Washington, D.C.)? If you tried to open a motor-home dealership in Montgomery County, Pennsylvania, you'd probably go broke, because people in this ring of the Philadelphia suburbs think RVs are kind of uncool. But if you traveled just a short way north, to Monroe County, Pennsylvania, you would find yourself in the fifth motor-home-friendliest county in America.

10   Geography is not the only way we find ourselves divided from people unlike us. Some of us watch *Fox News*, while others listen to NPR. Some like David Letterman, and others—typically in less urban neighborhoods—like Jay Leno. Some go to charismatic churches; some go to mainstream churches. Americans tend more and more often to marry people with education levels similar to their own and to befriend people with backgrounds similar to their own.

11   My favorite illustration of this latter pattern comes from the first, noncontroversial chapter of *The Bell Curve.* Think of your 12 closest friends, Richard J. Herrnstein and Charles Murray write. If you had chosen them randomly from the American population, the odds that half of your 12 closest friends would be college graduates would be six in a thousand. The odds that half of the 12 would have advanced degrees would be less than one in a million. Have any of your 12 closest friends graduated from Harvard, Stanford, Yale, Princeton, CalTech, MIT, Duke, Dartmouth, Cornell, Columbia, Chicago, or Brown? If you chose your friends randomly from the American population, the odds against your having four or more friends from those schools would be more than a billion to one.

12   Many of us live in absurdly unlikely groupings, because we have organized our lives that way.

13   It's striking that the institutions that talk the most about diversity often practice it the least. For example, no group of people sings the diversity anthem more frequently and fervently than administrators at just such elite universities. But elite universities are amazingly undiverse in their values, politics, and mores. Professors in particular are drawn from a rather narrow segment of the population. If faculties reflected the general population, 32 percent of professors would be registered Democrats and 31 percent would be registered Republicans. Forty percent would be evangelical Christians. But a recent study of several universities by the conservative Center for the Study of Popular Culture and the American Enterprise Institute found that roughly 90 percent of those professors in the arts and sciences who had registered with a political party had registered Democratic. Fifty-seven professors at Brown were found on the voter-registration rolls. Of those, 54 were Democrats. Of the 42 professors in the English, history, sociology, and political science departments, all were Democrats. The results at Harvard, Penn State, Maryland, and the University of California at Santa Barbara were similar to the results at Brown.

14   What we are looking at here is human nature. People want to be around others who are roughly like themselves. That's called *community.* It probably would be psychologically difficult for most Brown professors to share an office with someone who was pro-life, a member of the National Rifle Association, or an evangelical Christian. It's likely that hiring committees would subtly—even unconsciously— screen out any such people they encountered. Republicans and evangelical Christians have sensed that they are not welcome at places like Brown, so they don't even consider working there. In fact, any registered Republican who contemplates a career in academia these days is both a hero and a fool. So, in a semi–self-selective pattern, brainy people with generally liberal social mores flow to academia, and brainy people with generally conservative mores flow elsewhere.

15   The dream of diversity is like the dream of equality. Both are based on ideals we celebrate, even as we undermine them daily. (How many times have you seen someone renounce a high-paying job or pull his child from an elite college on the grounds that these things are bad for equality?) On the one hand, the situation is appalling. It is appalling that Americans know so little about one another. It is appalling that many of us are so narrow-minded that we can't tolerate a few people with ideas significantly different from our own. It's appalling that evangelical Christians are practically absent from entire professions, such as academia, the media, and filmmaking.

It's appalling that people should be content to cut themselves off from everyone unlike themselves.

16   The segmentation of society means that often we don't even have arguments across the political divide. Within their little validating communities, liberals and conservatives circulate half-truths about the supposed awfulness of the other side. These distortions are believed because it feels good to believe them.

17   On the other hand, there are limits to how diverse any community can or should be. I've come to think that it is not useful to try to hammer diversity into every neighborhood and institution in the United States. Sure, Augusta National should probably admit women, and university sociology departments should probably hire a conservative or two. It would be nice if all neighborhoods had a good mixture of ethnicities. But human nature being what it is, most places and institutions are going to remain culturally homogeneous.

18   It's probably better to think about diverse lives, not diverse institutions. Human beings, if they are to live well, will have to move through a series of institutions and environments, which may be individually homogeneous but, taken together, will offer diverse experiences. It might also be a good idea to make national service a rite of passage for young people in this country: it would take them out of their narrow neighborhood segment and thrust them in with people unlike themselves. Finally, it's probably important for adults to get out of their own familiar circles. If you live in a coastal, socially liberal neighborhood, maybe you should take out a subscription to *The Door*, the evangelical humor magazine; or maybe you should visit Branson, Missouri. Maybe you should stop in at a megachurch. Sure, it would be superficial familiarity, but it beats the iron curtains that now separate the nation's various cultural zones.

19   Look around at your daily life. Are you really in touch with the broad diversity of American life? Do you care? ◆

CRITICAL THINKING

1. When you were growing up, with whom did your parents socialize? Where did they live and what social functions were they likely to attend? Now that you are an adult, with whom do you chose to socialize? What is the demographic anatomy of your social group? Is it influenced by race and ethnicity? Is it influenced by common interests? Explain.

2. What does Brooks mean when he says, "Human beings are capable of drawing amazingly subtle social distinctions and then shaping their lives around them" (paragraph 2)? What examples does he give of such distinctions? Can you think of any "subtle social distinctions" in your own life that influence where you live and with whom you choose to associate? Explain.

3. What is "cultural affinity"? How does it influence the social and cultural values of a particular area? How is it reinforced, and how can it break down? Explain.

4. When we refer to the word "diversity," what do we usually mean? What types of diversity are identified by the author? What factors tend to influence people to find others like them?

5. What is ironic about the institutions that stress diversity (paragraph 13)? Why do they emphasize the need for diversity, and how do they fall short of practicing it? Explain.
6. Brooks states that he believes when we live with "people like us" we tend to be happier. Do you agree? If this is true, why do we tend to pay so much lip service to the idea of diversity but actually fail to achieve it?
7. Brooks begins his essay with the statement, "We don't really care about diversity all that much in America, even though we talk about it a great deal." Do you agree? Why or why not?

CRITICAL WRITING

1. *Personal Narrative:* Describe the neighborhood in which you currently live. How does it connect to the points Brooks makes in his essay? (A dormitory can be considered a "neighborhood.") Consider also in your narrative the reasons why you chose the college you now attend and the social groups with which you associate. Draw connections between your own "cultural cluster" and Brooks's observations on diversity in practice.
2. *Exploratory Writing:* In paragraph 11, Brooks discusses how the first chapter of *The Bell Curve* describes our tendency to connect with "people like us." Apply Herrnstein and Murray's hypothesis to your own life. Write down the names of your 12 closest friends and think about their socioeconomic backgrounds, race and ethnicity, religion, political leanings, and intellectual pursuits. Then consider them as a group. Write a short essay about what you discover about your own group and how it compares to the observations made in *The Bell Curve*. What do your results reveal about the multicultural face of the nation, especially as it applies to race?
3. *Persuasive Writing:* Write an essay in which you explain why you believe diversity is or is not important to the success of society. Is diversity more important in certain situations but less so in others? Explain your point of view while also making references to the text.

GROUP PROJECTS

1. In paragraph 5, Brooks observes that many neighborhoods have failed to be truly racially integrated "for whatever reasons." With your group, interview a diverse group of students on where they grew up. Name the region, state, city, or town—even the neighborhood—and ask them to describe their hometown's demographic profile, including social, intellectual, professional, and economic dimensions. Ask the people you interview for their impressions about why their family lived where they did and the cultural influences they experienced. Prepare a report on your findings. What did you discover about demographic clustering? What might it mean for diversity efforts in the next 20 years?

2. As a group, discuss how ethnic and racial differences divide and unite us as a nation. According to the report *Changing America by the President's Initiative on Race,* the gaps among races and ethnic groups in the areas of education, jobs, economic status, health, housing, and criminal justice are substantial. Read more about the report and the initiative at http://en.wikipedia .org/wiki/One_America_Initiative. Choose one subject area from its table of contents and read through that chapter and charts. Then, summarize what you have learned about the differences among racial and ethnic groups, and discuss how you think these disparities affect our chances of creating a society in which all Americans can participate equally.

CULTURE SHOCK

Look Legal

In April of 2010, Arizona Governor Jan Brewer signed into law the "Support Our Law Enforcement and Safe Neighborhoods Act" (Arizona SB 1070) Considered by many as the broadest and strictest anti-illegal immigration measure in recent U.S. history, it has been the subject of much controversy. U.S. federal law requires that aliens who wish to remain in the United States for longer than 30 days must register with the U.S. government and must carry this registration with them at all times. The Arizona Act allows law enforcement officers to ask for documentation during lawful stops or when there is "reasonable suspicion" that the individual might be an illegal immigrant. Critics fear the law encourages racial profiling. In June 2012, the U.S. Supreme Court upheld the provision requiring immigration status checks during law enforcement stops.

RJ Matson/PoliticalCartoons.com

THINKING CRITICALLY

1. What is the product being "advertised" in the cartoon? What does it profess to do?
2. What point is this cartoon trying to make? How effective is this cartoon at getting its message across?
3. What does it mean to be "American" and to "look legal"? According to this cartoon, what is the Arizona law supporting?
4. In what ways does this cartoon challenge racism? Explain.

Why Is the N.Y.P.D. After Me?

*Nicholas K. Peart**

> Racial profiling relies a great deal on stereotyping—generalized assumptions about groups of people based on characteristics such as race, ethnic origin, social class, religion, gender, or physical appearance. Advocates for racial profiling cite its usefulness in law enforcement, but they often skip how it marginalizes some groups and even persecutes them because of their ethnic background. The practice of racial profiling has created a sense of social and political distrust, to the extent that some parents give their children the "walking while black" warning, a version of which Nicholas Peart recounts below. What happens to the social contract when you cannot trust the institutions that profess to uphold the law? What if you are considered guilty of a crime before you even know the charges? In this next essay, student Nicholas Peart describes what it means to grow up afraid of the police in a society that stereotypes you as trouble solely because you are young, male, and black.

1   When I was 14, my mother told me not to panic if a police officer stopped me. And she cautioned me to carry ID and never run away from the police or I could be shot. In the nine years since my mother gave me this advice, I have had numerous occasions to consider her wisdom.

2   One evening in August of 2006, I was celebrating my 18th birthday with my cousin and a friend. We were staying at my sister's house on 96th Street and Amsterdam Avenue in Manhattan and decided to walk to a nearby place and get some burgers. It was closed so we sat on benches in the median strip that runs down the middle of Broadway. We were talking, watching the night go by, enjoying the evening when suddenly, and out of nowhere, squad cars surrounded us. A policeman yelled from the window, "Get on the ground!"

3   I was stunned. And I was scared. Then I was on the ground—with a gun pointed at me. I couldn't see what was happening but I could feel a policeman's hand reach into my pocket and remove my wallet. Apparently he looked through and found the ID I kept there. "Happy Birthday," he said sarcastically. The officers questioned my cousin and friend, asked what they were doing in town, and then said goodnight and left us on the sidewalk.

4   Less than two years later, in the spring of 2008, N.Y.P.D. officers stopped and frisked me, again. And for no apparent reason. This time I was leaving my grandmother's home in Flatbush, Brooklyn; a squad car passed me as I walked down East 49th Street to the bus stop. The car backed up. Three officers jumped out. Not again. The officers ordered me to stand, hands against a garage door, fished my wallet out of my pocket and looked at my ID. Then they let me go.

---

* Nicholas K. Peart, *The New York Times,* December 17, 2011

5   I was stopped again in September of 2010. This time I was just walking home from the gym. It was the same routine: I was stopped, frisked, searched, ID'd and let go.

6   These experiences changed the way I felt about the police. After the third incident I worried when police cars drove by; I was afraid I would be stopped and searched or that something worse would happen. I dress better if I go downtown. I don't hang out with friends outside my neighborhood in Harlem as much as I used to. Essentially, I incorporated into my daily life the sense that I might find myself up against a wall or on the ground with an officer's gun at my head. For a black man in his 20s like me, it's just a fact of life in New York.

7   Here are a few other facts: last year, the N.Y.P.D. recorded more than 600,000 stops; 84 percent of those stopped were blacks or Latinos. Police are far more likely to use force when stopping blacks or Latinos than whites. In half the stops police cite the vague "furtive movements" as the reason for the stop. Maybe black and brown people just look more furtive, whatever that means. These stops are part of a larger, more widespread problem—a racially discriminatory system of stop-and-frisk in the N.Y.P.D. The police use the excuse that they're fighting crime to continue the practice, but no one has ever actually proved that it reduces crime or makes the city safer. Those of us who live in the neighborhoods where stop-and-frisks are a basic fact of daily life don't feel safer as a result.

8   We need change. When I was young I thought cops were cool. They had a respectable and honorable job to keep people safe and fight crime. Now, I think their tactics are unfair and they abuse their authority. The police should consider the consequences of a generation of young people who want nothing to do with them—distrust, alienation and more crime.

9   Last May, I was outside my apartment building on my way to the store when two police officers jumped out of an unmarked car and told me to stop and put my hands up against the wall. I complied. Without my permission, they removed my cellphone from my hand, and one of the officers reached into my pockets, and removed my wallet and keys. He looked through my wallet, then handcuffed me. The officers wanted to know if I had just come out of a particular building. No, I told them, I lived next door.

10   One of the officers asked which of the keys they had removed from my pocket opened my apartment door. Then he entered my building and tried to get into my apartment with my key. My 18-year-old sister was inside with two of our younger siblings; later she told me she had no idea why the police were trying to get into our apartment and was terrified. She tried to call me, but because they had confiscated my phone, I couldn't answer.

11   Meanwhile, a white officer put me in the back of the police car. I was still handcuffed. The officer asked if I had any marijuana, and I said no. He removed and searched my shoes and patted down my socks. I asked why they were searching me, and he told me someone in my building complained that a person they believed fit my description had been ringing their bell. After the other officer returned from inside my apartment building, they opened the door to the police car, told me to get out, removed the handcuffs and simply drove off. I was deeply shaken.

12   For young people in my neighborhood, getting stopped and frisked is a rite of passage. We expect the police to jump us at any moment. We know the rules: don't run and don't try to explain, because speaking up for yourself might get you arrested or worse. And we all feel the same way—degraded, harassed, violated and criminalized because we're black or Latino. Have I been stopped more than the average young black person? I don't know, but I look like a zillion other people on the street. And we're all just trying to live our lives.

13   As a teenager, I was quiet and kept to myself. I'm about to graduate from the Borough of Manhattan Community College, and I have a stronger sense of myself after getting involved with the Brotherhood/Sister Sol, a neighborhood organization in Harlem. We educate young people about their rights when they're stopped by the police and how to stay safe in those interactions. I have talked to dozens of young people who have had experiences like mine. And I know firsthand how much it messes with you. Because of them, I'm doing what I can to help change things and am acting as a witness in a lawsuit brought by the Center for Constitutional Rights to stop the police from racially profiling and harassing black and brown people in New York.

14   It feels like an important thing to be part of a community of hundreds of thousands of people who are wrongfully stopped on their way to work, school, church or shopping, and are patted down or worse by the police though they carry no weapon; and searched for no reason other than the color of their skin. I hope police practices will change and that when I have children I won't need to pass along my mother's advice. ◆

CRITICAL THINKING

1. What assumptions do you have regarding our legal system? Do you believe that you will be treated fairly? That we are innocent until proven guilty? As you read Peart's essay describing the many times he has been detained by police, consider how your assumptions match his experience.

2. Have you ever been stopped by the police for any reason? What was the experience like? If not, what would you expect to happen, and how do you think you would react?

3. How do you feel after reading this essay? Are there particular points in Peart's narrative that seem more powerful than others? Do you find yourself becoming emotionally involved with his narrative? Explain.

4. Peart notes that at one point, the police tried to use his key to gain access to his apartment. Is this legal? Does it surprise you? Explain.

5. How is Peart trying to change police behavior toward "blacks and browns" in New York City?

6. Peart believes that he was unfairly judged by the officers involved in multiple detainments based on the color of his skin. What does he feel was most violated by his experiences? How does he appeal to his readers' sense of justice? Explain.

CRITICAL WRITING

1. *Exploratory Writing:* Nancy E. Gist, director of the Bureau of Justice Assistance at the U.S. Department of Justice, said in her forward to the resource guide *The Nature of the Problem of Racial Profiling,* "The guarantee to all persons of equal protection under the law is one of the most fundamental principles of our democratic society. Law enforcement officers should not endorse or act upon stereotypes, attitudes, or beliefs that a person's race, ethnicity, or national origin increases that person's general propensity to act unlawfully. There is no tradeoff between effective law enforcement and protection of the civil rights of all Americans; we can and must have both." Write an essay in which you build upon her statement, reflecting on Peart's experiences with law enforcement. Do you agree with her statement that there can be no "tradeoff" between civil protection and civil rights? Why or why not? How do you think Peart would respond to her directive? What about the NYPD?

2. *Research Writing:* Racial profiling for African Americans and Latinos is still of great concern. Visit the ACLU's Web site on racial equality at http://www.aclu.org/racial-justice and review the information on racial profiling. What are the most pressing issues concerning racial profiling today? Select an issue or case described on the ACLU Web site and research it in greater depth. Write a short essay summarizing the situation, the issue, and your position on it.

GROUP PROJECT

1. Visit the U.S. Department of Justice Web site and read the "Racial Profiling Fact Sheet" posted online at http://www.justice.gov/opa/pr/2003/June/racial_profiling_fact_sheet.pdf. Review the entire fact sheet and discuss it as a group. What is the government's official position on racial profiling? What exceptions does it make concerning racial profiling, and why? Identify any areas of the document that you find questionable or particularly compelling, and share them with the rest of the class as part of a larger class discussion on the issue of racial profiling and the racism that is connected with it.

▶ **Airport Security: Let's Profile Muslims**
Asra Q. Nomani *

VIEWPOINTS

▶ **Racial Profiling Is Poisoning Muslim Americans' Trust**
Sahar Aziz

Racial profiling is the practice by law enforcement or security officers of considering race as an indicator of the likelihood of criminal behavior. Based on statistical assumptions and stereotypes, racial profiling presumes that certain groups of people are more likely to commit, or not commit, certain crimes. The Supreme Court has officially upheld the constitutionality of the practice, as long as race is only one of several factors leading to the detainment or arrest of an individual.

For many years, the focus of the racial profiling debate has been on its impact on African Americans. Studies reveal that many police departments did indeed use racial profiling as a practice. As a result, many states instituted legislation prohibiting racial profiling of African Americans to ensure fairness for all citizens. In the case of national security, however, the issue of racial profiling is open to daily debate. The next two essays address the connections between racial profiling of Muslims and national security, especially in a post-9/11 world. Both essays in this section are by young Muslim women, but with very different viewpoints. Both raise interesting questions about racial profiling. Although it may seem unsavory, argues activist and journalist Asra Q. Nomani, how can we ignore past behaviors of a group of individuals bound by a common religion as we try to keep the citizenry safe? The other explains why it is never acceptable to profile—even when you think you are doing it for good reasons. Moreover, when law enforcement uses racial profiling to spy on citizens, she argues, counterterrorism agencies are wrecking their most valuable asset: Muslim American good will.

 Airport Security: Let's Profile Muslims
Asra Q. Nomani

1 For all those holiday travelers negotiating the Transportation Security Administration's new cop-a-feel strategy, there is a difficult solution we need to consider: racial and religious profiling.

2 As an American Muslim, I've come to recognize, sadly, that there is one common denominator defining those who've got their eyes trained on U.S. targets: MANY of them are Muslim—like the Somali-born teenager arrested Friday night

---

for a reported plot to detonate a car bomb at a packed Christmas tree-lighting ceremony in downtown Portland, Oregon.

3   We have to talk about the taboo topic of profiling because terrorism experts are increasingly recognizing that religious ideology makes terrorist organizations and terrorists more likely to commit heinous crimes against civilians, such as blowing an airliner out of the sky. Certainly, it's not an easy or comfortable conversation but it's one, I believe, we must have.

4   This past week, as part of a debate series sponsored by the New York-based group Intelligence Squared, I argued that U.S. airports should use racial and religious profiling. (Taking the opposite stand was a "debating team" that included the former director of the Department of Homeland Security, Michael Chertoff; Columbia University scholar of Pakistan, Hassan Abbas; and Debra Burlingame, a former flight attendant whose brother was a pilot of one of the planes hijacked on 9/11.)

5   I realize that in recent years, profiling has become a dirty word, synonymous with prejudice, racism, and bigotry. But while I believe our risk assessment should not end with religion, race and ethnicity, I believe that it should include these important elements, as part of a "triage" strategy that my debate partner, former CIA case officer Robert Baer, says airports and airliners already do.

6   Profiling doesn't have to be about discrimination, persecution, or harassment. As my debating partner, conservative columnist Deroy Murdock put it: "We are not arguing that the TSA should send anyone named Mohammad to be waterboarded somewhere between the first-class lounge and the Pizza Hut."

7   And more Americans, it seems, are willing to choose racial and religious profiling as one part of keeping our skies safe. At the beginning of the debate, 37 percent of the audience was for religious and racial profiling, while 33 percent were against and 30 percent were undecided. By the end of the debate, 49 percent of the audience was for religious and racial profiling, 40 percent were against and the rest were undecided, meaning that the motion carried. Of course, this "victory" in a scholarly debate doesn't mean that the motion would necessarily win any broader popularity contests.

8   In the debate, I said, "Profile me. Profile my family," because, in my eyes, we in the Muslim community have failed to police ourselves. In an online posting of the Intelligence Squared video, a Muslim viewer called me an "Uncle Tom."

9   But to me, profiling isn't about identity politics but about threat assessment.

10   According to a terrorism database at the University of Maryland, which documents 60 attacks against airlines and airports between 1970 and 2007, the last year available, suspects in attacks during the 1970s were tied to the Jewish Defense League, the Black Panthers, the Black September, the National Front for the Liberation of Cuba, Jewish Armed Resistance and the Croatian Freedom Fighters, along with a few other groups.

11   In each of these groups' names was a religious or ethnic dimension. For that time, those were the identities that we needed to assess. Today, the threat has changed, and it is primarily coming from Muslims who embrace al Qaeda's radical brand of Islam.

12   Data in reports released over the past several months from New York University's Center for Security and the Law; the Congressional Research Service, and the Rand Corporation reveal that over the past decade not only are many defendants in

terrorism cases Muslim, but they trace their national or ethnic identity back to specific countries.

13   According to the Rand study " Would-Be Warriors," the national origins or ethnicities most defendants came from was Pakistan, Somalia, Yemen, Jordan and Egypt, with a handful from the Muslim areas of the Balkans.

14   To be sure, according to New York University's Center for Security and the Law "Terrorist Trial Report Card," an analysis of terrorism cases prosecuted between 2001 and 2009 reveals that identifying race and ethnicity doesn't mean stereotyping according to country. Among the hundreds of defendants in the study, the largest number held U.S. citizenship. Law enforcement officials familiar with the cases said many of the Americans were ethnically connected to Pakistan, the Palestinian territories, Jordan, Iraq and Egypt. The study, however, didn't look specifically at the ethnicities of the U.S. citizens. According to the study, there were high incidents of cases of passport holders from those countries among the defendants.

15   The track record of Muslim plots against airliners and airports is clear, starting with the 1989 bombing of Pan Am 103 over Lockerbie, Scotland. After the first World Trade Center attack in 1993, Ramzi Yousef schemed with his uncle, Khalid Sheikh Mohammed, a Muslim of Pakistani Baluchi ethnicity, to blow up 12 jetliners traveling from Asia to the U.S., intending to kill as many as 4,000 people. The plan fell apart in 1995 after a chemical fire caught the attention of police in the Philippines, but a test run had already killed one passenger seated near a nitroglycerin bomb on a Philippine Airlines Flight.

16   Three years later, Osama bin Laden threatened to bring down U.S. and Israeli aircrafts through the International Islamic Front for Fighting Against the Jews and Crusaders, warning the attacks would be "pitiless and violent" and announcing that "the war has begun."

17   "Our response to the barbaric bombardment against Muslims of Afghanistan and Sudan will be ruthless and violent," he said in a statement. "All the Islamic world has mobilized to strike a prominent American or Israeli strategic objective, to blow up their airplanes and to seize them." A declassified CIA memo written in December 1998 warned: "Bin Ladin preparing to hijack U.S. aircraft."

18   In 1999, we had a "Millennium bomber," targeting Los Angeles International Airport. And, in a case that became very personal to me, on Dec. 24, 1999, a group of Pakistani Muslim militants hijacked an Indian Airlines jet from Kathmandu, Nepal, diverting it to Kandahar, Afghanistan, killing one newlywed passenger. In exchange for the passengers, India released Muslim militants, including a Pakistan-British Muslim militant named Omar Sheikh. Sheikh went on to mastermind the 2002 kidnapping of my friend, *Wall Street Journal* reporter Daniel Pearl, whom Khalid Sheikh Mohammed later confessed to killing.

19   After the Kathmandu hijacking, we had the 9/11 attacks. And since then, we've had the "Torrance Plotters," the "JFK Airport Plotters," the Glasgow, Scotland, bombers, and the "Transatlantic bombers," all targeting airlines and airports. More recently, there was the attempt by the "underwear bomber," Umar Farouk Abdulmutallab, who last Christmas attempted to blow up explosives in his underwear—a foiled attack that brought the pat-downs of today. In addition to the Portland plot, we had the package bomb attempt out of Yemen.

20   Victor Asal, a political science professor at State University of New York at Albany, and Karl Rethemeyer, a professor of public administration and policy at SUNY at Albany, have studied 395 terrorist organizations in operation between 1998 and 2005, and Asal concludes, "What makes terrorist organizations more lethal is religious ideology. When you combine religion and ethno-nationalism, you get a dangerous combination."

21   Asal, the son of a Tunisian father, says there hasn't been enough research done for him to take a stand on racial and religious profiling, but favors "behavioral profiling," which assesses risky behavior like buying one-way tickets with cash and flying without checked baggage.

22   As attorney R. Spencer MacDonald put it in an article in the Brigham Young University Journal of Public Law, we can have " rational profiling."

23   I know this is an issue of great distress to many people. But I believe that we cannot bury our heads in the sand anymore. We have to choose pragmatism over political correctness, and allow U.S. airports and airlines to do religious and racial profiling. ◆

 ## Racial Profiling Is Poisoning Muslim Americans' Trust
Sahar Aziz

1 In the same week, a 29-year-old Moroccan man was caught attempting to bomb the Capitol in a government-led terrorism sting operation and the NYPD was caught spying on Muslim students at Yale, the University of Pennsylvania, Rutgers, and other universities on the U.S. East Coast. These two seemingly distinct events epitomize the fundamental flaws in the government's counterterrorism policies.

2   On the one hand, the government, under both the Bush and Obama administrations, has expended significant resources to conduct "community outreach" meetings with Muslims across the nation. On the other hand, while Muslims are lured into trusting their government, they are systematically spied on, investigated, and sometimes prosecuted.

3   Millions of dollars are spent flying bureaucrats from various federal agencies to meet and greet Muslim leaders, most of whom are male, in an attempt to earn their trust. In those meetings, local and state law enforcement is invited to build long-term relationships with the Muslim communities in their jurisdictions. On the face of it, the meetings appear to be a good-faith effort to demystify Muslims and counter false stereotypes of Muslims as terrorists. In practice, the objectives are more duplicitous.

4   In a blatant violation of their trust, local and federal agencies are recording these community outreach meetings, as well as the names and personal information of the attendees. Even Muslim imams who have been engaging with the government for years have found themselves under investigation. Community outreach meetings appear nothing more than a tool within a broader fishing expedition of Muslim

communities nationwide. The strategy is that if there is no evidence of terrorism, then the government must go out there and create it through community outreach meetings that set the groundwork for sting operations.

5   In doing so, the government is alienating its most important ally, the Muslim community, which has been the most effective counter-terrorism tool the government has.

6   As witnessed in recent reports of the NYPD's long-term surveillance program, this information gathering is part of a much broader surveillance scheme targeting community leaders, Muslim students, and any other Muslim with the misfortune of interacting with an undercover agent or informant. Without any evidence of criminal activity, informants infiltrated Muslim student organizations at Yale, Rutgers, and other universities. The undercover agents attended student meetings, academic conferences, and participated in field trips. The attendees' names and conversations became the basis of personal files in intelligence databases and subsequent investigations.

7   Meanwhile, the government admits that "lone wolf" terrorists are currently the primary threat of homegrown terrorism in the United States. Despite the conclusions of a recent report by the Triangle Center on Terrorism and Homeland Security that terrorism committed by Muslims in America is declining, the government is focused solely on Muslims. To be sure, religious profiling is the least of the government's concern, especially during an election year when politicians earn political capital by Muslim-bashing.

8   Herein lies the paradox.

9   Assuming the government's conclusions are correct, lone wolf terrorists are very difficult to detect because they do not have co-conspirators or networks of support. They are often mentally unstable individuals at the margins of society. To the extent that the lone wolf terrorists who are Muslim seek to recruit other Muslims, they risk detection. This is explains the government's appetite for community engagement in hopes that Muslims will report such interactions.

10   But can we reasonably expect Americans who are themselves collectively targets of surveillance and suspicion to trust the very agencies spying on them? One need only study the experiences of African Americans systematically harassed, investigated, and prosecuted by police. The result is an understandable distrust of law enforcement—so much so that young African-American men go out of their way to avoid any contact with the police. Rather than view law enforcement agencies as protectors, they are viewed as persecutors. So long as the police engage in systemic racial profiling and attendant criminal punishments, community outreach is futile, as well as disingenuous.

11   Thus, American Muslims face a palpable dilemma. If they report suspicions about terrorism, they invite government scrutiny into their lives and are likely to become targets of informants, investigations and surveillance (if they are not already). This entails very serious risks to their liberty. If they avoid interacting with law enforcement to protect their civil liberties, however, they are accused of condoning terrorism and disloyalty.

12   Like any other Americans, American Muslims report terrorism about which they have knowledge. But revelations about the NYPD's surveillance program, coupled with proven surveillance of community outreach meetings, make one thing clear: no good deed goes unpunished for Muslims in America. ◆

CRITICAL THINKING

1. Why is Nomani called an "Uncle Tom"? What is an "Uncle Tom"? Look up the phrase and explain why this term was used to describe her position on racial profiling.
2. In your opinion, do you consider racial profiling ever justifiable? If so, under what circumstances? If not, why?
3. Nomani states that the issue of profiling Muslims to prevent terrorism should not be about "identity politics" but about "threat assessment." Can the two be distinguished from each other? Why or why not?
4. Evaluate each author's thesis. Analyze the supporting elements each uses to support her point. Based on the writing alone, who makes the more compelling argument? Explain.
5. Nomani provides two examples in her introduction that she claims exhibit flaws in U.S. counterterrorism efforts. How do these examples demonstrate the problems with racial profiling of Muslim Americans?
6. According to Nomani, why do "community engagement" efforts alienate Muslim Americans? What paradox do they create? What issues do Muslim Americans face if they do report awareness of suspicious activities? Explain.

CRITICAL WRITING

1. *Expository Writing:* We have all heard of racial profiling, but what does it mean to you? Is it something you have experienced? Is it something you hear about but doesn't directly affect you? Do you think something needs to be done about racial profiling? If so, what? Write an essay exploring your views on this issue.
2. *Personal Narrative:* Write an essay discussing your own family's sense of ethic or racial identity. What are the origins of some of your family's values, traditions, and customs? Have these customs ever been questioned by people who did not understand them? How would you feel if law enforcement made assumptions about you or your family based solely on how you looked or the customs you observed?
3. *Exploratory Writing*: Consider the ways in which Hollywood influences our cultural perspectives of race and ethnicity. Write an essay exploring the influence, however slight, film and television have had on your own perceptions of race and ethnicity, especially of people who have a different background from you.

GROUP PROJECTS

1. Since 9/11, many individuals who were or looked like they might be of Middle Eastern descent have found themselves facing greater scrutiny at airports, boarders, and public byways. As a group, discuss the issue of racial profiling and its use as a crime prevention tool.

2. Although much of the debate on racial profiling addresses legal and personal injustice, an often overlooked but important element is the impact of the practice on our collective consciousness. As a group, discuss the ways racial profiling can potentially harm a group of people. What impact might it have on them? Could it, as Aziz states, create distrust on both sides of the counterterrorism effort? Does it create an "us versus them" mentality? Explain.

CHAPTER
8

Family Affairs
Marriage in Flux

The American family is always in a state of change. How we perceive the very concept of family is based largely on where we come from and what values we share. We have a tendency to base our views on traditional constructs—models that are generations old and perpetuated by media archetypes. As a result, sociologists tell us that our vision of family is usually not based on realistic examples but on political ideals and media images. Yet the traditional family is obviously changing. Stepfamilies, same-sex relationships, single-parent households, and extended families with several generations living in one home all force us to redefine, or at least reexamine, our traditional definitions of "family."

From traditional models of a married nuclear family—with a husband, wife, and children—to cohabiting multigenerational stepfamilies and same-sex unions, this chapter takes a look at how our concept of marriage has changed over the last several decades. Divorce, for example, is a widely accepted reality of life that is no longer viewed as a deviation from the norm. Single motherhood is no longer ascribed the social stigma it had 30 or 40 years ago, with almost half of children born to mothers under 30 now born out of wedlock. Some states have legalized same-sex marriage. A census report issued in 2007 revealed that only 24 percent of households are made up of what many politicians refer to as the "traditional family" of husband, wife, and children. Clearly, the American family unit has changed.

We open the chapter with an examination of family from an academic perspective. In the Modern Scholar reading, "Family: Idea, Institution, and Controversy," Betty G. Farrell discusses the social and political structures that influence our concept of family, and how the institution of family is firmly entrenched in our cultural consciousness. She also explores the concept of the family in transition and why we seem to fear change when it comes to family structures, which are based more on nostalgia than on reality.

Not everyone agrees that marriage is best, however. Dorian Solot argues that marriage is an unnecessary institution altogether in "On Not Saying 'I Do.'" Solot wonders whether she missed the day in preschool when they told the little girls that the happiest day of their lives would be their wedding day. And sociologist Stephanie Coontz challenges the idea that marriage should be a goal. There is no way, she contends, that marriage can be reestablished as the main site of family and interpersonal relationships in our modern world, a view she defends in "For Better, For Worse."

Dennis Prager questions such views, however, in his editorial, "Five Non-Religious Arguments for Marriage." Prager argues that living together simply represents an underlying unwillingness to fully commit to another person, and anyone who says marriage is "just a piece of paper" isn't telling the whole truth.

The next reading addresses the growing acceptance of gay marriage, and what it means for thousands of gay and lesbian Americans. While the issue continues to be argued in religious, political, and social arenas, gay couples are flocking to make their unions legal in the eyes of the law. In "Why Gay Marriage Is Good for Straight America," Andrew Sullivan explains why the right to marry is more than just about formalizing a union—it is about personal identity and happiness.

The popularity of several television programs that focus on plural marriage has brought the issue of polygamy into our living rooms. Many Americans watch these programs with a sort of repulsed fascination, but the shows do raise some important questions about the nature of marriage as an institution. Should people be allowed to marry more than one person? What if only men are allowed to do this and not women? Libby Copeland explains why polygamy is not good for women, men, and society overall in "Is Polygamy Really So Awful?"

The instability of American marriage is often cited as the source of many childhood problems. Most of us have heard the statistics—over half of all U.S. marriages end in divorce. The next essay, by Lowell Putnam, explains that children of divorce may not be as scarred by the experience as politicians and the media seem to think. Having lived most of his life as a child of divorce, Putnam wonders, "Did I Miss Something?"

This chapter's Viewpoints section debates the benefit of remarriage versus cohabitation from multiple perspectives. First, in "Think of the Children," sociology professor Andrew J. Cherlin explains why cohabitating couples should think carefully before remarrying. On the other hand, public policy professor Sharon Sassler explains why second marriage presents more security for both the couple and their children than merely living together in "The Higher Risks of Cohabitation." Then Nicky Grist from the Alternatives to Marriage Project questions the meaning of marriage in today's society, and whether it is necessary anymore to categorize couples in this way in "Laws Should Reflect Reality." The final reading in this section is by W. Bradford Wilcox, director of the National Marriage Project, who argues that marriage plays an important role in our personal well-being, the successful rearing of well-adjusted children, and the economic health of society overall in "Why the Ring Matters."

Modern Scholar

Family: Idea, Institution, and Controversy
*Betty G. Farrell**

Although the family has always been in a state of transition, many politicians expound that the family is not just in a state of change, it is in a state of decline—to the detriment of society. And whether this is true or not, it seems that many people agree that most of society's ills are directly connected to the decline of the family. The truth is, the American family is more than an icon in our culture. It is an American institution, subject to intense scrutiny and criticism. In this chapter's Modern Scholar essay, professor Betty G. Farrell explores the importance of the institution of family in American culture and how this importance is inextricably linked to our social and political consciousness.

* Betty Farrell, *Family: The Making of an Idea, an Institution, and a Controversy in American Culture,* 1999

1   Q: What did Eve say to Adam on being expelled from the Garden of Eden?
2   A: "I think we're in a time of transition."
3   The irony of this joke is not lost as we begin a new century, and anxieties about social change seem rife. The implication of this message, covering the first of many subsequent periods of transition, is that change is normal; there is, in fact, no era or society
in which change is not a permanent feature of the social landscape. Yet, on the eve of
the twenty-first century, the pace of change in the United States feels particularly intense, and a state of "permanent transition" hardly seems a contradiction in terms at all.
To many, it is an apt description of the economic fluctuations, political uncertainties,
social and cultural upheaval, and fluidity of personal relationships that characterize the
times. For a large segment of the population, however, these transitions are tinged with
an acute sense of loss and nostalgia. Moral values, communities, even the American
way of life seem in decline. And at the core of that decline is the family.
4   In a nationwide poll conducted by the *Los Angeles Times* [. . .], 78 percent of
respondents said they were dissatisfied with today's moral values, and nearly half of
that group identified divorce, working parents, and undisciplined children as the key
problems. Only 11 percent of the respondents believed that their own behavior had
contributed to the moral problems in the United States, and a resounding 96 percent
believed that they were personally doing an excellent or good job of teaching moral
values to their children. Conversely, 93 percent thought that other parents were to
blame for the inadequate moral upbringing of their children. The sense of loss and
decline many Americans feel today is filled with such contradictions. Americans
want their families to offer unconditional love yet also to enforce and uphold strict
moral values. They want flexibility, mobility, and autonomy in their personal lives
but yearn for traditional communities and permanently stable families. When the
substance of the debate over families is this ambiguous and contradictory, it is important to look more closely at the underlying issues in this time of transition.
5   For most people in most eras, change seems anything but normal. Periods of
social change can evoke much social anxiety, because the unknown is inherently unsettling and because many people are stakeholders in the status quo. Those who seek
change generally want to effect a shift in the relations of power, either for themselves or for others. But such shifts are always unpredictable, and they can seem
treacherous to those who hold the reins of power, as well as to those who feel their
social, economic, or political power eroding. The groups with eroding power are the
ones most likely to resist, through active strategies and passive resistance, the ideas,
values, symbols, and behaviors associated with change. This describes such groups
in the contemporary United States as militias who see minorities, foreigners, and
new cultural values as a threat to the American way of life; whites who see blacks,
Latinos, and Asians as challenging their privileges and claim on limited resources in
a zero-sum game; pro-life advocates who see pro-choice supporters as threatening
traditionally defined family roles; and antigay proponents who see gays and lesbians
as subverting the gendered social order. Although social structural forces are ultimately responsible for the realignment of prestige and power among social groups
in any society, these forces are always complex, abstract, intangible, and invisible.
So those who symbolize or represent the forces of the new—women, minorities,
immigrants, the poor, and other marginalized groups—tend to be singled out and

blamed for the disruptions and upheaval associated with change. Social psychologists identify this process as scapegoating, the act of displacing generalized anxiety onto a conveniently visible and available target. Scapegoats have been identified in every era; but in periods in which the pace of change is particularly fast and a sense of unsettling disruption is acute, those social newcomers who challenge established values and behavior can all too readily become the targets of the rage, fear, and ambivalence of people feeling the earthquake tremors of social change.

Popular Perspectives on the Family

6 The family values debate has been generated against just such a backdrop in the late-twentieth-century United States. Fundamental changes in the expectations, meanings, and practices defining American family life have characterized much of the twentieth century, but especially the final 30 years. Consequently, concern about the family has moved to the center of the political arena. Threats to the family on the one hand and salvation through the family on the other are the two most prominent themes in the recent family politics discourse. That the American family is broken and in need of repair is a common assumption of many social observers. Its complement is that families are worth fixing, because making them strong (again) is the key to solving most of society's ills. Neither of these assumptions has been subject to much critical scrutiny, nor has the historical image of the strong, vital, central family institution of the past on which they rest. Longing for order is one of the impulses behind the current turn to family politics in the United States; and feminists, gays and lesbians, single-parent mothers, absent fathers, pregnant teenagers, and gang-oriented youth, among others, have all at one time or another been made the scapegoats for family decline in the United States.

7   Longing for a more orderly, mythic past is most commonly associated with the conservative position on the family politics spectrum, and it would be easy to caricature the nostalgia for a family modeled on the classic 1950s television sitcom as the sum total of this side of the family values debate. But if we assume that concerns about The Family, writ large, are only those of conservative politicians attempting to manipulate public sentiment, we would overlook the vast reservoir of social anxiety about contemporary family life that is also being tapped by many others from a variety of political and social perspectives: working mothers who are consumed with worry about child care; white Christian men who, by the tens of thousands in the late 1990s, attended Promise Keepers revivals that focused on renewing their traditional roles as husbands and fathers; adolescents seeking the emotional attachment of family ties among peers and in gangs when it is found lacking in their own homes; committed gay and lesbian couples fighting for inclusion in the legal definition of family even as they retain a skeptical stance toward this fundamentally heterosexual institution. Why such concern about the family? One reason is that the metaphor evoked by family is a powerful one. A family is defined not so much by a particular set of people as by the quality of relationships that bind them together. What seems to many to be the constant feature of family life is not a specific form or structure but the meanings and the set of personal, intimate relationships families provide against the backdrop of the impersonal, bureaucratized world of modern society.

That the American family is broken and in need of repair is a common assumption of many social observers. Its complement is that families are worth fixing, because making them strong (again) is the key to solving most of society's ills.

8   The core sentiments of family life that define the nature and meaning of this social institution for most Americans are unconditional love, attachment, nurturance, and dependability. The hope that these qualities are common to family relationships accounts for the shock with which we react to reports of violence, abuse, and neglect occurring inside the sanctuary of the private home. In popular culture, as in real life, stories of families beset by jealousy, envy, lust, and hatred rather than by the ideals of love, loyalty, and commitment provide an endless source of titillation and fascination. Family stories are not only the stuff of life we construct through our daily experience but the narrative form used to entice us as consumers into a marketplace adept at presenting all sorts of products as invested with emotional qualities and social relationships.

9   The widely promoted "Reach Out and Touch Someone" advertising campaign developed by AT&T in 1978 was a prototype of this genre. In this set of ads, a powerful multinational company hoped to pull at the heartstrings and the pocketbooks of the consuming public by promoting itself as the crucial communication link between family members separated by great global distances. The copy in the print advertisements told heartwarming personal tales of mothers and sons, uncles and nephews, and grandmothers and grandchildren reunited by AT&T's implied commitment to family values, albeit at long distance phone rates. The family metaphor works as an advertising ploy because there is widespread sentimentality in American society about family life. What makes families so compelling for those of us who actively choose to live in them, as well as for those of us who just as actively reject them as oppressively confining, is that families reside at the intersection of our most personal experience and our social lives. They are institutions we make, yet they are in no small part also constructed by cultural myths and social forces beyond any individual's control.

10   A desire for the kind of care and connection provided by the ideal family cuts across class, race, and ethnic lines in the United States. A commitment to family seems to be so widely shared across groups of all kinds in the hybrid mix that makes up American culture as to be nearly universal. It therefore comes as some surprise that the qualities many accept as natural components of family ties today—unconditional love, warmth, enduring attachment—were not the same expectations most American families had until 150 years ago. The historical variations in family life challenge the claim that the family, even within the same culture, has had the same meaning or has offered the same timeless experiences to its members.

11   Assumptions about American family life in the past are widely shared. These include the beliefs that families were large and extended, with most people living in multigenerational households; that marriages occurred at an early age and were based on permanent, unwavering commitment between spouses; that the ties between kin were stronger and closer than those experienced today; and that family life in the past was more stable and predictable than it is currently. These assumptions about the family of the past have collectively produced an image that one sociologist has called "the Classical Family of Western Nostalgia." It is the image

upon which politicians and advertisers, among others, routinely draw as they explain contemporary social problems by reference to family breakdown or as they tap consumer desires by associating a product with positive family values and warm family feeling. The family is a potent symbol in contemporary American society, because it touches our emotional needs for both intimate personal attachments and a sense of embeddedness in a larger community.

12   Is there truth to the fears that family values are weaker today than in the past—that children are more vulnerable, adolescents more intractable, adults less dependable, and the elderly more needy? In both popular culture and political discourse, sentimentality and nostalgia about the family have often prevailed, and a social and historical context for framing the issues has largely been missing. It is important to challenge the popular understanding of the family as an institution that is biologically based, immutable, and predictable with a more culturally variable and historically grounded view. Because families are central to the way we talk about ourselves and about our social and political lives, they deserve to be studied in their fullest scope, attached to a real past as well as a present and future.

Academic Perspectives on the Family

13 Assumptions about the nature of the family abound not only in popular culture but in social science as well. The disciplines of anthropology, sociology, history, and psychology all have particular orientations to the institution of the family that define their theoretical positions and research agendas. Among sociologists and anthropologists, for example, a starting premise about the family has been that it is one of the central organizing institutions of society. Its centrality comes from having the capacity to organize social life quite effectively by regulating sexuality, controlling reproduction, and ensuring the socialization of children who are born within the family unit. Many social science disciplines start with the question "How is society possible?" and they recognize that the organization of individuals into family units is a very effective means of providing social regulation and continuity. Through the institution of the family, individuals are joined together and given the social and legal sanction to perpetuate their name and traditions through their offspring. Whole societies are replenished with future generations of leaders and workers.

14   In the early twentieth century, the anthropologist Bronislaw Malinowski made the argument that the most universal characteristic of family life in all cultures and all time periods was the "principle of legitimacy." He had noted that the rules for sexual behavior varied widely across cultures but that control over reproduction was a common feature of every social order. Every society made the distinction between those children (legitimate) born to parents who had been culturally and legally sanctioned to reproduce and those children (illegitimate) whose parents were not accorded this sanction. The function of the principle of legitimacy, according to Malinowski, was to ensure that a child born into a society had both an identifiable mother and father. The father might, in fact, not be biologically related to the child, but his recognized sociological status as father was the affiliation that gave the child a set of kin and a social placement in that social order.

15   In addition to being the only sanctioned setting for reproduction, families are important sources of social continuity, because they are most often the setting in which children are cared for and raised. The power of social forces is such that parents normally can be counted on to provide long-term care for their dependent children, because the emotional closeness of family bonds makes them want to do so. Families are therefore particularly effective institutions, because they press people into service for their kin by the dual imperatives of love and obligation. Although it is possible that food, shelter, physical care, and emotional nurturance could be provided through alternative means by the state or other centrally administered bureaucratic agencies, it would require considerable societal resources and effort to ensure that these needs were effectively met for a majority of individuals in a society. What families seem to provide naturally, societies would otherwise have to coordinate and regulate at great cost.

16   To argue that families are effective or efficient as social institutions is not, however, to claim that they are necessary or inevitable. One common fallacy that some sociologists have promoted in studying the family at the societal level is the equation of its prevalence with the idea that it is functionally necessary. The assumption that societies "need" families in order to continue, based on the observation that some form of family exists in all known societies, ignores the range of variation in or the exceptions to this institution. Individuals and subgroups within all societies have constructed alternative arrangements to the traditional family of parents and their children. But the very fact that they are considered alternatives or experimental social organizations suggests how powerful the dominant family norm continues to be.

17   Another assumption that is shared across several social science disciplines is that family harmony and stability constitute the basis for order and control in the larger society. From this perspective, the family is a microcosm of the larger society, and social regulation in the domestic sphere helps promote order and control at all social levels. Individual social analysts might alternatively celebrate or lament the kind of control, regulation, and social order that was understood to begin in the family and radiate outward to the larger society; but the assumption that society was built on the foundation of the family was rarely challenged.

18   As a microcosm or a miniature society of the rulers and the ruled who are bound together by reciprocal rights and obligations, the family helps maintain social order first by its capacity to place people in the social system. It does so by providing them with identifiable kin and establishing the lines of legitimate succession and inheritance that mark their economic, political, and social position in society. Because individuals are located in an established social hierarchy by their birth or adoption into a particular family group, the nature of power and access to resources in a society remain largely intact from one generation to the next. Thus, one meaning of the family as a central institution of the social order is that it reinforces the political and economic status quo. Families ensure that the distribution of resources both to the advantaged and disadvantaged will remain relatively stable, since the transmission of wealth, property, status, and opportunity is channeled along the lines of kinship.

19   In another important way, families help to regulate the social order. Family life, according to both law and custom, prescribes roles for men, women, and children. Although these roles are really the products of social and cultural forces, rather than biological imperatives, and are therefore highly fluid in times of change, they appear

to most people to be prescribed by stable and immutable rules governing everyday life. The meaning of "traditional" family life is that people are conscripted into established roles. Everyone knows his or her place and tends to keep to it by the pressures of community norms and social sanctions. But such traditional family roles exact a toll as well. What promotes social harmony and order to the advantage of some produces severe constraints on others. Women and children, whose roles in the family have traditionally been subordinate to those of men, have sometimes resisted such prescriptive expectations and have led the charge for social change in both overt and covert ways. It is not surprising that in times of rapid social change the family has been identified as an inherently conservative institution, one that not only helps to perpetuate the status quo but is perceived as being oppressively restrictive to many of its own members.

20   Although many changes have characterized American family life over time, we should be mindful of important continuities as well. The most striking continuity is the importance that the family holds for so many people. The reasons that the family is important have varied historically, but there is no doubt that it has been a central institution, one on which people have pinned all manner of beliefs, values, and prejudices, as well as fears about and hopes for the future. Families reside at the intersection of private and public experience. We are all experts, since most of us have lived within one or more families at some point in our lives. Families can house both our highest hopes and our greatest disappointments, and their fragility or resilience therefore carries great personal meaning, in addition to social significance. The novelist Amos Oz has called the family "the most mysterious, most secret institution in the world." Its mysteries and secrets are not fully revealed in the social and historical record, but in reconstructing some of the patterns of family life, we can begin to understand why it has continued to play such a central role in American culture, as an organizing social institution, a lived experience, and a powerful metaphor. ◆

ANALYSIS AND DISCUSSION

1. Social scientists and family historians often comment that the American family is in a "state of transition." What do they mean? What is *transition*? Is it a positive or negative thing?

2. Farrell notes that in a poll on moral values, 78 percent of respondents said that they were dissatisfied with today's moral values, but that only 11 percent believed that their own behavior had contributed to this moral decline. What is your own opinion about today's moral values, and how does your own behavior fit in with these values?

3. Evaluate Farrell's opening joke about Adam and Eve. How does it connect to her material? Is it an effective means of drawing in readers and orienting them to her topic?

4. Farrell notes that Americans want their families to "offer unconditional love yet also to enforce and uphold strict moral values. They want flexibility, mobility, and autonomy . . . but yearn for traditional communities and permanently stable families" (paragraph 4). What, according to the author, is problematic with this yearning? Do you agree? Explain.

5. In her fifth paragraph, Farrell discusses our fear of social change. How does this fear of change connect to the practice of scapegoating? Identify some social scapegoats of the last century. For what were they blamed and why? Who represents "the forces of the new" today?

6. Farrell comments that our social concern for "The Family" is rooted in the "metaphor evoked by family" (paragraph 7). What does she mean? How does she define *family* in this paragraph, and how does this definition connect to our social concerns about the decay of the family in general? Explain.

7. How do we construct the institution of the family? What cultural myths and social forces contribute to our construction of this institution? How does nostalgia influence our view? Explain.

8. According to Farrell, what assumptions about family span many academic disciplines, such as anthropology, sociology, history, and psychology? How do these assumptions form the basis for the theoretical approaches of these disciplines? Explain.

9. How do families "help to regulate the social order" (paragraph 19)? How can this regulation "exact a toll" on certain members of society? Do you agree or disagree with Farrell's assessment? Explain.

RESEARCH AND WRITING

1. At the end of her essay, Farrell quotes novelist Amos Oz, who calls the family "the most mysterious, most secret institution in the world." Write an essay in which you explore this idea. How is the family "secret"? If almost everyone has a family and understands what the term implies, how can it be "mysterious"? Support your position with information from Farrell's article as well as your own personal perspective.

2. If you are a practicing member of an organized religious faith, research your religion's beliefs about family. If you are not a member of an organized religion, select one to research. Be sure to include references from news sources, journals, theologians, religious texts, and spiritual leaders of the faith. If possible, interview a religious leader for a summary of beliefs. Write an essay in which you describe the position the religious faith has on family and how these beliefs are "institutionalized" in the religion.

3. In a letter to a politician or public figure of your choice, discuss the current state of the family as it applies to the concept of family as an institution in American culture. In your letter, you should make specific references to the politician's own stance on the state of the family.

4. Design and administer a poll to people outside your class. Ask for opinions on the health of the American family versus its decline, the ideal role each family member should play in family structure, the desirability of day care, and so on. Also ask for anonymous information about each participant's age, economic status, education, political affiliation, religion, and race. After you have assembled the data you collected as a group, analyze the results. Do any groups seem more or less optimistic about the state of the American family? If so, in what ways? Are some groups more traditional? Explain.

CULTURE SHOCK

Marriage Trends in the United States

Several authors in this section note that marriage is on the decline in the United States. This graph below, based on 2004–2005 U.S. Census data, provides a detailed look at the numbers.

Percentage of All Persons Age 15 and Older Who Were Married, by Sex and Race, 1960–2005 United States[a]

	Males			Females		
	Total	Black	White	Total	Black	White
1960	69.3	60.9	70.2	65.9	59.8	66.6
1970	66.7	56.9	68.0	61.9	54.1	62.8
1980	63.2	48.8	65.0	58.9	44.6	60.7
1990	60.7	45.1	62.8	56.9	40.2	59.1
2000	57.9	42.8	60.0	54.7	36.2	57.4
2005[b]	55.0	37.9	57.5	51.5	30.2	54.6
2007	54.7	38.5	56.9	51.2	30.0	54.3

[a] Includes races other than black and white

[b] In 2003, the U.S. Census Bureau expanded its racial categories to permit respondents to identify themselves as belonging to more than one race. This means that racial data computations beginning in 2004 may not be strictly comparable to those of prior years.

Source: U.S. Bureau of the Census. Current Population Reports, Series P20–506; *America's Families and Living Arrangements: March 2000* and earlier reports; and data calculated from the Current Population Surveys, March 2005 Supplement

THINKING CRITICALLY

1. Is marriage an archaic institution, no longer practically functional in today's society?
2. What cultural factors could have influenced the numbers in this table? For example, do you think women's improved economic role outside the home has influenced their feelings about marriage? Could the social acceptance of divorce have influenced these numbers? Explain.
3. Are you more optimistic or less optimistic about the prospect of marriage after viewing this graph? Explain.
4. In your opinion, what is the long-term outlook for marriage? How do you fit into the outlook shown in the table?
5. If you could live together with a partner and enjoy the same benefits afforded to married couples, such as health insurance, inheritance rights, and retirement benefits, would you still get married? Why?
6. What cultural and social trends can you infer influenced the data in the table? Explain. If you were a social scientist, what predictions might you be able to make based on the data provided?

On Not Saying "I Do"
Dorian Solot*

Several of the essays in this chapter lament the decline of marriage as an inevitable—and regrettable—reality. The author of the next reading argues that marriage isn't all it is cracked up to be. In fact, people can exist in meaningful and rewarding relationships without marriage, and children can grow up in nurturing and emotionally stable homes. In this essay, a personal narrative, Dorian Solot wonders why such a fuss is made about getting married.

1   I must have missed the day in nursery school when they lined up all the little girls and injected them with the powerful serum that made them dream of wearing a white wedding dress.

2   From that day onward, it seemed, most little girls played bridal dress-up, drew pictures of brides, gazed in magazines at the latest bridal fashions, and eagerly anticipated their Prince Charming popping the question. More than anything, they dreamed of walking down the aisle and living happily ever after. I dreamed mostly of the cats, dogs, and horses I'd get to adopt when I grew up. When I was old enough to walk around town on my own, I remember my best friend stopping in front of a bridal shop window to point out which dress she'd like to wear someday, and she asked me to pick mine. I told her honestly that I didn't like any of them, aware even then that she would probably think I was weird, because that wasn't what girls were supposed to say.

3   In my early twenties, about three years into my relationship with my partner, Marshall, the occasional subtle hints that my family and friends were ready for an engagement announcement became decidedly less subtle. To keep their hopes in check, I announced what had seemed clear to me for a long time: I did not intend to get married. Ever. Be in love, sure. Share my life with this wonderful man, absolutely. But walk down the aisle and exchange rings—the tradition baffles me.

4   I didn't expect my small refusal to matter much to anyone. But I have quickly learned that in a society in which 90 percent of people get married sometime in their lives, lacking the desire to do so appears in the "barely acceptable" category.

5   Not being married to my partner has meant ending the conversation with a potential landlord after his first three questions: How many people? Are you married? When are you getting married? It's meant paying an extra fee—the unmarried surcharge, you might call it—to be allowed to drive the same rental car. And it's meant having my partner be denied health insurance through my job when he needed it, even though our four years together exceeded the relationship length of my newlywed coworkers who received joint coverage.

6   It's also meant answering questions that get frustrating. "Do you think you'll change your mind?" is a common one. I want to ask these people, "Do you think you might convert to a new religion? Do you think you might change your mind about

---

* Dorian Solot, *Nerve.com,* May 27, 2004

the ethics of abortion?" Anything is possible, of course, and I'm not so naïve as to think we all don't change our minds about things over the course of a lifetime. But the frequency with which I'm asked this question makes it less an innocent inquiry about a personal choice and more a suggestion that says, "Your position is so absurd you can't take it seriously for long."

7   I've lost track of the number of sympathetic strangers who've shared with me their incorrect assumption that as an unmarried woman in a long-term relationship, my partner must suffer from a severe case of commitment phobia. Women in newspaper advice columns and television talk

> *I've lost track of the number of sympathetic strangers who've shared with me their incorrect assumption that as an unmarried woman in a long-term relationship, my partner must suffer from a severe case of commitment phobia.*

shows are forever strategizing about where to find a man willing to get hitched and debating whether to leave the guys who won't marry them. Interestingly, though, every survey ever conducted on this subject finds that on average, men are more eager to marry than women are. The National Survey of Families and Households, for example, found that 24 percent of unmarried 18–35 year old men said they'd like to get married someday, compared to 16 percent of unmarried women the same age.

8   Eventually, frustrated that we couldn't find any group that could provide the support and information we needed, Marshall and I founded the Alternatives to Marriage Project. Judging by the number of emails and phone calls we received after posting a Web site, we weren't alone. There are growing legions of women who, like me, are not interested in assuming the role of wife. Books like *Marriage Shock: The Transformation of Women into Wives* and *Cutting Loose: Why Women Who End Their Marriages Do So Well* quote scores of women who explain how their relationships changed when they got married. Suddenly, they found themselves more likely to be making breakfast and less likely to be talking candidly about sex. As a result of this kind of research, some made the case for more conscious marriages with fewer gendered assumptions, and I think that's a great goal. But if marriage has that much power to change people's behavior, I'd rather invest my energy exploring alternatives, not struggling to reshape an institution that doesn't suit me.

9   To me, the issue isn't whether civil marriage should include same-sex couples. Of course it should; that's a fundamental matter of civil and human rights. The issue is the confusing tangle of meanings in the word "marriage," and how they do and don't correspond to real-life relationships and real people's lives. There's religious marriage, conferred by blessings; civil marriage and the legal protections it brings; and social marriage, the support of communities who give special treatment to couples they perceive to be married. (Having just bought a house in a neighborhood where no one knew us before, it's been fascinating to be treated as a married couple, even though our "marriage" is social, not legal.) On top of that, although the concepts of commitment, monogamy, and marriage usually go hand in hand, my work is filled with committed unmarried couples. And we've all read the tabloid headlines about married ones whose commitments don't last all that long. Among both married and unmarried couples, the vast majority chooses monogamy, while smaller numbers

choose polyamory or engage in infidelity. We have only one concept—marriage—that is used to divide the world neatly into two groups, married and not married. The real world is a lot messier than that. Our cultural inability to face that complexity leaves us in a state of collective bafflement about the status and future of marriage (Is marriage overvalued? Undervalued? Having a renaissance? Dying out?) and inspires confused debates about same-sex unions. The solution, I believe, is to encourage and support healthy, stable relationships and families in all their forms, instead of linking so many unrelated benefits to the piece of paper we call a marriage license.

10   There are joys to not being married. I love that I am not a wife, with all its hidden meanings and baggage. I love the consciousness of my relationship, day after day of "I choose you" that has now lasted 11 years and counting. I take secret pleasure in watching people wrestle silently when I mention "my partner," trying to ascertain my sexual orientation and marital status—as if it mattered. I love reading the headlines as one by one, companies, universities, cities, and states decide to provide equal benefits to the partners of their employees, regardless of marital status. I feel as if my daily life proves to those who say it can't be done—that unmarried relationships will fall apart when times are hard, that we can never achieve true intimacy, that we are doomed to lives of sin, sadness, or "perpetual adolescence"—that maybe the problem is theirs and not mine. There is an amazing diversity of families in this country; I hope one day society will be courageous enough to recognize and validate all of them.

11   I don't know how I failed to acquire a yearning for marriage. Maybe it's because of my feminist, hippie mom, who played *Free to Be You and Me* while I was in utero and encouraged me to have goals beyond marrying the handsome prince (and who, by the way, considers my handsome prince her son-in-law—or sometimes, affectionately, her son-outlaw). Perhaps it has to do with too many unhappily married people and the divorces I've seen, too many breezily pledged lifetime vows that lose their meaning long before the lifetimes end. Perhaps it has to do with my friends in same-sex relationships who can't legally marry (unless they live in the right city or state on the right day of the week), the fact that I already have a food processor, or my academic background in animal behavior, where I learned how few mammals mate for life. Or perhaps it's because I really was absent that day in nursery school. ◆

CRITICAL THINKING

1. If you decided to live with your significant other, do you think you would feel social pressure to marry after a period of cohabitation? Would your family approve? What are your personal expectations of cohabitation? Explain.
2. The author notes that although living together for a period of time is considered socially acceptable, deciding to maintain such an arrangement with no intention of ever marrying is not. What accounts for this view? If it is okay to live together, why isn't it okay never to get married?
3. Solot jokes that she missed the day the little girls were "injected with serum" that makes them obsessed with being brides and getting married. What does she mean? Explain.

4. What is the reaction of friends and family to Solot's decision not to marry? Do you agree that her decision appears in the "barely acceptable" category?

5. Why did the author decide not to get married? What are the benefits she cites about not being married?

CRITICAL WRITING

1. *Expository Writing:* Solot observes that many people live together before getting married. In your opinion, does this arrangement make sense? Is it better to test out a relationship before making a marriage commitment, or does it just make it easier for people to walk away from a relationship when the going gets tough? Would you live together with a sweetheart before making a commitment of marriage? Explain.

2. *Reader's Response:* Before you read this narrative, did you have any opinion on this issue? Did the essay change your ideas or give you something to think about that you had not considered before? Was Solot successful in persuading you to her point of view, if you did not already agree with it?

GROUP PROJECTS

1. Using free association and writing down anything that comes to mind, brainstorm with your group to develop a list of terms associated with the phrase *living together*. The list could include anything from "noncommitment" to "independent." Once you have developed a list, try to locate the source of the association, such as television, opinion editorials, government, political speeches, religion, and news media. Which sources are grounded in fact and which are not? What role does changing social opinion have on these associations? Explain.

2. Visit the Frontline Web site "Let's Get Married" at http://www.pbs.org/wgbh/pages/frontline/shows/marriage/etc/quiz.html and take the online quiz as a group. Have one person write down your responses before submitting the quiz for scoring. Review your score. Did any of the statistics surprise you? As a class, discuss your results.

For Better, For Worse
Stephanie Coontz*

As Betty G. Farrell explained in the first essay in this chapter, many Americans feel that the family and marriage in general are in a state of decline. Underlying this feeling is a sense of the loss of "traditional family values" that have contributed to the decay of marriage. How

* Stephanie Coontz, *Washington Post,* May 1, 2005

much of this belief is rooted in fact and how much is hype? Stephanie Coontz maintains that the problem is that we long for a social construction based on a false memory rather than fact. Culturally, we cannot "go back," and Coontz wonders why we would even want to.

1 [Y]ears ago, Vice President Dan Quayle attacked the producers of TV sitcom *Murphy Brown* for letting her character bear a child out of wedlock, claiming that the show's failure to defend traditional family values was encouraging America's youth to abandon marriage. His speech kicked off more than a decade of outcries against the "collapse of the family." Today, such attacks have given way to a kinder, gentler campaign to promote marriage, with billboards declaring that "Marriage Works" and books making "the case for marriage." What these campaigns have in common is the idea that people are willfully refusing to recognize the value of traditional families and that their behavior will change if we can just enlighten them.

2 But recent changes in marriage are part of a worldwide upheaval in family life that has transformed the way people conduct their personal lives as thoroughly and permanently as the Industrial Revolution transformed their working lives 200 years ago. Marriage is no longer the main way in which societies regulate sexuality and parenting or organize the division of labor between men and women. And although some people hope to turn back the tide by promoting traditional values, making divorce harder, or outlawing gay marriage, they are having to confront a startling irony: The very factors that have made marriage more satisfying in modern times have also made it more optional.

3 The origins of modern marital instability lie largely in the triumph of what many people believe to be marriage's traditional role—providing love, intimacy, fidelity, and mutual fulfillment. The truth is that for centuries, marriage was stable precisely because it was not expected to provide such benefits. As soon as love became the driving force behind marriage, people began to demand the right to remain single if they had not found love or to divorce if they fell out of love.

4 Such demands were raised as early as the 1790s, which prompted conservatives to predict that love would be the death of marriage. For the next 150 years, the inherently destabilizing effects of the love revolution were held in check by women's economic dependence on men, the unreliability of birth control, and the harsh legal treatment of children born out of wedlock, as well as the social ostracism of their mothers. As late as the 1960s, two-thirds of college women in the United States said they would marry a man they didn't love if he met all their other, often economic, criteria. Men also felt compelled to marry if they hoped for promotions at work or for political credibility.

5 All these restraints on individual choice collapsed between 1960 and 1980. Divorce rates had long been rising in Western Europe and the United States, and although they had leveled off following World War II, they climbed at an unprecedented rate in the 1970s, leading some to believe that the introduction of no-fault divorce laws, which meant married couples could divorce if they simply fell out of love, had caused the erosion of marriage.

6 The so-called divorce revolution, however, is just one aspect of the worldwide transformation of marriage. In places where divorce and unwed motherhood are

severely stigmatized, the retreat from marriage simply takes another form. In Japan and Italy, for example, women are far more likely to remain single than in the United States. In Thailand, unmarried women now compete for the title of "Miss Spinster Thailand." Singapore's strait-laced government has resorted to sponsoring singles nights in an attempt to raise marriage rates and reverse the birth strike by women.

7   In the United States and Britain, divorce rates fell slightly during the 1990s, but the incidence of cohabitation and unmarried child raising continues to rise, as does the percentage of singles in the population.

8   Both trends reduce the social significance of marriage in the economy and culture. The norms and laws that tradition-

Although some people hope to turn back the tide by promoting traditional values, making divorce harder, or outlawing gay marriage, they are having to confront a startling irony: The very factors that have made marriage more satisfying in modern times have also made it more optional.

ally penalized unwed mothers and their children have weakened or been overturned, ending centuries of injustice but further reducing marriage's role in determining the course of people's lives. Today, 40 percent of cohabiting couples in the United States have children in the household, almost as high a proportion as the 45 percent of married couples who have kids, according to the 2000 Census. We don't have a TV show about that yet, but it's just a matter of time.

9   The entry of women into the workforce in the last third of the twentieth century was not only a U.S. phenomenon. By the 1970s, women in America and most of Europe could support themselves if they needed to. The 1980s saw an international increase in unmarried women having babies (paving the way for Murphy Brown), as more people gained the ability to say no to shotgun marriages, and humanitarian reforms lowered the penalties for out-of-wedlock births. That decade also saw a big increase in couples living together before marriage.

10   Almost everywhere, women's greater participation in education has raised the marriage age and the incidence of nonmarriage. Even in places where women's lives are still largely organized through marriage, fertility rates have been cut in half and more wives and mothers work outside the home.

11   From Turkey to South Africa to Brazil, countries are having to codify the legal rights and obligations of single individuals and unmarried couples raising children, including same-sex couples. Canada and the Netherlands have joined Scandinavia in legalizing same-sex marriage, and such bastions of tradition as Taiwan and Spain are considering following suit.

12   None of this means that marriage is dead. Indeed, most people have a higher regard for the marital relationship today than when marriage was practically mandatory. Marriage as a private relationship between two individuals is taken more seriously and comes with higher emotional expectations than ever before in history.

13   But marriage as a public institution exerts less power over people's lives now that the majority of Americans spend half their adult lives outside marriage and almost half of all kids spend part of their childhood in a household that does not

include their two married biological parents. And unlike in the past, marriage or lack of marriage does not determine people's political and economic rights.

14   Under these conditions, it is hard to believe that we could revive the primacy of marriage by promoting traditional values. People may revere the value of universal marriage in the abstract, but most have adjusted to a different reality. The late Pope John Paul II was enormously respected for his teaching about sex and marriage. Yet during his tenure, premarital sex, contraception use, and divorce continued to rise in almost all countries. In the United States, the Bible Belt has the highest divorce rate in the nation. And although many American teens pledged abstinence during the 1990s, 88 percent ended up breaking that pledge, according to the National Longitudinal Study of Adolescent Youth that was released in March.

15   Although many Americans bemoan the easy accessibility of divorce, few are willing to waive their personal rights. In American states where "covenant" marriage laws allow people to sign away their right to a no-fault divorce, fewer than three percent of couples choose that option. Divorce rates climbed by the same percentage in states that did not allow no-fault divorce as in states that did. By 2000, Belgium, which had not yet adopted no-fault divorce, had the highest divorce rates in Europe outside of Finland and Sweden.

16   Nor does a solution lie in preaching the benefits of marriage to impoverished couples or outlawing unconventional partnerships. A poor single mother often has good reason not to marry her child's father, and poor couples who do wed have more than twice the divorce risk of more affluent partners in the United States. Banning same-sex marriage would not undo the existence of alternatives to traditional marriage. Five million children are being raised by gay and lesbian couples in this country. Judges everywhere are being forced to apply many principles of marriage law to those families, if only to regulate child custody should the couple part ways.

17   We may personally like or dislike these changes. We may wish to keep some and get rid of others. But there is a certain inevitability to almost all of them.

18   Marriage is no longer the institution where people are initiated into sex. It no longer determines the work men and women do on the job or at home, regulates who has children and who doesn't, or coordinates caregiving for the ill or the aged. For better or worse, marriage has been displaced from its pivotal position in personal and social life and will not regain it short of a Taliban-like counterrevolution.

19   Forget the fantasy of solving the challenges of modern personal life by re-institutionalizing marriage. In today's climate of choice, many people's choices do not involve marriage. We must recognize that there are healthy as well as unhealthy ways to be single or to be divorced, just as there are healthy and unhealthy ways to be married. We cannot afford to construct our social policies, our advice to our own children, and even our own emotional expectations around the illusion that all commitments, sexual activities, and caregiving will take place in a traditional marriage. That series has been canceled. ◆

CRITICAL THINKING

1. Is marriage in danger of becoming an obsolete institution? Why do people marry today?

2. Is marriage a goal for you in your life plan? Why or why not?
3. Coontz's opening paragraph begins with a reference to Dan Quayle and the television sitcom *Murphy Brown*. Why does Coontz start her essay this way? How does this example set up the points she makes in her essay?
4. What, according to Coontz, has contributed to the erosion of marriage?
5. Coontz states, "For better or worse, marriage has been displaced from its pivotal position in personal and social life and will not regain it short of a Taliban-like counterrevolution." Respond to this statement in your own words. Do you agree with her? Is it a generalization or a statement based largely on social fact? Explain.
6. Evaluate Coontz's use of statistics and facts. Do they support her points? Are they relevant to her thesis? Based on these facts, do you find yourself swayed by her argument? Why or why not?
7. Based on her essay, summarize Coontz's view of marriage. Cite specific areas of the text to support your summary.

CRITICAL WRITING

1. *Personal Narrative:* Write a personal narrative in which you describe the structure of your family during your childhood, focusing specifically on the role of marriage in your family. Were your parents married? Divorced? If you could have changed anything about your parents' marital relationship, what would it have been?
2. *Exploratory Writing:* Coontz notes that as people began to view marriage as more about love and intimacy, the divorce rate soared. Is marriage about love? Is it about family? Children? If a couple has children, but find that they no longer feel the marriage is a loving one, should they stay together anyway? Write an essay in which you describe what you think marriage is and what grounds individuals have to terminate it.

GROUP PROJECTS

1. As a group, make a list of the benefits of marriage Coontz cites in her essay. (Make sure you review the entire essay when compiling this list.) Discuss the list in terms of your own personal experience and perspective. Based on the list, decide whether marriage needs to be made more of a political priority.
2. Coontz asserts that "marriage has been displaced from its pivotal position in personal and social life." Working in small groups, discuss and compare the structure of family and the role of marriage within your own experiences. Think about the family you grew up in, families you have known, and the families you may have started. What marital structures do these families have? Compare your observations with Coontz's statement.

Five Non-Religious Arguments for Marriage

*Dennis Prager**

With the long list of celebrities living together and having children out of wedlock, coupled with a divorce rate at almost 50 percent, it would seem as if marriage is becoming passé. All across the economic spectrum, many couples prefer to live together rather than get married, at least for a while. In the next essay, author Dennis Prager gives five reasons why he thinks marriage is preferable to living together.

1 I have always believed that there is no comparing living together with marriage. There are enormous differences between being a "husband" or a "wife" and being a "partner," a "friend," or a "significant other"; between a legal commitment and a voluntary association; between standing before family and community to publicly announce one's commitment to another person on the one hand and simply living together on the other.

2 But attending the weddings of two of my three children this past summer made the differences far clearer and far more significant.

3 First, no matter what you think when living together, your relationship with your significant other changes the moment you marry. You have now made a commitment to each other as husband and wife in front of almost everyone significant in your life. You now see each other in a different and more serious light.

4 Second, words matter. They deeply affect us and others. Living with your "boyfriend" is not the same as living with your "husband." And living with your "girlfriend," or any other title you give her, is not the same as making a home with your "wife." Likewise, when you introduce that person as your wife or husband to people, you are making a far more important statement of that person's role in your life than you are with any other title.

5 Third, legality matters. Being legally bound to and responsible for another person matters. It is an announcement to him/her and to yourself that you take this relationship with the utmost seriousness. No words of affection or promises of commitment, no matter how sincere, can match the seriousness of legal commitment. Fourth, to better appreciate just how important marriage is to the vast majority of people in your life, consider this: There is no event, no occasion, no moment in your life when so many of the people who matter to you will convene in one place as they will at your wedding. Not the birth of any of your children, not any milestone birthday you may celebrate, not your child's bar-mitzvah or confirmation. The only other time so many of those you care about and who care about you will gather in one place is at your funeral. But by then, unless you die young, nearly all those you love who are older than you will have already died.

6 So this is it. Your wedding will be the greatest gathering of loved ones in your life. There is a reason. It is the biggest moment of your life. No such event will

* Dennis Prager, *TownHall.com,* October 3, 2006

ever happen if you do not have a wedding. Fifth, only with marriage will your man's or your woman's family ever become your family. The two weddings transformed the woman in my son's life into my daughter-in-law and transformed the man in my daughter's life into my son-in-law. And I was instantly transformed from the father of their boyfriend or girlfriend into their father-in-law. This was the most dramatic new realization for me.

> *If in fact "it is only a piece of paper," what exactly is he so afraid of? Why does he fear a mere piece of paper? Either he is lying to himself and to his woman or lying only to her, because he knows this piece of paper is far more than "only a piece of paper."*

7   I was now related to my children's partners. Their siblings and parents became family. Nothing comparable happens when two people live together without getting married. Many women callers to my radio show have told me that the man in their life sees no reason to marry. "It's only a piece of paper," these men (and now some women) argue.

8   There are two answers to this argument. One is that if in fact "it is only a piece of paper," what exactly is he so afraid of? Why does he fear a mere piece of paper? Either he is lying to himself and to his woman or lying only to her, because he knows this piece of paper is far more than "only a piece of paper."

9   The other response is all that is written above. Getting married means I am now your wife, not your live-in; I am now your husband, not your significant other. It means that we get to have a wedding where, before virtually every person alive who means anything to us, we commit ourselves to each other. It means that we have decided to bring all these people we love into our lives. It means we have legal obligations to one another. It means my family becomes yours and yours becomes mine.

10   Thank God my children, ages 30 and 23, decided to marry. Their partners are now my daughter-in-law and son-in-law. They are therefore now mine to love, not merely two people whom my children love. When you realize all that is attainable by marrying and unattainable by living together without marrying, you have to wonder why anyone would voluntarily choose not to marry the person he or she wishes to live with forever.

11   Unless, of course, one of you really isn't planning on forever. ◆

CRITICAL THINKING

1.   Many couples move in together without being married first but eventually marry later. Others never marry. Do you think people should live together before getting married? Should they marry at all? Why or why not?

2.   Why do people marry? What values and expectations does marriage carry in our culture? Are the values and expectations the same for couples who live together? Why or why not?

3.   Review Prager's second point, "words matter." What importance does he place on words? What words does he mean?

4. According to Prager, when one partner tells the other that marriage "is only a piece of paper," she or he is either lying or doesn't truly believe that the relationship is in fact forever. Do you agree with this assertion? Why does Prager feel it is a false argument against the importance of marriage?
5. In your opinion, which of Prager's five arguments is the strongest one? Which is the weakest? Explain.
6. Even though Prager is personally opposed to gay marriage, could his essay make an argument for legalizing gay marriage? Explain.

CRITICAL WRITING

1. *Persuasive Writing:* Argue the opposite viewpoint; in other words, provide five arguments for living together over getting married.
2. *Expository Writing:* If living together with a partner provided the same legal benefits afforded to traditionally married couples—such as health insurance, inheritance rights, and retirement benefits—would you still get married?
3. *Reader's Response:* Before you read this editorial, did you have any opinion on this issue? Did the essay change your ideas or give you something to think about that you had not considered before? If you did not already agree with him, was Prager successful in persuading you to his point of view?

GROUP PROJECTS

1. With your group, research the state of marriage in the United States today. Then in your own words, define what marriage is. You will have to discuss this as a group to come up with a definition that works for the majority. How easy or difficult was it to arrive at a definition that satisfied everyone?
2. Among the members of your group, describe the structure of your family during your childhood, focusing specifically on the role of marriage in your family. Were your parents married or divorced? Do you think the choices they made affected your outlook on marriage? Did they affect your life in general? How has your past experience influenced your future expectations of family life? Do you think the expectations of college students today about marriage and family differ from those of your parent's generation? Why or why not?

Perspectives: The New American Family

www.CartoonStock.com

"This is our daughter, my son from my first marriage, John's daughter from his second marriage, and I've no idea who the one on the end is."

THINKING CRITICALLY

1. What is happening in this cartoon? Who are the people in the picture, and what are they discussing?
2. What social or cultural situation does this cartoon depict? Can you relate? Explain.
3. What unique challenges do children of blended families face? Explain.

Why Gay Marriage Is Good for Straight America

*Andrew Sullivan**

Much of the debate about same-sex marriage hinges on how we define marriage itself—is it a partnership between two loving, consenting adults or a sanctified or legal union between a man and a woman? Many arguments supporting gay marriage focus on the issue of love: if two people love each other, goes the argument, they should be allowed to marry. Opponents to this view contend that marriage is more than about love: it has traditionally been a legal and social bond between a man and a woman, foremost to support the upbringing of children. To redefine this definition of marriage would be to undermine the institution itself and threaten the family. Should same-sex couples be afforded the legal right to marry? As state after state legally sanctions the practice, it would seem as if the country is leaning toward "yes." A longtime advocate for gay marriage, journalist Andrew Sullivan reflects on his own life, love, and pursuit of happiness—and why gay marriage is good for everyone.

1   As a child, when I thought of the future, all I could see was black. I wasn't miserable or depressed. I was a cheerful boy, as happy playing with my posse of male friends in elementary school as I was when I would occasionally take a day by myself in the woodlands that surrounded the small town I grew up in. But when I thought of the distant future, of what I would do and be as a grown-up, there was a blank. I simply didn't know how I would live, where I would live, who I could live with. I knew one thing only: I couldn't be like my dad. For some reason, I knew somewhere deep down that I couldn't have a marriage like my parents.

2   It's hard to convey what that feeling does to a child. In retrospect, it was a sharp, displacing wound to the psyche. At the very moment you become aware of sex and emotion, you simultaneously know that for you, there is no future coupling, no future family, no future home. In the future, I would be suddenly exiled from what I knew: my family, my friends, every household on television, every end to every romantic movie I'd ever seen. My grandmother crystallized it in classic and slightly cruel English fashion: "You're not the marrying kind," she said. It was one of those things that struck a chord of such pain, my pride forced me to embrace it. "No, I'm not," I replied. "I like my freedom."

3   This wasn't a lie. But it was a dodge, and I knew it. And when puberty struck and I realized I might be "one of them," I turned inward. It was a strange feeling—both the exhilaration of sexual desire and the simultaneous, soul-splintering panic that I was going to have to live alone my whole life, lying or euphemizing, concocting some public veneer to hide a private shame. It was like getting into an elevator you were expecting to go up, the doors closing, and then suddenly realizing you were headed down a few stories. And this was when the future went black for me,

---

* Andrew Sullivan, *The Daily Beast*, July 18, 2011

when suicide very occasionally entered my mind, when my only legitimate passion was getting A grades, because at that point it was all I knew how to do. I stayed away from parties; I didn't learn to drive; I lost contact with those friends whose interest suddenly became girls; and somewhere in me, something began to die.

4   They call it the happiest day of your life for a reason. Getting married is often the hinge on which every family generation swings open. In my small-town life, it was far more important than money or a career or fame. And I could see my grandmother's point: the very lack of any dating or interest in it, the absence of any intimate relationships, or of any normal teenage behavior, did indeed make me seem just a classic loner. But I wasn't. Because nobody is. "In everyone there sleeps/A sense of life lived according to love," as the poet Philip Larkin put it, as well as the fear of never being loved. That, as Larkin added, nothing cures. And I felt, for a time, incurable.

5   You can have as many debates about gay marriage as you want, and over the last 22 years of campaigning for it, I've had my share. You can debate theology, and the divide between church and state, the issue of procreation, the red herring of polygamy, and on and on. But what it all really comes down to is the primary institution of love. The small percentage of people who are gay or lesbian were born, as all humans are, with the capacity to love and the need to be loved. These things, above everything, are what make life worth living. And unlike every other minority, almost all of us grew up among and part of the majority, in families where the highest form of that love was between our parents in marriage. To feel you will never know that, never feel that, is to experience a deep psychic wound that takes years to recover from. It is to become psychologically homeless. Which is why, I think, the concept of "coming out" is not quite right. It should really be called "coming home."

6   In the end, I had to abandon my home in order to find it again and know the place for the first time. I left England just after my 21st birthday for America and its simple foundational promise: the pursuit of happiness. And I gave myself permission to pursue it. I will never forget the moment I first kissed another man; it was as if a black-and-white movie suddenly turned into color. I will never forget the first time I slept next to another man—or rather tried to sleep. Never for a moment did I actually feel or truly believe any of this was wrong, let alone an "intrinsic evil," as my strict Catholicism told me that it was. It was so natural, so spontaneous, so joyous, it could no more be wrong than breathing. And as I experienced intimacy and love for the first time as an adult, all that brittleness of the gay adolescent, all that white-knuckled embarrassment, all those ruses and excuses and dark, deep depressions lifted. Yes, this was happiness. And America for me will always represent it.

7   And that is why marriage equality is, to my mind, the distillation of America. If you're a heterosexual reading this, have you ever considered for a millisecond that your right to pursue happiness did not include your right to marry the person you love? And that is why, over the centuries, the U.S. Supreme Court has upheld the right to marry for everyone, citizen or even traveler, as a core, inalienable right, bestowed by the Declaration of Independence itself. The court has ruled that the right to marry precedes the Bill of Rights; it has decided that prisoners on death row have a right to marry, even if they can never consummate it. It has ruled that no limitations may be put on it for anyone—deadbeat dads, multiple divorcées, felons, noncitizens.

Hannah Arendt wrote in 1959 that "the right to marry whoever one wishes is an elementary human right ... Even political rights, like the right to vote, and nearly all other rights enumerated in the Constitution, are secondary to the inalienable human rights to 'life, liberty and the pursuit of happiness' proclaimed in the Declaration of Independence; and to this category the right to home and marriage unquestionably belongs." And, of course, after a long struggle, interracial marriage was finally declared a constitutional right, in perhaps the most sweeping ruling ever, with the court declaring that civil marriage was one of the "basic civil rights of man, fundamental to our very existence and survival." Barack Obama is a historic American figure not because he is black, but because he is the son of a black father and a white mother. He is the living embodiment of the pursuit of happiness that marriage represented.

8   I still didn't think it would ever happen to me. I thought I was too emotionally damaged, my emotions and sexuality severed by all those years of loneliness and arrested emotional development. I thought my heart had too much scar tissue, and I could live my life well enough with just friendship and occasional sexual encounters or dates. But when I first set eyes on my husband, I knew I had lucked out. Some things you simply know. And when we finally got married, a few years later, and our mothers walked us down the makeshift garden aisle, and my sister gave the reading through tears, and one of our beagles howled through the vows, and my father put his arms around me and hugged, I did not hear civilization crumble. I felt a wound being healed. It is a rare privilege to spend your adult life fighting for a right that was first dismissed as a joke, only finally to achieve it in six states and Washington, D.C. But how much rarer to actually stumble upon someone who could make it a reality. And to have it happen to me in my own lifetime! This joy is compounded, deepened, solidified by the knowledge that somewhere, someone just like I was as a kid will be able to look to the future now and not see darkness—but the possibility of love and home. That, I realized, was really what I had been fighting for for two decades: to heal the child I had once been—and the countless children in the present and future whose future deserved, needed, begged for a model of commitment and responsibility and love.

9   And that is why it has been such a tragedy that conservatives decided this was a battle they were determined to fight against, an advance they were dedicated to reversing. It made no sense to me. Here was a minority asking for responsibility and commitment and integration. And conservatives were determined to keep them in isolation, stigmatized and kept on an embarrassing, unmentionable margin, where gays could be used to buttress the primacy of heterosexuality. We were for them merely a drop shadow for heterosexuality. What they could not see was that the conservative tradition of reform and inclusion, of social change through existing institutions, of the family and personal responsibility, all led inexorably toward civil marriage for gays.

10   Yes, the main stumbling block was religion. But we were not talking of religious marriage and were more than eager to insist, as in New York state, on the inviolable religious freedom of churches, mosques, and synagogues to retain their bans on gay marriage. We were talking about civil marriage—and in that respect, religious tradition had long since ceased to apply. Civil divorce changed marriage far more drastically for far more people than allowing the small percentage who were excluded to be included. And no one doubted an atheist's right to marry, outside

of any church or any religion, just as no one doubted the marriages of childless couples, or infertile ones. In fact, every single argument against marriage equality for gays collapsed upon inspection. And when the data showed that in the era of gay marriage, straight marriage had actually strengthened somewhat, divorce rates had declined, and marriages lasted longer, even those who worried about unintended consequences conceded that the argument was essentially over. And that is why it remains so appropriate that George W. Bush's solicitor general, Ted Olson, would lead the legal fight against Proposition 8 in California; that a Reagan-appointed judge, Anthony Kennedy, would be the foremost Supreme Court justice affirming gay and lesbian equality; and that in Albany, in the end, the winning votes came from Republicans who voted their conscience.

11   Of course this is new and not so new. For a long time, gays and lesbians braver than I was were effectively married and lived together, risking violence and opprobrium and isolation. For decades these bonds existed, and we knew of them even if we never spoke of them. I saw them up close as a young man in the darkest years of the AIDS plague. I saw spouses holding their dying husbands, cradling them at the hour of their death, inserting catheters, cleaning broken bodies, tending to terrified souls. This proved beyond any doubt for me that gay couples were as capable of as much love and tenacity and tenderness and fidelity as heterosexual couples. And when I heard their bonds denigrated or demonized, dismissed or belittled, the sadness became a kind of spur. For so long, so much pain. For so many, so much grief compounded by stigma. But we did not just survive the plague. We used it to forge a new future. And in the years of struggle, as more and more heterosexuals joined us, we all began finally to see that this was not really about being gay. It was about being human.

12   Just like being gay is no longer necessarily about being an outsider. It is about being an American. ◆

CRITICAL THINKING

1. In your opinion, should same-sex couples be permitted to legally marry? Are you likely to be swayed by hearing different points of view on the subject? Why or why not?

2. Identify the primary points of argument Sullivan uses to support his case that gay marriage makes marriage overall a stronger institution.

3. According to Sullivan, why do homosexual couples want to marry? What motivates them? Do heterosexual couples marry for the same reasons as gay couples?

4. What does Sullivan mean when he refers to the "red herring of polygamy"? What arguments have been made against same-sex marriage and how are they dismantled?

5. Sullivan laments that marriage conservatives often cite religious reasons for being against same-sex marriage. Why does he feel such arguments against same-sex marriage are invalid on religious grounds? Explain.

6. What emotional and psychological toll is taken on gay men and women when they are denied the right to marriage? Explain.

7. Much of Sullivan's argument is based on his own perspective, feelings, and experiences. In your opinion, does this recounting of his personal history support or detract from his argument? Explain.

CRITICAL WRITING

1. *Persuasive Writing:* Write a letter to a minister, rabbi, or other religious leader. Explain why you think he or she should agree to perform a marriage ceremony celebrating the commitment of two of your best friends— a gay couple. Refer to comments made by other authors in this section as support for your case. Alternatively, you may write a letter arguing against such a marriage. Assume that you care about your friends, and know that your opinions can cause them pain, but that you still must advise against such a union.

2. *Exploratory Writing:* Gay marriage has been a prominent political and social issue over the past few years. What images of gay life has television presented to its viewers? How do the images correspond to claims that many gay men and women just want what marriage affords: social stability, anchors in relationships, and family and financial security? Write an essay in which you explore the portrayal of gay relationships in the media and how this portrayal may or may not influence public opinion of gay marriage.

3. *Persuasive Writing:* Will legalizing gay marriage increase or decrease the problems gay men and women now encounter in America in gaining social acceptance? What benefits might all gay people receive, whether or not they choose to marry? Do you think that a legal change in marriage will help to change the beliefs of people who now disapprove of homosexuality? Why or why not? Explain.

4. *Exploratory Writing*: Many of the arguments supporting gay marriage note that gay couples are in committed, loving relationships and wish to legitimize their relationship with a marriage license. Can you think of other, less idealistic reasons why people marry? Based on these other reasons, including the practical and the shady, could these reasons undermine the movement legalizing homosexual marriage? For example, what if two female heterosexual friends, one employed and the other not, wished to marry for health insurance? Could such alliances be avoided if same-sex marriage were legal? Explain.

GROUP PROJECTS

1. Working as a team using Internet resources, see what information you can find about same-sex marriages in California and in the United States overall. Assemble a list of resources and compare it with other groups in your class; then select a more narrow topic for each group to research online. Prepare a brief description of what Internet users might find at each site. What cultural and social conclusions about gay marriage can you make based on your research? Explain.

2. Should marriage be a public and civic institution? Should it be a religious, private, and moral institution? Should it have features of both? List the qualities that a marriage draws from each of these realms. After you have compiled your list, discuss with your group what marriage should be and for whom.

3. Design a survey that you will administer anonymously to other members of your class or students in the student union, asking for opinions on gay marriage. Design your survey to allow people to formulate opinions and express their views while incorporating some of the ideas presented chapter. Collect the surveys and discuss the results. How do the responses connect to the arguments presented in this section? Explain.

Is Polygamy Really So Awful?
*Libby Copeland**

The issue of polygamy, and more specifically, polygyny—the practice of one man having multiple wives—has captured popular awareness partly due to news coverage of polygamist leader Warren Jeffs' highly publicized conviction. Several popular televisions series have brought the issue into our living rooms. Many political conservatives often refer to the "slippery slope" argument when arguing against gay marriage. If marriage is about happiness, why shouldn't three or four people be allowed to marry? But a new study shows that despite what you see on reality TV, plural marriage isn't very good for society—for women or for men.

1 These are boom times for memoirs about growing up in, marrying into or escaping from polygamous families. Sister wives appear as minor celebrities in the pages of *People*, piggybacking on their popular reality TV show. And oh yes, we have a presidential candidate whose great-grandfather was an actual bona fide polygamist.

2 Americans are fixated these days on polygamy, and it's fair to say we don't know how to feel about it. Polygamy evokes both fascination and revulsion—the former when Chloe Sevigny is involved, and the latter when it is practiced by patently evil men like Osama Bin Laden and Warren Jeffs, the fundamentalist Mormon leader who had a thing for underage wives. At the same time, the practice of plural marriage is so outside mainstream American culture, so far in the past for many Westerners, that it has come to be regarded as almost quaint. What's so wrong with it, if it works for some people? In counterculture circles, the practice of polyamory, or open partnerships, is supposed to be having some sort of moment. All of which explains why, in response to the argument by conservatives like Rick Santorum and Antonin Scalia that gay marriage could be a slippery slope leading to polygamy, some feminists, lefties, and libertarians have wondered aloud whether plural marriage is really so bad.

* Libby Copeland, *Slate*, January 30, 2012

3   History suggests that it is. A new study out of the University of British Columbia documents how societies have systematically evolved away from polygamy because of the social problems it causes. The Canadian researchers are really talking about polygyny, which is the term for one man with multiple wives, and which is by far the most common expression of polygamy. Women are usually thought of as the primary victims of polygynous marriages, but as cultural anthropologist Joe Henrich documents, the institution also causes problems for the young, low-status males denied wives by older, wealthy men who have hoarded all the women. And those young men create problems for everybody.

4   "Monogamous marriage reduces crime," Henrich and colleagues write, pulling together studies showing that polygynous societies create large numbers of unmarried men, whose presence is correlated with increased rates of rape, theft, murder, and substance abuse. According to Henrich, the problem with unmarried men appears to come primarily from their lack of investment in family life and in children. Young men without futures tend to engage in riskier behaviors because they have less to lose. And, too, they may engage in certain crimes to get wives—stealing to amass enough wealth to attract women, or kidnapping other men's wives.

5   As marriage historian Stephanie Coontz has pointed out, polygyny is less about sex than it is about power. Rich old guys with lots of wives win twice: They have more women to bear them babies and do household work, and they also gain an advantage over other men. After all, in such societies a young man in want of a wife cannot simply woo her. There is too much competition, and he probably has too little to offer. So he winds up having to do work for a more powerful, polygynous man, bringing him gifts and tributes, in hopes of someday being rewarded with one of that man's many daughters. "Often the subordination of women is in fact also a way of controlling men," says Coontz, who was not involved in the study out of the University of B.C.

6   That polygyny is bad for women is not necessarily intuitive. As economist Robert H. Frank has pointed out women in polygynist marriages should have more power because they're in greater demand, and men should wind up changing more diapers. But historically, polygamy has proved to be yet another setup that screws the XX set. Because there are never enough of them to go around, they wind up being married off younger. Brothers and fathers, realizing how valuable their female relations are, tend to control them more. And, as one would expect, polygynous households foster jealousy and conflict among co-wives. Ethnographic surveys of 69 polygamous cultures "reveals no case where co-wife relations could be described as harmonious," Henrich writes, with what must be a good dose of understatement.

7   Children, too, appear to suffer in polygamous cultures. Henrich examines a study comparing 19th-century Mormon households, 45 of them headed by wealthy men, generally with multiple wives, and 45 headed by poorer men, generally with one wife each. What's surprising is that the children of the poorer men actually fared better, proving more likely to survive to age 15. Granted, this is a small study, but it's consistent with other studies, including one from Africa showing that the children of monogamous households tend to do better than those from polygynous households in the same communities. Why? Some scholars suspect that polygyny may discourage paternal investment. Men with lots of children and wives are spread

too thin, and to make things worse, they're compiling resources to attract their next wives instead of using it on their existing families.

8   Must polygamy always bring these social ills? Is it possible to be polygamous in a way that's good for you and everyone else? Maybe. Historically, problems have cropped up when polygamy is widespread in a culture with great disparities in wealth, and a few men hoard all the women. But it has worked in small cultures where there aren't a lot of differences in wealth and status. Coontz points to past Native American societies that occasionally engaged in what's known as sororal polygyny, in which a man married to one woman might also marry her sister, perhaps after the sister's husband died.

9   It's possible that even in a large, deeply stratified society like ours, rare instances of polygamy wouldn't foster gender inequity and roving bands of unhappy single men, provided those instances were spread out among a largely monogamous population. But it's hard to imagine that, because it isn't how it has played out here. Instead, American polygamy occurs in close-knit fundamentalist Mormon communities, in which young women often do appear to be subordinated and from which young men—the so-called "lost boys"—are exiled to reduce the competition for wives. Has fundamentalist Mormon culture shaped the expression of polygamy, or has widespread polygamy shaped fundamentalist Mormon culture? It's hard to separate the two.

10   And this is exactly Henrich's point: Polygamy may actually exacerbate inequities in wealth and gender that hurt societies, even if the institution itself appears neutral. Crime and chaos are threatening. Christianity may have brought monogamy to Europe and many other places, but those cultures succeeded because monogamy happened to suit them. In other words, as far as social evolution is concerned, the best form of marriage for a given society isn't really about what's moral, but what works. ◆

CRITICAL THINKING

1. List the problems with polygamy—as it applies to the marriage of one man to more than one woman—identified in the study. Why is polygamy not good for society overall?

2. Copeland observes, "Americans are fixated these days on polygamy, and it's fair to say we don't know how to feel about it. Polygamy evokes both fascination and revulsion." Why are we fascinated with the practice of polygamy? Why are we equally repulsed by it? Explain.

3. Copeland conjectures that, "It's possible that even in a large, deeply stratified society like ours, rare instances of polygamy wouldn't foster gender inequity and roving bands of unhappy single men, provided those instances were spread out among a largely monogamous population." What do you think would happen if polygamy were legally sanctioned? What problems might ensue? Would there be any benefits? Explain.

4. Why isn't it naturally "intuitive" that polygamy is bad for women? Why is it particularly bad for women in religious groups that recognize the practice? Explain.

5. How is polygamy harmful for children born into these family structures? Explain.

CRITICAL WRITING

1. *Persuasive Writing:* One common argument against gay marriage is that it opens the door to other marital arrangements, including polygamy. Write a persuasive essay in which you either argue against this position, or support its premise.
2. *Exploratory Writing:* Copeland states, "Polygamy may actually exacerbate inequities in wealth and gender that hurt societies, even if the institution itself appears neutral." Write an essay exploring this idea, drawing from information provided in her essay.
3. Watch one of the programs Copeland refers to in her essay—*Sister Wives* or *Big Love*—and describe the family dynamics of these relationships. Does the situation indeed seem to be more about power and less about sex? What sort of lives do the men and women in the program have? Does the program gloss over issues or elevate them?

GROUP PROJECT

1. Given the recent interest in polygamy as media fare, discuss as a group the ethical, moral, political, and social implications of the practice. Would polygamy be more acceptable if it existed outside of religious doctrine expressed by fundamentalist Mormon sects? Would it change if the focus were on allowing women to have multiple husbands? Discuss as a group and share the highlights of your discussion with the class.

Did I Miss Something?
Lowell Putnam *

Many of the articles in this section cite the increase in the divorce rate as one reason for the decline of marriage and the shifting shape of the American family. Divorce has become an American way of life. Nearly half of all children will see their parents' marriage terminate by the time they turn 18. And although society may shake its collective head at such a statistic, lamenting the loss of the traditional family, not all children of divorce see it as a problem. In this piece, student Lowell Putnam wonders why divorce is still such a taboo topic. Having known no other way of life, children of divorced parents, explains Putnam, simply take such a lifestyle for granted.

---

* Lowell Putnam, student essay, 2002

1 The subject of divorce turns heads in our society. It is responsible for bitten tongues, lowered voices, and an almost pious reverence saved only for life-threatening illness or uncontrolled catastrophe. Growing up

Growing up in a "broken home," I am always shocked to be treated as a victim of some social disease.

in a "broken home," I am always shocked to be treated as a victim of some social disease. When a class assignment required that I write an essay concerning my feelings about or my personal experiences with divorce, my first reaction was complete surprise. My second was a hope for large margins. An essay on aspects of my life affected by divorce seems completely superfluous, because I cannot differentiate between the "normal" part of my youth and the supposed angst and confusion that apparently comes with all divorces. The divorce of my parents over 15 years ago (when I was 3 years old) has either saturated every last pore of my developmental epidermis to a point where I cannot sense it or has not affected me at all. Eugene Ehrlich's *Highly Selective Dictionary for the Extraordinarily Literate* defines divorce as a "breach"; however, I cannot sense any schism in my life resulting from the event to which other people seem to attribute so much importance. My parents' divorce is a true part of who I am, and the only "breach" that could arrive from my present familial arrangement would be to tear me away from what I consider my normal living conditions.

2 Though there is no doubt in my mind that many unfortunate people have had their lives torn apart by the divorce of their parents, I do not feel any real sense of regret for my situation. In my opinion, the paramount role of a parent is to love his or her child. Providing food, shelter, education, and video games are of course other necessary elements of successful child rearing, but these secondary concerns branch out from the most fundamental ideal of parenting, which is love. A loving parent will be a successful one even if he or she cannot afford to furnish his or her child with the best clothes or the most sophisticated gourmet delicacies. With love as the driving force in a parent's mind, he or she will almost invariably make the correct decision. When my mother and father found that they were no longer in love with each other after 9 years of a solid marriage, their love for me forced them to take the precipitous step to separate. The safest environment for me was to be with one happy parent at a time, instead of two miserable ones all the time. The sacrifice that they both made to relinquish control over me for half the year was at least as painful for them as it was for me (and I would bet even more so), but in the end I was not deprived of a parent's love, but merely of one parent's presence for a few short weeks at a time. My father's and mother's love for me has not dwindled even slightly over the past 15 years, and I can hardly imagine a more well-adjusted and contented family.

3 As I reread the first section of this essay, I realize that it is perhaps too optimistic and cheerful regarding my life as a child of divorced parents. In all truthfulness, there have been some decidedly negative ramifications stemming from our family separation. My first memory is actually of a fight between my mother and father. I vaguely remember standing in the end of the upstairs hallway of our Philadelphia house, when I was about 3 years old, and seeing shadows moving back and forth in

the light coming from under the door of my father's study, accompanied by raised voices. It would be naïve of me to say that I have not been at all affected by divorce, since it has permeated my most primal and basic memories.

4   However, I am grateful that I can only recall one such incident, instead of having parental conflicts become so quotidian that they leave no mark whatsoever on my mind. Also, I find that having to divide my time equally between both parents leads to alienation from both sides of my family. Invariably, at every holiday occasion, there is one half of my family (either my mother's side or my father's) that has to explain that "Lowell is with his [mother/father] this year," while aunts, cousins, and grandparents collectively arch eyebrows or avert eyes. Again, though, I should not be hasty to lament my distance from loved ones, since there are many families with "normal" marriages where the children never even meet their cousins, let alone get to spend every other Thanksgiving with them. Though divorce has certainly thrown some proverbial monkey wrenches into some proverbial gears, in general my otherwise strong familial ties have overshadowed any minor snafus.

5   Perhaps one of the most important reasons for my absence of "trauma" (for lack of a better word) stemming from my parents' divorce is that I am by no means alone in my trials and tribulations. The foreboding statistic that 60 percent of marriages end in divorce is no myth to me, indeed many of my friends come from similar situations. The argument could be made that "birds of a feather flock together" and that my friends and I form a tight support network for each other, but I strongly doubt that any of us needs or looks for that kind of buttress. The fact of the matter is that divorce happens a lot in today's society, and as a result, our culture has evolved to accommodate these new family arrangements, making the overall conditions more hospitable for me and my broken brothers and shattered sisters.

6   I am well aware that divorce can often lead to issues of abandonment and familial proximity among children of separated parents, but in my case I see very little evidence to support the claim that my parents should have stayed married "for the sake of the child." In many ways, my life is enriched by the division of my time with my father and my time with my mother. I get to live in New York City for half of the year and in a small suburb of Boston for the other half. I have friends who envy me, since I get "the best of both worlds." I never get double-teamed by parents during arguments, and I cherish my time with each one more, since it only lasts half the year.

7   In my opinion, there is no such thing as a perfect life or a "normal" life, and any small blips on our karmic radar screen have to be dealt with appropriately but without any trepidation or self-pity. Do I miss my father when I live with my mother (and vice versa)? Of course I do. However, I know young boys and girls who have lost parents to illness or accidental injury, so my pitiable position is relative. As I leave for college in a few short months, I can safely say that my childhood has not been at all marred by having two different houses to call home. ◆

CRITICAL THINKING

1. In this essay, Lowell Putnam notes that people speak of divorce in hushed tones. If half of all marriages end in divorce, why does society still treat it as a taboo topic?
2. Is divorce detrimental to children or simply a way of life? Explain your point of view.
3. Evaluate Putnam's description of the way people discuss divorce in "lowered voices, and an almost pious reverence saved only for life-threatening illness." What accounts for this attitude? Do you agree with his assessment? Explain.
4. At the end of his first paragraph, Putnam comments that "my parents' divorce is a true part of who I am." Why does Putnam associate his personal identity with his parents' marital status? Discuss how parent relationships influence how children view themselves and their world.
5. Analyze Putnam's definition of what makes a good parent. Do you agree or disagree with this viewpoint?
6. Critics of divorce say it is a selfish act of parents who put their wants before their children's needs. Putnam contends that his parents divorced out of love for him, and their divorce was a kind of sacrifice. Evaluate these two perspectives. Can divorce be a positive event for children?
7. Putnam comments that his parents' love for him has not dwindled as a result of their divorce, and that he "can hardly imagine a more well-adjusted and contented family." Why do you think he uses the singular *family*? Explain. How would his meaning change if he had used the plural form, *families*?

CRITICAL WRITING

1. *Research and Analysis:* Using newspapers and newsmagazines, research a topic related to children and divorce. You might examine the issue of "deadbeat dads," the psychological aspects of divorce on children, or social perspectives of broken families. Write an essay analyzing the results of your research.
2. *Persuasive Writing:* Draft a letter to a pair of married friends with children who are filing for divorce to reconsider their decision, or to support it, considering the impact the new arrangement is likely to have on their children. Assume that both parents are working and they are considering an amicable divorce in which they intend to continue a close relationship with their children.
3. *Personal Narrative:* Putnam's essay is a personal narrative describing his view of how his parents' divorce influenced his life. Write a personal narrative describing how your parents' marriage or divorce has influenced your own life. Can you relate to anything Putnam says in his essay? Explain.

GROUP PROJECTS

1. As a group, design and administer a poll for your classmates to answer anonymously, asking questions about family status (divorce, remarriage, single parenthood, absentee fathers or mothers, etc.). Administer the same poll to a group of people a generation or two older than you, perhaps your professors or college staff members. How do the results compare? Are divorced families more "normal" than non-divorced families? Explain. What structures are more common among the different age groups? Discuss your results with the class.

2. In your group, discuss the effects of divorce on children. Further develop Putnam's idea that it is just another way of life. Compare notes with classmates to assemble a complete list of possible effects. Based on this list, develop your own response about the effects of divorce on children.

VIEWPOINTS

► **Think of the Children**
*Andrew J. Cherlin**

► **The Higher Risks of Cohabitation**
Sharon Sassler

► **Laws Should Reflect Reality**
Nicky Grist

► **Why the Ring Matters**
W. Bradford Wilcox

In April 2012, the National Center for Health Statistics reported that a rising number of first-born children have parents who are not married. The percentage of first births to women who were living unmarried to their male partner jumped to 22 percent. This figure applies to couples who are cohabitating but who are not married. In fact, over six million heterosexual couples live together unmarried, and the number is rising. With the divorce rate for first marriages holding steady at about 50 percent (the statistic varies when broken down among educational and socioeconomic lines), are couples opting not to tie the knot at all? With the increasing acceptance of cohabitation, why remarry?

The New York Times posed the question, "Is Marriage Passé?" to experts across the political, religious, and educational spectrum. If half of marriages are doomed to failure, and second marriages faring even worse, why "risk the nightmare" over again? This chapter's Viewpoints section explores the issue of the decline of marriage in America and whether marriage itself is becoming an outdated institution. Four editorial viewpoints are presented. Decide for yourself.

---

* Andrew J. Cherlin, Sharon Sassler, Nicky Grist, and W. Bradford Wilcox, *The New York Times*, December 20, 2010, to June 20, 2011

Think of the Children
Andrew J. Cherlin

1 When we refer to cohabiting couples, we tend to think of young adults who are trying out a relationship to see whether it might lead to marriage. There are large numbers of those, to be sure, but cohabitation is at least as common among people who have ended their first marriages and are looking for new partners.

2   In fact, about 60 percent of women in second marriages have lived with their husbands before remarrying (and an additional 9 percent have lived with someone and ended that relationship before remarrying a different partner). Other divorced individuals may have a series of cohabiting relationships without ever remarrying. Overall, cohabitation has become a much larger part of the "repartnering" process than was the case a few decades ago.

3   That people who have had an unsuccessful marriage would be cautious about starting another one makes sense. Some may have promised themselves that they wouldn't get trapped in a bad relationship again. Others may have good practical reasons for not remarrying: They may want to avoid being legally responsible for the financial problems like credit card debt that a partner may have.

4   They may want to preserve their assets for their children in the event of their death rather than having a large amount go to a second spouse who survives them. They may be receiving payments from an ex-husband that stop if they remarry.

5   But however cautious they are about remarrying, it's clear that previously married people are not being cautious about forming cohabiting relationships. The ease with which you can both start and end one makes it an attractive way to live with a partner while leaving the back door open for a quick exit. Surveys show that Americans tend to form new partnerships after a divorce faster than people in most other wealthy nations.

6   Is the growth of cohabiting relationships among the previous married a problem? Not necessarily, especially if no children are involved. If a mature adult, having already gone through a first marriage, decides that he or she would rather avoid the ceremony, the legal entanglements, or the lifetime commitment of another marriage, then so be it.

7   We are living in an era when marriage is simply less necessary than it used to be. One can live a respectable life without it. The Pew Center reported last month that when a sample of Americans were asked whether they thought that marriage was becoming obsolete, 39 percent agreed.

8   But adults who are repartnering often bring children with them. (More than half of all divorces occur in the first 10 years of marriage.) These children typically live with their mothers, but many spend at least a few days a month with their fathers. What children need after experiencing their parents' break-up is a stable living arrangement.

9   Studies suggest that experiencing a series of parents and parents' partners moving in and out of the household may cause difficulties like behavior problems in school for some children.

10   Unfortunately, cohabiting relationships tend to be unstable. Indeed, Americans' cohabiting couples break up in a shorter time than do cohabiting couples in most other nations. Children whose parents form new partnerships therefore face a high risk of seeing those relationships end, after which there may be additional partners coming and going.

11   So while it may be fine for divorced adults without children to explore new live-in partnerships without the commitment of marriage, those who have children would be wise not to enter into one unless they are confident that it will last. ◆

 The Higher Risks of Cohabitation
Sharon Sassler

1 Previously married people have probably heard the warning that divorce rates are even higher in second marriages. But I ask you, how could remarriage possibly be any worse? After all, 100 percent of marriages ended unhappily among the currently divorced. Second marriages on average cannot possibly fare any worse statistically.

2   Just as with marriage rates overall, remarriage rates have declined. Divorced individuals are increasingly choosing cohabitation as an alternative to marriage. Living together is sometimes believed to be a safer, if less formal, relationship.

3   But the reality is that dissolution rates are higher among cohabiting couples than remarried couples. According to results from the National Survey of Family Growth, only 13 percent of cohabitations remained intact (that is, did not make the transition into a marriage or dissolve) after five years; in contrast, 77 percent of couples that remarried were still together five years after the ceremony. The odds of remaining in a long-term partnership are higher when there is a legal tie.

4   As for those who are parents, remarriage is sometimes unfairly maligned for the impact it can have on children. It is often difficult for children to adjust to a parent's new spouse, and on average, research shows that children who spend time in step-families fare less well than those who grow up with married biological parents.

5   But on many dimensions children whose parents enter into second marriages have better outcomes than do children whose parents cohabit. They are less likely to drink or smoke, have higher levels of economic well-being, and as adults have better relationship quality than their counterparts whose divorced parents formed cohabiting unions or remained solo. Parents' intimate relationships serve as templates for their children, long after the divorce and its aftermath.

6   Finally, looking at those who do remarry reveals a well-kept secret.

7   Just as the advantaged are now more likely to tie the knot in the first place, they are also more likely to remarry following a divorce. Men, for example, are more likely to remarry than are women (especially if they are custodial fathers), and re-marriage rates are also higher for whites and the college educated. That suggests that marriage—even second marriages—confers social, legal, and personal benefits that those in positions of power or authority take advantage of.

8   Remarriage may be less beneficial among those nearing retirement age. Some recent studies have found that later-life cohabitations are more stable than those entered into by younger adults, though they are still less durable than remarriages. There may be other reasons to avoid remarriages among those who are retirement-aged; concerns with children's inheritance, reliance on a former spouse's pension, or a desire sometimes expressed by widows to enjoy the chance to do what they want without concerning themselves with another's wishes.

9   But for those interested in establishing intimate relationships with new partners, there are many reasons, well supported with the scholarly research, to put aside the fear of failure that divorce represents to many Americans, and engage in "the triumph of hope over experience." ◆

 ## Laws Should Reflect Reality
Nicky Grist

1   Marriage has too many meanings. Can we have a debate about marriage in which all parties are talking about exactly the same thing? Is it religious or civil? Economic or cultural? Should you marry for yourself, your children, your parents, civilization or the benefits? Should you avoid marriage because of politics, family history, world history, separation of church and state, or the costs?

2   Even more than first-timers, individuals considering remarriage may find at least one meaning of marriage unappealing. The popularity of civil unions in France demonstrates that couples are eager to be recognized and take responsibility, even while avoiding cultural, religious or family pressure to marry. People still fall in love and commit, but the diversity of relationship and family structure is increasing.

3   In the United States, only 49 percent of households contain married couples and 6 percent contain unmarried partners (2009 American Community Survey). So 45 percent of all households get left out of most debates about the costs and benefits of caring.

4   What should we do about that? First, lighten our focus on legal marital status. Second, strengthen our focus on the myriad values of diverse relationships between interdependent adults. Business and government policies that assume "a caring relationship equals marriage" are sorely out of date.

5   What if policies were based instead on the belief that diverse relationships are good for people and good for society? Governments would help people register their relationships and share resources (see Colorado, Salt Lake City, Washington D.C., etc.). Employers would extend health benefits to any household member (see Nationwide Insurance). Hospitals would let patients have any visitors they want (a new federal requirement).

6   These policies demonstrate that caring goes beyond coupledom. Helping diverse caring relationships is realistic, not radical and will make us all better off. ◆

Why the Ring Matters
W. Bradford Wilcox

1   Cohabitation is now an increasingly attractive option to many Americans—including middle-aged and older adults who have recently lost a spouse to divorce or death. We can debate about whether cohabitation is good for the adults involved, especially given the financial penalties often associated with marriage for low-income and older couples.

2   But a growing body of social scientific evidence strongly suggests that cohabitation and children don't mix, even though more than 40 percent of American children will spend some time in a cohabiting household.

3   Compared with children in married step-families, children in cohabiting homes are more likely to fail in school, run afoul of the law, suffer from depression, do drugs, and—most disturbingly—be abused. (Note that children in in-tact, married homes do best on all these outcomes.) In the words of a recent Urban Institute study, "cohabiting families are not simply an extension of traditional married biological or blended families."

4   Indeed, a recent federal report on child abuse found that children in cohabiting stepfamilies were 98 percent more likely to be physically abused, 130 percent more likely to be sexually abused, and 64 percent more likely to be emotionally abused, compared with children in married step-families.

5   There are at least three reasons why cohabitation is so risky for children:

6   1. **Unrelated males**. Cohabitation often puts children in contact with unrelated males, who are significantly less likely to invest in these children, and to control their tempers and rein in any sexual attraction they may have, compared with men who have made a public commitment to them and their mother through marriage.

7   2. **Instability**. While it is true that remarriage is less stable than marriage, cohabitation is still less stable than a remarriage. This is bad for children, who thrive on stable routines and relationships with caretakers.

8   3. **No norms**. Cohabitation doesn't enjoy the host of social and legal norms that lend marriage direction, stability and status. Consequently, children, grandparents and friends find cohabiting relationships more difficult to negotiate than remarriages.

9   So, if you are a parent and have lost a spouse to divorce or death, don't shack up. For the sake of your children, put a ring on it. ◆

CRITICAL THINKING

1. Why should people consider remarrying if they have children? What are the pros and cons?

2. Grist observes that the growth of civil unions in France means that many people are rejecting marriage and the many meanings it carries in favor of less-constraining unions. Do you agree with this view? Does the growth of civil unions mean people don't want to get married any more?

3. Grist asks, "What if policies were based instead on the belief that diverse relationships are good for people and good for society?" Respond with your own viewpoint.
4. W. Bradford Wilcox gives four reasons why children are better off being raised within a marriage than outside of one. Evaluate each of his reasons.
5. Does one of the four arguments about the pros and cons of remarriage resonate more with you? Which one do you find yourself agreeing with more, and why?

CRITICAL WRITING

1. *Exploratory Writing:* Do you feel that marriage is an important consideration for the rearing of children? Do you think cohabitation will confer the same stability for children as a marriage would? What factors influence your decision to marry or not to marry? Explore your perspective in a well-considered essay.
2. *Personal Narrative:* Write a personal narrative in which you describe the structure of your family during your childhood. How does your family compare with the family situations described in these opinion editorials? Are you more or less likely to follow the marriage and family patterns set by your parents? Explain.

GROUP PROJECTS

1. Working in small groups, discuss and compare the structures of families within your own experiences. Think about the families you grew up in, the families you know well, and the families you may have started. Evaluate the kinds of families you find. These may include two-earner families, traditional families, families with no children, blended families with stepparents and children, children raised by other relatives, and other groupings. Compare notes with your group.
2. Working in small groups, interview several people who have children under the age of 18. Describe the family units of the people you interviewed. Are they married with children, or are they living in a different family arrangement? What circumstances led to their family situations? Finally, how satisfied are they with their family arrangements, and what are their hopes for the future? After completing your interviews, compare your interviews with those of the rest of the group and write a short article reporting your results.

Brave New World

What Can Science Do?

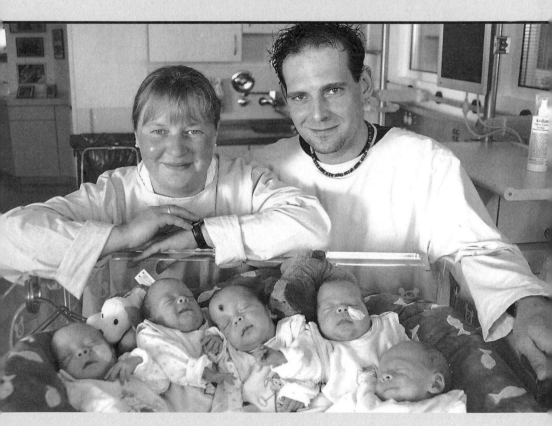

Biomedical science has ushered in a medical world that our great-grandparents could only have dreamed of. Today, human health has reached new heights, as medicine and surgery extend our lifespans and allow us to lead more productive lives. But with new medicine come new problems. We now have the ability to help infertile couples achieve a healthy pregnancy through reproductive technology. Egg donation, sperm donation, and gestational surrogacy raise new questions about what it means to be a parent. Organ transplantation means that thousands of people every year have a second chance at life. But the need for organs is greater than the supply. And while our health overall has improved, obesity, especially in children, continues to rise, undermining medicine's best efforts to keep us healthy. Finally, behind all of medicine's marvels is the buzz of health-care concerns in a country that is grappling with the legality and reality of universal coverage. This chapter explores a few such medical issues that Americans are dealing with today.

The chapter opens with four essays considering multiple issues connected to human reproduction. Reproductive technology has moved far beyond the world of test tube babies to the realm of science fiction. It is now possible to take an egg from one woman, fertilize it with sperm from a donor, and then implant the resulting embryo into still another woman. Technology is also allowing parents to select the sex of their babies and to identify genetic defects early in pregnancy or even before, raising tricky ethical questions. The first reading, "Girl or Boy?" by Denise Grady, examines how reproductive technology has skewed populations in China and India, and raises questions about what could happen if sex selection became easily available for everyone. Her essay is followed by an article by Mara Hvistendahl, who in "Will *Gattaca* Come True?" wonders whether we are reaching the point in that science fiction movie where we can genetically order "perfect children." Then, Alex Kuczynski provides a personal perspective on gestational surrogacy and some of its ethical nuances in "Her Body, My Baby." Jay Newton-Small presents a male perspective on the issue of reproductive donation in "Frozen Assets," in which he wonders: What rights do the offspring of sperm donation have later? Could 300 future children show up on a donor's door?

This chapter's Modern Scholar piece, "It's Not About Broccoli!" by Einer Elhauge, addresses one of the arguments regarding universal health care. Critics of "Obamacare" argue that it is unconstitutional because the government should not have the right to tell individuals what to buy. Sometimes called the "broccoli mandate," the argument posits that we enter a slippery slope in which government could tell us how to eat, what to buy, and how to live, all in the name of providing good health care.

The next essay explores the role Facebook might play in increasing organ donation. Bioethicist Art Caplan explains why he feels that the DMV is not the right place to encourage people to become organ donors in "For Organ Donation, Facebook Beats the DMV." Although this seems like a nice idea, is Facebook really the right place to increase the donor pool?

The chapter's Viewpoints issue explores the growing problem of childhood obesity. In July 2011, physician David Ludwig raised eyebrows when he asserted in a popular medical journal that severely obese children should be taken away from their parents due to the neglect that must lead to such a condition. His proposal came true in November 2011 when an 8-year-old boy was removed from his Ohio home by social workers after their attempts to have the boy's mother reduce his weight failed. The situation raises issues about who is responsible for childhood obesity, and does having an overweight child indicate poor parenting? Is it, in fact, child abuse?

Girl or Boy?
Denise Grady*

In only a decade, science has made tremendous advances in DNA and genomic technology. We can identify the genes that cause specific diseases and even warn parents of genetic risks to their future children even before they conceive of genetic risks to their future children. Although this technology holds tremendous promise, it also raises questions. We have heard of couples, for example, who use genetic testing to decide to end a pregnancy when the child's sex is not the one they want, a practice more common in countries where boys are the preferred sex. What if parents could *pick* the child's sex gender even before conception? It isn't easy, but it can be done. In this next essay, Denise Grady asks, if people want to choose their baby's sex before pregnancy, should doctors help?

1   Some parents would love the chance to decide, while others wouldn't dream of meddling with nature. The medical world is also divided. Professional groups say sex selection is allowable in certain situations, but differ as to which ones. Meanwhile, it's not illegal, and some doctors are already cashing in on the demand.

2   There are several ways to pick a baby's sex before a woman becomes pregnant, or at least to shift the odds. Most of the procedures were originally developed to treat infertility or prevent genetic diseases. The most reliable method is not easy or cheap. It requires in vitro fertilization, in which doctors prescribe drugs to stimulate the mother's ovaries, perform surgery to collect her eggs, fertilize them in the laboratory and then insert the embryos into her uterus.

3   Before the embryos are placed in the womb, some doctors will test for sex and, if there are enough embryos, let the parents decide whether to insert exclusively male or female ones. Pregnancy is not guaranteed, and the combined procedures can cost $20,000 or more, often not covered by insurance. Many doctors refuse to perform these invasive procedures just for sex selection, and some people are troubled by what eventually becomes of the embryos of the unwanted sex, which may be frozen or discarded.

4   Another method, used before the eggs are fertilized, involves sorting sperm, because it is the sperm and not the egg that determines a baby's sex. Semen

* Denise Grady, *The New York Times*, February 6, 2007

normally has roughly equal numbers of male- and female-producing sperm cells, but a technology called MicroSort can shift the ratio to either 88 percent female or 73 percent male. The "enriched" specimen can then be used for insemination or in vitro fertilization. It can cost $4,000 to $6,000, not including in vitro fertilization.

5   MicroSort is still experimental and available only as part of a study being done to apply for approval from the Food and Drug Administration. The technology was originally developed by the Agriculture Department for use in farm animals, and it was adapted for people by scientists at the Genetics and IVF Institute, a fertility clinic in Virginia. The technique has been used in more than 1,000 pregnancies, with more than 900 births so far, a spokesman for the clinic said. As of January 2006 (the most recent figures released), the success rate among parents who wanted girls was 91 percent, and for those who wanted boys, it was 76 percent.

6   Regardless of the method, the American College of Obstetricians and Gynecologists opposes sex selection except in people who carry a genetic disease that primarily affects one sex. But allowing sex selection just because the parents want it, with no medical reason, may support "sexist practices," the college said in an opinion paper published this month in its journal, Obstetrics and Gynecology.

7   Some people say sex selection is ethical if parents already have one or more boys and now want a girl, or vice versa. In that case, it's "family balancing," not sex discrimination. The MicroSort study accepts only people who have genetic disorders or request family balancing (they are asked for birth records), and a company spokesman said that even if the technique was approved, it would not be used for first babies.

8   The obstetricians group doesn't buy the family-balance argument, noting that some parents will say whatever they think the doctor wants to hear. The group also says that even if people are sincere about family balance, the very act of choosing a baby's sex "may be interpreted as condoning sexist values."

9   Much of the worry about this issue derives from what has happened in China and India, where preferences for boys led to widespread aborting of female fetuses when ultrasound and other tests made it possible to identify them. China's one-child policy is thought to have made matters worse. Last month, Chinese officials said that 118 boys were born for every 100 girls in 2005, and some reports have projected an excess of 30 million males in less than 15 years. The United Nations opposes sex selection for nonmedical reasons, and a number of countries have outlawed it, including Australia, Canada and Britain, and other nations in Asia, South America and Europe. Left unanswered is the question of whether societies, and families, that favor boys should just be allowed to have them, since attitudes are hard to change, and girls born into such environments may be abused.

10   The American Society for Reproductive Medicine, a group for infertility doctors, takes a somewhat more relaxed view of sex selection than does the college of obstetricians. Instead of opposing sex selection outright, it says that in people who already need in vitro fertilization and want to test the embryos' sex without a medical reason, the testing should "not be encouraged." And those who don't need in vitro fertilization but want it just for sex selection "should be discouraged," the group says.

11   But sperm sorting is another matter, the society says. It is noninvasive and does not involve discarding embryos of the "wrong" sex. The society concludes that "sex selection aimed at increasing gender variety in families may not so greatly increase the risk of harm to children, women or society that its use should be prohibited or condemned as unethical in all cases." The group also says it may eventually be reasonable to use sperm sorting for a first or only child.

12   Dr. Jamie Grifo, the program director of New York University's Fertility Center, said that he opposed using embryo testing just for sex selection, but that it was reasonable to honor the request in patients who were already having embryos screened for medical reasons, had a child and wanted one of the opposite sex. In those cases, he said, the information is already available and doesn't require an extra procedure.

13   "It's the patient's information, their desire," he said. "Who are we to decide, to play God? I've got news for you, it's not going to change the gender balance in the world. We get a handful of requests per year, and we're doing it. It's always been a controversy, but I don't think it's a big problem. We should preserve the autonomy of patients to make these very personal decisions."

14   Dr. Jeffrey M. Steinberg, from Encino, Calif., who has three clinics that offer sex selection and plans to open a fourth, in Manhattan, said: "We prefer to do it for family balancing, but we've never turned away someone who came in and said, 'I want my first to be a boy or a girl.' If they all said a boy first, we'd probably shy away, but it's 50-50."

15   "Reproductive choice, as far as I'm concerned, is a very personal issue," Dr. Steinberg said. "If it's not going to hurt anyone, we go ahead and give them what they want."

16   Many patients come from other countries, he said. John A. Robertson, a professor of law and bioethics at the University of Texas, said: "The distinction between doing it for so-called family balancing or gender variety would be a useful line to draw at this stage of the debate, just as maybe a practice guideline, and let's just see how it works out."

17   In the long run, Mr. Robertson said, he doubted that enough Americans would use genetic tests to skew the sex balance in the population, and he pointed out that so far, sperm sorting was more successful at producing girls than boys.

18   He concluded, "I think this will slowly get clarified, and people will see it's not as big a deal as they think." ◆

CRITICAL THINKING

1. What ethical concerns are raised connected to sex selection of babies? Why are people opposed to the practice? Why do people opt for it?
2. Several scientists point out that the few people who seek sex selection are not going to skew the population. In the light of what is happening in China and in other countries where boys are preferred, is this true? What about in a country where girls are preferred?
3. The author notes that currently, absolute sex selection via testing prior to IVF is very expensive—often $20,000 or more. Do you think if sex selection became more affordable, prospective parents would opt for it? Why or why not?

4. If medicine is able to offer new technology, such as sex selection, should it make it available regardless of the ethical considerations connected to it? Why or why not?
5. Grady writes, "The obstetricians group doesn't buy the family-balance argument, noting that some parents will say whatever they think the doctor wants to hear. The group also says that even if people are sincere about family balance, the very act of choosing a baby's sex 'may be interpreted as condoning sexist values.'" Why could aiming for "family balance" be "condoning sexist values"? Do you agree?
6. For couples in which sex selection is genetically important—such as in the case in which a particular disease is only carried by males—should health insurance cover the costs associated with the process? Why or why not?

CRITICAL WRITING

1. *Expository Writing:* Would you want to determine the sex of your first-born child? If so, what would you chose, and why? If not, explain why you would not want to pick your first child's sex. Is it a personal choice, or do you think this option should not be available to anyone?
2. *Exploratory Writing:* What is "family balance"? What do parents mean when they claim they want a child of a specific sex to achieve "family balance"? Write an essay in which you explore the validity of such a concept.

GROUP PROJECTS

1. Discuss with your group the ramifications of moving reproduction into the laboratory. With your group, develop a snapshot of what society might look like in such a world. What might the male/female population look like in different parts of the world?
2. With your group, develop a set a rules that set boundaries on how sex selection should be used and by whom. Under what circumstances could a couple chose the sex of their child? Should this technology be paid for by insurance? Why or why not?

Will *Gattaca* Come True?
Mara Hvistendahl*

For many years, the only glimpse women had of their unborn babies was via fetal ultrasound, which provided shadowy photographs of the fetus. Ultrasound technicians can often tell the sex of the fetus, as well as spot certain problems that may be present. But ultrasound and a blood test aren't foolproof. And we have all heard stories of women who have been

* Mara Hvistendahl, *Future Tense*, April 27, 2012

surprised to give birth to a boy after being told she was having a girl. More recently, however, genetic testing is providing a more accurate picture of the fetus—a genetic blueprint that can reveal the presence of certain diseases and genetic abnormalities. In this next essay, Mara Hvistendahl describes some of these noninvasive, early fetal tests, and how they may change pregnancy dramatically, while raising some ethical questions.

1   In 2003, back when such things remained unpredictable, a woman gave birth to a baby boy with Down syndrome. Her family was shocked. She had undergone the standard screening tests while pregnant—a blood test followed by an ultrasound—but the results had come back negative. Nor did she have the risk factors associated with Down, like advanced maternal age; she was 32. "She was not prepared for this," recalls Matthew Rabinowitz, her brother. When the boy died six days later, his mother was devastated.

2   The event left a deep impression on Rabinowitz. A young Silicon Valley entrepreneur who had recently left Stanford with a Ph.D. in electrical engineering, he had just sold the second of two successful IT startups and was casting about for a new venture. Current methods of prenatal screening carry a significant margin of error, and his sister's false negative suggested an opportunity. "I saw that we were applying our information technology and signal processing to various aspects of life, including cell phones and laptops, but not enough to the area of helping parents have healthy children," says Rabinowitz.

3   A scientist in Hong Kong had recently shown that a pregnant woman's blood contains a small amount of fetal DNA, and the prenatal screening world was buzzing about the potential of that discovery. Accurate blood tests, it was said, might soon reveal abundant information about the fetus as early as seven weeks of pregnancy. Rabinowitz drew on that excitement in 2004 when he founded Gene Security Network, later renamed Natera. Among the tests the company would develop was one to diagnose Down syndrome.

4   That test, called Parental Support, is currently in trials funded by the National Institutes of Health. Natera is one of several companies vying to commercialize fetal DNA tests, or noninvasive prenatal diagnosis (NIPD). A few years ago, a handful of these companies began offering NIPD to determine fetal sex and detect Rh-factor incompatibility—left undiagnosed, a woman with Rh-negative blood carrying an Rh-positive baby can produce antibodies that attack the baby's blood cells. Recently, we've seen a new wave of NIPD applications: Beginning last fall, the San Diego-based company Sequenom rolled out tests for Down syndrome and Trisomies 13 and 18, and Silicon Valley-based Verinata entered the market with tests for the same conditions in March. Rabinowitz expects Parental Support to be available by the end of the year. (He claims Natera's technology is more accurate than other tests.)

5   Now insurance companies are getting involved. Last week, Sequenom announced a partnership with the managed health care company MultiPlan, and others are marketing heavily to insurers. The tests currently available still carry a margin of error and thus can't yet be sold as a replacement for the likes of amniocentesis. Even as a supplement to existing methods, though, NIPD could be commonly used with high-risk women, predicts an article in the April issue of the insurance

industry magazine *Managed Care*. And as companies like Sequenom and Natera boost their accuracy rates, *Managed Care* says, NIPD "has potential to become a standard screening procedure." Because blood tests are less invasive than existing screening methods, and because they help insurers avoid the long-term costs of caring for people with expensive medical conditions and disabilities, they aren't a hard business sell.

6   The potential benefits of NIPD are many: elimination of the risks associated with amniocentesis, the replacement of aggravating probabilities with accurate information, and more time for expectant parents to make difficult decisions. But because insurance providers have an incentive to cover them, fetal DNA tests stand to be introduced before we have time to consider the slew of ethical and political challenges they will introduce.

7   Scientists have known for decades that the blood of a pregnant woman contains a few stray fetal cells. In the 1990s, labs began exploring blood-borne fetal cell testing as an alternative to amniocentesis, which carries a risk of miscarriage. But gleaning information from those cells entails the difficult process of distinguishing them from the mother's cells—and from fetal cells from earlier pregnancies, which can linger in a woman's blood long after a baby is born.

8   Then, in 1997, Dennis Lo, a medical researcher at Chinese University of Hong Kong, discovered that the mother's blood also contains floating strands of fetal DNA unattached to cells. Today scientists commonly believe the fetus contributes about 10 to 15 percent of the DNA in the mother's plasma. Lo licensed a technique of analyzing cell-free fetal DNA, or cffDNA, to Sequenom in 2005, and the batch of tests the company recently introduced are based on his technology.

9   Lo says an accurate Down syndrome test was originally considered the Holy Grail of prenatal diagnosis. But in the process of reaching that target, scientists also developed methods of determining fetal sex, which is one of the easier qualities to test for—and which became the first commercialized by companies looking to capitalize on Lo's discovery. While fetal sexing is helpful for couples with a genetic propensity toward sex-linked diseases like hemophilia, companies like Consumer Genetics, DNA Plus, and Prenatal Genetics Center now offer NIPD direct-to-consumer for parents simply intent on getting a girl or boy. In 2005, an early-generation mail-order blood test, Baby Gender Mentor, briefly inspired a media frenzy culminating in an appearance on the *Today* show—before it was found to be inaccurate. (Disappointed parents filed a class-action suit, and Acu-Gen Biolab, the company offering the test, filed for bankruptcy.)

10   The latest sex tests will almost certainly wreak havoc on countries with already significant sex ratio imbalances as they spread overseas. When news of Baby Gender Mentor reached India, for example, it sparked an outcry. Sex determination, whether through blood tests or ultrasound, is illegal in India, but many doctors flout the law. And if women can one day obtain results without the help of a physician or technician—by pricking a finger and sending in a spot of blood, as Baby Gender Mentor promised—gynecologist Puneet Bedi says India's sex ratio at birth would reach a "level unthinkable by any means so far." India's campaigners are prepared to fight the introduction of NIPD. But activist Sabu George says the fledgling anti-sex selection campaign is a poor match for the Goliath of the Western medical technology industry.

11   When Lo licensed his technology to Sequenom, he stipulated that it could not be used for sex selection. Rabinowitz says Natera won't test for sex at this point, either. But how long such provisions will hold is unclear. Meanwhile, NIPD's reach is expanding as the technology used to analyze cffDNA improves. In December 2010, Lo published a paper in *Science Translational Medicine* showing that in principle, at least, scientists can piece together the entire fetal genome from cffDNA. Lo says that exceeded even his own expectations: "If you asked me prior to 2008, I would have probably said that was science fiction."

12   At the time his paper was published, the process cost $200,000. Now, with the cost of DNA sequencing dropping faster than that of computing power, he estimates the bill may come to one-tenth of that—still expensive, but no doubt tempting for some parents. Lo wagers complete fetal genome testing might be widely available in a clinical setting within a decade. What fetal genes might one day suggest about a baby's eye color, appearance, and intellectual ability will be useful to parents, not insurers. But with costs coming down and insurers interested in other aspects of the fetal genome, a *Gattaca*-like two-tiered society, in which parents with good access to health care produce flawless, carefully selected offspring and the rest of us spawn naturals, seems increasingly plausible.

13   There are considerable hurdles to clear still before full fetal genome testing is available in a clinical setting. For the present, Lo envisions tailored packages targeting the 10 to 15 diseases most relevant to a couple's genetic history. But the ethical and logistical issues raised by accessing even portions of the fetal genome are tricky enough.

14   How to explain the test to patients is a particularly thorny question. Currently, genetic counselors are brought in only with parents who undergo amniocentesis or other diagnostic tests after finding out the fetus has an elevated risk of, say, Down syndrome. Widespread introduction of NIPD means all parents will need counseling, and without enough counselors to go around, the burden of explaining the test will most likely fall on the OB-GYN (though Verinata provides an in-house genetic counseling hotline). "You'll have a lot of women with OB-GYNs who are not really trained in genetics who are going to try to explain to them the implications of NIPD," says Jaime King, a law professor at University of California Hastings College of the Law. "And it's not just what happens when you get a high-risk result. It's: Do you even want this testing? And what do you want it for? And do know what you'll do with the results around a whole range of conditions? That's not something that women are currently prepared to decide—or that doctors are currently prepared to help them decide." That may be why in February, the National Society of Genetic Counselors adopted a statement opposing the routine use of NIPD for low-risk women. But since fetal DNA tests are risk-free, some doctors might offer them simply to ward off lawsuits.

15   More fantastically, the government might require testing. University of Texas-Austin bioethicist John A. Robertson recently outlined, for the sake of argument, a scenario in which states mandate that pregnant women undergo fetal DNA tests to avoid the costs of caring for the disabled people who might otherwise be born. There is constitutional precedent, he pointed out, in requiring suspected drunk drivers to submit to blood tests. (A state would have more trouble forcing women to hear or act on the results, he wrote.)

16   Marcy Darnovsky, executive director of the Center for Genetics and Society in Berkeley, Calif., notes that NIPD will provide women with "enormous amounts of information about the fetus that they're carrying at a very early stage. And it's available at a time when you can terminate a pregnancy with a pill." In one calculation by the Stanford Law School bioethicist Henry T. Greely, if just two-thirds of pregnant American women undergo NIPD, the number of fetal genetic tests done in the United States will jump from fewer than 100,000 a year to about 3 million. Just what that will do to the abortion rate is impossible to predict—but it probably will rise. (Some experts argue that an increase will be offset by our expanded ability to treat some conditions in utero.)

17   Even if the overall abortion rate increases, though, it may become more difficult for some women to get abortions. Anti-abortion activists are prepared for the new technology. Think Rick Santorum's tirade about amniocentesis allowing us to "cull the ranks of the disabled" was overblown? It was just the beginning. A recent LifeNews.com article calls NIPD a "seek-and-destroy mission against any life in the womb." For instance, pro-life activists might seek to ban Medicaid coverage of NIPD along the lines of the Hyde Amendment prohibition on the use of Medicaid funds for abortion—a change that would disproportionately affect poor women.

18   Just how soon the bulk of insurers will cover NIPD—and transform the discussion surrounding pregnancy and abortion in the process—is still unclear. A lot will depend on the accuracy rates to come out of trials like Natera's. If those cement NIPD as a replacement for amniocentesis, the new tests will undoubtedly mean less suffering for women like Rabinowitz's sister. But for the rest of us, things will get a lot more complicated. ◆

CRITICAL THINKING

1. The author points out that considering the current pace of medical advancements, fetal DNA tests stand to be introduced before we have time to consider the ethical and political challenges they will introduce. List some of the ethical considerations raised in the article and any others that come to mind.

2. Given the possibilities presented by noninvasive prenatal diagnosis (NIPD), would it be considered parental irresponsibility to allow a genetically imperfect child to be born?

3. One concern about genetic testing is that only society's "haves"—those with the financial means for good health care and, thus, access to testing—will have better control of preferable genetic outcomes, while the rest of society will have to go without. How could such testing widen the gap between the rich and the poor? Explain.

4. The author notes that bioethicist John A. Robertson outlined a case in which government-run health-care systems could mandate that pregnant women undergo fetal DNA tests to avoid the costs of caring for the disabled people who might otherwise be born. Respond to this scenario with your own view. Could it happen? If so, would the government have the

right to refuse to care for ill children? To demand that a woman terminate her pregnancy?

5. What is the opinion of the author of politician Rick Santorum? What bias, if any, might her opinion of Santorum have on the rest of the essay?

CRITICAL WRITING

1. *Exploratory Writing:* Watch the science fiction movie *Gattaca*. Is such a scenario possible? Do parallels already exist between the film and reproduction today? Write an essay in which you connect points raised in this essay with issues raised in the film.

2. *Research and Writing:* Indian gynecologist Dr. Puneet Bedi states, "India's sex ratio at birth would reach a 'level unthinkable by any means so far.'" Why does Bedi fear that NIPD used for sex testing will be abused in India? Research this issue online and write a research paper on the problem of birth discrimination in India and its possible implications on the birth rate in the future.

3. *Exploratory Writing:* In what ways, if any, could genetic testing alter the course of human evolution? Write an essay exploring the implications of this technology on the human race.

GROUP PROJECTS

1. Assume your group is made up of ethicists who consider the multiple, ethical sides of new technology and its potential long-term impact. In this case, specifically consider the pros and cons of using NIPD technology as it is connected to health insurance—both for private and government-funded programs.

2. Discuss with your group the impact the ability to determine a child's genetic makeup could have on future generations. Besides the medical benefits and potential pitfalls, discuss the social ramifications of such power. Include in your discussion points made in this essay—sex selection, disease eradication, selection for intelligence, and so on.

Perspectives: Meet My Mothers

www.CartoonStock.com

THINKING CRITICALLY

1. What issue does this cartoon raise? Explain.
2. In what ways is assisted reproduction complicating our idea of parenthood? Explain.
3. In your opinion, what makes a person a parent? Do we distinguish between different types of parents, such as stepparents, birth parents, and adoptive parents? Is one deemed more important than another? Explain.

Her Body, My Baby
*Alex Kuczynski**

It seems as if every week the celebrity pages announce another birth—born to an actress who used a surrogate instead of undergoing the pregnancy herself. In some cases, actresses have waited too long to conceive a child on their own. Others argue that because they rely on "perfect" bodies for their livelihood, they must have surrogates to achieve a pregnancy. Beyond Hollywood, more and more couples are becoming parents through gestational surrogacy—often using their own eggs. In this next article, abridged for this book, reporter Alexandra Kuczynski gives her personal perspective on the gestational surrogacy experience, and the conflicting emotions—and ethical questions—it raises.

1   At 31 weeks, my baby was kicking and stretching. On the sonogram screen, I could see that he was doing his customary sit-ups. The monitor broadcast the slushy sound of his heartbeat.

2   The technician varied from visit to visit. The previous time, we were lucky: it was the gregarious young woman named Gisele who wrote things like "Hi Mom and Dad!" over the cloudy portraits of the baby or, on one image of the baby's genitals, "I'm still a boy!" On this day, we got the terse woman who grudgingly wrote "foot" and "face," if she wrote anything at all. Then, she tore off the sonogram images and handed them to me with one hand; with the other, she reached down to wipe the gel off the stomach of the woman who was bearing my child.

3   I did not give birth to my son. He is the product of my egg and my husband's sperm. After half a decade of trying to become pregnant, sometimes succeeding but always failing to carry a baby successfully to term, I came to the conclusion that if we wanted to have a child who was genetically related to us, we would have to find a woman with a more reliable uterus to gestate and deliver our baby. That was in April 2007. I was 39 years old. Exhausted by years of infertility, wrung emotionally dry by miscarriage, my husband and I decided we would give gestational surrogacy— hiring a woman to bear our child—one try. It was a desperate measure, to be sure, and one complicated by questions from all the big sectors: financial, religious, social, moral, legal, political.

4   On May 11, 2007, my husband and I sent an e-mail message to a New Jersey lawyer who specializes in gestational-surrogacy cases. In July, a doctor coaxed eight egg cells—oocytes— from my ovaries and fertilized them with my husband's sperm. By the beginning of August, a substitute schoolteacher from Harleysville, Pa., named Cathy Hilling was pregnant with our child. On May 11, 2008, I was holding my 3-week-old son in my arms. It was Mother's Day.

5   The desire to be a mother—to give birth to a child, to care for that child—has always been rooted in me. I never doubted my ability to be a good mother. I had a

* Alex Kuczynski, *The New York Times*, November 30, 2008

charmed, happy childhood; I have a warm, loving, funny mother. Even so, I did not think of raising a child as a goal in itself. I saw motherhood as the natural outgrowth of a loving relationship. If I never met the man, I would skip the child.

6   I did meet the man, Charles Stevenson, when I was 32. Happily married at 34, I hoped that becoming pregnant wouldn't be too difficult. My husband—54—was older, but his sperm had a track record: he already had children from previous marriages. By the time I turned 35, nothing had happened, and after consulting a handful of doctors, Charles and I decided to start in vitro fertilization. Judging from several friends' experiences, we figured that I.V.F. would guarantee swift results. In the battle for my fertility, I wanted the big guns.

7   We started I.V.F. at Cornell University's Center for Reproductive Medicine and Infertility in New York City, the towering Emerald City of infertility. Every morning, patients waited for an hour or more in what came to me to feel like a hangar-size waiting room. A nurse would rattle off your name when it was time for one of the available doctors to peer at your ovaries. Occasionally, a name would ring out that you might recognize: someone's ex-girlfriend, an acquaintance. I was a reporter for *The New York Times,* so in my case the summons might lead others to remember a byline. Once, a fellow patient stopped me in the hall. "Don't worry," she said. "This is like A.A. We're not supposed to talk about who's here. Your secret is safe with me." Her silver sobriety bracelet twitched on her wrist.

8   I was taken aback. Her gesture underscored the helpless, self-enforced secrecy of the infertile. Couples often erect a barricade of privacy around the process to avoid the questions from friends and family members, and their ceaseless, useless volley of suggestions: You just need to relax. Did you try acupuncture? Soy milk makes you infertile. You're in front of your computer too much. What's the problem with all you career girls? Did this cycle work? Are you pregnant this time? How many shots? Where? A low whistle: Boy, you must really want a child.

9   You must really want a child. As if that were a bad thing.

10   The first three I.V.F. cycles failed. The eggs were good, but the resulting embryos didn't stick. I became ensnared in the terrible, wishful math of infertility. It went like this: I am 36 years and 2 months old. If I get pregnant today, I will have my baby while I am still 36....I am 37 1/2 years old. If I become pregnant today—this very day—I will have my baby when I am 38 years old....I am 38 years and 1 month old. If I become pregnant today—this very day, this very second—and manage to hold on to the baby, I will have my baby when I am 38 years old.

11   Celebrities offered hope, and still do. Halle Berry had her first baby at 41! So did Nicole Kidman, and two weeks later there were pictures of her wearing skinny white jeans. Not only fertile, but fit. Salma Hayek was 41. Marcia Cross, from "Desperate Housewives," was 44. John Edwards's sometime mistress had a baby when she was 44. Or was it 43? Who cares? That's way older than I am!

12   But after a total of 11 failed I.V.F. cycles and four failed pregnancies, stretched out over five years, actual hope becomes a mawkish pretense. So I abandoned hope. For myself, at least.

13   I can't remember when I first became aware of gestational surrogacy as an option, but it found its way into my brain after another pregnancy ended in miscarriage in December 2006. Doctors will recommend a gestational surrogacy if the

prospective mother doesn't have a uterus or if her uterus is malformed; if she has a medical condition that requires medication not compatible with pregnancy; or if she has had recurrent pregnancy loss or recurrent I.V.F. implantation failures. I fit the last two categories.

14   Before I.V.F. became a standard fertility treatment, about 15 years ago, the only surrogacy option available to infertile couples who wanted some genetic connection to their child was what is now called traditional surrogacy. That is when the woman carrying the baby is also the biological mother; the resulting child is created from her egg and sperm from the donor father. When the surrogate mother is carrying a child genetically unrelated to her, she is gestating the child, and the process is called gestational surrogacy. Now that there are hundreds, if not thousands, of doctors in the United States who can perform I.V.F., surrogacy agencies report that the numbers have shifted markedly away from traditional surrogacies toward gestational surrogacies.

15   There are no national statistics documenting this shift, however, or documenting much of anything about surrogacy. Shirley Zager, director of the Organization of Parents Through Surrogacy, a national support group, told me that there have probably been about 28,000 surrogate births since 1976, a figure that includes gestational and traditional surrogacies. Sherrie Smith, the program administrator for the East Coast office of the Center for Surrogate Parenting, a surrogacy and egg-donation agency, said that of the 1,355 babies born in their program since 1980, 226 were created through artificial insemination—traditional surrogacies—and the rest were gestational surrogacies, using either a donor egg or the intended mother's own egg.

16   "In the last few years, we've only done two or three cases of artificial insemination a year, which is way down from before," Smith told me. "The surrogates are happier, because they don't want to have a genetic connection to the baby, and the legal issues are much clearer." She added that it's much easier on the parents too. "It's one thing to say, 'Mommy's tummy was broken for a little while,' and another to have your child ask, 'Why don't I look like you?'"

17   Surrogacy is unregulated, and laws vary by state. In the states where it is legal, there is no box on the birth certificate to check "surrogate birth." In many states that don't expressly prohibit surrogacy—like Pennsylvania, where our child was eventually born—the genetic parents' names could be the only ones that appear on the birth certificate. If, however, our baby had been born in New York, where we live and where it is illegal to compensate someone for surrogacy, we would have had to adopt our biological child from Cathy, the woman who carried our child, and her husband. But our contracts were signed in New Jersey, and the consent form that Dr. Fateh had Cathy sign skirted any remaining legal issues.

18   In April of 2007, my husband and I met with a lawyer named Melissa Brisman at her office in New Jersey. Brisman handles gestational-surrogacy cases, and about 200 children are born as a result of her efforts every year. Brisman advertises for surrogates in newspapers, on the Internet, even on diner placemats. The typical cost for gestational surrogacy, she told us, would be anywhere from $30,000 to $60,000, all costs included—except for the retrieval and fertilization of my eggs and the transfer of the embryo or embryos into our gestational carrier. That would run us about $10,000 using our private doctor.

19   The fees to the surrogate would be paid out in monthly installments, not in one lump sum at the end. In this way the surrogate would be reimbursed for her monthly gestational responsibilities even if the pregnancy ended in miscarriage. No money ever changes hands directly between the intended parents (I.P.'s in surrogacy speak) and the surrogate. All the money goes into an escrow account set up by Brisman's office, and a third party pays out the monthly fees. I.P.'s and surrogates are discouraged from discussing money. This is partly to remove the air of commercialism from the proceedings.

20   Shortly after our meeting, Brisman's office started to send us profiles of potential surrogates. It felt strangely like getting a letter from the roommate who would be sharing your dorm room freshman year. They described themselves, their lives, their ambitions. Their household incomes were not, on the profiles I saw, more than $50,000. Most asked for about $25,000 to carry a baby, more for twins, and each made different stipulations: This one would not abort if the fetus was found to have Down syndrome, another one would.

21   The information in the packets provided by potential surrogates offered a rich picture of the country. There were married women and single women, women in their 20s and women in their 40s; women who would be willing to bear a child for a gay couple and women who would not; women from the Bible Belt, the Rust Belt, the Pacific Northwest and the industrial Northeast. Reports from social workers provided intimate details of their personal lives. The personal stories of the potential surrogates were deeply moving. One woman had given up her newborn for adoption rather than have an abortion; the experience led her to explore surrogacy. Most of the prospective surrogates were married and had children. Most had high-school educations, some had gone to college and some were college graduates.

22   None were living in poverty. Lawyers and surrogacy advocates will tell you that they don't accept poor women as surrogates for a number of reasons. Shirley Zager told me that the arrangement might feel coercive for someone living in real poverty. Poor women, she also told me, are less likely to be in stable relationships, in good health and of appropriate weight. Surrogates are often required to have their own health insurance, which usually means the surrogate or her spouse is employed in the kind of secure job that provides such a benefit.

23   While no one volunteering to have our baby was poor, neither were they rich. The $25,000 we would pay would make a significant difference in their lives. Still, in our experience with the surrogacy industry, no one lingered on the topic of money. We encountered the wink-nod rule: Surrogates would never say they were motivated to carry a child for another couple just for money; they were all motivated by altruism. This gentle hypocrisy allows surrogacy to take place. Without it, both sides would have to acknowledge the deep cultural revulsion against attaching a dollar figure to the creation of a human life.

24   In fact, charges of baby selling have long tarnished the practice of traditional surrogacy, and charges of exploiting women have lingered even as more couples opt for gestational surrogacy. We were not disturbed by the commercial aspect of surrogacy. A woman going through the risks of labor for another family clearly deserves to be paid. To me, imagining someone pregnant with the embryo produced by my

egg and my husband's sperm felt more similar to organ donation, or I guess more accurately, organ rental. That was something I could live with.

25   We had the money to pay. My husband is a very successful investor; I have made a healthy income for a writer. We were lucky in that we could afford to do what most infertile couples cannot. The questions for us were philosophical. I suppose I could have decided that it was my destiny to remain childless, that it was somehow meant to be. But I hate the phrase "meant to be," loaded with its small, smug assumptions, its apathy and fake stoicism. I believe that where things can be fixed, they should be fixed. In our case, reproductive technology could make it relatively easy for us to have our biological child.

26   And, at that moment, having a biologically related child felt necessary. What began as wistful longing in my 20s had blistered into a mad desire that seemed to defy logic. The compulsion to create our own bloodline seemed medieval, and I knew we could enjoy our marriage—our lives—without a child. Yet I couldn't argue myself out of my desire. A child with our genes would be a part of us. My husband's face would be mirrored in our child's face, proof that our love not only existed, but could be recreated beyond us. Die without having created a life, and die two deaths: the death of yourself, and the death of the immense opportunity that is a child.

27   My husband understood my desire: he had six children, mostly grown, from two previous marriages. No one questioned our wish to have our own child, but I found myself answering arguments of imagined critics: Should they be allowed to have their own baby when the husband already has children? Is their marriage stable? Think of the poor kid! All that baggage! I was sure such whispers lay ahead. Because for every person who told me surrogacy was a worthy, noble venture—just like the Old Testament story of Hagar, who gave birth to a son for Abraham when Sarah could not—there was someone else who brought up Margaret Atwood's dystopian novel "The Handmaid's Tale," in which fertile young women are enslaved as reproductive servants.

28   Charles pointed out to me that our marriage was not a dystopia, for one, and that while he had six children, I had none of my own. We have a happy, loving marriage and good relationships with everyone in our large family. The years of infertility were a burden, a period marked by weariness and despair. But they were also a reassurance, an affirmation that we are good companions. I do not advocate infertility as a way to strengthen the bonds of marriage, but five years of adversity pretty much proves the durability of your marital bedrock. Still, it was hard not to worry about what other people might think. Not being pregnant suddenly seemed like a public statement, one that left me feeling exposed and vulnerable.

29   When we came across Cathy's application, we saw that she was by far the most coherent and intelligent of the group. She wrote that she was happily married with three children. Her answers were not handwritten in the tiny allotted spaces; she had downloaded the original questionnaire and typed her responses at thoughtful length. Her attention to detail was heartening. And her computer-generated essay indicated, among other things, a certain level of competence. This gleaned morsel of information made me glad: she must live in a house with a computer and know how to use it.

30   Cathy told me that her motivations were not purely financial, although she was frank about the fact that the money would help with her two children in college. She

and her husband had taken in 17 foster children for short periods over the years; their new house was a bit small for more foster children. But the experience of having a baby for the New Jersey couple, Cathy said, provided her with a deep thrill, and the feeling that she was needed in a profound, unique way. There might always be other willing foster parents, she said, but there would not always be willing, able surrogate mothers.

31   I appreciated Cathy's warmth and straightforward manner. But there was something else that drew me to her—the same thing that caused me to see her computer-generated essay in a different light from the other women's hand-scrawled applications. She and her husband were college-educated. Her husband graduated from William and Mary. Her daughter Rebecca, then 20, wanted to be a journalist. They lived in a renovated mill house on a creek in a suburb of Philadelphia. They seemed, in other words, not so different from us. Later, during the election season, she and I were unaccountably pleased to learn that we were both planning to vote for Obama.

32   Cathy and I met at my doctor's office, where we would do the transfer. She brought her daughter Rebecca, who had been an egg donor to help pay her college tuition. The three of us were an infertility brain trust. I went for my 12th I.V.F. cycle, to make the eggs. This time, the cycle would be incomplete. There would be no transfer back into my uterus; my embryo would go into Cathy's uterus. On the day of my egg retrieval, I showed up for my operation with a sealed sample cup in my purse containing my husband's sperm. It was July. I struggled, as I did every time, to stay awake as the anesthesia pulled me under. As always, I woke up in the recovery room, with a cramp in my belly.

33   A few days later, Cathy's mother, Ann Peterson, a real-estate agent from Virginia, accompanied Cathy to New York for the embryo transfer. Cathy disappeared with a nurse. Ann and I did crossword puzzles. We made small talk. She ate carrots and celery from a plastic container. Cathy came out after resting for an hour with her legs elevated—after all that technology, they still make you put your legs up in the air—and beamed. "I think it worked," she said. "But then again, that's why they call me the Easy-Bake oven."

34   Two weeks later, we got the test back, confirming what Cathy already knew.

35   On a blustery October day, we went for the chorionic villus sampling, a procedure in which material from the placenta is extracted and tested for genetic abnormalities. It also tests for sex. Cathy held my hand as the needle went into her belly. We watched the baby jump at the intrusion. A day later, we found out we were having a boy.

36   Later in the fall, Cathy went to Las Vegas with her husband, who was attending a conference. I took the news badly. My tiny child—now that there was a sex, an identity, I could think of him as a child—was out there in Vegas at a craps table. I worried about the flight and whether the pressure would harm him. The thought crossed my mind to ask Cathy if it was really necessary to go, but I knew I couldn't. I had given her my baby, and I would have to give her my trust as well. I hated giving up control, but experience had proved that I had even less control over my own uterus, and trying to exercise any measure of authority over Cathy would cause both of us only grief. At the very least, Cathy's body was more reliable than mine. This was the pitiable truth I had to embrace.

37   And that wasn't always easy. When Cathy and I went for doctor's visits, she gave me the clearest sonogram picture to take home. I would drive back to New York, scan the image and send it out to family members and close friends—except that I would crop Cathy's and the clinic's names out of the frame. Even though they knew I wasn't the pregnant one, I didn't want them to be confused—who is this Cathy person? And for the forgetful ones: Why is Alexandra having her baby there? But more important, I wanted them to see my profile in the picture, not her name. It was immature, puerile, like a seventh-grade girl blacking out her nemesis' picture in the yearbook. I wanted her identity to disappear and mine to take its place.

38   What would I tell my son years from now? I was not able to produce you, so we outsourced you to someone with a better womb? Part of you came out of my tummy, but the rest of you came out of another lady's tummy?

39   Would I really be his mother? Was the key to motherhood carrying the baby? I had friends who had delivered children using donor eggs and friends who had adopted children, and they were certainly just as much mothers as women who had carried their own babies. But I worried that I was missing out on some great and essential preparation. I don't mean I should have been blasting Baby Mozart toward Cathy's belly. But a pregnant mother feels the child move and grow; she is preparing for motherhood whether she realizes it or not. What did it mean to not have this experience? Was a genetic connection enough? Would my child grow up and shout, "You can't tell me what to do—you didn't even give birth to me!"?

40   I tried to focus on the positive side. Of all the possible mothering paradigms I could count—birth mother, biological mother, child-raising mother, legally recognized mother—I would fill three of the roles. I had to settle for three-quarters his mother. That seemed like more than enough.

41   As the months passed, something curious happened: The bigger Cathy was, the more I realized that I was glad—practically euphoric—I was not pregnant. I was in a daze of anticipation, but I was also secretly, curiously, perpetually relieved, unburdened from the sheer physicality of pregnancy. If I could have carried a child to term, I would have. But I carried my 10-pound dog in a BabyBjörn-like harness on hikes, and after an hour my back ached.

42   Cathy was getting bigger, and the constraints on her grew. I, on the other hand, was happy to exploit my last few months of non-motherhood by white-water rafting down Level 10 rapids on the Colorado River, racing down a mountain at 60 miles per hour at ski-racing camp, drinking bourbon and going to the Super Bowl.

43   I had several friends around my age—37 and up—who were pregnant with their first children at this time, and I was amazed at how their feet swelled like loaves of bread. They were haggard. They seemed sallow and tired, and they let their hair go gray. I decided to call all of us Gummies—grown-up mommies—with the implication that some of us were so old we could have dentures.

44   I would soon be a Gummy. I just didn't have to do the hard part. I had the natal equivalent of a hall pass, a free ride, an automatic upgrade to first class. According to the expectations that govern modern womanhood, I should have been moaning to a shrink or to my girlfriends over cosmos about my inadequacies. But I tried hard not to see myself as a failure. I allowed myself the anguish of the moment when Cathy was playing my piano, and after that I vowed, not entirely successfully, to refuse

more self-punishment. I had been through so much—so much death and sorrow—that the gift of Cathy carrying my baby, shouldering the burden of the pregnancy, transferring all the fear of failure to her shoulders, was liberating.

45   As much as I tried to fight off the feeling, when I told others that I was expecting a baby—and this child was clearly not coming out of my womb—I would sometimes feel barren, decrepit, desexualized, as if I were branded with a scarlet "I" for "Infertile." At the height of her pregnancy, Cathy and I embodied several facets of femininity. She could be seen as the fertile, glowing mother-to-be as well as the hemorrhoidal, flatulent, lumpen pregnant woman. I could be the erotic, perennially sensual nullipara, the childbirth virgin, and yet I was also the dried-up crone with a uterus full of twigs. She got rosy cheeks and huge, shiny stretch marks. I went to Bikram yoga and was embarrassed to tell the receptionist—in front of the pregnant 20-something yogini in short shorts—to pull me out of class in case my baby was about to be born out of another woman's body.

46   Our baby was expected to be big—my husband and I were 10-pound babies—and we assumed he would come early. Two weeks before his due date, on a Wednesday, Cathy called to tell me her cervix was dilated three centimeters. I booked a hotel room near Cathy's house and Grand View Hospital, where she would give birth. I packed up my TomTom G.P.S., . . . and drove down to Pennsylvania with yellow "Baby on Board" signs affixed to the rear windows.

47   Birth is not a tidy business. As Cathy went into labor, my husband stood respectfully by her head to avoid being on the more visceral end of things. I found my son's birth to be a terrifying event. When the baby crowned and the top of his skull appeared, my brain did back-flips. There was the mind-bending philosophical weirdness of it all: there is our baby—coming out of her body. And then there was the physicality of it: the torture of childbirth, of being split open, of having your body turned, it seemed, inside out to produce this giant, beautiful baby.

48   At 3:49 p.m., Maxime came squalling into the universe. He weighed 10 pounds 10.2 ounces. In the delivery room, a crowd watched—a group that included Cathy, her husband, her two daughters, two nurses, a doctor and my husband. I cut the umbilical cord.

49   The previous winter, a Catholic priest, upon hearing of our impending birth and my plans to raise the boy in the same liberal Catholic tradition in which I was raised, sniffed and said to me, "You know, the church frowns on science babies."

50   After the birth, his comment struck me as terribly misguided. In my way of thinking, science is the ultimate expression of nature; nature and science derive from the divine. It is hard to suspend belief in the divine when you see my child. To me, he is astonishingly beautiful, with his bald cue-ball head and blue eyes and my husband's button nose. The miracle of his existence speaks to the generosity of humanity—and to the magical, unified coordination of more than a dozen people in the act of his creation.

51   I wish I could say that everyone's reaction to Max's birth was as generous. Most people were overjoyed for us. But extraordinary circumstances, I discovered, bring out extraordinary reactions in some people. I least expected jealousy. This from women who looked at me with tight smiles and said, "Well, thank God you didn't have to give birth to that huge child!" Or, glumly: "You're so lucky. Pregnancy is

overrated." One announced to a table of people at a dinner party: "My God, Alex. You've really gotten away with some stuff in your life. But this takes the cake!" It was as if I had performed some slimy trick and was still able to have my ticket stamped "Mother." Not only Mother, but Biological Mother.

52   Indeed, a month after Max was born, I was overwhelmed by the feelings I refused to acknowledge before his birth. In my fear of allowing anything to get complicated, I had suppressed every feeling of anguish and confusion for months, for almost a year.

53   I was sitting on our back porch in Southampton, N.Y. The baby was asleep. It was twilight. Suddenly, my chest seized, and electric impulses pricked at my skin. What had we done? Was it right to have circumvented the natural order of things? Why had I been chosen to miss out on the act of giving birth, to be left out of the circle of life?

54   My husband came out and sat next to me. He took my hand.

55   "You gave birth to our baby," he told me. "The doctors went in and took our baby out of you 10 months ago." He was casting back to the day the doctor removed my eggs. "It was like a C-section. They just went in and got him when he was very small. And now he is here, and as much a part of you as if he had come out of your body. Because he did come out of your body."

56   I recognized this version as a convenient twisting of logic. But it was true in its small, important way. Our child did come out of me, from us. Our bodies were married in a glass dish, and our boy was carried by another woman for nine months. He is our most vivid dream realized—the embodiment of the most blindly powerful force in the universe, brought to life the only way he could be. With a little help. ◆

CRITICAL THINKING

1. Kuczynski observes, "We encountered the wink-nod rule: Surrogates would never say they were motivated to carry a child for another couple just for money; they were all motivated by altruism. This gentle hypocrisy allows surrogacy to take place." What is the "wink-nod rule" to which she refers?

2. What is the difference between "traditional" and "gestational" surrogacy? What qualms, if any, does Kuczynski have about gestational surrogacy? Does she struggle with any ethical issues? Why or why not?

3. As the pregnancy progresses, what feelings does Kuczynski experience? How does she analyze these feelings? Explain.

4. What reactions do other people have when Kuczynski explains that she is expecting a baby by gestational surrogate?

5. Kuczynski notes that most surrogates do not have much money. Does it bother her that surrogates are probably doing it for the money? Why or why not? How does she feel about the surrogates who "apply" for the "job"? Who does she chose and why?

6. Why does Kuczynski feel that the Catholic Church's position on "science babies" is misguided? Why does the Catholic Church "frown" on them?

7. Did Kuczynski's personal narrative make you feel sympathetic to her problem and how she solved it? Why or why not?
8. How does Kuczynski's husband help her come to terms with the completion of the gestational surrogacy experience? Explain.

CRITICAL WRITING

1. *Exploratory Writing:* After reading this narrative, write an essay in which you respond to the ethical, moral, philosophical, or religious issues connected to gestational surrogacy. Remember that in most states gestational surrogates have no legal right to the baby they carry, because there is no biological connection.
2. *Research and Analysis:* Kuczynski notes that some people compared her situation to the Margaret Atwood novel *The Handmaid's Tale*. Read or research this story and explain why people would compare gestational surrogacy to this future dystopian society.
3. *Expository Writing:* The reproductive technology that enables Kuczynski and her husband to produce their biological child has met with controversy. Some critics argue that it exploits the poor. Others believe that it runs counter to God's will. Write an essay in which you explore these arguments while explaining your own position on this issue.

GROUP PROJECTS

1. Kuczynski wonders what the "key" to motherhood is. With your group, discuss this concept. Is pregnancy an important part of motherhood? Can you be a "full" parent without having experienced pregnancy? What makes a parent? How would the law interpret your definitions?
2. Research the practice of gestational surrogacy online. How common is it? Who uses it? Is it for infertile women only, or, as some pregnancies in the recent media suggest, for women who do not want their bodies "ruined" by pregnancy? Is one preferable to the other? Why?

Frozen Assets
Jay Newton-Small*

Assisted reproductive medicine offers opportunities that were once the stuff of science fiction. Today, donated sperm may be joined with a donated egg and implanted in still another unrelated individual to produce a baby. Although the outcome is usually a positive one for

---

* Jay Newton-Small, *TIME*, April 5, 2012

new parents, what about the children of these medical miracles? And what happens when dozens of babies are sired by one man? Hundreds? What about anonymity? Could a child later seek out his or her sperm donor father? What might seem like a good option to help a man pay for college just might come back to haunt him.

1 For Shari Ann, good Canadian sperm was hard to find. As a single woman in her late 30s, she wanted to get pregnant and knew she didn't have much time. When she began to hunt for the perfect donor, however, she was frustrated by the selection. In her hometown of Quebec City, she found only a few Jewish candidates—a must for Shari Ann (who asked to go by her first name to protect her family's privacy)—and none of them were suitable. So she called a clinic in Toronto that contacted a sperm bank in Virginia, and there she found her genetic Prince Charming: tall, athletic, smart, handsome and Jewish. She bought five vials of his sperm; her twin boys are now 7 years old.

2 Prince Charming's real name is Ben Seisler, though Shari Ann might have never known that, since U.S. donors can choose to be anonymous. But one day in 2005, Seisler grew curious about the results of his biological generosity. He plugged his donor number into the Donor Sibling Registry and was put in touch with not only Shari Ann's family but also at least 20 others. Overall, he counts more than 70 off-spring in the U.S. and abroad. Given the number of donations he made over the course of three years when he was in his 20s, there could be as many as 140.

3 Now 34 and married, Seisler broke the news of the scope of his procreation to his then fiancée Lauren on a 2011 Style channel documentary about sperm donors. Lauren—no surprise—was livid. And Ben—no surprise-struggled to explain his motivations: "I guess I was dumb."

4 Seisler might have picked a better way to fess up to his future wife, but in any case, a lot of American men will sooner or later be making similar disclosures of their own. Sperm is a growth sector in the American economy. From just a handful of vials 10 years ago, American sperm exports have grown into a multi-million-dollar business. The largest sperm bank in the world, California Cryobank, recorded $23 million in sales last year, and the U.S. industry overall does an estimated $100 million in business annually. As of late 2005, ABC News reported that the top four U.S. sperm banks controlled 65% of the global market. The U.S. currently exports sperm to at least 60 countries.

5 America's ejaculatory exceptionalism is not a result of American men's superior virility. Rather, quality control and wide product selection are the keys. The U.S. Food and Drug Administration requires testing for most sexually transmitted diseases. Sperm banks study a donor's family medical history going back three generations. Also, America has a very diverse population. So if you're a couple in a country like Japan, where third-party insemination is generally frowned upon, finding a match in the U.S. is easy.

6 What's more, the U.S. still almost always makes anonymity an option—and that's driving overseas customers into American arms. In 2004, after the U.K. passed a law forbidding anonymity, the number of sperm donors plummeted far below what was needed to meet domestic demand. Similar changes in Canada's and Australia's

privacy laws literally dried up local donations. Both countries now import more than 90% of their donated sperm. And for overseas shoppers who want to know the identity of the donor, there are plenty of American men like Seisler who happily come forward.

7   But the sperm boom gives rise to a lot of complicated legal and medical questions. Could a remote biological heir seek a paternity declaration against a donor father and later make claims against Dad's estate? When a donor settles down and finally has kids he wants to raise, will those children want to meet their scattered tribe of half siblings? Every young industry has its growing pains, but in the sperm game, those problems can be for life.

8   One thing that makes sperm such a profitable commodity is that the customer base is huge. The World Health Organization estimated in 2006 that there were 60 million to 80 million infertile couples worldwide. Thus far, most international sperm business has been for hetero-sexual couples with fertility challenges, but that is changing as more cultures accept lesbians and single parents—two groups that compose by some estimates up to 60% of the U.S. market.

9   While anonymity helps the U.S. tap this market effectively, it's the quality issue that really keeps overseas buyers flocking. Dads are profiled according to height, appearance and education level. A man with a Ph.D. can make as much as $500 per ejaculation. Lower-end donors, who still need at least a college degree and a minimum height of 176 cm, can earn about $60 a pop. Depending on how dense his sperm is and the mobility of his swimmers—critical to surviving the freezing process—a donor can make up to $60,000 over two years, the maximum amount of time most clinics use a donor.

10   "Prospective parents know more about these donors than I do about my husband's family medical history, and we've been married more than 30 years," says Trina Leonard, a spokeswoman for Fairfax Cryobank, the second largest facility in the U.S.

Taming the Frontier

11   Sophisticated as all this seems, we are still in the Wild West phase of global sperm sales. Lucrative pay has raised questions about sperm profiteering. Seisler donated to two clinics—one in Boston and one in Virginia—to help pay his way through college and law school. One man in Britain who donated for over 30 years has sired more than 1,000 children. Such stories prompted Britain to restrict the number of children a donor can spawn, including his own, to 10. The FDA has no limits on the number of offspring a donor may have, but most banks say they limit men to 25 or 30 children. That said, there's evidence that those guidelines can be loose, and banks have no way of knowing if a donor has visited several facilities. And there's nothing to stop individuals from starting their own endeavors. A 36-year-old California computer programmer has been in the news of late for fathering 15 children by giving out his fresh sperm for free—often inserted with a turkey baster. He claims to be a virgin.

12   More worrisome, donors could be unwittingly spreading genetic diseases. One Texas couple is suing a sperm bank in New England after their child turned out to have cystic fibrosis, a disease for which banks aren't yet required by federal law to screen. Another risk—that of an ethnicity mix-up for overseas buyers—is not just theoretical; it's happened. Finally, when a prodigious donor like Seisler produces lots of half siblings who grow up near one another, accidental incest could result. Shari Ann knows of two other children Seisler sired in Quebec and has been careful to track them. While it would be hard for foreign offspring to claim U.S. citizenship—unless their genetic fathers helped them—it's possible that sperm-donor fathers might be forced to take responsibility for them.

13   "Someone could show up—say, a 16-year-old whose parents died in France," says Arthur Caplan, a bioethicist at the University of Pennsylvania. "He may know his sperm father and say, 'I think you should support me.' American courts decide [such] issues to the child's best interest. They're not interested in promises from sperm banks. It may not make the child a citizen, but it sure makes the donor a dad."

14   For many sperm donors, like Seisler, the temptation to see what youthful folly might have produced can be powerful. In the Style channel TV show, Seisler explained what motivated him to reach out to his genetic offspring. "I want to be available to these families to be a resource for them," he said. "I'm curious as to what these kids are like. But I'm not looking for anything from them." When a friend replied that Seisler can't be hitting 70 Chuck E. Cheese birthday parties a year, he bristled: "I don't see them as my kids."

15   While that may be the boundary he wants to set, once the kids know who he is, it's up to them whether to honor it. He's been keeping in touch with dozens of families via e-mail—including Shari Ann's—but now that he and his wife are considering having kids of their own, he's maintaining a low profile. He refused to comment for this article.

16   Until the industry is regulated—and it may never be—it will remain a market that pushes boundaries. Some groups, like the Donor Sibling Registry, which has connected more than 9,000 biological fathers and siblings from 31 countries, are pushing to do away with anonymity, a move resisted by U.S. sperm banks, which fear the same kind of falloff in donors that other countries experienced. The banks instead favor an anonymous registry that could be used to ensure that donors aren't doubling or tripling their money.

17   In any case, genetic mapping makes things more transparent than they used to be, no matter what the anonymity rules are, and the timeless question—"Who's your daddy?"—is easier to answer than ever. What donor children and their biological dads choose to do with that information is helping redefine the concept of modern family and the global village. ◆

CRITICAL THINKING

1. Is the international exchange of sperm in any way similar to adopting a child from another country? Why or why not? Explain.
2. Newton-Small notes that one reason for the popularity of American sperm is that the United States is one of the few countries that still allow for

anonymity. What are the benefits and drawbacks of anonymity, for both the parents and the donor?

3. Newton-Small notes, "Could a remote biological heir seek a paternity declaration against a donor father and later make claims against Dad's estate? When a donor settles down and finally has kids he wants to raise, will those children want to meet their scattered tribe of half siblings?" Respond to these possibilities with your own viewpoint.

4. The author claims that the biological history of donors is meticulously gathered and passed on to the prospective parent. If biological history is already provided, what other reasons could a child produced from sperm donation have to track down his or her biological father?

5. What makes sperm suitable for donation, and why? Do the criteria to qualify reduce intellectual diversity? Explain.

6. Ben Seisler chose to publically tell his future wife about the number of children he sired through sperm donation on a television program. How would you react if your fiancé announced that he or she had donated eggs or sperm and that children were produced through the donation? Would it matter? Would the number of children produced be an issue?

CRITICAL WRITING

1. *Exploratory Writing:* Are there ethical and unethical reasons for sperm donation? Egg donation? Or is donor motivation irrelevant to the issue? Write an essay in which you explore the ethical issues connected to sperm and/or egg donation.

2. *Exploratory Writing:* Advertising for eggs and sperm often appears on the back pages of college newspapers—especially Ivy League schools. Write an essay in which you explore the ethics of reproductive donation as it applies to college students. Consider some of the ethical and legal issues of donation, both for the donor and any children produced as a result of donation.

3. *Personal Narrative:* Do children created with the assistance of sperm donors have a right to know their biological fathers? Is anonymity unjust? Many recent laws have paved the way for offspring of sperm donation to find their biological fathers. If you donated your sperm or eggs, how would you react if your biological child suddenly contacted you?

GROUP PROJECTS

1. Cryos International, a Danish company licensed in the United States, claims over 19,631 babies since 1991 (as of June 2012). With your group, evaluate their marketing strategy. Consider the social and intellectual components of their business. Are they commoditizing human reproduction? If so, is that acceptable? Why or why not?

2. This article notes that one reason sperm donation has "dried up" in many other countries is that donors may not remain anonymous should their off-spring later chose to locate them. As a group, discuss this issue. Would this possibility deter you from ever considering sperm (or egg) donation? Does it complicate the promises of assisted reproduction for infertile couples? Explain.

Modern Scholar

It's Not About Broccoli! The False Case Against Health Care
*Einer Elhauge**

One of the primary challenges against President Barack Obama's individual health-care mandate is that it allows the government to force us to buy something, even when we don't want it. Critics to universal health care argue that mandating insurance is like forcing Americans to buy more vegetables. In this essay, Harvard law professor Einer Elhauge explains why he feels their logic is so flawed—and dangerous.

1 The challengers of the health insurance mandate have focused on the Commerce Clause of the U.S. Constitution. As conservative Judge Silberman held, the text giving Congress the power to "regulate commerce" does seem to include a power to mandate purchases, given 1780s dictionary definitions of "regulate." The challengers argue that this plain meaning should nonetheless be resisted because otherwise the clause would lack any "limiting principle," and thus could be used to force us to buy GM cars, cell phones, burial insurance, or—their favorite bugaboo—broccoli.

2 But there *is* a limiting principle; it is the one the Supreme Court has actually articulated in its cases. To be justified by the Commerce Clause, a federal law must (1) involve economic regulation (2) that addresses a national problem (3) that affects interstate commerce. That is a broad power, but it is not a limitless one. It does not, for example, authorize a federal law against committing violence against women or possessing a gun in a school zone because those are not economic regulations, as the Supreme Court has ruled.

3 So the problem is not that there is no limiting principle. It's that the challengers don't like the limiting principle that exists. They want the justices to read into the Commerce Clause a *new* limiting principle, one that bars laws mandating the purchase of any product. But however attractive that kind of new limiting principle

* Einer Elhauge, *The Atlantic*, April 2012

might seem, it cannot be inserted into the Constitution by judicial fiat when it lacks support in the constitutional text, history, or precedent.

4   How does one address the terrible specter of a broccoli mandate? One response is that a broccoli mandate might not be valid under those existing limits, because there does not seem to be any national economic problem that has resulted from the failure of some of us to buy broccoli. But let us suppose one can concoct one by arguing that some hypothetical Congress might rationally think that the failure of some of us to eat broccoli makes us less healthy in a way that raises costs for others in our insurance pools. Let me further assume that, although such a hypothetical claim would be just plausible enough to meet the prevailing constitutional standard, a broccoli mandate would seem stupid to almost all of us. Does this ensnare us in a logical trap, forcing us to modify existing constitutional limits, to add a ban on purchase mandates? Not at all, for many reasons.

5   First, just because we may all agree that a certain type of law would seem stupid, does not mean the courts can insert a ban on such laws into the Constitution. The Constitution has no ban on stupid laws. The constitutional remedy for the enactment of a stupid law is voting out the stupid legislators who enacted it.

6   Second, if we all agree that a broccoli mandate seems stupid, then our political process will never impose it. Indeed, even the challengers admit that the states could adopt purchase mandates, and yet none of the 50 states has ever required us to buy broccoli, cell phones, cars, or anything else from the parade of horribles offered by the challengers.

7   Third, the challengers' argument would imply that the Commerce Clause must not give Congress any power to *ban* purchases of any product. After all, if Congress has such power, couldn't it enact outrageous laws *prohibiting* us from buying broccoli, GM cars, cell phones, or for that matter health insurance or even health care? The challengers' argument logically implies that because a power to prohibit could be used in these stupid ways, Congress's power to prohibit commerce also lacks a limiting principle. By that logic, judges should thus read new limits into Congress' power to prohibit commerce. But no one believes that would be proper constitutional law.

8   Fourth, suppose we imagine a future world where the political process has adopted one of the seemingly silly purchase mandates. If so, we might question our easy supposition that it was so stupid that the very fact of enactment would mean our democratic process had concluded otherwise. If the Supreme Court imposes its judgment that such a law would be undesirable, despite the lack of any constitutional basis, it will simply be allowing its preferences to trump democratic preferences.

9   Fifth, like any constitutional power, the Commerce Clause is subject to other constitutional limits. In particular, the constitutional right of liberty has been interpreted in a way that bans laws violating our bodily integrity. This means that even if Congress could make me buy broccoli, it cannot make me eat it. All it can do is make me pay money, a classically commercial act. Likewise, the health insurance mandate does not require anyone to actually undergo medical treatment. It just makes us pay money.

10   Sixth, because purchase mandates are just an obligation to pay money, they are really no different from taxes. Indeed, the challengers conceded that Congress could have imposed a financially identical requirement if it had just used the language of taxes and tax credits. Thus, the challengers themselves have no limiting principle that precludes any of their parade of horribles. Under their theory, Congress could still impose the dreaded broccoli mandate by just calling it a tax that one can avoid if one buys broccoli.

11 Seventh, while the challengers' argument relies on imaginary mandates that no one is even thinking of proposing, the parade of horribles on the other side is very real. Adopting the challengers' new principle banning federal purchase mandates would throw into doubt a long list of existing federal laws that mandate commercial transactions. One federal mandate requires corporations to hire independent auditors. Another requires that unions buy bonds to insure against officer fraud. Federal statutes also mandate that hotels and restaurants commercially deal with minorities and disabled persons. Federal antitrust law sometimes requires monopolists to supply their rivals. The list is endless. Are all such federal mandates now going to be the subject of new constitutional challenges?

12 The more fundamental problem with the challengers' method is that it asks judges to impose new constitutional limits based on their own policy preferences about how to treat various hypotheticals. This method is even worse than directly asking judges to create new limits based on their policy preferences, because it never confronts the question of whether the health insurance mandate itself is so clearly a bad policy. Instead, it invites the justices to create a new limit based on their policy preferences about hypothetical *other* laws like the broccoli mandate—laws that Congress is likely to never enact—and then applies that limit to laws like the health insurance mandate that are far less silly as a policy matter.

13 Worse, this whole "limiting principle" methodology itself has no limiting principle. One could take *any* Congressional power that is defined by existing doctrine and argue that the doctrine would have no limiting principle if Congress could use it to adopt stupid laws. Judges would have to limit Congress' power to prohibit commerce, because it could be used to adopt stupid prohibitions like a ban on broccoli or health insurance. Judges would have to limit Congress' power to tax, because it could be used to tax us all 110% of our income and then throw us all in jail when that proved impossible to pay. Judges would have to limit Congress' power to declare war, since it could be used to declare war on Bermuda if Congress didn't like Bermuda shorts.

14 The deepest problem with the challengers' method is thus the parade of horrible *judicial* decisions that would be unleashed by allowing judges to create new constitutional limits unsupported by constitutional text, history, or precedent in order to preclude imaginary laws no one wants to enact. I share the challengers' aversion to the "nanny state," but it would be far worse to replace our democracy with "nanny judges" who tell us which laws we can adopt. ◆

ANALYSIS AND DISCUSSION

1. Why is the "Commerce Clause" in the U.S. Constitution important to the health insurance debate? What does it allow, and what does it not allow? Explain.
2. Why do challengers to universal health insurance cite the issue of broccoli in their arguments? Is it an effective point? Or is it a red herring designed to steer us away from the real issue?
3. Why does Elhauge feel that arguments that focus on the commerce clause distract us from more valid issues to consider in the argument against universal health insurance?

4. Elhauge states in his first point, "just because we may all agree that a certain type of law would seem stupid, does not mean the courts can insert a ban on such laws into the Constitution. The Constitution has no ban on stupid laws. The constitutional remedy for the enactment of a stupid law is voting out the stupid legislators who enacted it." Respond to this point in your own words. Should the Constitution indeed prevent "stupid laws"? Why or why not?

5. What argument does the author provide for why a "broccoli mandate" will never really happen? Evaluate the validity of each.

6. Elhauge concludes, "I share the challengers' aversion to the "nanny state,'" but it would be far worse to replace our democracy with "nanny judges" who tell us which laws we can adopt." What does he mean by the term "nanny state"? What is a "nanny state"?

RESEARCH AND WRITING

1. In your opinion, if unhealthy behaviors raise the cost of health insurance for those who do not engage in them, should they be penalized in some way? Should the government make these individuals live healthier lifestyles? Write an essay in which you explore government's role in encouraging healthier lifestyles as it connects back to government-backed health care.

2. What is your position on universal health care? Should the government be allowed to make every adult pay for it, as the commerce clause seems to allow, regardless of their health or age?

3. Research the issues connected with the commerce clause and universal health care. Write an essay in which you outline, as Elhauge has here, the reasons why you feel the commerce clause applies to this issue.

For Organ Donation, Facebook Beats the DMV
Art Caplan*

In May 2012, Facebook announced that it would add "Organ Donor" as a Life Event on their pages. Currently, donor organ status is indicated on one's license, registered at the state level at the Department of Motor Vehicles. The idea of sharing one's organ donor status may be a good one—designed to increase participation and open the conversation about the importance of donation, but it also raises some questions. Is declaring "organ donor" on a Facebook page binding? How will the hospital know you have this status? And is Facebook really the best medium to advance such an important issue as organ donation? In this next editorial, bioethicist Art Caplan explains why he thinks it is.

1 Right now, nearly 114,000 people in the United States are waiting for organ transplants to save their lives. Tens of thousands more are in need of tissue, bone and cornea transplants to restore their mobility or sight. Facebook has decided to do something about the constant shortage of donors.

---

* Art Caplan, *Vitals MSNBC*, May 1, 2012

2   The company has announced that members can now declare their desire to be an organ donor on their Facebook page. According to a press release signed by Facebook CEO Mark Zuckerberg and COO Sheryl Sandberg, "…by simply telling people that you're an organ donor, the power of sharing and connection can play an important role."

3   I agree.

4   Donor cards and check-offs on driver's licenses work, but not well. Sixty-two percent of Colorado's licensed drivers and ID card holders have signed "yes," for instance. But in the rest of the U.S., many more Americans have not. For example, fewer than 15 percent have checked the driver's license donor box in New York State. Since most Americans say they do want to donate when they die—a Gallup study found 95 percent support organ donation—and since most families, when asked, do consent to donation by a loved one, why the poor donor card rates?

5   The answer, in part, is that the Department of Motor Vehicles is not the best agency to recruit organ donors. As I have argued in a recent article in the *American Journal of Bioethics* with philosophy professors Kyle Whyte and Evan Selinger, asking people to do something nice for others when they have been stewing in a long line, getting angrier and angrier while they wait is not conducive to altruism.

6   True story about my experience at the DMV: When I went to renew my license in Pennsylvania, I told the official at the counter that I wanted to be an organ donor. She frowned and said maybe that was not a good idea, since she had heard that people who check the wish to donate box might not get aggressive care at the hospital. She had heard wrong, of course. But the point is, being asked to donate by someone who does not know the facts, or, does not really care about them, while waiting in a crummy environment, is not the best way to identify donors.

7   Facebook can help. That's mostly because the power of a donor card really is to let others know about your wishes when you die. However, if for some reason your card is not found when you die, or your family and friends do not know you signed it, then your desire to donate might be unknown—or ignored. Facebook gives one more avenue for others to learn about your wishes—and that is all to the good.

8   Some might argue that it could be coercive to have your friends publicly state they want to be organ donors, especially if you are not sure. I don't think so. The choice is yours, but seeing that your family and friends have chosen to donate is a fact that might sway, not coerce, your decision.

9   So, good for Facebook for trying to help find more donors for those in need. Let's hope, for the sake of all those waiting for the gift of life, it helps. ◆

CRITICAL THINKING

1. Caplan states, "Since most Americans say they do want to donate when they die—a Gallup study found 95 percent support organ donation—and since most families, when asked, do consent to donation by a loved one, why the poor donor card rates?" Answer this question with your own view, adding whether you or your family members have officially declared your organ donor status.

2. One reason, Caplan proposes, for low organ donor numbers is that we ask people to do something nice for others "when they have been stewing in a

long line, getting angrier and angrier while they wait." Does your mood at the DMV influence your decision to be an organ donor? Why or why not?

3. What rumor does the woman at the DMV pass on to Caplan when he goes to renew his license? How can such rumors harm the organ donation effort? Explain.

4. Caplan argues that Facebook offers one more opportunity for others to learn your end of life. In your opinion, do you think Facebook would be a good way for your family to know you wish to be an organ donor? Why or why not?

5. Caplan admits that some critics of Facebook's movement could argue that "it could be coercive to have your friends publicly state they want to be organ donors, especially if you are not sure." Would you be influenced by your friends' organ donor status on Facebook? Could peer pressure make you indicate this status as well? Why or why not?

6. Does the fact that Caplan is a bioethicist enhance the validity of his argument? Why or why not?

CRITICAL WRITING

1. *Exploratory Writing:* Could an Organ Procurement Organization (OPO) use your Facebook status as legal proof of your desire to donate your organs upon your death? Could your Facebook status be more binding than your family's wishes? Write an essay exploring this dilemma.

2. *Persuasive Writing:* Write an editorial in which you, like Caplan in this reading, state your position on Facebook's decision to add organ donor status to its pages. Consider the pros and cons of the issue, and explain why you believe it is a good or bad idea.

3. *Persuasive Writing:* Bioethicist Summer Johnson McGee wonders, "Will those who aren't educated about organ donation believe that saying they want to be an organ donor on Facebook replaces signing up at the DMV or as part of a state registry?" Would you presume that setting your Facebook status to "Organ Donor" renders DMV registration unnecessary? Write an essay in which you respond to her concern, and offer any solutions for it.

GROUP PROJECT

1. Conduct a survey on Facebook's "Organ Donation" feature. Ask at least 50 Facebook users whether they have indicated this status on their Life Events. For those who have not, ask whether they are aware of this option, and if not, would they sign up? Finally, ask your respondents how they feel about this new feature, and if they think it will increase organ donation nationwide. Share your survey results with the class as part of a discussion on this feature and how effective it will be for increasing the organ donor pool.

VIEWPOINTS

► **The Debate Surrounding Removal of Severely Obese Children from the Home: An Editorial Commentary**
Martin Binks, PhD*

► **Childhood Obesity Warrants Removal of Child to Foster Care**
Susan Brady

► **Why Fat Cannot Make You Unfit to Parent**
Summer Johnson McGee

In 2010, the Centers for Disease Control and Prevention reported that Americans were becoming more obese than ever before. Over 65 percent of U.S. adults are considered overweight or obese as defined by U.S. body mass index guidelines. As of 2011, almost 20 percent of children were considered overweight. We know that obesity is connected to many diseases, including heart disease, diabetes, and certain cancers. In November 2011, child protective services in Ohio removed an obese 8-year-old boy from his Cleveland Heights home for "medical neglect." The mother of the 200-pound boy was charged with endangering her son's health. The case sparked national debate on who is responsible for the increasing girth of the nation's children.

In a country where school nutrition programs can count pizza sauce and French fries as vegetables to meet nutrition standards, is the government to blame? Parents? The fast-food industry? This chapter's Viewpoints examines the issue of childhood obesity. First, Martin Binks questions the controversial stand taken by physician and childhood nutrition expert David Ludwig and nutritionist Lindsey Murtagh who recommend that severely obese children should be removed from their homes if their parents cannot get them to a more healthy weight—arguing that a severely obese child is a neglected child. Binks is followed by two editorials exploring the ethics of removing an obese child from his or her home, and whether severe obesity is indeed a form of child abuse.

* Martin Binks, Ph.D., Obesity Society, August 2011; Susan Brady, *Health News*, November 28, 2011; Summer Johnson McGee, *Bioethics.net*, November 29, 2011

The Debate Surrounding Removal of Severely Obese Children from the Home: An Editorial Commentary

Martin Binks, PhD

1 Over the past several weeks there has been considerable public debate surrounding a controversial article published in *The Journal of the American Medical Association (JAMA)*. The article proposes that the State should consider removing a specific sub-set of obese children (above the 99th percentile) from the home and placing them in foster care temporarily as a remedy for their obesity.[1] It was suggested that this action could change the trajectory of the child's obesity by providing a period of time where they were exposed to healthy nutrition and reasonable activity levels. It was noted that during the separation parents could be provided with education to assist them in managing their child's weight. The central theme of the article is that this approach could be considered as opposed to more invasive surgical procedures. The article further states that under most existing child protective services laws, less intrusive interventions such as in-home social supports, parenting training, counseling, and financial assistance, may address underlying problems without resorting to removal of a child. In addition, the authors note that broader preventative measures are needed to adequately impact childhood obesity and that government could "reduce the need for such interventions through investments in the social infrastructure and policies to improve diet and promote physical activity among children." The authors, Lindsey Murtagh, JD, MPH; and David S. Ludwig, MD, PhD, are respected members of the academic and medical community (Department of Health Policy and Management, Harvard School of Public Health; and Optimal Weight for Life Program, Department of Medicine, Children's Hospital, Boston, Massachusetts; respectively) and have pre-sented a thoughtful analysis of this difficult topic. The purpose of this piece is not to summarize or even fully consider the entire debate. Nor is it to state any sort of offi-cial position of The Obesity Society. Rather we would simply like to add a few more thoughts for our readers' consideration.

2 As scientists we know that out of controversy often times comes innovation and that in considering unpopular opinions we sometimes find truth (the image of boats sailing off the edge of the earth comes to mind). As scientists we are also bound by our belief in objective analysis and fact-based decision making in considering all potential solutions to a problem and that often it takes a bold and controversial stance to ignite the type of debate needed to stimulate critical thinking. By its very nature the topic of obesity in children generates an emotional response. We as a society have agreed that protecting our children from harm is among our most primary re-sponsibilities. Deciding what constitutes 'neglect' to a degree that justifies removal of a children from their homes is among the hardest choices we have to make. So the

[1] Murtagh L, Ludwig, DS. State intervention in life-threatening childhood obesity. *JAMA* 2011; 306(2): 206–207. DOI: 10.1001/jama.2011.903

fundamental question raised by Dr. Ludwig and Ms. Murtagh is this: Does obesity in its most severe form constitute neglect and if so, what is the best course of action? This is a fundamental question that is clearly in need of discussion as the prevalence of obesity and related diseases increases rapidly in our society's most vulnerable population. It requires us to determine if as a society, in the case of our children's weight, we are failing in our fundamental responsibility to protect our children from harm. Childhood obesity rates have continued to climb and the medical consequences affecting our children have followed suit. Our efforts to tackle the issue on a large scale have been unsuccessful. The authors point out that the scientific community has identified a multitude of contributors ranging from the built environment and our continual proximity to calorically dense low nutrient foods to the influences of the human genome and our body's physiological adaptation mechanisms. Within this broad spectrum is our social environment. This includes our children's broader social environment (friends, school, and social gatherings) and their primary social environment (the family/home environment). Perhaps the most consistent argument heard against the notion of removing children who have severe obesity from the home is the fact that this approach singles out one among many contributors to the child's obesity and focuses too narrowly on the influence of the primary caregivers. While clearly parental influence is important, especially in younger children, in the context of broader influences on eating and physical activity the argument to remove children from the home is seen by many as perhaps placing too great an emphasis upon the influence of the home environment (especially in older children and adolescents) in the context of the child's broader food and physical activity environment. In fact studies have shown children are getting more of their food away from home in recent decades which may be limit the relative influence parents are able to exert.[2]

3   In making the point regarding the viability of removal of the severely obese child from the home, the article singles out adolescent bariatric surgery as a comparison/alternative intervention and suggests that surgical intervention is as yet unproven (although short-term results have been favorable, long-term outcomes are as yet unknown) and somehow potentially damaging to the family and individual due to the irreversible nature of the decision (vs. the 'reversible' situation created through temporary removal from the home). Both points are valid to consider given that the long-term physical and psychological impact of surgical weight loss for adolescents is relatively unknown. However, in considering this argument it is also essential to consider the fact that the impact of the proposed solution of removing the child from the home is completely unknown in terms of both efficacy in achieving physical outcomes (e.g. weight loss and health improvement) and the potential for permanent damage to the family unit and the child's emotional well-being. The assumption that placement in foster care, for a limited time, can have any meaningful long-term impact on the child's weight trajectory is unsubstantiated by the authors. However, even if we assume that a foster care placement will be able to effectively provide a healthy and structured food and activity environment (which

---

[2]Lin BH, Guthrie J, Frazao E. Quality of children's diets at and away from home: 1994–96. *Food Review* 1999b; 2–10.

is doubtful); the impact of this non-professional, limited scope 'intervention' on weight also remains unknown. By contrast, review of data show that surgical approaches (some of which are considered reversible) such as Laprascopic Gastric Banding) have been effective in reducing weight and comorbidities in severely obese adolescents.[3,4,5]

4   The issue of stigma and our society's long record of blaming victims for medical issues with behavioral components is also important.to consider (i.e. alcohol, nicotine and other drug addiction). What role does blame play in our debate over placing obese children in foster care? While we are not technically blaming the obese child, could it still be seen as blaming a secondary victim, the obese child's parent for being unable to combat on behalf of their child, the very same contributors to obesity we all agree are out of the direct control of any individual? Add to this the fact that we have a large proportion of parents of obese children who are, themselves, obese and we have what could be seen as blaming a primary victim on behalf of a secondary victim. Perhaps we need to step back a moment and consider what we each *TRULY* believe about who or what is to blame for obesity. Our professional consensus appears to be that environmental and psychosocial influences combine with our biological predispositions to impact adiposity in the context of our behavioral determinants. We often posit that those who are less biologically vulnerable are least likely to develop obesity or at minimum experience less severe forms of weight difficulty. Those individuals with the highest biological vulnerability are most likely to develop the disease in its most severe forms (including degree of obesity and comorbidities). Therefore, if we single out individuals with the most severe form of obesity for state sanctioned removal from otherwise loving homes, what type of society have we become? Is this an act of protection or one of discrimination based on biological vulnerability? The authors attempt to address issues such as unknown genetic disorders and biological influences in general; however they use as a basis of their initial argument for removing children from the home the following statement "Whereas typical children consume about 100 kilocalories per day more than requirements state, the energy imbalance for severely obese children may exceed 1000 kilocalories per day suggesting profoundly dysfunctional eating and activity habits." This statement clearly sets the tone that in order for a child to become super-obese they must be consuming huge quantities of food and furthermore in the context of the article, implies that those calories are being provided in the home. Given what we have learned in recent years about the influence of the broader environment on childhood obesity, coupled with the rapid increases in our understanding

---

[3]Holterman AX, Browne A, Dillard BE 3rd, Tussing L, Gorodner V, Stahl C, Browne N, Labott S, Herdegen J, Guzman G, Rink A, Nwaffo I, Galvani C, Horgan S, Holterman M. Short-term outcome in the first 10 morbidly obese adolescent patients in the FDA-approved trial for laparoscopic adjustable gastric banding. *J Pediatr Gastroenterol Nutr.* 2007;45(4):465–73.PMID: 18030214

[4]Al-Qahtani AR. Laparoscopic adjustable gastric banding in adolescent: safety and efficacy. *J Pediatr Surg.* 2007; 42(5):894–7.PMID: 17502207

[5]Treadwell JR, Sun F, Schoelles K. Systematic review and meta-analysis of bariatric surgery for pediatric obesity. *Annals of Surgery* 2008; 248(5):763–776 doi: 10.1097/SLA.0b013e31818702f4

of biological influences on energy balance, using such a broad assumption about feeding to justify removing children from the home due to their obesity, in the absence of other signs of abuse and neglect may not be an ideal solution.

5   It's easy to engage in intellectual debate on the merits of this issue. In fact it's easy to forget if we are not very careful, that the decisions we are discussing are not about some hypothetical family. We are talking about real people struggling with a complex multi-determined health condition. In fact it is very likely that this issue may impact the lives of our friends, colleagues, neighbors, and loved ones. These decisions carry with them a human toll. Think of your own colleagues, friends and family. Do they have an overweight or obese child? To what degree did the parent (your colleague, your friend, your family member) contribute to the issue through "neglect?" If their child happened to be unfortunate enough to progress towards severe obesity would you be willing to call protective services to remove their child from that home (with the same clear conscience you would have if you saw them beating their child) or is this issue somehow different? ◆

 # Childhood Obesity Warrants Removal of Child to Foster Care
Susan Brady

1 The controversy over childhood obesity has heated up after social workers removed an eight-year-old boy from his mother's home due to her inability or inaction to reduce his obesity.

2   The child, from Cleveland Heights, Ohio, weighs in excess of 200 pounds. The average weight of a male child of that age should be in the neighborhood of 55-60 pounds, with the high end tipping the scale at 78 pounds, according to growth charts from the Centers for Disease Control (CDC). Even accounting for the upper end of the spectrum, the child was more than 250 percent overweight.

3   Earlier this year I wrote an editorial on just this topic: Losing parental rights due to obesity. It was in response to an article in the *Journal of the American Medical Association,* which suggested that severe sanctions should be imposed on parents in cases where their children are morbidly obese and there is an unwillingness to make dietary and lifestyle changes to address the issue. In essence, it calls this type of parenting "child abuse."

4   This particular case is a good example of a morbidly obese child, where the mother did not take sufficient steps to reduce the weight, and county officials felt there was medical neglect. According to reports, the case was monitored for more than one year before social workers went to Juvenile Court to remove him from his mother's care. Childhood obesity can lead to a host of medical problems, both in youth and adulthood, most notably diabetes, heart disease, high blood pressure, and sleep apnea. Currently the child only suffers from sleep apnea, which is remedied with a CPAP device (continuous positive airway pressure).

5   Given the age of the child, the only way for him to have gained this much weight was with food purchased and/or prepared by his mother. In many cases, the lack of education or funds can lead to obesity, as starches are usually significantly cheaper than proteins and fresh fruit and vegetables.

6   But the mother is a substitute teacher and clearly has an education. The child was under a doctor's care, so lack of medical insurance or money to see a doctor was not the problem. There was clear incentive to help the child reduce weight, given the pressure and visits by social services, and yet it did not happen.

7   While there are surely facts about this case that have not been revealed, and we do not sit in judgment, this is a clear warning to parents about the consequences of their actions. Losing your child to the system due to an inability or unwillingness to control their obesity is a real threat. ◆

 ## Why Fat Cannot Make You Unfit to Parent

Summer Johnson McGee

1 An eight-year-old Cleveland Heights, Ohio boy has been taken away from his parents by Child Protective Services. An unfortunate, but routine occurrence in the world of CPS–but this time the case has an usual cause—this third grader weighs more than 200 pounds and in the judgment of some Cuyahoga County officials his parents are the cause of his abuse to his health and well-being.

2   But as the *Cleveland Plain Dealer* asked this week, "Is Obesity Cause Enough To Take Kids From Parents?" My answer is absolutely no.

3   Of course, it is a tragedy that an 8-year old third-grader weighs as much as a major league baseball player and that is almost certain that he faces a life of serious and life-threatening co-morbities of obesity such as diabetes, heart disease, depression and others. The issue is serious and has consequences that will effect this child throughout his lifetime. On this I agree with Art Caplan who has said, "A 218-pound 8-year-old is a time bomb." From a health perspective that is true. But will his health status be improved when he is yanked from his family and put into foster care? Almost certainly not, as studies have shown multiple negative mental and physical health consequences from being in foster care including 35% of children increasing their BMI while in foster care. Will the state ensure that his nutrition and physical activity will be better in his foster home than his previous one? They haven't said they will and it's impossible to see how they could.

4   Childhood obesity, no matter how severe, is no reason to take a child away from his family, whom we must assume love and care for him and provide for him well. Why this assumption? No other justification was provided for removing him from his family except for his BMI. But some may argue that his parent(s) are putting him in harms way, allowing him to eat and not to exercise in ways that certainly damage his health. This may be true, or it may be the result of socioeconomic and structural

factors that are beyond this family's control. Perhaps they live in a "food desert" and cannot get easy access to fruits and vegetables and perhaps even more likely they live on a meager income in a society where they are bombarded by commercials and billboards for 99 cent Value Meals.

5   Moreover, if Child Protective Services is going to get in the business of taking away children from parents who expose them to health risks repeatedly and with serious detriment to their health, the "stereo cops" had better start surveying every house to ensure that the volume knobs on teenage stereos are turned down, lest the parents allow them to get permanent hearing damage from their iPhones or car radios. Or the "tanning police" had better make sure that every child in America never gets a sunburn, because a parent who allows their child to be sunburned exposes that child to a significantly greater chance of malignant melanoma, just from one burn. I could go on and on, but you get the point.

6   Furthermore, there exist a wide range of details in the case not provided to us via the media: what is the BMI of his mother and/or father? Is obesity a problem throughout the home? Could education, behavior modification, or other interventions far short of taking away a child from his home help ameliorate this problem? Did authorities try these methods and warn the parents prior to taking away the child?

7   This case, as extreme as it is, does shine a light on an important issue in our society: childhood obesity. There are clearly better and worse strategies to deal with it. The worst would be to traumatize a child by removing them from their home solely because they struggle with their weight. The better strategy would be to have public health and social services unite to help children and their families who live in food deserts and who are the products of a society manipulated by food lobbies find ways to improve their health behaviors and their health outcomes. ◆

CRITICAL THINKING

1. Martin Binks questions the wisdom behind Lindsey Murtagh's and David S. Ludwig's extreme recommendation that severely obese children be removed from their homes. What response does medical ethicist Summer Johnson McGee have to this idea?
2. In your opinion, who is responsible for obesity in children? Parents? The fast-food industry? Schools? Who should be held accountable?
3. What factors contribute to childhood obesity? To what extent are these factors controllable, and in what ways are they beyond our ability to change?
4. How do children learn about nutrition and healthy food choices? From parents? School? Books or television? The Internet? In your opinion, what influences kids' views on eating the most?
5. In the case of the 8-year-old discussed in these editorials, it is mentioned that social services had worked for over a year with the boy's mother in an effort to help reduce his weight. Does this fact make the removal of the child seem more justifiable? Why or why not?
6. Whose argument seems the most credible to you and why?

7. Johnson McGee states, "'A 218-pound 8-year-old is a time bomb.' From a health perspective that is true. But will his health status be improved when he is yanked from his family and put into foster care?" Why does she feel that the child will not improve, and will actually be harmed from this experience? Do you agree or disagree with the decision to remove the child from him home? Explain.

8. Martin Binks, Ph.D., states that while his editorial is not meant to serve as a commentary on the issue, he does wish to raise some points for his readers. What concerns does he wish to raise? Do they influence the debate on whether children should indeed be removed from their homes if morbidly obese?

CRITICAL WRITING

1. *Persuasive Writing:* Prepare your own editorial on this issue drawing from the information provided in these readings. Explain why you feel that the decision to remove the boy from his home was a good or poor judgment on the part of child social services.

2. *Research Writing:* Go to the Center for Science in the Public Interest Web site at www.cspinet.org/new/200311101.html and view the CSPI report on the proposed connection between marketing and childhood obesity. Write an essay in which you explore the ways companies are contributing to the childhood obesity problem.

3. *Exploratory Writing:* Lindsey Murtagh, JD, MPH; and David S. Ludwig, MD, PhD propose a very radical and controversial solution to helping severely obese children improve their conditions. Read their recommendation in *JAMA* (July 13, 2011 issue). What other solutions might be offered? Or is their solution the right one? Explain.

GROUP PROJECTS

1. Together with your group, discuss the issue of childhood obesity. How common is it today? Why wasn't it as common in the past, and what do you think is contributing to its rise? What long-term social problems could result? (A good Web site on this issue is http://kidshealth.org/parent/general/body/overweight_obesity.html)

2. Brainstorm on ways to address the problem of childhood obesity, considering any impediments to your proposed solutions. How would you address the problem in schools? At home? How could the Internet and social media be used? Create a plan of action and share it with the class.

Photo Credits

Text Credits

"Annika Sorenstam Has Another Remarkable Year For A Lady," from The Onion.com, December 1, 2005. Reprinted with permission.

Margaret Atwood. "Debtor's Prism," from *The Wall Street Journal,* September 20, 2008. Reprinted with permission.

Sahar Aziz. "Racial Profiling is Poisoning Muslim Americans' Trust, from *The Guardian*, February 21, 2012. Reprinted with permission from the publisher.

Noah Berlatsky. *"'Twilight' vs. 'Hunger Games': Why Do So Many Grown-Ups Hate Bella?"* from *The Atlantic,* November 15, 2011. Reprinted with permission.

Martin Binks. "The Debate Surrounding Removal of Severely Obese Children from the Home: An Editorial Commentary," from obesity.org/publications (http://www.obesity.org/publications/the-debate-surrounding-removal-of-severely-obese-children-from-the-home-an-editorial-commentary .htm), August 2011, (c) The Obesity Society.

Luke Bobo. "Rap Artists' Use of Women," from RansomFellowship.org, © Luke Bobo, 2008. Reprinted with permission of the author.

dana boyd. "Streams of Content, Limited Attention, from *Educause Review*, Volume 45, Number 5 (September/October 2010): 26–36. Reprinted with permission of the author.

Susan Brady. "Childhood Obesity Warrants Removal of Child to Foster Care," from Health News, November 28, 2011. Reprinted with permission.

Jake Brennan. "Has Male Bashing Gone Too Far?" from AskMen.com, August 13, 2007. Reprinted with permission.

David Brooks. "People Like Us," from *The Atlantic Monthly*, September 2003. Reprinted with permission of the author.

Art Caplan. "For Organ Donation, Facebook Beats the DMV." from http://vitals.msnbc.msn.com/_news. Reprinted with permission.

Mary Carmichael. "Coming to a Lab Near You," from Frontline, "The Persuaders," November 9, 2004. Reprinted with permission.

Lakshmi Chaudry. "Mirror, Mirror on the Web," from *The Nation*, January 11, 2007. Reprinted with permission.

Andrew J. Cherlin. "Think of the Children," from *The New York Times*, January 20, 2012, The Opinion Pages. Reprinted with permission.

John Cloud. "Never Too Buff," from *TIME* Magazine, April 24, 2000. Copyright © Time Inc. Reprinted with permission.

Stephanie Coontz. "For Better, For Worse," *The Washington Post*, May 1, 2005. Reprinted with permission of the author.

Libby Copeland. "Is Polygamy Really So Awful?" from *Slate*, January 30, 2012. Reprinted with permission.

Jennifer L. Derenne, Eugene V. Beresin. "Body Image, Media, and Eating Disorders," from *Academic Psychiatry*, Volume 30, 2006: 257–261. Reprinted with permission.

Stephanie Dolgoff. "Tattoo Me Again and Again," from *Self*, September 2007. Reprinted with permission from Conde Naste Publications.

Avia Dove-Viebahn. "Feminism in a Mad World," from *Ms. Magazine*, Summer 2010. Reprinted with permission.

Tamara Draut. "Strapped," an excerpt from *Strapped*: *Why America's 20- and 30-Somethings Can't Get Ahead*. Doubleday, 2006. Reprinted with permission.

Robin Dunbar. "You Gotta Have (150) Friends, from *The New York Times*, Op-Ed. December 25, 2010. Reprinted with permission of publisher.

Roger Ebert. "Death to Film Critics! Hail to the CelebCult!" from *Chicago-Sun Times*, November 26, 2008. Reprinted with permission.

Einer Elhauge. "It's Not About Broccoli! The False Case Against Health Care, from *The Atlantic Monthly Group*, © 2012. Reprinted with permission.

Joseph Epstein. "The Culture of Celebrity," from *The Weekly Standard*, October 17, 2005. Reprinted with permission.

Niranjana Iyer, "Weight of the World," from *Smithsonian Magazine,* August 2006. Reprinted with permission of author.

Beth Janes. "Why I Rue My Tattoo," from *MSNBC,* October 4, 2007 http://www.msnbc.msn.com. Reprinted with permission.

Sharon Jayson. "Recession Generation," from *USA Today*, June 23, 2009. Reprinted with permission.

Allen Jenkins. "Inequality, Race and Remedy," from *The American Prospect*, Volume 18, Number 5, May 4, 2007. The American Prospect, 2000 L Street NW, Suite 717, Washington, DC 20036. All rights reserved. Reprinted with permission.

Brittney Johnson. "Lose Title IX Please, Boise State Wants Baseball." Arbiter Online, February 2, 2011.

Anya Kamenetz. "Generation Debt," an excerpt from book by the same title, Riverhead Books, 2006. Reprinted with permission.

Madeleine Begun Kane. "My Most Attractive Adversary," *PopPolitics,* December 2000. Reprinted with permission of the author.

Alex Kuczynski. "Her Body, My Baby," from *The New York Times*, November 30, 2008. Reprinted with permission.

Elizabeth Larkin. "Reality TV: Should We Really Watch?" from About.com, 2004. Reprinted with permission.

Glenn Loury. "Why Should We Care About Racial Inequality?" from *Issues in Ethics*, Vol. 10, No.2, Fall 1999, Santa Clara University's Markkula Center for Applied Ethics. Reprinted with permission.

William Lutz. "With These Words I Can Sell You Anything," from *Doublespeak,* 1989. Blond Bear, Inc. Reprinted by permission of the author.

Summer Johnson McGee. "Why Fat Cannot Make You Unfit to Parent," from *Bioethics.net,* November 2011. Reprinted with permission.

John H. McWhorter. "Why I'm Black and Not African American," from *Los Angeles Times*, September 8, 2004. Reprinted by permission of the author.

Jay Newton-Small, "Frozen Assets," from *TIME*, April 6, 2012. Reprinted with permission.

Asra Q. Nomani. "Airport Security: Let's Profile Muslims," from *The Daily Beast*, November 28, 2010.

Index

483